T0353988

ALMOST A SPY

ALMOST A SPY

Charles Petty

Former Political Section Head Of

Ministry Of Information Of Kuwait

authorHOUSE®

AuthorHouse™
1663 Liberty Drive
Bloomington, IN 47403
www.authorhouse.com
Phone: 1-800-839-8640

First published by AuthorHouse   01/03/2012

ISBN: 978-1-4685-2332-4 (sc)
ISBN: 978-1-4685-2333-1 (hc)
ISBN: 978-1-4685-2334-8 (ebk)

Library of Congress Control Number: 2011961954

Printed in the United States of America

Any people depicted in stock imagery provided by Thinkstock are models, and such images are being
used for illustrative purposes only.
Certain stock imagery © Thinkstock.

This book is printed on acid-free paper.

FORWARD:

This book is the first part of the planned two-volume series called "Almost A Spy." This portion being the almost-telling-all, the kinder, gentler part.

I have held back serious information as well as particular details of certain events. At this time going further may incriminate me or give others a chance to implement me for acts that I have not committed.

The experiences in this book are from my wife's and my endeavors abroad. I have altered some time periods and tinkered with various events to enrage those whom I had unpleasantries with. Otherwise, I hope to take you just beneath normal life and show you how easy it becomes to slip into the "sub culture of spying".

At present I am in failing health and terminally ill, but upon anything causing my untimely death or the injury or death of one of my close relatives due to my writings, such an act shall cause blistering documents and very damning information to be released. It is in the best interest of certain people that I not die by their hand.

Acknowledgements:

To Ivan Sopin, a young Russian whose genius and computer savvy transformed my manuscript into this published novel. Although Ivan, his wife Olga and their son Paul have super families back home, we feel they are truly our own.

To Betty Lippold, the gutsiest news woman I've ever had the pleasure to know. She boldly championed the causes of abused maids and many others as well as my own imprisonment in a guarded society where media is controlled. I will forever keep her in my heart and hope to always call her my friend. I also would like to thank Betty for the use of some of her photos in this book.

And to my loving wife Maia, who has lived many more adventures than this one with me. She has been there during the good, the bad and the indifferent, never wavering. My eternal love. Hopefully, in retirement she will get more of my best instead of all the rest.

CONTENTS

CHAPTER 1

Get the News Bearer

I'm half way around the world, lying on the cold marble floor of a Kuwaiti prison. I'm feverish and shaking profusely now, and sweating as if it were summer, when in fact, it is December. My body, mind, and spirit are nearing an end. I feel like I've already gone through the beginning phase of physical shut-down. I'm suffering from dramatic weight loss and a weakening heart. My pulse has alternately gone from racing to almost unintelligible. My whole bruised and busted body can't take the brutal punishments any more.

Keeping track of days and nights—or days from nights—has been almost impossible because police and guards almost never leave me alone, dragging me from room to room and floor to floor. They often start out by dragging me by the hair on my head. If a clump of that gives way, they usually reach for the ears. I know most of the cartilages from my ears must be shattered by now. Some time ago, my belt was removed for "my own personal safety," as they said. I guess they must have thought I would have the energy to commit suicide, before they beat me to death. I need that belt now because losing nearly fifty pounds in just over three weeks has created this new Jack-LaLanne waistline that doesn't allow my pants to stay where they ought to be.

I guess if it weren't for all the swelling, I'd look anorexic. Food is now a thing of the past. I haven't been able to digest or take nourishment since my throat got messed up in a drop kick by an overly zealous Kuwaiti policeman who surprised me during a nap. Talk about kicking a man while he's down and asleep! My legs and hips have swollen to the point I can no longer remove my pants over them, and the fever raging within my body has grown more and more dangerously. Most of the time, I just lie here, drifting in and out of consciousness. Surely this isn't the way my life will end, or is it?

There's a lot of irony in my story. For instance, I'm imprisoned in Kuwait, the country my own nation so generously helped in defeating that ferocious Iraqi dictator Saddam Hussein and his half million strong—but dumb—occupying army. One day, I was working for one of the most powerful men in the Middle East, and the next I was arrested and thrown into a filthy overcrowded prison cell, sharing the same fate as all other expats who dared complicate the lives of these lazy oil-rich Arabs.

My dilapidated substandard prison cell is unfit even for criminals. There's been neither trial nor confrontation by my accuser, and no impassioned concessions made on my behalf for all the things I've done for Kuwait's Royal Family as well as several Kuwaiti Ministers, for whom I've directly been working.

I'm still a bit dazed by the rapid acceleration of events that led to my imprisonment, but hardly surprised or shocked. I've felt it coming for a while. As probably the only outsider who really knows Kuwait's overall sinister picture, I should have expected no more and no less of them. Kuwaitis' cruelty to their servants, women folk, and those who don't follow their every whim with adulation, is legendary; still I dared to double cross those arrogant white robed ingrates with my own version of personal combat. There came a time when being bought off was no longer a priority of mine. I had to begin waging my own personal war on His Highness and others, the only way I knew how.

Now, my plan is simply preservation, instead of the usual self promotion and financial success. My lust for money be damned for now. My mind and energy have to be focused on resolving the huge crisis unfolding between me and them, before it gets further out of hand, and either leads to a confrontation between my country and my host nation, or my destruction.

I knew when I went up against such influential men inside their own country, there would be a price to pay, and I'd have to be dealt with sooner or later; of course, much later would have been preferable.

My hosts had planned to kill some of my fellow countrymen, a group of Ranger soldiers who were on desert maneuvers in Kuwait. I couldn't let that happen. Some of these same soldiers could have been a part of that massive coalition of military forces that fought so valiantly to liberate Kuwait. And now some of Kuwait's top generals have sanctioned a plan to kill the Americans and make it look like the Iraqis did it in a cross-border missile attack.

I've continually reminded the Generals from the Minister of Defenses' Office and several other plotters at our nightly dewaniya gatherings, that I am an American. Just because they pay me a great salary, I can't let my silence be mistaken as loyalty to Kuwait. I've reminded them that I have residency in Kuwait, not citizenship. My loyalty remains with my own country and countrymen, now and always. Their indiscreet discussions on how to kill American soldiers makes my blood boil. They seem to think of me as one of them, but I'm not. And that has to be understood.

The way Kuwait would kill the American soldiers was discussed on several occasions within an ear shot of me, and probably on many more occasions before I had actually heard of it. The tape recording I turned over to a sub-committee of the United States Congress somewhat crudely outlined the steps necessary for the attack. The list included the Kuwaiti Generals' names to most likely be selected to oversee the covert operation. On the tape recording, the Kuwaitis also suggested how to slip some scud missiles back into Iraq from Kuwait soil through the demilitarized zone as well as spoke of their satellite photos of the targeted area and desirable grid areas for launch. Other necessary information on routine American Airwac reconnaissance time frames and scheduled activities within that border region were also verbally supplied on that recording. Most importantly, they emphasized the missile attack would occur the month prior to Kuwaiti troops joining the Americans in the desert exercises.

The taped Kuwaitis also reveal which munitions storage facility within their country has the confiscated Iraqi scuds needed. They go into detail how they should be taken back through UNSKOM, United Nations-Kuwaiti border lines. Next, and not least of all, the discussion included how to target the largest concentration of American soldiers on maneuvers; the plans stretched even so far as to prepare several specific ministries within Kuwait on how they would react once the terrible news of the incident and deaths was released.

These ministries were to condemn the Iraqi terrorists, and aggression, and then call for a timely unilateral response against Baghdad from the United States, Gulf Cooperation Council States, the Arab League and the United Nations.

The Kuwaitis have for some time wanted to reignite a war between the United States and Saddam Hussein, and this plot was but one discussed. The Kuwaitis would enlist extreme elements within their own military, bring in a few ringers from al Qaeda, to kill the American soldiers and make it look as though the attack came from the Iraqis. The Americans would then be forced to go back into Iraq and kill, or remove Saddam Hussein. In turn, the plan would rid the Kuwaitis of their menace to the Northwest and save them from having to pay for continued arms purchases and huge protection expenses from former coalition partners, and the United States in particular.

This information was so extremely sensitive and privileged that I handled it with kid gloves, for all the good that it did me. The news of my treason acts against Kuwait reached their ears even before my plane departed from JFK, New York, back to Kuwait City.

It's somewhat surprising that I've been arrested, and even more so that I've been incarcerated, rather than silencing me with a bullet to the back of my head, or worse yet; beheading me within the walls of the

Governorate building in downtown Kuwait City, as they did with many others before me. Sure, they say beheadings stopped in 1972; but ask families of the expats that have just gone missing in Kuwait, about what their friends really thought or heard, had happened to them. Where's Amnesty International when you really need them? They should be on their knees with little forensic test kits checking the area within the Governorate's inner courtyard. I can show them just where to look. After all, I know the place well. As a part of my punishment, I had to kneel with my white death robes across my arms, just a dozen feet from the guys being beheaded each Friday, following prayers at the nearby mosque. My captors would then say to me that next Friday, "it'll be my turn."

Those riding high against me in Kuwait, some members of the Royal Family, the Minister of Information and the Crown Prince's henchmen have been especially perturbed recently at what they're saying is my proven disloyalty to them. During my eight years here, I've openly and often strongly expressed many opposing viewpoints to them, at times in less than subtle tones; but I've always remained diplomatic and respectful of my host country and the many Kuwaiti friends I've made in high places here.

Until recently, I had never ratted on them for their many past indiscretions, but now I have no choice. So I ratted on them in the biggest way I could, exposing their murderous plot against American soldiers by flying back to the U.S. and telling everything I knew to a New York Senator that I trusted at the time, then several days later to a sub-committee chair person that was to take the information before Congress, I thought.

It seems the United States Senator from New York was working on some pretty big financial investment packages with the Royal Kuwaitis and others. He just happened to let them know that I had gone to New York and libeled them terribly. Needless to say, my reception upon returning to work at the Ministry of Information, and then again at Dasma Palace was less than welcoming. My arrest wasn't immediate, but quickly enough, the boom was lowered and the noose was tightened, literally.

Each following day thereafter, I wondered what would be their ultimate pleasure: a noose around my neck, a firing squad, or my head on the chopping block.

Breaking the confidence of my influential moneyed political and military Kuwaiti friends, and then exposing them for what they intended to do, had to be done. No one else from the American government had privy to such damning information against Kuwait as I did; certainly no one from the U.S. Embassy with all their political might and ass-kissing power, could or would do it.

Without coercion and before the beatings started, I owned up to what I'd done in recent months against Kuwait. Well, not everything; there were quite a few more surprises, following my "first interview" and the many interviews that followed. After all, I've been here for eight years and we've barely scratched the surface of what I've really been doing over a much longer period of time than they will probably ever realize. I've provided them with just a little fodder to feed on, knowing that if the real can of worms was opened, I would probably; though I can't see how, be in even worse shape than I'm in now.

My confessions to all the interrogators haven't been apologies; especially to those arrogant bastards that really thought they could get away with killing American soldiers and starting another war with Saddam just to remedy what they called "the Americans bleeding their pocketbooks."

For some time, the Kuwaitis have suspected that the Americans lied and showed them old altered satellite photos, supposedly proving Saddam's army was poised for invasion again, when in fact, they were not. It was simply a technique used by the Americans during intelligence briefings to make the Kuwaitis increase their annual spending to around two and a quarter billion dollars for protection by patriot missiles, jet aircraft, maintenance, joint military exercises, ass-kissing, building contracts, and many other things.

Most of what I've done I remain proud of, even some of the shocking ways I went about doing them. Since early last year I've continued endangering the safety of my wife Maia and myself while keeping in mind one thought: "If I leave this predatory den of lions now, who will take my place? "There's no other American or even westerner in sight who can be the eyes and ears for our side. The Central Intelligence Agency and National Reconnaissance Center, an umbrella of intelligence gathering agencies would tell you that only someone trained behind a desk in Virginia, or in a Colorado facility, could be in such a position of "know," but it ain't so. (The NRC is the biggest "bad boy" out there, and most Americans have never even heard of it. They're bigger than the CIA, the FBI, and many other intelligence organizations combined. Like the others though, they too do not like sharing information.)

I haven't seen any spooks around me except the British. Those two at the American Embassy must have some strange priorities because I've never seen them taken into confidence within the Royal Family or by the Kuwaiti Generals. No other westerner within Kuwait has had such expansive access to the power hungry men who use their money; positions and religion to put strangle holds on the United States and other western nations like I have. I certainly can't leave it up to the American Ambassador (who now shuns me) or other diplomats who hear and see only what the Kuwaitis want them to hear and see. Both the diplomats and the Ambassador don't want to hear or see anything that might get between them and their objectives in the Middle East, especially the lucrative arms deals and building contracts, strategic military bases, and of course oil.

Here amongst these ever wavering and almost always embattled Arabs is black gold, and the Ambassador and other westerners know why they're here. It's like the Ambassador told me before he alienated me, "we go to poor countries to have them kiss our ass while we give them money and aid, and buy their United Nations vote. We go to rich countries to kiss their ass and seek lucrative contracts, airbases, seaports, and arms agreements."

Kuwaitis are well adept at wooing the West with all the above vices, or sometimes they just do like other countries do, they woo us to do their dirty work for a price in hard cash. After all, don't Americans fancy themselves as the policemen of the world?

Worldwide, our dignitaries from the United States and other western countries are greeted by a day of good will and handshakes. What they don't seem to realize is that sooner or later they'll end up paying dearly for those donations and contracts. Either they'll have to support those arrogant bullies in times of crisis and war, and they'll do it with American lives and tax-payers' dollars or through having to significantly reduce those countries' past due loans; bolster their governments' economies and resupply their militaries with hundreds of millions of dollars in used military equipment, clothing, and training, like we've done to Egypt, Israel, and Jordan to name a few.

Kuwaitis, as other oil rich Arab nations are known for not paying their debts; at least not until they've had time to delay, renege, or cheat on all their prior commitments. With a Kuwaiti, you're never going to get what was agreed upon, even with their signature on a contract.

Since the 1991 Gulf War and the ousting of Saddam Hussein from Kuwait, the American Government is still owed billions of dollars by the Kuwaitis, who have been dragging their feet on payments for arms purchases and maintenance contracts. They seemed surprised many purchases like aircraft didn't come with free maintenance contracts. They assumed they had perpetual care, like cemetery lots. Kuwait is not just in debt to the United States, but too many other coalition partners who saved Kuwait's palaces and gold as well. They also still owe deployment expenses to other coalition governments for troops who came to their rescue.

In my near eight years here, I've done my share of groveling; not to the extent that diplomats do because I've always had something else to sell, and they bought it pretty readily, and for a lot of money. I learned to serve Kuwait's big boys with their own little covert needs packages. Indeed, I am and have been a "yes-man and their own well paid "step-and-fetch-it" And in years past, I've been the "token" American they've invited to parties, cultural events and holiday trips, births, deaths and weddings.

Clearly, I've had my own agenda all along. It's been dominated by money, seconded only by my curiosity to know things I shouldn't. The little parts I played early on, evolved into international matters against Iraq or Iran, and even Bahrain. Ah, but once I started my own little payback war against the Kuwaitis, I used some of the same information back against them to bite them in their ass.

For the most part, I've been liked by Kuwaitis. I've been considered a kindly peacemaker by some, fun and witty by others, and just an all around well connected grape on the vine of information. I could deliver a polite slap to the hand of a fellow peer and verbalize an awkward message to a member of Kuwait's Parliament on behalf of my government, or from the Brits, or even someone else. Anything coming from me could truly be bullshit, but from my lips could sound like an official policy by any Government.

Through most of my time here in Kuwait, I've remained neutral, helpful, enthusiastic and a real solid sounding board to my superiors, until the time when they crossed that line I had drawn in the sand, so to speak. When I was arrested, one of the first things the Crown Prince said to me was, "How could you have reported things that were said here in confidence? I pay you a great deal of money and I demand your loyalty." To which I promptly replied "You pay me a lot of money for a job well done; my loyalties are with my own country. They're not for sale." I guess the loyalty in question is now what they've been beating out of me in prison for the past several weeks.

For more than six of my past seven and a half years in Kuwait, I've done my job with great zeal and pleasure, but how have things gotten so bad now? Everything has gone so wrong. I've stayed too long for them and for me.

For the past twenty four months, since I met with that New York Senator and another member of congress and I got the cold welcome back to Kuwait by my employers, things have really gone downhill. There's been quite a war between them and me over pay as well as over what I know, and what they think I know, and even things they're afraid I know. They've admitted they have no idea what to do with me. The American Ambassador has distanced me, His Highness the Crown Prince suspects I got him in trouble with the London tabloids, but isn't sure what I did, and the deal he had with Iran was somehow sabotaged, probably by me. It is true I furnished the head Royals of the Bahrain Government with documentation that Kuwait would stay indifferent to any destabilization inside Bahrain that might be instigated by Iran.

I've remained in Kuwait City only to show them I'm as much an advisory now as I had been a friend in the past. The Minister of Information and His Highness, the Crown Prince's advisors and cronies all know that I know the Generals names involved in the cross border scud plot. They suspect, and rightly so that I've been taking names and kicking ass.

From some of the top offices in the country to the inner circles of power, including their intelligence briefings and censoring of news, I've been there, at the center of it all. How strange is it to imagine that I was even promoted to the Political Section Maodiir (manager) of Radio newsrooms at the Super Station, censoring Kuwait's news and events from their own people. Ah, such vestiges of power while I've been having fun doing the news and weather on radio and jumping on every piece of important information that I could get my hands on.

I've traveled with their big boys, shopping and gambling with them, eating with them, and drinking the "Islamic harum" alcohol with them; I've been on sex junkets to Bangkok with them, even meeting secretively (on my part accidentally) with some Kuwaitis immediately following the first Gulf War, who spoke of removing Kuwait's leadership, prior to the rearrival of the Royal family back into the country. Years later, I listened to their arrogance and unthinkable decision to allow neighboring Bahrain to be destabilized by sympathizers to Iran. They've tried unsuccessfully to convert me to Islam, but were more successful at corrupting me with their wallets and jailing me.

It's ironic how having been in prison for the past days and weeks has given me an eerily long hind sight of crucial events and information that needs to reach the outside, so called, "infidel world." For now, however, it appears that the sheiks have it; 1-0 in our latest round of "tit for tat."

CHAPTER 2

Going on the Offense

Now I speak harshly of Kuwait, but in reality, Maia and I were enjoying our time and friends in that country for several years. It was not until 1994, after our comeback trip from the United States, when everything started going wrong, and the Kuwaitis and I began attacking each other. First, it came only from their side. When over time I felt that enough was enough, my gentile nature took a back-burner, and a more vigilant side of me had to come forward. I've always been called Chuck, Charlie, or Chuckles. I'm quick to laugh, tell a joke or sing while walking down super market aisles. I don't ever remember a time in my entire life that I would have been considered an advisory to anyone.

Kuwait's Royals, some Ministers and advisors have liked me enough to keep me in Kuwait this long, but have also feared me enough to refrain from reigning in controls over me. However, some pretty serious warnings and accusations have flown at me from inside the Ministry of Information and Dasma Palace, and from me back at them lately. Now they're obviously as confused as I am on how we're going to resolve our numerous disagreements.

On several occasions, they've threatened me with putting on trial for spying or espionage, yet we all knew what a can of worms that would open up. I've even told them that they wouldn't have to pull my fingernails out, as I'll squeal like a pig if they just say they're going to do it. Later, of course, that is exactly what happened, only in the true Kuwaiti way:

My first conviction was in a closed court room. I was never notified of the trial, and no one was there to represent me. Obviously, I was convicted of espionage in absentia. What a surprise.

Nonetheless, I'm not guilty of espionage. What really makes them think charges of that magnitude can stick? Almost everything I've done for all of them, including the Royals, the United States, the Brits, or whoever else was mostly done outside Kuwait and inside Iraq on their orders. What's that expression . . . "I serve at the pleasure of . . ." Well, that's me. It still amazes me that as the token American nearly at the top of the heap in Kuwait society, a man that has been led around by the paw into the tigers' den and I've seen everything the tiger has to offer. I've been led around and introduced by all of Kuwait's "big boys," their society's most powerful men. They've shown me a lot of places and let me know a lot of things that I should perhaps never have been privy to, but until now, I've never had any intention of using any of it against them. Espionage would surely mean that my plan all along was to use the knowledge they were giving me, for ill purposes against the state of Kuwait. It ain't so.

Verbal threats and accusations haven't been the only posturing directed against me, prior to, or since that clandestine trial. My personal motives towards Kuwait had never changed to malicious or threatening, nor had any malice truly entered my mind until things got a lot stickier; such as when I returned from the States, having reported that Kuwait was going to kill American soldiers. My pay then started getting withheld; our penthouse was broken into; and Maia and I had three bomb threats. After that, we knew a great change was in store for us. Still, I kept working and hoping for weeks on end that things would return to normal; sadly, they never did.

Each time one or more of my opponents acted, I had to reassess my position and the passive role I was taking and then wait to see how things continued, before moving further along with my reaction. "Just wait a little longer," I'd tell myself. "This will all soon blow over and things may return to near normal again." Surely, my exposing their sinister plot in New York hasn't deserved such consequences as being life-threatening. Each day though, I've been feeling a little more like road-kill, and some pretty big buzzards were circling. It was about this time I had to start defending myself. The escalation on my part had now begun. It was time to take the conflict back to those who were constantly coming after me. I made that final turn against them and moved into the offensive position.

Before my captivity, I was probably the second or third most well known American in Kuwait, falling behind only the Ambassador and my disc jockey partner at Kuwait's Superstation 92.5, a smooth-talking girl by the name of Linda. Linda is a really great gal as is her husband and children. Their marriage has lasted for more than seventeen years, a not-so-easy feat when you are the daughter of a prominent American doctor in El Paso, Texas, and your husband is the son of a Bedouin from the desert in Kuwait. Linda and Badran live in the mostly poor Kuwait City suburb of Al Jahra, known to be heavily populated by the country's more religious zealots and fundamentalists, as well as former desert dwelling families like Badran's.

As former desert wanderers, Badran's family is considered third-class citizens of Kuwait. His family for the most part has remained settled in one place for as long as whole generations but still not officially given citizenship. Neither Badran's family nor his family with Linda is part of the nomadic lifestyle that is considered stateless, the Bedouin. Bedouins, some of whom also live in, or near, Al Jahra, usually remain loyal to tents rather than apartments or houses. They're the lowest class or stateless people, who still wander the deserts regardless of territorial borders.

Linda while wearing the traditional black abaiya "looks the role" of the conservative Muslim wife during routine daily life in public, except in the presence of others within her home or at the Ministry with me. Her wearing of the black abaiya is used during driving commutes and shopping only. She's a gregarious soul with quick humor and a loud contagious laugh. Linda's enthusiastic radio shows are geared toward the lively pop cultured youth of Kuwait. Her shows contain hits from all the top western performers of the day such as Back Street Boys or Boyz II Men. Her dialog sounds no different than any DJs you might hear on better stations inside the United States. She's popular and her request line and faxes pour into the Super Station, day and night. Her fans adore "LINDA LOU."

Linda and I face each other during broadcasts, through a huge sound-proof glass window. Contact between us is usually done through microphones or by jumping up and opening the thick metal door that separates our rooms. During broadcasts, the contact is very limited, unless one or the other happens to bring donuts from that great American establishment Krispy Kreme. We're here at least six days a week or in such cases that my sleuthing in Iraq takes me away from the studio, there is need for me to tape my portion of the next day's broadcast. I do the news, weather, sports, and sometimes international stock markets; and Linda takes care of keeping the listeners happy for the rest of the hour. Linda is not only my work associate but later played an important role following the Iraqi invasion.

Being on the air most days of the week and meeting repetitious daily schedules makes me an easy person to find. My part time cover job at the radio station puts me on the air waves every day at 7 a.m., 9 a.m., and noon. The rest of the time, I'm at Dasma Palace in the Crown Prince's office or atop mine and Maia's penthouse along the beach.

How strange it seems that the Justice Ministry says that they have been unable to find me to serve papers.

That hearing at the Justice Ministry alleged my involvement in espionage on more than forty counts; but from what I understand and though I was not represented by counsel, the U.S. State Department intervened and rebuked Kuwait for having brought me up on such severe charges.

It would be some time, weeks, in fact before those original charges would be lifted and assault charges put in their place. With the lesser charge of assault stemming from an incident between me and a Kuwaiti some seven months earlier, the Kuwaitis knew the American Embassy would be hard pressed not to get involved.

If I had been openly put on trial for espionage, I would have, without reservation, gotten on the stand and spilled my guts. I would not only have confessed my role in some earth shattering vendettas and simply bad dealings between notable Kuwaitis, but also told of things they've done against allies. I could have also managed to trigger some infighting that would hurt or even damage the Royal line of succession in this sandy, penis-sized nation.

Since they've turned so harshly against me, any court appearance by me will cost them. One day Kuwait may be my country's enemy, so at this point, I guess there is some truth to the charges of espionage. I have lined up coordinates on the Magellan Global Positioning Satellite for future targeting of Kuwait's secret palace hideaways, top ranking military bunkers, and at least three of their clandestine German built tunnels. I have recently become that bad boy they thought I was before.

I've out sourced to third parties security and access codes to Ministry complexes, duplicated sensitive keys to high ranking offices and planted some future surprises inside the Ministry of Information Complex, not to mention I've written detailed dossiers on as many high ranking Kuwaiti officials and military leaders as I could. Once you've been labeled bad and you've had to fight for your life, I guess it brings out the worst in you. Look what I've become. Now I'm actually living up to most of those former false allegations.

I can say that all information I now possess, so do several other sympathetic below the radar organizations; some friendly, some not so friendly. Following my first arrest, I made sure my knowledge got spread around. Some of that information has gone to radical anti-Islamic groups that would have no qualms using it if something terrible happens to me, or if I disappear. Many documents have been put aside for my own safety. If I'm killed, several hundred documents will be released or utilized against Kuwait or people within the Royal family, or within their Government as retaliation.

Being confined to a prison cell gives me plenty of time to rethink my past fortunes and misgivings. Naturally, now I'm thinking how these sniveling Kuwaiti ingrates will get what's coming to them one day, if not from me, then from Saddam Hussein's armies again; or if he's dead and out of the picture, then maybe from neighboring Iran. Iran is my bet.

Kuwait should be scared! If they only look internally at thousands of their own fundamentalist Bedouins who are not happy, then include the 450,000 Palestinians that were expelled from their long time homes in Kuwait after the Gulf War, the Kuwaitis should really be scared. With the signing of one document, Kuwait's Parliament voted to expel all Palestinians as well as their families including some who had lived in Kuwait their entire lives. They had to shut their businesses, leave their jobs, abandon their homes, quit their schools, and forsake their friends to be kicked out of Kuwait "en masse." Most took to the isolated desert highways toward Jordan. Where was the world when all this was happening? Has anyone in America ever heard of such a massive move of people from one country because of the Gulf War? Remember, that was 450,000 people, elders and children alike.

Not that I'm too sympathetic. Some of those Palestinians were my friends, but for the most part they sided with Saddam Hussein against coalition forces. Mind you, they had good reasons to side against the Kuwaitis, just not against the United States and the coalition of forces.

Most Palestinians, some Jordanians and even some Egyptians, Pakistanis and Filipinos sided with Saddam Hussein philosophically during the invasion of Kuwait. But next time they will probably be marching alongside invading soldiers. I'm not now, nor have I ever been a threat to Kuwait, yet they are looking over the heads of those who really are. I am just one man, cornered like a rat, who's going to fight back for his life.

Had there never been plans to kill the American servicemen and had that New York Senator remained more loyal to our own soldiers than to Kuwaiti businessmen, I would have never used my time and energy to gather such destructive information and documents about Kuwait as I have now; nor would I have ever used such despicable tactics in obtaining them.

Imprisonment comes as little surprise and I'm sure all the monkey wrenches haven't stopped falling yet. This newest charge of assault against a Kuwaiti that owed me money is a rather dumb one, but true. Although the charge stems from a real incident, it is highly inaccurate and blown out of proportion.

Following the assault not by me but by the Kuwaiti, I was convinced by my attorney and higher-ups that the best thing to do was to let the incident rest The Kuwaiti man involved owed me a debt I intended to collect after one year of owing it to me. He attacked me but since only his side of the story was told, it made it sound like I assaulted him because he didn't come around with the money. Instead he was outraged that I would have the nerve to collect. He walked over and banged me in the back of the head following my turning to head to the door after a screaming incident. It involved me and a debt collection against the head of Kuwait's Criminal Investigations' son so the father would go to any length to protect his sons' lying and cheating. It was true that I fought with the son after he hit me in the back of the head. It should have ended there. It was the only actual fight that I've had with anyone in twenty five years. I was proud I kicked his big six-feet-four-inches ass.

It was possible that my arrest in some distant way could have been related to that fight, though I still believe whole heartedly that all charges and imprisonment is the brain child of the Minister of Information His Highness' first cousin. The Minister of Information is a Sheik of the Royal household in his own right and it was he who carried out his threats and a vendetta to halt my snooping against Kuwait's Islamic fundamentalists.

Kuwait is the true image of a victim in the eyes of the world, and the Minister of Information is the one who wants to keep it that way.

Nonetheless, he knows, and I know, that it ain't so. He's still playing a role he created as Kuwait's Ambassador to Washington during the Occupation and subsequent Liberation of Kuwait, back in 1990 and 1991. Of course, he has another agenda too, making me stop digging for proof positive information, from files within mosques and other places that show Kuwait's big boys being heavily involved in financially supporting fundamentalists and militant organizations inside and outside the Middle East, such as Al Qaeda, al-Aqsah Martyrs, Hamas, and Egypt's Brotherhood. Remember, even Ramzi Yousef, who bombed New York's World Trade Center in 1993, had just arrived from Kuwait where he received funding. He told me over and over, to leave them alone.

I didn't go back a long way as friends with the Minister of Information, as opposed to many other Kuwaitis. Like cats marking their territories, we each established our own territory very early on, and both continued frequently scenting our ground over the years that I worked for him. Once, he and I almost had a "knock down, drag out." It was over a headline in a Kuwaiti newspaper that read "DEATH TO AMERICA." I marched in and said, "Since we're very strictly enforcing the censoring of news on television and radio, how is it that a Kuwaiti newspaper can get away with printing statements like that, unless you gave your blessings. After all, you as an Al Sabah (Kuwait's Royal family), control all media, don't you? "

I was raging, while angrily reminding him that a lot of Americans died for his freedom, and that all his other fellow Arabs and neighbors had failed to come to his aid. Before the British and Americans vowed to rescue them and save all their oil riches, hence allowing them to regain their marble palaces again. "Such a headline of DEATH TO AMERICA is a slap in the face to all Americans."

I went on by saying, "With that irresponsible type of headline and attitude, why should anyone spare Kuwaitis from the wrath of Saddam Hussein's armies. It just shows the world that Kuwaitis are bad boys too, with a reputation for back stabbing, cruelty and cheating. After all, who should ever believe what Kuwaitis say when they continue writing things like that and screwing neighboring countries, say, stealing oil from Iraq or helping Iran to destabilize Bahrain? Why should any other countries ever come to their rescue again? The world, and especially the United States, should consider any future invasion as 'an Arab affair'. We should stop the use of those American 'world policemen,' and let the Kuwaitis suffer their own consequences." But unfortunately, they know, and I know, that the United States will do anything for money, bases, or oil.

The more I lived in Kuwait, the more reasons I found for the Americans not to have saved those sandy butts. Since I've remained for the almighty buck, too, I'm really no different than the Brits who have done it since 1939, or the Americans who have filled a few money coffers as well.

Despite making great money over here, I am yet angry that American soldiers, who aren't paid much, still have to go to Kuwait and fight or even die to participate in the Liberation of some pretty shady characters. After all, I reminded the Minister that I had been present before invasion, at the conference in Jeddah, Saudi Arabia, when His Highness the Crown Prince and his cronies agreed they had no choice but to play their trump card against the United States, which ended up getting a lot of Americans killed. Surely, everyone in America has the right to learn the real reasons we're now supporting Kuwait.

It was actually Kuwaitis themselves who instigated the situation that lead to Iraq's invasion of their country. The Kuwaitis then played the guilt card against the Americans and lured them on to becoming their ally by flashing gold.

Remember, until now the United States had been supporting Saddam Hussein to the tune of hundreds of millions of dollars a year. That money was used to line Saddam Hussein families' pockets and his war efforts against Iran. So, it wasn't just Ambassador Glaspie's diplomatic blunder back in July of 1990 in Baghdad that leaned us toward Kuwait and away from Iraq. The offer of a seaport and airfields and lucrative contracts inside Kuwait helped too.

Kuwait in effect, had over the past twenty years been stealing oil through lateral drilling across Iraq's border, which created the hostility that resulted in Saddam Hussein setting out to right what he saw as a wrong of their country. Kuwaitis then made the United States feel guilty for their small role (or assumed role) in allowing the invasion to take place before the Kuwaitis dangled money in front of our Defense and State Departments' noses to close the deal.

After seven years, the United States may have forgotten what brought them half way around the world to fight the "Gulf War," but the Kuwaitis haven't and I haven't. I am the one now caught between these Arabs carrying a grudge and their virile attempt to show their muscle against the United States, who, they think, planned and caused the war and raped their cash boxes of billions of dollars.

CHAPTER 3

Prisoner Swap

Like slaps in the face and punches to my stomach, surprises were around every corner. Now I'm sitting in jail, awaiting transfer to prison. This morning I was chained and ironed, and summoned to the upstairs of the Detention Center, General al Gharieb's office then told that charges against me had been formally prepared now, and a more severe sentence of three and a half years of hard labor was rendered in my absentia. I numbly sat before him General Gharib as yet an even stranger story poured from his lips. It was just too far fetched. Did the Minister of Information stay awake at night thinking these things up? The prison sentence almost sent me to the floor, but that wasn't the big news. I was to be used in A PRISONER SWAP—a Kuwaiti for an American. I would be released if, and when, the American Government intercedes on behalf of a Kuwaiti imprisoned in Boston for slavery. Until such time, my sentence will be more than triple his.

Everyone knows that life expectancy in a Middle Eastern prison is only a few years at best, so who's fooling who? My counterpart Kuwaiti will await whatever lies ahead of him inside an air conditioned or heated cell. He's got color television, no doubt a sink with clean running water, and a hygienic toilet. (No meat loaf in American prisons though. Meat loaf is what I used to get fed by my mother while we were growing up, but that's considered inhumane treatment now.) He'll have movie nights, and work out areas and cigarettes, if he wishes. I'll be having none of that inside a prison cell in Kuwait.

If the prisoner swap goes sour, then all bets are off. They'll probably make it appear that I escaped late one night into the desert and can't be found. That would make some generals, ministers, and royal bubbas happy. The American held prisoner back in Boston would only have to tough out his conditions for a bit longer. Meanwhile, I'd be out of their way more permanently. Problem solved.

For more than four years, I've quietly watched my employer manipulate visiting American diplomats and presidents, other dignitaries and heads of state, tycoons of industry and worldwide oil production alike, playing them all like pawns and getting them to buy into the "victimization of Kuwait," while fleecing their pockets or reneging on deals. The lengths the Minister of Information would go to have everything his way, are no less far reaching than Saddam's "Scorched Earth Policy."

The Minister of Information and his lessers at the Ministry have been quite influential in my evolution, into both the "person I use to be and the persona non grata I've become. With me, as with many others before me, the Kuwaitis point fingers at others, instead of themselves, for their own misdeeds. They never assume blame nor accept responsibility for any of their own actions. Even they will tell you, it's the "Kuwaiti way." I've tried the best I could to give the finger back to them.

The Minister of Information himself often sent me on little assignments inside Iraq that were opposed to by many of his own country's policies; yet, he has probably had a lot to do with putting me in prison. He was tired of my trying to get paid for services already rendered. (The act of withholding money for services rendered is very anti-Islamic, but is also one of Kuwaiti's most abused religious laws.)

The Minister of Information, like most men of great wealth and power, uses his money to influence others who'll do their bidding for him (like me but on a grander scale), at home and abroad, especially in Washington where he remains at all times above reproach. In Washington, he was former Ambassador from "the victim state of Kuwait." "It's so nice to see you again, your Excellency."

At home, he is looked upon as being a high ranking member of the Al Sabah Royals, part of that sanctimonious group of people their own nationals are not allowed to find fault with. Someone with his credentials would have no trouble or conscience about having me arrested, then imprisoned at hard labor or even taken on that night trip into the desert and shot; whichever is more convenient or efficient.

I was already in trouble because of all the information I turned over to the Senator in New York, and again the Minister of Information has become verbally abusive to me after learning of, or guessing that my latest night forays have turned within, and against him and his country rather than outside the country toward Iraq. On several prior occasions, his lackeys from the Ministry of Information told me of his displeasure at my trying to connect Kuwaiti purse-strings to Muslim fundamentalist groups in which a Kuwaiti from one of the country's most influential families sits as speaker of al Qaeda's elite board, right next to Osama bin Laden.

It has been easier proving some Kuwaitis' financial ties to Palestinian groups like Hamas and Fatah, but more difficult trying to get inside numerous mosques' files to check on the more extreme elements, like the al-Aqsah Martyrs organization, known for sending children into Israel with bombs attached to their bodies. Some Kuwaitis condone the practice as well as their own financial support of some of the Martyrs' families, but don't want to leave a paper trail.

At times, I wonder whether our American Ambassador, whom I believe is probably the smartest man I've ever met, is really as gullible as he seems or is he just trying to avoid getting in the middle of something that may offend his Kuwaiti hosts. If the Kuwaitis do get perturbed, they may halt financial payments to the United States Government. There's a little hard ball being played here but I'm just not sure who is at the bat.

This morning, for the first time it became official that the disturbance I had been hearing down the hallway from my prison cell were representatives of the United States Embassy. They were shown into a private room while

I was transferred into another iron clad jail cell where I was chained, handcuffed, and then shackled into the leg irons placed around my ankles. I was then led in toward my waiting visitors.

It seems the American Ambassador has been told by attorneys of the slave holding Kuwaiti college student in Boston's prison, that his family wants the United States Government to free him in exchange for me, and in addition, a second stipulation has been attached. The Kuwaiti, a fight with whom many months earlier led to the assault charge, is to be paid $185,000 for the discomfort the buffoon suffered at my hands. My fight opponent's attorney says they have forensic reports saying their dim wit, six feet four inches tall idiot of a client is now suffering a 3 percent permanent disability to a fingertip due to his fight with me. For all I know, he hurt his bird finger while digging his nose. Of all the things I could accurately be accused of, this is probably the truest but surely the most ridiculous.

Poor ole Ghassan, my Palestinian-Jordanian friend who was arrested and imprisoned with me; he still hasn't figured out what's going on or why he's in jail too, except that he witnessed my fight with the Kuwaiti seven months earlier. He has no idea of the whole mess that is encompassing his and his family's life. It's far more involved than he can imagine. It's a little late now to start coming clean with him. What he doesn't know may kill him, but if we're both lucky, it won't.

I'm growing weaker in quicker stages now. The unspeakable things they've started doing to me hurt me physically and psychologically, and yet, these are not the type of things you bring up in conversation with a coworker or visitor who might come to see you. I'm remaining asleep or deep in thought for longer periods of time. It could be either from my weakened physical condition or depression. For parts of each day, I care less what happens to me. The beatings, all those night time injections, the chain wrappings and the subsequent hangings from my stomach, and of course my biggest most embarrassing secret the nighttime rapes. The pain, the smells, the brutality will follow me the rest of my life. My body is in constant pain from the slightest movements or touch. All I have is time for sleep and reflection and a hope that the pain will soon just go away.

This whole present prison mess began on the day of my arrest. All hell started breaking loose shortly after my Swedish American wife Maia prepared for work. Later that same day, we were to depart Kuwait for our annual Christmas vacation back to the United States. We were booked on a late evening Air France flight from Kuwait City to Paris, then on to Savannah, Georgia, via New York. We were so excited. It was December 7, 1995, a day that will forever live in my infamy.

In Georgia, my mom was scheduled for heart surgery as soon as she became strong enough. Aunt Ethel was awaiting our arrival in New York for a quick visit there first. We'd try to make it home before mom's operation so Maia and I would be able to help take care of her and Dad. Hopefully, the surgery would be soon, so we'd be home during part of Mom's recuperation.

Maia and I never take more than a month holiday in the U.S. because I work for a foreign government, which makes me tax free. Maia pays U.S. taxes because she works for the American Embassy. The thirty days time limit doesn't apply to her.

It looked like this holiday season was going to be especially busy for us and we looked forward to being around all our loved ones. Our bags were already packed and we'd made arrangements for Samir Yousef, a great twenty six year old Lebanese friend of ours who has a liberal work schedule to look after our penthouse and the cats, here in Salmiya, Kuwait.

Samir looks a lot like American movie star George Clooney but is probably a foot shorter. Working for his grandfather's clothing company allows him the freedom of arranging his work schedule in any way he wants. He can stay at our place and use it as his personal bachelor's pad at night and he can return several times during the day to check on our three cats Eric, Sweetie and Baby.

I had a day off on December 7, electing to start my vacation the day before, December 6; but Maia still had to put in a few hours at work. Like the start to all other mornings, the Islamic Call to Prayer blared over the loud speakers from all the mosques throughout the city. Just before dawn they called out "Allahu Akbar, Allahu Akbar,"—"God is Great, God is the Greatest," and other than a bit more dust than usual in the air, the day seemed just that.

With the rising sun not yet coming over the horizon, tens of thousands of local Muslims were awakening for their earliest of five daily prayers. Following the religious rituals of washing up and praying, they'll hit the bed again for a short nap before rising for the day.

While I continued sleeping, Maia got up and dressed, covered her honey-blond hair with an Islamic head scarf, leaned over, and kissed me goodbye. The chauffeur then took her to work as usual. That kiss was the last moment I would see my wife for a long time.

Several hours later, I received a telephone call asking if I'm Charles Petty, and would I tell the man on the telephone how to get to my apartment. I said, "Yes, I'm Charles Petty, but before I give my address over the telephone, which are you and what the purpose of this call is?" He replied he is a policeman and I have an unpaid parking ticket he wants to collect personally. That sounded very fishy to me and I responded. "That's not true." "I've never had a parking ticket in Kuwait, and I can't believe a policeman would come to my home to collect the fine." He continued demanding I meet with him, so I agreed but several doors away at the taxi office, not our apartment.

I had a strange sixth sense, and warning bells went off in my head. The day Maia and I had feared for a long time was about to happen. Will today be a repeat of the standoff in the Crown Princes' office a while ago, immediately following my return to Kuwait from seeing the New York senator? In that one, all was well that ended well. The whole intense incident lasted a few hours, while the National Guardsmen surrounded me. That showdown ended when I agreed to vacate the main position I held at Dasma Palace, that of giving the Crown Prince an occasional intelligence briefing, which should have been done by a Kuwaiti anyway.

One topic of the conversation that morning in His Highness's office still remains fresh in my mind. While surrounded by all the National Guardsmen, the Crown Prince sort of made a statement and a question at the same time. He said, "I have been told that you have been taking documents from this office for your personal use. Is it true? "I said "Yes" without further elaboration. He jockeyed momentarily with a former advisor to His Highness the Emir and a good friend of mine, Issa al Asfoor, then again began addressing me. "You can't read Arabic well enough to understand what's here. How many documents have you copied? "My reply shocked him a little and reddened his round, black cherub face. "Everything," I said, again without elaborating. "How did you get out of this office with any of my files?" he said. "First of all," I told him, "I didn't have to leave with all the documents under my shirt. Some I did take out that way while others I copied and faxed." After all, he should have realized, as I did, that he owned probably the best fax machine in the country as well as the best copy machine in the world.

I sheepishly replied, "have you ever checked your phone records or seen any of these same guards frisk me?" Surely he hadn't, and they wouldn't have dared; I had been to most of the Guardsmen's weddings, births of their children, and wept with them over a dead family member's body. Why would they ever search me? I'm sure mental wheels in that room kept churning for a long time, but the incident was over and points made, so we both moved on after the intelligence briefing decision was made and accepted.

On the morning of December 7, before I met the strange caller, I called the United States Embassy and told Maia what the man said, and how strange I felt about the way the man phrased his questions. Maia knew of the tension between the Minister of Information and me, and warned me to be careful. We had heard many times of foreigners inside Kuwait being met by Kuwaiti secret police and never being seen again. Surely those were just stories. I proceeded downstairs to wait within the walled area below our building, to see who arrived at the nearby taxi office. I hadn't seen anyone go into the office yet, but I did notice a car with two Kuwaitis sitting in the parking lot across from it.

Since I'd been the target of a car bomb attempt several months earlier, which was probably tied to my snooping, I had remained extremely cautious. Now, I had that cold feeling something was very wrong. I waited till the taxi office manager stood in his doorway before walking toward him, making sure he saw me. "Salamu alaykum—alaykum salaam," we greeted each other, finishing up with the regional expressions, "slonik, kaif halik."

Several men opened their car doors and began running toward me. I dove into the taxi office, where I grabbed a telephone and dialed Maia's number at the American Embassy. As soon as she answered, I hollered our own secret code word, "SWEEP!" The last thing I heard before the men tackled me was Maia's scream.

CHAPTER 4

Bail Denied

Mine and Ghassan's bail hearing was denied, which to the Kuwaitis meant more than it should have. For them it must have signaled the "go-ahead" to begin putting us through the rigors of prison life. All was well, so to speak, or at least it seemed so until later, shortly after midnight. Three Kuwaiti prison guards entered our brightly lit cell and gently encouraged me to stand and come with them. Before exiting the lock down unit's second set of iron security doors, one of the security guards bent down to shackle my feet in irons while another pulled handcuffs from the back of his trouser waistline and clamped them around my wrists.

Walking in chains for me was not without its limitations, but I continued trying to keep step with my uniformed escorts through the main entry hall and then out the front doors. I thought to myself, "Was this the night my captors would take me for my last car ride in the desert, or could there be some other reason for this midnight rousting?" Once in the parking lot of the Criminal Detention Center, I was led towards two cars; one I assumed was a CID (Secret Police) car, the other was undoubtedly one of the burgundy colored, armor plated, Royal motorcade vehicles, and often seen escorting upper members of Kuwait's Royal Al Sabah family through the streets of Kuwait City.

Somewhat relieving but still puzzling was why I hadn't been shoved inside one of the waiting vehicles, but rather positioned face down over the trunk of the other, plain white vehicle, instead. My pants were quickly unzipped and dropped around my shackled ankles. "Bend over" is common terminology between Kuwaiti men, yet I felt sure that for me they had something else in mind. Either way, with the reputation of Kuwaiti men for sex with other men and boys, no phrase starting with "bend over" could be good.

The foremost thought in my mind was obviously not the same as those of the white robed CID men. They had a little surprise for me that created quite a skirmish between me and two of the CID secret policemen. With their assistance, someone resembling a doctor came along and offered up a double-handful of syringes for one of them to hold. The first of at least twelve that I was administered that night contained a yellowish substance, almost the urine color. For the next few seconds the pain was so great I wasn't sure which would have hurt worse, that syringe or an Arab suitor.

It took more than a minute for the syringe's content to be fully emptied into my buttocks, and it felt as though a hive of bees had just opened me up to lay their larvae. The process continued over and over again until my buttocks had become quite numb but somehow still in great pain. Fears raged within me as I wondered the truth, what this Arab-Nazi like doctor had just given me AIDS, cancer, tuberculosis, and other diseases, as he had smilingly told me following each needle he drove beneath my skin? This was one ugly look at Kuwaitis I had always heard about but never seen.

With a pat to my rear and a few chuckles from the so called doctor, who obviously loved his job, I was carried semi-unconscious to my cell. As if I didn't already have enough to think about before, now I had to worry about surviving prison and taking home a disease that could sooner or later take its toll on me or my family.

My body riveted and quaked as the contents of the now-emptied syringes rushed through my blood stream. The contaminants seemed to heat and expand as they raced towards my heart and brain. All the languishing pain was soon followed by feelings of exhilaration and euphoria, and finally with an awkward sleep. My thoughts the next morning were at first clouded by some dizziness and incoherence; however, my mental clarity resumed shortly after and I was able to refocus on the circumstances that had lead up to my incarceration and the predicament I was in now.

Only a year ago, Maia and I were having the most exciting time of our lives and surely even greater years were still to come. We were on our way to having everything we ever wanted for ourselves. There was money, travel, excitement and intrigue. I had become a trusted insider to Arab politics and power in the Middle East, and enjoyed all the privileges that came with it.

Within the confines of my office, Arab wire services spat out their regional news while Intelligence agencies gave me files with secret satellite photographs and messages to review. Not two but three Governments requested my ground observations and I was both directly and indirectly in the employ of the Kuwait Royal Family, who were also the recipients of the majority of my labors. In those days, I led a clandestine parallel life right before everyone's eyes, including our closest friends, and I enjoyed it immensely.

To most people I was the radio broadcaster they heard three times a day reading the news, weather, and sports on Kuwait's Super Station FM 92.5. To others, I was the go between intelligence services and the country's Royal Family. To one of Kuwait's Royal Family Ministers, I was chief political writer and censor of news; yet for the other, I carried out minor covert intelligence operations against Saddam Hussein inside Southern Iraq. Kuwaitis helped my career and in return I helped them.

During that same spoofing and sleuthing time period, Maia and I had a tightly woven group of friends with whom we shared both good times and bad. Many of our friends were from faraway exotic places on the other side of the world while others like Barbra, Betty and Linda were from back home in the United States. It was with these friends we partied, traveled, celebrated, and cried. They're people we hope to have the pleasure of knowing for the rest of our lives. It is from these very same friends and from others with whom we worked that Maia and I have continued to hide the real reasons we remained in Kuwait long after danger warnings sounded.

Looking even further back into my past, prior to these seven and a half years in Kuwait, life has been anything but a straight road forward. Since my wimpiest days of childhood, I have packed in more than one lifetime; from a pansy to a cactus flower; from that once easily intimidated youth to the brazing mercenary I've now become.

20/20 hindsight is indeed clearer. With all the time I now have on my hands during confinement in jail, there's plenty for reflection. Now I can more clearly see all that's passed and possibly much of what's to come; maybe it'll be a long life of filth and hardship in an Arab desert prison, or perhaps a short life and quickened death by abandonment in the drifting sands surrounding this moneyed kingdom. Maybe it'll be the quickest remedy yet, beheading. Illegal in Kuwait? Aren't many other things? Like the infidels from the West that they so despise, Kuwaiti Muslims do whatever they wish; they just condemn others who do it more openly.

Until now there had been little time for retrospection of the man I am, or how I got to this point in my life. I didn't just one day leave my upbringing in Savannah, Georgia, and end up the next day dining with members of Royal families and partying in their palaces or aboard their yachts. I've had to pay my dues and even do a little selling of my sole to get this far.

I've never been thought of being brilliant or terribly smart. I was never qualified to boost the oil production of Kuwait or any other country, or to advise Middle Eastern rich sultans on investments or banking or anything else. However, in one of life's strange ironies, I've become a man who straddles two worlds, trusted in one where I have no allegiance, and living far away from the other where I owe and fully pledge my loyalties.

How strange it seems even to me that I've been able to go further and accomplish more in a place that one day will probably be enemy territory than at home, in my own back yard, so to speak. Keeping this in mind, I've worked alongside Kuwaitis, getting to know them and the way Arabs think and act. The longer I stayed within their midst, the more untrustworthy and deceptive I found many of them to be. My catering to their needs and doing their dirty work must be akin to an Islamic Fundamentalist knocking on doors in the United States passing out Seventh Day Adventist literature.

As a young man, I used to hear about Russians being schooled in a town in Siberia where everyone spoke English and lived like Americans, so they could be better spies when they came to the United States for purposes of espionage or whatever. I guess I'm the American version of those spies, except that there was no schooling that prepared me for the kind of life I've been living here. I just learned a few words of Arabic before coming to Kuwait and really knew nothing more about the people or their economy beyond that there was enough money to go around. Purely and simply I came to Kuwait to make money. Who knew in what direction that would lead? I thought I would come to Kuwait for one year then go back to America to the same life style I had left, hopefully with more financial security than I ever had before.

Perhaps if I had known several years ago what I would be doing now, I would have trained better, including finishing a university. Certainly, no job I ever had before taught me how to gather intelligence or kiss Royal butts.

Some of my past jobs included being a Sports Director on the cruise ship M/S Boheme in the Caribbean, Second Purser and Assistant Cruise director on the Song of Norway and Sun Viking cruise ships out of the Port of Miami. I also owned Grand Canyon State Tours and Convention Services in Arizona. All were exciting but nothing neither earth-shattering nor remotely resembling what I've been doing in Kuwait. Only during my time in the United States Air Force had there been anything in my life that foreshadowed a future in foreign intrigue.

While in the United States Air Force, my first exciting job was to get between a Turkish Chinese spy called Ikute and our military soldiers working at TUSLOG Headquarters in Ankara. That was around 1969. I had to befriend him and feed disinformation to him all the while carrying out my real job, which was supplying parts for communications and troposphere radar sites around Turkey. Just before the end of my four year hitch in the Air Force, I fell into a serious situation involving the attempted overthrow of the Turkish Government by the Dev Gen party. One of the anti-American acts in that attempt was the kidnapping of several of my close military friends, who at the time were returning from work at a secret communications site on Dikman Hill near Ankara. I guess you can say that from there things went downhill for all-American military personnel in Turkey. We stood by as their Government fell. From then on, though, I was hooked on the excitement and risk of living on the edge so I began seeking it out at every opportunity.

Following my four years enlistment in the United States Air Force, I went to seek fun and fortune in another direction; a life totally unfamiliar to me that might also involve the joy of travel. I persisted and got what I wanted though I had no particular skills to offer or qualifications needed for my new jobs. I was however persistent and presented myself well to those who were to employ me.

When I left the Air Force, I went to Miami, Florida, where I decided to work on luxury cruise ships in the Caribbean. I had never been on a ship bigger than a nine foot row boat, but as I watched the ships leaving the Port of Miami for several days, I knew that was exactly what my next job would be.

First, I did the same as everyone else. I applied for jobs at all the major cruise lines offices. None called me back, so it was time for more drastic action. Someone once said to me, "If you want something bad enough, you'll stay in their face until they're forced to at least to consider you." I had also heard, "If you want to get a job a lot of other people also want, you have to do something different that will draw positive attention to yourself."

My personal appearance was neither uglier nor more handsome than other people's applying for the same jobs. If anything, I wasn't as intelligent as them nor did I have as many qualifications as they had but I possessed two things they didn't, "balls" and "drive."

I decided to be different from everyone else by researching names of owners of ships and their top executives to find out whether any of them lived in the Miami area or not. I then started my door knocking campaign. Most doors were slammed in my face while saying, "What right have you got coming to my house looking for a job on my ship?!" "If you want to work for me, go to the office and fill out an application like everyone else." This went on for several days and a number of doors until I hit the right one.

I'll never forget it. A man by the name of Rafael Ordonez lived in Coral Gables, a suburb of Miami that I was only slightly familiar with. Fortunately or not, I approached his door about ten o'clock in the evening. Mr. Ordonez answered the door himself. I said, "Mr. Ordonez, I'm Charles Petty and I'm here for a job on your ship." He gave the same response as all the others, but I could tell he was laid back sipping a cocktail, so I didn't recede with the "No" answer. I said, "You may think I'm crazy but I don't care." "I'm starving and in need of a job desperately. I want to work for you." He replied, "You don't look like you're starving." I said, "OK, you got me on that one but I just got out of the Air Force, so I'm not starving yet but will soon."

Mr. Ordonez asked, "Have you ever worked on a ship before?" I said, "No," to which he said, "How do you know you won't get sea sick and throw up all over the passengers?" I answered, "I'm a born Viking with Norwegian heritage and I wouldn't dare get sick." He returned, "You're crazy." I said, "Probably, but I want a job so much, I'll even swab your ship's decks after hours for it."

Rafael Ordonez said, "Are you looking for a job as a purser or what?" "Yeah. That's it," I answered. He said, "What skills do you have for purser duties?" I said, "OK, you got me on that one too; I don't even know what a purser is." He said, "You're a real nut case. What makes you think I should hire you? "I said, "Because I have a tremendous desire to work on a cruise ship, and I promise I'll do my very best." Mr. Ordonez resumed, "Charles sometimes in life you have to lie just a little bit. You've already told me you can't do any of the jobs on my ship, so I'd be a fool to hire you."

Mr. Ordonez thought for a minute and said, "You have been overseas for a while in the military; did they ever teach you how to use a camera and develop film or join a camera club or anything like that?" I said "Yes." He said, "Charles, you're lying to me." I followed with, "Yes, and I got it from a good source that I should do so." He said, "If you can learn photography as quickly as you've learned how to play me, I guess I've got a new assistant photographer." Of course, I was elated when told to report to the Port of Miami at the Commodore Cruise Lines office on Thursday. I'd be sailing that afternoon.

Mr. Ordonez told me he had a photographer named Argentino Boo. He was a great photographer but lousy in public relations. If a woman said, "Sir, I wasn't wearing that dress the night that this photograph was taken," Tino would tear the picture up or tell her she was a "stupid bitch with a bad memory." I was to intercede whenever possible, while following Tino around like a puppy dog, learning everything I could about the photography concession on the M/S Boheme.

When I got on the ship, Tino was thrilled he had a new assistant, and showed me where the dark room and film were located below deck. Within a few hours I was to return to the dark room, load the cameras and come up for the "bon voyage." At that time we'd take pictures of passengers coming aboard the gangway and standing on either side of a life preserver with the ship's name on it. In a few days these pictures would be for sale.

As the ship pushed away from the dock, I panicked because it was time to be taking the "bon voyage" pictures. I hadn't been able to find my way back below decks to the dark room, much less gather up the cameras and load film into them, to shoot gangway pictures. I resolved the matter by hiding in my room until the ship was well off the coast of Florida, and the evening's dinner was over. I figured I'd at least get one free cruise out of it, even if Tino fired me right away.

As expected, Tino was very angry when he found me. He was about five feet four inches tall, and foaming at the mouth. With his dark hair, he looked like a cross between Clark Gable and Daffy Duck. I just started hysterically laughing at this little guy spitting out ten dollar vulgar curse words in English, which was his second language. He said, "You're fired and you can get off the ship when we get to San Juan." I said, "You can't fire me, Tino; I was hired by Rafael Ordonez and he told me you were a little bastard with a foul mouth that's costing him money in the photography concession."

Tino said, "He told you that?" I promptly replied, "He did, but Tino, he also said, you're the best photographer he's ever had, but you need to wear a muzzle." He wondered, "Why did he tell you something like that?" I said, "It's quite obvious, Tino. If you teach me how to load those cameras, take pictures and develop them, I'll always assist you well. I'll also walk between you and any customer you're getting ready to eat up. Deal? "He said, "OK," and we got along great from then on.

Within a few months Tino was taken off for an emergency Appendectomy and I had no trouble running his entire concession. I was, however, very happy when he finally returned and retook much of the workload from me. We stayed friends for the short while we worked together, but for some reason he always called me Mike, even after I visited him years later at Discovery Cruise Lines out of Fort Lauderdale, Florida, where he was an Operations Manager while Rafael Ordonez owned the company.

One of my two brothers later remarked how lucky I was to have such a good job with great pay, and to wear tuxedos and tennis outfits and getting to sunbathe on beautiful sandy beaches in the Caribbean and South America. I reminded him that there was indeed a little luck involved in that job, but the fact was that no one picked my name out of a telephone book five hundred miles away and announced I'd be the next Assistant Photographer and Assistant Cruise Director of a Luxury Cruise Ship out of Miami. Later, of course I did just that; becoming in that order Assistant Photographer and Assistant Cruise Director for one of the largest Cruise lines in the world.

Through all my faults and inexperience, it was my ability to surmise a situation quickly and act upon it that always got me where I wanted to go, with Rafael Ordonez or with a Turkish spy or a Sheik in an oil rich Arab kingdom. My creativity and bluffing got me there, whether I qualified for the new job or not.

Many years later, similar approaches thrust me straight into the middle of some very important and influential Kuwaiti all male discussion groups, where toppling the present Emir was discussed, as was reigniting another Gulf War between Kuwait's western allies and Iraq's Saddam Hussein.

I first became valued at Dasma Palace and the Crown Prince's offices for my uncanny ability to make fast accurate observations and then act on them with finesse and fairness as though each party won. I inadvertently saved a few Royal asses and even managed to patch up differences between a few of them who had been feuding for quite a while. A year or so later, I was readily accepted at the Ministry of Information for doing what they said Americans do well, "speaking straight." I became part of reorganizing, writing, and broadcasting radio news and weather and sports shows to Kuwait's English speaking community: the British, Americans, Australians, Indians, many Europeans and young Kuwaitis.

The perks from knowing Royals just kept getting better: yachting weekends, cash, and more personal contact with some of Kuwait's Royals, their residences and their trips. To them I became a sounding board on Americans' thoughts in politics, morality, the Middle East, Arabs in general and knowledge of great vacation destinations.

I had become close with His Highness the Emir's advisors, the Crown Prince Designates office, and many Ministers. They trusted me to speak my mind but with diplomatic restraint when certain persons were involved. I traveled with them to meetings in Switzerland, France, and Beirut. Some of the so called "meetings" in Monte Carlo, Cairo, Hong Kong, Bangkok, Singapore and Manila were more play times than business.

In the beginning, my desk in Dasma Palace was in an office wing, not even in the same building as His Highness the Amir; and it was left out in a hallway alone at that. Later, as I became more trusted, I was more included in the all male Diwaniya discussions and moved to better and better desks, finally making it across the courtyard, into His Highness' office building, the Amiri, and better yet; into an actual office. I could only go up from here.

Any time a Kuwaiti proposal that needed American approval or at least notification was formulated by the Emir or his top Ministers, I was brought in, and it was read and talked about to me first. Often I would tell them their presentation was unclear, or their written proposal was in all English words, but due to their phraseology, it didn't make any sense to me. They would continue refining the copy, often with me at their side, until it satisfied all of us. Even if a meeting was held among all Arab neighbors or partners, they would ask me to attend. Through me, the Americans and British were kept up to date, and if further clarification was needed, I could help give them a better understanding of what went on at the Arab meeting.

Once, there was discussion whether Kuwait would try to force neighboring Dubai United Arab Emirates to close a "free port" called the Baghdad Dock to the Iraqis. The Iraqis were importing arms from China through that port, whereas some influential Kuwaitis were also using it for less than above board imports as well. Through that same Baghdad Dock yet another Kuwaiti was making a lot of money from deals concerning illegal whiskey. He used leverage with Kuwait State owned oil exports to gain control of several operations there. He was so high up in the government of Kuwait that he was able to reroute Chinese arms shipments through the port of Shuwaikh near Kuwait City, so he could add another tax to the vessel before it continued on to the port of Basra, Iraq, Kuwait's own enemy.

The Iraqis, who were being fleeced, held a negotiation with China once again and rerouted the arms shipments back through the "free port" at Dubai, UAE again eliminating Kuwait. The Kuwaiti middleman was angry that he wouldn't be making money off the shipments, so he pressured his cousin the Emir of Kuwait to cool relations with Dubai until the Iraqis were forced to look for another port, possibly through Iran.

The Americans got word of Chinese arms coming into the region and wanted Kuwait and the Emirates to explain all they knew. The Kuwaitis tried their explanation out on me first. They contended that Kuwait caught the Iraqis trying to purchase arms shipments from China and tried to confuse the issue with a paper chase through ports of several countries. When the Kuwaitis found their port was being used, they forced an end to the arms coming into Kuwait which left the Iraqis little choice but to seek another port. This sounded good to me and was first drafted and then sent through American Embassy channels on to the United States Government.

I would often sit next to the Emir or the Crown Prince and speak with them about reasons Americans felt the way they did about Palestinians, radical fundamentalist movements like Hezbollah, Hamas, and other factions and why radical Islam is scary to us. We agreed and disagreed on a lot of issues but they always enjoyed my perspective. Several times each day I was summoned into someone's office for my opinions.

CHAPTER 5

A Night-Time for Secrecy

It seems as though it was twenty years ago, when in fact, it's been just a little more than five since the good times started rolling for us. Times were good then but are grand now. Money flowed like Maia and I had our own well; marble palaces and embassies were just other places to work and be seen; yachts were where holidays and weekends were spent, unless we were on safari in Africa or on a Royal Indian train roaming the Asian subcontinent. Paris, Rome and Zürich were extensions of home.

It seems like I heard something similar before, "When times were good, they were very good, and when times went bad, they got dangerous." One minute you're atop the world and the next, the world is weighing you down. Anyway, it was back on one of those typical really good days that an advisor under His Highness, the Crown Prince, and Prime Minister stopped for a quick blow of sandal wood on the hookah with me. Nothing seemed out of the norm for a regular searing hot summer day in the kingdom of Kuwait, other than a Kuwaiti was sitting here with me. That could in fact never be an average day because in summer there are no Kuwaitis in their own country. They're oil rich and the palaces they occupy here are but humble digs compared to the ones they live in London, Paris or Cairo. It would be ludicrous for them to endure heat when servants can run their country in their absence. I of course was one of the latter, though pretty high up on the totem pole.

The morning started with the usual call to prayer. The holy men throughout Kuwait raised their voices in homage to Allah. With the calls from every mosque in the city still echoing in my ears, I heard a knocking at our Penthouse door. I rarely have one, but today was my day off and I was still sleeping in. Even rarer was to see a Kuwaiti at my door this early. It was the advisor to His Highness the Crown Prince, Abuhalif, who came in and sat nervously awhile with me before asking if I'd care to attend a meeting in Jeddah, Saudi Arabia. A whole delegation of Kuwaitis would be attending. Since most of the attendees will be arriving from other destinations, there will be room on the plane for me, and there may even be a side trip elsewhere, following Jeddah.

From the sound of the invitation, I thought it may be a day of meetings in Jeddah with a big party at gambling casinos in Cairo or relaxation in Geneva to follow. It had been awfully hot in Kuwait this summer, well over 120 degrees Fahrenheit most days, with the occasional dust moving through from the Southwest; so I could enjoy a little rest and recreation, though Maia had to stay and work.

Since coming to the Middle East, it was fairly common for Maia to go for dress fittings in Hong Kong or Paris with the girls, while I would join the boys on their forays to different parts of the world. After all, these are Muslim countries and these are my Muslim coworkers and counterparts, and the way they do things.

Repercussions from this late July 1990 "meeting" would be felt by millions of people around the world. But, of course, I had no way of knowing this beforehand. I had been in the service of the Royal Family in one position or another for about a year and a half. I was not briefed on the reason for the Jeddah meeting nor its participants ahead of time, which really meant nothing to me. They never let me in on a lot of the venues or happenings before time. It was always, SURPRISE; we thought you would enjoy this.

I remember doubting there would even be a meeting at all, because many of our other excursions had also been slated as "meetings" but turned out to be surprise destination "parties"; so I just packed my clothing and boarded the private Royal Kuwait Airways jet, "Kazimah," that had been readied on the tarmac nearest to the Royal Reception Terminal of Kuwait City's International Airport. I carried aboard one small briefcase and a gym bag. Inside my other travel bag, in the luggage compartment below was a tuxedo, several sport jackets and all the accessories I might require for meetings or frolicking.

It was an unceremonious departure even though the country's second Royal was to be aboard. Just outside the Royal terminal looking toward the tarmac was less than a full company of Kuwait National Guardsmen in attendance and even less Color Guard. Just minutes after my boarding, His Highness and several Ministers arrived and quickly made themselves at home within the sitting lounges of the forward compartment. Conference rooms, offices and the more private quarters are on the upper level; but for now the Crown Prince and others stayed below.

To my amazement, the number of Kuwaiti Ministers and Royals among us this day while temperatures soared under the rare shade tree to 125 degrees Fahrenheit meant that something was amif. The red carpet had been rolled up and the auto driven staircase pulled away seconds after His Highness boarded. Though the control tower warned of take off problems that could arise from the extreme heat on the tarmac, the "go-ahead" was still given. I guess they figured that whether it would take five thousand feet of runway or one third of the desert floor to lift off, there was really nothing in the way of His Highness's jumbo jet. The engines reached their high-pitched scream and we taxied out and up.

The more than two hour flight to Jeddah, Saudi Arabia from Kuwait City had been uneventful and unrehearsed, as though the meeting we were to attend, if any; was relatively unimportant. His Highness the Crown Prince and Prime Minister, Sheik Saad al Abdullah al Salem al Sabah, who headed our contingent, never returned to the forward cabin during the entire flight. Most of the Ministers and close friends aboard spoke naturally, not tense; several even nodding off for a few minutes sleep.

One of the only times I spoke during the flight was while being instructed in protocol. I was to make myself a little scarce after landing in Jeddah, because I was not cleared for entry by King Fahd's declaration. I just relaxed and leaned back in the oversized crème color leather recliner and waited for the bevy of Kuwaiti flight hosts to cater to their most important guests, then closed my eyes and slept most of the flight.

During the flight, His Highness had a continuous flow of visitors from our cabin up to his suite but I wasn't one of them. I barely woke to see several of his friends on their way back to retake their seats before landing.

The Crown Prince is the picture of an Arab sheik. He's never seen in western clothing, only traditional flowing Middle Eastern robes. He's a big man, considered kind-hearted and often jovial, but he does have physical problems, the heart being one of them. He is very dark-skinned, fiftyish, with a jolly round cherub's face, but sporting a non-cherub-like black mustache. He stands about five feet ten inches tall, weighing in around 235 pounds, of which about forty is overweight. Both illnesses and weight make him tire easily. There have even been rumors of colon problems and diabetes. Usually, once His Highness sits down, he's there for some time. He's a very gentle man, a kinder and more loved man than the Emir. At times he shows biting humor that is also quite unlike the more reserved Emir.

I personally like watching the Crown Prince and Prime Minister at State functions because of the regal way in which he carries himself. My favorite time being around him is when he's reviewing the troops or walking through reception lines on the tarmac of some nation's airport where he's a pro, disguising his shortness of breath and still appearing as though the future head of state should look. His appearance is more the part of a world leader than the Emir whose posture and gait are extremely poor. The Crown Prince may be fifteen to twenty years younger than His Highness the Emir but they are even further worlds apart in their differences.

The seventy year old Emir has dyed black hair, very black eyebrows, a mustache and a goatee. His posture is abominable and whether walking or sitting, he slumps forward. A terrible unintentional comparison of his piercing eyes is to Charles Manson for those who might recall him from the 1960s or 1970s.

During formal receptions or gatherings, both His Highness' The Emir and The Crown Prince always wear brown state robes with real gold brocade trim with full matching brown transparent muslin over garments which cover their traditional Arab white pantaloons and tee-shirt. In colder months the more traditional dishdasha or flowing robe may be worn under the state robe.

In Jeddah, I waited until His Highness departed the plane, followed in succession by the next most important in Kuwaiti affairs. I followed at the rear, barely making it to the motorcade's last car as the police and first cars began departing for Saudi Arabia's Royal Guest Palace.

July 30, 1990, 8:15 p.m., Jeddah, Saudi Arabia. I was soon to find out that the stakes to be played for tonight, here and now, will be more costly than all the poker games played in the history of the world. Where else but a super rich oil nation could host such an event. The Iraqi dictator, Saddam Hussein's henchmen are here too, but everyone else attending will soon wish they weren't.

By evening only a Holy man's cries from a mosque on palace grounds and hundreds of other surrounding mosques echoed through the city breaking the silence. There were no sounds of traffic, no children at play or birds readying their nightly perch. There wasn't even the slightest hint of a breeze to wisp away the sweltering 122 degree heat of the day which by now, 8:30 p.m., had only managed to drop to 106 degrees. Jeddah's streets were quiet except for the occasional scurry of a taxi; not that the people of Jeddah were asleep, because they weren't. Saudis are a night people just like Kuwaitis, but also like Kuwaitis, most Saudis aren't in their own country during summers either. The ones that are home are between dinner and time to go shopping or visiting relatives' homes.

The Kuwaiti contingent and I had arrived through a non-ceremonial gate behind the Guest Palace and were quickly shown to our own full building, a full marble palace unto itself. Ours alone housed an unknown quantity of hospitality suites, each with its own adjoining security quarters, meeting rooms, and of course luxurious accommodations fit for a king, which in this case there would be several.

This evening was to be informal, if you can ever call any foreign diplomatic mission to another country in which you're housed in a palace as such. Many of Kuwait's sixty some delegates meandered between one another's suites for a while, as others freshened up for dinner and our first meeting with some of our hosts. Still, there was no conversation about the reason for our visit nor was there any sign its outcome could have very permanent and devastating consequences.

The evening moved along, with the Crown Prince missing through most of it. I heard later he was being received by several prominent guests from an Egyptian delegation in yet another Palace Guest House here on the grounds.

That night, we dined on foods laid out in chafing dishes, buffet style, but even at eleven o'clock p.m. it was too early for most of the Kuwaitis to eat. A few of them nibbled at the food as I did but we all thought there would be plenty of time for grazing after tonight's meeting, if there was going to be one. Surely, we'd be back to ravage the tables before or around midnight, much more the customary time for eating dinner in the Middle East.

For the majority of us, there was no meeting, so we visited each other for a while before eating and going to our rooms. I couldn't sleep, so I walked the ever unfolding manicured palatial grounds checking out the architecture, fountains, and foliage, but tried not to wander too far. I didn't want to take the chance that a meeting might still happen during these early morning hours without me.

It was during this time alone that I began to relax and sense the refreshing sounds and sights surrounding just one of the many Saudi Family's Royal Palaces. Now that the hustle and bustle has ended and everyone has pretty much gone their own way, the air was cleared of people's sounds. Now, I could start hearing the splashes of cascading water from the numerous sculpted fountains, the sprinkler heads turning on and off after spritzing droplets over probably the only green lawns in the city. I could also now hear the occasional sounds of the high pitched cicadas.

Walking these palatial grounds seemed no different than those at Dasma Palace, Bayan Palace, or the other three palaces in Kuwait, except these seemed to be manned by an awful lot of zealous and touchy National Guardsmen. They weren't pushy or rude, but hardly derelict in their duty of keeping an eye on me. For that matter, guards seemed to be everywhere.

I nonchalantly kept checking out my surroundings while the guards on the rooftops kept checking me out. Several zero-horizon, blue mosaic-tile fountains were interesting as were the poodle-trimmed olive trees nearby. These trees were unusual because in countries like Kuwait and Saudi Arabia where they grow a lot of olives, the trees are deemed more work-horses and producers than landscape artistry. I'd never seen any cut like that in Kuwait.

I had just about turned to retrace my footsteps and get some sleep when I noticed there had been a definite increase in the number of cars and motorcades entering the palace's southern and western gates. From a distance, I could barely distinguish yet another group of automobiles traveling at more than speed limit, as they too approached the side gate. These cars like the others were using only parking lights that barely cut the night's darkness. Also like the others, a majority of the vehicles sped farther down the drive, beyond the Royal emblem gates, while several other sleek black Mercedes' near the motorcade's center gained an almost perfect stealth entry into this privileged domain.

Within a few short minutes, another group of parking lights came toward the same gates. This time several palace security vehicles escorted two more black limousines inside. The limo's tinted windows were as dark as the black paint on the exterior of the car. Even though I couldn't see inside, I had the feeling it was someone of great importance and most likely the reason we were all here.

Once inside, this motorcade like all the others made a brief pause to unload its secret passengers. Also as the others, these guests departed with great haste into the massive ornate-stone carved doorway beyond the port-cu-tiere. The now vacant limousines in quick succession drove farther up the Palace drive and bled into the night.

Every movement went off like clockwork. Each motorcade approached, the Palace's welcoming committee hurriedly received their guests and then their limos rapidly disappeared up the drive. The last two processions, without a doubt carried the most influential people so far; but the arrivals weren't over.

While still a great distance away, I could see rotating red and white lights of police and escort vehicles that were unmistakable. The latest line of more than fifteen cars was approaching at a high rate of speed. The increased activity they caused actually scarred me. Everywhere I looked, everybody was doing something. It was like "lock and load." I pictured in my mind a helicopter suddenly appearing overhead and black ops troops with rifles dropping on rope ladders above me. My heart pounded loudly in my ears.

Once more upon arrival, a bevy of men began exiting the stone doorway, nearest the drive, each at a speed just under a full run. Some began filling their ceremonial positions outside, along the drive. Others remained near the entry, while several headed out as far as the Palace's walls and gate. A group of dark-suited western-style security men, armed with machine guns, exited the doorway and assumed positions on both sides of the driveway's overhanging Ramada. Two persons, one a westerner, the other a Saudi in white dishdasha with red and white Ghutra head covering, stood near the busy gate, speaking into their hand-held radios. With his right hand circling in the air, the Saudi moved quickly to one side, while the westerner backed toward the wall.

Powerful motors glided open the palaces' huge iron gates. Without the loss of precious seconds, two chains of pagoda lights lit both sides of the drive like an air strip. Two fast approaching Saudi police cars flashed their blue lights, then screeched to a diagonal halt, blocking the possibility of oncoming traffic. Behind the regular Saudi police came a steady stream of red and blue flashing lights atop a burgundy-colored Chevrolet Suburban security wagons which continued their parade inside the gates and up the drive toward the palaces' main entrance, where they abruptly halted. Special security agents hurled themselves from each of the security wagon's doors, and then ran towards the now-entering pack of limousines, which comprised the main body of the fifteenth car motorcade. Each limo, in turn, halted adjacent to the building's steps.

The security agents, many of whom carried rapid fire handguns, scrambled alongside the newly arrived limos' passengers and quickly ushered them towards their hosts and the doors that led to the rotunda.

There had been a lack of National or Ambassadorial flags on any of the limos and no hint of who the special guests were. In retrospect, about all I could remember of those arriving was flashes of white robes, armed Saudi militiamen and armed men in western-style suits. So much of what I was seeing this night was reminiscent of motorcades I had seen and been in with the Royal Family of Kuwait, except for the amount of arms surrounding these guests and the zest in which they were hastened inside.

In Kuwait too, Royal motorcades begin with numerous police on motorcycles, then police cars, followed by some of the same style burgundy, Chevy Suburban, steel plated, security wagons that hug both sides of the Royal Family's or guest dignitary's limos. It's customary for the steel-plated Suburbans to flank front, rear and both sides of each limo and travel at their exact same speed, blocking all but a quick glimpse of the long black armor plated cars they protect.

I've had the chance to ride in several of the Kuwait Royal Family's limousines and the specially equipped Chevrolet Suburban escort vehicles used in flanking those Royal entourages. The Suburbans, like the main limos, include an additional three thousand pounds of steel armor plating, and also contain three inch bullet proof windows, tear gas launchers, ignition bomb scanners, non-penetrable gas tanks, and an additional storage place for more weapons.

About the only thing that can successfully "take one of these vehicles out" is a heavily packed outwardly directed explosives launcher with a light beam activated trigger such as that used on November 30th, 1989, against a German Industrialist. A ninety degree target impact carries the most deadly result. Neither the Suburban's nor the limos' armor makes much difference against such a powerful precision strike as that. Two of the more successfully blocked assassination attempts, against Georgian President Eduard Shevardnadze and Sri Lanka's Chandrika Kumaratunga were thwarted due to their armor, though both those vehicles were Mercedes.

Tonight, I'm seeing a larger concentration of such vehicles than in all my past years combined. Something big is happening. This trip is not just a gambling junket to Cairo or Monte Carlo. Whatever is happening has got to be really big.

Now that the streets outside the palace's walls have fallen silent, the temperature inside the palace was starting to heat up. The gathering guests and hosts alike spared little time with salutations, but rather spoke in quieted tones, more like one would do at a funeral.

That night as I lay my head on the pillow, my thoughts contained more questions than answers. What was really going on here and who was really involved?

CHAPTER 6

A Message from Saddam Hussein/ Emergency Jeddah Conference

For the majority of our delegation, including me, the new day, July 31, 1990, didn't begin until mid afternoon. Of course I didn't know that a lot of behind the scenes meetings and communications had been going on earlier that morning, the night before, and for days and even weeks prior.

About three-thirty in the afternoon, a small group of Saudis in traditional flowing white dishdashas came to our Guest House to escort all of us to the Palace Conference Center. Upon entering the Center's massive hewn wooden doors, we came upon the grand foyer. No more wood from here in. Everything discernible was marble, except for side by side father and son portraits of His Highness Prince Abdullah and His Highness King Fahd ibn Abdul Aziz, the monarch and Custodian of the Two Holy Mosques.

In the rooms before us, lay a near sterile environment of nearly five different tones of marble. Upon marble; upon marble. Nothing says "hi honey, I'm home" like marble. Marble floors, marble inlays, marble walls, and marble stairways.

Once we moved through several anti rooms and closer to those where we would join our hosts, the harshness of the décor softened. It was still marble, upon marble but more than half the floors' surfaces were now covered in exquisite, museum quality Persian and Oriental carpets, several depicting scenes reminiscent of horsemen and warriors of the former great Persian Empire to the North.

Several smaller silk Oriental throw rugs of brighter reds, blues, and browns in the adjoining twelve feet wide hallway weren't too shabby either. As several entourages of men walked on them, their thick tightly woven tuft crushed beneath their feet like new snow does under boots. The silks' shine changed hues during each visitor's passing step.

Alas, we reached the actual receiving line. As is the custom in the Middle East, most guests leaned forward and kissed both cheeks of their Arab hosts. A few of those in attendance were Saudi Nationals who easily stood out from the rest. Instead of air kissing His Highness' cheek, they leaned upward as he bent forward and kissed his forehead. I refrained from my instincts and didn't shake hands but rather went with the protocol and air kissed both cheeks while gripping his hands in mine. "Salam Alaycom Your Highness," I said as my turn came.

From another direction, a large crowd of men were following a senior member of the Saudi Royal Family. They meandered towards a large elegantly appointed meeting room. The lead Royal's dishdasha ballooned slightly out as he passed from one room to the other, baring at least a slight resemblance to Marilyn Monroe's famous air vent scene.

Another Saudi Prince, a very young one whom I believe to be the half brother of Abdullah and second in line to the throne, made his way around air kissing. Once again the Arabs paid the "more" respect befitting his position and kissed his forehead, while I shook his hand.

The meeting room we meandered into was grand of course but less so, looking more like an upper end corporate board room.

Glasses filled with orange juice and water was on the usual hospitality table with only a slight difference: there were also gold rimmed Middle East chai glasses for tea. The mid afternoon's sun streaming in crystallized the glassware but garishly accentuated all the silver serving trays that lay atop the banquet table.

The room's richly appointed chairs were ornate, high backed and gold gilded with one inch trim in off silver and burgundy silk that screamed "no expense spared." Like the carpets throughout, all furniture was surely museum quality as well. The largest piece of furniture, a giant six pedestal marble table appeared to weigh half-a-ton or more. The prized imported conference table's pink—and brown feathered marble top was the same as the Palace's magnificent floors and had probably been mined in Pakistan or Iran near the border of Afghanistan where the Emir of Kuwait's most prized marble comes from.

The two towering alabaster torchères, each standing about eight feet tall had shades that were translucent. They allowed only passive light to escape during daylight hours. Instead of drapes, the room's giant multi-pane window was covered floor to ceiling by intricately carved dark mahogany mushrabiya (spooled wood carvings). All in all, everything I'd seen in the entire Palace so far, except for the carved woods was of a perfectly tuned pallet of pastels. While I was visually taking it all in, the security contingent had quietly exited the room.

All guests took their appointed seats along each of the table's sides, about 20 chairs in all. Four chairs remained empty at the far end from our Saudi host, His Highness Sheikh Abdullah ibn Abdul Aziz, the Crown Prince and First Deputy Prime Minister. He is the middle aged half brother to the older King Fahd. Sheikh Abdullah assumed his rightful place at the head of the table. I had been briefed only slightly before entering the meeting room. "Remember," said Abdul Rahman, "Prince Abdullah is really the man in charge in Saudi Arabia and it's he who has most of the power in the country, not the King." Sounded like Kuwait's Crown Prince and Emir to me.

Those in attendance from the Prince's right were one of my bosses, His Highness the Crown Prince and Prime Minister of Kuwait, Sheik Saad Abdullah al Salem al Sabah and three of Kuwait's representatives, including the Minister of Oil, al Ameeri and me. All of us lessers began sitting to the Crown Prince's rear. One of my Crown Prince's Under Secretaries sat to my side. On the other side of the table, to Prince

Abdullah's immediate right were Saudi Arabia's Foreign Minister, Sheik Saad al Feisal and two senior members of Saudi Arabia's Military and Defense Ministries. Continuing along their side of the table was a representative of the Gulf Cooperation Council States, followed by Chedli Klibi, Secretary General of the Arab League, and two members of Jordan's delegation, including that country's Foreign Minister, Marwan al Qasim. The United Arab Emirates' Oil Minister was seated next to Morocco's President Zine el-Abidine Ben Ali. Finishing out our side of the table was the Egyptian delegation. Their President Mubarak was pretty much the emergency sessions' organizer along with King Hassan of Morocco, who was also attempting to play a significant role. Most of Kuwait's other sixty members had earlier been escorted to a room across the hall where they waited.

There were, of course, several other persons in our meeting room assuming chairs behind and to the outside of the table's prominent participants, the same as me. Some of them were to take notes, some, like me, probably just to bear witness, while others would use stenographic machines and tape recorders to preserve the meeting for posterity. I never found out exactly where I fit in or why I was included, probably one of those just to bear witness.

I looked around the room trying to place who everyone was. It helps in the Middle East to know what color head scarves or ghutra, each wears in his land of origin. In most cases, red and white check is Saudi and Emirates, pure white for Kuwait, black and white for Jordanians and Palestinians and so on. Next I listened for how each person was addressed during introductions.

A hushed silence fell over the room when His Highness Prince Abdullah began speaking. He began by welcoming each one personally for their attendance and bid Allah give all those present strength to see this meeting through to a peaceful solution. Prince Abdullah conveyed best wishes to each attendee from Saudi Arabia's Ruler, His Highness, Fahd ibn Abdul Aziz, Custodian of The Two Holy Mosques.

The Prince began speaking; first, Prince Abdullah asked all participants to be prepared to stay within these humble confines for as long as it takes to resolve this most disturbing issue. He said, "Please, there should be no interruptions for a while as I help you become more aware of why you have been summoned here today."

Of the two men standing to the rear of Prince Abdullah, one leaned forward placing several documents into his hands and then returned to his upright position. After glancing briefly at the top paper, Prince Abdullah said, "Four other persons will join us now. Bear with me while they present this serious problem in their own words. I ask that all of us remain as restrained as possible but begin entertaining ways we may all work together." He nodded his head and immediately the second gentleman in white dishdasha and black and white check ghutra moved forward through the room towards a door at the far end. As though at a funeral, this man spoke in quieted tones to four gentlemen who were now entering. He then escorted the men, two of whom were wearing military uniforms, and others in dishdashas, to their awaiting chairs. Now we were really getting down to business and finding out about all those other mysterious arrivals and security.

Iraq's President Saddam Hussein's group of four was led by Izzat Ibrahim al Doori, Vice Chairman of the Revolutionary Command Council, who was followed closely by Saadoun Hammadi, Iraq's Deputy Prime Minister and two others I didn't recognize. Rather than sit, al Doori paced back and forth closely behind his chair. When the mustached Iraqi stopped pacing, he began leaning against the table with his hand balled into a fist.

Al Doori began speaking firmly but with a slight tremble in his voice. He gave his regards to all those in attendance and then said, "Allah's presence this afternoon in this room will help right a terrible wrong to the poor people of Iraq."

Saddam Hussein's messenger personally eyed each of his Arab brothers but more quickly glanced past each of us lesser journeymen further away from the table before glancing back towards his own fellow countrymen.

"I have no time to waste on salutations and condolences. Time is running out." He came straight to the point, in sharp contrast to the way Arabs usually speak. Staring directly at his Saudi host, al Doori said, "We have a tremendous problem here. I have been told by my President Saddam Hussein to tell you that our troops are on the border of Kuwait. We have tens of thousands of men prepared to enter and to overtake that country. Many of you at this table are no doubt aware of the massive buildup of which I speak. Some of you in this room know through spy plane capabilities from your western allies that this is true. Most of you also know my President is a man who has the ability to carry out his will."

"This day, I bring you the solemn message that in three days time our armed forces will march into Kuwait, annihilating anyone and anything in our path. I pray you don't dismiss my President's warning."

Al Doori then began a long rambling speech about oil and stolen wealth by a brother nation who rationed out a pittance of welfare in return. He said, "This brutal thievery has continued unabated for more than twenty years. Kuwait has always managed to buy silence and subservience by returning tiny sums for Iraqis to look the other way. Your Muslim brothers and sisters suffer while Kuwait stuffs their coffers at their expense. Kuwait with their superior technology and financial capabilities has not only drilled their lucrative oil fields in the North, but has tapped those of the poorer, less educated people on the other side of the border inside Iraq." Now looking directly at His Highness Kuwait's Crown Prince and Prime Minister, he said, "First you drilled your own wells; then with each new technical advance, you found ways to drill laterally and then horizontally far into the rich fields of Iraq." He then rambled some recent wording Saddam Hussein had used during his now infamous meeting a week earlier with American Ambassador April Glaspie about "his people bleeding rivers of blood."

By now the somewhat embarrassed Kuwaitis at the table looked downward as if a horrendous secret had been let out of the bag. Immediately when the Kuwaitis saw the Iraqis, they thought the subject matter would be quite different than it was. The tables for once were turned.

Next, al Doori went on with admonishments to all Arab brotherly states that his country and his country alone fought a hard victorious battle against Iran for eight years. This battle against fundamentalism was in the interest of all Arab states, especially in the Gulf region and Saudi Arabia. "Now, what does Iraq get for it; each one of you is now demanding repayment of contributions given to Iraq during that time of crisis. The United Arab Emirates and Kuwait in particular have once again slapped the Iraqi people in the face by overproducing their oil, cutting its price at the world market place and taking food from our children's mouths. Your overproduction alone damaged the Iraqi economy by more than a billion dollars a year in lost revenues; yet Iraq is still expected to repay war loans."

Of course this was old hat to the Kuwaitis; they had heard it all before but not so dramatically, and in such a dressing down fashion in front of such a distinguished audience. All the talk at this meeting, as well as all the speeches, admonishments and threats for the past several months, boiled down to the Iraqis finally coming to the table. However, they did not come to bargain, but rather to find out how much other Arab nations were ready to concede both to Iraq's new role as dominant power in the Middle East and to Iraq financially. There probably was never any doubt in the Iraqi President Saddam Hussein's mind that the invasion of Kuwait was already "on."

Iraq was ten billion dollars in debt and Saddam Hussein's game of chess had begun in earnest on May 28, 1990, with a war of words and tactical challenges in attempt to unite Arabs. He would begin by using rhetoric phrases against Jews and freeing Jerusalem from Israel. Next he increased border tensions when he warned Kuwait and United Arab Emirates for the first time about their oil overproduction during his July 15, 1990, speech. On that date, a letter from Iraq's Tariq Aziz to Secretary General of the Arab League accused Kuwait of stealing oil from the Rumailah Oil

Fields and encroaching, even over occupying the border between the two countries aliened by the Arab League in 1961.

With little response returning from Arab leaders, he again went on the attack on July 17, 1990. This time Saddam Hussein threatened Kuwait with military action for the first time. The situation was now accelerating rapidly. Just one day later, on July 18, 1990, Saddam Hussein demanded $2.4 billion dollars in compensation and the return of the oil fields from Kuwait (which Kuwait's Cabinet immediately rejected on all terms). On July 22, 1990, Iraqi troops mobilized and headed for the border with Kuwait; President Mubarak of Egypt tried to avoid military action between the two Arab States by shuttling between Iraq, Kuwait and Saudi Arabia.

President Mubarak continued his efforts to stop an upcoming war by getting all parties to meet. The first of such meetings was instigated by the United States at the Presidential Palace in Baghdad. That became came the now infamous meeting between Saddam Hussein and Madam Ambassador April Glaspie of the United States in which the supposed "green light" was given by her for Iraq to invade Kuwait.

During our Jeddah meeting, Iraq's Vice Chairman of the Revolutionary Command Council Mr. al Doori continued his admonishments by trying to drive a wedge between the newly strengthening alliances of Saudi Arabia and the United States. Iraq's al Doori now addressed all those at our Jeddah meeting by paraphrasing Ambassador Glaspie's assurances to Saddam Hussein that the United States would not get involved in such a situation between two brotherly Arab States. He emphasized over and over again that President Bush has made it clear that he desires friendship with Iraq, not confrontation and that Ambassador Glaspie made remarks possibly backing remuneration of funds and properties back to Iraq by Kuwait.

Most of those in the room who heard the words from al Doori later spoke amongst themselves questioning the legitimacy of al Doori's words. Was the American Government actually going to stand by and support such outright extortion and aggression? Who here had access to what was really said at that meeting about a week ago other than Tariq Aziz, American Ambassador Glaspie, and President Saddam Hussein? Could there possibly be an accurate transcript that was kept of that meeting as evidence? Ambassador Glaspie is now back in Washington and may have to be contacted for her personal interpretation if the Iraqi's are unwilling to supply such evidence of the meeting.

Immediately following al Doori's rambling speech, often in tones that Arabs reserve only for warlike conditions, Kuwait's Crown Prince and Kuwait's Minister of Oil appeared truly disturbed but defiant. They looked at each other, spoke only above a whisper to each other and starred at Saddam Hussein's messenger al Doori, then around the table at other participants. My quick glance around the table revealed the Kuwaitis weren't the only ones feeling the tenseness. Most persons present were slightly tapping their pens on the marble table, twitching their necks or rearranging their bodies in the chairs.

Al Doori became stiffer and slightly louder as he continued "I tell you tonight, we are prepared for all out war. We are prepared to destroy the nation of Kuwait if they do not abide by the terms my President gives them in your presence. We demand two billion four hundred million dollars to be set aside immediately through third country governments. It must be secured for the people of Iraq from the coffers of Kuwait. I tell my brother His Highness the Emir of Kuwait Sheik al Ahmad al Jaber al Sabah, this you must do to prevent the chastisement that otherwise will soon follow."

"INVASION." Now I could read it on everyone's face. Invasion had never been a serious consideration before, had it? Most people were now sitting rigidly in absolute silence. Others were fidgeting briefly but no one even reached for the juices, teas, or waters that still sat untouched since the beginning of the meeting. One of the Kuwaiti delegates turned to me and backed his chair slightly from the table as he grasped his crotch and pointed his finger under the table at al Doori. I think this was to signify "Screw the Iraqis."

As fast as Saddam's delegation entered the room, they were gone, with only one of the four Iraqis remaining seated at the table of players. Tariq Aziz's assistant had long been the whipping man for all of Saddam's quests or in some cases, conquests. Tariq Aziz always managed to smooth over all Saddam Hussein's messages before and his assistant was quite adept at handling himself in much the same way. He was trying to put a firm but softer more tolerable edge on the words of his maniacal leader.

The assistant began, "I believe you now see we have a very serious situation at hand. I'll now with the permission of my President give you the timetable for invasion; then I will leave you alone to discuss amongst yourselves what will be the proper outcome of this meeting. I stress to you, Your Highness Sheik Abdullah, you must encourage our Muslim brothers to do what is right. Do not push us into a position that will result in war. Before I leave you in the next minute, I will describe to you what our plans are in the event these monies are not secured."

"We will cross the border of Kuwait within the next 72 hours and proceed to secure Kuwait's Rumailah Oil Fields and the farming communities of Umm Qasr and Abdaly. We will proceed to all Rawdatain Oil Fields and those of Sabahiya and will overrun Kuwait City to seize the very banks that have refused to pay our rightful due. We will obliterate any military opponents that stand in our path and destroy any other encumbrances as they occur. We will remerge Kuwait's territories into the 19th province of Iraq. This I promise you." Saddam Hussein's henchman then rambled some religious paraphrase quite out of context to the situation and then said, "I will return to this table at your convenience."

Prince Abdullah, whose Saudi title is "Sheik," spoke quietly as he looked directly at the representatives from Kuwait. The Sheik used both hands to flip his long red and white head scarf back from both sides of his face to a more comfortable position, like long hair hanging down his back.

This allowed him better visibility out the sides of his eyes especially in the direction of the Kuwaitis. "What is your response?" One Kuwaiti with a strained grin on his face and gritting his teeth nearly chuckled while throwing his head scarf back in much the same manner and said, "What they speak of would be an illegal action, and God, Allah himself will chastise any such act of barbarism against the peaceful peoples of Kuwait."

"There will be no monies now or anytime in the future. No blackmail demands by an aggressive dictator will ever be met. This self important dictator defiles and disgraces the very land and people he rules. We'll answer neither his demand nor welcome his marauding troops if they enter our sovereignty."

He continued saying "I now ask that representatives of Saudi Arabia, Jordan, Egypt, Morocco, and the United Arab Emirates, as well as the Secretary General of the Arab League to assist us in pushing this crazed madman back from our borders."

Within moments, Sheik Abdullah, who is also the head of Saudi Arabia's National Guard turned to the Intelligence community of his own ministries and said, "What are we prepared to do if Saddam's armies cross into Kuwait?" His Generals thought briefly and began speaking quietly together before answering. "Your Highness, it will take months for our troops to be in position to hold back any such incursion. We're totally unprepared at this time and in the near future to prevent such a march into the brotherly state of Kuwait."

Immediately, the Saudi Arabian military General spoke saying that for days and weeks the Americans and British have photographed the Iraqi buildup and their continued movement toward Kuwait's border. He says "for a fact, we know that many missiles are now below the 35th parallel. Armored tank divisions and other heavy artillery are continually being massed and reinforced only miles beyond the entire length of Iraq's border with Kuwait. We believe at this time, as far as Britain is concerned, there's no way of holding Saddam and his forces back."

The General also noted that certain military and diplomatic agreements between the United States and Persian Gulf States haven't allowed any deployment of equipment, troops or weaponry near enough to the region to be of value at this time. It'll take several months at the earliest to force the Iraqis back across the line. This is on the presumption the Iraqis will already be held up in heavily populated civilian areas of Kuwait. It may even take years of intense preparation to keep casualties to a minimum."

There was only one possible solution that could delay Saddam's troops at least for a while. Each attending country could jointly pay for any delay bargained. The discussion then moved back to the table head, Sheik Abdullah who bluntly asked the Kuwaitis again what they could "commit to" today to help themselves. He reiterated, "Time is running out." The Kuwaitis continued sitting steadfastly. One spoke literally restating what they all had said earlier, "Allah will punish those who act in such a barbaric way. We have nothing to say to them and we have nothing to give them. For many years we've given Iraq charity and built those same forces that now threaten us. We provided defense and security for the Iraqi people against the armies of Iran and this is how they repay us."

After a long silence in the room, one of Egypt's representatives spoke up saying, "I believe Saddam Hussein is an evil man to be reckoned with. I believe he will do exactly as he says. I believe my meeting with him earlier did not make clear either his correct intentions or ours. It's best we sit at this table now and come up with a solution and we need Kuwait to be a large part of the remedy." The Kuwaitis continued their silent unmoved stares.

The representative from the United Arab Emirates iterated that all of us were just sitting there repeating over and over in different ways that we know of no other way to break the 72-hour deadline. From the body language around the table that was precisely what was being said. Muffled conversations could be heard around the table. Everyone was speaking to his neighbor, but overall the conversations seemed to be drifting farther from the subject rather than trying to resolve the issue at hand. It was at this point in the dialog that someone raised the question, "What if we give the "go ahead" to Saddam's forces to take the Romailah Oil Fields in Northern Kuwait and allow the Iraqis to hold them and continue pumping and selling oil while the whole matter is taken to the World Court. The matter would not be settled for maybe 4-6 years; during such time the Iraqis would be rebuilding their near stagnant economy and feeding their people. Kuwait would save what could turn out to be a human tragedy in lost lives and economic destruction."

The Kuwaitis couldn't believe what they were hearing and reacted with hostility in their voices and by standing, one literally ripping apart his strand of worry beads while another accidentally knocked his chair over backwards.

A Saudi General spoke to the Kuwaitis, "How would you resolve it; you can't hide it; it's not going away. There is no possible way for our troops or yours or those of several different armies to get into position within two days to block forces of such great numbers. Any such attempt will allow them to be wiped out within hours. This crossing, this invasion into Kuwait's sovereignty, if it happens, cannot be halted."

The Saudi General continued speaking, "You know Kuwait can't even ready its own military forces because most of them are outside the country on holiday with their families thousands of kilometers away. We here in Saudi Arabia are no different. We have the same problem as do all other friendly states in this region. Among all of us present here tonight, perhaps we could only muster half the planes needed to defend Kuwait and perhaps less than half our artillery can be readied for battle. I say, put your militaries on alert, call in your personnel, notify the civilian population of Kuwait, and place whatever obstructions you can in Saddam's path at the border. If enough is there, the Iraqis may reconsider at what cost they want to pursue another war."

"Their eight years war with Iran may have been enough for them and maybe right now they're just saber rattling to get money. If so, we'll have to find a way to barter and delay this deadline. We may then have more time to approach the Iraqis with dialog and diplomatic maneuvering until more military manpower can be brought to the region. At least sit with us now and discuss all options." The Saudi Minister of Defense spoke again and laid it on the line saying to the Kuwaitis, "The time to spend your money is now, while your people and nation are still intact, rather than in a short time you may be mourning your dead and trying to rebuild your nation and its economy. The cost of war will perhaps be as great as the two point four billion dollars, oil fields and forgiveness of debts demanded. In terms of human life, a war is the costliest of scenarios. At what price do you put the lives of your citizens? At what price do you put the lives of the Saudis, Americans, British, French, and others you urge to fight in your place?"

Again the subject of Ambassador Glaspie's meeting with Saddam Hussein was broached and what impression she might have given Saddam Hussein.

Someone at the table asked for further clarification on what Saddam Hussein had spoken of in his televised speeches about "Iraq's oil" being latterly and horizontally pumped and shipped through Kuwait's pipelines. Possibly how many fields is President Hussein talking about? "No one present had the expertise to get detailed with drilling procedures except Kuwait's Oil Minister al Ameeri, who was sitting almost in front of me, but he wasn't speaking. Few persons attending had any doubt Saddam Hussein's claims are not only possible but probable. It's not the first time the Saudis had heard of the situation now being spoken of, but on that last occasion at the Arab League Conference in Cairo the subject seemed inconsequential and fell on deaf ears.

The British discovered the first oil in Kuwait in 1938, and since then the Brits and Kuwaitis have eagerly developed large fields of high quality and quantity together. Research monies are always available for learning and developing the latest in technology toward drilling bigger and better oil fields. These research monies are readily implemented and, yes, there is and has been for a long time lateral and horizontal pumping going on. The Kuwaitis and British are eager to capture as much of the world's oil market as possible. The British have always been obligated to rescue the Kuwaitis from any political situations or antagonisms on their borders but the Americans have always stayed at arm's length.

By now, Kuwait's delegation felt broken and angry. So far nothing had been resolved and they felt hurt, betrayed and as if they had lost their friends and allies. No additional time seemed to be needed; their situation was hopeless. Their Arab allies and even some of the world's superpowers couldn't and wouldn't help, at least for now.

Most of the main players at the table had more than seventy two hours to try to resolve the situation. The Kuwaitis, I found out later, as well as all the others had been informed about the content of the forum beforehand, but few thought it was as serious a situation as it turned out to be.

Some say American Ambassador April Glaspie felt her meeting with Saddam Hussein on July 25, 1990, inside the vast Presidential Palace in Baghdad was only Saddam's way of feeling her out about such a move. According to one of his sons-in-law, Saddam Hussein exited that meeting with Ambassador Glaspie saying that he had given her a lesson in diplomacy the United States won't forget for a long time.

According to Ambassador Glaspie, transcripts from that meeting between her and Saddam Hussein were later delivered to the Reuters Wire Service and Arab Wire Service offices in Baghdad. On the Arab copy, Saddam Hussein himself had highlighted in yellow magic marker remarks made by Ambassador Glaspie which indicated that Washington would not intervene in a conflict between Arab States. Saddam Hussein interpreted this as a "GREEN LIGHT" for the invasion of Kuwait.

Assuming this information was correct; one also had to assume that Ambassador Glaspie said what Washington was feeling. She had probably already spoken with the United States Secretary of State earlier and sounded him out on American views. If this was the case, there had been even more than five days time to know that the situation had already moved into a crisis phase, not that this would have been common knowledge by any means.

Saddam kept his invasion intentions so secretive that Iraq's own Defense Minister later expressed surprise that an invasion by his country was underway, much less having known there was a meeting on the July 25 between Saddam Hussein and Ambassador Glaspie. Iraq's Defense Minister also says he was surprised yet again to find out there had been yet another meeting in Jeddah, July 30 and 31, 1990, which brought together many concerned Arab representatives. Little did he nor I nor many others know that there had been many other out of view meetings held between Arab heads of State, including Morocco's King Hassan II, Palestinians, Turks, Syrians, Jordanians, Egyptians, Emiratis, Saudis, Kuwaitis and Iraqis, many of whom are here in guest palaces meeting amongst us now.

Inside Saddam's own country, he kept most of his true plans secret even from many of his top in command. To most, everything was considered normal, just another build up along Iraq's border with Kuwait. The Iraqi Defense Minister later said that he heard about the actual invasion from radio. Saddam's intent was so classified that only several members of his immediate family knew what was going on. Several of those, including two of the sons-in-law at this meeting were later killed by him. I've been told that one of the sons-in-law was executed shortly after he defected to Jordan.

The Jeddah meeting concluded with the Kuwaitis not wishing to speak on the subject of reparations to Iraq any more. It was time for them to return home, notify their families and take whatever precautions they could: make financial transfers outside the country, get their family members and households to safety, and do a lot of praying. All this had to be done within the next 65 hours and 40 minutes.

Still, that short time frame was not cast in iron. What if Saddam Hussein and his "mad" forces actually started moving well before the set time with preemptive strikes against Kuwait's near sleeping forces? The Kuwaitis at the meeting lost little time in expressing their disappointment with the situation and in all other participants. In a hurried blur of briefcases and white dishdashas, they, with me in tow, exited the conference room. Rapidly on their heels, the remainder of our sixty person entourage followed as ducks lined in search of water. Much had to be done when Kuwait's Crown Prince, Oil Minister al Ameeri and the other sixty delegates to the Jeddah meeting returned to Kuwait City.

We had barely arrived at the Jeddah airport for the return trip to Kuwait when His Highness the Crown Prince and Prime Minister came directly to me. He said "Charles, you and Sheik Al Ameeri's Under Secretary will leave aboard King Fahd's plane immediately to Baghdad. You are to bring me copies from the Wire Service offices in Baghdad of the meeting Ambassador Glaspie had with Saddam Hussein. I'm sorry to say it but this whole invasion thing, if it happens, may lie on her shoulders. If these documents are what they may appear to be, I will hold the United States responsible for any incursion along our border with Iraq or anything else that might transpire from her "green light."

His Highness and the others went their way while the Oil Minister's Under Secretary and I went ours. Both the Saudi Arabian and the Kuwaiti Royal jets were already warming up alongside each other, neither of whom felt time should be lost.

I arrived in Baghdad in the very early morning hours. By the time Diplomatic phone calls and maneuvering had concluded which lined up our transportation into Baghdad and the opening of the Reuters Office to get a genuine copy of Madam Ambassador April Glaspie and Saddam Hussein's meeting, daylight was nearing the horizon. Though al Ameeri's Under Secretary and I slept a little on the flight from Saudi Arabia to Iraq, we were still very tired and wanted to get home. Neither of us wished to waste time in Baghdad.

We barely walked through the doors of Reuters when we were met by three men, one in military clothing, another appeared to be a Reuter's employee and the third probably a cleaning man. Few words were spoken. Brief salutations were uttered, a letter pouch was passed to my right hand, and I reviewed the paperwork briefly before we departed back to the airport in the same transportation that had brought us downtown.

Since there were fourteen hundred members of the Kuwait Royal Family, but few of them inside the country, many tasks from banking to gathering valuables had to be tended to quickly. The few al Sabah family members inside Kuwait had only two and a half days to take care of all tasks for their numerous households.

It's not known whether the decision not to notify the general population was made at this time or who made it or whether it was made shortly thereafter. To this day those in top government positions refuse to answer the question why a command was given to disconnect the Impending Danger Warning or air raid sirens throughout the city and keep the impending invasion secret. Those same sirens had blurred their deafening sounds daily for years in a rehearsal for just such an event. It was also interesting that only the Royal Family was told of the impending danger, so as to keep the civil population off the Fahaheel and Maghreb motorways leading to Saudi Arabia. After all, Family members didn't want the inconvenience of fighting traffic or waiting in line at the Saudi Arabian border checkpoint with common people while doing something as inelegant as fleeing.

As for me, I was told to keep silent about the meeting I had attended as well as the Baghdad trip that followed. I had managed to collect copies in Arabic and English of Saddam Hussein's meeting with Ambassador Glaspie. Imagine, I even had the original one on which Saddam Hussein used the yellow magic marker to highlight American Ambassador April Glaspie's words that America wouldn't get involved in a fight between Arabs.

Though I didn't realize it at the time, those same high-ranking Kuwaiti officials who told me not to worry were like rats fleeing the sinking ship during the night. They had told me several things were being done behind the scenes to insure the invasion wouldn't happen, but they weren't waiting around to find out if what they were telling me was true. They even had the nerve to order me that I was to tell no one of what I had seen and heard in Jeddah. I should not be the one to cause a panic in this country. I was stupid. I trusted them.

CHAPTER 7

Clouds of War

Mine and Maia's first year in Kuwait had been a harrowing one but good in many ways. Those days were long before the world knew about Saddam Hussein and still almost a year and a half before CNN showed missiles flying through downtown Baghdad.

I had gone to Kuwait to work and Maia was soon to follow. Reminiscing those times now, one must touch upon the good, the bad and the ugly. Surely at no time in my past has there ever been a more memorable time than the invasion and occupation of the country I was in. This wasn't the actual Gulf War itself that most Americans do have some knowledge about, but the prior acts of the lunatic dictator and his half million strong army that led up to the Gulf War.

Kuwait is a tiny desert country, not much bigger than the Atlanta metropolitan area. Both its neighbors, Saudi Arabia and Iraq are giants in comparison; and Iraq just happened to want little Kuwait for its oil resources, so it stepped over the line and took it. The next seven months that followed for me and for the country of Kuwait qualifies as "the bad."

It was just days after our Jeddah conference and I had settled back down to my normal daily routine. I continued my silence and continued to believe Kuwaiti, American and British sources that said no invasion would happen. Everything was to be just fine and even though the whole Royal Family was departing, Saddam Hussein would listen to reason and take the money the U.S. and Britain was offering to buy time. For being gullible, I'd be the one who would later pay. Though none of us knew at that time, the countdown to invasion had started.

From inside Kuwait's Ministry of Information Complex—early August, 1990—56 hours before invasion.

"Good Afternoon, Kuwait. This is the Super Station FM 92.5 News and Weather. It's three o'clock, 50 degrees Celsius, 122 degrees Fahrenheit; I'm Charles Petty."

(And so goes the first of two news, sports and weather broadcasts of the afternoon for me. I normally have the 7:00 a.m., 9:00 a.m. and 12:00 noon shows five days a week but today I switched, due to the Jeddah meeting and my trip to Baghdad that followed. As of tomorrow morning, I'll return to my normal broadcast times.

The Ministry of Information Complex in Kuwait City where I work daily, when not working for His Highness' the Amir or Crown Prince at Dasma Palace, is the eyes, ears and voice of the State of Kuwait. The Government tightly controls all media within the country except newspapers but even mandates some censorship policies on them. While working on radio or writing for television, I work directly for the Minister of Information who is also an al Sabah, part of the fourteen-hundred members of the Kuwait-ruling Royal Family who own and live in this tiny country. Kuwait's population is just over a million and a half with the greater half being servants from other countries. Before the Palestinians were expelled, they were by far the second largest group within Kuwait. Now the population has become more multinational with the majority of migrant servants imported from lower third world countries; those immigrants are less educated, less affluent and easier to contain.

The Minister of Information for whom I work in the mornings, is a cousin to both His Highness the Crown Prince and Prime Minister and His Highness the Emir, one for whom I work the latter parts of most days. Half of my day is spent at the Ministry of Information Complex on First Ring Road writing censored news and broadcasting radio shows. For the second half of my day, I head to the Amiri at Dasma Palace, the residence and offices of His Highness the Emir of Kuwait, the King, Sheik Jaber al Ahmed al Salem al Sabah. The offices, but not the residence of the Crown Prince; His Highness Sheik Saad Abdullah al Salem al Sabah are also there.

Sometimes I go to the Crown Prince's residence at Sha'ab Palace to work, but on most days he comes to the Amiri office complex at Dasma Palace to be near the Emir, government advisors, communications and so on.

The Minister of Information, who runs all television and radio broadcasts, is a Sheik like most of his titled cousins and uncles, controlling all positions of significance inside Kuwait. "Sheik" in this country is translated "Prince." This Minister is a Sheik as are all other male members of his family, including his sons. The Ministers' girl cousins and sisters are Sheikhas (Princesses) but can't have positions of power like their male counterparts. Al Sabah men control the Ministry of Information, the Interior Ministry, Ministry of Defense, Prime Minister and Premier as well as the Ambassadors to the United States and several other prime postings throughout the world. Of course, the head of Kuwait, the Emir is also the number one al Sabah and patriarch of their clan.

Kuwait does have a Parliament which acts much like the American Congress; however, it's ironic that members of the Royal Family are forbidden from running for Parliamentary seats or other lesser positions because they already control or heavily influence all outcomes anyway. Kuwait, I guess you can say, is a little off center of a benevolent dictatorship. There's little opposition to Royal Family policies in Parliament or anywhere else.

Coming to work was almost unbearable today. I had to leave Jeddah, Saudi Arabia in the wee hours of the morning to head straight for Baghdad, so I'm still very tired. The Minister of Oil's Under Secretary and I gathered English and Arabic copies of the transcripts of Saddam Hussein's last week's meeting with Ambassador Glaspie from the Wire Service offices. Then we immediately flew back to Kuwait. The transcripts seem to bear out Saddam Hussein's claim that the United States won't interfere if one Arab nation goes against another, such as Iraq invading Kuwait.

The men turning the documents over to me and the Under Secretary said that Saddam Hussein took great pleasure in attaching a special note to the outside of the Arabic transcript for the Americans and the Kuwaitis to read.

I carefully bound the small leather pouch with a string before putting it inside my tan briefcase. We were then off for the return trip to the airport outside Baghdad and then on to Kuwait City. I had some inkling the papers I carried were possibly very damaging to the United States for use as blackmail, but who really ever thinks they're the one carrying such documents. These of course were of great importance and could result in the great tragedy. I didn't. I remained convinced that the Americans and the British especially were going to resolve matters with Saddam Hussein even if the Kuwaitis refused to. Invasion and a real war resulting from last night's meeting in Saudi Arabia was never something I contemplated seriously.

That late July 1990, night and early morning still held little significance for me other than I had just flown several hours as an important passenger in a real rich King's private jet. The Under Secretary, whose name I still didn't know (because we weren't all wearing name tags or anything like that) re-boarded Saudi Arabia's Royal aircraft in Baghdad very nonchalantly, still quite unimpressed by the feat we had just accomplished. Looking back, I guess I should have gotten the other man's name, but everyone acted like we were already supposes to have known each other. I felt as if I were standing next to a king and you wanted to reach in my pocket and hand someone the camera I brought, but didn't.

During our two and a half hour flight over Iraqi air space to Kuwait, I stared at the terrain below wondering if the people living in the tiny little dots of houses would actually be going to war with us soon or whether their spokesmen at the Jeddah meeting were bluffing. I thought the latter.

King Fahd's pilot was a very personable man who knew the importance of our mission perhaps even more than we did. The three of us, the pilot, the Under Secretary and I spoke briefly several times during our wait at the Baghdad airport and again once airborne, but by now I was really tired and less than interested in long conversations. The pilot did seem well informed about our satchel cargo and pressed me for detailed information, but I avoided more than two sentence replies each time the subject was brought up. I had a feeling he was not just a pilot but a member of the Saudi Royal Family and possibly even an intelligence agent for their government, but it still didn't matter. I just needed some sleep.

The Kuwaiti Oil Minister's Under Secretary was even less concerned about the papers than I and only once even mentioned them. He was a typical Kuwaiti, content to let someone else do everything for him. He just went along for the ride while I spoke to the Iraqis and hurried our schedule along in Baghdad. The only real conversation between the two of us was less than ten minutes after we lifted off the tarmac in Jeddah. He asked my opinion whether I thought the Americans would be impressed enough by the papers to allow them to be used as blackmail. He said he believed his government would have no qualms about using Ambassador Glaspie's assurances to Saddam Hussein that the United States wouldn't get involved in a war between Arab neighbors. I replied, "Who knows what the American Government will say about the papers. Maybe they'll say the entire conversation was taken out of context or they'll deny Ambassador Glaspie even met with Saddam privately. All I know is Saddam Hussein has quite a history as a war monger. I wouldn't put it past him trying to invade Kuwait, but personally believe it's a bluff." I said, "Saddam just wants some money to rebuild his country after their eight years war with Iran, so he's just a saber rattling to get some attention and money. As soon as the Americans and British put some money in a Swiss bank account. Saddam will back down and quietly go his own way until he needs some attention again."

I said, "Personally, I believe Saddam Hussein would use any cash he gets for some other unique egoistical project like his fifty-story Saddam Tower now being built in downtown Baghdad, instead of rebuilding his country's economy. Once the new project is financed by hook or crook, he will no longer be interested in war but will be rebuilding his power base with his son Huday as his second in command instead of Tariq Aziz."

By nine thirty on the morning of July 31, 1990, the Oil under Secretary and I had completed our side trip to Baghdad and were back in Kuwait City. King Fahd's plane continued its flight back to Jeddah.

As soon as we hit the tarmac at Kuwait International, we were whisked through the Royal Terminal into an awaiting burgundy colored, armor plated Chevrolet Suburban Security vehicle belonging to the Amiri Guard. The security vehicle we traveled in is the same as those used by the Saudi Arabian Royal Family's protection. Our small three cars motorcade arrived at the rear entrance of the Emir of Kuwait's residence, Dasma Palace about 10:15 a.m. Within five minutes of rolling through the palace gates, we were unburdened of our documents and told to go home and get some rest, which of course didn't happen. Like it or not, I was instructed by telephone minutes after walking through my door to report to work on the afternoon shift at the Super Station. The call had been made by someone of little importance and quite uninformed of the deed I had just accomplished.

The rest of my day was normal. I edited and wrote the news then broadcast the three and six o'clock news and weather shows instead of relaxing, resting or sitting around the Crown Prince's Diwan hearing what had been going on in the Palace since the crushing results of the Jeddah meeting.

Today is the last day of July, which has no significance at all other than it is still hot. The region's normal hot temperatures haven't changed and won't be changing for many months to come. High pressure will continue sitting over the entire area for several more months, thus preventing daytime temperatures from dropping below the hundred degrees mark until the third week of October. Kuwait isn't like the Sahara in Africa or the American southwestern deserts, which are very hot but dry. Kuwait can reach temperatures in the shade of more than 135 degrees with humidity from the Persian Gulf remaining around 50 percent. That is far more unbearable than anywhere else I've ever lived including the interior of Somalia and the desert town of Apache Junction, Arizona. Even Phoenix may reach 122 degrees a couple times in a hot year but the humidity there drops to 3 percent or slightly more. It's not cool but you're not sweating profusely.

Working for His Highness, Sheik Saad as a confidant, go-for, and political strategist or whatever he referred to me as at the time, left me with far too much time on my hands and nothing to do, especially in the summer. I asked for and was given a second job at the radio station to add a little more excitement to my life. Actually, the job I asked for was disc-jockeying the "Oldies and Goldie's" 50's and 60's hit shows for English-speaking expats. Somehow, I let the Minister of Information news people rope me into doing the news, weather, and sports on the FM band instead.

Don't get me wrong: I liked the new job at FM 92.5. The position gave me "hands on" access to wire services and news events around the world in "real time" as they happened, which also fit nicely with my ever expanding knowledge of the region.

There were only about five hundred Americans in Kuwait in 1990 not counting the six Marines at the United States Embassy. No American military personnel were in Kuwait because no agreements had ever been signed between Kuwait and the U.S. Until now no base or port was used by the Americans, thus allowing no American support equipment to set a foot on Kuwaiti soil. The United States had tried for years to get a port or base in Kuwait but had continually been denied by the Royal Family and Parliament, who had the British to protect them if anything went wrong between Kuwait and their neighbors.

There weren't many Americans in Kuwait but there were many other English speaking Europeans, Indians and Australians who wanted and needed someone to program or disc jockey the music for them. A sweet Indian lady named Brenda from Goa was doing an outstanding job programming all the tunes of the day, but the station lacked "on air" personalities, disc jockeys, news persons and others who would also be native English speakers. Later, other people would come such as an American disc jockey Linda, who married a Kuwaiti, as well as several other half Kuwaitis who would disc jockey contemporary hits. All in all, before the invasion Kuwait radio was laid back and less than informational or entertaining.

44 hours till invasion.

My job started and ended before the real heat of the day. That morning before daybreak, about five o'clock, I stepped into the 87 degree stagnant heat and felt like turning around and going back to bed. The day's first call to Prayer was just echoing throughout the countryside. The fine dust in the air made it chokingly uncomfortable.

Daily, my work started only a few hours after most Kuwaitis went to bed. I drove through empty streets and arrived at the huge Ministry of Information Complex where no one really mans the fort. Even the Kuwait National Guardsmen who supposedly maintain security are usually sprawled out behind their reception desks asleep.

The Ministry's sprawling complex has three major buildings and half dozen smaller prefabricated types rimming its fortress style, guarded walls. My jobs at the Amiri and Ministry were both within heavily guarded fortified complexes, the only difference being that the Ministry of Information's National Guardsmen were usually asleep. At the Palace Amiri, they'd have been shot for the same offense.

Within the Ministry of Information Complex, the center building is by far the largest. It has fourteen stories of administrative offices and communications gear. The Minister's office occupies the entire top floor. To each side of the Administration Building are three story matching bookends. On one side is Kuwait's two television stations, on the other are four radio stations. The radio building contains an English station where I work, two Arab stations and one Farsi station broadcasting to the Iranian labor force here.

The television stations are Channel 1 Arabic and Channel 2 English. The three main complex buildings are joined by neat enclosed glass skywalks on the second floor level. The small trailer-like prefab buildings skirting the inside complex's fortress walls are used as security billeting for the National Guardsmen who protect it. One prefab at the front gate has a small office for screening entering persons and issuing passes to visitors. The other at the rear gate merely checks identifications of workers as they enter from the parking lots. I've heard it said that a "chain" or "security" is only as strong as its weakest link. If that's true, there was no security at the Ministry of Information most of the time, especially during early morning hours.

It wasn't unusual for me to walk all the way through two security posts, gain entry into the Communications buildings of either television or radio without once being asked if I belong there. I've made it several times all the way to the outer part of my office without even seeing a Kuwaiti National Guardsman. It is not unusual to hear that other unwelcomed guest have been found wandering Ministry hallways looking for DJs or friends. Little guess as to why my office/on-air studio has two dead bolts. Other studios have the normal flashing ON-AIR lights too but that has never stopped people from just walking in off the street and starting to talk to the person who's ON-AIR at the time.

The Information complex's fortress walls have six gun turrets, barbed wire running along the tops of the walls and jersey barriers that create a security maze at the Ministry's front entry; but why bother with all the barricades if you can just walk through the gates while everyone's asleep?

The first thing I did each morning was go to the communications Wire Services Room within the central tall tower to pull all news items that had come in during the night from both Reuters and KUNA, Kuwait News Association.

August 1st appeared as though nothing of great importance were happening worldwide. That always made my job a little more difficult. I had to search much harder for a story. When a major story hits the wires, it's easy to have plenty of copy to read. Reuters and KUNA are both usually full of interesting details but that day they weren't.

Daily after reading the news from the wire services, I assembled the stories I thought most interesting for my listening audience, then rewrote and reduced them in size to fit my fifteen minutes time slot, and then continued the same routine two more times each day before my work at the Ministry of Information was finished. In between news writing and broadcasting of each, I jumped into my car and headed to Dasma Palace for intelligence briefings by CIA and MI6 British outside intelligence. Next, I returned back to Kuwait Radio, finished up there and then returned once again to Dasma Palace where I combined both intelligence reports for His Highness. After that briefing I headed home, usually arriving a little after one thirty in the afternoon. Back in the days preceding the Iraqi invasion, some Americans in Kuwait received their local newspapers from cities back home in the States but for the most part they relied on anything they could get from Kuwait Radio, Television, or the English-Arab Newspapers of which all were censored.

Following the usual "Good Morning Kuwait," the station identification and my name, I provided the temperature conversion from Celsius to Fahrenheit, the "allowable" world news, weather, sports and stock market information.

To begin the "on air" production, I programmed the computer to go to "Live Studio," which followed the last song nearest the top of the hour. I waited a few moments while easing the music sound bar down and the news typewriter ticker-tape volume increased. The news theme with typewriter ticking grew louder as the regular music volume dropped. A phase bar then allowed me to phase out both as I brought up the volume of my microphone. (Now I stared at the clock . . . 3-2-1 . . .)

"Good Morning, Kuwait, you're listening to the Super Station FM 92.5. It's nine o'clock, 34 degrees Celsius, 93 degrees Fahrenheit on a day that will be climbing to 53 degrees Celsius, 128 Fahrenheit; I'm Charles Petty with the news."

Since I didn't require technicians, no one else was inside the building with me until just before my second broadcast at 9:00 a.m. During Kuwait's long summers news writers' and broadcasters' jobs are much easier. The work load is cut by half. After all, we didn't have to write for English television because no one was in the country to watch it. After my noon radio broadcast, I was out of there. Another hour or so at Dasma Palace and again I was free for the rest of the day.

During the hot part of the day on 1st of August, 1990, I rested. It was the typical dusty hazy 122 degrees. Though evenings always remained hot too, that would be the times I would head out to the shops in Salmiya where I lived or over to friends' homes. I did have a few other options though: I could have played night tennis with Abdullah on the lighted courts at the Safir International Hotel or watched our two best cable television channels in this part of the world, the Star Channel from Hong Kong or the Indian Channel from Bombay (now Mumbai). Both had American, British, and Australian programs like "Bay Watch," "Oprah Winfrey," "Neighbors," and "The McGregors."

To play tennis with Abdullah in the heat even during the late night took too much energy. If I weighed fifty pounds more than I did, maybe it would have been worth it because Abdullah would have kept me running all over the court, losing the match and weight at the same time. Even thinking of playing tennis in the summer was too much for me; I've always looked great on the court fashion wise but, I'm not good at the sport. I've always had the best looking tennis clothes and snow ski outfits of anyone I knew but was also the least accomplished athlete. I liked being at the event and wearing great clothes but really couldn't have cared less about the physical exercise. A statement that sounds even ridiculous to me, knowing that I walk or jog three to five miles a day along the Salmiya beach front. I then go to Hyatt Gym with my friend Saleh to meet up with another of our friends, a Sheik in the Royal Family who also owns the gym.

After speaking to my Palestinian friend Gus (Ghassan) and Ruba earlier that first day of August, I promised to stop by their apartment in the evening for at least a few minutes before they headed on vacation over the desert to Amman, Jordan. Gus was saying how much better it was to travel during the night without the heat on the tires, fan belt and radiator. They were heading to Amman to visit both their families, since Gus's brother married Ruba's twin sister a year after Gus and Ruba were married. Both sets of parents also live in Amman. The eight hour car trip is tiring for them, but for the most part it's on good roads through Northern Saudi Arabia.

As luck would have it, that afternoon turned out to be a little more eventful than watching television or playing tennis with Abdullah. I had been invited to a pool party at the home of our good British friends Guy and Shari. They wanted some of our gang to get together for the rest of the day to play games in their pool and have a few drinks under their shade trees. Other guests invited were from the British and American Embassies.

Guy and Shari's home in Ahmadi Township, fifteen kilometers south of Kuwait City was about as close as you can come to a southern plantation outside the United States. Their home was a full sized Tara, complete with the white elegant two story columns, circular drive, fireplaces, dainty sweeping staircase and sun porches. Guy and Shari were provided the estate as one of their benefits from Guy's employment. Before the Iraqi invasion, he was the top British executive with KOC, Kuwait Oil Company. KOC built the home six years earlier and furnished it with all but the personal effects each tenant would bring to make it their own.

Shari was a great hostess and reminded me of Loretta Young the way I remembered her in the old movies of the late forties and fifties. I could see Shari as Loretta swooping down the staircase, her dark hair tightly pulled back, full lips, thin waist and elegant full crinoline skirt. Guy on the other hand was the stereotypical Brit. His complexion looked as though he'd seldom seen the sun. His face was lean and staunch but his hair perfectly kept. Guy reminded me a little of a lighter complexioned Prince Phillip, always dressing so well that often I thought that when I got rich, I'd have Guy choose my clothes and develop my gentlemanly manners. It was from Guy that I learned exclusive tailors actually ask men the question, "Do you dress right or left," referring of course to where your family jewels and maleness is placed inside your briefs. I told Guy that in the American military, we had the command "Dress Right Dress" but certainly didn't have any similar meaning. We both could picture the soldiers throwing their male genitals from one side of their under briefs to the other in unison each time the command was given. The phrase "Dress Right" or "Dress Left" kept us roaring with laughter on more than one occasion when either of us would shout the command after seeing someone showing his "maleness" in too tight dishdashas as they like to do in this part of the world. The male's genitals are often seen while white dishdashas blow in the desert wind.

The only part of Guy and Shari's estate that was unlike Tara was the swimming pool with its full service bar. Both the pool and bar were prizes to be envied in this hot country that also forbade the use of alcohol or women in swimsuits on the beach. Their bar was stocked extremely well, though it was against the law for consumption outside embassy walls. Certainly Guy's bar was only slightly better than ones in many Kuwaiti homes. It wasn't unusual in those Kuwaiti homes to even "tap a keg" if enough people were present. Though Kuwait is a strict Muslim country, there are also many who have fallen outside their religion for the forbidden drink.

Following work and then several hours of rest, I arrived and rounded the front driveway of Guy and Shari's home in my Ministry of Information vehicle and parked under the trees at the far west-side lawn, nearest the swimming pool. I wasn't the first to arrive. There were already a number of other vehicles parked out near the street and a few others inside the estate's fence. By late afternoon most people had finished work so their recreation room and pool side became standing room only. There was plenty of food and drink, a fully stocked bar and fifties' and sixties' songs resonating from four huge speakers.

By mid afternoon, quite a nice size group frolicked in the sun and played water volleyball. One voice that rose above the merriment of the crowd was Bob and Liz's six year old son Marc. He was first on one team and then the other. He got a lot of attention that day because he used some Prell concentrate shampoo on his hair that morning and as soon as he hit the water, the chlorine made his hair turn green. Now the little Martian boy was playing to the hilt his new hair color and the attention it got him.

Marc's mom and Dad, Liz and Bob were British expats who had been living in Kuwait about half Marc's life. Bob was an intelligence officer for the British Government in the Middle East and Liz was a tall light brown haired, late thirties, aristocratic type sometimes filled in as a secretary for British firms working in the oil industry.

It was now 35 hours before invasion.

Looking back, I couldn't remember seeing anything that led me to believe Kuwait's leaders had already thrown up their hands against Saddam Hussein's threats and had begun emptying their safety deposit boxes and rounding up their last remaining family members still inside Kuwait. I still believed what I was told following the Jeddah conference a few days earlier that there was going to be ongoing negotiations that would prevent an invasion.

Work at the Ministry and the Amiri Diwan in the past two days seemed quite normal because in the summer time, I wouldn't expect to be seeing many of the Ministers or Royal Family anyway. And I didn't. If anything was wrong, my host, Guy would surely have pulled me aside to compare notes with me. We both scoffed when I told him of the Jeddah meeting and he added that officials at Kuwait Oil had barely mentioned they may need additional security in the oil fields. Not once did Guy ask for further information or act concerned that anything like an invasion could happen. Even Bob, the British intelligence officer, laughed and swam with his family. Surely if he had known negotiations had broken off and something as life threatening as an invasion was soon to happen, he would have been acting differently. He wouldn't have jeopardized the safety of his own family at the pool that day.

I later told Bob the only premonition of anything strange happening was when I encountered the Minister of Information's car sitting at the entry of the central Ministry's building just before I left work at 12:15 p.m. I thought he was out of the country! He had met us at the Jeddah Conference only to depart on a different plane, supposedly for a different destination. The Ministry's gates were still open and there wasn't even one Kuwait National Guardsman at the back gate checkpoint where I came in every morning and left each afternoon.

At Guy and Shari's, everyone moved under the large blue and white striped canopy pool side and proceeded to feed themselves from the chafing dishes on the buffet table. The food line was the perfect place and time for many of us to mingle and find out what everyone else had planned for the upcoming weekend, which in the Muslim Middle East starts on Wednesday evening. After all, today was already Tuesday. An Arab Thursday is the same as Saturday in most countries and Friday is like Sunday.

There's not much choice as to where to go for summer-time leisure activity around Kuwait City, but at least we had the Khiran Resort and Failaka Island. Khiran was about another 20 miles south along the Persian Gulf toward the Saudi Arabia border, and the chalets or detached vacation duplexes on Failaka Island were about 5 miles to the Northeast out in the waters of the Persian Gulf. Of course there were also Bahrain and Dubai, two lush rich green modern Arab paradises, one and two hours flight southeast of Kuwait, correspondingly. Since everyone, expats and Kuwaiti alike wished to live there; we all tried to go as often as possible.

In Dubai, United Arab Emirates and Manama, Bahrain there are drinking pubs or bars unlike in Kuwait. There are also nightclubs and dancing and women are allowed to wear regular bathing suits to swim in hotel pools and on the beaches. In Kuwait, women are not allowed in any water unless of course they wear a full length black abaiya.

Dubai and Manama also have super duty free gift shops, and their gold prices are better. Sometimes we buy pork, bacon and ham—also illegal items in other Muslim countries to bring back to Kuwait by plane. When we pass through customs at the airport, we call it British meat or pink turkey. Though Manama and Dubai are Muslim, they appear more like Southern Florida with their American made automobiles, palm lined boulevards and strands of high rise white beachfront hotels. They are in sharp contrast to Saudi Arabia which lies just a few miles at the other end of causeways from both countries.

The enjoyable day at Guy and Shari's passed into night and everyone moved inside to the air conditioning. The rich cherry wood wall inside their study was unlike any others in Kuwait. The richness of cherry wood always made me feel at home, so Guy and I and almost everyone else once again ended up in there to escape the heat outdoors. When the chairs and sofas were full, the rest of us sprawled on the floor on Arabic throw pillows. Bob, of Bob and Liz was really a burly looking Brit with dark hair and mustache. He sat on the floor to my left and started a political conversation rolling for the first that day. Liz, Shari, and several other people involved themselves in conversations about when to use certain Arabic words and who'd be giving the next party. Politics were usually the order of the day between Guy and me. And now Bob was fully a part of it.

The three of us were sort of a first line of intelligence information for our "friend's network" of what was happening in Kuwait. I had plenty of information pass my desk that few other people inside or outside Kuwait ever had the privilege of seeing. Bob got quite a lot of intelligence reports through the British, and though he doesn't divulge a lot of specifics because of his job, we talk, sometimes almost in code. He sort of always lets me read between the lines of what he's saying.

Guy had an unusual perspective to add to ours. Because of his job overseeing oil production in Kuwait for the British, he had to take extra security precautions in times of crisis, so he had the privy to things we probably wouldn't hear. Another occasional person that sits in on our conversations gives us an additional feel for what the average expat without inside knowledge is thinking, or rumors they've had been hearing.

In confidence, I told Bob and Guy that I didn't like what I had seen in Jeddah but I believed the Kuwaitis were taking care of the matter, or somehow the British or Americans would impede Saddam Hussein from sending his armies across the border. Bob said he had heard of the meeting but was told things became better after the Kuwaitis left and the others put their thinking caps on. They talked with Saddam Hussein directly by telephone from the conference room in Jeddah for several hours after the Kuwaitis stormed out the room.

Guy reiterated there had been no Ministry of Oil decision for additional security at this time. He was told however that after American Ambassador Glaspie's meeting with Saddam Hussein on July 25, the Kuwait military had been placed on partial alert. All of us laughed at what we thought the Kuwaitis could do to defend themselves against the hardened war experienced Iraqi soldiers. Even if Kuwaitis were inside their country instead of being at Disney World in Orlando or their apartments in Cairo, what could they do?

Just as the last guests left, Guy pulled me to the side and asked me to come with him. He had someone who wanted to meet me. We returned to the cherry wood study where I saw someone sitting in the big easy chair that I hadn't noticed earlier. He was good looking, distinguished and dark: an Arab man in his late thirties with slight salt and peppering to his hair. He stood and then started to kiss me on the cheek the Arab way but then backed off as though suddenly he realized I was a westerner. His name was Nabil. He shook my hand and said Guy had told him about me, and he'd like to have my thoughts about a situation he was "in" right then.

He really wanted to know the name of a good attorney Americans would use if they got into trouble with Kuwaitis. I told him for the most part the Embassy gave them little advice if any. Usually they were on their own and most likely they'll end up leaving the country; and if the situation was bad enough, they would leave the country inside a mail pouch which is diplomatically free from inspection. If there was a confrontation between an American and Kuwaiti, the Kuwaiti usually runs to the American's company sponsor (another Kuwaiti) where the American works and then puts pressure on the company to terminate the American employee unless things are settled exactly the way the Kuwaiti wants.

I had had many friends of other nationalities who needed legal advice, but none of the Americans or Brits I knew personally who ever needed an attorney. One American and one Brit in the past disappeared in Kuwait and were never to be heard from again. In those cases, the Kuwaitis with whom they were at odds were suspected of killing them and disposing of their bodies, but no one could prove it nor thoroughly investigate it since the Kuwaiti families had solid Royal Family connections and investigators ran into brick walls at every turn.

Nabil told me that he and Guy became friends when Guy took a sideline job as a consultant to a construction company. Nabil, a Jordanian, owned the construction company that was the main contractor for the job. Nabil and Guy became fast friends as did their wives. Nabil's sponsor was a Kuwaiti who'd married into the Royal Al Sabah Family. Nabil was running into many problems going up against a man with such powerful and influential family ties.

Nabil had been in Kuwait for more than fourteen years. He and his family had lived peacefully in Hawali until just under a year ago when his eleven year old daughter's school called urging Nabil and his wife to come take their daughter home because she'd been hurt. When Nabil arrived at the school, he found his daughter still lying in a small pool of blood in a central hallway. She'd been beaten on the head with something by two older Kuwaiti girls. A witness said they even continued beating and stomping her after she was unconscious.

Nabil started hollering for someone to call an ambulance but the school said the other two girls mothers wanted their girls left out of this and wouldn't allow a doctor to get involved either. They warned Nabil against taking his daughter to the hospital. When Nabil snatched his daughter up in his arms and proceeded to take her to the backseat of his car, he was accosted by the two Kuwaiti mothers who had come to their daughter's aide more than twenty minutes before Nabil was called, almost a full hour before he arrived on the scene. All they would keep saying is that his daughter was in the wrong because she had been rude to the two Kuwaiti girls. These two Kuwaiti mothers were more for placing blame than in allowing the girl to get medical attention. The mothers fought with Nabil, slapping and hitting him and trying to pry his arms from around his daughter. Finally Nabil sped away to the hospital with the two Kuwaiti mothers' car in close pursuit behind him.

At the hospital, the scene was much the same. When Nabil grabbed his daughter in his arms to carry her into the emergency room, the women again fought him. Even one of the Kuwaiti's Indian drivers busted Nabil's lower lip in the attack and one of the mothers clawed him down the side of his jaw with her long fingernails. Two doctors in the emergency room immediately came to the girl's side but were soon in the middle of the fight. The doctors had to fend off the Kuwaiti women and try to calm them down. Nabil's young daughter lay on a gurney for several more minutes before the doctor came over to Nabil to tell him he's sorry he's unable to treat the girl. The doctor would rather Nabil took her home and come back in a couple of days after this mess dies down. He said he'd clean the head wound and sew it up but wouldn't take ex-rays or give her an examination. He said, "You know how it is. I work for them in their country. If I don't listen to them, I'll have a heavy price to pay. My practice here will be terminated." The women finally left the emergency room after shouting further warnings at Nabil and trying to find out who his Kuwaiti sponsor was. Nabil took his bloody limp bodied unconscious daughter and again laid her in the back seat of the car for the ride home.

Nabil had always heard that Kuwait's health care laws cover Kuwaitis and expats working in the country but has always been told to seek private doctors rather than ones at hospitals. His family had never required the service of a hospital before; even his daughter, who was now lying here, had been born in Jordan while Nabil and his wife were on a planned maternity vacation. He now said he knows when Kuwaiti authorities say "adequate care" is taken of all nationalities within the country. The key word was "adequate."

Late that night the little girl regained consciousness for a short while and seemed pretty good except for being disoriented, though she never got out of bed. She again went to sleep. The next day, she seemed to still be resting comfortably, so they didn't try to awaken her. By the third day Nabil and his wife were panicking. They knew they had no choice now but to take her to a hospital in Amman, Jordan, eight hours away by car. The doctors at the Kuwait hospital repeatedly over the past two days had refused to see her again. A private physician, who was consulted, came to their apartment and said he feared for the child's life. She must be put in a hospital immediately. The doctor was also a foreigner, a Croatian, so his word also meant nothing when he called to try to have the girl admitted to the hospital under his orders.

Nabil and his wife knew this trip from Kuwait through the desert to Jordan would not be good for her but it would be her only chance.

Nabil ran into trouble again when he tried to get his exit papers from his Kuwaiti sponsor. His sponsor said it wouldn't be good for public relations to take the injured girl to a hospital in Amman. Though both countries are Arabs and Muslim, Jordanian newspapers had already been blasting Kuwait for their inhumane treatment of Palestinians and Jordanians working there. "No", Nabil's Kuwaiti sponsor would not sign exit papers.

When all other reasoning had failed, Nabil spoke the key phrase that rang with dollar signs in the Kuwaiti sponsor's eyes. Nabil said "I'll do anything you want but please let me take my daughter to the hospital in Amman." The Kuwaiti immediately set about having papers drawn up. The next day, he called for Nabil to come over and sign them. Several months earlier the Kuwaitis had been demanding Nabil renegotiate a higher percentage of Nabil's company, so this paperwork would now give him the leverage he wanted. Nabil had to sign a paper stating that he had denied his Kuwaiti sponsor a higher percentage for a long time and that the matter would be settled retroactively to a date agreed upon by the two before Nabil and his family could leave for Amman.

No one can set up a company or do business in Kuwait without paying money to a Kuwaiti for the privilege. The Kuwaiti doesn't ever have to do anything, but for the duration the new company is in business, the Kuwaiti draws an income that could range as high as fifty one percent. The foreigner who is setting up the company will now always be at the Kuwaitis discretion on business matters and how much money the Kuwaiti wants to take from the company. The sponsor literally becomes a partner of the business without putting up any money, setting up the new company and never has to work there. The Kuwaiti does nothing but draw free money.

Because Nabil's sponsor was considered a partner, Nabil was forced to sign a "Power of Attorney" that would allow the Kuwaiti to run the company and collect all normal fees and monies as long as Nabil was in Jordan with his injured daughter. After the Kuwaiti sponsor was satisfied with the "Power of Attorney," Nabil was free to leave the country with his barely conscious daughter again lying in the back seat.

After Nabil reached Amman, doctors told him the child would need extensive surgery if she was to survive. She had to be airlifted to London. Only two hours after they arrived in England, the little girl died.

Nabil and his wife returned to Amman with the girl's body for a family funeral. After the grieving process had covered nearly a week, Nabil headed back to Kuwait leaving his heart broken wife with relatives. When he arrived at the Kuwait border check point, he was told his residency papers had been canceled and he couldn't reenter Kuwait. Nabil went to a nearby town in Saudi Arabia to call his sponsor, who told him he was no longer welcome in Kuwait. Though Nabil was the owner of the company, if he came back he would be placed in prison for absconding with company money.

Nabil called our mutual friend Guy to get an attorney to represent him in Kuwait. The one inside Kuwait would have to work with the one Nabil hired in Jordan. It had been more than two months since the girl died of her injuries, and now Nabil was back in Kuwait on a visitor's visa.

The first thing Nabil did was to return to his apartment. It was empty. The landlord and the Kuwaiti sponsor had split the furniture and belongings up. Even the little girl's clothes and the wife's jewelry that were lying on the dresser in their bedroom had been taken. There was nothing left. The Kuwaiti sponsor took half because he said it was to pay for the attorney he had to hire to fight Nabil. The landlord got the other half because the sponsor never paid Nabil's rent as instructed during his absence.

At a meeting in Nabil's Egyptian attorney's office in Safat, downtown Kuwait City, he was handed an ultimatum. Either he signs his entire company and all its assets over to the Kuwaiti sponsor or he would be immediately taken to prison for having stolen from the Kuwaiti. Nabil said the sponsor had planned ahead even bringing a couple of policemen with him to the attorney's office. Nabil had no choice but to sign away about million and a half dollars in assets just to stay out of prison. Nabil knew, as we all know, that in Kuwait it is not necessary for a Kuwaiti to bring charges against a foreigner to have them imprisoned. They often use what's considered an administrative imprisonment. You can be held without charges and without knowing when your time will be up. You may stay for years. According to law, Kuwait denies this can happen. (Kuwait has many unwritten laws in which many fortunes have changed hands from expats to Kuwaitis.)

Nabil believed he has a good case and would like to have gotten a good attorney to fight his sponsor's action, but so far no one wanted the case. Nabil would be staying at a local hotel one more day before his visitor visa was up. He must leave the country with nothing but the clothes on his back. As one final insult, his Kuwaiti sponsor was holding his passport to be picked up only before being escorted to the border day after the next day, which would be August 2, 1990.

I sat through the whole story dumbfounded but not surprised. I'd been living in a world of privilege in Kuwait, but I've heard similar stories more often that you can imagine. I guess the shock of this one was that it was the first time I'd actually stood in front of a real live person it was happening to. Nabil was such an articulate and demonstrative man; I really saw the pain in him. If I knew anyone who could have helped this man I wouldn't hesitate. My conversation with Nabil and my inability to help him really brought my spirits down after such a great afternoon.

I still had to go to Gus and Ruba's that evening, but I wouldn't tell them anything of Nabil's story because even though they're Jordanians, the same as Nabil, they'd feel his hurt and depression the same as I did. It would take the edge off their happiness. They'd been anticipating going home to their family in Amman for so long, they were ecstatic, and I didn't want to mess that up.

At that time, there was certainly no inkling of tens of thousands of enemy troops lying in wait only fifty two kilometers (less than thirty miles) away. In less than 30 hours they'd be descending on us with tanks, machine guns, and mortars.

Chapter 8

Like Sitting Ducks

On my way home, I stopped by Hawalli to see Gus and Ruba. Hawalli is a predominant Palestinian and Lebanese township at the center of greater Kuwait City. It's on a mostly vegetative wasteland as looks go, but is a vibrant part of the city cramped between four freeways. Thousands of bland—and beige colored four to eight story slightly decaying apartment buildings, jammed side by side, dominate the horizon, block after block in all directions in an area two by two miles. There are shopping strands in Hawalli with Kentucky Fried Chicken restaurants, corner video shops, furniture and appliance stores as well as living areas with schools and playgrounds. In its booming business district, there are giant neon signs mounted atop taller buildings like a miniature New York's Times Square. What's most apparent by day is the disrepair of perhaps 90 percent of all the buildings within this rich country.

No one from another country other than Kuwaitis and seven other Gulf Cooperation Council States' citizens may own property in Kuwait; so, expats, even upper pay scale ones like Gus and Ruba are allowed to reside in anything other than these crowded dilapidated, townships similar to Hawalli. Americans, Brits, Dutch, Aussies and just a few others may be allowed to rent in better parts of the city. For the most part, Kuwaitis house their expat workforce in districts amongst people of their own kind, and then pull high revenues from each building without maintaining the structures. Rent runs double to triple what we'd pay for similar housing inside the United States. Wages for Americans and some other westerners are high in Kuwait, but for Palestinians, Jordanians, and other middle and low end laborers, even those with university degrees from the United States and Britain, wages are quite low; less than half their equal counterparts in America.

Gus and Ruba Abu Omar are both from well to do Jordanian families. They own a large number of tractor trailer trucks, bulldozers and other heavy equipment, and have lived in Kuwait all their lives but still are not allowed to become citizens. In Hawalli, as in many other expat enclaves in Kuwait, many family members live together while building a nest egg of gold and heavy machinery which they are allowed to own.

In Kuwait, it's not uncommon to visit someone who is considered upper middle class or well to do yet they are prohibited from finding accommodations equal to their station in life. In Kuwait they are forced to live in such substandard buildings that lack plumbing pipes and electricity cables inside the walls. Exterior paint has long ago peeled from the outside of Gus and Ruba's building, and the once concrete stairs have eroded to such disrepair that the chicken wire inside the concrete is now mostly exposed. Water trucks are still in use in Hawalli because this area and its hundreds of thousands of residents have been bypassed by city water and sewage systems in favor of Kuwaitis only communities further from the center. Only about half the streets of Hawalli are paved, and no parks have trees or bushes; quite the contrast from Kuwaiti neighborhoods. The private non-Kuwaiti school system is almost non existent for most residents, so Gus and Ruba have had to enroll their children in expensive American and English schools for safety and better education.

This evening, Gus and Ruba greeted me at the front door and as usual ushered me in where a small group of mostly Jordanian, Lebanese and Palestinians were conversing. After customary kisses on the cheeks between me and the other men, I greeted Ruba and the other ladies present by just speaking. Only one presented her hand for a shake. None of the women present wore headscarves. Everyone was strewn throughout the apartment's two small main rooms and the kitchen. In homes in the Middle East, chairs and sofas line most of the walls of the living room; theirs was no different. Usually Oriental or Persian throw rugs cover the floor, but Gus and Ruba opted for wall to wall blue carpeting. Two coffee tables and several smaller glass top individual tea tables in front of the sofas were already full of snack and dessert plates.

There are no pictures on the walls of any of these homes because I'm told Muslims feel the same way about pictures as they do about statues: if you put them in a room, they're like shrines. Muslims in this part of the world think westerners worship them. This is especially true in Kuwaiti and Saudi homes, though Gus and Ruba are far more sophisticated than that; but still within Middle Eastern tradition they have opted for no pictures on the walls and no dining table in the dining room, just a television area.

A dining table and chairs are of course of little consequence since most Arabs eat on the floor over spread newspapers anyway. I can list more than a few Royals who do the same. Fortunately we didn't eat on the floor at Gus and Ruba's; we sat on the living room furniture and ate from the tea tables.

Ruba had been cooking most of the evening and dinner was served about 11:00 p.m. Arabic and English was spoken by everyone present, from Ruba's father, a chemist to the visiting children who had come along with their parents to see Gus and Ruba and their oldest daughter Lu Lu. Everything was a delight as usual and certainly days and evenings like this helped fill a family gap in my life.

My wife and family were still home in the Tempe, Arizona but would soon be joining me in Kuwait in the near future. My wife Maia met Ghassan several years ago while we were attending a conference in Southern California. They also liked each other. Now that Ghassan has married Ruba, I'm sure Maia will enjoy her as well.

For the next two hours I sat in Gus' and Ruba's living room and ate lots of food and drank lots of hot tea from brass and glass chi cups. We joked about what the child would look like when Ruba bears their second, hopefully a little boy named Hassan. Surely with Ruba's Sophia Loren looks and sharp features, her genes would overpower Gus's hairy face and course hair. Ruba gave way to one concession though: her nose was slightly bigger than Gus's. That night was very pleasant, and I never spoke to them of the Jeddah meeting or of anything from my earlier discussion with Nabil.

Much too late, I went home. Work came only four hours later. I not only had to be fully awake for work but had to be lively enough to go on the air as well, and do my version of "Good Morning, Vietnam; Good Morning, Kuwait" speech. Gus says their plans for driving to Amman are delayed by a day because Ruba wants to consult her obstetrician about the trip first.

Driving back to my penthouse in Salmiya, I had to fight traffic on both the Fahaheel Motorway and the Fourth Ring Road exit before finally arriving home. It was now well past midnight, yet the streets were still crowded. So many people are out late every night in Kuwait because it's the only time the weather is slightly tolerable. The restaurants were still full; shoppers still crowded the Sultan Center market and the beach side jogging and walking path that runs parallel to Gulf Road was crowded with large groups of lounging Palestinians, Indians and other expats who are used to summer nights in Kuwait.

Invasion is now 25 hours away.

Still unknowing that invasion is near. My working companion and fellow DJ Linda Lou and husband Badran live in the mostly Bedouin community of Jahra. They sit right in the path of Saddam Hussein's half million strong army and Kuwait City. Linda, an American from El Paso, Texas, met and married Badran, a stateless man who always considered him Kuwaiti. His family has stayed in one residence for years and hasn't wandered the deserts in tents like most other Bedouin families. They married while he was serving as a Kuwait Army officer at Fort Bliss, Texas. Badran's expertise was missiles: deploying, repairing, and launching.

Linda is quite rotund and has always carried some mental scars from young American boys who never gave her the attention she rightfully needed and deserved. Often in America we hear "she has a pretty face and wonderful disposition but she's so heavy. "If she could only slim down." Well here it is again. Linda's a sweet, loving and thoughtful woman who didn't just get sweet over night; she's always been that way. I'm sure she had too little attention paid to her in formative years because of her weight. Kuwaiti or rather Arab men in general really do admire and want to marry big women. It's a pleasure to see a culture that doesn't turn and stare because they're big and ugly but rather they're thinking to themselves, "I want some of that."

Badran, a six feet tall dark haired olive complexion man is good looking as well as thoughtful and kind. It's nice to see that he and Linda found each other. Unfortunately, there's a lot of baggage that comes with a bicultural couple, especially with such diverse backgrounds as Linda's and Badran's. After twelve years of marriage and being transferred by the military to exotic places like Honolulu, Hawaii, Austria, Germany, and California, Linda and Badran resettled in Badran's hometown, Jahra, Kuwait.

The township of Jahra sits at the edge of big ever moving and expanding sand dunes in the desert just west of Kuwait City. Linda left a comfortable life as the daughter of an American military doctor to join a foreign man who wined and dined her and gave her presents. Badran's a good man, an officer and a gentleman who has great loyalty for the Kuwait's government that has spent so much money on his career and training.

Most other Bedouins live in poverty as nomads in the desert, changing residences with the seasons between Iraq, Saudi Arabia, and Kuwait. They have camels as work animals for carrying loads and also as meat for the dinner table. Most tribesmen have unusually large families and own a very good population of sheep as well. Their living quarters range from tents in the dunes to walled three to five room one storey, mud adobe styled buildings in Jahra similar to the adobe dwellings of the Indians in the southwestern part of the United States. Rooms are in line or an L-shape with all doors except one gate emptying into a dirt courtyard. The women's wash is hung on the roof to dry and the cooking is done on the ground outside or on the floor within a small kitchen.

The adobes make shift kitchen cooker is a gas plate and a large ten liter butane tank. No windows are allowed to face outside the dwelling so the fundamentalist veiled women and girls cannot be viewed inside their private surroundings. The full black abaiya and veils can be taken off within these walls, unless visitors are present. Meals are served on the floor on newspaper when available and cloth when not. Smaller families may sit together but most have one area for females and a separate one for males; children may again be separated. Most ladies eat behind a veil of mushrabiya (carved wooden spindles) or in another room. Even many weddings and restaurants in Islamic countries, such as Kuwait and Saudi Arabia have secluded areas separated by these beautifully lathed decorative pieces.

The culture shock for Linda and her little girl Miriam was devastating when they first arrived in Kuwait. Badran's father and his four wives who by now had 36 sons and nobody counted the daughters resisted Linda and the half breed daughter from America. Everyone lived and slept in an L-shaped, six room adobe bungalow. Each of his four wives had a separate room they shared with their smallest children. As sons get older, they all sleep in the same rooms no matter which mother bore them. Daughters of approximately the same age do the same.

Most of Badran's oldest brothers are unable to work because of their Bedouin status so they tend the family's sheep, goats, and camels. Little actual money is brought in other than one brother driving a taxi and some other brothers taking odd jobs; Badran and Linda have to turn over their entire paycheck every third month to his father. To complicate matters even more, Badran had another wife before marrying Linda and was the father of her three children. Yes, Linda did know this before she married Badran.

We, Americans find Badran's marriage situation inconceivable but as is the Muslim custom, Badran may possibly end up with four wives and many more children. He's a caring family man. Every four nights he switches bedrooms to the other wife. Usually an agreement is made between the two women before the second marriage takes place. Later this type agreement will be reached with the third and fourth wives. In Linda's case, she had Badran all to herself in the United States and several other locations before he returned to the situation with his first wife who never traveled with him. "Do the wives of such families living in the same household fight?" Some do and some don't. In the case of Linda and Badran's only other wife, they hated each other and had to be moved to separate but equal households.

Badran's pay from the Kuwait military has to be split three ways, equally between the two households and with his father. This leaves no way for one family to go on vacation to Europe or back to America visiting relatives without the other receiving equal money. Not long after I had given Linda a sectional sofa, I visited her only to find that part of it too had gone to the other family.

Linda and her daughter Miriam have withstood abuse by some of Badran's family members and lived in near impoverished conditions to "stand by" their man. Miriam attended her first few years of school in America and Europe but is now unable to go to school because her spoken Arabic is at a basic level, and Bedouins didn't want this half-breed American in their fundamentalist culture.

Miriam's a beautiful young girl, obviously from two good looking parents. She certainly melds the features of both together in a stunningly elegant look even at this young age. She's thin and statuesque like her father with a fabulous olive complexion and has the gorgeous silky brown hair, eyelashes and Linda's mouth. Miriam a few months ago began wearing the Muslim scarf to cover her head and long black dresses as is customary with girls when they have "first blood." This time in a girl's life while she's beginning to develop womanhood is so proud that they can hardly wait for everyone to know. She and her mom go shopping for new clothes and undergarments and of course, they choose the finest scarf to cover her head; it doesn't have to be black like the abaiya she'll wear over everything out in public.

Miriam is no different than other young ladies in the Middle East in loving all the hoopla that even the male storekeepers make about her new womanhood while they shop. She was given another present by her mother and father as well. Miriam will be pampered at a special shop where ornate designs and patterns are carefully drawn all over her hands, fingers and wrists in henna, a reddish dye sometimes used on the hair and often by celebrating Arab women on their hands, feet, and ankles.

For Linda and Miriam, their worst incident happened soon after arriving in Kuwait from the United States for the first time and meeting Badran's family. The father had the other sons beat Badran unconscious while he personally attacked and beat Linda. Both required hospitalization for a few days, but of course this is not a crime in Kuwait. It's a moral issue to be settled within the family structure. Had death resulted, the situation would still have been condoned and supported as a prerogative of the family. Linda's a strong woman and survived the incident still shouting the tremendous love she has for her man. Behind closed doors and amongst friends, Linda and Badran are often seen strolling hand in hand and affectionately cuddling and speaking. This is not the case between him and his other wife. Badran has come through as a strong man, not following the cycle of abuse. Not once has he lifted his hand at Linda or Miriam.

Often, while I'm speaking with both of them, I go off on a tangent saying "why can't you just pick up your belongings and head back to the United States and forget this family? Do it for the sake of Miriam." But their resolve to assimilate into this culture before going back to the United States to retire is their choice and besides, legally Badran would have to divorce his other wife to receive proper papers to live and work in America. I hope everything works out well for them whatever their course in life might be.

Linda and Miriam have always kept very good contact with the American Embassy, mainly because of the never ending paperwork the Kuwaiti government constantly demands of her, so at least they have some attachment to their old world.

The community of Jahra is virtually void of trees or grass, but has become a full fledged city in the desert with vibrant shopping districts, wide motorways, modern schools and government complexes as well as hundreds of five and six storey apartment buildings. Many of those buildings are owned by Muslim fundamentalists who allow no cable or satellite television or even telephones on the premises. Linda lives in one of them but clandestinely carries a cellular.

In less than 24 hours, Jahra would be Kuwait's first populated battleground by the invading Iraqi armies and Linda and Badran's family would one of the first to suffer.

Most of Kuwait's military bases are within shouting distance of Jahra, only fifteen miles from downtown Kuwait City and about one third of the way to Iraq's border. Jahra is the last populated area before the massive expanse of desert to both Iraq and southwest towards Saudi Arabia. More than two hundred thousand residents of Jahra have a view of the only large sand cliffs in the country. Mutla Ridge, as they are known, is where the desert meets the waters of the Persian Gulf. northwest of Jahra, lying just below the cliffs is a cloverleaf of merging highways where more than half Kuwait's main roads start or end. This would prove invaluable to invading Iraqi forces due to the invaders' ability to fan out from there in all directions as others could come from air and sea. The highway that leads east from the cloverleaf into Jahra comes near the United Nations base and the now American seaport at Doha. Two others begin there as Fifth and Sixth Ring Motorways, both doing as their name indicates, ringing Kuwait's heavily populated capital and surrounding suburbs with super highways. From the cloverleaf, the roadways heading southwest aim towards some military bases before continuing on to the farthest regions of unpopulated desert wastelands in the direction of the borders with Saudi Arabia and Iraq.

One highway heading north goes through 38 miles of open desert before reaching the small Kuwait farming community of Abdaly on the Iraqi border. That highway also passes through several large oil fields, long the contention by Saddam Hussein to be the ones where the lateral and horizontal drilling is going on. To the northeast, just 34 miles up another desert road winding around Kuwait Bay lies Umm Qasr, another small farming village and naval community, also on the Iraqi border. At this point Umm Qasr Naval Base is only one mile to the Iraqi town of Umm Qasr and less than 50 more miles to the border of Iran.

I was awakened this morning at four o'clock, not by my alarm that's set for that time but by mother calling from the United States at 8 p.m. EST. She had seen on the television evening news that Iraqi forces were building up in the southern part of that country. She wanted to know if I was in any danger. I reassured her that I work for the Minister of Information. If anyone would know anything, I would. I wasn't going to alarm her with any partial knowledge that I had, but I did tell her we were aware of the buildup and everything seemed OK. We spoke more about whether my wife was coming to Kuwait before Christmas or whether I would be going home to bring her back with me in January. Our conversation then moved on to other family matters that develop when you're separated by half a world.

After hanging up, I got dressed slowly while nibbling a bagel and cream cheese and drinking a glass of orange juice. Of course, the first thing I always check every morning is the weather. By walking towards my floor to ceiling windows that dominate three sides of the penthouse, the weather outside would be hard to miss.

On this morning, as I peered out, nothing looked different, the traffic or weather. The stars were brighter today because for the past several days we've had a thin layer of dust covering the city. At least this morning was clear. Even though it was still dark, I could see almost the entire city.

Visibility was pretty much unlimited and if it were daylight already, I'd be able to see the twin smoke stacks of the power plant at Doha to the southwest, Failaka Island, to the north and all the way up to the gas burn-offs in the Romailah Oil Fields on the Iraqi border.

This morning, I went to work and parked in the back lot of the Ministry of Information Complex and then entered the rear prefabricated guard post. After speaking briefly with a guardsman who was only partially awake, I walked the next fifty yards to the main Administration Building.

Again as usual, there was no guardsman present at this entry, but I figured he was asleep on the floor somewhere in the vicinity of the main lobby. Just before I reached the elevator, I spotted him in a sleeping bag behind a reception desk.

Once inside the building, I headed to the communications room where I ran into a man in dishdasha minus his head gear. I had never seen him before and became concerned why he would be sitting inside the wire service room pulling and tearing the lengthy rolls of copy that had come in overnight. He said he had to pull copies for the Minister, and then politely handed me most of the rolls of red border copy I usually get. It was immediately obvious that much of my overnight wire service copies were missing.

The main roll appeared to have been torn at different intervals throughout the night. No one had ever cut or pulled my copies before. I protested about his messing up my information and told him I'd be talking to someone about it when they came to work later this morning. I then proceeded out the tall Administration Building through the second floor glass skywalk and over to my own office/studio in the smaller bookend radio building.

The seven o'clock and nine o'clock news casts went well, and since it only takes just over an hour to prepare the one for noon, I decided to head over to Al Muthana Mall in front of the Meridian Hotel; after all, today was just another hot steamy day in Kuwait.

While at Al Muthana Mall, I decided to stop in at the travel agency to check on my Christmas reservations. Usually reservations have to be made quite far in advance because of connections through Europe. Often the actual flight you want will be difficult to get due to the amount of people in Europe traveling at the same time or weather conditions the further north you go.

After twenty five minutes or so, the travel agent finally had it straight. This year I'm not going via the Netherlands to New York and then on to Savannah, Georgia, but will instead be going through Istanbul and Rome to Miami, where I'll meet my wife Maia and my mother and father for a cruise in the Caribbean. This route allows me a few vacation and shopping stops as well as keeps me from landing at northern airports. I very much dislike northern routes during winter season because of snow or deicing.

Al Muthana Mall is one of the three largest upscale shopping centers of Kuwait City. There, I ran into Ghassan and Ruba coming out of the bookstore. They had purchased a new Road Atlas for the United States. They said, hopefully, they'll be seeing me in Miami in January while I'm passing through on my way back to Kuwait with Maia. They'll be heading to Miami, the Keys and then on to California for the remaining days left of the two months they will be spending in America. They're going to combine Christmas, New Years, and the Muslim Holy month of Ramadan. I knew what they were doing and I didn't approve. They were going to do like many other Arabs and nationals do by having their new baby in the United States. Usually, at the expense of the American people. I didn't cause a scene but told them my concerns and we each departed in our own direction.

Ghassan graduated with an engineering degree from the University of Southern California and had enjoyed living there for five years. He loved it so much he wanted Ruba to get to like it too because one day he wants to have a home there. They're Muslims whose religious holiday Eid is in February at the end of Ramadan, so Gus's father decided to give him enough time away from work before and during the holiday season to allow them to really enjoy the United States. They appeared busy this morning and eager to leave tonight for Amman, Jordan to see their family. I polished down a burger and fries at Hungry Bunny in the Mall before running in to the next person I knew, Melanie.

About the only thing I knew of Melanie was her age, forty two; and that she was an American woman with a Liberal Arts Degree (emphasis on liberal) from Louisiana State University. The rest of what I knew of her was rumor and innuendo. This was her fourth year in Kuwait, the first two of which she spent literally as a captive of her former Kuwaiti Sponsor.

Melanie now works designing cornice moldings and ceiling tiles and commissioned art for a company in Kuwait City's suburb of Shuwaikh. Street word has it that no man from the ages of fourteen to forty five who has known her intimately will ever forget Melanie's experienced hands. Those same rumors say all that molding of wet clay on the pottery wheel has paid dividends to Melanie's suitors.

She and I spoke pleasantries and then said our good byes in about five minutes. I headed back to the Ministry of Information Complex. I finished my noon radio show before going back to my penthouse in Salmiya to rest and escape the intense heat of the day.

It's now 12:30 p.m., nine-and-a-half hours before invasion.

I got a good rest that afternoon and didn't wake up until I got a telephone call from a Kuwaiti buddy, Saleh Marafie about 4:30 p.m. He wanted me to meet him at 9:00 o'clock this evening at the Sizzler in the Fashion Way shopping mall within a hundred yards of my apartment. Next, my Filipino maid Jeanette knocked at the door. She was running more than two hours behind on cleaning her other client's apartment so she was just arriving to give mine the once over before ending her long day.

Jeanette's a very timid type, not someone you would expect to drop her whole life in the country she was born and raised in and to follow her man half way across the globe to make money. She, like many other expat laborers, came to Kuwait to bare the loneliness and inconvenience of living here, just so their three kids left with grandma back in the Philippines would be able to attend better schools and have a decent home to live in. Jeanette and her husband Jamie also hoped to save enough money while working in Kuwait to build their retirement nest egg. Jeanette came because Jamie had already come with a manpower company for construction work six months earlier.

Jeanette's sister Emily had also recently come to Kuwait. She was employed by a Kuwaiti family as a domestic, a maid. Since she didn't have a husband or children, she lived with her employer's family. Kuwaitis have complete control over their domestic helper's entire life. What Emily had thought was a wonderful chance to come to Kuwait for a job and be near her sister hadn't happened. She hardly ever got to see Emily. Jeanette says her sister tried to quit working for the Kuwaiti family because of their physical mistreatment of her and because they withheld much of her pay.

Jeanette has on several occasions had to take hygiene supplies over to her sister because after several months her host family hasn't paid her wages or furnished her with personal supplies. They claim she's still paying for her return air fare trip to the Philippines just in case the employment agreement doesn't work out between them.

I had just finished dressing to go out for the evening and meet Saleh before the doorbell rang. Ali Chougli, an Indian bank manager with the Commerce Bank of Kuwait arrived with his seventeen year old son Sunay. It's a pleasure seeing them. Ali and I met when our mutual Kuwaiti friend was trying to set up a business venture and bring an American company over. The venture didn't work out but our friendship did and has steadily grown.

Ali is about my age, mid-forties, successful and well-traveled. He doesn't have quite as thick an accent as most Indians do. His daughter, who attends University in England, maintains the apartment in London that Ali and his wife purchased for family holidays.

Sunay, the teenage son doesn't look Indian but rather a bit more Kuwaiti. His sharp features and hair are less dark than his father's. The European and American fad clothing he wears shows tremendous influence by his Kuwaiti and foreign peers. He really appears more like one of them than one of his own people. Since he's lived in Kuwait most of his life, Sunay also speaks fluent Arabic with a Kuwaiti accent. Tonight as usual we settled into some trivial conversation dominated by how good the pastries were they had brought me and a new restaurant downtown that one day we'd have to try.

I've learned to enjoy Indian curry chicken, Lebanese cooking and other exotic foods since coming to Kuwait, so Ali and I as well as other locals and American friends dine out a lot. We're always on the lookout for another new food experience. I couldn't help but notice that Sunay was busy the whole time his father and I spoke. With binoculars in hand, he stood before my massive living room windows checking out all the cars coming down Gulf Road, occasionally turning his head as if following some of them into the Sultan Center parking lot. "What else?" he said, but seeing if any girls were arriving. Ha, little chance he had with them. Even Indians can't speak to most girls in public in Kuwait, but at least his Indian high school is co-ed. Soon Ali and his son were off and so was I. Jeanette, my maid, would lock the apartment up as usual and I wouldn't expect to see her again until next Tuesday.

It's now one hour before Kuwait's border checkpoints are destroyed in the first minutes of invasion.

Its 9:10 p.m., and Saleh, my Kuwaiti gym buddy just turned in from the street towards the front gates of my building. "Jump in, Charles," he said. "I want to run by the gym for a minute." We stopped at the Holiday Inn Fitness Center and then, having missed the guys there, we went to Hyatt Fitness Center where we met up with the Sheik and several other mutual friends. We found out what their plans were for tonight; then we were off again foot loose and fancy free.

Saleh, who's from one of the wealthiest families in Kuwait, but not royal is a lot younger than me, yet age hasn't posed a problem for us. We have many mutual friends and interests. We're compatible but not alike. Saleh and I met at the gym several months earlier when I overheard a conversation between two Kuwaitis talking about the American Universities they had attended. Saleh had attended a college in a small town in Arizona called Prescott. I listened for a while and then joined their conversation stating I too had lived in Arizona prior to coming to Kuwait. I owned and ran Grand Canyon State Tours in Scottsdale and Tempe, suburbs of Phoenix. He said he had attended college in Prescott about eighty miles north of Phoenix for two years before transferring to another university.

Saleh and I felt an instant bond through humor, enjoying strolling the shopping districts of Salmiya in the late evenings and going to the gym. We didn't share the same interest in the consumption of alcohol or chasing women. I, like other Americans and foreigners in Kuwait had our own what we called "bathtub stills" to make wine and other alcoholic beverages, but for me, I seldom partook of my own creations. I offered and Saleh drank several glassfuls of wine on each visit to my apartment. It was some time later that his mother and I spoke about his drinking problem and I formulated some ground rules about when to have a drink around Saleh and when not to.

There are two things all Arab youth in Kuwait have, and that is porno tapes and access to someone who can get alcohol. At first I gave Saleh my homemade brew of white and red wines but later stopped offering. I became really concerned he'd have a second auto accident like the one he had in the United States, and this time he would be killed. I didn't want anything like that to happen. Since I only drank on rare occasion, it was only then that I would offer it to him.

The strikingly handsome Saleh is fairly light skinned, about six feet two inches tall, has a big weightlifter's upper chest and arms but scrawny bird legs. Most of the time Saleh wears western clothes, not cowboy but western; in the sense of being from the West, European or American. On this night, however, he was wearing the traditional white dishdasha and head gear but not sandals like everyone else. He wore penny loafers.

Saleh has this thing about trying to secure my apartment some day to bring his girlfriends over but so far that hasn't happened. I don't like to vacate my place for others to make it their bordello. He apparently has little trouble getting the ladies because his mobile phone rings constantly. With the limited amount of Arabic I know, I usually listen in on his conversations with these young ladies and rib him about his harem, even though having one until he's married is forbidden. That statement sounds nonsensical but, in fact, in this region of the world is nearer the truth. If the Arabs have a Don Juan, Saleh is he.

It was amazing how normal everything in Kuwait still was before invasion. This evening showed no signs of being different from any other, yet destruction and death loomed over our heads and for many, it was only a precious few hours away.

While at the gym tonight, Saleh was told that some of our other buddies would be taking their boats and jet skis over to the Failaka Island Touristic Enterprise chalets tomorrow, so he made plans to meet them over there. They wanted me to come along as well, but I was one of the few people in Kuwait who had to work at least five or six days a week, so tomorrow would be out for me. My weekend wouldn't start this Wednesday night, like everyone else's, but afternoon tomorrow. Maybe I'd make it over to Failaka Island later on one of the last Hydrofoils leaving the Ras al Ard Salmiya Port about a mile and a half from where I live.

Saleh and I headed back to the eastern section of Salmiya through ever thickening traffic. Parking in Salmiya, Kuwait's most popular shopping district on this night or any night is almost impossible to find. We returned to my apartment building and parked in my other space. Even though Kuwait's extreme heat forces many people out of the country at this time of year, Salmiya's sidewalks, streets and shops remain the country's busiest. In the one strip of eight to ten blocks nearest where I live, there are countless upscale boutiques, gold jewelry brokers, malls, less expensive clothing, jewelry arcades and more than 30 fast food and ethnic restaurants: Italian, Chinese, Indian and Arabic as well McDonalds, Burger King, Pizza Hut and others.

In Salmiya, as in more than ten other Kuwait City suburbs, the local gold souks (markets) are in strip malls where there are many shops, not just for purchasing jewelry but for browsing as well. It's normal that almost every time you go out to walk, you'll stroll through at least several souks with near endless quantities of gleaming gold.

Imagine a store, only two to three times the size of an average American living room, packed with more gold of 18 and 22 Karats than you've ever seen in all the American jewelry stores you've ever been in. There's gold hanging from the walls, necklaces like Cleopatra might have worn and belts that weigh more than a pound each hanging over wooden dowel rods. Counters are filled with solid or filigreed rings, chains by the hundreds, lockets, pendants, earrings, and complete dowry collections worth tens of thousands of dollars each.

The dowry pieces are usually purchased by the parents and family of the groom to be for their new daughter-in-law to be. The young lady, her sisters and mother usually go to the shops, find what they want, then tell the groom's family the location of the store and the piece or collection desired. In this way, the groom's family learns how much the new daughter-in-law is expecting as only one of the marriage gifts. This practice is also not limited to wealthy Kuwaitis but for many other Arab nationalities as well.

The only thing missing in these gold souks is jewelry for men. It is against Islam for men to wear gold, but they're allowed to carry gold-writing pens, a favorite present that may cost anywhere from a hundred to a thousand dollars or more.

Saleh and I walked the half block from Pizza Hut to Fashion Way mini-mall where the Sizzler Steakhouse Restaurant is located on the second floor. While we sat overlooking the sea, Saleh's telephone rang constantly—women, of course. It's a wonder he's ever finished a meal. By 10:40 p.m. we did finally finish and both Saleh and I went our separate ways, he to who knows where, and me to my friend Janelle in the wealthy suburb of Mishref.

Invasion would soon begin just forty five miles away.

If it sounds like I did a lot of running around and visiting, I did. That's what is done in Kuwait. Almost every night of the week, you're gone. Maybe you'll stay home one night and everyone will drop in to see you.

On this night, the air still hung heavy and sultry; the crowds still filled the late night streets and still none of us knew that a quarter million men with tanks and tens of thousands of tons of deadly weapons were literally coming for us. Everyone would awaken to a different world tomorrow. No one would ever be the same again. Some out for this evening of leisure with their families will die before another sun rises. Tomorrow there will be many new widows and some of these same children, laughing, dining, walking hand in hand and buying toys tonight with their parents will be newly orphaned; some even before it is time to rise for breakfast.

When I arrived at Janelle's house, it was very late evening, but according to local custom it was dinner time. She, some of her family members and several of our mutual friends were just sitting down to eat. Janelle ran over to me and planted a big double cheeked kiss on me before flittering away like the social butterfly she is.

On this evening the fully energized Janelle wore a typical Middle Eastern long red teardrop sequined lounging gown. Though she always cooked for a full day before her guests arrived, she'd still be the life of the party and the grand hostess.

Janelle, an American born to Lebanese parents living in California, met and married a Kuwaiti student attending the University of Southern

California. She returned with him to Kuwait where they had three children and everything went well enough, except his family didn't particularly like his choice of bride. He was supposed to have returned home and then married into another influential Kuwaiti family.

The tanned Janelle is overweight but only slightly so; she wears her brown hair medium length and slightly frosted and is one of the most kind, generous and loving people I've ever known. And smart too. She studied alongside her twin sister and received a degree in law in the United States before marrying and moving to Kuwait.

Though he was from a wealthy family, Janelle's husband became a commercial airline pilot for Kuwait Airways; they built their first home in Kuwait and had three children and life seemed full and happy; however, their fairy tale didn't continue long enough to end in happiness as he died of a massive heart attack at the age of forty two.

The in-laws that Janelle thought had been somewhat receptive of her and the children over the first years while her husband was alive came over and kicked her and the "half breed" kids out immediately after the funeral. They were given airline tickets and said "return to America; there's nothing in Kuwait for them."

Prior to August 2, 1990, when the Americans were called to come to their rescue, Kuwaitis always considered the Americans disgusting infidels to be disliked and distrusted. Her in-laws were only echoing the same sentiments the majority of Kuwaitis felt.

Janelle did return to the United States and continued her pursuit of international law. She went back to Kuwait seven years later and proceeded to reclaim her children's rightful place in society and the monies they were entitled to as heirs to a large family fortune. One day I'd love to see a movie made of her terribly long and tedious struggle that finally led to the kids winning their place in Kuwait society and securing financially for the rest of their lives.

Janelle's in-laws laid traps almost as deadly as land mines, but Janelle maneuvered around them and persisted with a vengeance. Her father in law became her personal target. She bound his assets in Kuwait, which is no simple task for an outsider. Within a few years the other members of that family were begging her to take certain assets to halt the crazy vendetta. Janelle persisted finally getting her biggest breakthrough soon after the old man, the head of the clan, died.

Janelle heard someone mention that the dead father in law had another wife in Spain. Only Janelle would have gone to find her and became friends with the woman. She told the Spanish woman the old man was now dead and wanted to know if she had been taken care of properly. After learning the woman got very little, Janelle and the old man's secret wife formed a partnership that would span the next couple years and three continents. Janelle probed the Spanish wife's memories of trips to other countries and whether she and the old man had stayed in a hotel or an apartment. Was it owned by the old man or leased? Did they bank there? Where else had the old man opened accounts? They soon uncovered another wife in Morocco and then documented and froze tens of millions of dollars more in assets. Even the rest of the old man's Kuwaiti family knew nothing or little of all the squandered wealth that had left their grasp.

Then the big agreement came. Janelle laid out the legal work and proceeded to divvy up the found monies. The other wives received a decent settlement; Janelle's kids received a more than fair share and the old man's closest relatives were even allowed their share, contingent of course on settling with Janelle's children for their father's rightful share of everything in Kuwait and abroad. All total, it looks like Janelle's fight packed more than a hundred twenty million dollars into her children's American accounts.

Janelle kept everyone laughing all the way through dinner, later passing out Tums antacid tablets to help everyone digest the twenty dishes of tasty chickens, rice, corn, beans and other things I didn't recognize.

She then proceeded to the large living room as everyone trailed behind her like some kind of gypsy queen. The Arabic style dancing she began performing requires shaking her ample bosomy top flirtatiously but not vulgarly, while cupping a long scarf below her buttocks before tying it around her thighs and below her rear end. She then raised her hands upward toward the ceiling making hand motions like hula dancing and began moving very rhythmically through the room toward each guest. She continued the dance while slinging her shoulder length hair round and round in Arab fashion. I've seen this dance many times before and it's usually done very sensuously but with Janelle it comes off more as a comedy routine, not unlike the dance of Tu Tu in American Hawaii. Soon after midnight, I made my exit for home for a couple hours sleep before work. Janelle was still dancing when I left.

August 2, 1990, 4:15 a.m. Iraqi troops are already approaching Kuwait City by land, air, and sea.

As I still lay sleepy eyed, beginning to awaken, my alarm sounded. More than four hours had passed since I left Janelle's and those late hours were making it even more difficult to climb out of bed. The darkness of just past four o'clock in the morning wasn't making it any easier either.

Reluctantly but dutifully I dressed, grabbed a cup of tea and a bear claw roll, jumped into my van and drove to work. I had seen some tracer fire over the horizon toward Camp Doha but that was not out of the ordinary in Kuwait. Usually, someone celebrating a wedding or just wanting to shoot upwards does so with little fear of police arrest. How often in newsreels have we seen celebrations with Palestinians or other Arabs shooting their rifles into the air almost straight up. Don't they realize the bullet has to come back down somewhere? What we haven't seen on American television is the end result. Often a guest or member of the wedding party or someone from a group of celebrants is injured or killed by those same shooting outbursts, yet they continue unabated.

I arrived at the back parking lot of the Ministry of Information Complex about 5:15 a.m. and passed two almost asleep National Guardsmen as

I went through the identification checkpoint still unimpeded by any security as usual. Not only did the guards not check me but didn't even really open their eyes to see who I was. After passing the second guard post, I entered the main administration building without seeing a guard there at all; the guard was probably sleeping behind his reception desk or in a sleeping bag around some corner. I went upstairs and tried to enter the wire services room but for the first time since going to work there it was locked.

I needed access to the information that came in overnight on the wire services to make the morning's news. Now what would I do for today's news stories? Months earlier I had tried to get the Ministry to buy computers to link our radio studio up with the incoming wire services but that didn't happen. That would have at least allowed me access to the wire services even if someone over in the administration building had mistakenly locked the door and wouldn't be in until later to open it.

I passed through the glass skywalk connecting the second floors of both buildings and proceeded to my radio studio. After sitting for a few minutes trying to figure out how I would handle not having any information for the early broadcast, I decided to return to the administration building to the Arab section that assembles and writes news for Arab language television. The Egyptian writers at Kuwait Television One usually come to work about the same time as I do, but there was no one at their typewriters or even in the room. I thought, "What's going on?"

While walking through the building, I rounded the corner straight into one of the legal department's attorneys, an Egyptian named Mohammed. He inquired what I was doing there and proceeded to tell me to get out and go home or to the American Embassy or anywhere I'd be safe.

CHAPTER 9

The Iraqis Are Here

The Iraqis are here. They've invaded Kuwait.

I stood silently for a moment without even thinking of a question to ask before the Ministry of Information's lawyer rapidly departed. Somewhat stunned, I headed toward the first floor to exit the building when a bomb exploded towards the upper floors. I quickened my pace through the empty hallways from the center building crossing, once again back through the glass skywalk to the radio building. About middle way through, I heard cap gun sounds and looked down towards the pavement in front of the building where the sounds seemed to be coming from. From my perch in the glass skywalk, I saw two Kuwaiti guardsmen running, then stopping, squatting, taking cover, then running again to get into the ground floor snack bar. Several Iraqi soldiers with AK47s ran quickly in succession after them. When shots were fired inside the snack bar, a degree of reality said I had just witnessed some of the first casualties of a "real" war.

The pounding of my heart quickened. The rush of adrenaline pumping within my body at high speed made me euphoric and brought flushness to my face. I thought surely it's not a real war like in the movies, but when several closer gunshots ricocheted as if they hit the bottom of the skywalk's steel below me, I became a believer and wasted no time getting back to my soundproof, yet not bulletproof studio. I stayed in the relative security and comfort for a few minutes before feeling trapped with no way out.

The journalist within me kept thinking of "getting the story" and doing a live broadcast, but I wasn't really sure if that would be all that was alive after the broadcast. After all, I'm just a want to be journalist not an old veteran who would die for a story.

I continued thinking the craziness of war couldn't be happening. That attorney I ran into in the hallway couldn't be right. Iraq wouldn't have the nerve to invade Kuwait after negotiating with the Americans and the British and whoever else. Still, I remembered the determination in the faces of those five Iraqis attending the Jeddah meeting. I suppose the defiance the Kuwaitis showed at the meeting, coupled with the "go ahead" they perceived given by Madam Ambassador Glaspie should have left me no choice but to believe what I was seeing.

It was still difficult for me to realize the Iraqis actually followed through with their plan to invade Kuwait instead of opting for continued financial and other support from the United States as they have for years. I still remained hopeful that the British and Americans were taking care of the situation even if the Kuwaitis weren't. I've never been in a war condition before and never thought of what I would do if something that far flung ever did happen. Really now, don't things like war always happen to other people, not us?

After fleeing the temporary refuge of my soundproof studio, my next inclination was to go somewhere else, see what's really happening. Even a Neanderthal could surmise that if I have no weapon and there are all these Arab soldiers running around that look alike, it's hard to say who would recognize me and who would shoot me. I do know that the odds don't favor me because the Iraqis are half million strong, and the Kuwaitis in summer don't have enough soldiers in country to battle each other for Pizza Hut, much less the Government.

Only if you look carefully can you tell which country's soldier is which. Kuwaiti soldiers wear Rolex watches and Gucci penny loafers with their uniforms tailored, but Iraqis don't. I'm not crazy enough to halt running soldiers to check who's wearing what.

As the sound of rapid machine gun fire grew closer and closer, I knew the situation was becoming even more dangerous for me. I headed towards a downstairs basement doorway about the time gunshots again ricocheted, this time off the stairwell walls nearby. Now with real purpose, I headed through the Ministry's basement door, down another flight of stairs and through partially darkened empty warehouse rooms.

I remembered an old equipment hallway on the second level basement where we stored some stuff from the old radio studio during its remodeling process several months ago. I headed for there with great haste, as though my life depended on it because it probably did. I felt reasonably safe there for several minutes before deciding to move on. I began exiting my second place of modest security and started to return back to my studio when I heard several more nearby shots. That did it for me. The reporter in me was completely gone now and I became a person solely concerned with my own health.

This time, I backtracked through the second level basement and followed the corridor I had been told went under the rear parking lot. Once there, I realized what I'd been told was true. The corridor did indeed go below the Ministry of Information's parking lots and over towards the Governorate Building next door, nearer my car; but that's a government building also and since the Iraqis are here, chances are they're there too. What if I surfaced right into the barrel of a rifle?

I quickly relieved myself of my Arabic Palace ID cards and the Ministry of Information Political Section ID, stuck them into a cracked mortar opening between two concrete blocks in the tunnel walls and then headed through the mostly darkened corridor to the other side.

What I had been told wouldn't happen, did. American, British, and Kuwaiti officials right to the end refused to say an invading army of fanatical, radical, fundamentalist and most importantly, armed Iraqi soldiers with instructions to murder, loot and occupy Kuwait were now on their way. Even the Kuwait Royal Family denied it to everyone but their own, whom were probably still scurrying to empty their cash boxes and hide their valuables before fleeing across the border into Saudi Arabia. With few exceptions they could sit the whole situation out comfortably at King Fahd's mountain summer palace in Taif, Saudi Arabia. The rest of us were prey.

At two o'clock on the morning of August 2, 1990, the first column of Republican Guard troops crossed the border from Iraq into Kuwait.

Barely an hour and a half after I exhaustedly crawled into bed the night before, and those two hours that followed when my alarm clock rang; reconnaissance units of the first Iraqi invaders had begun crossing into Kuwait. Iraqi General Iyad El Rawi ordered his troops first to shell the Abdaly passport checkpoint and then overrun it. Other than a short bombardment, the actual fighting that followed was more of a toy pistol fight by the Kuwaitis than an impediment to Iraq's invasion forces. Simultaneously, the checkpoints at al Salmi to the West and Umm Qasr to the east came under similar attack. The destruction of the Customs Center and police post at Umm Qasr opened the way for thousands of Iraqi troops to overrun Kuwait's largest naval base. All combined, Al Salmi, Abdaly and Umm Qasr took no more than one hour to eliminate.

Though this attack should have been anticipated, little effort had been made by the Kuwaitis to impede such a cross border advance. Kuwait had put only half its troops on red alert more than two weeks earlier, yet did nothing to beef up security along border posts or bases or even issue an order for the Kuwait Army to stand and defend itself. Kuwait had even failed to recall their vacationing troops. Kuwait had not recalled one tank driver, one missile technician, or even one pilot to defend the sovereignty of their beloved homeland. For Kuwait's top military leaders or the Royal Family who head almost every aspect of life in the country, it would have been inconceivable to make someone leave vacation in Europe, Egypt or Walt Disney World. The Kuwaiti commander at Umm Qasr base on the border with Iraq made two calls within the first minutes of attack. He made one call to the Minister of Defense and the other to His Highness the Crown Prince, both in Kuwait City, about forty miles to the south. Both were warned of the Iraqi crossing and possible movement toward Kuwait City. "They're coming, I can't believe it, they're here" said the Commander of Umm Qasr. I continued sleeping while calls to various military units went out in all directions from just down the road at Dasma Palace and across town at the Defense Ministry.

By 3:00 a.m. the Iraqi pathfinder soldiers in two vehicles with six armed troops in each had already arrived deep in the heart of Kuwait City. They randomly shot at storefronts and small groups of people in the downtown Safat district around the corner from the Ministry of Information Complex where I work. These Iraqis were already cruising what most cities would consider their "main" street, Fahd Al Salem.

By 3:30 a.m. some guardsmen who had been home secure with their families had begun arriving at their duty stations.

Well inside Kuwait territory, the Iraqi Republican Guard ran into their first real skirmish with Kuwaiti armor about twenty miles south of where they had begun the invasion; however, Kuwait's Sixth Brigade was quickly overrun. There would not be another unit fighting back until ten miles northwest of Jahra where Linda and Badran live.

Kuwait's 35th Brigade moved rapidly to halt the onslaught of Iraqi tanks; troop trucks and heavy armor moving south along the Abdaly highway toward Kuwait City, Kuwait's insignificant five armored vehicles was no match for the hundreds of tanks and thunderous troops approaching. They nonetheless stood their ground as long as they could by ordering air support from Ali al Salem Airbase just a few miles to their southwest.

Iraqi helicopter gunships next smashed and quickly disposed of the small 35th resistance and continued their advance toward Kuwaiti Air bases and the populated areas. Minutes later four Kuwaiti jet fighters struck back at the advancing Iraqi column, doing some damage but they too were insignificant in causing any obstruction to the massive and murderous Iraqi onslaught. The Kuwaiti jet fighters quickly withdrew to the protection of an airfield in Dhahran, Saudi Arabia.

The first defenses inside Kuwait had crumbled and had been overrun almost as fast as a tank could drive without being impeded by so much as a speed bump in the road.

At 4:30 a.m., within three miles of where I was riding along in my van towards work and quite unknown to me, amphibious landings were taking place along the coast of Kuwait City.

Many Iraqi amphibious landing crafts came out of the waters of the Persian Gulf and swarmed the foot of Kuwait's proud symbol, the Kuwait Towers and their prime target, the Emir's home at Dasma Palace just the other side of the towers. A second major landing from the sea with thousands of soldiers came less than a mile around the bay near the Amiri Hospital. This second landing provided the Iraqis a full flank to the rear and side of the Emir's residence at Dasma Palace. A third amphibious landing was to the heart of Kuwait City's seafront at Seif Palace. Four out of five Kuwaiti Palaces are on the Persian Gulf and they were all attacked from the sea and the air within the first hours. Only Bayan Guest Palace is inland and came under attack later. The Iraqis faced no major battles for the palaces either. The amphibious landings had support from Iraqi fighter planes and helicopter gunships that bombarded and overwhelmed their security perimeters and sent the few Kuwaiti National Guardsmen running for cover.

The Royal Family had quickly removed them and was no longer at Dasma Palace, Sha'ab Palace, or any other royal residence because they were already on their way to Taif, Saudi Arabia, under the protection of King

Fahd ibn Abdul Aziz. The Emir of Kuwait's younger brother, Fahd, was the family's only member still on palace grounds. He was shot and killed by a sniper as he tried to flee a rear gate.

Still at 4:30 a.m., Iraqi bombers hit Kuwait International Airport. The majority of destruction was just east of Terminal Two.

More than one hundred British and multinationals had already boarded a British Airways Boeing 747 airliner and were awaiting takeoff when the air raid by Iraqi helicopter gunships occurred. The cockpit pilots received continuous delays from Kuwaiti air traffic controllers in the tower who couldn't make up their minds what to do. First, the tower halted any incoming traffic. Second, the runway lights were extinguished. Then several more delays cost the "ready and boarded" plane crucial hours. The Iraqis actually had time to capture the airport, the British Airways 747 still sitting ready for takeoff with all passengers aboard.

The passengers and crew were taken hostage and the plane was blown up on the tarmac. When the passengers reentered the terminal, it was not the same place they left hours earlier. Many of the large plate glass windows had been blown out; Iraqi soldiers were everywhere with AK47 rifles; and the passengers were no longer free but prisoners of the semi-barbaric armies of Saddam Hussein.

For me, the terror and possibility of getting killed hadn't really sunk in yet, even though I was at work in the middle of the buildings and complexes being bombarded. Sure, there had been two massive explosions on the upper floors of the building I was in and I had personally witnessed Kuwaiti Guardsmen being pursued and probably killed by Iraqi troops, but my mind wasn't ready to accept we were at war yet. Though I still hadn't accepted it, I had instinctively started taking action to secure my own butt. I confronted the enemy, watched a brutal execution of Kuwaiti soldiers within Ministry walls, saw a Filipino get his head almost cut off by an Iraqi soldier's bayonet, fled through the streets getting shot at twice and made it all the way home to safety.

From home, I planned the best way to escape the country if things got really bad for me, but I still hoped I'd wake up and find the whole thing would have been a scary dream. Surely, it would have been a very vivid dream if all the friends I had talked with on the telephone in the last few minutes were also in it.

Being home in reasonable safety gave me a chance to regroup my thoughts and go over the events that led to the run for my life through downtown Kuwait City's streets. I remembered the tunnel I escaped through and the experience I had at the other end. What if it had been only a rumor that the Ministry of Information Complex was linked underground to the Governorate Building?

Now I'm beginning to realize that the earthquake of sensations I experienced while tucked away in my soundproof radio studio much earlier really were bombardments and tank fire from the war raging outside. The very complex of buildings I was in had been under attack from the air and ground. By the time I made the decision to get out of the studio because it may become an isolated tomb, Iraqi troops were inside and outside all the Ministry's buildings. Getting to my vehicle without encountering some death defying moves had been nearly impossible. My one and only hope was to go with my hunch of a secret unused tunnel that supposedly linked underground the Main Administrative building of the Ministry of Information Complex and the Governorate building or City Hall less than two hundred yards away. At least until now my luck had been great.

To get to the Governorate, I still had to maneuver my way through the Radio building and down several stairways to the basement of the main administrative building. It was just before I exited the second floor stairwell of the Radio building when I encountered my first dead soldier. He was a young Kuwaiti kid that I had seen around but never actually talked to. Several bullet wounds ran perpendicular in his body, through his chest and abdomen. No doubt he had been caught in a volley of high-powered rapid gunfire, probably from an AK47 which most of the

Iraqi soldiers were carrying. Blood covered the young man's upper torso and pooled in a large area beneath him on the floor. The gruesome picture of the dead boy raced through my mind many times for the next several hours, replaying like a video recorder left on repeat. Again and again, my brain reshowed me the blood oozing from his ears, nose and mouth and the bloody holes across his body.

I was too busy to offer anything more than a "God bless you" before I was off alternating between running and crawling to find the tunnel or storage facility if there really was one. Fortunately, this was one rumor that turned out to be true. Entering the below ground passageway from the lower basement was a little difficult in that its opening had been cluttered by broken unused office furniture and almost totally hidden from view, but it was doable. Once I saw it, I had no doubts where it would lead.

The tunnel looked better than I thought it would. I pictured raw concrete with no lighting at all; instead, the tunnel was more like a hallway with light gray tiles on the floor and large fluorescent tube lighting in the ceiling; however, I couldn't find a light switch, so I just tried to close my eyes and refocus. After I closed the door to the Ministry and began walking forward, my eyes adapted to the darkened environment more, so I could make out distant intervals of light streaming through. Daylight was coming from the air vents in the ceiling approximately thirty feet apart all the way through the tunnel.

I walked rapidly through the passageway for several minutes, keeping track of where I might be by the vents in the ceiling. I couldn't see any cars in the parking lot above but I was sure I was directly below them. Momentarily, I heard the roar and felt the rumble of this giant heavy object over me. "Oh God, is that a tank up there with nothing but some concrete ceiling between me and it? The vibration was horrendous. What if the ceiling wasn't thick enough to hold the weight? I continued scurrying through the tunnel, now even faster than before, listening for anything that might tell me what was happening above and whether the tank was headed in the same direction as me or not. If it doesn't fall through, I hope it leaves the parking lot where my car is before I get up there.

When I reached the end of the tunnel, the doorway leading up and towards the Governorate Building was filled with old typewriters, broken desks, chairs and old banged up file cabinets, much the same as the other end. At first I sat quietly in an office chair that was missing one roller while listening to all the sounds surrounding the building and atop the tunnel; there were plenty. I thought to myself, almost murmuring the words aloud, I could either go out and face the music or wait till later when the Iraqis would probably be even better entrenched than they already are. I wondered where that tank was. I couldn't hear it rumbling anymore, so it must have been gone or sitting still.

The next sound I heard was another thunderous explosion. I guess I had a pretty good idea where that tank was now. Once again the bombardment sounded as though it hit the Ministry of Information complex. I visualized the blast in my mind, a fiery explosion ripping away at the facade of the Ministry of Information building.

I was reluctant to exit the tunnel because from my position I knew Iraqi troops were also all over the Governorate Building Complex too, but I didn't want to get trapped below ground either. From my secret hiding place, I listened intently for a while trying to disseminate which sounds out there were within this complex and which were probably out in the lot where my van was parked. In general, the whole outside sounded like war movies I used to watch on television, a chaotic mass of tanks rumbling and firing and soldiers running, ducking, and shooting.

At one point though, it became time to leave my third security and comfort zone. I decided to get out of my underground passageway and confront the next situation head on. By tugging at a metal door, opening it and walking about fifteen feet, I found what appeared to be just what I was looking for, an exit. I carefully and quietly began climbing the steps up to ground level where the final obstacle lay. Even before I had completely opened the door, the smell of smoke from tank fire and burning buildings billowed in.

Just great! My luck! I was literally poking my head out of the doorway into a group of Iraqi soldiers taking time out for a cigarette break. The first two who spotted me grinned from ear to ear like someone who might have seen a cute prairie dog appearing from his hole. There sure were a lot of Iraqis up here. They seemed friendly enough, even offering me a smoke, but I wasn't so relaxed as to take advantage of it; besides, I don't smoke anyway. I declined, feeling reasonably sure they wouldn't shoot a man just because he refused to smoke with them.

Instead of fearing for my life, they put me at ease right away by starting to ask me questions. Where did I work and why was I there on Thursday (the Arabic week end)? They were amused by my ability to speak moderately good Arabic with them, since most Americans don't bother learning it. They took me over to meet some other soldiers like I was a toy they had just found, not someone they captured.

During the time I was with them, I saw from the corner of my eyes a firing squad. Several Kuwaiti soldiers and three Indian servants had been lined up against a wall. Within seconds of the men being placed against the wall, machine gun fire rang out and then fell silent. Only the three Indian cooks or kitchen staff remained. The Kuwaiti soldiers now lay splattered in their own blood at the foot of the red and white wall. Moments later the Iraqi with the machine gun motioned for the servants to get out of there. They ran so fast that had I blinked my eyes, I would have missed them.

The Iraqis I had been led around by quickly found something else to do other than talk to me. Their next in command hurried them off to the Ministry of Information Complex where I had just come from, for an all out assault I supposed. Without thinking, I asked where they were going. They said "Shoot, kill Kuwaitis."

In Olympic events, I had always wondered how they measured tenths and hundreds of a second in time; surely these minuscule amounts were insignificant. Now I knew how fast that really was. In less than a second I surmised that my congenial time with the Iraqi invaders was over and my life again was in full danger. I made a dash toward the parking lot, literally running alongside the Iraqi soldiers. They were running in an assault charge on the Ministry and I was running to my vehicle that lay in their path.

Much like you do when you're nervous, I fiddled with the car keys in the lock so long I wasn't sure I had already unlocked it or not, but went through the motions of opening the door as fast as I could anyway. Several more Iraqi assault soldiers continued running past me and to my rear, looking in my direction but never slowing or taking aim.

I jumped in the driver's seat and thanked God before strapping my seat belt around me for what I was sure would be a bumpy ride home. As I backed away and drove toward the exit, another company of soldiers, I couldn't tell which side, were less than a hundred yards away and running in my direction. I took my shirt and undershirt off, tied the white T-shirt to the car's radio antenna in a sign of surrender and put my top short sleeve shirt back on. I kept the windows rolled down with my arm out so anyone seeing the fleeing vehicle would also see a pale arm that obviously was a Westerner instead of a Kuwaiti.

Several soldiers glanced at me, but fortunately they seemed to be carrying out their assigned agenda. None appeared the least bit interested. No one followed as I drove my car from the parking lot onto Fahd al Salem Street. I passed in front of the Meridian Hotel, not bothering to stop for the traffic light between there and the downtown Kuwait Air building before turning onto Gulf Road. Within the next mile, it was apparent that Seif Palace was under siege, so I turned back on to other downtown streets again instead of hugging the coastal Gulf Road.

I began cutting over a few sandy desert lots amidst the high rise buildings, changing from street to street without as much as one Iraqi soldier in pursuit. I kept driving along sides of buildings when possible rather than out in the center of the streets. After all, it was broad daylight and it was possible some near sighted Iraqi couldn't see my shirt and might open fire on me from any direction.

The journey home was a long intense one. I still had to pass Dasma Palace, where I work the other part of my day for His Highness, as well as passing the American Embassy Complex nearby. As I got nearer to Dasma Palace, there was no doubt in my mind that it was taking heavy fire. Helicopter gunships continually strafed it from the air amid tanks, troops and troop carrier trucks everywhere. More reinforcing Iraqi soldiers were jumping from those personnel carriers to join the assault. Fire and smoke raged from every military complex, palace and government building I could see. Any time a low flying plane or helicopter came overhead, I stopped so I wouldn't draw attention.

Once again, I had to avoid getting too close to the full blown assault, so I continued cutting further south through construction of what one day is to become First Ring Road. I bumped and jerked through the sand and dirt piles and over the new concrete until I made it safely to my next obstacle. The American Embassy in B'neid al Gar District was surrounded by tanks, but there was no overhead firing from helicopter gunships like at the Palace and Ministry locations close by. It didn't appear to be under assault from the ground either, but I avoided it regardless.

After cutting through some back roads behind the high rise buildings where most American Embassy personnel live, I came under rapid fire by a machine gun. Without thinking, I threw the gears in reverse and backtracked around the corner from the Continental Hotel. With my main concern being getting shot, I continued screeching around corners across open lots and down alleyways until I passed the Al Salam Maternity Hospital.

It was at this point that I checked from the corner of my eye the bullet damage to the rear and side of my vehicle. I had taken several gun shots to the trunk and back windshield of the Ministry van but I still wasn't going to stop to do a full inspection. I drove like a maniac out of B'neid Al Gar District and into the next line of fire. Tanks and helicopter gunships were everywhere in front of me now as I neared a place near and dear to me, Sha'ab Palace where the Crown Prince lives. Massive portions of the palace's green tile roof were ablaze.

With still another three miles to go before reaching my apartment, I kept my eyes peeled in all directions for all things. Helicopters were firing live rounds from above and troops and tanks were doing the same from ground level. Mostly, fighting was concentrated over and around the green-tile roofs of Sha'ab Palace. I could see dark billowing smoke coming from inside the complex near the rear of the Palace's grounds. The street to the rear was full of Iraqi troops and my only other option, Gulf Road, on which I live, had become a thoroughfare for tanks.

Every place I needed to get past was already filled with Iraqis. I kept turning more inland, taking lots of small side streets and empty sand lots until I once again worked my way West of Sha'ab Palace, next to the Fahaheel Motorway. At Istigal Street I became trapped.

Now there was no place to go except straight forward into a road block. Within seconds, that confrontation with Iraqi soldiers I had so dreaded had come. The Iraqi soldiers pointed their rifles at me and motioned that I pull to one side, turn the car engine off and wait as they checked my ID. All I had left on me since ditching the Arabic ones in the underground passageway was my Arizona driver's license in English. I knew few of these Iraqis were educated and probably couldn't read their own language much less mine, so I wasn't worried. My unmarked Ministry of Information van was sitting in silence while the sounds of my heart made up for the missing sounds of the motor. Surely the soldiers could hear my heart too.

The soldiers didn't seem really concerned with me and even managed a little laughter about my shattered rear window and the bullet holes in the trunk. Their main concern continued being several other vehicles pulled to the same side of the road as mine. These had Kuwaitis in them. At least a few did. The soldiers had detained several trying to flee, but instead, the Kuwaitis had ended up face down on the cement, sprawled on the roadway with their legs spread far apart and their hands back behind their heads.

The Iraqi soldiers waved me through and for just one moment I relaxed enough to look up from the roadblock to the penthouse where I live. It seemed much farther than just another mile and a half or two and may still turn out to be impossible to get to, especially since I could see what appeared to be yet another road block between me and my building. In another feeble attempt at outmaneuvering the invaders, I took off on one more side street, skirting the road block but coming under fire from a lone Iraqi soldier guarding a group of men near the taxi office two doors from my building. Little did I know at the time, but that bullet also pierced my vehicle's right side window putting a hole through the back seat just behind me.

I got home in time to see the German Embassy family from the fourth floor of my building being loaded into a guarded van with a small amount of luggage. They said "officially" the Iraqis have invaded Kuwait. Now didn't that come as a surprise to me! I filled them in on my Ministry and Governorate escapades and a Reader's Digest version of my street running adventures before they were off. At least they're being evacuated over land to Saudi Arabia, the opposite direction from Iraq. One thing they said though stuck in my mind. "There's going to be a big clamp down by the Iraqis, so I had better get out of the country right away."

I pushed the elevator button for penthouse and, as the doors closed, sighed relief for how lucky or unlucky I was right now. Lucky I guess that the run for my life was successful, but unlucky that I was in the middle of a war.

The first thing I did upon entering my apartment was to grab a pair of binoculars and head straight to those huge floor to ceiling glass windows my penthouse is known for. I began checking out everything. I looked back over the route I had traveled to get home and then tried to analyze where all the fires in the city were.

I could see several large plumes of smoke and fires, mostly in the downtown area where I had just come from and on the far West side of town towards Jahra, Sulaibikhat, the Doha military base and the Ministry of Electricity Complex on Fourth Ring Road. Within the next several hours, I made a lot of telephone calls asking others what they knew so far and told them of my experiences as well as everything I could see from my perch above the city. I then made plans to get food and money as well as throwing some clothes together in a suitcase just in case I had to run. I wondered if the Iraqis had gotten to the bank. I guess I should've gone there first.

A few hours after I arrived home, I began formulating a plan on how I could get to the border of Saudi Arabia if things got worse. I honestly didn't think it would ever come to that though. For the most part, I believed Americans and most foreigners would be left alone but may sometime in the future be told to get out of the country.

I sat the binoculars aside for another minute and tuned into the television and radio stations as if by magic I was expecting to see someone reporting the day's events and giving explanations. Of course television and radio were both off the air. Now how could that have been a surprise! I should have been the one on radio.

Everyone I called said they had been listening for me at either the seven o'clock or the nine o'clock broadcast times and became concerned when I didn't come on. They had already started hearing through the grapevine that Iraqis had invaded the country. Most of my friends though were still inside their own homes and hadn't seen an Iraqi yet; but they weren't going out to look for them either. Some people like Janelle, who sleeps late, hadn't even heard the country was under siege.

I ventured over to the Sultan Center Market and ran into an American Basketball coach from Glendale, Arizona. He was employed at one of the Kuwaiti only sports clubs and had brought his whole family to Kuwait to live. He indicated that he and his family were ready to evacuate to Saudi

Arabia within the next couple of hours after going to the bank, packing and rounding up supplies. I told him I have no idea what I'm going to do yet, but I'm taking a few precautions. We both stopped momentarily to speak to other Americans and Brits in the Sultan Center Market before going our separate ways.

Few people were in the store. I guess most were staying home until they found out exactly what was happening and how serious the situation was. I left the market and carried all my food stuffs plus newly purchased portable radio, extra batteries and candles home. I had shopped like a hurricane was bearing down on me, in great quantity.

Now from my huge windows with almost 360 degrees view, I watched a full invasion unfold. I felt a bit like Nero watching Rome burn. Iraqi tanks and troop carrier trucks were coming down Gulf Road in an almost unbroken procession. There were hundreds of them. They were coming towards my apartment and running along almost every other street I could see too.

Major battles were now taking place in the desert, southwest of Jahra, at the Jabber Air base and Ali Al Salem Air base. At 5:30 a.m., the Communications tower in the suburb of Sabahiya had taken a direct bomb hit and was toppled by an Iraqi fighter plane air raid.

By 6:00 a.m. the Crown Prince's palace on Gulf Road in Sha'ab took shells from two bombing sorties. Within the same time period, the residence of Crown Prince Sheik Saad, one of my employers and the next designated ruler of Kuwait, was surrounded. This was also the location of the roadblock where I had been stopped earlier. My boss, The Crown Prince Designate and a few members of his family had come back to Kuwait to conclude some banking business and to pack very personal possessions. They still managed to safely exit the country only hours before Iraqi helicopter gunships attacked their Sha'ab Palace. So far, the only member of the Royal Family caught by the Iraqi invaders and then killed was the Emir's younger brother at Dasma Palace.

As Sheik Fahd, the Emir's younger brother got into his car and moved towards the ornate rear palace gates, he was shot to death by a sniper who was crouched atop the old museum building outside palace grounds. His murder was only hours before I passed nearby on my frightening run through the city's streets. A lot of rumors flew as to why Sheik Fahd remained behind. Some say he partied too much the night before, as was normal for him on a Wednesday night, the beginning of the weekend. There was still another rumor saying he stayed to fight. Either way, he was killed in his white Lincoln Town Car while trying to flee the Emir's residence at Dasma. The young Sheik was one of the most loved Royals and the head of Kuwait's Football Federation and Kuwait's Olympic teams.

At 6:00 a.m., Kuwait Radio announced on the Arabic Station, "The Tyrant of Baghdad has invaded Kuwait." Whoever made that announcement had to have been in the Ministry of Information Complex the same time I was.

This morning, General Khalid Abdullah Boodai, who received a call from the Crown Prince only moments before he fled at 2:30 a.m., ordered additional armored vehicles to defend the Emir's Dasma Palace and his own Sha'ab Palace; but of course this was far too late and to no avail. Protecting the two Royal residences from the massive onslaught from the sea and air would have been fruitless either way. At least the Emir and his entire family of wives and offspring were already in hiding or on their way to the mountain top palaces of Taif, Saudi Arabia; and the Crown Prince and most of his gang were already there or en route as well.

The largest battle of Kuwait started around 8:00 a.m. at Jiwan Camp in Sulaibikhat suburb, just West of downtown Kuwait City. Jiwan Camp, the Military College, and the Ministry of Defense Complexes are all grouped nearly together there. My friend Robert, a University professor, lived near there and called to tell me that all hell was breaking loose nearby. Of course we didn't know exactly what was taking place till later, but it was obvious to him that a major battle was under way.

The Iraqi military had taken up several primary lookout points to aid them in their bombardment of the tri-complex. The main lookout was on the roof of the occupied 11-story Ministry of Electricity and Water building across the street from Jiwan Camp. Another lookout was atop the Islamic Medical Center Mosque dome on the complete opposite side of the tri-complex. From here, the Iraqi command guided the horrific assault on all three complexes: Jiwan Camp, Military College, and Defense Ministry.

From the Orthology Mental Asylum Hospital grounds a quarter mile away, tanks, mortars, and artillery rained down on Jiwan and the others. From the Sabah Hospital grounds came more cannon fire, and from the Doha wetlands a little further to the northwest came the big guys, the 156 mm shells. All the ground assault was reinforced by helicopter gunships, Iraqi jet fighters and a battery of tanks.

I watched from my windows the massive clouds of smoke billowing from that part of town as my friend Robert continued calling and filling me in on huge blasts. He said the Ministry of Defense was ablaze but didn't know the Military College had already fallen. The battle for Jiwan Camp raged for just under ten hours from 8:00 a.m. till almost 6:00 p.m. At one point many wounded Kuwaiti guardsmen who had good chances for survival were put in vehicles and sent to hospitals in other suburbs such as Farwaniya and Adan. Few could know that within a couple more hours those hospitals too would come under Iraqi siege.

Kuwait's lack of preparation, supervision, and decision making was again proving costly. At Jiwan Camp in the early hours, the Kuwaiti Operations Room Commander made the mistake of instructing all his troops to lay down their weapons. He ordered no fire be directed at the oncoming Iraqi military. His surrender continued until another of the camp's commanders arrived and promptly countermanded the order. Resistance by the Kuwaitis resumed too late and with only 50 mm automatic weapons left to fight with.

The order made no difference in the end because the camp had to fall. The odds were grossly in favor of the invaders, perhaps somewhere between 30-1 and 50-1 in numbers only; and the Kuwaitis were ill equipped to make matters worse. Kuwait didn't have a chance. Their arrogance at the meeting in Jeddah cost them in the eyes of their friends and allies, and now their arrogance was costing them in lives and property. Their "ever so beloved" country was now falling to the mercy of the crazed madman Saddam Hussein.

Shortly before 5:00 a.m., the industrial area of Shuwaikh, the ports, al Salam Palace, the Ministry of Interior, and the Ministry of Foreign Affairs were overrun. All around town the conquering Iraqi soldiers were executing Kuwaitis and others who dared stand in their way.

Most of Kuwait City was under full siege within hours after the first tanks crossed the Iraq-Kuwait border. People living in the suburbs hadn't actually seen any invaders yet because the invaders were still busy blowing up Kuwait's infrastructure. Only those living in high rise apartment buildings were seeing the billows of smoke and watching the newly arriving armies taking up positions.

My building in the busy beach side community of Salmiya faces one of the widest and busiest thoroughfares in Kuwait City, Gulf Road, and a perfect perch for seeing everything happening for miles around. Each apartment, except for those in the basement, was seven thousand five hundred square feet of marble and luxury. And then there was the playhouse on the roof, ours.

Everyone living in our building was either a diplomat with a family or an expat worker like me, with a little money that could buy the best views in the city. Within our building's basement lived three couples, one Dutch and two British. The other floors were single family occupants of the whole floor. On the first floor was a design center for elite homes and palaces; on the second floor was a German Embassy family; the third floor housed a Canadian businessman and his family; and the fourth floor was another German Embassy family, the one I saw being whisked away. The fifth was a member of the royal family, but only a part time resident of Kuwait who had married another nationality. The husband never returned to Kuwait with her, but the Sheikha and several of her children came back often. She didn't want her children staying with their more Royal cousins and grandparents in a palace and I understand the arrangement was mutual. Her family, as most others, was out of the country for the summer when invasion came.

Between the Sheik's floor and my penthouse were two others, both empty since the two former Italian Embassy families gave up their leases.

As I stood peering from my windows, the whole situation outside looked pretty ludicrous. There was something wrong with the whole picture. I was standing in my penthouse surrounded by a world of materialism, Persian carpets, and chandeliers, yet I was calmly standing watching a nation being destroyed and people's lives ending. Logical or not, I continued grasping to some false security, peering at the real war through tinted plate glass windows and binoculars.

Chapter 10

Like Nero Watching Rome Burn

By noon the sky was full of gunships, both helicopter and fighter jets hovering and screeching over the city. There were sounds of bombardments near and far and the smoke at times lay as low as fog. Throughout the afternoon, the occasional thunder of jets became the rule rather than the exception. Their sounds blocked out all other sounds except my own thoughts. None of the aircraft were actually firing at targets anymore but showing their strength in numbers. Most helicopters within my view continued circling patterns around the Kuwait Towers and Dasma and Sha'ab Palaces.

The waters of the Persian Gulf remained busy all day. Several Iraqi sea landing craft filled with troops headed down the coastline past my building towards the port of Salmiya, just over a mile away. Other craft a little further out in the bay looked as though they were heading towards Failaka Island eight miles to the northeast.

Occasionally, I had to put aside the binoculars to answer the telephone. Surprisingly, one of the people calling me was Nabil, the Palestinian whose daughter died of injuries received at school. He wanted to know what was happening from my view. After relaying all my news to him, he in turn told me he was scheduled to leave Kuwait today for Amman, Jordan because his new visitor visa expired. His Kuwaiti sponsor had already ended up with Nabil's company and now told him he had washed his hands of him. An invasion was on so he didn't have time to mess with Nabil, give him back his passport or see that he exits the country safely.

I could sense further entrapment, hostility and tremendous despair in Nabil's voice. He said nothing out of the ordinary to me but I had the feeling he felt it was time to pay his former Kuwaiti sponsor a visit. As for the Kuwaiti sponsor who had stolen more than a million and a half dollars from Nabil, it was still too early in the war for him to have learned any lessons. His timing for further abuse of anyone was over, yet he continued. He was now a hunted man inside his own country by invaders and most likely other people like Nabil who had genuine grievances to settle.

Bombardments of the city were lessening but fear throughout the land had begun taking a hard grip. With each telephone call, rumors and news of recent atrocities, unfolding events took on lives of their own. All information and supposed information spread person to person and via our telephone grapevine network because all radio and television stations were still off the air.

At first, Kuwait television broadcast patriotic songs and still pictures of the Emir and Crown Prince but was soon switched over to a silent picture of Saddam Hussein. Later I learned there was a remote television studio being set up in a suburb of Kuwait City, away from the hands of the Iraqis, but that too was only rumor. I kept my television tuned to CNN almost all the time. After a short while they announced little more than "There appears to be an invasion in progress." This was all the information I was able to obtain at such a crucial time? Soon, we would have no more CNN or any other communication with the outside world.

While standing in front of my windows, binoculars in one hand and iced tea in the other, I glanced down at one of several ongoing commotions. Several soldiers from someone's army; I assumed Iraqi invaders jumped from the back of a troop carrier truck and ran past the empty lot at the foot of my building. Again, their automatic weapon fire sounded fake like quick volleys of shots from cap pistols out of the direction of

Pizza Hut and to the rear of Hungry Bunny. Moments later, a death squad dragged out two squirming but still alive teenagers towards a waiting vehicle where they were stood and held spread eagle. Both shoeless boys in dirtied and bloodied white dishdashas remained standing facing the truck with their hands in the air while one soldier from above used the butt of his rifle to smash down hard into one of the kid's faces, causing the youngster's head to crack like a hammer to a pumpkin. Quickly now as one body fell like a tumbling bag of potatoes to the ground, the other met his fate at the hands of the savage Iraqi killing machines.

The second young man had entered death as cruelly as the first. Then the young boy's bodies were riddled in a hail of bullets like in a scene from "Bonnie and Clyde." Both lay quietly in the dead calm that followed, while the new occupiers of Kuwait laughed lit cigarettes and reenacted the exciting event.

The inhumanity of the day's events left me physically unscathed but certainly emotionally scarred and drained. From the time of those executions on, finding an escape route was no longer an option for me but rather a priority. I never thought the Iraqis could outsmart me on escape routes, but they could shoot me if they happen to already be where I was trying to get to. I had done a television report some time ago about crossing the desert and survival in it, so I knew to let some air out of my automobile tires to aid driving over loose sand. I knew where the worst sand drifts were between here and Saudi Arabia and I knew where the least traveled roads were. I thought I could make it by car or even boat in the Persian Gulf if I had to.

One of my plans was to wear dark clothing, carry some water and dried fruits, and walk down towards the docks in Salmiya only a mile and a half from where I live, just before dark. My thinking was that the invaders were still occupied with securing their foot hold on the main land while they could secure the sea at a later time. From Ras Al Ard Port, I'd grab a boat that I was familiar with, row quietly and slowly onto open water until I was away from the coast and then continue heading just offshore enough until I spotted Kafji, Saudi Arabia, about forty miles away. I could reach safety there.

I still thought of the escape routes as alternatives because I hoped they wouldn't be necessary. Some part of me still wanted to believe the troops would suddenly withdraw from Kuwait after being checkmated by the super powers. I really knew this probably wouldn't happen, but in such a desperate situation I still wanted to hold on to some hope. None of the people I called seemed to have formulated any plans of action yet, but I could tell they were already thinking of possibilities. Some said they were planning what they should take if they drive to Saudi Arabia. Others talked about the airport; yet others said they would just sit it out, hoping they'd be safe at home. After all, the Iraqis just wanted the government, not individuals.

Surprisingly, stores still had food, and banks still had everyone's money. As far as I was concerned, sitting tight was about the only thing to do until an actual plan could evolve or something even more drastic happened.

My thoughts were still of both fascination and guilt. Everything in my mind seemed contradictory. I should've been able to broadcast but would probably have been killed if I did. I wanted to stay to witness a war firsthand but didn't want to be one of its casualties. What, if anything, would the Iraqis do to Americans if they clamped down? Would they round us up and take us to prison? Would we end up on the run? I opted to take each hour, as it came, calmly. I had to admit I felt invigorated like I was playing a dangerous game I liked.

The bank was no problem. Though Kuwait National Bank was closed, only one block away was the closest ATM. I put my card in to withdraw the maximum amount, 750 KD ($2,500). Now I had money and food. Again, it was almost too easy. The Sultan Center Market was busy but there was no panic. It wasn't like someone said there will be an invasion tomorrow and we all need to shop for food. The invasion had already happened and the troops were here. With a little more forethought though, everyone would have to come to the same conclusion. Those thousands of marauding soldiers out there had no soup kitchens and would have to get their food from somewhere.

My good friend Saleh called and said some expats were rounded up in Safat district, downtown Kuwait City. They were taken to the Sheraton Hotel near the Ministry of Information Radio and Televisions Complex. He said his brother was told that other expats were being taken to the Orthology traffic circle for some reason, maybe detention. At this time no one had any idea whether any of those detainees were American or British. I told him I still couldn't believe any harm would come to expats, because the Iraqis I encountered this morning were unconcerned with me. Through each step of the way they could have captured or killed me and they didn't. Instead, they had allowed me to pass through the road block with no hassle at all, perhaps because Saddam Hussein was still receiving money and support from the United States.

Saleh's family was in great danger because of their wealth and ties to the Crown Prince and had to begin taking extreme caution. He didn't say whether they were going to stay to defend their home or would be fleeing the country, like most other Kuwaitis that happened to be in the country at the time of invasion. He did say, however, that he may be unable to contact me again for quite some time.

Embassies were of little help to their countrymen when the time of crisis came. The people in the basement apartment below me called the British Embassy and were told, "Listen for any announcements made over radio and television; then weigh the truth for you." I was sort of told the same thing by the United States Embassy who had contingent plans to evacuate their own staff and dependents, but no one in the American community outside their employment would be taken to safety.

News continued mostly by word of mouth, but many of us had satellite television and was kept informed by CNN as well as BBC. At least, we felt the world was aware something was going on in Kuwait as long as there was still communication. CNN would occasionally break in their usual telecast day but really said nothing about the full scale invasion and the massive destruction that had already started and was still taking place.

No matter what my decision would be, to flee or stay, I had only one more necessary chore that had to be taken care of, and that was to fill my automobile gas tank and as many other petrol cans as I could. The government owned stations were still pumping and weren't overly busy. There were two well armed Iraqi soldiers standing out front of the one I went to, but at the time they didn't seem to have any orders to do anything but stand there. While a Bangladeshi filled my tank and cans, I heard several more muffled bomb blasts, like they were coming from the west side of town where most of the smoke was earlier in the morning. Strangely, the only roadblock I hit was less than a half block from home but once again I was waved through. Nothing in my life ever prepared me for a situation like the one we were all experiencing in Kuwait. Your brain had to work overtime, and there was never any time for it to stop. Stopping or not thinking or planning correctly or just wrong timing could cost you your life. It was like my brain was a computer trying to call up information that was never stored there. In just one morning of my life, I watched Kuwaiti guardsmen run for their lives and lose. I met the invaders face to face, darted through city streets, running for my life and stood and watched a city burn. The excitement and fear I felt and the adrenalin rushes I experienced were little different than when I was getting pumped up as a kid because some big bully was supposed to meet me after school to beat my puny little ass. I was a little pansy, half the size of all the other boys my age, and I felt one third the size of the big boys.

This time my fears could possibly have more deadly consequences than getting my butt kicked after school. Perhaps now I was either braver or crazier than I thought. Nonetheless, I sought out danger by going into the streets when there was little reason to be out there at all.

I was constantly in touch with one of my Kuwaiti friends living in the Zahra mid rise building next door to mine. Mishal was a great source of news from Arabic television and radio via neighboring Bahrain, just to the southeast of Kuwait. Mishal told me the latest news and I told him what I had seen and heard, because my place was higher and had a better all around view than his.

Another part of our newly forming communication network was my Lebanese friend Samir, residing in Hawalli, who went onto the rooftop of his eight story apartment building and fed information back inside to his wife who then relayed it to me and several other people. I was doing the same thing from my place back to Samir and friends in other suburbs.

Unfortunately, I was unable to call Linda and Badran because they lived in that Islamic fundamentalist building in Jahra that didn't allow telephones (the landlord had gone so far as to take Badran's mobile phone out of his car), and Linda wasn't answering her cell. Jahra was Kuwait's first populated area in the path of oncoming Iraqis, so information from there would have been extremely valuable. From them, we could have learned quantities of troop movements entering the metropolitan area from the main highways linking Kuwait with Iraq.

Our mouth to mouth communications "friends' network" was enlarged when we linked up with Nabil at his hotel in Messila Beach as well as other contacts in other suburbs. Another friend of Mishal had a radio and began screening a barrage of short wave broadcasts concerning Kuwait.

Several men of multiple nationalities in Salmiya who had no view like mine, wandered over to the beach to look back on the still burning city and all the helicopter activity. When I recognized two of them as fellow joggers, I motioned for them to come up for an even better view. Within an hour their group had grown to eight. During that impromptu assembly on the roof, an Iraqi helicopter flew right past my terrace at almost the same level. We all stood like bumps on a log and could have been picked off easily as it passed, but it showed no interest and didn't fire. It was so close; we could see the men inside and almost made eye contact with the one hanging from the open doorway.

I served hot tea and microwave popcorn to my excited roof top guests as everyone rotated use of my binoculars and telephone, calling their families and friends to tell of our "narrow escape."

All afternoon, ships from about four miles off the coast continued ferrying smaller landing craft towards the Kuwait Towers and Dasma and Seif Palaces. Closer in, we saw a Kuwait Touristic Enterprise hydrofoil heading from the Ras Al Ard Port in Salmiya towards the main beaches of Kuwait City. That was not a usual route for tour boats, so we knew the Iraqis had already appropriated the hydrofoil too. Its normal route was back and forth between Salmiya and Failaka Island in the opposite direction.

One topic of conversation that came up on my outside terrace was the same everyone everywhere was asking. "Why was there no warning from the air raid sirens that had sounded every day without fail for years, and today of all days it was silent?"

Even seeing the almost non-stop procession of tanks and other military vehicles speeding down Gulf Road past my building and feeling the ground rumble beneath me, I still didn't feel the war was personal.

The telephone rang again. It was Janelle; she had just awakened and said several people had called her about a war or something. I told her all I knew and what I could see. She was thankful that her two young boys, Mishal and Haythem were in California. She said she was going to get her face together, then call our British friend Joy and her long time male friend Heyman, and see what they know. Joy years ago had been married to a Kuwaiti pilot like Janelle and their close friendship has continued through some sad years, both becoming widows with small children, losing their husbands at early ages. Now Joy and Janelle became part of our communication "friends' network."

I stayed put the rest of the afternoon because of my almost 360-degree panoramic view of the entire city, Kuwait Towers, the Palaces, the Persian Gulf, the beaches, offshore islands and the main thoroughfare

Gulf Road that runs right next to my building. Surely my view was one of the best, if not the best in the whole city. From my apartment I watched one country swallow another.

Occasionally a few more tanks with their outpouring of noxious exhaust scurried along Gulf Road but there was almost no normal traffic. I guess because people were already hearing rumors about executions and car stealing at road blocks around town. Once in a while though, I would see a car bolt far in excess of the speed limit down Gulf Road and then hurriedly turn off before encountering columns of Iraqi tanks or roadblocks.

Another American friend just happened to be wandering around my neighborhood and dropped in for the view. When he saw a group of tanks and troop carrier trucks approaching on Gulf Road, he said, "I wonder whose they are." With a slight sense of biting cruelty, we both burst into simultaneous laughter because we both knew they couldn't be Kuwaiti tanks as it was the weekend. Even the Kuwaiti Army couldn't get someone to drive a tank then!

By late afternoon, the telephone was still ringing, often. By evening, the first day of invasion, wispy gray and black smoke and the smell of fire from other parts of the city lay over Salmiya, cutting the overall visibility. Now since just one morning's dawn, the only thing that seemed normal were the mosques' calls to prayer. Some shops didn't open in the afternoon at all, and the ones that did had no customers. The normally bustling Sultan Center Market was doing fair business with mostly Europeans and Americans buying groceries, stocking up in case things got worse. Even the normally busy parking lots at the upscale boutiques of Fashion Way remained almost empty. There were no customers at Sizzler Steak House, Pizza Hut, Farah Restaurant or any of the local eateries. The city was already taking on a ghostly appearance.

Each time I went to my windows, I couldn't help but wonder how many people died out there today? What was going to happen to us all? What other countries—were doing diplomatically or otherwise to help rescue us? I also wondered whether the next time I came face to face with an Iraqi; would he shoot me? I wondered how the smug Kuwaitis from the Jeddah meeting were feeling tonight while they lay safely tucked away in their apartments in Cairo, palaces in Taif and other places far from Kuwait. They left the rest of us here to face the results of their greed and inability to make decisions at that meeting. I thought they should have lost face with all their allies after storming out of that meeting. It's funny how loyal allies remain when great sums of oil and money are at stake.

How could the Americans, British and even Saudis view Kuwait's leaders as anything but greedy cowards after watching them in time of crisis? In my mind, I already knew the Kuwaitis would probably use their trump card, the transcripts of the Glaspie/Hussein meeting as blackmail into getting someone else to do their fighting for them. God, how dumb was I in securing those papers from Baghdad and personally handing them over to the Kuwaitis.

As night began to fall, many people from Salmiya, men, women, and children alike, braved the darkness to come to the beach for a view of the glowing smoke clouds downtown across the bay. I watched all of them below as I somberly packed an emergency suitcase and watched points of interest with my binoculars.

It had been a full day. Earlier, about four o'clock in the afternoon, I rounded up all my valuables, a couple of gold items I bought to take back for Maia at Christmas, my best watch and the majority of the $2,500 I withdrew from the bank. I dug a hole in one of the dirt planters on the balcony, placed the valuables inside a glass container and sealed it in a Saran wrap. After the dirt and plant were replanted, no one could ever dream that anything of value was hidden there. I really had no reason for doing this, but if I did leave my apartment in a hurry or got detained at a roadblock or searched and taken away, no one would get my most expensive things. I also thought that the rumors may be true and the Iraqis had started breaking into Kuwaitis houses, beating them up and rounding up foreigners.

I awoke around 8:00 a.m., August 3, 1990; just 34 hours after invasion came to Kuwait City. I made this a stay at home keep in touch day. Our tight knit "friends' network" had now become a well informed rumor mill. I made several calls back to the United States letting everyone know the latest local events and told them the next call they got from me could be collect from Saudi Arabia. They of course were extremely concerned for my safety and their response was for me to head directly to the airport to get the first flight out. I explained that the airport was seized early yesterday, even before I left work. Most of the fifteen remaining commercial aircraft had been blown up on the tarmac or at their terminal gates. There wouldn't be any more.

On the 4th of August, two full days following the invasion, the onslaught of Iraqi tanks continued pouring into the country, securing their hold on every segment of life. I watched cable television most of the day and night to see what Washington and other capitols were saying. It wasn't much. I was not allowed to go to work anymore so I started sleeping longer each day. This morning I awoke to the roar and rumble of tanks once again, hundreds of them lining Gulf Road in both directions. They drove east and south in all six lanes, both sides of the median as far as the eye could see, some playfully crossing into the median, crushing concrete planters, shrubs and small palms as they went. The normally clean beach drive was now entirely muddied and marked by the broken concrete where ever the tank's steel track teeth dug in.

I couldn't imagine where the tanks were heading because there was nothing of military value, bases or Ministry complexes on the Salmiya peninsula, only a bedroom shopping beach community. Gulf Road, however, winds around the entire coast through several other suburbs to the south, before eventually reuniting with Sixth Ring Road. The only place of any interest at all would be the Touristic Enterprises Port here in Salmiya where all the ferry boats, hydrofoils, yachts, and smaller boats are anchored. Maybe the Iraqis intended to load all those tanks on the several small ferry boats at Ras Al Ard Port to transport them over to Failaka Island.

Our "telephone-informed sources" said that during the night other columns of tanks had rolled down Fifth and Sixth Ring Roads and the Fahaheel Motorway southward, beyond Messila Beach, securing the Iraqi's southern flank between Kuwait City and Saudi Arabia. They also said all the tanks were continuing to move southward reinforcing the ones that were firing on the oil refineries and ports of Fahaheel, Mina Abdullah and the Khiran Power Plant that lay within the path to the border of Saudi Arabia.

It was an unusual sight to see hundreds of hostile tanks coming down the street but even stranger seeing hundreds of the so called modern Iraqi soldiers sitting on the rock jetties in their underwear, washing and pounding their only uniform clean in the sea water.

My Kuwaiti friend Mishal in the next building came up again for a better look at the tank columns. I asked him about the signs the Iraqi tanks were flying and some of the soldiers were waving. He said they were "V," for Victory. At first, we were both a little puzzled but Mishal said he had heard from friends in Hawalli District that Iraqi soldiers were waving the same type flags over there, while telling the local Palestinians they were happy to come save Kuwait from its internal revolution. I told Mishal that statement was almost as ludicrous as the ones I heard the morning of invasion. One version came from the Iraqi soldiers who spoke with me just before they stormed the Ministry of Information Complex, and another version came from my Indian friend Ali Chougli.

The Iraqis told me they came to kill Kuwaitis. They obviously knew where they were and why they were here, but the ones who spoke with Ali Chougli while he was stopped at a road block in Rumaithiya, replied they came to Amman, Jordan, for a practice invasion as the first step to invading Israel. When those soldiers were told to look around at all the destruction, they had invaded Kuwait, not Amman, they were surprised and shocked.

The Iraqi soldiers said they had been loaded aboard transport trucks in the middle of the night and told they were heading for Amman, Jordan where they would do a mock invasion of the city with the permission of the Jordanian people. From the exercise, the Iraqi troops would learn better how to invade Israel. The real assault would come one month later.

One of my friends shopping for groceries at the Sultan Center Market heard several people saying they had just been kicked off Failaka Island. They said the Iraqis took a couple ferries over to the island the first day after invasion and began rounding up all the food in the stores and homes. They took all of it to the Kuwait military post on the north side of the island, in the baron region near the coast. Officers of the Iraqi Republican Guard told all the civilians to be off the island within three days. If they did not leave Failaka, they'd be imprisoned or worse. Each family exiting was also instructed to pay a thousand dinars ($3,300) to the Iraqi guards controlling the port or they would be left behind and in lots of trouble. Most Failaka residents wasted no time in heading for their bank accounts at the few local automatic tellers or banks on the island then left.

Tonight, like last night and the nights before, I fell asleep watching cable television waiting to hear news about what other governments were doing about the situation in Kuwait. Each day I called home to family members and friends discussing what they had heard and what I knew.

On the morning of the 5th of August, about 80 hours after the invasion, I got up and went over to the Sultan Center Market, not because I needed groceries but because I wanted to be around other people. Everyone over there was talking about the Umm al Aish Earth Satellite Station north of Kuwait City. The giant dish was hit by Iraqi air strikes sometime during the night. It seemed without this big dish all microwave transmitters in the city were useless. It would no longer be possible to make telephone calls outside the country. Literally, Kuwait had become cut off from the rest of the world.

CHAPTER 11

All Communications Are Cut

Though the al Aish dish was destroyed and communications to the outside world were no longer possible, communication within the country was still OK. Later we learned that some suburbs such as Ahmadi on the far south side of town and a couple of the suburbs on the far west side had lost telephone use altogether.

None of our friends' phones had been affected by the interruption in local service so our "friends' network" was still our vital link with each other. Of course, when I got home from Sultan Center Market, I immediately wanted to find out if the new information I had obtained about the Umm al Aish Dish was true; so I tried to call the States and got less than half way through the dialing process before the phone started beeping. It was true. We had been cut off from the outside.

As soon as the war and invasion started, it seemed to be over. The positive report came today as Mishal, many neighbors and I watched from his apartment next door. The televised message was of the utmost importance from Saddam Hussein to the people of Kuwait. He announced that, beginning tonight, there would be an orderly withdrawal of Iraqi troops from Kuwait. Of course everyone in the room shouted and screamed.

The occupation of Kuwait was over and it only lasted three full days. Everyone was relieved. Many people in the country were celebrating by pouring into the streets of their suburbs and into Salmiya's shopping district for the first time since the Iraqis came. I think we all rested better that night and prayed for everything to get back to normal.

By the next morning, a second broadcast was being shown on Kuwait Channel One Television, and we all rushed to our sets to watch it. Our bubble of happiness burst as we watched the latest puzzling and troublesome announcement. When it was over, Kuwaitis and expats alike weren't sure what had just happened. The broadcaster announced names and showed pictures of a new provisional government for "Free Kuwait." No one in our room seemed to know any of the people who were now the heads of the government of Kuwait. Some people outright laughed as the broadcast showed a local accountant assuming the position of President of Kuwait. One guy in the room made comments like, "See, in Kuwait every man can grow up to be President just like in America."

It's true that most Kuwaitis don't like America, yet this slur was not directed maliciously at the United States but was merely a funny analogy. At the end of the program, more videos followed showing ecstatic Iraqis in Baghdad and Basra reveling in the streets at news they had liberated Kuwait from their internal revolution.

After watching television, we tuned to the Arabic radio. All channels were still off the air as was my English station but a makeshift station had been set up by resistance fighters who began making announcements at varying times from different locations each day. So far, the Iraqis had been unable to find out who was running the rogue station or where it was coming from. Yesterday the station told of many Kuwaitis' homes being broken into by the occupying armies and women being raped. Some heads of families had also been taken away by Iraqi soldiers. The radio also read a list of names of those they were calling martyrs, who had refused to cooperate with their captures and were executed in front of their families.

Many people I knew were talking about having good parties to celebrate the Iraqi retreat, but that last information coming from the rogue radio station quickly put a damper on everyone's mood. Now once again we were confused and unsure what to do next.

Kuwait Arabic television returned on air showing insignificant uninformative broadcasts and that was all. The rest of the time it showed Saddam Hussein opening new schools in Baghdad and passing in review of his troops or a test pattern of the Iraqi flag and the singing of patriotic songs.

If it was true that the Iraqis were leaving, it would be interesting to see reports on damage done in the country since occupation began. I hoped I'd be called to do some of the documentation. I called my supervisor from the Ministry of Information to ask when we might be returning to work. He said that if things went as expected, probably in a few days. First they'd get Arabic television and radio back on the air properly and then work on the English station. Hopefully, I would soon return to work at the Ministry of Information, but it looked unlikely I would be able to return to the palaces since much reconstruction had to be done to them before members of the Royal family could return.

On the 6th of August everyone was looking for signs of the Iraqi withdrawal that Saddam Hussein had promised but we weren't seeing any evidence of it. We wondered if perhaps the big armies outside the city were withdrawing first, before the troops within the city would leave. Some people went so far as to say the whole thing was a big hoax by Saddam Hussein and the Iraqis weren't really leaving at all. They were digging in.

Over the first few days, a lot of residents of Kuwait City fled to Saudi Arabia, but soon we heard through our "friends' network" that Iraqi soldiers soon forced the closure of the Nuwaiseeb Customs Checkpoint near Khafji and the other one south of Wafra. There was no other way to get out of the country except over the sand through the deserts. One of the people that had gone to some border post said that when the Iraqi troops finally succeeded in closing the gate to Saudi Arabia, some of the thousand cars still waiting immediately deflated their tires a little, and then headed out through the sand to bypass the checkpoint. Thousands of cars, mostly Kuwaiti had already managed to pass through the same border crossing over the past three days before the border station was closed. Thank God all the Rolls Royce's carrying tons of expensive stashes of the Royal family had already crossed through.

Driving over the desert's sand was dangerous, but for some it was the only way left to get out. Families loaded into vehicles stuffed with personal belongings and relatives. Cars were seen heading over the open desert towards the West and Southwest with three feet high luggage racks filled to capacity. They had extra gas cans tied atop the trunk and bumpers and the vehicle tires slightly deflated to aid travel through the blowing sand's changing depths. The daytime heat of the desert reached extreme temperatures of nearly 150 degrees; so many families chose to travel at night. Fortunately, most nights were clear, and the stars and moon provided more light than at first expected. Not all fleeing families reached the border in their vehicles; however, some had to abandon them in the drifting dunes where the wheels couldn't make enough traction to proceed any further.

Most of the people that hadn't left yet said they wanted to leave Kuwait as soon as they could figure out how to do it safely, but the Iraqis were clamping down tighter every day, as I personally witnessed with a second Iraqi roadblock set up on Gulf Road in front of my apartment. Both checkpoints remained permanent throughout occupation.

The daily calls to prayer from mosques' loud speakers continued coming in loud and clear five times a day. I'd never been fond of the calls personally; however, they were now a semblance of order amongst all the other chaos. Many mosques had come under siege and had become dangerous places to go because inside most, the Iraqi military had taken up residence and were making sure the religious leaders weren't instigating resistance.

Starting about 3:30-4:00 every morning, according to sunrise, I heard simultaneous calls from the loud speakers from about seven mosques, blaring clearly, "Allahu Akbar, Allahu Akbar" (God is Great, God is Great).

On August 7th all final phones, including the last local lines, went dead in the whole country. The situation became quite scary. The loss of our "friends' network" was a great blow to our personal freedom and to our security. We were unable to speak and share information with each other and now had to resort to word of mouth, which made rumors worse. We were hearing lots of tales of Kuwaitis being murdered by Iraqi troops and by Palestinians settling the score with their unjust Kuwaiti employers, like, I think Nabil had done. Many abused Indian maids had also turned in their bosses to Iraqi soldiers and gruesome stories were told of what had happened to them. There were even a couple stories of people assisting the Iraqis in torturing or killing the Kuwaitis.

It was only a couple hours later that I learned that my maid Jeanette's sister Emily had killed her employer and had in turn been killed by the Kuwaiti's wife. Emily had turned her employer in to the Iraqi soldiers who came for him on August 5th. She had run away from the Kuwaiti family the day after invasion and had gone to live with Jeanette and her husband. Emily went back to the Kuwaiti home once more to try collecting all the money they owed her for almost a half year's work but was unsuccessful. She wanted her passport and to use the money to go home to the Philippines.

When she returned to the Kuwaitis home to collect the money, her master/employer beat her badly, broke her nose, busted her upper lip and tore a big chunk of hair from her scalp. The Kuwaiti also kicked her in the stomach several times while she was down.

In rage Emily found Iraqi soldiers nearby and begged them to return with her to the house. When they arrived, the Kuwaiti slapped Emily in front of them. One soldier opened fire on the Kuwaiti who then dropped to the floor in a hail of bullets. The Iraqi soldiers stepped over the bloodied dead body, ransacked the house and took money from the mistress, giving part of it to Emily. The other half they kept.

The man's wife armed herself with a 9 mm pistol and followed the soldiers and Emily out the door, opening fire on Emily, fatally wounding her with a lucky shot to the back of the head just before she reached the gate. The shocked Iraqi soldiers rushed back inside the house in pursuit of the Kuwaiti mistress and gunned her down in front of her children.

Neighbors had been listening to the gunfight and soon came to gawk at Emily's and the Kuwaiti's lifeless bodies. They were heard to comment, "That Philippine tramp had them killed. Both Kuwaitis were peace loving, law abiding family people. Now they were dead because of a silly maid." Emily's bloodied but calm looking body remained near the gate like garbage for several days while the bodies of the Kuwaitis were quickly gathered and buried in Muslim tradition hours later.

Cars all over the city were being stolen with more frequency, mostly by Iraqis at road blocks who were daily becoming more demonstrative and authoritative. They were now acting with impunity, slapping or beating anyone they wished and raping whoever they pleased.

What a difference a week made, and in some cases even a day. When we lost the telephone, we lost touch with our friends. From that time on, I knew of no one who ventured out more than a block away from their home or apartment. Rumors became even more rampant, and it was obvious to everyone that the Iraqis were not leaving but rather the feared clamp down had already begun.

Telephones were of no use any more and local television and radio stations continued being of little use. All they served up was propaganda, Iraqi patriotic songs and pictures of Saddam Hussein shooting weapons or waving the Iraqi flag. Satellite television service was also knocked off the air, so television could be turned off without feeling you were missing anything. More and more we began listening to the rogue Kuwaiti radio station and to shortwave broadcasts from Radio Bahrain and the BBC, which were both great sources of information because they broadcast about Kuwait most of their scheduled days. The small independent Arab country of Bahrain is about the same distance from Kuwait City as Atlanta is from Savannah, Georgia, 260 miles away.

Every night I watched rifle tracer fire coming from several different locations around the city and sometimes saw a new building ablaze. Of course, all fires now burned without fire engines responding. Firemen were also forbidden to go to work.

We were all stunned on the seventh day of occupation when Kuwait Television broadcast news from Baghdad that Saddam Hussein's Revolutionary Command Council had annexed Kuwait as the 19th Province of Iraq. Kuwait was now called Kazimah.

By the eighth day since invasion, August 10, opposition to the Iraqi takeover had grown. People, both Kuwaiti and expat alike had become more openly vocal. Word of mouth had it that several Iraqis had been killed by a resistance movement. Word of mouth also said Iraqi soldiers retaliated by burning some homes and executing some heads of households nearest where the bodies were found.

Most Iraqi soldiers were housed in neighborhood schools with some of the upper ranks quartered inside Mosques. Every neighborhood, perhaps a fifty in all had areas where large numbers of Iraqi troops camped out. The Iraqis had not only established many roadblocks but patrolled every neighborhood on foot and guarded every market, gas station, bank and store; anywhere groups of people might congregate.

Iraqi soldiers walked into any store and took what they wanted. Meat stores were hit especially hard. Iraqi troops walked out with as much as they could carry without paying. They went to people's residences demanding money and food as well. Most people at first didn't think this was a serious problem, but food supplies soon dwindled. By the time the numbers of Iraqi soldiers had increased to almost a third of a million who all needed to be fed (not counting the country's normal population), there was little or no food left. The Iraqis had interrupted shipping and trucking into the country; therefore no other foods or commodities were arriving. All food warehouses in town had been emptied and Baghdad was unprepared to continue supplying their million man army within Iraq and down in Kuwait.

While Iraqi soldiers patrolled the neighborhoods, they hassled and roughed up everyone they came in contact with. Roadblocks became ambush places for modern Jesse James's in Iraqi uniform. They had within their power to rob, steal or kill without having to answer to anyone but God above.

I just heard from Mishal that there was a women's anti-Iraq occupation rally today in the big open lot near Mubarek Al Kabir Hospital in Jaberiya. He said a friend of his wife told him that Iraqi troops opened fire on the women, killing at least one of them. Many others had been wounded and carried over to the hospital. He said the women had been marching and carrying portraits of the Emir and the Crown Prince. I told Mishal that I heard there was another spontaneous rally somewhere in Rumaithiya, the mostly Indian district where Ali Chougli lives but I hadn't heard if gun shots were fired there also.

My British friends from Ahmadi, Guy and Shari with the "Tara" home were awfully brave or stupid today. Without fear of the Iraqis, they decided to go for a ride to visit friends in several parts of town. They were showing amazing bravery as far as I was concerned. I had journeyed outside on an occasion but never again with my van. Even when I walked alone or with others along the beach, I wore a plain Egyptian cheap cotton style dishdasha for disguise with a red and white head wrapping, similar to that worn by Aunt Jamima. My American clothes apparently worked as well, but I felt safer in some sort of disguise. Iraqis didn't hate Egyptians, so chances were they would never harass one. Dressing down like an Egyptian quickly distanced my looks from that of a Kuwaiti or a westerner. So far no Iraqi ever glanced at me a second time.

Guy and Shari's new found bravery was unbelievable to me, especially since they were driving their new British Land Rover. Earlier, Guy and Shari went to their Palestinian friend Nabil's hotel room. During their visit together, Nabil said he would no longer be in touch with them nor me the rest of the time he remained in Kuwait, and that our fears of a confrontation between him and his sponsor had already come. Nabil had taken two Indians who also use to work for the same Kuwaiti sponsor and they settled the score once and for all.

Nabil said he and the Indians held the Kuwaiti sponsor at gun point for several minutes while they pressured him into signing documents relinquishing Nabil's million dollar company back to him. Nabil figured these documents would allow him at least enough time to strip the company and to retrieve as many assets as possible and get them to Jordan. In the event there was to be any worldwide response to the Iraqi invasion of Kuwait, Nabil and his family would be long gone. Crossing the borders of Saudi Arabia or especially Iraq would be easy with these legal papers and his equipment would be relatively simple since Jordanians like Nabil had sided with Saddam Hussein.

The Kuwaiti, of course, initially refused to give back Nabil's company or even extend sympathy Nabil's daughter had died of her injuries and delays caused by him and other Kuwaitis. Nabil coaxed the Kuwaiti into signing the legal papers only after shooting him once in each kneecap. With the signed documents in hand, Nabil walked out and never turned back; the two Indians still had issues they needed to settle with the same sponsor.

During Guy and Shari's hour long visit with me, they said they had heard on BBC Radio that Saddam Hussein had gotten the "go ahead" to continue occupation of Kuwait twice, the first time by American Ambassador April Glaspie and again at the Arab League Conference in Cairo earlier today. Guy said the Arabs at the conference were divided on the issue of Iraq's occupation of Kuwait, but in typical Arab style they failed to reach any resolution for Saddam Hussein to get out. Guy said that BBC shortwave told of film footage of Iraqis taking to the streets in Baghdad in celebration of their Arab League Conference victory.

To hear that Arabs were indecisive at the Arab League Conference in Cairo at such a crucial time was no surprise to Guy or me. Kuwait's leaders should know only too well of their own indecision at the Jeddah meeting that resulted in invasion and occupation. Kuwait would have no allies if they weren't bought and paid for.

Guy and I both spoke about the likelihood of a group of Arabs ever reaching decisions on anything promptly, unless they have someone as a backup they can blame when it goes wrong. Kuwaitis especially choose to stay "not liable" for anything that happens in their lives.

Their reckless indecision can be seen while driving down any street in the country. While following a few car lengths behind a Kuwaiti, you'll see them almost miss the same street they've lived on for years. You or I would have begun getting into the right turning lane and lowering our speed some distance before the turnoff, but a Kuwaiti usually nears the intersection in the passing lane at full speed, then without the use of a blinker tries to pass all other cars before cutting across the lanes in an attempt to make the right turn. They're also notorious for always straddling two lanes. For them, the hood ornament is used to align on the white lines in the middle of a thoroughfare. One wheel must always be in another lane. If someone dares honk at them, they will come back on the street to chase the honker through 12 miles of city streets.

Once I asked a Kuwaiti friend, why do they make everything so difficult? He said that even in Kuwait they tease each other about this. He said they say a European or American will eat with a spoon going straight from the plate to the mouth. A Kuwaiti will put the spoon in the right hand but will wrap his arm around the back of his neck trying to reach the plate from the left side.

On the 10th of August, the same day the Arab League met in Cairo, the occupying Iraqis took full control of Kuwait's hospitals. Since most nurses in the country were Filipino, word of mouth passed from my maid to me. She said in the first days following invasion the Iraqis had already stolen most of the equipment from the nurseries, operating rooms and kitchen freezers. Now they were in control of all hospitals and systematically wiping them out.

In their first staff meeting, the new Iraqi military hospital chief said nothing would change but within hours his men were forcing mental patients out onto the streets without prior notification to family members.

Today's biggest announcement came via Kuwait Channel 1 Arabic Television. The Tyrant of Baghdad, Saddam Hussein announced the appointment of his cousin as Military Governor of Kuwait. Ali Hassan al-Majid, the same ruthless character that Saddam placed in charge of the Kurdish areas in Northern Iraq in 1988; the same man who unleashed chemical gases on the population there would now be our new Governor. What would he do in Kuwait after having already killed thousands of men, women and children in his own country? Immediately, every household began creating safe areas within their apartments or homes to hide in the event there was a gas attack.

I finally decided the situation in Kuwait had deteriorated to a point that it was in my best interest to get out of the country. So far, I felt really lucky the war had passed me by and not once had I felt true danger since the first morning's run through the streets, fleeing my work place. Rumors intensified that many foreigners had been rounded up and the Iraqis were forcing people street by street to start listing the occupants of each apartment in each building and their nationality. That sounded to me like a harder clamp down was coming soon. I was of no use in Kuwait anymore. I couldn't work at the Ministry of Information or at the palaces for the Royal Families.

On August 11, nine days after occupation began, my neighbor got a news flier that said the resistance movement wanted everyone to go to their roof tops at midnight and yell "Allah Akbar." The flier also said everyone including women and children should continue the call airing their grievances against occupation for thirty minutes.

From the terrace that night, just off my bedroom, at two minutes to twelve I heard hundreds of voices begin piercing the night air. People were standing on their balconies at the nearby high rise Zahra Complex just to the east and rear of my building and on the grounds of the Italian Ambassador's residence below me. On the roof tops to my south were probably more than a hundred people. The Dutch couple from our basement and one Brit from next to them stood with me on my terrace for a full thirty minutes doing some yelling of our own. We hollered, "Get out of Kuwait, Saddam!" and "We hope Saddam gets his ass kicked by the Americans and Brits."

We didn't speak to people atop other buildings but we got some stares in our direction from those who understood what we were yelling. The strange demonstration sounded like thousands of voices screaming in the darkness of night, coming from all directions except the sea.

From the darkness and pale of the moon, you could barely see but easily hear, women, probably covered in black abaiya and veils, their children and men folk, all animated as they stretched their arms skyward in chant. The midnight rebellion was a resounding success, a triumph for organized resistance by the masses against Iraqi occupation. It did nothing physically to the occupying Iraqi armies but was a great morale booster to the rest of us.

As the next day unfolded, we heard new stories of young Kuwaiti boys as young as eight years old being tortured and executed by Iraqi soldiers in front of their families. It was a very sad situation. The horrible was happening. Still, Kuwaitis have always been known, even by other Arabs as untrustworthy, belligerent, often cruel and for the harshest treatment of expat workers of all countries in the Middle East. It was terribly hard hearing some of those stories about the suffering and indignities happening to them, but it was even harder drumming up sympathy for Kuwaitis anywhere except in the United States and Britain, where there was an underlying monetary reason.

Everyone but westerners knows that if a Kuwaiti feels he's been wronged, someone is going to get hurt. Whether someone doesn't render sex when it's wanted, that person gets beaten. If a Kuwaiti wants your assets, you're going to jail. There'll be no papers and no charges; it's an administrative hold that can last until the Kuwaiti feels better or you give in. Records are not kept and sweetly handed over to human rights organizations, so proving such wrong doing has been difficult. One must always remember that Kuwaitis are "clever."

What was seen following invasion with workers turning in their sponsors and bosses was perceived by almost everyone but the Kuwaitis themselves as a well deserved backlash from all those who have suffered at the hands of the Kuwaitis. Their record of inhumane treatment of others was one of the big reasons people of other nationalities sided with the invading armies. Few put their own safety on the line to help them. None of the foreign labor groups liked Saddam Hussein or his armies but they felt whatever happened in Kuwait and to Kuwaitis had to be better than the past.

The Iraqis became the ones fabricating all the charges against Kuwaitis. I too felt that I could have done more to help Kuwaitis, but I was only employed by them to do a particular job, not part of a mercenary army that would come fight their battle to save their asses for a dollar. It was true. I felt sorry for the families of Kuwaitis being tortured and killed. No amount of abuse Kuwaitis perpetrated on others justified the way they were being treated by the Iraqis, but what could I do.

Fortunately, Kuwait's younger generation seems to have a better hold on humanity and I do foresee a better future for them. It sounds as though I don't like Kuwait or my Kuwaiti hosts, which is not true at all. I am entitled to my opinion about them, the same as they and so many of their Muslim brothers are concerning westerners and the so called infidels I represent.

I had been cooped up in my apartment and nearby surroundings so long, I really needed to get out and see friends. I slid back into the seat of my van, just like Guy and Shari had done and headed out without concern or fear of the Iraqis. I drove my personal van over to visit Janelle for a while in Misref and was stopped only once for a routine roadblock with no trouble. While in that section of town, I stopped to do a little grocery shopping at the Coop in Bayan District near the Guest Palace before going to see other friends nearby. I had heard that coop was one of the only few in the country that had some supplies left. I was shopping when call for prayer came over the loud speakers from all neighborhood mosques. All Arab men went to one part of the store to pick up their customer courtesy prayer rugs as the women left the building to wait outside. All the men got down on their hands and knees in the aisles facing Mecca for prayer while I continued my business. I didn't kneel but listened intently. The right thing to do was what I was already doing. I tried not to step over someone praying, so I continued shopping while doing a little praying of my own.

During the time I waited for the cashiers to return to the checkout registers, I picked up an Arabic leaflet from the floor. It was the same as one handed to me by an Iraqi C. I. D. Officer (not so secret police) as I entered the store. These Iraqi intelligence people are spies on society, much the same as their plain clothed Kuwaiti secret service counterparts, but with a far more deadly agenda than looking for youngsters holding hands or kissing, liquor use or sexual activity.

The Iraqi leaflet headlines were easy to read, but I had to ask a passer by to read the detailed parts for me. He said the handbills announced ten new laws that all Kuwaitis and other people living in Kuwait will have to abide by as of August 16, next week. Some of these new regulations are

—All military servants from the Ministries of Interior and Defense will report to work. Kuwaitis will surrender all weapons; those found with guns will be liable to execution.

—Any house from where shots are fired will be demolished together with surrounding properties.

—Civil servants failing to report for work will be sacked in accordance with a Revolutionary Command Council instruction.

—All Kuwaitis must take their automobiles seventy or more miles away to the Basra, Iraq Traffic Department for new number plates or their vehicles will be seized.

Word came from several sources indicating the Iraqis wanted full control of everyone exiting Kuwait. At first I pondered whether I should get involved in such a scheme. Should I go through regular channels to exit or should I strike out alone as previously planned? Several other Americans had been told by the American Embassy that it was organizing a convoy for those wishing to leave. Many other embassies were doing the same.

According to the new Iraqi regulations, Filipinos, Indians, Pakistanis, Bangladeshis, and Sri-Lankans would go north into Iraq, to the Port of Basra where they would be boarded on ships for India from which they may get air travel home. Several South Koreans who worked on Failaka Island would also leave in that group. Kuwaitis wishing to leave, Jordanians, Lebanese, Palestinians, Syrians, Egyptians, Americans and Europeans would head north to Baghdad where air transportation and buses would be waiting to repatriate them to their homelands or wherever they wanted to go.

When Kuwaitis signed transportation papers to exit their own country, they had to turn over their Civil Identification Cards to the Iraqis. These of course bore the Kuwaitis addresses, which later aided the Iraqis in ransacking and pilfering any valuables left behind.

I really had to mull my situation over carefully before committing to heading to Baghdad in one of those escorted convoys the American Embassy was sanctioning. Saddam Hussein and his boys hadn't exactly played by the rules so far. What if they got us all there and then held us prisoners or everyone got shot in an accidental gunfight on the way to Baghdad?

Liz and Bob said they'd be taking this route, as would my Egyptian lawyer friend Mohammed. The British couple in our basement was going this route as well. My Palestinian friend Ahmed and his family were driving their own cars through Iraq to Jordan, but they should have no trouble. Technically, most Jordanians inside Kuwait were really Palestinians, but since they don't have a country, they carry Jordanian passports which allow them to travel. Many of their independent cars would be following the escorted bus convoys to Baghdad then over to Amman.

I decided to make the trip through Iraq by bus. I would make the necessary arrangements, fill out the paperwork and secure my van in the basement of the Zahra Complex. I then set about the task of rounding up whatever I needed to take with me and secure the doors and windows of my apartment.

I decided to take all the money I withdrew from the bank with me, putting some in each sock, pocket and in my underclothes as well as in my wallet. The night before I was to leave, about 2:30 a.m., I gathered my second most valued belongings and carried them downstairs to an area near the swimming pool at ground level. I dug a hole and placed my foot locker containing things like photos, a few valuables, a few nice antique books I bought at Friday Iranian Market, videos, audio tapes, a radio, some bags of wine yeast, coins and paper money I collected from several countries in the region and an expensive silk Persian rug that was very small but cost more than $1,200. I carefully covered the trunk with a tarp and dirt and placed some of the century plants nearby atop the freshly packed soil.

Everything was in place for me to leave Kuwait at 10:00 a.m. The bus and convoy would have an armed Iraqi escort and would be meeting with other buses being loaded in other locations throughout the city. Jahra would be our last stop.

As I arrived at the open field between Salmiya and Rumaithiya, where our bus was loading, I noticed several cars filled with families and their belongings bulging over the rooftops. They were allowed to follow the buses out of Kuwait. Iraqi patrols in jeeps were assembled in front of our lone bus. They were to escort the convoy to Abdaly on the Iraqi border and then relay with other Iraqi soldiers to guard the entire convoy on to Baghdad. The trip was to take about nine hours. I suppose the extra time was for people having to use bathroom facilities somewhere along the way. I asked if we were going to be taken straight to the Baghdad airport and the answer was, "I think so."

After our final pick up point of one other bus and three more cars in Jahra, the convoy was again on its way. As we passed through the cliffs of Mutla Ridge, our departure began to feel more real. We motored along the thirty something miles of desert sand to the Iraqi border where a quick hand wave of the border guard permitted our motorcade of four buses, a dozen cars and six Iraqi jeeps to roll toward the enemy's capitol, Baghdad.

CHAPTER 12

A Line in the Desert Is Drawn

Force was to be met by force. None of us in Kuwait doubted it. In the months following Saddam Hussein's invasion of Kuwait, the world had begun amassing a coalition of armies that would take the fight back to the Tyrant of Baghdad. Early on, the civilians living in Kuwait, both the Kuwaitis and expats alike knew the invasion was only the first round. There had to be a second round, the liberation was yet to come. That was scary. With little accurate information and rare communications from the outside world, we worried "are we going to be invaded?" The Iraqi army's entrenchment into Kuwait's population was so complete; we wondered "how would they separate them from us while bombing?" Now about a third of a million of his murderous troops were in control of literally every segment of life in Kuwait. And then there is Chemical Ali, he may gas us and the coalition will probably bomb us.

Instead of heeding coalition warnings and retreating before the first bombs began dropping, Saddam Hussein dared enlarge his war in the Persian Gulf by spreading his armies past the borders of Kuwait and into neighboring Saudi Arabia. That was definitely the last straw, because at that time while Saddam Hussein was pummeling the town of Kafji, Saudi Arabia, he awoke everyone to his full ambition of forcefully taking more than a quarter of the world's oil.

Unfortunately for Saddam, more than thirty worldwide militaries were already taking better positions from which to force his armies into retreat. The coalition's forces, mostly comprised of dreaded infidels wouldn't stop until they were within spitting range of Baghdad itself.

When Saddam moved into Kafji, the timing couldn't have been worse for him. Agreements had been finalized between the government of Kuwait in exile and the Americans, British and others. The normally penny pinching Kuwait Royals were now ready to pay everyone and anyone that would come to their aide.

Since Kuwaitis are not known for standing by their agreements, billions of dollars had to be put in special foreign accounts that would pay the salaries of all "bought and paid for" coalition armies, or as the Kuwaitis later referred to them as "mercenary" armies. Additional agreements gave the Americans access to Kuwait's bases and ports which they had wanted for years and the British got reinforced agreements that had been deluded by squirming Kuwaitis not wanting to pay their old obligations.

Many Americans especially, thought we went there for Kuwaiti oil, which wasn't true at all. Americans have never gotten oil from Kuwait but our allies the British, Germans, Dutch, Japanese and others have. We were in it strictly for the money, not for moral convictions that concerned the United States position in policing the whole world in the name of "good". We were there for money and the guilt trip Kuwait put on us because Ambassador Glaspie's faux pa was perceived as giving Saddam Hussein the "green light" to invade Kuwait.

Almost three weeks before the Liberation of Kuwait began, its capitol, Kuwait City and the rest of the country suffered it's most fearful and destructive days; even worse than those that followed the Iraqi invasion just over six months earlier.

On January 24, Iraqi troops blew up all state of the art oil terminals along Kuwait's coast. The spewing of huge flows of oil into the Persian Gulf contaminated water and covered beaches and sea bottoms for hundreds of miles downstream in Kuwait, Bahrain and Saudi Arabia.

Since Iraqi leaders had come to feel there was no chance of holding Kafji, Saudi Arabia or Kuwait, they began a campaign of systematic destruction. They ended Kuwait's fresh water supply by blowing up the desalinization plants and storage facilities, dynamited all the power plants and electrical sub stations and began planting millions of land mines. The burying of land mines was a bid to expand the environmental disaster from the sea to the deserts using the mines as their first line of defense.

Saddam Hussein's troops had moved against Saudi Arabian and Qatari military units near Kafji but progressed no farther. The Saudis and Qataris managed to beat the Iraqis back to a stalemate while air support from coalition partners aided the halt. Now it was time for what Saddam Hussein was calling "The Mother of All Battles".

Saddam's forces were well entrenched all the way down Kuwait's coast to Kafji but now it was the coalition's turn to select the time and place for battle.

The Liberation of Kuwait started in the morning at 3 o'clock Kuwait Time, Thursday, January 17. On the East Coast of the United States it was 7 o'clock in the evening January 16, 1991. The "Go" signal had been given and coalition bombers roared their engines from the decks of aircraft carriers in the Persian Gulf and from desert airfields inside Saudi Arabia. All high altitude planes and a barrage of outbound cruise missiles were aimed for simultaneous strikes against Baghdad and Kuwait City. CNN broadcast to a worldwide viewing audience with up to the minute live coverage from Baghdad, whereas Kuwait City's plight remained in a full blackout.

Both Kuwait City and Baghdad were soon alight with thunderous explosions from the air and Iraqi tracer fire from the ground. Though some collateral damage, re: civilian human lives was expected, it was to be kept at a minimum in Baghdad and with even far more concern in Kuwait City where tens of thousands of Iraqi soldiers had their anti-aircraft gun positions atop apartment buildings and homes still occupied by Kuwaitis and foreign workers.

Iraqi occupied air bases in the surrounding deserts west of Kuwait City were the hardest hit that dawn by United States Navy A-6 intruders that bombed all morning and during each of the following days, while U. S. Air Force F-16E bombers struck by night.

Most Kuwaitis had built bomb shelters inside their houses months earlier when rumors flew about possible Iraqi gas attacks against the civilian population. Some built shelters inside small cement rooms and basements, while others used cement blocks in areas under the already reinforced concrete stairways. Many Kuwaiti houses are solid concrete pours, even all the interior walls, while most other dwellings contain cement block interiors. You'll find none of the wood stud walls like most American homes are built from.

From about 10 o'clock in the evening of January 31, until February 1, Kuwait's populated coastal communities suffered major bombardments by coalition ships at sea. Most came from the cannons of United States warships outside the reach of Iraqi cannon batteries on Failaka Island. More horrific assaults on Kuwait's coastline and inland regions came via allied bombings from the air. Between these January and February dates came Kuwait's second most bloody time frame; the first having been the ten hours both sides of Muslim New Years, when the country rumbled and blazed almost without end.

Kuwaitis knew the Iraqis would have to depart soon because no one could withstand that kind of pressure very long. The Iraqis were under almost continuous fire day and night at their command posts and bases in the deserts as well as all their living facilities throughout Kuwait City and its suburbs. By February 7, drinking water for the Iraqi occupying army and the civilian population alike had run out. Also by February 7, there was no bread, dairy products, potatoes, rice or other staples left in the stores. Each family was on their own for food, often pooling what they had from their vegetable gardens with other families, friends and neighbors.

In a final stage of planned destruction, the Iraqis moved their mine planting efforts from the deserts and beaches to the oil fields, burying nearly five million mines all total. Thousands were planted surrounding the base of each of the more than seven hundred oil platforms, above ground pipelines and as a line of defense even wider expanses of the desert.

On the first night of the Gulf War, everyone in the United States including my wife Maia and I stayed up all night watching CNN's coverage by Peter Arnet from the El Rasheed Hotel in Baghdad as tracer fire and explosions lit the night skies. We watched in amazement as a lone cruise missile barely missed the hotel.

Only those in Command bunkers in Saudi Arabia knew that until Arnet got off the air, essential Iraqi telephone and communication lines could not be severed by allied air strikes. The top military command center in Riyadh, Saudi Arabia where General Swartzkopf and others were, watched and listened to Arnet's last words as he signed off the air. Within seconds of concluding that broadcast, coalition bombers and cruise missiles smashed all the main communications networks in the country. From then on everything was satellite feed.

For Maia and me the news of the first bombings of Baghdad has become a memory etched in our minds forever. It was late afternoon at our home in Tempe, Arizona, almost the exact half way point around the world when all major television networks broke from regular scheduled programming to bring a "SPECIAL REPORT". They said, "Latest reports from the Middle East indicate and have confirmed that war against Iraq for the Liberation of Kuwait has begun."

Along with the rest of the world, we watched nonstop coverage showing illuminated tracer fire from Iraqi ground positions throughout Baghdad as they tried in vain to reach high flying coalition bombers that were smashing their defense systems, command headquarters, bridges, scud missile batteries, military runways and Republican Guard units in a reign of terror from the sky.

By now my wife and I were glued to our comfortable sofa in Arizona watching every report but still wondering what was happening inside Kuwait. Live satellite feed continued from Baghdad but none came from Kuwait where all communication with the outside world remained destroyed.

The Iraqi's had now been in Kuwait for six and a half months but there had been only partial lootings and robberies. Within the next two weeks, however, Saddam Hussein set forth his plans for retreating from Kuwait which included ordering his troops to conduct a massive "Scorched Earth Policy". They would now blow all the oil wells, rob all the banks, smash and destroy shop windows everywhere and torch Kuwait City on a more grand scale than they had done during invasion.

British and American bombers including the new stealth B-1 bomber and F-117 stealth fighters attacked Baghdad and military installations throughout Iraq and Kuwait. The massive air strikes were named "Desert Thunder" and the yet to come ground battle would be named "Desert Storm."

I anxiously awaited every televised picture of anything from the region, but especially wanted to see Kuwait and verify with my own eyes what the reports weren't saying. We knew the oil fields have been blown and the deserts were ablaze. Reports on television said soaring torches of fire spit flames hundreds of feet high from some wells, while hundreds of others have been blown without catching fire. They created lakes of oil, drowning the mines and making it even more impossible to remove the hundreds of live ones that remained surrounding each well base. That's what reports were saying but there was still no live feed showing it to us. CNN and the other networks showed only satellite photographs of Kuwait covered in darkness as billowing oil clouds blackened the land and air.

The Gulf war started with tremendous ferocity. The nonstop bombing of Iraqi installations within Kuwait and up into Iraq were firstly to eliminate scud missile sites, anti-aircraft firing positions and as much of the Iraqi

Air Force as it could; then move on to military installations, ground forces and the destruction of Iraq's communication centers.

After three weeks of chastisement from the air, coalition forces began Desert Storm by moving in with tank units and ground forces for the short fight and even quicker mop up operation. The great ground battle lasted a mere ninety hours and the dictator Saddam Hussein and the army he called the greatest and most powerful in the Middle East had been miserably defeated with tens of thousands dead and hundreds of thousands taken prisoner.

We all then sat back in anticipation for Saddam Hussein's fall. We watched the final tank battles, the final prisoners being rounded up and the final move that had to come toward Baghdad, but never did. Like most other people, I had followed all allied victories with great pride but all along I had the sinking feeling the final job of dealing with Saddam Hussein would remain unfinished and it did. There would be no killing or removing him, nor even the toppling of his government.

President Bush and British Prime Minister Margaret Thatcher had said all along they'd liberate Kuwait but it was neither the job of the United States, Great Britain nor any of the other allies to actually take out Saddam Hussein.

Since quite a few Israelis died in the scud missile attacks on Israel, I personally hoped they'd turn the Israeli military machine or Masaad loose on Saddam and let them hunt him down and execute him, but of course they didn't. I didn't think our governments would hold back on the antiquated Viet Nam "no assassination" policy but they had.

In the United States we still suffer from that Viet Nam era guilt complex when assassination of undesired leaders was planned in the top corridors of our government. Public outcry against such policies in the 1960's flew back in the face of our politicians who later had to answer for them. This time the American public cried to "get" Saddam but now the politicians were covering their own asses by refusing to do so.

The government of Kuwait in exile promised to finance a large share of the war's costs but the United States and other allies would also split a big share as part of the guilt trip. No one should forget that the blame should be well spread around to the Americans and many of their United Nations allies as well as the Kuwaitis and Saddam Hussein.

Kuwait should bear most blame for the human lives lost and the destruction of their own nation and its economy due to their own arrogance at the Jeddah meeting and for almost twenty years of stealing Iraqi oil. Both Kuwait and the United States supplied Saddam Hussein with money to perpetuate his eight years war with the Iranians.

The Americans and other allies should be blamed for supporting Saddam Hussein for years and supplying him with billions of dollars in cash and military hardware, plus training their scientists and providing germs and chemical warfare knowledge to Iraq.

The British even trained the Iraqis and Jordanians in laying mine fields and then were awarded lucrative contracts removing them from the deserts of Kuwait and Failaka Island after the war. As for the French, they'll sell anything to anybody at any time. Little needs to be said about France, the country I so vehemently dislike and distrust. I knew they would continue supporting Saddam Hussein even if he lost the war because of the billions of dollars in oil contracts they would continue holding for many years to come. Even French mine teams were rewarded lucrative removal contracts inside Kuwait following the 1991 Gulf War. Their Sofreme Company had part of the deal to mop up piles of mines and money.

I do think Washington had something to do with a "green light" to invade Kuwait. Let's see; the U.S. had supported Saddam Hussein for eight years against Iran and that came out as a draw. We needed ports and bases in the region and we needed to get paid billions this time instead of handing out billions of dollars. OK Madam Ambassador "here's how we'll do it." "Give Saddam the green light on all oil fields in dispute between

Kuwait and Iraq; no, better yet, tell him it's a go on Kuwait but warn him against going as far as Kafji, Saudi Arabia".

While home in Arizona, I told several influential people about Kuwait and the meeting I attended in Jeddah, Saudi Arabia but no one ever believed me. I later tired of talking about the subject and allowed them to believe it only after they heard about it again during the Congressional inquisition of former American Ambassador Glaspie more than a year later. Congress wanted to hear what happened at the meeting she attended with Saddam Hussein in Baghdad on July 25, 1990, and the one I attended in Jeddah the last night of July 1990.

The United States has always soft handled the Kuwaiti's roll in antagonizing the situation over there. The U. S. Department of Commerce foresaw a huge financial bonanza in a Middle Eastern war and the State Department fully supported their reason for cleaning up Kuwait's image while building them up as "the victim". Here's where my boss at the Ministry of Information who use to be the Ambassador to the United States came in. He could play an important role in giving the ports and bases up to the Americans and he would get "victim" status that he could play for many years to come. But remember, Mr. Ambassador, it is also a pay as you go program.

The United States military was happy the situation between Iraq and Kuwait deteriorated to the point of war. They loved having a battle mission that aided our militaries in receiving an even larger budget from Congress. So many American bases had been closed and others still being eyed for closure that the U. S. military needed another war, and fast. President Bush's ratings weren't insignificant either. He and his party looked forward to escalating his poll approval rate as a President at war.

Immediately following the meeting in Jeddah, Saudi Arabia the end of July 1990, there was a coin toss. We, the United States could continue pouring hundreds of millions of dollars into Saddam Hussein who wasn't the biggest aggressor in the Middle East yet or we could bring money back into American coffers by supporting Kuwait with whom we had never had a relationship or alliance in the past. Kuwait at least had money and lots of it. Kuwait's assets prior to invasion were $200 Billion. The coin toss of course came out in favor of bringing money in. Besides, it was an easy public relations sell to get everyone at home and around the world to hate a mad man like Saddam Hussein.

The Kuwaiti arrogance at the Jeddah Meeting allowed the situation to turn into a war and everyone who wanted to take advantage of it did. It was a spur of luck for the western powers that they should be rewarded financially and received the military bases and ports they had long wanted near Iran and the Middle East as bonuses. The Kuwaitis were also big winners by having hired other countries militaries to fight their war.

A war has to have losers too. No one told the parents and spouses of those who would be killed that everyone else would be in it strictly for the politics and business potential. Statistics later downplayed the losses of American lives as minimal and lucky that they stayed so low. The American Government said that was the price we paid for war. To the Kuwaitis the death factor never entered into it. It was as simple as hiring other people to fight and die for them; strictly financial.

The beginnings of war as seen live through the eyes of CNN from Baghdad were vivid. Tens of thousands of rounds of illuminated tracer fire and anti-aircraft shells pierced the night sky in search of coalition planes. That image on television looked much more familiar to me than to most other people. I had seen the same army in action up front and at close range a few months earlier.

It was apparent from watching television that the Iraqis were a much more formidable foe to our forces than the Kuwaiti military was against them. Saddam put up some real resistance but of course, it was minimal against such military hardware as the United States and other allies had. Saddam Hussein could never have imagined military tanks whose outer shells could burst away from them if hit by Iraqi fire sparing the soldiers inside from serious injury or super fast tanks that had wide earth pushing blades on them that could bury the enemy and their tanks as they lay in wait in their trenches.

One of the most helpful American military weapons used was a new device that calculated incoming shell trajectories. As soon as the Iraqis would shoot a shell from their cannons, our equipment would hone in on it, calculate the coordinates from which the shell was fired, then our tanks would return fire to the same coordinates, annihilating it before it could ever send a second shell.

The United States M1-A1 tank can cross the deserts at speeds of 40 miles per hour and shoot deadly shells at the rate of one every 4 seconds.

Like most Americans, Maia and I were watching our first "real time" war while sitting in the comfort of our living room. In this televised war, the two eager participants, Baghdad and the multinational coalition forces put on an excellent show. Our side not only had far superior equipment and technology but well groomed Generals, politicians, spokesmen and strategist telling us, the viewing audience what had been done or should be done or might yet be done as satellites in the heavens beamed all the bombing and the talking back to us while we were eating popcorn.

Could you imagine the scene in our living room one day when three elderly women came to visit us while war coverage was on; these old ladies sat back sipping highballs as they talked with some authority on Iraqi inability to communicate between headquarters and their commanders in the field and about where Iraqi antiaircraft shells would fall back to earth after not finding their targets.

Prompting that last little ole ladies debate was a televised report on Iraqi shells falling back to earth on their own cities. Our Stealth Bombers were too high flying and were already departing the area before the Iraqis began firing their surface-to-air missiles. The next day's television coverage would show mosques and civilian buildings supposedly hit by our bombs when all along their own shells were crashing back to earth with horrendous consequences, literally bombing themselves.

Between the times we watched the war on television and the time I had gotten out of occupied Kuwait through Baghdad was just under five months. I could only imagine the destruction in Kuwait after that much time. At first I got on with my normal life but as soon as the war of liberation broke out, my every thought returned to my life in Kuwait and the people I knew there.

Many of our friends and acquaintances had also gotten out of Kuwait. My radio station friend Linda who was married to the Kuwaiti soldier Badran called us from Washington, D.C. She and their daughter Miriam escaped from Kuwait after Badran was taken prisoner by Saddam Hussein's army. She was one of the only ones we heard from.

From our home in Tempe, Arizona my wife and I watched the war while sitting on a beautiful, tuft sofa surrounded by big adobe walls, courtyards with fountains, gardens and a baby grand piano, three sets of French doors, a family sized barbeque grill and a Cadillac in the drive. Watching the war unfold on television in such comfort, seemed not so different from when I stood in my penthouse windows in Kuwait City; watching the invasion unfold in front of me. Both times I witnessed man's most aggressive acts against another as I sat in the lap of luxury eating microwave popcorn as if they were fictional movies or videos in an arcade. Somehow through the mass media experience, we lost a lot of the sadness that should have been there.

Daily Maia and I screened every CNN broadcast very carefully. We couldn't believe the exacting coverage of the bombing of Baghdad and we enjoyed watching most military and political discussions, however, there were some that pissed me off. Maia could see me get very upset each time a professor from one University or another would be interviewed on what course of action they thought Saddam Hussein would take next. Of course they would have all this educated, logical thinking rolling off their tongues and I wanted to puke. There is no way we can even begin to think like Saddam Hussein or any Middle Eastern Arab for that matter. They defy our logic much of the time.

Most of the time I would leave the room when those "know it all professors" were on television, but I never stopped watching all the other reports. Maia and I stayed awake almost all night every night listening to every word, watching every picture. To me the scenes were not just around the other side of the world but were only too real and familiar from the place I'd been calling home for more than a year and a half.

Before the war, I'd been to both Baghdad and Basra and all points in between and spent a lot of time driving through the deserts and cities that were now being hit by coalition forces. Each detailed description of targets released by United States military spokesmen fit an image in my mind of places I'd been. CNN showed aerial photographs of offshore oil terminal spillage along the coast of Kuwait and the ruins of a small sea port on Failaka Island that I was especially familiar with.

We watched the bombing go on for almost a month before I decided it would be over soon and I should get back to Kuwait. Maia decided to stay in Arizona while I tried to reenter Kuwait to make some money rebuilding after liberation. Only twice since I returned had I been able to talk to someone in the Royal Family. They were all living pretty high In Taif, Saudi Arabia in the summer palace of King Fahd, but one day I received a call confirming my identity before the second voice came onto the telephone. It was Kuwait's Emir. His Highness Sheikh Jaber al Sabah was calling from an aircraft somewhere en route to Phoenix for business. I said I would like very much to see him while he was in Phoenix if his time permitted. He said that would be pleasant and he'd try to make time.

The next call I got from his party was while they were staying at the Phoenician Resort on Camelback road. His Highness was in final negotiations to purchase a large share of the new resort that was having financial difficulties. He would later remark that if all else fails in Kuwait, perhaps he would be spending more time in Arizona because it would allow him to be close to two nephews who were attending Arizona State University. Their families would love to stay with him for an extended period of time there, "Ansh Allah" (the most used of all phrases in Kuwait), "God Willing". That phrase and "bookra," meaning "tomorrow," are both used every few sentences.

His Highness the Emir Sheikh Jaber and I met twice, both times over dinner at the Phoenician while talking. He said speaking of Kuwait, which most of these conversations were, the country would remain in a state of chaos for some time to come but once Kuwait is liberated, I would be his eyes and ears around the palaces and the Americans before his delayed return. Surely, as an American I would be more able to get around town than a member of the Royal family might be in those first days. I assured His Highness I would help in whatever way I could and would look forward to being in his employ again.

In less than a week, I was aboard a flight to Cairo, Egypt where I waited an additional three weeks in the fairly nondescript Pharogypt Hotel for further visa and paperwork to be cleared. Most rooms in the city were already occupied with Kuwaitis and their children who were also waiting out the war's end.

The Gulf War continued with the ground armies of more than thirty nations mopping up and capturing tens of thousands of beaten, rag tag, apologetic Iraqi soldiers but not before nearly one hundred thousand of them had lost their lives in the trenches and desert's sands.

From January 17, 1991, the day the actual Gulf War began to the day Kuwait was liberated by ground troops February 26, was only 40 days. Following the liberation of Kuwait City, the last battle of the war would still be a week away. On March 2, 1991 no less than a thousand Iraqis died in the final battle for the Romaila Oil Fields on the border between Kuwait and Iraq. On that day in the very small Iraqi village of Safwon, terms of surrender were given Saddam Hussein by General Norman Swartzkopf and the allied armies. Most surprising of all though was that still no formal surrender was ever demanded nor signed!

CHAPTER 13

"Scorched Earth"

Two days after surrender, March 4, 1991, the Iraqis turned over all seventy seven coalition forces that had been captured as prisoners of war. Though it was no easy task for our side to hand over Iraqi prisoners to their government; after all, there were more than eighty six thousand of them. Kuwaitis awaiting their captives to be returned from Saddam Hussein's armies would wait in vein. None of their six hundred would ever be heard from again.

The war over and the Iraqis driven from Kuwait allowed the United States and allied armies to secure all land areas they thought may cause safety concerns for incoming civilian flights. Permission was soon given for Kuwait Air and several other carriers to resume operations on a very limited basis. I would be among the first to reenter. I had special permission to be on the first flight but it wasn't to be. Someone in His Highness' employ in Taif, Saudi Arabia had faxed to me in care of the Giza Sheraton Hotel in Cairo, a peace of paper with His Highness' stamp confirming my flight priority; however the Kuwait Embassy in Cairo from which I also had to have another stamp was swamped by throngs of Kuwaitis and servants trying to get authorization to reenter the country. I couldn't even get near the front gates so I missed the maiden flight.

To secure a seat by another method was my only chance. I immediately taxied to the airport and began lobbying officials. It worked, but only after two days and one night sitting in unsanitary conditions without returning to my hotel for as much as a shower or shave. Fortunately, one airport official volunteered to take my travelers checks all the way back into Cairo to clear my hotel charges while I boarded the plane.

The reason I didn't manage to get on that first flight was due to lack of the embassy stamp and because every Royal had a cousin who had another cousin who had a brother that needed to be on that flight. I fortunately made it on the second one though. Just two hours after I boarded the nonstop Kuwait Airways flight from Cairo to Kuwait City we neared the country's air space. Within the next few minutes, my whole Kuwaiti adventure came full circle.

Saddam Hussein hadn't left Kuwait easily. His retreating "Scorched Earth Policy" had been labeled the most devastating environmental disaster ever caused by man. I soon saw it first hand from the air, then by land. My flight descended from 16,000 feet, bumping gently a few times on approach toward Kuwait City. Everyone on board knew soon after we pierced the clouds we'd be seeing something few people in the world had seen. For all those aboard, our anticipation was extreme.

This second commercial flight back into the country since Kuwait's airport reopened was mostly filled with Kuwaiti men and Embassy men returning at their earliest opportunity. Amongst us though were a few reporters and a couple Kuwaiti women, but no children.

We weren't sure what we'd find once we got there because there was still only a minimum of communication coming from inside the country. All major network television reports said it was dark all day every day from oil fires and the Iraqis had literally destroyed every-thing. The last thing Maia and I heard on CNN about Kuwait International Airport was the story about the British Airways 747 awaiting takeoff when the airport was overrun during the first day of invasion.

When I left Kuwait the first of September last year, I voluntarily boarded one of the Iraqi soldier escorted buses from Kuwait City to Baghdad. The trip to Baghdad was on one of Kuwait City's stolen city transits, crowded, dirty and smelly. It was hardly like one of those luxurious Prevost I used during my ownership of Grand Canyon State Tours and Convention Services in Phoenix.

The fifty nine other passengers on that bus and I had to endure almost nine hours on something less than comfortable, but at least it was a ride in the right direction and hopefully toward freedom.

My buses at Grand Canyon State Tours had seats that would slide into the aisle to give each person more sitting space. They also had five color televisions, VCRs and a galley with a microwave oven and refrigerator. Aboard this city transit bus, the air conditioning didn't even work.

It wasn't bad enough that we were over crowded like sardines with many passengers without seats and sitting on the floor, but among those who did make it aboard, several had forgotten to bathe before coming. Once the shoes came off, forget it. It smelled like a gymnasium wet mopped in soured arm pit sweat. Hygiene was thrown to the wind as people ate and dropped their garbage at their feet and spit and shot nose goobers into the aisles. Children cried and screamed as they nibbled goat parts, and mothers became overly protective of the small spaces they held, occasionally slapping at and arguing with fellow trippers.

The only westerners on the bus were three Europeans and me with the majority of other passengers heading home to Syria. Personally, I like Syrians to a degree, though more physically attractive than most other Arabs, they're a little more uncouth and less clean than their neighbors. Syrians have a lower standard of living than most Middle Easterners and are always on guard against Americans, believing we're all spies. I couldn't stand the smell on the bus any longer so I reached into my shaving kit and took out my cherry lip balm. I didn't have cracked lips but the smell of cherry had to be a thousand times better than dirty feet and armpits. I took my finger and squished a glob of the lip balm up both sides of my nostrils and breathed through my mouth. This was a much better arrangement. At least I couldn't taste the stench of my fellow passengers any more.

The only problem with this solution resulted hours later when the heat of my body began melting the lip balm up my nose and it started running down into my mustache. I had no handkerchief to blow my nose in, so I quietly picked at it and rubbed it on the bottom of my seat.

This unfortunately was not my only mishap during the trip. Our convoy of cars, buses and Iraqi soldiers arrived at a little village where everyone got off the coaches, stretched their legs and used the toilets. Since Arabs use only a hole in the floor and wipe their butts with their hands dipped in water, a new smell came aboard. A bottle of lemon juice was passed around and poured sparingly on each person's hands which did diminish the smell just a little.

When my turn to stand over the porcelain hole in the floor came, I stood directly over it and aimed but missed. How embarrassing and what a mess! My feet had been positioned on the porcelain correctly, but for some reason my posture had been improper and the poop didn't hit the hole. My first attempt failed leaving an ever so little bit deposited on my left shoe's heel and still I hadn't finished. With the next try, I moved my feet along the porcelain feet imprints, changed my aiming position, leaned forward then backwards, grunted and missed again. This time as I strained, I lost my center of balance. Finished or not, I was through. With my own toilet paper I wiped myself and the soil from my shoes.

I was able to clean all but the sewn ridge along the back of my shoes, where the soles met the leather. The American in me was embarrassed enough to at least make me want to clean the place up a little. I did so with a little bit more of the personal toilet paper I had brought. I wadded it all up together and heaved it toward a little square window above and to the left of me. This window however turned out to be a small fan that in turn through the whole mess back in at me.

I then rode the rest of the trip believing I could smell it and so could everyone else. Fortunately, no one else seemed to notice as it was mixed with the smell of arm pits, rank feet, with a twist of lemon and cherry.

Four hours later, around twilight, we arrived before a barricaded government building in Baghdad and disembarked as it began to rain. Two other refugee buses that had passed us on the road arrived earlier and had already unloaded their passengers. Once inside the building most people sat with their belongings at their feet and let the children run wild. Old men sat together on the floor lighting horse shit cigarettes while women fiddled with their purses and carry on bags.

An announcement in Arabic indicated the groups would soon be separated once again, with those departing for Syria in one section; while those going back toward Iraq's Persian Gulf port of Basrah and ships eastward in another, and finally our group for overland travel to Amman, Jordan or the Saddam International Airport near Baghdad in the third, much smaller group.

I of course opted for the airport to try to get aboard any flight heading to Europe or Cairo, Egypt, although I wouldn't have minded staying in Iraq's capitol just a little while. From what I could see, Baghdad was much prettier than Kuwait City and the Iraqi Capitol had a metropolitan touch that Kuwait didn't have. There were a lot of trees, bustling traffic congestion, sprawling bridges over the Tigres and Euphrates Rivers and colossal monuments everywhere.

I remember thinking, I wish the clouds of war weren't hanging over our heads because I would like to have taken a tour of Baghdad, or just walked around a little. The Iraqi Capitol's wide boulevards and seemingly sociable people certainly presented no picture of a city or country that could soon be torn and destroyed by war. I liked this seemingly undisturbed capital that had already been at war with Iran for more than eight years.

At the airport just outside Baghdad, I only had a few hours to sit in protective custody before a seat became available on the eleven o'clock p.m. flight to Geneva, Switzerland. From there I made a connecting flight to New York and on to Arizona.

Just six months after fleeing Kuwait, I was on a plane heading back there. I was already within fifteen minutes from touchdown on approach to Kuwait City and there was still little evidence of the smoky conditions we were suppose to be seeing. The sky was still bright and blue and I was able to follow the desert terrain, highways and occasional dwellings below us. So far there was no sign of the infamous oil fires.

We started our descent into Kuwait International Airport a few minutes later and only then did a hushed silence fall over the cabin as we saw the ominous, dark, oil clouds appear on the horizon, just ahead and below us.

After dropping a few thousand more feet, wispy clouds began passing the plane's windows, at which time the passengers became audibly louder. As we descended even further, all passenger's interests peeked and those nearest the aisles began straining for views of the fires, leaning as far as they could over the persons next to them to catch their first glimpse of post war Kuwait.

For several minutes the plane heaved and roared back at us as if being robbed of its power while we continued slicing through layer after layer of ever thicker, darker smoke outside. In reality, it was still mid day but we were as sightless as if someone had ordered us to wear blindfolds. Momentarily though, our vision began repairing itself and as if by magic, our extreme anticipation was rewarded. Before us lay a ghoulish hell, a fiery inferno covering hundreds of square miles. The largest land and sea environmental disaster of modern time and the whole scene was predicated by just one mad man as payback for thwarting his crazed ambitions for world oil domination.

I could now recognize land marks of the desert terrain and coastal region south of Kuwait's populated areas. Even the ground appeared darker than normal or perhaps the ground was now mimicking the oil clouds the way water does. The small lightless village below us lay in contrast to several nearby dozen or so oil fires that raged billowing plumes of black smoke. I calculated this to be the town of al Wafra and the Wafra

Oil Fields, still several miles south and west of the Gulf's waters. Next in view came the Nuwaiseeb Customs Check point on Kuwait's border with Saudi Arabia and the Burgan Oil Fields about twenty miles south of Kuwait City.

While our descent continued, I visually followed the Fahaheel Motor Way north and the spur highway that becomes the Magreb Asafar Motor Way a mile or so inland from the waters' edge. We continued this flight path until the motor ways intersected the Ring Roads of Kuwait City.

Along the way I noted nothing was in abundance below except oil fires; not cars, not lights, not bushes nor trees nor any signs of human life. The desert sands even lay dreary, grey and lifeless.

Next we flew over the town of Ahmadi where Guy and Shari lived in Tara and the oil fields there before flying above Seventh Ring Road on our final approach into Kuwait International Airport. As our wings dipped and veered slightly west the excitement became overwhelming. We were coming to earth amongst endless fields of fires lit like giant contrail plumes of smoke spiraling from the space shuttle after liftoff. The normal brilliant lights of Kuwait City's former million and a half residents no longer existed. I looked in all directions, from Mina Abdullah Oil Terminal and the community of Fahaheel and out as far as Jahra to the west and Kuwait City to the north. It looked like dusk, but in reality it was now only 2:15 in the afternoon.

The normal heavily traveled and lit motor ways lay motionless beneath us as uninhabited endless strips of concrete and asphalt. It was as if Kuwait City and its suburbs had no surviving citizens. It appeared like the movie "The Day After".

As we glided above Airport Road, I could see makeshift runway lights modeled from tin cans of fuel set afire, running parallel down both sides of our approach. With a little bumping and stomping of brakes, our Kuwait Air flight slowed to a gentle drive atop the bullet riddled tarmac near the airport's only terminal able to be opened to business.

Arabs in the Middle East always clap when they touch ground but never have I heard it so loudly nor go on for so long. There were also several cries of "Allah Akbar," "God is great" from passengers throughout the plane.

The two and a half hour flight from Cairo had been uneventful except for the past several minutes, but had been considerably more tense and felt longer than the nonstop eight hour flight I had taken three weeks earlier from New York to Cairo, Egypt.

Kuwait's Terminal Two building had no electricity but was relying on many roaring generators near the control tower and around the main facility. Bomb and fire damage was everywhere. Quite evident was the fact that at least one raging battle had been fought at the airport, almost fully destroying some hangers and most normal passenger areas of all terminals. Several nearby aircraft also lay scorched and gutted in ruin.

As our plane swung in toward the terminal's remains and temporary outside gate, I peered in the direction of the Royal Terminal but because of its location at the opposite end of our approach, I was unable to see it.

Though we officially deplaned at Terminal Two, the old passenger Terminal Two as I knew it was gone. The structure was still there but the main concourses to passengers' departure and arrival gates were destroyed. Very little of the terminal's front facade or plate glass windows were left either. The whole place was now mostly comprised of pieced together 4' x 8' sheets of plywood. All the airport terminal's metal roofs and hangers alike were riveted with millions of bomb shrapnel wholes.

We deplaned our Kuwait Airways flight via a portable stairway more than a hundred feet from the main building itself. Kuwait National Guardsmen instructed us to follow them toward a crudely built, small ground level entry that led to an even cruder, endless hallway of even more 4' x 8' sheets of plywood. Once inside the lower section of the terminal that had once been baggage claim, was where we all first felt and smelt the remnants of a real war close up.

This former baggage claim area's floor and the terminal's multilevel lobby bore little semblance to what they had once been. The once gleaming marble floors and walls were fire scorched and cracked; the roof had partially caved in but had been meticulously removed. The baggage carousel was inoperable so a small military pickup truck trans-ported our bags from the plane to a cleared area just inside the building's front entry.

The gathering of my bags and foot locker and clearing Customs which under normal circumstances would have been tedious went unbelievably fast.

Since I had ten year residency in Kuwait, it was a lot easier for me to go through Immigrations and Customs than for businessmen and reporters arriving for the first time. As usual, Customs agents questioned everyone whether they carried alcohol or any illegal substances and wanted to know if anyone was in possession of religious articles, magazines or unsanctioned meats like pork products which are forbidden under Islamic Law. This time, as on other occasions before, I heard a National Guardsman request a businessman to remove the crucifix from around his neck. On another such occasion, I was the one who had the crucifix around my neck ripped from me and thrown to the floor. So much for Islam being a tolerant religion.

As I walked past the last Custom's check point, the National Guardsman said to me "Salam Alaycom," then in English "welcome," I replied with the customary "Alaycom Salam, Kaif Halik, sloanik", "How's it going" at which time his face lit up with a smile ear to ear.

Kuwait has never been a pretty country and now that I was back in post war days, the scenic value had certainly not changed favorably, nor anything else for that matter. I questioned myself as to why I had really returned at all. No one had ever come to Kuwait expecting a tourist destination, beautiful swaying palm trees, waterfalls, resort hotels or even pretty beaches; so now that oil fires stifled the very air we breathed and raw crude fell from the skies and the normal already dead, ebbing desert sands were now clogged in massive oil lakes, there was even less reason for me to be here. You have to come to Kuwait for a reason and of course mine was money, at least this time.

I had to keep telling myself this reason over and over, otherwise; I would have reboarded the same plane and headed back to Cairo where there was life, excitement and purpose.

Only minutes after departing the terminal's front doors, I made several observations that wouldn't prove different in the days, weeks or months to come. Within those first few minutes, my white dress shirt became speckled with tiny droplets of oil raining from the hovering smoke clouds. Oil now covered all ground surfaces in the entire country, the deserts, parks, beaches, highways, the near lifeless trees, grasses and bushes, as well as the sides and roofs of all former white and sand colored buildings.

Looking above, the sky was black with oil but to the east and west I could see sunlight radiating on the far horizons like during winter months above the Arctic Circle. To the north and south in the directions of most oil fields, everything was as black as midnight. The strong smell of oil overwhelmed all other senses. Over time, the blowing and drifting sands combined with oil to create grit along the roadways and sidewalks like a slushy gray mixture of snow and dirt.

I encountered one of the several aggressive taxi drivers sitting in front of the terminal exactly where they use to be in the old days. All Palestinian, Indian and Egyptian taxi drivers were ecstatic about their renewed possibilities of making money again and fought over every customer leaving the terminal. The one that got me said the airport was beginning its first day of business and the cars being used for transport were those seized from Palestinians and others who sided with Saddam Hussein's invasion and occupation of Kuwait. I spoke in broken Arabic to the driver, so he was even more eager to tell me whatever I wanted to know. Because I don't speak Arabic really well, I'm sure I missed a good part of what I was supposed to have understood, but the conversation lasted all the way to my apartment.

Things that were supposed to look familiar to me still did in a way, but the stillness, the dirtiness and the deadness of everything felt strange and disorienting. Uncollected garbage was strewn and blown into the streets and the desert's sands were reclaiming the desolate City's roadways, parks and parking lots all the way home. I almost never saw a living sole. No pets, no birds, no people.

The first light I saw other than the one at the airport control tower emanated from the guard post of Bayan Guest Palace. The royal gates themselves appeared to have been badly damaged during occupation but what little of the palace I saw from Fifth Ring Road appeared to be ok. Several months later however, I was asked to tour the palace and observe all the destruction first hand. The entire palace complex had suffered greatly from hand grenades, firebombs and gunfire. Ceilings were scorched and burnt through to the next floor. Windows were smashed, marble on the walls and floors was scorched beyond repair and most stairwells and the grand chandeliers had been blown out. All furniture and carpets had been looted by Iraqi soldiers and sand lay inches thick on the floors of the once lavish palace rotundas.

Of course simple fixtures like smaller chandeliers and mirrors were only shattered images of themselves. The priceless, exquisite Persian carpets that use to cover massive areas of each of the Guest Palace's floors were all missing and had probably been sold in the markets of Baghdad.

The palace's exterior that use to appear as a lush, green mirage amidst the surrounding desert, looked like someone had gone over each foot of the ground with a blow torch. There was almost nothing left. Without water for irrigation, the desert was rapidly reclaiming the land.

My taxi turned onto Gulf Road one block before my apartment building. During Occupation, I remembered this intersection as one of the biggest Iraqi roadblocks in my neighborhood. From here I looked up at my once beautiful, modern, white building that dominated the skyline. The whole building now had a dirty face of sand and oil. My building and all the others surrounding it were dull, brown and gray. Its once striking green double pane windows were filthy and looked more the color of a paved roadway.

I didn't waste a second. After paying the driver and putting my luggage down at the bottom of the stairwell, I ran all the way up to the penthouse. There was no electricity so obviously the elevator didn't work. The whole building appeared deserted. My full glass front door had been shattered and left partially open and the carpet in the foyer was full of blown sand and foot prints. The same was true of my penthouse's two other full glass doors that opened onto my rooftop terrace.

On my terrace facing the sea were hundreds of concrete blocks that were built into a rooftop antiaircraft position for shooting at allied aircraft. Also, a few long green wooden boxes of surface-to-air missiles still lay next to my satellite dish. Because the rooftop anti-aircraft guns had been used quite a lot, their explosive vibrations had shaken loose the top layer of concrete blocks of every wall throughout my apartment. The roof had literally been lifted and set back in place several hundred times.

As for the interior of the apartment, the wall to wall carpet was still there but that was about all. Almost all the furniture was gone with only two large wardrobes and a box spring from a mattress set remained. The refrigerator was there as was the stove, but all the smaller appliances and kitchen utensils were gone. From the bathroom, the sink, storage cabinets and shower accessories were gone but the bidet, toilet and tub remained but were broken.

All in all I'd been wiped out. Even the light sockets and under sink drain pipes had been pried away, the water taps from all kitchen and bathroom sinks had been broken off and all lighting fixtures were gone. Since there was no water, no electricity and nothing left, I guess I didn't live there anymore.

My second day in Kuwait was a real eye opener. First I went to the basement of the Zahra complex and found my van still sitting where I left it. It was very dusty but not nearly as bad as it would have been had it been left outside for almost seven months. On the way back to my apartment, I passed the exact place I saw the Iraqi death squad kill the young boys. All proof of their bullet riddled bodies had long since been washed away except in my mind.

I spent much of that day and the next couple of days wandering the streets downtown looking at the devastation, row after row of stores, hotels, the Iraqi Embassy, the al Sabah Family palaces on Gulf Road and the place of my former employment, the Ministry of Information Complex.

Much of the country was badly damaged or fully destroyed. It ranged from partially scorched to fully gutted. Dasma Palace, the other place of my employment for His Highness had been bombed and torched as had the Crown Prince's residence, Sha'ab Palace near where I lived. I guess I not only didn't have a place to live or work anymore but obviously they didn't have one either.

The hundreds of shops along the main Fahd al Salem Street in Safat District, downtown Kuwait City were only skeletons of what they had once been. The al Muthana and Souk al Kabir Malls were looted and blown up by hand grenades which had blown out their glass showcase windows, ceilings and display cases.

Even though I was prepared to see destruction, I guess I wasn't prepared for anything on such a grand scale. The shops I use to stroll through in Salmyia were all destroyed as were the shops in almost all other suburbs. Instead of the usual heavy smell of incense, every shop smelt of charred lumber and garbage.

Destruction was thorough. Even the sidewalks were destroyed. In the United States sidewalks are poured in long stretches of concrete, in Kuwait they are not. Theirs are constructed using one foot square concrete pavers at a time, inset and compacted in sand. The Iraqi soldiers had removed millions of these pavers and used them to shield themselves from the future enemy that would come from the sea. By stacking them six feet tall bunker style on roof tops and by removing sliding glass doors from apartment buildings and filling them in with concrete pavers with just peep holes for sniper fire, the soldiers were able to fortify key buildings seaside and along motor ways. The remodeling was so systematically done that it was apparent the Iraqi soldiers had been schooled in these fortification techniques.

Though there was little left of my apartment, I still liked the view from the terrace. I continued returning there time and again without making a final decision whether it was worthwhile cleaning it up or not. I spoke with the Kuwaiti landlord in Cairo and he said the minute I begin sleeping there again, I would have to make the full rent payment each month. He even talked about how I would have to pay all the back rent as well. Greedy Bastard, where are all the Iraqis when you need one?

The Kuwaiti landlord in no way accepted responsibility for any cleanup nor even putting glass back in the front door yet I was expected to pay full rent and rebuild the place for him at my expense. In Kuwait all maintenance costs are borne by the occupant who is why most rental units are dilapidated and have never seen paint or repairs before. Most buildings eight years or older look fifty or they've already fallen down.

The Kuwaiti landlord should have paid for his own rental units to be rebuilt because the Kuwait Government had vowed to pay returning Kuwaitis full compensation for all losses, and a healthy fee for rebuilding.

Last night I was very alone. I hadn't connected with any friends yet so I didn't have any other place to stay except the ruins of my own apartment. I did what was necessary to clear a dust free place to lye down on the box springs before settling into a quiet, lonely, very dark, non electrical evening. All I really needed for the night was a thermos of water or something to drink and I was set. If I had to pee, I'd go outdoors on the rooftop terrace.

How strange it was to see so few lights and almost no cars in Kuwait City. I didn't even see one car on Gulf Road where just a year ago I sat in traffic jams more than twenty minutes long without moving, and during Saddam Hussein's invasion of Kuwait, the same road was crammed in all directions from horizon to horizon with Iraqi Army tanks.

On my third day back, I went to the Sultan Center Market to scrounge for any non-perishable food items I could get, and then drove around trying to locate any friends who might still be in the country. I was surprised to find pay phones working and even more surprised to find the American Corps of Engineers had done the emergency work to get them turned on. The Americans were already in place reestablishing Kuwait's electrical, water, sewage, etc. infrastructure.

Finally, I was able to contact my first friend on the telephone. Ali, my Indian banker friend was glad to hear from me and said he had many stories to tell. I was anxious to hear his first hand account of occupation following my departure, and of course, Liberation. He came by my apartment about 10:30 a.m., and we stood on my city view terrace talking about what we were seeing and what happened in the different locations he pointed to. Ali said he had returned to my apartment with his son and another friend once while it was still in good shape. The doors were still locked and unbroken so they walked around the outside terrace to look at the panoramic city view.

Ali and I began staring down at the beaches and main part of the city across the bay. It was an amazing sight. The city under siege lay revealed before us. The entire length of beach was strung with barbed and razor sharp concertina wire. Also, full length of the beach was hand dug trenches for Iraqi soldiers to take up positions in the event troops liberating Kuwait would come from the sea. About every forty feet inside the trench were concrete paver bunkers with gun barrel openings in the direction of the Persian Gulf. Boats of all sizes littered the sand. Most had their sides or bottoms torn out and none had motors. I guess the Iraqis had stolen them and they too like everything else were sold in the open markets of Baghdad.

Pelican and other bird carcasses floated bobbing up and down in the water and lay along stretches of sand nearest the water.

As Ali and I drove around the city, he showed me the remains of several of our friend's homes and palaces torched or destroyed by grenade attacks. He also showed me the remains of Saddam Hussein mosaics and pictures everywhere. Most of them had been des-accreted by coalition soldiers or mobs of expatriate laborers and Kuwaitis who burst into the streets the morning after the Iraqis fled the country. Most portraits of Saddam were now beyond recognition.

One of the first things we both noticed was the amount of Iraqi military helmets, boots and gas masks lying everywhere. We kept wondering about that for more than a month before I remembered President George Bush's speech telling the Iraqis to leave Kuwait with nothing but the clothes on their backs. Our President told them to put down their weapons and walk out. The advice was sort of taken; they were heading out all right but doing the exact opposite of what he said. They shed their military clothing but got into Kuwaiti national dress, the dishdasha to blend with the locals if spotted by American or coalition soldiers.

The tens of thousands of retreating Iraqi soldiers then stole every vehicle in sight, loaded them down with stolen goods then headed for the Iraqi border. During the seven months of occupation, the Iraqi Government or their army had systematically stolen most police cars, ambulances, garbage trucks, city buses, school buses etc; but still just a few remained. At nearly the final hour of occupation, the vast majority of vehicles left in the country were stolen by fleeing soldiers.

Now in their stolen automobiles and wearing stolen civilian clothes, they acquired the final thing needed to insure their safety. They grabbed a Kuwaiti hostage. In the event they were stopped by any advancing foreign troops, they could bargain their way out, or so they thought.

The Iraqi departure was as hurried as their arrival. Beginning late night February 25, and the first hours of February 26, 1991, Iraqi soldiers inside Kuwait began gathering at road check points and traffic circles throughout the city. From here, the remaining school buses and city buses still inside the country were loaded with thousands of troops for their hasty retreat back to Iraq. At the traffic circles (or in Kuwait they're called round about), the Iraqis gathered and waited until official word came. About 2:00 a.m. on February 26, the mass exodus began. Tens of thousands of Iraqis with several hundred hostages jammed the roadways heading north and west. Little could they have known that soon, almost all of them, soldiers and captives alike would be dead?

They withdrew from Kuwait City and most points south, heading westward through Sulaibikhat and down Fourth, Fifth, and Sixth Ring Roads (Kuwait's freeways). All highways come together just west of Jahra and that's where the culmination of their lives would also come together. It is here that they would die.

The rag tag army was now looking quite different from seven months earlier when they poured in as one solid unit of death and destruction. The retreating convoys of buses, trucks, Rolls Royce's, Mercedes Benz and Chevrolet Caprices narrowed into a lonely, tight desert pass called Mutla Ridge.

CHAPTER 14

Valley of Death

Clothed as civilians with hostages and car loads of booty in tow, the retreating Iraqi soldier's met their fate. Twelve ears shattering American fighter aircraft screeched through the night skies bombing all those who traveled below. Over and over again the aircraft unleashed tens of thousands of rounds of ammunition and incendiary bombs on the trapped Iraqis trying to flee through the totally inescapable double walled pass of Mutla Ridge. Our bombers continually strafed the two lane desert highway that squeezed through that natural barrier ridge that divides Kuwait's populated areas near Jahra from the unpopulated expanses of desert sands that lead all the way to Iraq.

The Rolls Royce's, fire trucks, school buses, city buses, dump trucks, Toyotas, Chevrolets, Mercedes Benz, police cars and every other kind of transportation you can name were trapped within the tight, two lane cliff opening. The bombing sorties came again and again, killing the fleeing Iraqis and their captives, melding their flesh and blood into carnage nearly inseparable from the twisted, charred steel wreckages.

For the fleeing Iraqis, there was nowhere to go but to hell. Probably none of the soldiers that dark, cold morning knew the name of the place they'd die. No one escaped Mutla Ridge now known as, "The Valley of Death."

After the first batch of Iraqis laid dead and burning at Mutla Ridge, it was time for others to continue forward and meet their destinies. With no other way to get through the cliffs, the next group of vehicles tried to go around the flaming wreckage of the first, then they too were trapped and torched by the angels of death that continued visiting from the sky again and again; until not one car, truck or bus was left untorched. The allied bombers had done their job only too well. In all, the carnage of vehicles and dead bodies spread more than one hundred fifty feet wide and almost a mile long. Entire convoys of man and machine lay intertwined and beyond recognition.

There has never been a toll set on the amount of souls that died that night and early morning at Mutla Ridge, but surely it was many thousands. And for many Kuwaitis who had been taken hostage in the last hours of occupation, they too died in that inferno.

Several months after the rebuilding of Kuwait had begun, only a narrow path between mutated vehicles had been cleared to allow a single lane of passage. As I drove my car through the masses of twisted steel, I could feel the five to fifteen feet high walls closing in around me. It was hard to distinguish what some vehicles had been, steel chassis missing, top carriages mangled and buses standing on end; jammed so tightly together, they were unable to fall to either side. A bare few were identifiable as vans or police cars, but most weren't. They all had one more thing in common. They were all filled with booty, clothing, VCRs, televisions, furniture, lamps, children's toys, cooking utensils, carpets but no human body parts etc.

As is the Muslim custom, dead people are to be buried by the next sundown. These invaders or what was left of them were no different. Bedouins, the stateless desert wanderers who live near Jahra performed the unimaginable task of trying to separate and gather all those body parts of friend and foe alike to bury.

My fourth day back in the country was spent touring Kuwait City's bullet riddled streets. I strolled through old familiar neighborhoods that were anything but. Everywhere I had been to dinner, where I had shopped and where I met friends had all been destroyed. The gold souks in Salmyia were nothing but burnt roofing timbers and three feet deep shards of glass and debris. Hand grenades had been thrown into the revolving restaurants atop the famous Kuwait Towers, the al Sharq Restaurant and all other choice eateries around town.

At Ras al Ard Salmyia, near the ferry port to Failaka Island, all the tourist boats and private yachts had been sunk where they moored. Expensive, long excursion craft, yachts both small and large were lying at the bottom of the Persian Gulf. Only a glimpse of some white hulls from the undersides of the Touristic Enterprises shuttle boats showed just below water level. Their Yellow and white striped roof canopies had broken or been torn away and now lay bobbing in the water and atop rocky barriers near by. Children's carnival rides at the beach side Showbiz Pizza were destroyed. The Showbiz structure itself was almost unrecognizable. Even the concrete flower planters out front had been set afire.

Once more I returned to the beaches. The entire length of Kuwait's coast line was a horrific mess. Not that they had gotten much of that oil spillage reported on CNN, they didn't; but what a mess the half million Iraqi' soldiers had made digging in and setting up their line of defense. They were sure the allies would begin liberation by storming the shores of Failaka Island eight miles off the coast, northeast of Kuwait City. Then, they'd surely head to the beaches of main land Kuwait.

The razor sharp concertina wire the Iraqis stretched, covered the length of the coastline twice, one line well into the water, the other thirty feet further back on the sand. The thousands of Iraqi trenches and fox holes along the city's beaches and deserts made the sands of Kuwait look more like prairie dog holes out in the vast wastelands of Texas.

Perhaps I was a little surprised to see the waters of the Persian Gulf along Kuwait's coastline in such good shape. When the Iraqis blew the first oil cap at Mina al Ahmadi Oil Terminal off shore, we all thought Kuwait's beaches would become the wash up area. It was not the case at all Saudi Arabia and Bahrain, from sixty miles to two hundred miles down flow received the worst oil pollution.

Kuwait's oil pipelines travel in long straight lines atop the desert sands all the way to the sea. Once seaside, they go below water and rise again at designated platforms about a mile offshore. Large oil tanker ships of a quarter million tons can load from these terminals without docking at ports on the mainland. These sea oil terminal caps were the first blown.

Khafji, Saudi Arabia became the worst environmental disaster beach wise. Some oil did sink locally coating Kuwait's seabed and coral reefs off shore but never on the beaches themselves.

The environment of Kuwait's deserts and populated areas didn't fare so well. To say everything was in shambles would be an understatement. Saddam Hussein's Scorched Earth Policy lit more than seven hundred fifty oil fires that billowed thunderous flames hundreds of feet high, while about a third of them gushed oil fifty stories into the air falling back to earth, creating massive oil lakes surrounding their base. Smoke and droplets of oil blocked all sunlight from the sky. Noon looked like dawn or dusk. Most of the northern oil fields toward Iraq were northwest of Kuwait City where the predominant wind currents blew from. Therefore, most of the dark oil and smoke raging skyward from those fields blew over Kuwait City. Another similar area of severe obscured visibility and obstructed breathing was further south toward the Saudi Arabian border at Nuwaiseeb. That's where the Ahmadi and Burgan Oil Fields blackened the main highway connecting the two countries. This highway was often impassable due to dense fog like conditions of oil clouds.

Motorists returning home via the Saudi-Kuwait highway protected the paint finish on their cars by saturating the outside of the whole automobile with 10W30, processed oil from a can. This prevented the misty waves of crude oil that road the wind currents, from damaging the paint. Of course oil falling from the sky also coated the roadway which in turn built up under some automobile undercarriages causing fire hazards.

Since few vehicles were left inside Kuwait and hundreds of nomad camels had been killed by war and blown up in mine fields, we were truly in a transportation starved wasteland. The balance of man and animal seemed near. For a while I saw people several different times atop camels on down town city streets. Within the first weeks of returning, I saw less than a hand full of vehicles, and only about twice a week did I ever see an eighteen-wheel truck loaded with cargo roll toward the city.

Dead, bloated camels littered the country's deserts as often as did Iraqi fighting vehicles and tanks. Often, baby camels stayed nearby their dead mother and continued wandering through live mine fields. It was hard imagining the changes a few months and a few hundred thousand, maniacal troops did to Kuwait.

First post war images of Kuwait were hard to describe and even more unfathomable was the massive manpower and huge amounts of money it would take to rebuild the country.

The next morning, I walked four miles along the beach from my apartment to Kuwait towers and the American Embassy compound around the bay. I didn't walk on the sand, of course, because there were still buried mines and others washing in from the sea. Mostly, I walked out in the middle of Arabian Gulf Road which now looked like a giant six lanes wide sidewalk, much of which was sand filled, tank scared and bullet riddled from aircraft.

Arriving at the United States Embassy appeared to be the least of my problems. I had a hard time getting someone inside to answer my pounding on the main entrance guard shack. Finally, a Palestinian came through a back door and slid the small Arabic sign away from the lower front of the bullet proof glass. She leaned forward into the small half circle window from which someone could slide their passport beneath. I told her I wanted the names of any American companies wishing to set up business in Kuwait, and if they had arrived yet? "I don't know" she said abruptly and asked why I was in Kuwait now. She told me it was far too early for anything to start and I should leave and return again in a few months.

Dissatisfied with the answer I got, I strolled over to the 17 storey Kuwait International Hotel in front of the American Embassy and was amazed to see how badly time, oil and occupation had been to it. This was the hotel used by CNN and the Iraqis to look down into the strangled, isolated American Embassy Compound. The Iraqis had shut off the water and electricity to the U. S. Embassy, trying to force it to move to Baghdad as they had most others. The Americans inside which included Ambassador Ghnem and the Marine guards held fast, even having to drink water from the swimming pool to survive. Iraqi soldiers could have reined bullets down onto the one and two storey buildings within the complex if they had wanted, but still feared the Americans enough that they didn't.

Unlike most other hotels, the Kuwait International Hotel stayed in operation throughout the seven months of occupation and took on a history of its own. Iraq's top officials stayed there, often meeting with lower ranking field commanders in the lobby. The Hotel remained undamaged for quite some time until a brave young Kuwaiti woman in the resistance movement finally smuggled a bomb inside. Several of her comrades set off the explosion which eliminated quite a few high ranking Iraqis and totally destroyed most of the second floor lobby. Now entering the hotel had to be done through a tremendous amount of reconstruction and like the airport, many walls of 4 x 8 ft. sheets of plywood.

I went to the Kuwait International to spot any Americans that may have come in on the two planes that had arrived since mine. Hopefully, some would be businessmen or contractors committed to the rebuilding effort. Surprisingly, there were quite a few people huddled in small groups throughout the lobby and taking care of business at the hotel's new temporary front desk. By far, the busiest place was the international pay telephone room. No less than three dozen people were waiting for their chance to call outside Kuwait.

I spotted a man, late fiftyish, blond turning gray hair, rugged looking. I found out his name was Sonny and that he was a "good ole boy" from Alabama, here with a partner to set up a camp. We spoke for several minutes about the possibility of my employment and I stressed the point, "I'm already here and other Americans may not want to leave the comfort of their homes and families to come to oil clouds and mine fields." "Why not hire me?"

Sonny's partner Bob, a less patient man in his mid forties, looked more like Al Gore than Al Gore did. He was pacing at all times instead of sitting. He too was agreeable that I may be of use to them and I should contact them within the next two days here at the hotel. Before departing, I forced myself to use the restroom; truly a luxury at this time in this country.

For the past couple days, I had peed out doors on several occasions and I went to the Sultan Center Market several more times. The real porcelain western style toilet at the hotel was sheer pleasure. The Sultan Center didn't have real toilets either but at least they had water and they flushed. They had the typical two porcelain steps you put your feet on while sticking your butt toward the back wall. Using one of these facilities was not a nice "des a vu" experience. Even the Sultan Center had no toilet paper, but I was long over that problem and was ready and eager to use my hands if necessary. Most of the time, I carried toilet paper in my pocket. Since Arabs use a can of water or a long shiny hose to spray their rear ends while they use their hands to wipe, I made it a personal policy to shake hands as seldom as possible. I'd rather "air kiss" or kiss their cheeks any time than touch their hands.

Now that I'd met Sonny and Bob, I decided to double my efforts in getting a job, so next I headed to the American Corps of Engineers Headquarters in Kuwait. I found the fourteen storey, brown building in the downtown Safat District of Kuwait City near where I use to work. I thought, since the Corps was rebuilding the electricity, water and sewage for the entire country, maybe they'd have some position for me if Sonny and Bob didn't.

I never did get to see an American at the Corps of Engineers office. Much like at the American Embassy, I was interviewed by a Palestinian. The rest of that entire floor's staff were Filipinos, Palestinians, Lebanese and Indians who were less than interested in an American who wanted to work there. They barely wanted to talk to me. Finally, I filled out an employment application, attached it to my resume and left; never to be heard from again.

After several hours seeking employment down town, I returned to a Kuwaiti friend's home where I could stay until I made other arrangements. Ahmed al Adsani's house in Bayan, near one of the palaces was quite nice, but when he offered to let me stay there I didn't realize he was thinking of me more as a servant than guest. I didn't mind cramped quarters or little food. Those things would get better with time for me and them. What I did mind was Ahmed, who thought he was my new Master coming in telling me to help his gardener till the ground before planting season, then asking me to wash down patios and his car. I told him he'd have been really at home in the Old South as "Master", but I'm a carpetbagger and it was time he laid his business proposition on the line, which was the pretext for why I decided to stay with him in the first place.

Ahmed wanted to involve me in a new business venture once Kuwait started rebuilding. I agreed to weigh his proposition but he'd have to let his other slave, an Egyptian do all those other chores.

I felt very ill at ease at Ahmed's home. He and his wife stayed alone inside the big house with seven bedrooms. The Indian maids, the Egyptian driver and I stayed out in a one room concrete block shanty out back. Ahmed's children remained in Cairo at their apartment one block from the Nile River near the Sheraton Giza Hotel.

The food at Ahmed's was insufficient for third world employees so I brought in as many groceries as I was able to purchase from the still partially stocked store shelves. The cleanliness of where I was staying was less than hygienic and no where even close to Godliness, yet Ahmed wanted me to stay there while we discussed business ventures. I had little choice so I spent my days rambling around town and my evenings with Ahmed and my banker friend Ali Chougli, sitting outside in the heat where the garden use to be.

Ahmed finally presented to me his long awaited proposition. He'd like to go into the Kindergarten business in Kuwait, American style. He raved on and on how it would be so simple to do with my knowledge of the way Americans do things and with my ability to hire someone and my ability to find the right building, and my ability to finance the first year of operations and supplies. I ask him what his part in this venture would be and he said he would have to legally own it in his name and pay me a salary; a pretty good salary or part of the business, whichever I thought best. He said this was the "Kuwaiti way." I firmly in the "American way" told him the Kuwaiti way sucks. I guess he could see the veins in my neck throbbing so he backed off and I packed my things.

How stupid of me, I had for a while forgotten how Kuwaitis conduct business. They'd learned nothing during seven months of occupation, maybe it should have been seven years. Ahmed was a clown in Kuwaiti robes. He was the kind of person I had come to hate and disrespect in Kuwait before invasion and here he was trying to pull the wool over my eyes after his half million dollars home and fat ass were just saved by infidel forces from my country and many others.

I set my suitcase and footlocker off his property onto a nearby roadway near my car and started packing. I'm going back to my apartment. Ahmed followed me like a hurt puppy. He still persisted, saying "look even if you work somewhere else in Kuwait, I will give you sponsorship and all you have to do is give me 15 percent of your salary." "Isn't this a good deal?" I couldn't believe this man just survived a half million occupying troops looking for someone like him to kill. I soon returned to his home to flatten his tires with a tire iron.

A few weeks later, I met with Ahmed again when he tried to make me feel a little more his equal than a slave. No mention was made of the tires. We went to a Parliamentarian friend's home nearby and I sat through an informal meeting discussing of all things the possibility of assassinating the Emir. The country would then be under the rule of the Crown Prince and Prime Minister, my former boss, whom they liked. Their main reasoning for such a plot was to get rid of the Emir whom they blamed for running out and staying hidden until the country was freed. Even now they blame him for not planning his return any time in the near future.

To them, the Emir was also to be blamed for several financial scams that he had pulled on his constituents, concerning some satellite purchases. From what I heard, all the money disappeared, no satellites were purchased and many Kuwaitis lost millions of dollars. The Emir was also blamed for several other financial schemes as well as many other short comings in the country. Several of these men also resented the Emir for down playing their part in resistance and liberation. I knew several of their grievances weren't true, but who was I to extinguish internal strife. Living at Ahmed's house would surely have been risky now, and I was glad to be rid of him.

One of the things I learned within the past couple years living in Kuwait was how Kuwaitis had to have a free ride on everything. Everyone owes them a life because they were chosen by God and rewarded with riches from the earth. Their government social welfare state has prepared them for a life of no incentive, relaxed leisure days and no reason for higher education other than it was a fad to go to university (college is a term they use for trade schools and is frowned upon).

Kuwaitis know they'll probably never have to fall back on education but truly need the subsidies their welfare state provides for them from birth until death. I use to think such a lifestyle would be wonderful, but when I saw what it did to Kuwaitis over a period of time, I knew it wouldn't be worth it.

I met my Indian banker friend Ali, and as luck would have it, his wife and son had just caught a flight to Mumbai (Bombay), India. Aircraft were now arriving and departing about three a day at Kuwait International Airport and many of those trapped for so long inside occupied Kuwait, were now making use of the renewed flights to get out for some well deserved relaxation. They were seeking hot water and electricity and I didn't blame them. Kuwait had been in total shambles for the past two months since Saddam Hussein began his retreat and invoked his "Scorched Earth Policy."

Ali's apartment was pretty much like most American ones. He had a sectional sofa in the living room, a dining room suite with blue wall to wall carpeting and matching draw drapes at the glass sliding doors. Most of all, his toilet was western style and his building had water and a generator for electricity. That meant the toilet worked. Ali's Kitchen was well stocked with utensils to cook with, and he had a bottle of butane gas for the stove. The small Indian market below Ali's apartment had some staple groceries but no milk, butter, creams etc. I paid for a few things that would at least show my host I appreciated his hospitality then met his brother-in-law who also was temporarily living there.

The brother-in-law's family left for India a month after invasion so he had long ago surrendered his apartment, so he moved in with Ali's family. The three of us got along famously. One evening while we were talking about invasion, occupation and personal experiences, I asked Ali "how did you keep your "almost new" car when everyone else around lost theirs?" He laughed and said he continued using his vehicle for work for almost the entire occupation. At one of the first Iraqi roadblocks he encountered, they issued him a pass to put inside the window. It stated he was a bank official and required the car for work. He said, for whatever reason the Iraqi had in mind for later, possibly to use him, it never happened but he did always get through roadblocks easily.

Ali said as Liberation approached, it became harder to hold onto the car. Most Iraqis wanted it to drive home during retreat. Ali realized cars were being appropriated with alarming frequency, so one night late during curfew; he took his car to an empty lot in the middle of his neighborhood. There, he and his brother-in-law and son jacked it up on blocks, removed the tires, removed the front hood, threw lots of newspapers and other clean garbage inside to make it look bad, then covered a lot of the car with canned oil, threw cans of dirt and sand all over it and quietly proceeded to break out one head light and one tail light. They popped off some of the aluminum chrome detail strips along the side, and the car was complete. It looked pretty undesirable, especially with a few torn up clothes, oil and dirt put under the hood, even the engine looked bad. The car sat there untouched for the next six weeks before Liberation.

Following Liberation, a little bit of time spent cleaning and reassembling it and it bore no resemblance to the way it must have appeared in the vacant lot. He still had one broken head light and tail light but it was one of the nicest cars in Kuwait. Obviously, Ali was one of the smarter car owners in the whole country.

Ali also told me of his son's run in with the Iraqi soldiers. One day while the teenager was hanging around several other kids, an Iraqi soldier grabbed him and wanted to know where he lived. When he told them Rumaithiya, they didn't believe him because that was an Indian community and he looked very Kuwaiti. They slapped him around a little and then made him take them to his home. Once at his parent's apartment, it took a lot of convincing and documented paperwork to actually believe this child had two quite dark parents who were obviously Indian. The boy didn't even have the same accent; after all, Sunay had been schooled in Kuwait all his life and ran with trendy Kuwaiti boys.

While the Iraqi and Sunay were in Ali's apartment, the soldier waved his AK 47 automatic rifle around several times and then demanded some aspirin for his headache. Ali and his wife catered to the soldier until he fell asleep sprawled on the couch. Ali's son and wife left the apartment for their own safety and Ali remained alone with the Iraqi. When the soldier awakened, he was more civil only asking for tea, then he left.

Ali said the Iraqis allowed Indians, Filipinos and Palestinians a lot more freedom than Kuwaitis, and usually didn't loot their homes either.

I remained at Ali's apartment for three days before going to work for Sonny and Bob at their Marr Bell Company camp at Messila Beach. From the Kuwait International Hotel Bob, Sonny and I headed southeast about 8 miles out the Fahaheel Motor Way.

The Kuwait City suburb of Messila Beach is one of the more affluent neighborhoods in a town where affluent neighborhoods are plentiful. Several Royal Family residences and small palaces share the nearby shoreline with several other very rich Kuwaiti's homes there. In Messila, Long private docks jut into the sea from each beachfront residence. One mansion looks a lot like the one used on the television's BEVERLY HILLBILLIES.

Some of the huge fifteen and eighteen bedroom homes were of fabulous Middle Eastern architecture with domes, arches and walled court yards, and others were like three storey modern glass office buildings. Almost all had giant fountains, circular drives and stately entry gates. As Bob, Sonny and I neared the neighborhood; we could see many of these estates in partial disrepair with their former lush gardens dead, windows broken, gates broken down, and their mansion's facades awash in oil. I'm sure Messila Beach was, and will one day again be a beautiful place to live.

CHAPTER 15

From the Rubble

Sonny, Bob and I drove down a formerly affluent suburban street in the Kuwaitis only neighborhood of Messila Beach. Soon we arrived at a stretch of sand between one of the fine homes and the Kuwait Oil Company's Beach Club. How Bob and Sonny secured this prime land to build a fully self contained prefabricated camp for foreigners was beyond me. Later I heard Bob say at least a thousand times "this damn property cost me a million dollars." He was full of it. Through time, I heard the same exaggerated mumble jumble about everything from the cost of bunk beds to kitchen supplies and company vehicles.

Their camp had already been under construction for just under a week when I got there. About dozen prefabricated 10 X 24 feet buildings had been placed near the beach in two separate rows. Within the next weeks, a beehive of activity would result in a real camp with ten times more buildings and several more rows. This camp would continue expanding and later became "main camp" with two others, then three and four more to follow.

Filipino engineers, laborers from India, Sri Lankan, Pakistan, Bangladesh and Thailand continued pouring in. Prefab housing units arrived from Saudi Arabia, furniture from Italy, bedding and cooks from India, vehicles from the United States, generators from Germany and England and confiscated water tanks from Iraq while concrete pavers and gravel came from inside Kuwait.

As the self contained camps came more alive, our workdays grew longer and hotter. The only thing positive about the thick oil clouds hovering above, was that they moderated Kuwait's usual intense heat. The clouds didn't create any nuclear style winter or anything, but temperatures were at least twenty full degrees cooler than normal.

Daily, we three western engineers had cranes off load and set into place new housing units. The Filipino engineers and their work crews rapidly added electrical and plumbing services to the camp and the Thais and Indians dug sewage spills toward the waters edge of the Persian Gulf. A mandatory air conditioner shop was set up, as were administrative offices and two dining rooms, one for the British and Americans and another for the TCNs (third country nationals).

The camp became relatively comfortable fast and though it didn't have the creature comforts I enjoyed before invasion at the Royal Palaces nor my penthouse, this Royal Ordinance camp soon became the best place to live in the entire country.

Each arriving prefabricated living quarters had a single bath opposite the front door and two bedrooms, one at either end of the building. Unlike anything else in Kuwait at 220 volts, the electricity in our camps was strictly American 110 volts. Each air conditioned housing unit had American toilets and showers and huge amounts of bottled; drinking water was flown in with our weekly food supplies.

Ernie and Stevie, both engineers like Sonny, were Johnnie Walker, whiskey drinking, rednecks from Alabama. Ernie was a nondescript balding, forty five year old, fat wasted rugged man with a true southern drawl. Stevie, the impish one was a thin, humorless, small framed little guy that looked a little like Mel Tillis, but Stevie didn't have the stutter problem, just a testicle or lack of them problem. Stevie whose uncooked turkey complexion with pimples made my skin crawl so every time I was around him, I just wanted to slide him into the oven and bake him.

Stevie was pussy whipped and in great financial difficulties back home in Mobile when Bob I assume rescued him and promised him the world to come to Kuwait. Stevie was a mama's boy that had probably never been away to Boy Scout Camp so he was finding life not so perfect in Kuwait. He whined incessantly about everything.

Our camp had grown from about sixteen people to about fifty in just the first couple weeks. Even then it was becoming a bee hive of activity with construction underway 360 degrees around the property. Cooking and dining facilities were moving along well except the menu was extremely limited. I remember the first week; all we had to eat from our Indian chef was Indian curry chicken and rice cooked over two open fires in the sand. We were afraid to try any of his other real Indian dishes but were content to eat the curry chicken and rice three times a day, every day until enough was enough.

Each morning noon and night were the same, two big kettles over an open fire with us sitting around in the sand eating Indian food from paper plates and drinking non iced bottled water from plastic cups? Of course the added spice came from crude oil fumes and droplets from the great outdoors. The setting was picnic like, but quite something else.

More prefab housing, dining and recreational units continued arriving. Daily I would drive Bob's six pack Toyota truck to the Saudi Arabia Nuwaiseeb border checkpoint to escort several flatbed trucks ferrying our supplies in. I went to the border checkpoint each day of the week except Thursday and Friday, the Muslim weekend.

Some flatbed trucks were fully loaded with building materials, others with new generators for back up electricity, cable of various construction sizes, food supplies and furniture. With each day, new crew members arrived and the camp grew to become so comfortable that we retreated farther and farther from the dark world of Kuwait and more into our own blossoming camp life.

One day, Bob returned to camp and announced our Client, Royal Ordinance of Great Britain would be arriving within the next week. Everything had to be ready. We had never had a slack day yet but our fastest pace began following the announcement. Royal Ordinance was a British mine and bomb ordinance division of the company that also owned Rolls Royce and other large corporations. They'd be bringing hundreds of their own staff and experts to remove explosives from Kuwait and Failaka Island off the coast.

Bob was given new specifics for accommodations and support facilities which included a laundry facility, two larger dining halls; each capable of catering to hundreds of men which had to be built, furnished and staffed along with two recreational halls with vcrs, televisions, pool tables, table tennis, a reading room and darts.

For the tcn's, third country national's modular housing units were assembled together into three long, 40 room barracks, capable of housing hundreds of men. Their three barracks and one recreation facility and dining hall became our Camp Two, about a block away from the Main Camp in Messila Beach.

Establishing another camp meant more generators had to be installed, more sewage, plumbing, below ground electrical cables, water tanks, warehouses and another motor pool repair shop. Another laundry facility was also added and staffed.

One week later, more than a hundred British ordinance guys arrived, as did the first of their hundreds of laborers, more Indians, Thais, Bangladeshis, Pakistanis and Sri Lankans. The new tcn laborers didn't work around camp but started immediately assisting the Royal Ordinance Brits with mine and bomb removal along the coastline of Kuwait, and in the deserts. They hand carried tens of thousands of defused mines back to trucks for transport to safe bunker storage facilities back amongst us where we slept. The mines were saved for future use by the Kuwait military.

These new manpower arrivals came fast and furious. The second, then third groups of almost identical proportions arrived two weeks apart. The British mine clearance experts were housed in the original main camp with Bob, Sonny, Ernie, Stevie and me.

Royal Ordinance corporate executives instructed our Marr Bell Company's higher ups that anything their guys asked for, they were to get. They wanted their men to have comfort, good food, recreation, and clean clothes, always. They were not to have any worries other than their job of mine removal. With the strenuous, nerve racking task of disarming live explosives, nothing else in their life should be a hassle. Marr Bell provided everything from maid and laundry services for British housing, roadside repair service (our own AAA) for tire repair anywhere at any time, and even tea boy room services for the new Royal Ordinance (RO) administrative offices in the main camp. Meals, said RO, should be cooked by a new premier chef. They should always be on time and excellent. Soon, every day eating became like dining in a fine hotel.

Donald St. Pierre, a nice young Cajun guy in his late twenties from New Orleans, Louisiana was busy setting up our Mobile, Alabama investor owned company's; on-property administrative office in the main camp.

Royal Ordinance came in with more than twenty new Land Rover vehicles to be used by their mine clearance teams, and additional large troop carrier trucks for hauling tcn's into the field and bringing defused mines back to the storage facilities. They also brought dump trucks and other heavy equipment like "960" loaders and backhoes. The Brits called this stuff "Plant."

A surprise was to find out who had been hired in England to oversee "plant" for Royal Ordinance in Kuwait. It was Bob from Bob and Liz, my old friends with the green hair son from parties and swimming at Guy and Shari's Tara home in Ahmadi.

Marr Bell employees were extremely busy building and manning vehicle maintenance shops, adding more fuel storage tanks, increasing the number of generators and backups, adding to the water storage facilities and establishing a whole realm of support shops. They included shops for air conditioner repair, electrical, carpentry, plumbing, storage, grounds maintenance and automobile servicing. We now had incoming supply warehouses and underground bunkers for storing the deactivated land mines and other explosives, all in our own complete self contained village.

We became the only people in Kuwait who had unlimited supplies of drinking water and food, including milk, butter and eggs as well as transportation and air conditioning. We even had our own satellite dish, courtesy of RO.

While Kuwait remained slapped into a dark sleep, we at the Marr Bell-Royal Ordinance Camp had few worries greater than whether the ice machines were producing enough or whether the RO guys preferred their meals cafeteria style or from chafing dishes buffet style.

Kuwait lingered in limbo for several more months before the actual rebuilding effort started. Everyone wanting to come into the country to do anything was delayed until all mines and explosives were removed from the deserts and seaside. The American munitions experts, CMS, didn't arrive for almost another year. Kuwaitis were reluctant to rebuild because they were still unsure if Saddam Hussein would come back in the future.

For Royal Ordinance and us, being the first to arrive in Kuwait, other than the American Corps of Engineers was bold and daring, exciting, dangerous, fulfilling and lucrative. It was a good life that came with a price tag. The price paid wasn't in money only but in lives lost.

We had more than a dozen of our men, our friends and coworkers killed or maimed by exploding mines while making Kuwait's sands and sea safe.

The RO guys earned three hundred forty five dollars a day, seven days a week, and thirty days a month. Their insurance policies covered loss of life and loss of limb. The loss of limb clause got very technical and was unfortunately used too often. Insurance payments distinguished between loss of a finger, a forefinger or partial hand. The clause asked, "Did the person just lose use of the finger or hand or leg or foot or was it missing or partially missing?" A Lost life was worth a million dollars. All other body parts were proportionately less.

Money was of course why most men had come to Kuwait. They sought the same thing all of us wanted, a better life for our families; not from insurance God forbid, but from the daily high wages earned. Each man just had to pray everything would go well, and one day he could go home to help spend the money he'd made.

I must admit, when the first explosives teams arrived, I was impressed. They were not the men I thought they'd be. For the most part, they were articulate, well spoken, well groomed and well educated. I suppose I had the image that someone who messes with mines or bombs must be a little off balance. Not so. As we sat together in the evenings, I heard their stories. "Why were they in Kuwait?" Some told of their impending marriage, some of their impending divorce and others of hardship or illness within the family. This was a good chance for them to earn more money to start their married life or pay off loans or finance a better lifestyle for their family.

One of the RO guys, John told me he had a small son who was severely retarded. The boy was in a special school not paid for by the British Social Welfare program. Another RO guy, Ken told me his first wife died of Cancer, he remarried a woman who was taking care of his three small children, but his new wife had sent his children away to live with their grand mother while he was here. The wife was keeping the house and moved her new boyfriend in. When he returned, Ken was going to get his children back and rebuild their lives in a new town.

Probably the friendliest RO guy in camp, Chris was a really funny person. Everything he said was witty. He could never keep a straight face while telling you something, and if it was straight, you knew to watch for a punch line or a gag at the end. Chris just wanted a better life for his family, better schools for the kids and a better home. This story was by far the one I heard most of all.

There were a few lost soles that joined the group as well, like Ringo. Ringo was in his mid thirties, still lost and didn't know what he wanted to do or how to do it. Perhaps he really was talented with explosives, but I cringed each time I thought this man was into anything more dangerous than a cap pistol. In my opinion, he was a pathological liar, a thief and as explosive as any pyrotechnics he worked with. I never asked him how he felt as he defused a live mine because, I was sure to him it was at least a little ecstasy. I was also sure it was probably only practice for what he may do some day, like blowing up a Post Office or going to work for the Irish Republican Army. Perhaps he was just waiting for the big bang which would kill him as his last, big, ultimate high.

Kenny beat them all. Kenny was twenty eight years old, six feet seven inches tall, and a burly guy with a nice smile for everyone. He was quiet, but not too. He was by far the biggest eater in camp who could put away more food than anyone I'd ever seen. He wasn't fat, but managed to pack all the food in somewhere. I got the Filipino carpenters to build Kenny a special, extra long bed. I liked him and John, and Chris and many of the other guys very much. What a place and time for male bonding!

Gus, Ghassan my Palestinian friend from way back in my Ministry of Information and Dasma Palace days; was hired by Bob to work in procurement for Marr Bell. The last I had heard from him was when he and his wife Ruba headed out from Kuwait through Northern Saudi Arabia for Amman, Jordan the night of invasion.

I learned later, they went from Al Salmi border checkpoint into Saudi Arabia and literally bypassed the whole invasion of Saddam Hussein's forces. They never saw the Iraqi soldiers or tanks that were huddled in mass only about fifteen miles away on the Iraqi side where the three countries almost meet. Gus and Ruba never heard a word about the invasion until several hours after they reached Amman. They were awakened from their sleep and told by family members that Kuwait had been invaded and that they were lucky they were out of the country.

Gus' father's heavy equipment company made it through occupation all right, but was seized by angry Kuwaitis just a few weeks before Gus began working for Marr Bell. The Kuwaitis were once again lashing out at Palestinians or Jordanians because their country supported Saddam Hussein's invasion and the fact that Palestinians weren't harassed by his troops during occupation. Now, the Kuwaiti's took Gus' fathers' company to help make up for their losses. Ghassan became unemployed until he was hired by Bob.

Ruba had not returned from Jordan yet. She was waiting until life in Kuwait got back closer to normal. Gus was living in their Hawalli apartment alone with Ruba's father who was a chemist by profession. He had worked for many years in Kuwait so he was back hoping to get work. Gus' father's business was almost defunct since Occupation and Liberation anyway, so Gus remained in Kuwait to try to regain what he could of the vehicles and equipment. He found out about Bob and Sonny about the same time I did. His new job was trying to procure additional linens, bunk beds and whatever car parts might be needed for Marr Bell and Royal Ordinance. His role expanded as the company grew and Kuwait returned to life.

Ghassan said newspapers in Amman printed all positive news about the takeover of Kuwait and held the line, "the whole thing was Kuwait's fault". He thought nothing of returning to Kuwait with Ruba to resume their normal lives but Ruba decided to stay with family in Amman a little longer. It was after Gus returned to Hawalli that he saw all was not well. Their apartment had not been sacked by the invaders. Iraqi troops allowed the Palestinian and Jordanian community in Hawalli to go about business, almost as usual. It was considerably later when Kuwaitis became more empowered, that their revenge against Palestinians became frequent. Gus said he was allowed the luxury of feeling safe from the Iraqis in his own apartment without probability of soldiers coming there during the night. Hawalli was truly a safe zone if there ever was one in that war. Ruba returned to Kuwait through Baghdad during occupation and said they were allowed to shop and get gasoline when needed. She didn't leave again until the Iraqis began pulling out and sabotaging the electrical and water supplies.

Marr Bell and Royal Ordinance both had to have Kuwaiti sponsors to set up inside Kuwait. It was from Marr Bell's sponsor that we heard more stories of Palestinians turning Kuwaitis in to Iraqi soldiers during occupation. He said Palestinians would escort Iraqi troops to Kuwaiti homes, and then while the Kuwaitis were being interrogated, the Palestinians were rewarded with household items they wanted. We also heard the same thing about Indians and other nationalities in Kuwait during occupation. Former maids like Jeanette's Sister Emily, turned in their bosses and got them killed. We were told barbers, seamstresses and clerks turned in some westerners as well. Those who turned in Brits and Americans received rewards of cars, appliances and furniture.

Many of our friends told of other payback vendettas against Kuwaitis for the way they had been treated in the past. I even heard it from Nabil, who soon after occupation began, made a deadly move against his sponsor. His retaliation was against the Kuwaiti who seized the opportunity to steal Nabil's construction company after he wanted to leave Kuwait to seek medical help for his dying daughter. The Kuwaiti stole the company and showed no concern that Nabil's daughter had died of the injuries she received at the hands of the Kuwaiti girls. For many others of various nationalities, revenge against abusive Kuwaitis seemed justified. In the hunting sense, "open season on Kuwaitis" lasted seven months; "open season by Kuwaitis" against other nationals had lasted many years.

For as many stories as we heard about Kuwaitis and westerners getting turned in, we heard an equal amount of stories of other nationalities harboring and helping Kuwaitis and westerners at penalty of death, if caught by the Iraqis.

There are always weak people and strong people in all societies and at every economic level. What happened in Kuwait could happen any where else in the world. After seven months of occupation by the Iraqis, most Kuwaitis returned to the country and immediately began ill treating their "inferiors" as they always had in the past.

Kuwaitis appear to have learned nothing. In Kuwait, there's a strong sense of the animal kingdom where those with money and power rule and prey on those less fortunate and weaker. They do this without shame or guilt.

I'm sure if there is another invasion of Kuwait in the future, not only the few Palestinians left inside the country, but all the Indians, Bangladeshis, Egyptians, Syrians and possibly even some Americans will again turn against them.

Following the Liberation of Kuwait by allied forces in Desert Storm, Kuwaitis went on vengeful witch hunts against Palestinians and others in Hawalli. Stories abounded of Kuwaitis back in control and Palestinians being dragged from their shops and homes, never to be seen again. Others were murdered by gangs of young Kuwaitis putting ropes around their necks and being drug through the streets of Hawalli.

Even Kuwait's lower class Bedouin community had turned against the first class Kuwaitis. These nomads of the desert have for hundreds of years roamed the vast deserts of Iraq, Kuwait, and Saudi Arabia. They had never been harnessed by any border. For many, their seasonal movements continue to this day. For many others however, they've settled and continuously lived in one home and one village for fifty, sixty or more years. Though these people share a bloodline with Kuwaitis, they're not allowed to become citizens. Some Bedouins even have grandparents who have lived in Kuwait all these years, bore large numbers of children, who in turn had more children, and none are citizens because they did not feel the need to fill out paperwork. Some have managed through occasional circumstances to become Kuwaitis, but only second class, unlike oil sharing Kuwaitis.

Bedouin communities turned against Kuwait and sided with Saddam because of their ill treatment by the government and first class citizens in their own land. The Iraqi invasion was made easier by such communities who felt they had been wronged, and used for many years and didn't mind being used one more time against the Kuwaitis.

Kuwait's disputed border with Iraq had been a bone of contention for many decades. It had been marked and remarked on paper, and after each dispute with their neighbors, Kuwait always seemed to end up with more land. The invasion of Kuwait in 1990 wasn't the first time Saddam Hussein had invaded Kuwait. The last time his forces came was more than ten years ago, just before his eight years war with Iran. The Americans were still considered by Kuwaitis as "bad infidels." The Americans were neither asked, nor did they volunteer to go to Kuwait's rescue; but the British who were instrumental in establishing Kuwait as an oil power didn't want to lose their vital interests, so they did. They came to Kuwait's aid and threw Saddam Hussein out and pushed the line of demarcation between Iraq and Kuwait even further north and west.

Following Desert Storm and the Liberation of Kuwait in 1991, the demarcation line was again moved further north and a buffer, demilitarized zone was established for even greater protection, once again in Kuwait's favor.

Bob, of Bob and Liz, spoke with me only a few minutes after coming to work with RO. Later we talked about what happened to them since I saw them at the pool party in Ahmadi at Guy and Shari's Tara home. Bob had worked in "plant" heavy equipment as an intelligence cover for years. Now, he came to work for RO. Liz was still recuperating in England with their son Marc. Bob said he and Liz and their son were taken hostage by Iraqi troops during the expat roundup. He said one day they heard a commotion of trucks and troops downstairs and were alarmed to hear Iraqis rounding up other expats on the floors below them. It was only a matter of minutes before the three of them were also seized. They were being taken down stairs by two men with AK 47 machine guns when their son Marc, the rowdy little kid at the swimming pool with green hair, bit one of the Iraqis on the thigh. Liz had to break his turtle hold on the soldier by smashing together Marc's jaws.

The soldier was screaming and pointing the rifle at Bob all the while they were being put aboard a bus for transport to Baghdad. They were not well treated in Iraq at the beginning, but as time went by, Liz and the little boy were separated from Bob, but their treatment got better. They were "guests" on Saddam Hussein's televised broadcast to the world, when in fact; they were "human shields". Of course, on television and later in magazine photos, their pictures were too small to recognize. Their family was held for three weeks before being released unharmed. Bob had been held in a factory, probably thirty miles outside Baghdad while Liz and Marc were held in an underground building for a while, somewhere inside Baghdad, and then thrown into a large communal room at one of Saddam Hussein's palaces. When they saw each other at Saddam Hussein's broadcast, it was the first time they had been together in eleven days.

CHAPTER 16

Mines Bombs and Royal Ordinance

Most of the munitions experts who arrived to work for RO were men who had seen more than one war. Royal Ordinance's men poured in to our new "main" camp. Most were British who served as soldiers or mercenaries in several wars in Africa and the Far East. Some had been mercenaries in Rhodesia until it fell and in Cambodia, Laos and Thailand. Others had been with the British military fighting against Argentina down in the Falklands. They all came together in Kuwait with their counterparts, the British Gherka soldiers from Nepal. This combination made for great tales around the dinner table. All of them came in trade, service for money.

Marr Bell's Bob was in charge of hiring construction personnel only but began hiring people of questionable nature to work within our company. They were all Americans from the United States but some were totally without any skills that I could see. I wasn't an engineer but carried my full work load well as a project manager. Some of these other guys seemed to have no job at all and sat around all day and night drinking and talking of their former football glory days or their female conquests.

I enjoyed my job and made my share of the money also. The only thing I didn't like was the roommate I ended up with at Marr Bell Camp One. This man was another Alabaman whom Bob must have owed money to or to the man's father. The thirty two years old man was scared of his own shadow and had an I Q only about double his age. He stayed awake late every night trying to talk because he didn't want to fall asleep. Oddly enough, he often left the room to walk around camp at night. Our houseboy, Missan said he had to make the bed up every day around a large Bowie knife he kept under his pillow. Several times after he walked around camp at two or three in the morning, he awakened me and told me of vehicles parked nearby. He was sure they were assessing the camp for a terrorist attack.

Once when we had a drive by shooting, it didn't help this man's fragile state of mind. Other times, he came in and said a fishing boat without any lights was sitting just off Messila Beach and he supposed they were sending landing parties ashore for various reasons. Later, his night outings became so frequent that he slept all day then kept me worn out trying to talk to me all night. I needed my sleep. After all, I had to work about fourteen hours every day in the heat and oil. One day he just disappeared. No doubt he had caught a flight back to the United States. Often we laughed about him and another of the next people Bob hired.

Colonel Dan was a former U. S. military officer who had retired as soon as the Gulf war was over. He'd been in Kuwait during the war and remained instead of returning to the United States to retire. He made several important contacts, one of whom was Marr Bell's Bob. Colonel Dan wasn't my roommate but he was a real Colonel. When his roommate spoke, it was like des a vu. I could hear myself telling about the character who shared my room.

Colonel Dan demanded the room's overhead light be left on all the time. He had a dog with him that he found starving shortly upon his return to Kuwait. This dog had a bladder problem and left piddles of pee all over the room and even on Colonel Dan's bed. Houseboy who had lived in pretty backward conditions in his homeland couldn't believe Colonel Dan's an American who lives like an animal. Colonel Dan was supposed to help win contracts for housing and support from the American military, I think, but there were never any results that paid. He later moved on and then years later developed cancer and died.

Several of Bob and Sonny's other sales managers or whatever title they assumed, came with questionable pasts with an even more questionable present. Bob was the one attracted to the world of secrecy and deception. Before becoming Director of Marr Bell in Kuwait, he had been in the FBI. Some of the stories we heard about him had to do with the Carlos Marcellus organized crime family in Louisiana. Bob supposedly put the main man in prison, then had to seek safety elsewhere to keep from being killed. Bob believed in his own mind, and some others believed also, he was CIA. He's a very intelligent man who can spot a financial error at a glance and has one of the best methodical minds I've ever known, but was a ruthless penny pincher, a bully, a driven man who had bouts of manic depression and headaches. Bob flew in and out of Kuwait with airline tickets that said one route and returned having gone a whole different way. He mostly frequented India, and Nepal, two of his favorite crash points. He threatened people, made demands, got loud and had fits of anger but we learned to accept that, that was Bob.

Bob often stayed awake all night, then called meetings for the whole staff to attend at two or three o'clock in the morning. He sat behind his desk wide awake lashing out at one thing, then another while everyone else sat passively in their chairs, not really hearing or participating in Bob's lone rantings. He was a good man to be in his position. He was impersonal and uncaring and as long as he had a percentage of the business based on profits, the business would do very well. By hook or crook, the business made a lot of money.

Bob never spoke of jumping in the sack with women and showed little compassion for his own wife when she called telling him she had cancer. Their four daughters were forced to live some place other than with his wife, but it didn't shake him, at least that we could see. Business went on as usual. Bob was kind to me a couple of times, but I was so leery of him I couldn't enjoy those few moments. I had every respect for his brain; too bad we couldn't use him like a computer by taking away his ability to speak or interact.

My loyalty to the company, Marr Bell, was a different story, they looked after us, kept the money, excitement and jobs rolling in and I liked the majority owner Mr. Marr. Mr. Marr was a short five feet seven inches tall, overweight, sixty year's old man from Mobile, Alabama but not a redneck. He came to camp in Kuwait twice and most people feared him. I liked him and respected him immediately. He was a man who could laugh, drive a hard bargain, differ with your opinion and win you over. He was tall in character.

About the only thing I liked about Bob on the other hand was that he knew Tom Marr was his superior and he never forgot it. Blond haired graying Sonny who had the complexion of cracked elbow was loyal only to himself and on a bad day, he lashed out at anyone and everyone in sight. He was thoughtless and careless and consistently menacing. He loomed like a sand shark, not qualified to be one of the big boys of the sea, but he could get his teeth into anyone he considered weak prey. Sonny had been a construction contractor in Montgomery, Alabama or Birmingham, I forgot and didn't care. I heard he drank so much before straightening up that he was losing everything he had ever built for his family. His wife was now running the company in his absence, and doing quite well I heard.

Sonny probably also had money invested in Marr Bell or he wouldn't have been in Kuwait. I take that back. I heard him lay a sales pitch on the Kuwait manager of Blount Construction Company. He told that manager about the equipment we had and the facilities we controlled and I thought he was speaking about a completely different company. His line of bull shit did land a few contracts later. I guess he paid his way.

Marr Bell's relationship with Royal Ordinance grew sounder and more lucrative. Within the next six months, we had more than three hundred fifty people on our payroll, and RO had grown to more than four hundred. Both RO and Marr Bell brought in more foreign TCN (third country nationals) laborers to work on several new desert mine contracts. Our offices had expanded as had Royal Ordinance's. We added to their existing camp and we purchased new prefabs for our use as well. Donald, Marr Bell's accountant/manager was now running a tight ship financially and just screwed me out of several hundred dollars to Bob's benefit. Donald was normally a good man, but he has a character flaw that also runs along money lines. He's actually quite talented in arbitrating between Marr Bell and Royal Ordinance disputes but he botched this one with me.

Bob was always trying to rip another dollar from his client's pocket and sometimes got caught. Donald always had to make it better. Bob often created ways to take financial advantage of RO and didn't mind creating a tiff between contractor and client. Donald had on several occasions pulled Bob's ass out of the frying pan. Bob never considered a client a future partner on ventures in other places in the world but rather the client was someone whose pockets had to be picked "now". A one time client was all he wanted.

Marr Bell now had more than one hundred twelve housing buildings and an array of maintenance and storage facilities. The main Camp One had around one hundred seventy five British and Americans living in its ninety four buildings. The TCN camp had grown to more than seven hundred Thais, Filipinos, Bangladeshis, Indians, and Nepalese living in three main barracks and a few smaller ones at Camp Two. We also had some smaller camps.

I gave notice to Donald I was taking vacation, going home to get my wife who was now in Savannah, Georgia. She would be returning to Kuwait with me. He voiced some interest in hiring her to assist in the office but Bob voiced concern and didn't like that I was bringing my wife back to Kuwait, so I told him I'd move off camp when I returned the next month.

I returned to Savannah to my parent's home, where my wife was now waiting to go back to Kuwait with me. She rented out our home in Tempe, Arizona and put our furniture in storage. We spent three weeks vacation together with my family before returning to work. In that short time we enjoyed Christmas, celebrated our wedding anniversary and rang in the New Year.

That vacation time flew by, while we visited with everyone in our extended family and they all wanted to know all about Kuwait. There had been several months of almost no contact with the family after I returned to help rebuild Kuwait and now everybody wanted to know everything. They wanted detailed descriptions of the destruction caused by Saddam Hussein's armies and the rebuilding effort that was now going on. They wanted to know how much money I was making and all about the oil fires and land mines.

For Christmas presents, I brought "Desert Storm" war gifts of Iraqi helmets and gas masks for the guys, but sense no stores in Kuwait were open yet; the ladies had to settle for money. Before leaving Kuwait, I combed the streets and deserts rounding up many gas masks, helmets and pictures and put them in two large foot lockers to carry on the plane with me. I had several different kinds of hand grenades and other artifacts that were rendered FFE, "free from explosive" by Royal Ordinance munitions guys. In order to get the war items through United States Customs, I had to carry papers aboard the plane with me that described the pieces and their disarmament.

At both Kennedy International Airport in New York and the Atlanta airport, the trunks caused quite a stir. Hordes of custom and security officials waited for their turn in line to view the trunks' inside gifts. I was an immediate celebrity, or at least the contents of my foot lockers were.

I enjoyed every moment home with the family and I was happy to have my wife Maia returning to Kuwait to live with me. Just before we left Savannah, a female friend of my brother's wanted to meet us to see if there was any way possible she could join us in Kuwait. At that time, I had no intentions of taking anyone else back with us.

When I went to Kuwait just after Liberation, I took a friend named Keith Harvey who also wanted to work in Kuwait and earn some big money. Keith was a great guy, but it was hard for him to leave his wife and children. He did so, but almost turned around at Kennedy Airport in New York.

Over the telephone, his wife was having a hard time saying goodbye and said she had become ill. He was so broken up that I expected he would board a plane back to Savannah before boarding our flight to Kuwait, which was scheduled to leave at eleven o'clock in the evening. Keith stayed strong for a while and made it all the way to Kuwait. After a few days looking for a job, he decided Kuwait wasn't for him and booked passage home. Within a week he was back with his children and wife and quite happy.

Everyone else that said they'd like to come to Kuwait with me was all talk and no action. When it came down to the final moments, they backed out. All the work I put into getting them visas and a sponsor (no easy matter), and different company information for future employment and ran up telephone bills, they dropped by a simple phrase like "Oh well, I decided not to go."

Now someone else was saying she wanted to go with us. This time, I wasn't going to allow her or anyone else to hit me with that line again, but I did. There was whining and boo hooing and "please" and many other sweet phrases. She said she would be company for my wife, since the two of them would be about the only expat women in Kuwait. I relented. Margaret, a late blooming twenty two year old childless divorcee, was aboard.

Margaret's sad story about how she had run up huge college debts should of told Maia and I how extravagant her lifestyle was and we'd probably get caught up in here money woos. We right away fell prey to her next schemes and as her next victims. She was sure that working in Kuwait, making good money would allow her to start life anew.

From day one in Kuwait until about day ten, everything seemed fine. Maia and Margaret came to work at Marr Bell with me. They both had good jobs working with Donald in the office. Both were smart and easy to catch onto their new positions and Donald was grateful. The relationship between my wife and me and Margaret soon started falling apart.

Margaret lived with us in our three bedroom apartment. She had her own bedroom with its own bath in the Kuwait City suburb of Mangaf. She began entertaining the boys from RO scheduling them like chores, one following the other through most every evening and night. Three guys were regulars with an occasional change if one of the regulars went back to Britain or on vacation elsewhere. She turned our apartment into Margaret's "love nest."

Margaret kept telling us she had been celibate for so long, she wasn't use to having a man. This gave way to terrible conversations about her vagina which she called "the baby's playpen." Now that the play pen was being used frequently, the more she has to take care of it; and that she did. She became obsessed with finding a plastic surgeon Stateside that would do what she called "hoo ha rehab" for a new "designa vagina". The first thing she did was throw away all the toys and batteries she brought. There seemed to be enough there to run a Caterpillar generator.

Before two many months passed, Margaret owed us more than a thousand dollars in telephone calls and never put her part into the kitchen or even watered the plants while we were away in Egypt, Russia or Sweden.

"Margaret does Kuwait" was the phrase we started hearing from the guys at camp. Her nick name was "Thumper" for someone screwing as often as a rabbit; Maia and I simply referred to her escapades as the trolip's frolics.

The woman wasn't paying her fare share of the rent or anything else and even had the audacity to become paranoid that Maia and I were spying on her activities or somehow enjoying them. She demanded and I gave her a lock on the inside of her bedroom door. I told her it would be better to put an electric revolving door there instead.

We barbed back and forth but it was difficult to throw her out because she really had no options of a new place to live. We carried her for a few more months in which she became almost engaged to a banker, then was pretty sure she was going to marry a guy from Royal Ordinance and then there was a sure bet, the guy from Texas who had lots of money and owned his own business back home. For her it was always a sure bet that she would soon land in the lap of luxury and her big move to Kuwait would have paid off; but of course it didn't exactly happen that way. The first guy she went with who wanted to marry her was a short dumpy American from CMS, the munitions company in Kuwait for dismantling bombs and mines in the American Sector. She said he was hung but not so much cock wise, but had a bucket of nuts. From the first night we met him, Maia and I started referring to him as Planters.

The second fellow, the banker apparently didn't like Margaret as much as she liked him and took some one else on his trip to Paris instead of her. The fourth guy, the one from Royal Ordinance was pissed that she had called him while he was back home in the UK visiting his family and Margaret had made sure that his wife knew she was screwing her man in Kuwait. He came back and dumped her.

The guy from Texas suddenly disappeared one day and never took her home to meet his mom and dad. Margaret was up to her nipples in men, but no husband. The field was narrowing.

Margaret's trip to Dubai, United Arab Emirates with four guys went well. This gave Maia and me the opportunity to pack her goods and prepare her for life at a different location. This move on our part was not because she owed us so much money but rather more because our nerves were shot and our building's manager said he was fed up and was going to report this third roommate of ours to the CID Secret Police. All her money was going for expensive clothes and gold jewelry, not rent or food.

Arabs in other apartments in our building were calling her "whore" and saying we ran a brothel. In an Islamic country, this is punishable by law, if the law had come back to Kuwait yet. Fortunately, it hadn't and Margaret moved out of our place and in with a different four guys than we had ever seen. We later heard she married. Soon "Margaret does Kuwait" was a closed chapter in our lives, and only once in a while did we hear sneering remarks about "Thumper" for the next six years. Maia and I learned our lesson and never allowed anyone else to come overseas to work with us again.

CHAPTER 17

Ali Baba Runs

Kuwait rewarded Desert Storm coalition partners by giving lucrative arms and reconstruction deals for rebuilding the country and high paying contracts for mines and ordinance removal. The first of all companies and armies to arrive was our own client Royal Ordinance of Great Britain. Later, Kuwait would again reward the Brits and other liberating coalition governments by purchasing billions of dollars in self protection arms, especially from the United States, Britain and France.

Parcels of the Kuwaiti map were divided up and handed out according to each ally's strength and participation in liberating them. As with the rebuilding contracts and arms sales, areas of Kuwait with the heaviest concentration of mines went to the biggest allies. The Americans were given the Kuwait Saudi border region near al Wafra in the southern desert. The parcel ran at a triangle, northeast from Fahaheel Motor Way, south to the Nuwaiseeb border crossing, back again toward Khafji, Saudi Arabia.

The British received several locations. They got mine removal contracts for the main beaches of Kuwait, Failaka Island and the British sector which was in the deserts north of the American sector. All over Kuwait, each ally, France, Germany, Egypt, Russia, Bangladesh, Pakistan and others received their share.

The first to begin mine removal was the Brits. Royal Ordinance won the contract with the Kuwaitis and we won the housing contract from them.

We at Marr Bell dutifully and very profitably housed and catered to all their needs. Royal Ordinance began mine removal within two months of Liberation. The Americans didn't start until one year later.

The British moved carefully foot by foot along the majority of beaches in Kuwait City during the first clearance, which was again followed by two more quality control walks on the same beaches by Bangladeshis and later even by the Kuwaitis. The most heavily populated beach areas, parks, roadways and urban areas around Kuwait City were the first to be cleared.

For the first several months, about a dozen people per month, most of them children were killed or maimed by mines that were just lying around or partially buried. Later, the toll continued to rise but with less frequency. Mines washed up on the beaches and children found them and played with them. Sometimes with deadly results.

Each British mine removal and disposal team was composed of about a dozen men in protective gear walking in a straight line, shoulder to shoulder. Some used mine detectors while others were spotters, by eyesight only. Any mine discovered was dismantled by the team member nearest it. To insure there were no mines left, the beaches were cleared the second time at the lowest tide of the season.

Bangladesh's soldiers were given quality control, so it was they who followed the Brits about a month later. The Kuwaitis then followed the Bangladeshis and posed for pictures with headlines that read in the next day's newspapers: KUWAIT SOLDIERS CLEAR BEACHES. The articles exclaimed the expertise of the Kuwaiti soldiers, never mentioning the other nationalities. "The beaches are now declared safe for use", the papers would say.

A Kuwaiti mine removal team came one day while Maia was peering out our living room windows in Mangaf. The beach was our front door. She brought me to our picture window shouting "Look down at the Kuwaiti mine removal team." More than twelve men were shoulder to shoulder walking the beach, the same as the British; except the two Kuwaiti soldiers holding the mine detectors were following behind the others.

Along with Failaka Island and the coastline of Kuwait City, the southern area near Saudi Arabia was where Saddam's forces thought an allied attack would begin. This was where the Iraqis planted the heaviest concentration of mines. Our troops would later call the area, "The deep kill zone", where enormous Iraqi mine fields stretched mile after mile after mile along the desert floor.

As I traveled along Wafra road that separated the British Sector from the American Sector, I looked into the desert in all directions. Mines lay in rows and patterns all the way to the sandy horizon. To a novice, they appeared to grow like pineapples dotting the barren landscape. Often they were not just one type of mine. There were combinations, like rows of "Bouncing Bettys" with a few "Anti Personnel" mines, and "Antitank" mines in between.

The name "Bouncing Bettys" gives a hint as to what they do. When contact is made, they jump crotch high and explode. Their force will vaporize the lower torso and sever the extremities (arms, legs, genitals). V.S. 50's, antipersonnel mines are little more than the size of the palm of your hand, but will probably blow a leg off and make you bleed to death. The most powerful antitank mines are about the size of a frisbee but several times thicker. Every one of these mines and the rest of the five million within the deserts had to be removed with the lowest injury and death toll possible.

While most of the RO guys were sent to work in the British Sector of mainland Kuwait, many of them came to Failaka Island, to the last part of Kuwaiti soil where the Iraqis surrendered. On March 3, 1991, more than four days after Kuwait's Liberation, fourteen hundred and five Iraqi soldiers led by an Iraqi Brigadier General surrendered to coalition forces.

The fifteen miles long and three miles wide Persian Gulf island of Failaka was a thriving tourist retreat for Kuwaiti citizens prior to Iraqi Occupation.

Hundreds of private homes and beach bungalow rentals and even a few private walled farms lie amidst the baron wasteland that encompasses most of the island. Vegetation, trees and bushes are limited to the main town area only.

Since Occupation and Liberation, Failaka seemed more than eight miles out to sea. It felt hundreds of miles away, totally cut off from the mainland of Kuwait except for underwater telephone cables and water lines. Out there, there was no sewage, no electricity and no live people except ours. Even all the animals except about two dozen cats were dead.

Stevie and Ernie the other Project Managers from Marr Bell had gone to Failaka Island, checked it out, and determined where the RO mine removal camp could be set up for the British explosives teams and the hundreds of expat support laborers.

Both men selected a kindergarten school with lots of spare room, a gymnasium that could be used for a dining facility and kitchen. The school was not the best choice around, but was adequate. It had several maintenance rooms that they quickly converted to a mechanics stall, plus a tire repair shop, an air conditioner repair shop, electrical, carpentry, and plumbing shops.

Royal Ordinance sent their first sixty men to the island then continued sending more at intervals of a dozen at a time until Failaka was fully manned at more than three hundred British ordinance men and third world laborers. In addition to mercenaries, soldier of fortunes, corporate warriors and other ordinance guys that had arrived at Messila Beach main camp and Failaka, Royal Ordinance brought in the 2-5 squadron of the British Army to aide in mine removal and detonations.

Ernie came back to Messila Beach and Stevie stayed on the island literally crying each day as he talked to the office or to Bob. He was lonely, he missed his wife and kids in Alabama, and he is going to have a nervous breakdown. This continued until he was considered useless over there and they invited him to return to main camp. He bitched if a ferry load of supplies didn't arrive on time, then he bitched if the ferry did arrive and he had to off load it. He bitched at cats storming the buildings for food, and bitched about whatever else he could. Finally, Bob asked me to go over to replace him and run the camp. I told my wife farewell, boarded the eight o'clock morning, infrequent ferry from Ras al Ard Salmyia and took the two and a half hour ferry trip over.

While on Failaka, I made friends with the nine Kuwaiti guardsmen housed at the ports and got on very well with the RO guys, the British army troops and the Indian and Bangladeshi laborers including the Third Country Nationals under my command. Being on Failaka was certainly remote if nothing else. I also looked at it as peaceful and serine. I would like to have had Maia on the island with me but she would have gone out of her mind from boredom. It was best she remain in the Mesilla Beach Marr Bell administration office with Donald.

During the Iraqi withdrawal from Failaka, they blew up the only two electricity sub stations on the island, the water storage area, sunk all the Touristic Enterprises boats in the harbor and sacked hundreds of residences. They looted the few stores and blew up the island's two gas stations and bus station. All Kuwait's two story, London style tour buses had earlier been taken to Iraq as had Failaka's police cars, fire trucks, water trucks and all other service vehicles. In their place were foxholes, mined ports, barbed wire beaches, abandoned tanks and hundreds of large artillery cannons. The cannons had been put in place by the Iraqis to target American and allied warships offshore in the Persian Gulf.

The Iraqis had destroyed most living areas on the island and moved prairie dog style into partially buried 10 feet X 20 feet ISO metal shipping containers. They were in the sand dunes everywhere, all over the island. Those Iraqi soldiers who took up residence in the small town of Failaka lived in the schools, mosques and hospital.

Iraqi tanks took up guard positions throughout the small vacation community and along the islands only central road. Like the iso metal shipping containers the soldiers lived in, the tanks also lay partially hidden in mounds of sand with only their barrels visible above ground. Most tanks still remained in these positions, even after the war was over.

Unfortunately for history, some of the tanks were even crudely dug into archaeological digs of a three thousand year old ancient Greek civilization.

Failaka Island's history can be traced back through several major empires, the Persians and the Greek, Alexander the Great was here as well as the Turks of the Ottoman Empire. Iraq's barbarian soldiers had no sense for the island's historic value and destroyed whatever they felt necessary, including looting and tearing apart the ancient museums.

Several 2-5 British soldiers and I spent a lot of time in the destroyed library searching for information about the whole place from the only English language encyclopedias we could find amongst the ruins.

Within the first few months following the Gulf war Failaka again became a tourist attraction, but this time for military Generals, Colonels, Corps of Engineers officials and persons from many Embassies as well as our own company owners. I became part time tour guide and knowledgeably showed them the Iraqi war destruction, looting and devastation the island sustained during Occupation and following its Liberation. Not just a little of the damage was caused by our allied bombing raids.

Since Iraqi soldiers occupied all the six schools on the island as barracks, they all became prime bombing targets. The allies hit the Iraqis where they lived. Our bombers took out the few factories on the island and someone, either our side or theirs, took out the Ministry of Electricity and Water's main materials warehouse. The only hospital on the island took a direct hit of a 2,000 pound bomb directly into the cafeteria.

The girls boarding school that we later moved our personnel into, had taken a two thousand pound bomb into the gym. I rebuilt all the main buildings into comfortable quarters which included recreation rooms, dining facilities and housing. The facility became billeting for not only Royal Ordinance and Marr Bell but also for other companies like Blount and Morrison Shand who became tenants when they came to rebuild the island's infrastructure.

All main buildings on the island had been bombed. American war ships or planes "smart bombed" the television station, the communications building and telephone company; then regular bombs took out the police and fire stations, the hospital, all six schools, the banks, three factories, the Ministries, a shopping center, several housing areas and the bus terminal.

Of the seventeen thousand "smart bombs" and two hundred ten thousand normal, "dumb bombs" used against the Iraqis during Gulf Storm, there were probably fifty or more "two thousand pounders" delivered to Failaka. These did the most damage but several other types of bombs reigned on Failaka causing massive destruction as well, like tens of thousands of small rockei. We knew "smart bombs" had hit Failaka because the communications centers had been wiped out, yet their towers were left in tact.

When Royal Ordinance bid the contract for munitions removal from Failaka, they did so from an aerial survey flying over in a helicopter. Their calculations were tens of thousands of pounds underestimated so Royal Ordinance almost lost money on the contract. They couldn't believe how many still unexploded, mines, blue 77 rockei cluster bombs and even two thousand pounders remained unexploded and stuck in the dirt and sand.

The island had been subjected to almost daily bombings by allied aircraft during Desert Storm. Every time planes flew to Iraq to bomb Baghdad or anywhere else, they flew back over Failaka and unloaded all undropped ordinances. After all, a plane cannot land on an aircraft carrier still loaded with explosives. Failaka had become the dumping ground.

There was no Kuwaiti civilian population to contend with on the island since the beginning of Iraqi occupation. The only inhabitants left during the Gulf War were Iraqi soldiers, so the entire island was fare game. One large Iraqi Republican Guard unit was based on Failaka and was preparing a missile base for use against possible liberators, but they never got to use it.

The only other living beings on Failaka Island besides soldiers from Saddam Hussein's armies were cats. Those that survived were veterans of hunger and knew what survival took. They had lived through bombings, lack of food, no care and the hostile, oily, wet and hot climate.

After we arrived and set up dining rooms, the cats staged attacks against our men for their food. A few cats conducted air attacks by dropping from the partially destroyed dining room ceiling onto the table to get it. Goats kept for sacrifice by locals at their residences before the war, had all died of starvation. There were no dog deaths, because no dogs were ever allowed on the island due to a local belief in a curse.

One of the most pitiful sites I came across was that of a small tiger striped, rust, colored kitten about five or six months old. She had starved to death. Her body was extremely emaciated, with her ribs visible through her small furry coat. With one final effort in life, she crawled up into the comfort of a furry, teddy bear on a child's bed, and died. I found her snuggled so tightly between the teddy bear's legs that it appeared they had settled in to their final sleep together.

Our engineer, Felix and the other Filipinos had Stevie's orders to kill all surviving cats. When I got there, I rescinded the order and fed the ones still left. These cats had managed to stay alive in the most horrid conditions following invasion, occupation and liberation, so I felt they had earned respect and the right to life.

Following Liberation, the Kuwait Government forbade the civilian population to return to Failaka Island, so it remained distant and dark except for our camp, the cats and a few Kuwaiti soldiers. The cats under my protection were promptly given names and catered to. There was my favorite Groucho, who had the same black mustache marks above his mouth and cheeks that the late entertainer, Groucho Marks had and there was Marilyn, a beautiful long white hair Persian who had a black beauty mark above and to the left of her mouth like Marilyn Monroe. The other favorites were twiggy, maniac and bag lady. Bag Lady was so pitiful, but a special favorite of mine. Her long brown paper bag colored hair was unkempt, dirty and had caught fire. In some places along her body the skin was bare and others terribly matted. She had been burned in a fire or bomb blast and her eyes were so sad. They seemed to have extra skin covering them. Three of her paws had dirty white on the tips of the feet as if she was wearing three boots. I had a special place to feed her away from Marilyn and the others who were real scrappers.

Royal Ordinance divided Failaka Island into two sections. Some British Army Two Five Squadron soldiers were assigned the deserts and beaches for mine and explosives removal in the deserts and beaches while the other Two Five Squadron men removed all explosives found in the town and inhabited areas. According to surveys, there were three minefields on the island's beaches. Two on the north beach and one on the south near the Failaka Touristic Enterprises chalets otherwise there were numerous two thousand pound bombs still "live" out there, and tens of thousands of "live" rockei embedded in the sand and dirt.

A flail machine was brought in to help clear the beaches mines. This equipment looked like a road grader sitting below a small bullet proof cab, with a snow plow up front. The machine had an armor plated undercarriage and rows of steel chains on wide rollers placed underneath, much the same as air craft wings. The lone operator sat behind a single, very small, square, bullet proof window barely able to see where he was going. The flail's wide, wing like cylinders extended out more than seven feet to each side. Attached to the cylinder were heavy duty steel chains about every eight inches. When they rotated at a high rate of speed, they impacted and dug down into the sand about one yard below the surface. If a mine was there, it exploded.

Occasionally my friend Kurt, the flail's operator would finish work early because a mine had escaped unexploded as it passed beneath the flail's chains, but did explode directly under the cab section just as the vehicle's small steel wheels rolled over it. This left the cab more vulnerable and Kurt was hit by the flash and sound of the exploding mine. His hearing was impaired for a while and he appeared to be in slight shock but the next day, he was out in the mine fields again making $435. dollars a day.

Big Kenny, the big Brit I liked from Messila camp was now on Failaka with RO, the Two-Five and me. He was eating the camp out of house and home but the cooks appreciated him so much they cooked him anything he wanted. His and the cook's specialty were french fries. The cooks soaked the long cut potatoes in freezing cold water then threw them in the deep fry grease and "voila", salted, peppered and perfect. Kenny had been known to eat two baskets full in one sitting.

Kenny's face was of constant interest to me and I finally asked him about the small but long black scars imbedded in his face and neck. They looked like holes with pencil lead in them. He said when he was working in Cambodia, locating and disarming mines; he reached through some tree stumps to see if a mine was in there, about the same time someone else leaned into the bushes to get a better standing position. A mine went off, the Cambodian next to him was killed and Kenny caught fragments everywhere in the front of his body. He was hospitalized for a short time then went back to work. (If I had come that close to being blown up, I think that would have been enough warning for me. I wouldn't be hiring out to clear mines any more).

Kenny and I talked often, and on real boring evenings we took small cases of hand grenades out to a desolate beach area near the old Alexander the Great ruins near the port of Failaka. Kenny and I sat back in our lounge chairs, the ones we confiscated from the Touristic Enterprise's ruins and threw grenades. There were some beautiful evenings. (Joke.) The moonless sky filled with oil clouds, the sea filled with the smell of oil and the stench of rotting birds and fish carcasses, along with the loneliness of this island literally wiped off the map by Iraqis and allied forces bombings.

These were just simple nights. Kenny and I alone with three types of hand grenades and the noise they made as each exploded. We threw some grenades at little dirt mounds and others at cans. Sometimes, we threw in precision like acrobats, seeing whose would detonate first. We talked about family and life at home, then pulled the pin and threw. BANG! We spoke of places we'd still like to go in the world—pulled the pin, threw it. BANG!

Sometimes we did this for more than an hour before walking the five or six darkened blocks back to camp half deaf. These evenings were far more dangerous than I ever knew. It was only later that I learned some Chinese, Russian and Eastern European hand grenades, especially those aged from weather and deterioration were unpredictable. They could explode at their predetermined time lengths after the pin was pulled or they could explode the instant the pin was pulled, or any time in between. We had both been very lucky because we had thrown hundreds.

The city streets on Failaka Island were eerie in the day but far more so at night. Most of the blue 77 cluster bombs had been removed from the main streets and sidewalks but the walk back to camp was still spooky. There was no sound. The trees had no leaves, hundreds of homes lay destroyed, roofs were leaning, walls had been blown away, cars were blown upside down and metal television towers broken and lying on the ground, shop windows blown into thousands of pieces of sharp glass and shop shelves lying fifty feet from the building's foundation. There were no lights, no people, no birds, no wind and no moon.

While Kenny and I walked back through the dead streets, all RO and the 2-5 squadron guys were watching videos or settling down in their rooms to read. All the TCN laborers were in their television lounge watching Indian videos or playing board games.

One night during the Gulf War, my wife and I watched CNN coverage of allied forces bombing Iraqi gunboats in one of the two small ports on Failaka. Our camp was now located one block from that small port.

Failaka Island took the most damage of any place outside of Baghdad. There had been a much wetter winter than normal in the Gulf region during the occupation of 1990 and early 1991, so much of the sand and caliches, salt like soil, was very soft. When bombers flew over Failaka and dropped their cluster bombs by the thousands, some blew on impact and some didn't. Since so much of the island is desert, tens of thousands of these unexploded small rockei explosives stuck out of the earth everywhere.

Before being dropped from bombers, these cluster bombs are encased inside white, cigar shaped hollowed, fiberglass tubes about five feet long. The casing separates in mid air, into two separate pieces, allowing the cargo of hundreds of small foot long, deadly, dart like missiles to fall through the air indescrimanently. Some casings were larger than others. The larger ones with one yellow stripe contained three hundred fifty cluster bombs. The other smaller version contained two hundred fifty cluster bombs.

Most of the thousands of rockei cluster bombs that fell on Failaka's neighborhoods exploded upon impact as they hit hard objects, but the ones that fell in the desert or in people's yards just stuck in the wet, muddy sand without exploding. In town, the cluster bombs destroyed large areas of concrete block structures, roofs and roads. We even found live rockei in the air conditioner units of buildings we remodeled to live in.

When RO or the Two Five found live explosives near our camp, the surrounding area was evacuated; then the soldiers placed a white wad of clay like plastic explosive called P3 against the rockei or mine to be exploded. Next, this P3 was attached to a long wire that went to a detonating trigger. The explosive was then blown up alone or in series with several other explosives found nearby.

When Marr Bell arrived on Failaka, it was near impossible to drive down a street without blowing a tire due to the amount of shrapnel everywhere and live rockei on the roads and along curbs and gutters. It was absolutely necessary for all vehicles to carry extra tires. Within the camp, we had our own tire service center just like "Pep Boys" stateside.

Within a short time, munitions removal on Failaka became more organized and Kuwait granted a military helicopter for emergency standby in the event anyone got hurt in an explosion. The chopper arrived every morning and departed when the last ordinance guys quit work for the day. Usually, they stopped shortly after noon, before the worst heat of the day. One of my side benefits was the luxury of being permitted the use of the helicopter, so I began shuttling back to my wife on the mainland of Kuwait more often or having Maia flown to me. Prior to that time, I lived on the island more than five months and only went home once a week, if I was lucky.

It was a real pleasure taking the ten minutes flight from the island to the mainland, from one camp to the other; instead of the former two and a half hours from port to port by ferry boat or the much improved trip by private military boat that had started only a couple months earlier. The quicker boat was dubbed the "Lollypop" by the Brits. Perhaps the name was derived from the "Good Ship Lollipop", I don't know.

The "Lollypop" was a former Iraqi gun boat that RO converted into a quick ferry directly from the Messila Beach Camp on the mainland to Failaka Island. The sixty foot long boat had been abandoned in a hurry during Iraqi withdrawal from Kuwait. The Kuwait Ministry of Defense removed the guns and allowed RO the use of the gun boat for trips to and from the island as part of their bomb and mine removal contract. It was used almost daily ferrying RO and Marr Bell troops and laborers to and from camp on their days off and also for much needed supplies in support of everyone at the Failaka Camp.

Due to the Ministry of Defense contract, RO and Marr Bell was allowed to utilize anything left on the Island with the stipulation that none of it be removed to the mainland. Early on, this phrase took on broad meaning as we needed more and more supplies that were either unavailable through our supply channels on the mainland, or were needed in quick order to continue RO's support without delay. More often that not, rough seas in the Persian Gulf prevented the ferry boat from arriving for two weeks or more. According to schedule, the large car ferry was supposed to come every third or fourth day. In many cases, it didn't run at all so we ran short of food supplies and fuel. Later we learned to horde as much as possible in freezers also appropriated around the island for just such emergencies.

First it was freezers, and then came the need for fuel. We, mostly Felix our Filipino foreman, sunk siphon lines down into the local gas station's underground tanks. We siphoned what was needed to keep the generators for the camp running. Then we needed tires. Our men began combing the desert, stripping destroyed Iraqi military vehicles to establish a tire shop. We then needed longer or thicker cables for the generators, so we found the old Ministry of Electricity and took what we needed. This continued with paint, furniture, floor tiles, kitchen cabinets, cement, etc.

The Kuwaiti soldiers on the island didn't approve of us utilizing these things but they did well for themselves. They had sofas, carpets, heaters, generators, heavy blankets, televisions and VCRs they had appropriated from houses; but they were leery of our guys doing the same thing. The Kuwaiti soldiers weren't beyond approaching me or my men wanting to sell some of their booty though.

The Kuwaiti Army had little to do with guarding the island, so most of the time they spent tagging along behind our occasional pickup trucks, harassing us while we were out on requisitioning runs we called Ali Babbas.

The Kuwaiti soldiers were jealous of our control of the island but enjoyed occasionally dining with us and constantly calling on us to fix their tires or tow their vehicles that had broken down. I think they didn't understand the Defense contract wording on "appropriating" necessities needed for our camp. So, we carried out these Ali Babba runs. Knowing the Kuwaiti guards were watching videos or asleep, we drove from our camp under blackened moonless skies in darkened vehicles without the use of lights.

One day, following a problem with one of our generators, time was of the essence. We needed a simple part to fix it immediately. The only two other generators found on the island so far, had been destroyed. We had, however, run across a third one that still had the much needed part attached. It was out in the desert near the Iraqi missile launching pad on the north side of the island. That night without incident, we drove at low speed through the small town's streets and over dirt roads into the desert to get to the launch site. After removing the piece, we carefully drove back to camp safely.

Because of the moonless nights, any night was hazardous to go out. We could have easily driven over a live rockei or mine. For safety purposes, we stationed two men on the hood, one over each headlight. The headlight of course wasn't on but these men were spotters for the driver who watched the road, foot by foot. A night of Ali Baba and we were exhausted. With the generator part in place and running, that night's deed was accomplished.

There were several nights when Kuwaiti troops in their vehicles chased us through darkened streets but we knew where the explosives had been removed and where they hadn't. We just took off over stretches of desert where the Kuwaitis were afraid to follow. We didn't really fear them. It was more a big game to us and a break in the boredom.

CHAPTER 18

Munitions for a Princess

During our long stay on Kuwait's Failaka Island, I got to know the British Royal Ordinance mercenaries and Two-Five squadron soldiers quite well. Especially, from our nightly gatherings at the dinner table. Many evenings I listened as they glorified their own and each others political kills in Cambodia, Laos or on Africa's sub continent in Rhodesia. A few even spoke of being imprisoned on Africa's Gold Coast over a diamond mine dispute.

John, Kurt, Kenny, Chris and several others were wonderful conversationalists and I learned so much from them. Some things I shouldn't have. They were far more intelligent than I ever expected and they played mental games far over my head. Several of them subscribed to Mensa Magazine and often debated articles in recent publications. They also often took turns playing head games while sipping an evenings hot tea.

One that I remember in particular had to do with two midgets riding on a train in a boxcar. There was one other man present in the boxcar as well but of normal stature. When they arrived at a rail yard one of the midgets was dead. The police pulled his body from the train but couldn't arrest anyone for murder because the death was ruled a suicide. Only a small ruler with twelve inches marked on it, was the main clue. Why did the midget kill himself?

Everyone at the table then quizzed the story teller. In the end, it came out the midget who was still alive knew he was two inches taller than the other and would never have the career of being the world's smallest until the other fella was dead. He carried with him a fake ruler that only had eleven inches on it but it was made to appear to have only ten. The two midgets debated about their height and used the measuring stick on the taller of the two midgets to prove to the shorter one that he, the taller one was actually shorter. When the smallest midget saw the measurement, he assumed he was no longer the smallest man in the world. His career was over, so he killed himself. This was only what I think I remember, really they were talking over my head and I only believe I got the gist of the story.

Two of the newest guys at our dinner table on Failaka were mercenaries of the highest caliber. I found both quite refreshing. Russ, the one everyone had been waiting for had arrived. For weeks prior to his arrival, he was the talk of the camp. Everyone kept saying this biker type killer was coming. He was now under contract to RO for clearing munitions and headed to Kuwait. When he arrived, I summed him up right away and liked him. He had a great personality shoulder length sun bleached blond hair like a California surfer and the look of a normal high school jock. He and I became friends after foraying on an "Ali Babba run one night, to get a particular boat he had seen at the other end of the island's small town. Even after Iraqi invasion, the sixteen foot speed boat was still complete with motor, which most weren't.

To get it out from under the Kuwait militaries eyes, we stole through the night, without lights, in a large troop carrier truck. I drove and Russ sat on the hood as "mine look out." We were followed through the darkened desert by our camp's huge, loud crane and Pakistani driver. Within minutes after arriving at the boat's site, the Pakistani crane operator hoisted the boat, and then lowered it onto the truck bed while Russ and I guided it down.

On the way back to camp, Russ sat inside the truck cab with me instead of lookout position on the hood. At one point, he thought he saw the dark shadow of a Kuwaiti military truck in pursuit and shook my shoulder. I promptly slammed on brakes, sending the boat forward, knocking out the truck's rear window and putting a bowed crease in our roof. We dropped the boat off next to the water near camp and called it a night. The next day everyone in camp wanted to know how the truck's cab had gotten split down the middle but no one who knew, talked.

Russ, as did many of his peers conducted several good classes later in the week on "stalking." Only then did he tell of our "Ali Baba" run and how we had done so many things wrong.

RO guys were great and I've spent many hours looking back on some of my adventures with them. They, the soldiers and laborers alike called me "Mr. Chuck, (I'm about ten years older than most of them and twenty years older than a few). After my wife arrived and went to work at Marr Bell's office with Donald, she became known as "Mrs. Chuck."

Fortunately, there were no deaths or injuries to our people or RO's on Failaka but soon after the guys returned to the Messila Camp on Kuwait's mainland, Chris lost his leg and John was blown to pieces. Several others not as close to me also died in land mine accidents in the Kuwaiti deserts.

I remember the day at Messila Camp, we lost our gregarious, joking, friend John. Many of the ordinance teams were returning early but none was their normal, rowdy selves. Word quickly spread from the main RO offices outward. John had blown up in the British section near Wafra Township. You saw no tears but no one was speaking, not even to their own team members. The camp felt the pain. Even the laborers moped around. The administrative offices accomplished far less that day than they normally would have while we all carried on the whole day in hushed tones. Dinner time came and went with an almost silent dining hall. It took time to get over John's sudden parting from us, but time did pass and work did go on, beginning the next day.

As for Chris losing his leg, the RO guys took it in stride and went to see him in the hospital before he was airlifted back to England. Chris was lying in bed, obviously still dazed and in pain. He appeared mummified wrapped in bandages covering far more than the leg stump. The guys lightened the mood when they entered with a fake parrot on one guy's shoulder and a hand carved peg leg for Chris to wear.

Our worst catastrophe occurred one day in the British Sector of Southern Kuwait. Several TCNs were assisting an RO team in hand carrying the disarmed anti tank mines back to a truck for storage. Storage was one of two ways mines were disposed of in Kuwait. They were either destroyed in place or disarmed and saved for possible future use. On that particular day, one of the TCN laborers stopped to pick up a live mortar as he walked past it. He carried it back to the truck where several other men also continued loading explosives that were now disarmed but not "FFE" free from explosives. He thought the mortar he was carrying was not dangerous and put it up in the truck to bring along for disposal with the other defused mines. When the work day was over, several men piled into the truck cab and the rest sat on the defused mines in back. While riding to the storage facility the man began playing with the live mortar. That Bangladeshi and four others were killed as it and several mines went off. The big troop carrier truck was disabled and the driver and two other TCNs riding up front were also severely injured.

The Kuwaiti Coroner refused to handle one of the dead boys' remains. His torso was so badly destroyed that one of Royal Ordinance's explosives experts had to go to the morgue and check inside the destroyed body for more live explosives. The body had to be declared "FFE," "free from explosives" before it could be sent home.

After this horrible incident, the TCN camp down the street from our main camp took on the appearance and sound of death. The worst part came when the Kuwait government denied RO permission to ship the boy's body home. The Kuwait Government was just now beginning to return to the country from exile and of course the "red tape" was now returning with them. Red Tape is the only thing Kuwaitis are really good at.

Kuwaitis returning back home hampered everything. In every aspect of life something was now delayed or became far more expensive. The Kuwaitis were more concerned with whether our electricity cables were of the right load bearing and the panel boxes were located correctly on the lot than they were at assisting the rebuilding effort. They would come into our camp and shut down the generators to conduct tests, then leave to have tea and didn't come back to perform the tests for several hours or several days. The entire camp for mine removal teams would come to a halt with no air conditioning, ability to iron, cook, and work in the offices or in the maintenance shops until the Kuwaitis had their tea or decided to return.

It didn't stop there. Their game of "I'm in charge" took on deadly proportions. They rounded up and seized all RO walkie talkies because a new Kuwait law said walkie talkies could be used in sabotaging the country (though these were being used to clear mines from their country). Soldiers and land mine removal experts in the field were now in great danger. Two men severely wounded and dying of blood loss could not be helped because their team members were prevented from using radios to bring emergency medical assistance. Help could have come from ambulances or from a helicopter flying to the site of the explosion, but instead, the wounded men had to be gathered up by their own team members, then driven to a hospital near Kuwait City more than thirty miles away before getting treatment. In a couple cases, the Indian laborers did not receive care fast enough and bled to death.

Accidents and potential accidents were a fact of life in an arms camp. Some men became quite blasé about the danger that was ever present. A humorous, British RO friend I called Little Bob came to me one day and continued talking for a period of no less than twenty minutes. We laughed and talked until I said "Bob, what have you got in your hand?"

"A live grenade," he responded and I was in shock. "What the hell are you doing with that in your hand while you're talking to me? Damn it, get rid of it." He casually walked over by the camps front gate to a sandbagged foxhole and dropped it in. "Look out Chook" he said as the thing exploded.

There were so many incidents that happened inside and outside camp. One night someone about a mile away in a Kuwaiti neighborhood shot high caliber rifles into the air toward our camp. One of our TCNs lying on a top bunk was hit in the chest. The metal roof and corrugated ceiling board wasn't enough to stop the bullet so he was hit while asleep. The bullet didn't even break his skin but he was badly bruised and from that night on, there were very few TCNs who would sleep on the top bunk again. It was a full job to disassemble hundreds of bunks so everyone could sleep ground level. Little did they seem to notice that now with no one up top, everyone was vulnerable. At least in their logic, they were satisfied with the beds remaining on the floor, wall to wall for quite some time.

TCN laborers were a different world for me. I had maids and tea boys before, but I never had to literally care for their needs; and now we had more than a thousand, third country nationals. One of the problems I had was in teaching them how to use a western toilet. Our prefab housing units had only western style porcelain commodes. We tried toilet paper but they removed it and carried it for their noses only. When one of our barracks' chiefs walked in to inspect, he was almost overcome by the stench of poop. The Indian and Bangladeshi TCN's were use to squatting in a jungle or standing on porcelain feet prints. This western toilet that had a seat with a hole in it, and a flap and a flush handle was a little beyond them. Shit was everywhere.

Their efforts with this kind of toilet echoed my personal experience with the Arab toilet. While gagging with a face mask, I would stand over the dormitory maids until everything was hygienic again. This went on several times too many before I felt the need to do a personal demonstration. I would show them exactly what to do with a toilet.

I assembled about six hundred TCNs into their dining hall and had a new unused toilet brought in. I stood in front of the crowd of people packed a dozen or fifteen deep, some standing, others sitting on the floor. I brought translators for each language and dialect to the front with me. I turned the toilet sideways for them to get a good view then proceeded to show them how to pee. You bend forward; lift the seat flap and pee. I didn't actually pee but I did unzip and make the sound. I then simulated the flushing of the toilet. This accomplished, I asked if anyone had questions. They were giggling but unspoken. Everyone seemed to know how to do this now. O K, next we made sure the seat was down, we drop our pants and (for this purpose I wore some funny looking undershorts) you face forward as you sit. With bowel movement sounds and the use of a little toilet paper, I demonstrated the clean up. They roared with laughter but no one ever shit on the seats again and most of the time the toilets even got flushed.

Kuwait after the war was full of explosives everywhere. Millions were laid by the retreating Iraqis, others were dropped from allied aircraft, and others were in large warehouse depots or disbursed throughout neighborhoods around Kuwait City. Every street had a few small storage facilities. Usually they were in basements of confiscated homes or palaces. Inside even the smaller facilities were cases of hand grenades, long green cases of surface-to-air missiles, mortars and hundreds of thousands of bullet clips, or boxes of bullets for rifles and pistols.

One day it was raining terribly hard and most people knew they couldn't work so they just stayed in bed. I was about the only one to enter the mess hall for breakfast and had sat alone for a short period of time before little Bob jumped inside, slamming the door behind him. He was in a rain slicker but as he started removing his jacket and rain boots, I could see that every square inch of him was wet, shirt, pants, socks and all. After seeing me so dry, Little Bob hollered, "Chook, I don't know how long you've been here but I shouldn't think you'd want to go out there because it's raining puppies and pussys."

Shortly after the weather slacked off a little, I used the time to go exploring again but this time closer to home base. Across the street from camp was a three story marble mansion. I plundered there until I stumbled across a massive amount of Iraqi arms and explosives. The mansion's thirty rooms plus full basement had undoubtedly been used as the neighborhood arms depot. Some of its contents would soon become my own personal arsenal, secretly stored for further use by me if an Iraqi invasion happened again.

The house's architecture resembled an insurance company in suburbia America more so than a private home of a Sheikha (Princess) of the Royal al Sabah Family. The interior in its entirety evolved around a central marble staircase that wound from bottom to top. The floors were also marble and the walls were concrete with no interior wood trim or sheet rock.

This is the way almost all homes in Kuwait are built. They have all the glitz of expensive materials but they're usually cold and unfeeling. All chandeliers inside were broken and the furniture from each room had been thrown down the central staircase to the basement. In most Kuwaiti homes, you don't find things like books, wall paneling, fire places, beautiful cabinets or indoor living plants. Those things are not part of their culture. If there are books, they are few and far between, with the exception of religious material only.

The kitchen of this million dollar mansion was equipped more like a cabin in the United States would be. It had cheap industrial metal cabinets with a long, single piece, stainless steel sink and counter top and plain, exposed, florescent tube lighting.

The whole mansion appeared to have been lived in by Iraqi troops during occupation because several piles of dark green wool Iraqi uniforms were still on the floors of several rooms as well as piles of defecation and urine stains. Burnt stains were also present where Iraqi soldiers had built fires atop the marble floors on which to cook.

The mansion had been looted and destroyed systematically, the same as all the residences and businesses on Failaka Island and the rest of the country. Work from that same Iraqi handbook on pillaging and destruction had been carried out to the "t". Even the wall plugs, the light switches and plumbing had been torn from the walls. Someone had used a pick ax on the marble floors and marble kitchen walls. Toilets, bidets, sinks and windows were all busted. Paver stones at the front and rear doorways were removed and taken to the roof to build anti aircraft gun positions and one car in the carport had been blown up and burned. An Iraqi military jeep engine was still on rigged pulleys inside the living room. The biggest surprise was in the basement.

In the basement was a munitions depot surprise. It was completely filled half way up the walls with cases of rifle shells, unexploded mortars, SAM, surface-to-air missiles and an interesting looking bazooka gun. Wooden mortar cases covered entire rooms that were more than 20 feet by 25 feet. Cases of tens of thousands of rifle bullets and cartridges filled another room equal to the first two. There were so many cases of hand grenades that Royal Ordinance lost count while removing the stock pile. More than two hundred fifteen cases had actually been counted before counters were distracted by someone hollering from another room of yet another find.

A lightweight, plastic bazooka gun weighing about four pounds was the most interesting article down there. I held it for quite some time studying it. To an inexperienced weapons handler like me, it appeared to be empty because I could see from front to back through the tube. I came to the conclusion that it was a toy made to look like the real thing so I took it back to camp as a souvenir.

Royal Ordinance's funny little Bob saw me carry it into the dining hall and promptly came to usher me back outside. After checking it for a minute, he said it was the real thing, and loaded. The safety had even been taken off. It would have destroyed the entire dining hall and killed many of those inside, had I pulled the trigger (harder). Little did Bob know, and I never told him that I had already pulled the trigger but it felt stuck. It was very difficult to pull and I never got it to work. The last thing he said to me about the Bazooka was, "It's hard to pull the trigger for a reason". The whole weapon was considered disposable after one use.

I spoke to a few people about my incident but for the most part, shut my mouth; because I felt I had recklessly endangered so many lives that I'd refrain from telling anyone else. I soon learned that in war, many weapons are made of plastic and are considered disposable after a single use.

It took Royal Ordinance munitions teams two days to remove the huge cache of bullets, mortars, and weapons found inside the mansion before declaring the building FFE, free from explosive, minus of course, the three small Mitsubishi truck loads of arms and ammo that I had removed during nights prior to my reporting the find.

I first had to find an empty twenty foot long, metal, iso cargo container before loading it with my personal booty. My container remained for several weeks on the other side of the Kuwait Oil Company Recreation facilities less than a hundred fifty yards from our camp until I could relocate it elsewhere, well beyond prying eyes. From that location, I continued stocking it with more and more weaponry found at other locations. Chuck's arsenal could now arm and resupply a small resistance army for some time. Even after moving the container to several other relocations, I continued stock piling as time and supplies permitted.

The tally was impressive: more than 20 surface to air missiles, more than sixty five cases of hand grenades, 220 AK47 Kalashnikov rifles, probably a ton of bullets, 1 bazooka, over 100 huge artillery shells full of gun powder, two dozen 9mm pistols, 300 anti tank mines, 408 vs 50 anti personnel mines, 18 bouncing Bettys, twelve boxes of explosive pins of some kind and various other items, I didn't even know what they were.

To this day, the loaded container remains buried within sight of a mosque near the fork of the Asafar Magreb Motorway and the Fahaheel Motorway between Kuwait City and the Saudi Arabia border at Nuwaiseeb.

Marr Bell/Royal Ordinance became a pretty fair sized camp site containing a few thousand people within the much larger million and a half residents of Kuwait City. Even though our main camp was by far the smaller of the two, Marr Bell/RO shared the Lion's portion of important visitors. First, the "Iron Lady" of Britain herself, Prime Minister Margaret Thatcher came to visit. She, of course, played a very important role along with President George Bush in bringing the Coalition Forces together and carrying out "Desert Storm." Without her power and international stature, George Bush would have had a much harder battle ahead. The outcome may also have been much different.

Kuwait showed great respect for the Prime Minister and invited her to come to Kuwait to receive their personal appreciation. Marr Bell's (rather Royal Ordinance's) camp was one of the places on the Prime Minister's agenda. The munitions teams of Royal Ordinance got the big morale boost they deserved by having their Lady Thatcher visit and recognize them for the crucial services they had already and still were performing.

The morning of her arrival at camp was one of dressing up and dressings down. Sonny was dressing me down at every turn, making sure I had made everyone do everything that was supposed to be done. Sonny was in one of his body shaking withdrawal type symptoms alcoholics go through after a binge. People in the RO head office were barking commands right and left as well, while the rest of us were putting the place in order. The itinerary was that Lady Thatcher would be "going here," "doing this" and "walking past that" and "departing from here."

After a delay of more than two hours, her motorcade arrived. Everyone was standing in position. First to arrive were several Kuwaiti police cars that pulled to the side, staying outside the camp's gate. The next sets of vehicles were in a series of black, and then white Chevrolet Caprices bearing part of the Kuwaiti security entourage. Next came cars bearing

British Embassy personnel and more security. Margaret Thatcher's car was about four-teenth in the procession. Lady Thatcher accompanied the British Ambassador to Kuwait in a black Jaguar. Upon exiting their car in front of the Royal Ordinance Headquarters building, they and several other top ranking officials quickly moved inside to meet with RO's top people in country. They stayed there about twenty minutes.

The Prime Minister and a group of about twenty people including the RO hierarchy then came out and began walking slowly along a pathway of flagstone that I designed and TCNs built. It lead to the recreation building where tea and or'douves were readied. Before entering the Recreation Hall, Prime Minister Thatcher passed an exhibition of all the different types of mines found so far in Kuwait. I built a slanted hard sand pit that an RO munitions expert filled with the ordinances. On view were several large caliber artillery shells, many rockei types of blue 77's and pods from cluster bombs. There were vs 50 small antipersonnel mines and larger antitank mines and "Bouncing Betty's." The usual three types of hand grenades were represented as well as a couple SAM surface-to-air missiles.

Lady Thatcher greeted and was greeted by the upper echelons of RO and gracefully passed by the rest of us as though we were not there. I guess it was hard to focus on everyone, everywhere. She seemed to all of us to be a tough ole gal who also had "balls." She appeared not at all the giant I thought, but rather a gentile Lady who must have a tough streak within her that doesn't show through her clothing. After the tea and walk around, the huge motorcade quietly withdrew from our compound, with neither a siren nor honking horn.

When Princess Anne, Britain's Princess Royal, visited Marr Bell-Royal/ Ordinance Camp, not a lot was different from the Margaret Thatcher visit. The motorcade was as long, the time waiting felt the same and the RO participants were the same. Even the same exhibit of munitions was done but this time; I had scoured the desert and found real "pink" sand. One pickup load of "Pink" sand covered over the other hardened beige sand in the previous munitions exhibit. Most people probably didn't notice or may have barely noticed my little coup. To me it was "special" and I didn't come by the pink stuff easily. Not to mention that it had taken an "Ali Baba" run at night to whisk it away from the construction site of a small palace being built in the desert on the outskirts of town.

For this visit as in the other, Sonny, Bob's partner again showed his ass and kept barking commands for people to do things, especially for me to take care of things that had already been done hours ago. He had probably been sleeping off a drunk or something right up to the time the Prime Minister arrived. He said he didn't drink any more but he looked and acted like a twitching, angry, unclean man with bloodshot eyes.

For Princess Anne's visit, my wife Maia and Chris Marr, the wife of our company's owner were decked out in their bright red blazers and lay in wait to shake her highness' hand. Of course, Mr. Marr, Marr Bell's Bob, and Sonny were on hand as were Gus (Ghassan) and Ruba, another Palestinian office worker and dear friend Mona and her American fiancé Neal Spring and Brits Bob and Liz (who over saw the tea), Donald, Captain Thappa of the Ghurkas, a new project manager, a Britt, Robert Barnett and me, Mr. Chuck.

Two other things were strikingly different about the Princess Royal's visit from that of Prime Minister Thatcher. As soon as the Princess Royal exited the RO main building to take the walk through camp, a bagpiper whaled from the recreation room patio. He wasn't a Scotsman like you would expect but a Nepalese Ghurka who was working with RO to remove mines. He was decked out in his official Ghurka uniform of dark green with a dark plaid kilt. On his head was a dark green beret with some kind of insignia I couldn't see well. The piper played several tunes but none seemed livelier than the other, however, he played well I was told. He certainly looked the part.

Ghurka security men still serve Great Britain, the same as they have for many years. They're well disciplined remnants of a colonialist power that is no more. Until recently, they have been headquartered in Hong Kong not Kathmandu, Nepal.

Princess Anne, sister to Prince Charles of England and daughter of Queen Elizabeth was dressed in a pink two piece suit with a thick dog collar choker of pearls around her long, long, thin, svelte neck. As I gazed at this moneyed lass, all I could think was, it was a good thing her mother owns a yacht like Britannia and castles because she was well onto the homely side. Had her descendant Anne Bolin had that very long, thin, neck, it would have draped over the chopping block as far as the basket. When I made my remarks initially, both Mrs. Marr and Maia admonished me but for the rest of the Princess Royal's visit, I was captivated and stared at that long neck and pictured all the money she was worth.

The other thing different about the Princess Royal's visit was that she was not allowed to walk up steps if possible. As a convenience, our steps were done away with at the recreation room and I had an incline built. The biggest job was to make an incline that was more than six feet wide and about eleven feet high which would go over a wall nine feet high. I had loads of hardened sand brought in and sculpted at a slight rise over more than sixty feet. The incline made it easy for the Princess Royal to traverse with ease the high wall from our camp onto a vantage point at Kuwait Oil Beach Club so she could watch a demonstration of munitions being detonated. Of course, all the pavers for the walk came into our possession via another Ali Babba run.

After watching the explosive display, like Lady Thatcher's motorcade, Princess Anne's also slipped away without use of sirens, just the screeching tires of its front running police escorts.

When there weren't important visitors to tend to, we had to get back to the real business of the day. I had been asked by Bob to scout an area near the Northern Kuwait border for a place to build a United Nations camp sometime in the future if our company received the contract. I knew the border fairly well before the war having gone to Baghdad several times, and during official plundering or snooping visits for the

Minister of Information or His Highness the Crown Prince. For me, the trip back on familiar sand was a pleasant break in routine.

Instead of my former Ministry of Information vehicle or my own personal Chevy Astro van, this time I drove a red RO Land Rover with British flags painted on the side and an oil field pass in the front window next to an ordinance sticker taped inside the front window.

On all occasions in past years, I had to slip into Iraq under cover of darkness and through the vastness of desert sand but this time I sort of had clearance. The first day I got stopped at each of the roads three border checks. By the third day I had figured out the easiest way to sail right through all three between Mutla Ridge and Iraq by pretending to be speaking on the car radio and having no time to be stopped by the guards. It worked well on each successive visit.

This continued as the easiest way to head unimpeded through Kuwait and across its northern border into Iraq. One of my Filipino workers named Ray always followed me in a second identical vehicle. This made our little scouting party look even more official. We had no trouble going anywhere. I knew my way over most of the main roads and now thanks to my exploring, most of the back roads on both sides of the Iraq-Kuwait border as well. I, of course continued seriously looking for the best site possible for erecting a United Nations camp for housing UNSKOM troops, but I was also enjoying seeing what remained from Desert Storm along the border. There were hundreds of destroyed Iraqi tanks and other vehicles dotting the sandy, treeless, desert landscape for many miles in all directions.

I could look in all directions and couldn't see one person, nor distinguish where the border of Kuwait stopped and the border of Iraq began. One day the region was to be patrolled as a demilitarized zone but for now, there is only isolated desolation. I roamed through the Northern Kuwait farm land and Southern Iraqi desert with Ray in tow, most of those days and again a week later.

On October 6, 1991, the second time exploring for Marr Bell inside Iraq, I continued much further than I realized because the journey and road conditions were just too easy. I never ran into anyone for a while. Later, I became disoriented because of the oil clouds and ended up facing in a different direction than I thought. I drove and drove with Ray always following my every turn. I finally radioed Ray telling him we needed to stop at the buildings just ahead. They were probably the first United Nations buildings being set up.

The camp of about a dozen, white, portable buildings sat on a sandy hill. I drove right up to the front door of the building I assumed was headquarters, while Ray followed in his RO Land Rover then parked beside me. The building was the headquarters all right. I spoke with the men inside but they seemed ill at ease with me and Ray. I spoke in Arabic as much as possible but they still seemed bothered. I sat with the man in command as he of-fered hot tea in the small Arabic chi glasses, and we downed several as we talked. Finally, I said, "this is the last place before Iraq? He in turn said "no, this Iraq." I said "oh, this Iraq," pointing in the direction of the other side of the building. He said "that Iraq, this Iraq." In Arabic I said "oh shit, Where Kuwait?" He formed his hand like a bird and said "over there Kuwait."

I hesitated for a moment as tension built in the room. I then tried to put him off guard by saying "you in big trouble." He and his now crowded office was full of men laughing and saying Arabic phrases exactly the broken way I had phrased mine "you too in big trouble." I sat and looked at Ray for a moment and realized they knew not one word of English so I told Ray, I'll keep them on the defensive rather than ever allowing them to take the of-fensive. I stood up, put my hands on their leader's desk and said "big mistake, I'll be going now." He said a superior officer was on the way and I wouldn't be going anywhere. Again, I turned to Ray and said "when I say get out of here," turn and with great authority stand and walk toward the door. Don't look around and never show fear. He agreed but only if I'd go first. I jokingly told him, what good is he? "Wouldn't you take a bullet for me?" He said "hell no. You're crazy."

Within moments, another group of about five men joined us in the cramped room. One, I believe was the Iraqi Major the other officer had been waiting for. He also seemed more amused at the situation than worried, but as we spoke, I could see worry entering his mind. I told him we must leave now and he said "no," "his" superior had been called. I jumped to my feet and hollered directly in his face. I said in Arabic "we leave now!" "This big mistake, you in big trouble." "I go Baghdad, you be dead." "America and Britain bomb you." I used the English word bomb because I didn't know it in Arabic. I don't think the way I said it left anything for interpretation though.

The Iraqi officer thought carefully for a moment as I sensed his weakness. I stood and told Ray to get up. He did so and we proceeded to leave the room, Ray followed almost up my butt. I knew since the Iraqi soldiers had not drawn one weapon they would probably continue reacting the same way. I went to my car and got in. Ray got into his vehicle and our engines started at the same time like at a drag strip. As I backed out, the Iraqis only half heartedly ran along beside me for about fifty feet. No one pulled a gun on us and we were soon gone.

We continued on until about two hours later when we came straight over another sandy hill and into another camp. I told Ray to look at the flag. It was also Iraqi. It has red, white and black thick stripes with three green stars running through the middle white. I radioed back to Ray saying "you want tea" and he said, "I want to go home." We had begun backing up when some soldiers, very rag tag looking in sock feet came up beside our cars with rifles pointed. I spoke in Arabic very nicely to them and they appeared not to overreact. They asked if we were British and I lied and said "yes." One soldier also asked me what was in the big thermos I had beside me in the seat and I replied "iced tea." They laughed and said whiskey. Mistakenly, I said "La, Ameriki oreed chi wa thelg". Americans like iced tea not Arab hot tea." He missed my slip of nationalities and said "give it to me." I handed it to him but he was afraid to open it. He said, "haram" which means "forbidden." I said "come, I'll open it and show you Ice in tea." They were fascinated, but didn't want to drink any of that stuff. We spoke courteously for a few minutes before saying good bye. They waved and I pointed my movie camera at them while I sped away. Again, Ray followed in quick pursuit.

Still another half hour or more passed before we spotted a white vehicle in the far distance. I thought it might be a United Nations car. It was, and we sped toward it and the Kuwait border as he continued flashing his lights about twenty times. I pulled up next to him and he asked in a Russian accent of broken English, had I been to Iraq? I said, "Yes" and he wanted to know what they said. I said, "I only went to have tea. I have to get back to Messila Beach now, good bye." I left him in a cloud of dust. We drove hard and fast back to Kuwait City and showed everyone our astounding little video tape backing our story.

CHAPTER 19

Repairing Life and Lakes of Fire

I went to Iraq three more times in the next month and each time, either outran the United Nations vehicles or never saw any. On one trip, I plundered several bombed Iraqi munitions storage facilities just north of the Kuwait border village of Abdaly. One facility had many underground shelters, each containing cases of rifles, mortars, sam (surface-to-air) missiles, bullet clips and the regular three kinds of hand grenades. I learned to tell the difference in Kalashnikov rifles, Russian, Chinese or Czechoslovakian. I also learned to tell the difference in grenades from the same countries.

The Iraqis lost the Gulf War while still having tremendous amounts of unspent munitions a couple kilometers outside Kuwait's border.

During one of my explorations, I had already gone down in several Iraqi fox holes looking for small 9 mm pistols, and good AK 47 automatic rifles as souvenirs. The first places I always looked inside a bunker or foxhole was next to, or above the exit. It was usually there. Any rifle would be left so the soldier could rapidly grab it on his way out. RO's little Bob had given me that information.

I entered one bunker and while I was prying open several wooden cases, I felt something hit the back of my shoe. When I looked, a shot of fear penetrated my head and my eyesight was momentarily darkened. For a couple of seconds, I thought I would end my life by a grenade exploding at my feet inside an Iraqi munitions bunker. Instead and thank-fully the grenade's pin was still in tact. That experience shook me up enough that I quit plundering places where visibility was limited.

Probably my biggest mission during that time period was to retrieve a huge semi-truck trailer that was an Iraqi chemical lab. The trailer had a single, eight-inch thick, vault-like door in the rear and a similar one forward on the right side. Inside were shelves and special protected florescent lights. All lights were housed within some kind of protective tube, glass encasement. Also, there was a steel safe and a small but inadequate looking sink in the trailer lab. It had only one small window and it too was encased in thick steel with bullet proof glass. The truck was empty of chemicals or munitions of any type but nearby I found yet another fairly large munitions dump that I thought might still have chemical weapons.

I walked around filming the area and the trailer until I decided to try to haul the massive heavy lab truck back to Kuwait City. There were several glowing phosphorous looking shells at that same site. Some were broken, others bent and yet others were still in good shape. I think an allied bomb had hit near enough their storage shelter that the explosion tossed some of the huge live shells up to fifty yards away.

Ray and I returned to Kuwait City from our foraging and pillaging trip in Iraq but had to wait several more days before we would attempt to change all the flattened tires on the lab trailer and try to retrieve it all the way back to Kuwait City; about fifty miles away over not the best of roads.

I brought some of my Pakistani drivers back with a convoy of two red Land Rovers, a large crane, a dump truck and two low bed trucks to retrieve the chemical lab trailer and two nearby twenty foot, steel shipping containers.

The entire trip back to the border region, up and back couldn't have gone smoother as far as the three Kuwaiti checkpoints were concerned. Right under Iraqi troop's noses, we dug out the two large 10 X 20 feet metal ISO shipping containers and put them on our Syrian driver Henry Magarin's low bed truck and one other. After inflating the tires, we then hooked up the Iraqi Chemical lab trailer to the big dump truck. I noticed the last time I was up there, the trailer needed several tires. Some were low and others appeared blown, so this time we brought the right size and amount of tires needed to get it on the road as well as a compressor to pump up any that needed air. We got the trailer as far as Jahra Interchange, just west of Kuwait City when the dump truck pulling the chemical lab trailer overheated.

We uncoupled it and headed home. Bob refused to let me go back for the lab trailer even though I showed him the video of what I considered an important find.

Several days later, I called some people in the Ministry of Defense I thought might find it of interest and gave them permission to haul it away. They were extremely appreciative and several days later called me saying the trailer had caused quite a stir in the right circles. I told them I was going under cover to Baghdad within the next week on my two days off and if I see the "thing" they earlier asked about, I'd check its location with my Magellan then give them the coordinates. Magellan is what the British call their Global Positioning Satellite service equipment, a piece of equipment that would in future months and years be my best friend.

It was a short time after the chemical trailer run when I heard the news. One of our ole Marr Bell friends, Chad was caught behind Iraqi lines. I couldn't believe it. All my persistent forays and he was the one getting caught. Bob had even shown Chad some of my films and made him aware of the exact locations of all facilities and soldiers I had charted. Chad was held for a million dollars ransom by the Iraqi government, payable through the American Embassy in Baghdad. Bargaining went on for a couple of weeks if I remember clearly, and then Chad was released unharmed from the Iraqi Abu Ghareeb prison on the outskirts of Baghdad.

When I saw him at the Sultan Center Market in my suburb of Kuwait City, about a month after his release, I told him how surprised I was to hear he had been captured. I wanted to know whether he had pissed them off or something. He said he was fine until they checked his vehicle. He had been caught red handed with quite a few 8 X 10 inch photographs of many of the communications sites and bridges in Baghdad, bombed during Desert Storm. He had forgotten they were in a briefcase under the passenger seat. Daa aah.

I don't know why Chad would carry those things around, but several of us had these same photo copies. We use to collect them and trade them like baseball cards. We had them for so long, I too had forgotten they were at home in a box. I later heard through the grapevine, the Iraqis had been paid a hundred thousand dollars for Chad's release but never got the rest.

The oil teams from Texas began arriving in Kuwait about the same time as we were setting up camp for Marr Bell. The first teams were housed in two, twenty eight story buildings in the Kuwait City suburb, Abu Halifa. We didn't get to see much of these guys because we were involved in pretty heavy schedules, as were they. Occasionally, we ran into a couple of them in Salmyia at the Baskin Robbins ice cream parlor.

Baskin Robbins was the first actual fast food place to reopen. Since the Sultan Center Market was right next door, the two stores became our main, if not our only hangout. Around eight o'clock in the evening, we all sat eating ice cream. Hunks of men, killers, oil men, spies and explosive experts, all sitting at cute little striped parlor tables in sweet, frilly, little, wire chairs.

At first, the Kuwait government contracted the teams of Red Adair from Texas, to extinguish the more than seven hundred fifty, raging oil fires. The first estimate of time putting all the oil fires out was more than a year. The government and the Emir soon grew impatient and nullified their exclusive deal. I think the original oil contracts specified payment by the day while on the job, rather than by the fire extinguished. The blazes seemed pretty tough to put out but the whole process was taking the Americans too long, or so my Kuwait Minister of Information boss later told me. Kuwait's new agreement, open to aspirants from around the world was payment upon completion per well.

Open oil capping brought in some great crews and some dogs. They came from the Far East, the Near East and the Mid East. Teams came from Africa, Europe, America and Australia. The ones that came in on shoe string budgets had the most unique if not the best techniques. The Chinese came in with huge bull dozers and started a safe distance back from the blaze. They continually piled up dirt atop dirt, continually moving the mountain as they moved forward. They finally arrived at the site of the well atop the mountain of dirt then pushed the mass onto the oil fire, extinguishing it. Then they had to uncover the well, and cap it.

The Bulgarians or the Romanians, (I forgot which) proved to be the toughest act to follow. They took old red fire trucks that looked little different than extended long pickups with a twin axel in the rear. They had adapted a jet turbine to the flat bed and pointed it at the gushing, fiery well then ignited the jet turbines. The roaring turbines blasted the well with such intensity, it put the fire out. Their guys then ran out and capped it. They could do one oil well a day, whereas the Chinese would take a month and the Americans, several days. These Eastern Europeans were closing down the blazes and raking in the money. From what I was hearing around town, Red Adair was getting ready to buy another super yacht for himself but had to rework his game plan if he was still going to get any more of the lucrative payoffs from capping wells. All in all, the fires were put out far ahead of schedule and at far less cost than the Kuwaitis first thought.

Everyone stateside and in Kuwait thought putting out oil fires was tough but good paying. They were right, but it was a very hazardous way to earn your pay. I never wanted anything to do with those fires. When Saddam Hussein decided to retreat from Kuwait and put in motion his

"Scorched Earth Policy," most people really didn't understand what he meant.

He had Iraqi and Jordanian soldiers lay British style patterns of mines throughout the oil fields. They had already placed mine fields along the beaches and in Kuwait City so they were experienced and fast. They sewed thousands of mines around each oil well before blowing the well itself. This meant the thousands of gallons of crude continued spewing, forming oil lakes around each well. Putting out the fire was secondary to removing the land mines from beneath the surrounding oil lakes.

Some of our RO guys returned to camp completed soaked in oil; even their faces and hair were covered. I asked why they had to get so dirty. They said imagine having to get down on your hands and knees, crawl through oil neck high until you felt a mine with your hand. Then you had to carefully disarm the mine that you couldn't even see without getting blown up. Some times in order to get into the right position, you had to take a deep breath, submerge your whole head into the oil, and then disarm the mine without tripping its trigger. Under the oil, they couldn't attach plastic explosive next to it like above ground then run a line to a detonating trigger. This all had to be done by hand.

I told little Bob and Kenny that I coveted their big salaries once in a while but there was no way I'd do their oil job for any amount of money. Many people both in camp and back in the United States later marveled at the video films I made of oil fires and mines being disarmed. I trusted my RO friends so implicitly that I actually followed in their exact same footsteps, through the live mine fields, filming the entire time. I leaned over my friend's shoulder to film his hands as he disarmed an antitank mine. Occasionally, I still look at those videos but think what a fool I was.

Those films and several others, also show me burying dead Iraqis on Failaka Island. They proved so vivid that I didn't send them home. Rather, I brought them home with me at Christmas time. I knew I should be with them when they were shown. My mother and wife would have gone crazy if they had gotten them in the mail and thought they were regular home movies.

Again as usual, when the last oil fire was being put out, the news reels showed Kuwaitis manning the equipment and one of their officials turning the wheel, screwing on the last cap. Well, I guess that was OK. They paid for that opportunity.

I was going through a difficult time with Bob, my boss at Marr Bell, and it no longer appeared we could work together. There was a slight difference of opinion but it was enough to make me feel that the end of my employment with the company had come to an end. After I quit, I never for one moment regretted it. I had several offers of work immediately in other companies including Sofreme, the French ordinance company that had just arrived. My Palestinian engineer friend Ghassan had moved over to Sofreme after Bob pissed him off. The American CMS ordinance disposal contract office was also just setting up, that was another possibility.

Two months before quitting, I contacted an agency that had liked a little work I had done for them in another country at another time. With them, I could make some good money; have more free time to work a part-time job and travel. My wife and I talked it over and I began working for the intelligence gathering organization right away. This secretive job was going well, but wasn't as fast paced as I liked and needed. The job was fun and also didn't interfere with our vacation time that had already been planned.

Maia and I scheduled two of our trips to become one. We went to visit her family in Sweden, following my business trip to Russia, where I met with some American Chevron Oil people in Moscow. They were getting ready to expand their Kazakhstan facilities. We left in late June 1992, for a week in Moscow and ten more days in Stockholm, Sweden.

We landed in Moscow amidst their massive economic time of woes. Every corner of life there was influenced by hard times, the darkened airport, unlit boulevards, hotels, food, and travel prices. Just walking through the airport terminal was quite a contrast from other international airports we traveled through in America, Africa and Europe. There were only a few drab snack bars, but no souvenir shops or modern passenger lounges. Maia found it depressing and expressed her concerns about going into Moscow proper and about getting back on another Aeroflot plane again.

From our seat aboard the Aeroflot plane, we could see holes in the cabin floorboard that looked down to another layer of floorboard that was probably the roof of the baggage compartment. I was having a ball thinking this was so exotic. The windows were so scraped we could barely see the landscape below, and the food service stunk. The stew-ardesses were exactly like an American commercial we saw several years later; big boned types with light hair and round, full faces with rouge smeared on each cheek. It's like they came out the 1940's in America; stuck in time. They wore small, polka dot print dresses like those mom use to wear when I was a child.

We arrived late in the evening downtown Moscow, and we had already been told we would be mugged if we went out at night. We were staying at the Ukraine Hotel across the river from the Parliament building the Russians call the White House. The Ukraine Hotel was a tall building of Stalinist 1930's architecture. This meant the entire building was quite ornate and somewhat Gothic like old European buildings. The center tower rose twenty five stories but the two ends were only about twelve stories each. Our room was on the twelfth floor, right below the section that continued rising skyward.

Some of our friends that use to live in Moscow while attending University said this was the hotel where several questionable foreigners had jumped from the roof top or room windows to their deaths.

Since the Ukraine Hotel was being remodeled, the lobby was a mess. Supposedly they were changing out the marble in the floors and installing better lighting. One of the other American guests was Huge O'Brien, the actor from several western movies and the "Wyatt Earp" television series. He was with a group of young people on an exchange program.

We said our "how do you dos", and went on our way, but did manage to bump into him again several times in the next couple of days. Though he had numerous youth in his exchange program he always seemed like he wanted to talk. One evening we ask him for cocktails and it became a nightly thing.

Because of the taxi drivers warnings, Maia and I decided to take everyone's advice and stay inside the hotel the first night. I looked around our room for anything that could be a microphone bug or camera, but didn't see any. That didn't keep us from talking directly to the walls and mirrors the rest of our stay, anyways. We freshened up and changed into dinner clothes before going down stairs.

Once again it seemed as though we had stepped back into the 40's. The hotel's dining room was in a large old hall that reminded me of a scene from World War Two. The tables and tablecloths were dull and quite eccentric. The decor of the room was battleship gray, with a touch of army green. The floors were wooden and unpolished and the room's old-time chandeliers with cloth shades made me feel like we had stepped into the pictures we had seen of our parents. Absolutely not one word of English was spoken by anyone anywhere in the hotel, restaurant or bar.

The menu was presented to us without a word spoken. Maia and I looked at pictures and ordered by pointing. We had checked into the hotel a few hours earlier and weren't quite sure how much we were spending, but it had to be cheaper than Stockholm would be. We thought we saw a picture of steak but it could have been something else. When the food arrived, we had ordered enough things that we could pick and choose from more than a dozen plates in case some of it was not to our liking.

The steak turned out to be excellent and through hand signals, I ordered another to go. The rest of the food, from or'douves; to dessert were fabulous. The waiter had continued to try telling us how expensive the wine was and seemed to be asking again and again were we sure we wanted it. We insisted. The bill came and it was to our amazement, both dinners were $1.85 US and the bottle of wine was almost $3.00. What a wonderful surprise. Several years later at a restaurant nearby the bill came to $68. Per person.

We continued dining while a western sounding band played on a stage at the far end of the room. We both remarked several times how we felt we were in a time warp scene before either of us was born, circa 1945.

The next morning, Maia and I joined some new friends for breakfast in the same dining hall. I had met the guy in the hotel's bar late last evening while Maia stayed in the room washing her hair. The guy, Igor, was a twenty five year old Russian who looked like he stepped from the cover of GQ Magazine. Igor was not what I thought a Russian would look like. He was more than six feet tall, dark hair, perfect olive complexion, trim and very handsome. Igor had a square jaw like a Turk.

Igor and I spoke last night through an interpreter. I learned he was an attorney who was very active in sports, especially Tai Kwan Do. He showed me in the bar how far up the wall he could kick his foot. I made a mark on the wall with a pencil to the place he kicked, about seven feet up. The mark made from my kick was around four feet up. Even that almost caused me to rupture myself.

When Igor arrived the next morning, his wife was with him. She was as beautiful as he was handsome. How is it that we had probably found the two best looking people in the whole country? Both were dressed "to the nines" in the latest European style clothing. Igor and Jana had been married about five years and had a little girl, Mila, of whom they promptly showed us several pictures. We then headed off sightseeing. To our surprise, Igor was driving a white Mercedes Benz, a new one. He said this one was his, Jana had an older one.

Our hosts were great fun and we bought matching English-Russian phrase books and pointed to the phrase we wanted to say. We all laughed a lot and they showed us the Kremlin, Lenin's Tomb, Red Square, the Bolshoi Ballet Company, McDonalds Restaurant, and several beautiful Orthodox cathedrals.

In the middle of our touring, Igor stopped the car, went inside a restaurant and returned a few minutes later. He urged us to wait a few more minutes as we continued watching people leave. When we went inside, there were no patrons left. We were the sole customers. There was a strolling violin and a staff that snapped to attention as we passed. They obviously had known Igor from before, and welcomed him and us like he owned the place. Maia and I now really wondered who he was. The food was in amazing quantities and kept coming for more than an hour and a half. We made it back to the hotel in the late afternoon following several hours of shopping with Igor and Jana in Russia's biggest department store, GUM. GUM was actually a mall not a store. It was three stories high branching out in several directions, more than two city blocks long and wide. It was right beside Red Square.

Maia mentioned there was to be a "Three Tenors" concert that night in Red square. Naturally, when she mentioned it to Igor, it took him only a few minutes before he had tickets. We also heard from Hugh O'Brien that the tickets were being scalped for three hundred dollars each, but Igor said he only paid equivalent to fifteen dollars each. We went to the "Three Tenors Concert" in Red Square that night and almost froze. The Three Tenors of course are Pavarotti, Carrera and Placido Domingo. Maia was in heaven watching and listening to her favorite singers on earth, though it was a cold heaven with snow flurries.

Because Moscow is so far north, it didn't get dark until after eleven o'clock at night and even then, it was more dusk than dark until one o'clock in the morning. The temperature fell to 40 degrees Fahrenheit on the Fourth of July and by next morning had to be in the low to mid thirties. We left before the concert was over because it clouded up and the winds picked up. After several times of returning to Igor's car for heat, then back to the out door concert, we decided it was time to go.

The next morning, Igor was busy so I made contact with the Chevron Oil company executive I was to meet in Moscow. Chevron was getting ready to build camps in Kazakhstan and I had spoken with several of their people by telephone from Kuwait at their New Jersey offices. They wrote me saying they wished to meet with me in Moscow. This was a difficult time for them to get away because they were at a crucial stage of negotiations with the Russian and Kazakhstan Governments. There were lots of blueprints and numbers to look over and during our meeting; I must have made thirty pages of notes. They and I decided there was more work to be done before our next meeting.

The Chevron people tried to show Maia and me around Moscow, but I told them we had wonderful guides, and they were pleased. That evening Igor and Jana took us to the most exclusive restaurant in Moscow, The Peking House. It was a lavish huge place with magnificent, palatial walls and ceilings. The Chandeliers were massive, oriental pagodas and the carpets were exquisite. Again, the meal seemed to go on forever, dish after dish. Our food and company were as exquisite as the place we dined.

On the third day, Maia and I met Igor and Jana in the hotel lobby and again headed out for a full day of touring and buying. I had mentioned to Igor that Maia would like to buy a fur coat since she had almost frozen to death the evening before. Since we were living in Kuwait and it was summer, there had been no reason to think of bringing a heavy coat with us. Maia wanted to get a nice fur now. Igor said shopping at his friend's place would be the best buys in town, and we would love his furs.

Earlier in the day we were in Arbat Shopping District and saw some men's vests made of fur. One we stood and laughed at for quite some time. It was a really bad pelt that had shed most of its hair. I said to the man standing behind the table "dog" and he replied back by saying "hungry bunny", a phrase we recognized from the restaurant chain in Kuwait. It was the only way he could say rabbit.

Now that we were in Igor's friend's shop looking at real furs, we would occasionally find one we didn't really care for and either he and Jana or Maia and I would say "hungry bunny" and that meant to laugh and move on to the next one. The live models continued showing furs to Maia and

Jana while Igor and I looked at men's fur hats. He kept saying no problem every time I asked a price. After finally nailing down the price on a full length sable coat, I told Maia that "I will never tell you this again in either of our lifetimes," "buy any coat in the store you want." "Get the sable one and she did".

We shopped in that store for several hours and came out with more than a few boxes. I even got a big Russian style Mink hat for myself. Maia did well for herself too She and Jana enjoyed modeling our new purchases the rest of the day, leaning against light polls like ladies of the night, gracing staircases as people stared, standing in front of fountains and anywhere else a model might pose.

Later that evening, Maia and I took a taxi downtown to the largest McDonald Restaurant in the world. We stood in a horrendous line that began more than a block away. We finally arrived at the counter inside, got our orders and paid just over four dollars each. McDonald was too expensive for most Russian's wallet but you could never tell by the hundreds of people waiting in line. We arrived late in the evening and left just before closing. That line never stopped. When the restaurant finally did close, it was interesting to see long banquet tables being set up along the street curbside. We were told, and later witnessed long strands of cars pulling up to purchase already bagged McDonald meals from private entrepreneurs, long after the restaurant had closed.

Igor always carried a gym bag everywhere. We'd stop to park the car, he would run around and pull the gym bag from his trunk, and then we were off to shop. Finally, I asked what he carried in the bag. He smiled a grin from ear to ear and opened it. I almost fell over. It was cash. They were all American one hundred dollar bills in bank wrappers. There was a lot of cash. He said it was more than $100,000 US. From what I could understand and only slightly remembered from his friend the first night we met, Igor moves United States money around in Syria, Lebanon and United Arab Emirates. This was not an easy thing to figure out. Maia and I were still trying to figure it out during the flight from

Moscow to Stockholm. Several more wonderful days like the ones we had in Moscow and it would have been impossible to leave the city and our new friends.

Igor and Jana had shown us one of the best times we ever had in our lives and to them we were eternally grateful. We were never permitted by Igor to spend money on meals, transportation or their wonderful companionship. If we were part of something illegal, we didn't know. We certainly never gave them information of any kind and they never asked any questions of us, other than about how Americans live.

The next day, we shopped by taxi for a special gift for them. We found an exquisite set of crystal pitcher and glassware that was truly the most beautiful we had ever seen. It seemed a small token for what they had given us.

Our trip continued another couple weeks visiting Maia's relatives in Stockholm, Sweden and we did the normal tourist type things and paid a bundle of money for it up there. We had been to Stockholm on numerous occasions and enjoyed it but we didn't have as much fun time with her relatives. Nothing we did in Sweden could come close to the enjoyable time we had in Moscow. Upon returning to Kuwait, we spoke often of our wonderful hosts in Moscow and were completely taken aback when Katrina, our Russian KGB agent friend told us Igor's father or Uncle Olaf Kalugan was the head of the KGB. This man who spoke perfect English was one in the same as the friendly, round faced man with the slight turned down mouth on one side, and the wrinkle on only one side of his forehead that we had been introduced to and had dinner with.

Several weeks later, we returned to Kuwait. Bob didn't ask me face to face but wanted to know if I would go to Somalia for the company. I accepted, and boarded a flight that went via Dubai, United Arab Emirates to Nairobi, Kenya. From there, I boarded another flight to Mombasa, Kenya to make my connection for Somalia.

CHAPTER 20

Force Feeding Somalia

Last week, CNN invaded the coast of Somalia, several hours prior to the amphibious landing of some twenty nations in an operation to be known as RESTORE HOPE. The network's bright spotlights were already in place to brighten the beaches, so people back home in America and around the world could see their loved ones as they stormed ashore, like invaders to save the poor starving people of that country. Our military men jumping from the sea's landing craft were all wearing night vision goggles. The stadium bright lights of world television networks totally blinded them. Thousands in the landing party fumbled onto the beaches as they tore the goggles from their faces. Few times in history have so many brought gifts with such force.

Thank God all the local Somalis that night were getting a good laugh, because the first showdown between locals and outside forces would be only three days later, and not too much longer before both sides would begin killing each other. United Nations forces were seen by the Somalis as unwelcome guests, prying into their internal war lord struggle. Congress should have known this before they coerced the world body into taking part in an African Bosnia just to prove our government isn't prejudice.

The original intent of the billion dollars a year relief operation was to provide food and aide to those in need, and to avoid clashes with locals. Of course, the outcome would prove far different. The multinational peace keeping forces came ashore in the wee hours of December 10,

1992. It was January 8, 1993 when I boarded a Kuwait Airways plane from Kuwait City to Dubai, United Arab Emirates, where I had a five hour layover before boarding a Kenyan Airways flight to Nairobi. I had been to Africa on several prior occasions but never that far south, so I savored every moment. The only image I had of middle Africa was instilled in me during childhood by Hollywood films. Of course, that image was only of boats in swampy waters infested with crocodiles and scantily clad natives saying "ungawa".

In the old films or in Tarzan flicks, we never saw starvation and ugliness, like the tribal war now enveloping most of Somalia's six million people. Hollywood's Africa and Tarzan movies killed off or captured the bad guys just minutes before the show ended thirty minutes later. Good ole Hollywood even lied to us about where Tarzan lived. It seems they misled us into believing it was on the African continent, when in fact; those adventures according to comic book legend took place in the jungles of South America. Nothing I saw in Somalia was like anything portrayed in Hollywood features or comic books.

My Somali adventure actually started when I landed at the Moi International Airport on the outskirts of Nairobi, Kenya. It was wonderful, colorful, tropical, green and quaint. From the huge, modern Terminal One, I exited and walked a short half block to Terminal Two, which looked a little more Hawaiian. Terminal Two contained few exterior walls. It mostly contained several ticket counters under concrete canopies surrounded by palm trees, bougainvillea vines and other tropical vegetation. Unlike Terminal One that had mechanized accordion ramps that coupled with all aircraft, Terminal two passengers boarded and disembarked by walking out to the plane on the tarmac.

As I summed up where I had to return tomorrow, I began picturing myself boarding a small prop plane to make the next leg of my venture, flying treetop level all the way to Mombasa. Surely I'd be peeping through a small porthole, watching herds of elephants and spotting lions as we passed over the grasslands. It turned out to be far less visually exciting.

Now that I felt comfortable about where I needed to return to tomorrow, I flagged down a zebra striped courtesy van, to whisk me down some not so modern thoroughfares into Kenya's bustling capitol city, Nairobi; about twenty minutes away. The closer I came to the city; I was taken more aback, seeing several quite tall high rise buildings that could have been in any major American or European city. Nairobi's wide, tree lined boulevards with flowering mimosa trees, tall palm trees, purple Jacaranda, multi colored bougainvillea, and pink oleander bushes gave me temporary thoughts of being on vacation instead of heading for work in yet another destroyed country.

The Hotel Intercontinental where I was staying, appeared to be a 1970's style, concrete block structure, ten stories high on a fairly busy roadway, near the city's center. It was within walking distance of the carved wood market, banks, night clubs and other hotels.

The first thing the desk clerk told me was not to go out onto the streets at night, and certainly never go out alone, even in the daytime. He said if I want to go night clubbing, make sure a taxi drops me at the front door and waits for me to go inside. His thoughtfulness made me feel a bit unsafe but I was no wimp. I had just come from one bombed out destroyed country, and was on my way to another. As long as I wore my canvas safari vest with all the film or bullet pockets I looked macho. I could handle anything.

Anyway, I did go shopping alone, and that night I went to a local club. I took the hotelier's advice however, asking the taxi driver to wait until I was safely inside the club's front door. As I exited the car and took my first steps, the driver was already turning right onto another thoroughfare, about a half block away.

The club was jamming, living up to its name Jambo, which in local Swahili means hello. Though I was the only white guy there, no one paid me any attention. All the black locals I could see, looked as western as me. They weren't at all what I expected. I thought they'd be dressed in dashikis or African clothing, wearing braids in their hair and wildly, colored, cloth headdresses. Instead, they were wearing clothes that could have been purchased in New York, London or Paris. The Africans in America obviously were blacker culturally oriented than the Africans in Africa.

For a January night, the evening was quite pleasant. The temperature remained in the upper sixties Fahrenheit. Before my paranoid walk home from Jambo Club, I had a great time listening to an international mix of tunes and watching the local's dance style.

The next full day, I spent wandering the streets, getting acquainted with my new surroundings. I found nothing intimidating other than, I lost three hundred dollars in a money scam that I had been warned not to do. The hotel desk clerk the first morning, said "people out there will try to rip you off for some big American bucks, so don't fall for the money exchange rate game. They will ask if you want to purchase money on the black market at a lot higher rate than banks give, so try not to get sucked into their scam."

Try as they did to discourage me, I got hooked into one where the man showed me all these Kenyan Shillings and the great exchange rate I'd be getting, then proceeded to trade me a few shillings wrapped around a lot of cut blank pieces of paper. By the time I summoned a policeman, I think the perpetrator was in Mombasa lying on the beach about an hour plane ride away.

That first night, I had a great dinner inside the hotel and after returning from the club, I settled in, savoring the good life. I knew the not so good life was coming tomorrow.

Instead of flying a domestic air carrier to Mombasa, I traveled aboard the VIP International Red Cross executive jet, a plane I would become quite familiar with over the next couple months. Each time I traveled aboard it, I felt more like a fortune five hundred CEO than a mercenary with a job title heading into a war ravaged country. Just over a comfortable hour flight away, my plane landed at a Kenyan military air base within sight of the Indian Ocean.

After deplaning, I checked with the Canadian and American joint Base Operations Center, where I was told there would be no plane to Mogadishu until the following day. They answered my next question by telling me to bunk in with the soldiers of both countries, in their temporary tent accommodations adjacent to the runway. They told me tomorrow there would be quite a few military transport planes taking all of them to Somalia as well.

The rest of the day, I watched movies in the entertainment tent, ate chow with the rest of the guys, and rested on an Army cot while listening to the never ending roar of huge aircraft propellers and turbines. As the only civilian around, I was a novelty and the soldiers couldn't wait to share their experiences of Somalia with me. Most of them insisted I must be CIA or mercenary or something because none of them had seen anyone else like me flying military aircraft and made comfortable by high ranking military officers. Most of the guys and some ladies had been there since the amphibious landing and reinforcements arrived a few weeks earlier and were already returning from a few days rest and recuperation on the beaches of Mombasa.

From these veteran's of Somalia, I got the impression our friendly gesture of giving food by force to the starving people in Somalia was already in trouble. Most of the soldiers were adamantly opposed to either Canadian or American forces being there any longer. They said the humanitarian end of the gesture was already gone and sniper fire was around every corner. They spoke of the Somalis who'd rather fight than eat, and our effort to force feed them or kill them was wrong.

The next morning, I climbed aboard an American C-130 military aircraft with about thirty other men, all in uniform. The Australians, Americans and Canadians carried their duffle bags up the plane's rear ramp and took their seats, length wise along the fuselage, facing each other in two long rows. Some C-130's were set up for cargo but this one was for troop use only, however several pallets were on loaded just before the ramp closed.

Commercial transports like this C-130 have no inner insulated walls, just the same steel shell that is both the inside and outside of the aircraft. Electrical wiring and cables are fully exposed and run the length of the plane's interior. The all metal seats were portable fold down types, with no cushions, backrests or windows.

Within a few minutes, the engines roared and the aircraft thrust upward and out over the Indian Ocean. All uniformed passengers passed around a chewing gum like pink ball they stuck in their ears, then got into their Mae West life vests before settling down in the floor, or stretched out atop the metal seats for the flight. After sticking some of the chewing gum in my ears as well, I grabbed the other end of a soldier's duffle bag and lay on the vibrating floor like many of the others.

We touched down on the Mogadishu Airport tarmac amidst desert vegetation, sand dunes and thousands of international military tents. To one side was a bombed out terminal building and a large destroyed hanger, and to the other were tents all the way over the sand dunes as far as the eye could see, to the Indian Ocean.

In all directions, there were military vehicles with strange insignias, flags and oddly dressed soldiers. Hoisted high in the air in all directions, blowing in the hot desert like breeze were flags of every color and size, each baring the signatures of Command and Operations tents from every participating coalition nation?

Within seconds of deplaning and to my great surprise, I was met by one of my old friends from Marr Bell days. Lalit Zadoo, a native of Kashmir, an area in dispute between India and Pakistan. He stood before me in all his splendor, round faced and died red hair. As a tradition, Zadoo men of Kashmir, dye their hair an orange like red color similar to Lucille Ball's.

Zadoo was different from anyone I had ever known in my life. In Kuwait, he joined Maia and me at our home many times. Many of our international friends use to come over to have cultural and inquisitive discussions about each others lifestyles. Zadoo was one of those fun guests.

He use to tell us of his days of plenty and days of lean; from the life of a privileged educator's family, to the time when he became a monk and begged daily for his meals, from local villagers while sleeping in caves at night. Zadoo was well educated, articulate, never a bore and spoke English as his first language.

At Marr Bell, Zadoo was a Third Country National or (TCN) Project Manager. His job title was the same as mine, but was not paid a fraction of my salary, nor afforded the normal American standards of comfort that I was. He had voluntarily gone to Kuwait to help keep his family in money, while the Kashmir region was being destroyed by a territorial war between India and Pakistan. So far, he has been able to send plenty of money home and get a few more experiences under his belt as well.

Zadoo and I embraced for a quick moment on the tarmac before he walked with me toward the bombed out terminal building where my transportation awaited. Of course along the way, we had a few laughs at Bob's expense. Our former boss in Kuwait was again our boss for this project in Somalia. Gosh, the bombed out buildings made us feel like home.

Zadoo placed me in the safe hands of my driver escort with Marine shooters, then bid me farewell as he boarded the same C-130, heading back to Mombasa for a few days at Marr Bell's field Business office. Our company had changed names once again and now we were called Disaster Recovery Company. Disaster Recovery had been awarded some lucrative contracts to provide support to American and international forces in Mogadishu, and would also be involved in a few side ventures. The American company Brown and Root out of Houston, Texas was one of our largest contracts in Somalia.

My U. S. Marine guard escorts ask me how I liked the destroyed surroundings I was seeing at the Mogadishu airport and were surprised to hear I hadn't even noticed them. These ruins didn't appear any different than Kuwait to me. I was unimpressed. Bombed out buildings, twisted, charred steel, bullet riddled runways and walkways; I felt as though I had touched down in Kuwait two years earlier. My only thought was "oh yea, it looks like Saddam was here too".

An American Marine grabbed the other end of my foot locker and helped me throw it into an Army Humvy. The Humvy, a super wide jeep that seats six comfortably and eight closely, had space in the rear for my trunk next to a marine sitting at a mounted M-60 caliber machine gun. Up front were two soldiers sitting with automatic rifles. I sat in the second cab seat alone, flanked by these machine guns and dead serious Marines in all directions. My guards gave me a bullet proof vest and a helmet to wear before we began rolling out from the secured airport, toward what they called "sniper alley".

My driver blew his horn, put the Humvy in gear and began moving forward, but no longer alone. We were now the center of three armed vehicles. I sat importantly at the center of the small but heavily armed convoy. At first, I was still perplexed about why we needed so much protection to help feed a starving nation, but those inexperienced first notions quickly vanished after taking three bullets to a radiator on my inaugural trip through town.

Our three vehicle convoy sped out the airport's heavily fortified gates and headed into some crowded streets. The gunner just behind me said, "As long as our vehicles move rapidly, you don't have to worry; it's when they slow down almost to a standstill that tensions rise".

Our small heavily armed convoy rounded a pitted and broken concrete traffic circle known as K4, when the guards became very tense, poised to strike back with their weapons if needed. They kept their eyes peeled for snipers as we turned southwest, into sniper alley, an area already known for locals taking aim at the care givers.

K4 was the busiest traffic circle in Mogadishu and it was difficult to go to the airport, seaport or American Embassy Compound without first passing through it. Here, the four choices of roadway forked with one leading to the sea port, a second toward the airport, a third to the former American Embassy Compound and the fourth toward the opposing war lord Mahdi's territory.

Today again, sniper fire rang out and our guys shot several rounds of rapid fire back toward some rooftops, about seventy five yards away. The ambush came so fast, I didn't even have time to react. By the time I did, the confrontation was over. Our lead Humvy had taken three bullets to the front. My guards remained with their fingers on their triggers and tense, while I remained crouched down the remainder of the way to the former United States Embassy Compound; still four miles away.

My Marine "shooters" as I came to call them, would continue being a great source of protection for me over the duration of my stay in Somalia. They always kept their eyes peeled for anyone in the crowds who might try to shoot us, jump on the vehicle, attempt to stab us or who might throw a hand grenade at us. The "shooters" were not there to fire as much as they were as deterrents and intimidators. Most times, we made it through without incident.

Within the next couple months, we'd do this same trip another sixty times or more. Sometimes we weren't as lucky as others and took bullets to the radiator or lights. Twice we were physically attacked by gangs of Somalis who grabbed at our helmets, sunglasses and even the Marine's weapons.

About midway along a mile stretch of white wall, our convoy slowed briefly while a flurry of uniformed Turkish and Italian troops cleared the way of the former Embassy Compound gates for us to enter. The fortress like entrance quickly opened, allowing our three vehicles to pass without hesitation, yet still not leaving enough of an opening for any of the local Somalis to gain entry. A glance to my rear revealed several other armed humvys and a Pakistani tank securing the compound's entrance from the opposite side of the street.

The original American Embassy in Mogadishu was set up as a three walled compound. The inner most walls, surround the embassy building itself, while the second set of walls several hundred yards out, include a former golf club house and several small guard billets. The outer wall covers a distance of approximately one square mile. Within the third walled area there used to be a nine hole golf course, but of course over time, severe drought had reclaimed it, so there is nothing now but sand. The grass within all three walled areas had long ago dried up and the property reverted to its original barren sandpit.

The compound's club house is now a partially destroyed or partially rebuilt military Command Center for the United States Army in Somalia. Several warehouses formerly on the property are now nothing but concrete slabs of burnt and twisted metal frames. That's where our company, Disaster Recovery was designated to build a camp.

Like the airport, everywhere I looked within the American Embassy Compound walls were encampments of other nations. Supplying food to the starving people of Somalia truly had become a multinational endeavor. Flags were flying from more than thirty countries inside this compound alone, and there were more up the street at the University Complex and at the sea port and airport. Each had their own Command tent plus several more sleeping tents, dining halls and satellite dishes. Everywhere I looked, I also saw soldiers in camouflaged fatigues and dark green or tan tee shirts.

Vehicles within these multinational forces' camps, included hundreds of personnel troop carrier trucks, jeeps, tanks and helicopters. The most curious vehicle was a riot control, tank truck from the African country of Botswana. It was configured like a bird house, high atop four big semi truck tractor wheels. It looked more like the American Civil War submarine, the "Merrimac", with port holes to shoot from and a solid steel door on the backside.

The extent of my conversation and welcome that first day was by Marr Bell's asshole Sonny, when he stuck his head out a tent flap and said "welcome to Somalia, you need to go relieve our new man who's been at the sea port for six hours."

Sonny, from Marr Bell and a couple of the other guys were already housed in small three to five man tents on concrete flooring of destroyed warehouses, within the embassy compound walls, just across from the Army's Operations Center. The pitched tents had a minimum of conveniences, bathrooms, air conditioning and cooking facilities weren't among them. The company's new Dutch cook made dinner on a campfire, reminiscent of old postwar Kuwait days, when our Indian cooks made curry rice for breakfast, lunch and dinner.

Somalia's heat was horrendous and there were no creature comforts like ice or cold drinks. Troops had only come ashore in Somalia less than two weeks prior to my arrival; so many supplies were still arriving in a continuous flow of cargo planes and freighter ships.

As soon as dinner was over, Bastard Sonny told me to head to the port before darkness fell. Sonny's man at the port was supposed to get a shipload of a million bottles of drinking water offloaded. What neither Sonny nor I knew was that the new guy's attitude and inability to hire local labor, fork lifts and trucks had already pissed off the American Harbor Master in charge of the seaport. Sonny's ship was being sent back out this evening to make room for priority military ships arriving.

I now had to be hurried through the dangerous streets at dusk, to the safety of the seaport's fortified gates and walls by another small convoy of heavily armed escorts. The guards dropped me off alone and unfamiliar with my surroundings at the sea port and without Sonny making any provisions for my food, drink or supplies of any kind. I hadn't been informed what to do, who to talk to, nor informed I was expected to spend the night dockside.

This new Marr Bell British character Jeremy, I was to relieve, said I could take over because he had been there almost seven hours since the ship first docked, and the military people running the port had been uncooperative about getting our ship offloaded. The Harbor Master's story was quite different. He said Jeremy had wasted the whole time the ship was docked, sipping Johnny Walker with the cargo ship's First Mate. The only thing they both agreed on was the story about the ship's contents. Jeremy and Harbor Master said the ship had hit a storm at sea and the cases containing a million bottles of potable drinking water had broken loose from their pallets. Tens and tens of thousands of loose bottles had filled the entire lower storage deck of the ship. Jeremy said it was a mess, "take care of it".

It took several hours to speak with the Captain and assess the cargo's condition for myself, before the ship put out to sea. I had to bargain with the Harbor Master for more time and for another return trip. The port's priority was for Military ships arriving, not commercial vessels like ours. Commercial ships were allowed to tie up at the small number of sea port berths for only short periods of time, when no military ship was due in.

Harbor Master Ed Johns of San Antonio, Texas was the civilian in charge of the Port of Mogadishu. He was about six feet two inches tall, forty two years old and had light brown hair and mustache much like the Marlboro Man. Funny that I would describe him like that because that's how people describe me. Others say I look like Dennis Weaver.

I believe I look more like Dennis Weaver because, once in my early twenties when I was back packing around Europe with Canadian hockey player Gordon Dornstauder, young people especially use to follow me down the street and peer in restaurant windows thinking they had seen Dennis Weaver. At first they called out "McCloud". I hadn't been in the United States for a long time and it was weeks before another American told me they thought I was McCloud from a Dennis Weaver, weekly TV series. I suppose the series ran while I was in the Air Force in Turkey.

Harbor Master Johns had been brought in from his duties as the civilian in charge of a Port in Saudi Arabia. In Mogadishu, he was to oversee the arrival and departures of the vast amount of international ships arriving at the port, to off-load supplies for all the coalition troops that were bringing aid to the Somali people.

Within moments of our meeting, Harbor Master Johns set me straight about Disaster Recovery's other man. He said that man was a jerk and he had purposely not allowed our ship to stay in port because when he allowed it to berth earlier, this Jeremy character farted around and never got one pallet off the vessel. He spent all his time trying to tell a young American lieutenant how important he was with the Disaster Company, and the rest of his time was spent drinking Scotch whiskey.

I assured Harbor Master Johns I was there with a job to do and I would do what had to be done to get the cargo off the ship and trucked to the United States Embassy Compound grounds. It was agreed; our ship could come in at sunrise the next morning if I could prove I was ready to begin handling the cargo.

Harbor Master Johns then introduced me to Somali George, a strongman in the Mohammed Mahdi's war lord camp and one of the three former enforcer's of Somalia's exPresident Mohammed Siad Barre. After the fall of the Siad Barre Government, George's group and two others creamed off as much as half of all food aide organizations shipments arriving in the country through the port.

George and I got along well right from the start. It was he who would be furnishing me about sixty stevedores who would help offload our early morning arriving vessel.

Our ship arrived at the RO-RO ramp before six o'clock in the morning and it was a mess. The million bottles of drinking water for the international militaries was in a pile about seven feet deep, covering the entire lower cargo hold and the upper deck of the vessel.

After attempting every method to offload, including fork lift and hand carrying, it was evident the whole mess could only be emptied by an "ant moving method". I would have to employ hundreds of people to form ant chains to pass bottle after bottle and carton after carton from the ship, until the final smashed pallets could be removed.

Somali George was a man of his word. Though he was making a truck load of money for his efforts, he made things happen. I proposed we hire three hundred fifty people to work the human off load chain, and he was to make sure he had enough supervisors in place to keep everyone working. Harbor Master Johns said we had the entire day and over night if needed, but the ship was to be out of harbor by sunrise when a military cargo ship was do to berth at that same RO-RO ramp.

Our carry and pass along method of bottle removal was working fine but taking a lot longer than expected. Somali George was true to his word and had all three hundred fifty laborers there on schedule. I had the American Military Police form lines that would search the laborers for weapons or the, before entry into the ports facilities then pass them along to me, where I would organize them into colonies of movers.

Harbor Master Johns, during one of our many conversations, told me the seaport was allowed to open because an agreement had been reached between the country's two war lords that had previously divided the country and the city of Mogadishu into two loyalties. One Clan led by former President Mohamed Mahdi and the other under Mohamed Farah Aideed. Since I had awarded what was considered a contract for labor to the Mahdi faction, I had to enter into negotiations with the other war lord Farah Aideed's people to award a contract for providing the thirty to fifty, eighteen wheel trucks and trailers required to move our bottled water supplies to a warehouse, crossing the hostile green line that divides the two warring factions.

Mohamed Farah Aideed's financier and second in command, Osman Ali Hassan Atto was a man who had gotten rich in oil exploration before the country's collapse into anarchy. It was with him, I negotiated a ninety five thousand dollar deal for truck carriers. The trucks were at my disposal for as long as I needed to get the job done, even twenty four hours a day if needed. It was also agreed American Marines in fully armed Humvys would be providing protection for me and my convoys through both territories. These agreements were difficult, argumentative and had to be carried out diplomatically. They took far more money but far less time that I had expected. Within the first hours of my arrival I had already accomplished something few men could or would do; meet with both warring factions and reach agreements with both.

Osman Atto took great pleasure in telling me about the opposing faction's Somali George at the port. He was the man who cut the throats of all the ship Captains who had refused to pay his war lord exorbitant amounts of money, to get their ships out of the harbor after the Mahdi camp forcefully overran the port. Osman Atto's clan overran the seaport and the Embassy compound grounds but that seemed ok with him.

Hostilities between the two warring camps was evident to me from the beginning and it was a little unnerving to have to visit both camps within the space of hours. Agreements had to be made though, and they were. The task of unloading all the bottles of water took more than four days in all and Harbor Master Johns was gracious to let our ship return time after time, as long as no military ships were awaiting berths.

During those three and a half, four days, I formed pretty good relationships with the Mahdi's war lord's strong man George and the opposing Osman Atto from the Aideed camp. My relationship with George came down to a first name basis, he called me Papa Chuck and I called him Cut Throat. George really got a kick out of that. Later we shortened the name even further to "my George".

Though I was only in my mid forties, out of respect, Osman Atto and his men always called me Papa as well. I received great respect from both sides of the warring clans but of course I knew it was mostly the money, the American dollars that were buying it.

For the rest of my time in Somalia, I became a person who could, and did go between the two camps with impunity. Much like Kuwait, I had wooed my way into friendships that were exciting, colorful and dangerous if nothing else.

My camp life at the United States Embassy Compound was less exciting and more hostile than the environment outside the compound's gates. Bastard Sonny, Marr Bell's second in command was the company's front man for the Somalia project and his toxic attitude and abusive qualities were in superior form. He and the new jerk Jeremy cleaned rifles all day and played cards by night, while others did the work and got kicked in the ass for doing so. After not sleeping more than seventy six hours at the seaport, I returned to the Embassy Compound to a Sonny who demanded I not sleep until I found a typewriter somewhere in the four square mile compound on which I'd type all the reports needed to make his job easier. The Bastard was relentless and talked incessantly about his maneuvering through the streets of Mogadishu to the Olympic Hotel bar where he and Jeremy had dinner two nights in a row, and most assuredly had several drinks too. The Olympic Hotel was about the only place left standing in the country that was still open for business. It was frequented mostly by foreign journalists.

Sonny's bitching and moaning was a daily preoccupation and he would have been unable to comprehend the amount of times I was unguarded on the streets of Mogadishu or flying down "sniper alley" all alone. I never once permitted him to go to either war lord's camp with me because I thought he'd say something stupid and we'd be impaled by the natives, or I would forever more have to listen to his war stories about when he came face to face with those warlords or their seconds in command.

My first deed in Somalia accomplished, I went to sleep. For thirty seven hours I slept in a tent infested with ants in ungodly temperatures and humidity. Bastard Sonny was prepared for battle when I finally awoke and my next assignment was to try to soothe tempers between he, Jeremy and Disaster Recovery's second largest subcontractor, Brown and Root. The Texas company is probably the largest contractor in the world and Sonny wanted to mingle with their "in field" hierarchy but had instead managed to piss them off. Disaster Recovery was suppose to be building a more permanent camp for Brown and Root, much like we had done for the British Royal Ordinance, British military and United Nations in Kuwait but he never submitted a plan for the housing or placement of the shipments of prefab buildings our company had already ordered. Our prefabs were running over two weeks behind schedule and Sonny and

Jeremy could no longer keep the contract without making some pretty heroic moves. They didn't and the contracts were canceled. Brown and Root finally accepted some of our buildings after their arrival, but had already gone around Sonny and ordered ship loads of prefab buildings, air conditioners, generators, vehicles and other supplies from a Saudi Arabian outfit called Red Sea.

Guy and Shari's Tara Burnt by Saddam Hussein

Royal Ordinance & Marr Bell Camp I

Betsy Gorlay

Reporter & Friend Betty Lippold

Gus and Ruba Omar

Abdullah

Chuck on Superstation 92.5

Disc Jockey - Linda Lou

Chuck on air with news, weather and sports

Dedication New US Embassy
From Left: Thomas Farley – FOB, Prime Minister His Highness Sheikh Saad Abdullah
Al Ahmed Al Sabah, President George H.W. Bush and U.S. Ambassador Ryan Crocker

July 4th Celebration: Barbara Vaughn, Maia, Betsy, Chuck, Ambassador & Mrs. Crocker

From Prison to Hospital

Maia & Chuck at Marine Corp Ball

Betty McNaughton & Marine Escort

Chuck with South African Pres. Nelson Mandela

Lyle & Regita Ditmar with Maia

Princess Anne of Great Britain with entourage touring our Royal Ordinance Camp

Maia & Chuck at Pyramids of Giza

Kuwaiti men playing card games at a home diwaniya

Royals at Camel Races

Betty Lippold and member of Royal Family

Traditional Kuwaiti Sword Ceremony

Chuck & Michael Budran with Kuwaiti Colonels

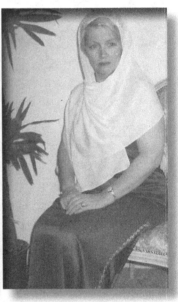

Chuck with President George H.W.Bush   *Maia*

this is Maia   *this is Chuck*

Chuck with Mirror Image

Chuck Petty and wife Maia

KIH Ghosts and Goblins

Autumn season's costume get-together

THE autumn season abounds with warm sunny days and cool breezy nights. As October gave way to November, the transition was made with the help of Ghosts and Goblins. Costumes of every possible creation was adorned by child and adult alike before, during and post Halloween. Americans, Chuck Petty and his lovely wife Maia (top) as Sheriff and "flapper" hosted a get together for American companies here in Kuwait at their home in Salmiya. One of the scary, unlikely greeters was a "witch" with green hair.

• The Kuwait International Hotel sponsored a buffet and costume contest for their 350 employees. It was difficult to select five winners among the terrific characters: K. Narayanan, Engineering as an "alien" Sylvestre Fernandes, Personnel as "Ramses II"; Aziza Khan, Sales and Marketing as "sultan" rebel; Estrella Rueno, Accounts as "witch" and Kabir Hussein, Housekeeping as a "ghost." Also, 136 raffle prizes were given out through such sponsors as Al

Annual Halloween Party at our Penthouse

Chuck & Maia at Formal Dinner Party

Arab Times Headlines

Chuck in the field

Chuck in His Office

Chapter 21

Cozying Up to Some War Lords

Marr Bell's top man in the Middle East, Bob Isaksson arrived in Somalia to take control of the camp situation temporarily and resolve issues with Brown and Root and look for other business. He landed several other contracts in Somalia during that brief visit, so we wouldn't have to leave the country after Brown and Root gave us the boot. We began providing buildings to house the top international military Command General's and porta toilets for the tens of thousands of troops at the Mogadishu airport, sea port, American Embassy compound, University compound and the Swedish hospital. Either Bob or Sonny pulled another hat out from their sleeve and won a contract from a "Save the Children type charity" to dig water wells in remote Baidoa and Bardera, Somalia.

Bob's first words to me after his arrival were that we should have refused the cargo load of a million bottles of water and claimed the insurance. He said "piss on the M–F–s that needs to drink it. Bottom line says we probably would have made money by settling for an insurance claim. So went all the thanks for busting my butt.

Cut Throat George and I were bonding and he began bringing me presents of all sorts, collectable Somali money, dinner invitations, carved wooden statues and some old post cards that showed what Mogadishu used to look like before years of war ravaged it. Harbor Master Johns was happy the relationship was going well and encouraged it. He said there had been too many problems with George in the past and if he finally found someone he could like, go for it. Please help make everyone's life a little better by keeping George in check.

Everyone loves a pay day and George's people were all looking forward to their first real money earned in almost three years. I knew it would be nearly impossible to sort each persons pay out and hand it to them but George insisted. In a war ravaged country, security for the huge payout would be a major problem no matter how it was handled, but our company's accountant Donald St. Pierre and I had a plan. We arranged for an open air bank to be set up under some trees near the Embassy compound main gates, within the secured walls, and under heavy guard. I gave George a time and the place and told him to have his people there.

Several hours prior to the payout, many hundreds of Somalis began converging on the embassy compound gates. United Nations forces, mainly those from Italy, Turkey and Pakistan became uneasy at the prospect of trouble. Access by so many locals had to be handled very carefully. Several more guard units were summoned to the front gates and dozens of additional mounted guns were put in place behind sand bag walls. The plan was to allow no more than one single file column of twenty Somali laborers in at a time. The column would further be broken down into five units of five persons between two guards at all times. Donald and I would be sitting under the trees with bales of Somali money to be handed to each laborer as he or she passed.

We hit only one snag and soon rectified it. Most Somalis like Arabs have similar names; therefore it would be impossible to check any written list to see who really worked or who didn't. Most Somalis, who neared me, clasp their hands together in recognition and said "papa" and we knew they were part of our three hundred fifty who had to be paid. Others were dazed and not sure why they had come other than they had heard the Americans were giving out free money. Obviously, we had to have several lines going off the side to filter out those who had no idea why they had come.

Out of hearing range from other locals, one at a time, the Somalis were asked why they were here. The ones that said they came to get paid for working offloading a ship was paid and the others were led down a very long exit corridor, out the back side of the compound's grounds so they wouldn't be able to rejoin the line or gain access to those who got paid.

Even though Somali money denominations were 1,000 Shillings and 10,000 Shillings, it took bales like hay to pay the laborers and for three and a half hours, each of them carried away rubber bands full of bills the size of loaves of bread. When the money was nearly exhausted, so were the demands for it. It worked out as exact as any miracle would have allowed. From those coming to our open air bank, I also selected more than thirty hard workers for longer lasting jobs within the compound walls of the former American Embassy for the Americans, Turks, and Italians. About another fifty were to meet me for my next project again at the seaport in two days. There was another ship arriving and it too had to be offloaded.

The only truly starving person I met in Mogadishu was a young boy about fifteen to seventeen years of age. When he came to me asking for a job offloading the ship, he appeared ready to faint. He was obviously too weak to help but I couldn't refuse him. I asked him through an interpreter how long had it been since he had eaten. A day or more, two days, three? He didn't know. He said his grandmother and sister were all that was left of his family and they had no money or food.

I told the young boy I wanted to hire him to work on the dock and in camp but he would have to get stronger to do that. I gave him the equivalent of twenty American dollars and told him to stay home with his grandmother and sister and all of them eat for three days as much as they could, then come back to me and he will be working for me as long as I'm in the country. I would pay him every afternoon after work so he would have money for food every night. I personally didn't think he'd ever come back but I hoped he would. I left word at the Sea port gate that no matter when he arrived, he was to be shown to Mr. Chuck where he would start working with me immediately.

For the next several days, I didn't think much about him because I was too busy, but on the fourth day, he arrived back and ready for work. Main gate security at the Sea port sent him all the way to me at the embassy compound by jeep escort and I was happy to see him. He joined my other group doing janitorial services, maid cleaning, garbage removal, etc. He was as good a worker as I was to my word. He was paid daily and grew stronger as the days passed. Everyone at camp, the Somalis and the Americans knew him as Chuck's boy. No one dared push him around or treat him badly. I didn't see him often but he seemed happy and always waved no matter where he was when he spotted me.

I never knew the young man's name. Each time I asked, he bowed his head and said it so softly that I didn't press further. It was unimportant, there was a good sole in there and no name was needed. His supervisor was always commending his work and always made sure the money was there for him.

The only other young man that stood out was about twenty one or two years old and had clearly more distinguishing facial features than the Somalis. His nose face and jaw line were sharper and his English was almost impeccable. Obviously he was far more educated than any of the others. One day he told me "thank you for letting me work here". He said he was a Christian in a Muslim country and that his family had been broken up and fled because Christians weren't tolerated in Somalia, at least around Mogadishu. He said if the others find out he's a Christian then they would kill him, even if they had to do it at work. So often I heard from a Muslim how tolerant Islam is and yet so often I found it to be the contrary. It seems strange that the exact word "tolerant" is used by all Muslims as if programmed or taught.

This man was also a great worker and I kept him in my employee for the whole time I was in Somalia. Before I left, I turned him over to the Italians within the Embassy compound and they were happy to have him.

One day, he came to me with a small envelope with something inside. He was so proud to give it to me but a little embarrassed also. He said he wanted to thank me and though it wasn't much, he hoped I would like it. Inside the envelope was a piece of paper with a note on it and a small very thin wash cloth. The small gift was overwhelming and I almost cried. I told him I appreciated it very much and I would always hold on to it and remember my time in Somalia and him. It was all he could afford but it was enough for me. The cloth and note mean so much that I still keep it with my coin collection in a bank vault in the United States.

Osman Atto, the owner or controller of all the low bed trucks and second in line within the Mohamed Farah Aideed war camp and I began to share many evenings together at his spacious walled, compound about a mile and a half from the former U. S. Embassy grounds. Otto was a snappy dresser, for a man who lived within the ruins of an entire nation. He came to each meeting or dinner in cleanly pressed white or light blue short sleeved shirts, black firmly pressed trousers and polished black or white shoes.

Osman Atto's manner and speech were diplomatic and careful but also inviting and most gracious. He too, like Somali George, showed me their best sides. Often we dined at a table where food was aplenty and the family setting could have been anywhere in America. Each member (males only) came to the table well dressed and well mannered. Only a wife and the possibility of daughters were missing. Osman Atto later told me his wife was in Canada with one of his older sons and she rotated back and forth to two of her other children in Glasgow, New Jersey where they attended school.

Another agreement had to be made between me and War Lord Mohamed Farah Aideed so the next time I went to Osman Atto's walled compound, we met under quite different circumstances. I had been taken to the street where he lived and had to wait several hundred yards away while word was sent for him to come meet me. Atto's compound was only two blocks from the main Bakara Market Street but was a world away in terms of security. From the turn at the corner, there were armed guards everywhere, from the rooftops to lookout posts atop ten feet high walls. His house on the dirt street was a fortress. I was plenty intimidated while being talked down to by gunmen high above on the roof. I simply told the men I would be right back.

When I returned just over an hour later, the odds had been evened a little. My escorts this time were four humvys full of U. S. Marines ready to hunt bear. This time each vehicle contained the usual driver and front seat shooter, with a Marine at the mounted 60 caliber machine gun in the middle and two shooters in the rear seat. My concern was more for protection than going over there to out gun the other side. Though I needed intimidation on my side, I needed to have it without making the War Lord or his second in command feel like war was coming to his own back yard. During the hour I was gone, I sent word via one of my Somali's that I would be returning within the hour with a business proposal for use of all the trucks under Mohamed Farah Aideed's ownership or Osman Atto's control.

As my Marines and I rounded the final corner and turned onto Atto's dirt street, we proceeded slowly and cautiously. Near the fortress walls, partially covered with blooming bougainvillea bushes, we came to a halt. The main single six foot gate at the center of Osman Atto's compound opened and the well dressed man himself appeared with only two others to his side. Neither they nor he appeared armed.

Osman Atto spoke English in a loud voice for all to hear and said, "Please, my friend there is no need for such show of force here." "Everything is fine and you and I will talk." With bullet proof flap jacket on and a helmet on my head, I climbed from the Humvy and moved slowly toward the center of the street where he too was making an effort to meet me half way. His two sidemen had stopped walking and only he and I met in the center. We both instinctively turned side by side and began walking together. First we walked about fifty feet up the street in one direction, then about fifty paces in the other direction; then back and forth again and again, until this first meeting was over. We had come to an agreement for the truck rentals. Papers would be signed with a handshake the next day. He asked that our meeting be more pleasant the next day and expressed the hope that I would come less heavily guarded. I expressed my concerns that all protection was in his favor. If his men were expected tomorrow, mine would be too.

The next day, the tense atmosphere from the first day was much better. After working all night at the Ro Ro ramp at Mogadishu Sea Port attempting to unload the broken water pallets, I was happy for the interruption and even looked forward to seeing Osman Atto again. This time without War Lord Aideed at his side, he welcomed me as an old friend and we again walked back and forth on the street. Children down the street watched us both only slightly as they played tag, chasing each other around while others waved to us trying to get our attention.

On this day, I brought two humvys of shooters for security and peace of mind but I neither felt intimidated nor tense as Osman Atto and I approached each other face to face. A mutual respect from strength had been reached and we both felt it.

I was not the only one who came to realize that in the first four days of my arrival in Mogadishu, I had already met two of the main players in Somalia's inner conflict. Word passed rapidly amongst the American Marines of mine and Osman Atto's meeting and volunteers as guards started popping out of the wood work. There would be no trouble getting an escort from now on. All U. S. Marines were curious and I was constantly being asked would I accept them as volunteers for my next face off. With the permission of their superiors, most of my original shooters continued escorting me until I left the country. Months after I left Somalia I continued hearing the U. S. military wanted to capture Aideed or Mahdi. This came as such a surprise to me and I imagine the Marines that often protected me. If the U. S. wanted Aideed, they could have told me to stab him with a fork at dinner at one of the four times he dined with Osman Atto and me. As for Mahdi, he was a little scarcer but twice sent for me and cut throat George to join him at his residence on the side of town where the stadium is.

One evening about two weeks later, Osman Atto invited me to Mr. Oakley's home for dinner. Mr. Oakley, the former Ambassador was now serving as United States Special Envoy to Somalia. It was Mr. Oakley who worked out agreements with both warring factions to allow the multinational peacekeeping mission into Somalia.

Mr. Oakley was a sixty one year old man of slight build, high cheek bones, slightly graying hair over the temples and a modest dresser. He too, like Osman Atto always wore short sleeve shirts and light weight trousers but Mr. Oakley appeared a little more middle of the road America. Comfortable looking, but putting on no airs of importance, nor of any fashion sense; certainly none was needed in this country.

Mr. Oakley, Osman Atto and I dined on another healthy dinner, and then talked for hours on a garden terrace under a huge canopy of trees. My accompanying shooters (eight this time) waited inside Mr. Oakley's walled, stone paved courtyard near his automobiles and their humvys. That night through normal conversation, it came up that before the UN peace keepers came, he was in control of the American Embassy compound as well as the University and other places we were utilizing. Now he's receiving rent payment for those same facilities that he admittedly overran to keep War Lord Mahdi's forces from taking them. He seemed quite pleased with his accomplishment, and went on to tell me that one of the homes he was now living in, as well as several others now under his control were Chevron and Amoco Oil executive homes before factional fighting split the country apart.

The more we talked, the clearer the picture became concerning the war lords and which side we were on. Of course, I still remained confused about many issues concerning the whole internal struggle thing but the peace keepers definitely leaned in Aideed and Atto's direction. One clan held the airport, the other the sea port, both had main markets that were separate, the city's main ball field was held by one clan, the

University the other and we supported both sides by supplying them with money for truck rentals and favors.

How innocent those first days, weeks and months were for me. Later, it would be Osman Atto that would pose the real danger to me and become the biggest thorn in the side of the Americans and UN troops whom he would later fight against the hardest. Also, in the not too distant future he would switch sides, favoring War Lord Mohamed Mahdi and lead to the hostilities that caused the death of his former War Lord Mohamed Farrah (Farrah means happy in Arabic) Aideed, his old Godfather.

Being called Papa by all sides was not totally new to me, but struck me strange that everyone thought of me that way. In Kuwait, the hundreds or even thousands of laborers at Marr Bell had called me Mr. Chuck and occasionally Papa with only the Indians calling me bapu, but in Somalia even the higher ups like cut throat George and Osman Atto called me papa.

In actual age, I was probably less than ten years older than Atto or George, but I may have had that worn out rugged look because of all the long hours and days I was putting in out in the sun. I, however, still thought of myself looking a bit like my old days as a male model wearing Khaki pants and shirts with epaulets. Some of my best modeling pictures had been wearing the attire I was now wearing daily in Mogadishu.

I felt little different, but even I now found my old $900 a day modeling jobs of the late 1970's and early 1980's light years away from what I was presently doing. No more Marlboro ads or print work for Saks Fifth Avenue, Holiday Inn hotel brochures or layouts for computer companies or Case Tires. My small Toyota truck in Somalia and my Humvy transportation were worlds apart from the Registry Resort ads I had done in Scottsdale and Phoenix with Rolls Royce. I have to admit though, the Marlboro ad I originally did and was more famous for, was almost a joke. It was during the time when the advertising agency was doing more test ads and was putting little money into the ad campaign. My pictures were only frontrunners for the Marlboro men who would later grace bill boards and go on to make small fortunes from each ad campaign and spokesman tour.

Three quarters of my print work, modeling and television commercials work had come from Plaza Three Modeling Agency in Phoenix and the rest divided between the West Coast and New York. Those days were long gone and almost forgotten except for a few reminders around our apartment in Kuwait and home in Arizona. Now of course, I'll be adding pictures to my portfolio of war torn Somalia in flack jackets and helmets.

There were a lot of things happening in Somalia and within our own company. We began shipping in prefabricated buildings similar to those we had in Kuwait and established quite a modern creature comfort base for ourselves within the Embassy Compound walls. From here, we headed up water drilling operations, drinking water distribution and sales and most importantly, porta toilet and toilet paper operations. Few can imagine a heavily populated country like Somalia without sewers or even toilets in the whole country.

In Somalia, it had been common practice since the country fell into anarchy in January 1991, for the entire populous of millions of people to defecate and urinate behind bushes or in fields or streets. Nothing worked any more. After a few months and few years with little water to dilute it, things got ripe.

For the first couple of weeks, none of the United Nations or American military units had adequate toilet facilities either, so it was our job to import them, set them in place, continually restock the toilet paper and pump the toilets contents. For this, we had what we called the "shit patrol". It was made up of college and university students from Alabama with ties to our original Marr Bell Company. These kids replaced all the smudge pots the American and other armies had been using. Now everyone got clean, fiberglass porta toilets maintained on round the clock schedules. The importance of these toilets and those maintenance men was immeasurable. When one of the porta units wasn't emptied in time, word came from the Commanders them-selves to attend to it with all urgency. Our one and two whole poopers were probably the biggest success story in Somalia.

There were many food relief agencies from around the world operating in Mogadishu and throughout Somalia. Those stockpiles of food in less secure areas were often hit by gangs of gunmen in the night. Here in the capitol city of Mogadishu, people weren't starving like the hoards of people we had seen on television. Other than my boy at camp, I never really saw anyone in bad shape, anywhere near us. There were flourishing markets, one in each war lord's territory. Canadian soldiers I spoke with on the plane said northern cities of Somalia, like Belet uen and others had never seen starvation and still had some semblance of city government with a stable population.

Nightly, as many of us gathered inside the Army's Operations building to watch television, we'd howl at CNN's broadcast of the starving, fly infested faces of small children dying in Somalia. The CNN encampment was right here amongst us and we kept trying to find out where they were shooting, but they were withdrawn and stand-offish from everyone else. Their self importance was as far from reality as those scenes of starving babies they kept showing the world.

Once, I went in the lead truck of a food relief convoy to Bardera and Baidoa. CNN and many multinational forces accompanied the tons of food supplies aboard our thirty two trucks as they rolled through the interior countryside all the way to the Kenyan border. We drove hundreds of miles through parched, semiarid land filled with only wandering shepherds with thousands of healthy camels and goats. Neither my driver nor I could fathom people starving if so many well fed goats and camels were allowed to live. Why wasn't someone eating them? Even in the deserts of Saudi Arabia and Kuwait, with all their wealth, I had never seen so many camels and goats.

The camels and goats were the only measure of wealth in this Somalia. They were never to be killed or eaten. Only blood from slits in the sides of their necks could be used for drinking. A man would let his own family die of starvation before he would kill any of his herds for their food. But, even far outback we saw no starving people.

When we returned to Mogadishu, we were all busy telling everyone we knew about the herds of unslaughtered animals. We also continued our nightly visits to the Operations Center to watch television and the CNN coverage. Little was seen for the next two nights but on the third, we all had to sit up straight in our chairs while CNN aired the convoy trip to the starving people of Baidoa and Bardera. They again showed lines of starving, thin people with flies on their faces and hands outstretched for food. I couldn't hear what was being said because everyone around me was hissing and booing too loudly.

I was with one of my Marine escort Captains that night when we confronted CNN's cameraman and woman reporter. The Captain asked where the CNN crew had been to get those pictures of long lines of decimated people receiving rice and milk substitute. A crotch scratching female reporter responded it was actually across the Kenyan border in a remote village just beyond where the rest of us had been. We both inquired when had they slipped away from the convoy, and how did they get truck loads of food out from under our noses all the way to the other location? They said they took a few trucks there and made it back before our scheduled return to Mogadishu.

By the end of our confrontation, several more civilians and military men joined in taunting the CNN crewmen about giving false impressions to the world. We all voiced our opinions of the misleading film and took a few extra minutes to thank them personally for lighting up the beaches so well during the amphibious night landing, more than a month earlier. Most soldiers felt their lives were in great danger that night and just wanted the spotlights turned off as their landing craft came ashore.

Where we had been in Bardera and Baidoa, only several dozen people even showed up to get rations of food. Most of the population just kept walking indifferently, along the streets staring at the convoy. They appeared neither malnourished nor eager to have intrusions of soldiers or civilian aid workers in their midst.

Disaster Recovery had progressed a lot since our original first week in Somalia, and the camp offered just about all the luxuries one would need; hot showers, private bathrooms, two men to a room, air conditioning, a real kitchen and a dining hall with ice maker, teas and juices, even a telephone set up to call anywhere in the world we wanted.

My family back in the States had watched most of the CNN coverage and was very worried about me being involved with American troops that were gunning down local Somalis. I tried to explain the real situation to them, but it was difficult when all they were being fed were half truths or lies on television. It's true, there really was a lot of danger out there, but soldiers weren't gunning down innocent locals.

As for Somalia's War Lords, they never felt it was in their interest to have other nationalities from around the world inside their country medaling in their internal affairs. The War Lords still preferred a "winner takes all" position. The only reason they allowed all these foreigners certain freedoms and access to their capitol was out of greed. These foreign governments were bank rolling many local projects, rebuilding some of the infrastructure and providing money to keep their war going on. Mahdi's man George at the seaport and Aideed's man Atto and his truck rentals all benefitted from deals made by me and paid by my company.

Daily, opposing Somali War Lord controlled radio broadcasts instilled hatred for the opposing clan and preached anti American and anti United Nations rhetoric. The Somali people would stand in line for food handouts and then while still carrying the goods in their arms, curse us as Colonialist.

All westerners had to be guarded. Our troops were both guards and escorts because of the hostilities we faced each time we traveled from one location to another, whether off loading food into warehouses for the Somali people or on trips to the garbage dump. If they weren't after us individually, then they were after our trucks. Even women and children carried bayonets, pistols or rifles. Children twelve years old often raised their rifles against soldiers who were too caring to mow them down with their 60 mm mounted weapons.

The same War Lords who were making money from us also put bounties on American vehicles. Each time we moved through the streets of Mogadishu, it was an invitation for gangs of Somalis to try to collect on that bounty by pulling you from your vehicle or overtaking you any way they could. They wanted the trucks and jeeps and sometimes they got them. If a soldier was too slow to open fire on men, women or children, then he ran the risk of being hurt or killed, or at least to lose his vehicle.

Without armed troops, no assistance to Somalia would ever have been possible. The people of Mogadishu especially, were at war with each other and us. For them, war had long ago become a way of life. We were just the newest players in the game. Their violence between each other was not as bad as toward us because they had more to win from us.

The destruction of Somalia was worse than anything I'd seen in Kuwait. Even if the Iraqis would have stayed in Kuwait seven years instead of seven months, no army could have caused more destruction than Somalis had caused to themselves, tearing apart their own country's infrastructure into the smallest of pieces.

In Somalia, every building had been stripped of wire and cable. Even the walls had been pulled apart for the wood studs. Anything that could be stolen sold or used to burn had been. There were no door frames or window frames, no kitchen appliances or sinks or tubs, no glass and even most roofs had been disassembled for use as firewood. People lived like cavemen in concrete shelters of walls and floors with everything else gone; including the bushes, trees and grass in their yards.

There was no infrastructure at all. There were no banks, factories, police stations, post offices, bus companies, city or state governments, no jails, no corner grocery or pharmacies, no electricity, water, telephone, gas stations, sewers or anything else left but hostile natives. For them, there was no real access into, or out of the country. No mail, no trains and no flights other than those for the United Nations and relief organizations.

Because several powerful men became greedy and wanted everything their way, they allowed the whole country and everyone in it to be destroyed. The same men were still fighting each other when we came, and they'll still be fighting when we've gone. From us however, they did manage to get extra provisions of food and money to support a more prolonged war.

Everything in Somalia was not doom and gloom. One day my spirits were lifted and I chuckled while watching the interaction between an American soldier guarding the sea port and a young Somali boy. As I stood along side my latest arriving ship, I saw the best pantomime I had ever seen.

The American soldier was atop a wall of huge metal shipping containers patrolling for snipers who may shoot into the maze of stevedores, army men and ship crews working nearby. A very black little boy in red short pants and bright yellow tee shirt stood perhaps a hundred yards further away on the beach. They carried on a quite clear nonverbal conversation.

The little boy motioned, "I come there?" the American guard used a hand signal saying "no". The little boy next said through sign language "you go gate, sign me, and go to you". The Marine again used his hands to say "no". The boy grew bolder and signed "I dig gun from sand, shoot you". The soldier next gestured "I kick your ass". The little boy's hand movements said "I shoot your ass, you fall down, I laugh."

This was only one of the conversations I saw between the two over the next couple of days. It was not unusual for the Marine to come on duty and immediately start searching the beach with his binoculars for the little boy with whom he enjoyed their unusual rapport.

Several situations occurred between Americans and Somalis that weren't fun and didn't end well. When any vehicle rode through the streets, extreme caution had to be taken. Windows had to be up and doors had to be locked. On several occasions, a vehicle or group of vehicles would be at a stand still waiting for another convoy to pass. Entire crowds of Somalis would turn on them and attack. The drivers would be beaten and robbed and occasionally badly injured. Simple things like truck windows didn't stand in any ones way very long, before the driver was soon fighting for his or her life. Swarms of locals descended on them with machetes, sticks and bare hands. There were grenades and mortars too, but those were mostly held for harassing military compounds at night or for breaking into offices of the UN or charity organizations for the money and supplies they held.

On several occasions, I witnessed American Marines or Pakistani troops opening fire above the heads of locals, to rescue their own. CNN reports leaving the country remained sensationalized and unconstructive as usual. The friendly, starving Somali people were being shot to death by the armed peace keepers and food bearers.

Within weeks, everyone I talked to thought there was no reason for anyone to be in Somalia any longer. "Let them go back to their own war and we can monitor it from highflying satellites", was their sentiments. From the commanders who sat with us in the evenings, to Osman Atto and Cut Throat George, all views were the same. No outsiders should be in a country they weren't invited into, no matter what their purpose was.

One day on a simple routine trip to the garbage dump, a band of Somalis ambushed two of our Disaster Recovery vehicles. While our men were dumping garbage, they were ambushed from all sides by machete toting locals who probably wanted their vehicles. Just moments before a machete ripped into the skull of one of our guys, the Marine shooters opened fire and took two Somalis out. Again it was reported "American soldiers killed several locals".

One night, about a dozen American and Canadian military commanders sat around with us in Headquarters Building on the Embassy Compound grounds. As we watched CNN, the conversation turned to why were their soldiers still in Somalia? Their only sensible conclusion was the same I had come to earlier. Congress was committed to not showing partiality between races, what was good for Bosnia was good for Africa.

Bosnia, Kuwait and Somalia are all Muslim countries where other religions are either not tolerated at all, or are barely. More simply, I felt the problems could have, or should have been resolved by other very rich Muslim countries; or at least by the largest power brokers in those regions. Americans should stay out of it.

In the case of Somalia, there were far more deserving African nations that should have been helped. The decision for intervention in Somalia was a poor one at best, and several people had to die and tens of thousands had to live with that decision as best they could.

It didn't take long for the climate, the hostility and the long work hours in Somalia to get to you and rest and relaxation was well earned and deserved. It was time for mine and I planned it via our satellite telephone with my wife. Since one of us was already here, we decided to take the opportunity to visit more of Africa. We would enjoy an exotic holiday on the continent somewhere else instead of settling for just memories of Somalia. We decided that Maia would join me in Nairobi, Kenya and then we'd spend five more days together on a safari.

Disaster Recovery needed operating money in Somalia to convert to Somali Shillings for laborer's pay, hiring trucks and to pay berthing fees for ship arrivals. Since banks were non existent, Maia was to bring a cool hundred thousand dollars in cash with her to Nairobi. One of Disaster Recovery's office personnel from Mombasa would fly in with me, accept the money, and then return with it while the two of us went on holiday. Little did we realize at the time that this new side job of Maia's money running would soon open another chapter in our already soap opera lives.

CHAPTER 22

Sleeping With the Lions

Several telephone calls back and forth between Kuwait and Somalia and Mine and Maia's rendezvous in Nairobi and our safari plans were complete. She would arrive barely more than an hour after me at Moi International in Nairobi; we'd catch a taxi together and stay at the same InterContinental Hotel I stayed in the last time I was there. Our company's Filipino money handler, Kitts, from Mombasa was already in Nairobi awaiting the hundred thousand dollars in cash from Maia.

Maia had carried the wrapped packs of hundred dollar bills from our office in Kuwait through Dubai, United Arab Emirates, where she had a six hour lay over and a plane change; then onto her longer flight to Nairobi. Throughout the trip's twelve hours, she never let her guard down long enough to sleep or rest while holding the treasury in her lap.

It frightened Maia to know how much money she was carrying and even more thinking of the penalties she faced in the event one government or another's Customs agents would check or confiscate it.

Maia's plane was delayed by several hours so I just stuck around the airport. Upon her arrival we wasted no time to get Maia and her shattered nerves to the hotel. She had arrived money in hand you might say and now it was time to turn it over to Kitts and begin our holiday together.

Soon would be mine and Maia's first night together in months. She looked gorgeous. Her cat-like green eyes bore a single tear as she outstretched her arms to reach around my waist just as I pulled her in to a full teddy bear hug. Our first night in Kenya was to be as special as any we had known. The next morning, we departed on our first safari, five days in Southwestern Kenya's Masai Mara region.

In our small touristic animal camouflaged van, we drove for almost five hours through mountains and forests, through wide expanses of vegetative wastelands and into national preserves. Our tiger skin, painted van continually passed other zebra striped and giraffe spotted vehicles on their return trip back to the country's capitol city.

Very near but still outside Masai Mara National Preserve, we began running into huge herds of zebra; hundreds of them chewing on the low lying grasses of the region, like horses on a big ranch out West in the United States. Some wandered across our narrow roadways bringing us and other traffic to a halt in both directions. They were beautiful and dazzling. We couldn't believe that within our first fifteen minutes near the park, we had already seen more zebra than we had seen in a life time, on television or in zoos.

Further down the road, there were almost as many wildebeests as there had been zebra earlier. These strange horse like, moose like animals had blue tinted butts and long black tails just like the fly swatters we had seen back at our hotel's gift shop. These animals were big and gangly but moved quickly away from our vehicle as we neared them. No doubt these animals had some sense of propriety and security because we never saw any fences that stopped them from wandering out of the preserve, onto adjoining pasture lands or local communities.

Kekorok Lodge where our accommodations were for the next four nights was delightful, rustic, exotic and most enjoyable. All the modern conveniences of hot showers, excellently prepared meals, gift shops, swimming pool, free public cultural lectures and happy hour bar were provided in tasteful style. Dinner the first night in the Masai Mara was scheduled for seven thirty. The dinner hour was set to accommodate enough time to reload into our vans and catch a glimpse of wild game in the park, before settling into our room and cleaning up.

I had booked us into a romantic, movie like safari tent but within seconds of Maia seeing it, that deal was off. As soon as our hotel escort led us about a hundred yards from the main lodge to a concrete slab with a tent on it, Maia was silent but eyes wide open. Our bellman unzipped the front of the tent revealing comfortable looking twin beds and a lot of curved stick bamboo and rattan furniture. Her eyes grew bigger and now the mouth opened too.

I was pleasantly surprised at the tents amenities and even thought the kerosene lanterns for night light was a great touch. By the time our bellman unzipped the rear exit of the tent though, and pointed to the outside bathroom, Maia's mouth began verbalizing all that she had been thinking. It was pretty evident that if I stayed here tonight, I would be alone.

It saddened me a little that Maia immediately headed for the main lodge and booked us into what she termed "more suitable" quarters for the duration of our stay. This time, our luggage was moved to a private duplex cottage just off the main lodge, beyond the swimming pool. The place didn't appear Kathryn Hepburn-Humphrey Bogart like, but it did look storybook and I must admit, was a lot more hospitable.

The cottage's Dutch door opened to reveal exquisite wood paneled cherry finished walls, a double, four poster canopy bed with an oversized, white mosquito net overhead. The room had two beautifully constructed his and her multiflowered over stuffed armchairs of matching print with the drapes. Between the two chairs was a Victorian silver tea serving set with an assortment of fine teas atop a Queen Anne table. Instead of a straw rug like in the tent, this one was a thick broad Turkish Byzantine pattern. The room looked as though it had come from a gentlemen's hunting quarterly.

We dropped our bags, freshened up about fifteen minutes, reloaded into our stripped van and in quick order with others following, headed out to watch our first "kill". The roof of our van had a canvas top that pulled back so each of us on the tour could stand in the vehicle with our arms shoulders and heads sticking through the roof. Just seeing Maia sticking her head through the roof like that, knowing we were in the middle of Africa and seeing her honey blonde hair blowing in the breeze was enough to melt me away.

The only obstructions to our close personal views of wild animals in the park were by other tour-ists heads and vans in front of us. From one spot to another, all our vans raced over the grasslands to other locations as drivers conversed with each other via walkie-talkie. We heard, "Water buffalo spotted near the brush to your right", "Wildebeest to your left," "Cats just ahead".

Finally, we settled in to a hushed silence in a high grassed field, where most of the animal colored tourist vans had turned off their motors and rolled gently in unison into a parallel parking lot. Our invasion force was there to watch the big cats move in on their water buffalo dinner; a tasty thing to watch just before your own.

This evening just after six o'clock, approximately two hundred yards from the front of Kekorok Lodge's entry was our big sighting of "cats". Tourists and guides alike were now communicating in hushed tones as we watched the barely visible lions' manes creep through the high grasses, nearer and nearer the water buffalo. Suddenly, all twelve to fifteen lions lunged toward the water buffalo as they systematically tried to peel the weaker and younger ones away from their adult protectors. Several cats roared and circled the bigger animals keeping them busy while the other cats closed in on the ones they had selected for dinner.

As rapidly as they had lunged, the hunt was over. As if a bell rang and the hired actor lions were returned to their corners, the hunt halted. The water buffalo went in one direction and the cats in the other. No dinner at seven for these cats, maybe later they'd hunt again while we weren't stalking the stalkers.

We returned to the lodge and dined from a huge buffet, well plied with carcasses from our natural surrounding habitat, as well as the usual steaks, roast beef and chicken. It was good to be dining inside near the fireplace because night time in the Masai during March gets cold and damp. Even the monkeys playing pool side earlier had retreated to warmer refuges somewhere else where they could stay warm.

After dinner, the hotel manager announced that everyone should remember they were on a wild game preserve and the animals outside mostly stalk their prey during nighttime hours. "There are no fences to keep them away from the lodge, nor armed guards for individual protection, so please, once you have been escorted by a guard to your room." "Stay there".

That little speech was followed by a British accented gentleman guide coming to the front of the dining room, announcing that more than twenty lions, probably many of those we had seen earlier are now roaming the grounds of the lodge. "Please wait a short time before having our armed escorts take you all to your rooms." Maia was slightly alarmed but for me it was the same as most nights in Somalia where the humans stalked us after dark.

While other tourists stayed and smoked old stogie cigars by the fire and shopped for film and souvenirs from the gift shop, Maia and I got a guard to walk us from the main lodge to our bungalow, where I watched her intently disrobing while drawing her bath. Afterwards, she dabbed and wiped herself dry before sacheting over to her side of the canopy and striking a pose in her surprise uniform of the night; some not so lady like thong panties and a cheetah, sling shot bra. Following the day's safari and the night's jungle activity, came the lions' roar. For several hours, the cats continued playing their actors' role for the tourist. Round and round they went. To the front, side to side, and to the rear, the cats walked relentlessly around our accommodations, all the while continuing that God awful low toned growl.

Maia finally nudged me saying, "If we were still in that tent, I'll bet you wouldn't go out side to pee would you"? My response was, "The cat roars are probably surround sound tape recordings played nightly by the Lodge to give guests a more authentic feel of the safari experience. Now go to sleep.

For the next several days, we took two or three short safaris a day. The options were one in the morning before breakfast, one in the afternoon and another just before dark. These safari treks were within a boundless territory where roads meant nothing. Tourist vans ran at all angles through waist deep grasses and over hills and dells. Occasional patches of trees interrupted the landscape but more often than not, they stood alone amidst the far away morning or daytime mists. We'd spot a giraffe's silhouette munching from the top of a tree on a far away hillside, then head from point A to point B without any care of what we had to cross to get there. Once there, the narrative started, "Here we have an orphan giraffe, not because he is really, but because his type migrated to this reserve from yada yada yada.

While not bouncing through the lowlands on photographic hunts, we attended lectures by native Masai tribes men back at the lodge. One such lecturer was the very dark, very tall, very thin, sharp chisel featured man named John. He told us about his people, what their daily lives were like and who did what in the family.

John said, "Mama builds the huts and the boys and daddy take care of the cattle. The girls make the clothing and cook." John said "Masai are known for being very tall and slender and of course, exceptional hunters". He then said, "Traditionally, the Masai always wear their tribal color red, not as an accent piece, but every garment from head to toe is red."

It was not easy listening to John, not because his tribal accent was difficult to follow but be-cause he habitually twisted his elongated ear lobes. They were long enough to stretch around to the other side of his face, then hook onto the opposing ear. John explained that to get the ear lobe this large, an earring sized whole had to be pierced, and then made bigger throughout the years. First the size of a dime, then quarter, half dollar and eventually large enough to have a dessert plate pass through it.

I asked John whether he was ever fearful the lobes would get caught and pulled. He answered, "Only while hunting or running; at which times he usually wraps each lobe around its own ear, then puts little clips through to keep them in place.

The day following John's Masai tribal lecture, we, meaning Maia, I and the rest of the tourists from Kekorok Lodge visited John's village, where we toured their huts, sampled their food and watched colorful but monotonous dancing in which red clad men and women jumped up and down in sync with each other, face to face for long periods of time. These dark, tall, thin, people jumped up, down, higher then lower, then up, down, and higher, then lower again, again and again; over and over and over. The drum beat wasn't catchy either. It was as monotonous and without highlight as the dancing was.

The object of the whole athletic exhibition was to see which male and which female could jump the highest, the longest while remaining the most rigid. The Masai girls wore beautiful, elaborately beaded, disc shaped necklaces tightly bound around their necks. With each jump, the discs flapped up past their chins in front of their faces, then dropped again and again back below their necks to their breasts.

On the third day of our safari, we moved on to Tanzania where everything, vegetation, culture and wild game remained much the same, only a little farther south from the Equator, a little wetter, and a little colder.

Here in the Serengeti, the monkey and hippopotamus' populations tripled while being joined by herds of wild elephant.

While journeying through the outback, crossing from one country into the other; we came upon a worn down pyramid shaped, cement mile-marker standing about four feet tall. Our guide told us the wearing down of its concrete was due to elephants stopping to rub their butts as they passed through the brush.

Following our first five days in the Masai Mara and Serengeti, we traveled to the foot of Africa's highest mountain; the massive snow covered Mount Kilimanjaro where we actually spent no time at all. The region's never ending; cold misting rain had created huge mud bogs that made travel almost impossible. Animals were nearly invisible since most had migrated north, escaping the mountains winter. It was rainy and muddy at the bottom and severe cold and snowy further up. It truly amazed me though how much snow we saw on the equatorial 14,000 feet summit.

After returning to Nairobi and spending another night at the Hotel InterContinental, Maia flew back to Kuwait and I took the executive International Red Cross jet back to Mogadishu.

I could tell that Maia was more relaxed on her return trip because she was no longer carrying the money, just a few inexpensive souvenirs.

Though Maia looked rested, she was actually in the beginning stages of an allergic reaction to her immunization shots taken prior to departing Kuwait.

On my flight back to Somalia, my mind wasn't on the locals who would be shooting at me or trying to drag me from a vehicle, but rather mentally reviewing the largest feast I had ever indulged in. For me normally, food has little meaning except as substance for life or to squelch an occasional hunger pain. This was but one after effect of my head injury many years earlier, that I had been left with almost no sense of taste or smell. For me, green English peas taste little different than M&Ms.

The buffet layout at Kekorok Lodge in the Masai Mara was great but Carnivore's Restaurant in Nairobi had the most magnificent exotic game buffet that I had ever seen or tasted. At Carnivore's, there were huge chafing dishes of animal carcasses like monkey, gazelle, wildebeest, zebra, crocodile, water buffalo and many others that I didn't dare guess.

But other than being a visual treat, the whole thing was wasted on me. I ate fish and french fries.

By the time I returned to Somalia, the peace-keeping mission had begun faltering badly. The sit-uation had become increasingly dangerous for American and other nation's soldiers and aide workers. Even worse though, tensions were near boiling point between the locals themselves. Several international aide organization's food storage compounds had been raided and their workers taken captive. Some had even been killed.

Work wise, we at Disaster Recovery still had contracts and reason for remaining in Somalia, though Brown and Root had jerked their housing contract away from us. Our company had received the contract to design and build the camp for coalition Generals within the Embassy Compound walls. Fourteen portable buildings like the ones we used in Kuwait were shipped in and assembled within a large oval ring, much like circling up the wagons in the Old West. These General's quarters were attached to the rear of the main American Embassy building itself, which was being rebuilt by another contractor.

So the Generals wouldn't have to walk in shifting sand or mug if we were lucky enough for it to rain, we built sidewalks of wooden planks and bunkered up the undersides of the General's prefab buildings with sand bags. Aesthetically, the camp looked pretty good and the Generals and their staffs moved right in with great haste.

The noisy generators supplying electricity to the General's camp had to be silenced or at least muffled by building huge sandbagged walls, nearly surrounding each of them. Without those sand bags, the noise level would have been almost unbearable. Nightly, I and other senior staff members of Disaster Recovery took periodic readings from the generators so the Generals would never be inconvenienced by loss of lights or air conditioning.

Daily, safety warnings came down from Army head quarters within the compound for everyone to take great precaution at all times, in all places. This meant that Bastard Sonny and Jeremy would not be heading to the Atlantic Hotel bar again any time soon. The machismo of those two were in their eyes only. Continuously, they sat telling war stories and cleaning rifles all day, seldom venturing out into the wilds of Mogadishu where they could possibly get shot or axed by machete or bayonet.

My work continued unabated for another six weeks or more, running back and forth to the sea port, the air port, the war lord compounds and trips to far away towns like Bardera and Baidoa. My odds for having a bad event befall me were getting to be astronomical and my false sense of security in such a war torn place as Somalia finally came to an end.

One day, I was anxious to get to the sea port while my Marine shooters carried out their commit-ment to another duty. I left the Embassy Compound anyways and headed for the port alone. Just me and my five ton flat bed truck. On Market Street in the middle of Aideed territory, I ran into a roadblock. I had done everything correctly except take an armed escort with me. My windows were rolled up, my doors were locked and I was trying not to slow down unless I had to avoid a slow moving pedestrian.

That day, the market was teaming with locals and both sides of the street were packed as was the middle of the roadway. The locals were all carrying chickens or sacks of coal, or other items to barter because they had no legal currency. For me the situation became very tense, very fast. It was impossible to tell who was carrying a weapon or who wasn't.

Less than a mile from Embassy grounds, I began frantically searching for an escape route if it became necessary. Ahead, not more than a hundred yards was the rear of an American military convoy. They were separated from me by only a few overloaded taxis and about a hundred people lulling around. I had always felt safer with an armed escort, but didn't always take such precaution. On a day like this, there could be hell to pay.

I was sure I was close enough to the rear of the military convoy that I could tie in to the back of it. I continued moving at a snail's pace, trying to get closer and closer. With a lot of careful maneuvering, I was able to pull to the rear or their last Humvy, but unfortunately for me, it was dangerously poor timing.

The Somali locals had either carefully or spontaneously orchestrated an attack. The rear Humvy that was in front of me was the first to fall prey. Their rear seat M-60 gunner failed to open fire fast enough to save them. They were quickly over powered as the rear gunner sustained a crushing blow to the back of his neck by a thick, rounded stick. Who knows what the gunner was really thinking, maybe his reluctance or second guessing came from all those CNN televised reports of Marines killing local Somalis. This time, his delayed reaction had catastrophic consequences. Gangs of Somalis, many of them armed, drug him and two other soldiers from their vehicle and began beating them with everything from machetes to walking sticks. All I could see was blood every where. Momentarily, I too came under surprise attack and my vision and concentration became temporarily clouded by fear. What should I do next to save myself from the swelling numbers of local Somalis who were already descending on my truck?

There was no way for me to reverse my vehicle or exit to the rear. It appeared I would become their next victim. Most assuredly, bands of Somalis were now attacking the convoy's forward vehicles as well. My heart pounded so loudly my own ears could hear it. I quickly checked to make sure I was wearing a bullet proof vest that I didn't actually remember putting on. All I could picture was being dragged from my truck, laid on the road and sharp machetes slashing across every inch of my body. I was as scared as I had ever been in my life. A rush of adrenalin pumped through my veins as the inevitable began to happen. I was next.

The military convoy of lumber, tents, generators and other materials must have been too tempting for the local Somalis to pass up. Through the mass hysteria and attacking Somalis, I saw what I thought were several more of those overloaded taxis stopping to block the path of the six

Army vehicles that were trying desperately to escape. Other taxis began pulling along either side of the convoy, boxing it in. The whole ambush came within seconds but lasted many terrifying minutes. American soldiers were fighting for their lives and for control of their weapons and vehicles. Fortunately for me, the Somalis were less interested in me and my empty flatbed truck than the booty that lay ahead so they continued their full assault against the convoy.

Automatic gunfire rang out from several different directions. I couldn't tell if all of it was coming from the convoy itself or whether it was coming from nearby rooftops as well. I ducked slightly behind my steering wheel and continued trying to slowly run over anyone between me and that rear Humvy. My heartbeats soon drowned out the sounds of gunfire.

Within seconds, the swarm of people moved in my direction targeting me and my truck. A hard metal object began slamming against my driver's side window while simultaneously crucial blows were being delivered to my front window in several places.

Through one of the holes of my now shattered front windshield, I could see a blur of camouflage clothing jump on to my right passenger foot board. A soldier held a death grip to the door handle and my truck's side mirror. With great panic in the bleeding soldier's voice, he yelled and motioned with his rifle for me to move forward. I did with as much speed as I could. The Somalis, except for a few hangers on were reacting to the gunfire and were now running in all directions away from us. The rear Humvy had been abandoned and its mounted M-60 automatic weapon was now being controlled by the enemy. Timing could really prove deadly now. By the time some Somali figured out how to use the humvys gun, we'd either have to be out of there or dead.

Moments seemed like hours but my hitchhiking soldier and I were finally in the clear and heading toward the sea port. We finally spotted the rest of the ravaged military convoy ahead of us. It had also spotted us and halted momentarily to allow the soldier hanging on to my right cab to climb over to one of his own. They hollered for me to follow them but in the turmoil of the moment, they apparently didn't notice I still had problems of my own. Someone had his hands around my throat and I was getting banged in the jaw.

A Somali had broken the glass on the driver's side window and had reached both his arms inside. Momentarily, his grip released from my throat only to grab at the steering wheel. I fought violently to tear his hands away and to shove him off the truck's running board. I couldn't. He again turned to fight me and began ripping at my ear. This time, I did the only thing I thought would save me. I allowed him to gain some control over the steering wheel and assisted him in turning the wheel toward himself. The front side of my truck impacted with another oncoming truck; metal against metal, truck against truck; wiping out the guy. So I thought.

Another block or so away, while rapidly moving toward the safety of the sea port, I heard screams of pain. They were coming from my trucks flatbed just behind the cab. I couldn't see who was there but I didn't have to make many guesses. My final attacker was badly injured and crying for help, but help wasn't going to come from me. I speeded up and drove erratically, trying to bump him off. I even made several vain attempts at hitting big potholes as well as going off the road to throw him from the truck's bed. Nothing seemed to work. I soon entered the sea port's main gates with the injured man still aboard.

The bloodied and wounded military convoy barely made it through the port's gate before me. Guards waved them through, and following a quick judgmental call, me too. As our vehicles came closer to the side of the Army hospital tent, military personnel came running from all directions to help us. Some assisted what remained of the other six convoy vehicles while others proceeded in my direction. People from the tent and nearby began helping the wounded soldiers out of their vehicles and moving them toward the hospital tent's side entry.

I told the first few who reached me that I was carrying a Somali in the back that had attacked me. It was obvious the market attack on the convoy had been fairly serious. While giving all of us first aid, the rest of those present began inquiring as to whether anyone had been left behind and yet a few more removed the Somali from the back of my truck.

The dented side of my truck and the broken out windows told a lot of my personal story as did the blood splatters and scrapes along the driver's side door.

I supposed my attacker had been moved to another section of the port's hospital but I never asked. The Somali's condition, or whereabouts never came up again and I didn't care. My injuries appeared worse than they really were. I was quite bloody and bruised but not seriously injured. A few stitches to the lower ear and lobe where they're attached to the face and I was fine. Some of the convoy's troops weren't as lucky. Two were unconscious and others were bloody and obviously in pain.

For several hours following the attack, about twenty of us sat around outside the hospital tent, talking and checking on the wounded soldiers as they came from being treated. Everyone voiced the same opinions; mob mentality had taken over and once the sharks began attacking, everyone wanted their piece of the prey. We were still unable to rationalize how the Somalis could do this to the same people who came to help them? We asked ourselves what rationale dictated that temporary loot and bounty was better for them than long lasting food and assistance?

Though we sat rationalizing, we also knew that none of us had ever been in such desperate circumstances that resembled anything like what the Somalis had endured over the past half decade of internal war. Even after all that happened to us, we had a hard time really blaming the average Somali citizen. We did however have plenty of words against their War Lords of whom we were filling their cash tills.

Strangely enough, I still felt more empathy toward the Somali people than I did toward the Kuwaitis, around whom I'd lived for considerably more years. Kuwaitis are egotistical, brutal and viciously into power games. They rape, murder and steal with impunity; yet they have all that money can buy.

Sure we knew that there were plenty of Somali men and women like those who attacked us in the streets, and we also knew there were equally as many Somalis like those working for us on the docks and at camp who were good people trying to exist through extremely hard times. At both our work sites, it was these people who were always smiling and singing. The same song no less, but always singing.

One day I asked several laborers what was that melodic but monotonous tune they sang from early morning to mid afternoon every day. They replied "I don't want to work any more, I don't like to work. I don't want to work any more, I don't like to work; again and again and again. The melodic but repetitive way they sang the song made it sound much more pleasant than the English translation.

CHAPTER 23

Staged for a Kidnapping

Bob, our company's main man in Kuwait and Somalia made frequent trips between our Marr Bell office and our Disaster Recovery office in Mogadishu, each time creating and leaving behind little fire storms that had to be put out by surviving members of the team. Bob just happened to be in Somalia when my truck and I got attacked and his reply was simple, everyone, the soldiers and me made mountains out of molehills. He said, "One of those f—Somalis gets in your way, just knock the shit out of him, or run over him, damn it, get on with your business".

Of course, Bob, like me, always wore a bullet proof vest. Unlike me, he seldom left camp and never without shooters with him. Before Bob left the last time, he ended up creating another very volatile situation by trying to maximize the company's profits. He decided to make only a few partial payments to Osman Atto for those truck rentals I negotiated. Of the ninety five thousand dollars, he drug the payments out for months then suddenly decided not to pay any more at all.

I told Bob that could be a big mistake but his reply was only "Fuck that war lord, let him come after me". I reminded Bob it would be me they would come after. Once again Bob laughed and said "that's very dramatic Chuck". He however did decide to meet with Osman Atto one final time to clear up the matter.

Obviously the meeting didn't go well because Bob came back to camp, said not to pay them another f—cent, then without telling a soul, he boarded the next available aircraft back to Kuwait. He left me like a sitting duck. It was Osman Atto who sent word for me to come to him again. At that meeting he was very adamant that as the financial man to Clan leader Mohamed Farah Aideed, it was his head that would roll if the money was not paid. He requested urgently that I make the Marr Bell office in Kuwait well aware of the importance of the final balance of almost forty thousand dollars. At my next meeting with Osman Atto, I didn't tell him that Bob's latest words on the telephone to me from his comfortable desk back in Kuwait were, "Chuck, go over there and tell that son of a bitch we're not going to pay him another damn dime."

Several days and weeks passed with Bob absent from Somalia and the War Lord Aideed demand for the money kept getting louder. Bob finally decided to come back to Somalia to clear the matter up once again by trying to renegotiate the entire agreement. He had learned something from the Kuwaitis. He was telling me and Osman Atto that the trucks had cost too much and should have been negotiated for a much lower price. Atto reminded Bob that his trucks were the only ones in the country and that the more than thirty, eighteen wheel flatbeds running between the storage facilities and the sea port for at least eighteen hours a day round trip for more than a week was a good deal.

By the time Bob had returned to Somalia this time, I had spent twenty evenings or more with Osman Atto, mostly at his secured compound. At least half of these dinner dates were spent trying to placate Atto's demands. The strain between Osman Atto and me grew more evident at each meeting. Toward the end, I was back to never approaching Atto's compound unless I was with a full compliment of well armed United States Marine escorts. On almost every occasion, the walls of his compound were ringed with snipers while I beefed up my escort to no less than six vehicles. Still Bob played his game of one upmanship.

For Bob, this stunt of non payment or reneging on a deal was no different than those he had pulled with Royal Ordinance or other clients. But before, he'd always gotten away with them. This time, I knew he was dealing with someone a lot more dangerous. To Bob, it was all still a "profit/loss" game.

Cut Throat George at the sea port didn't like the way Bob treated him either and often jokingly said "one day I kill him." If he was waiting for me to say no, he shouldn't, he wouldn't hear those words from me. In fact, I went so far as to line Bob up for George to kill. Kidnappings and even executions were not unheard of in such an anarchist land as Somalia and Bob should have remembered that. Here, everyone plays for keeps.

Bob's arrogance and lack of concern for my safety put me in a state of anger so much so that I told Cut Throat I wanted him to kill Bob at the port if possible, but if he would rather do it elsewhere, I'd help get him there. Without hesitation, George wanted to do it that same afternoon. Now things were really stacked against Bob and he couldn't see it. Cut Throat George from the Mahdi Clan at the sea port hated him and wanted to kill him and Osman Atto and Mohamed Farah Aideed wanted to settle the score.

Several hours later, Bob was sitting with me in the cab of one of our trucks at the sea port and I told him I could have him killed. He said "sure Chuck, you're so full of shit" "You're not that kind of guy". That was my only warning to him. I really wanted it done and the sooner the better.

About four o'clock that afternoon, Cut Throat came to me and said he would do it soon but I convinced him to wait another day or so. I didn't really have cold feet but I really didn't want to be the one to line Bob up. If Cut Throat went ahead on his own, I would have been fine with it. I just didn't want it to be at my command.

By the time I got back to camp at the Embassy Compound, Bob had unexpectedly gone to the airport and caught an early flight out. Of course, to this day he would say he left as scheduled but he and I both know the real truth. He left me in harms way to face the mess he couldn't stand up to.

One day, Cut Throat who was a rival of the Aideed, Osman Atto Clan said, "papa, Osman Atto goin da kidnap you for da money". I asked where he heard that. Had he heard it from one of Atto's men? He just said, "Papa maybe you get killed".

His warning was not lost on me. How could Cut Throat from the opposing Mahdi Clan hear such a warning? The sea port and the airport as well as the Embassy Compound were separated by warring clans and neither side nor their people spoke casually to each other. Later that same day at the airport, yet another warning was passed to me. This time by another Somali from War Lord Aideed's own clan.

I immediately hurried back to camp and packed my clothes. I was going to get out of Somalia too. I was so angry at Bob and these new threats that I jumped into one of our small six pack Toyota trucks and headed straight to Osman Atto's compound without armed escort. I literally stormed the gates as a one man army. His men knew me so well they tried to head me off but never got rough with me. They just kept saying "papa, Mr. Osman sleeping, he talk with you later." I told them I didn't give a damn that he was sleeping; I demand to see him now. They never let me get through the courtyard near his front door, so I requested a piece of paper that I could write a message to him.

Dear Osman,

Twice today people told me you were going to kidnap me because Bob would not pay you the the money he owes you. I want you to know what I'm planning and the position you and Bob have put me in. I have taken precautions to exit this country. I called my brother in

America and told him all the information he needs to know about your children and their school in Glasgow, New Jersey. My brother can be a bad man like Mr. Bob and I have in—structed him to get your children. Their safety is now tied to mine. Shortly after you read

This, I will be in Mombasa, Kenya emptying your bank account if possible. If anything happens to me, you will have your own hell to pay.

Mr. Chuck

During the many evenings Osman Atto and I spent together, I learned all about his children, wife and where they had homes outside Somalia. Once, he gave me his bank account numbers in Mombasa and requested me to put the money into his account while I was at our field office there. I used these pieces of knowledge as the only leverage I had. I wasn't bluffing.

It wasn't an hour before Osman Atto came to the front gates of the American Embassy Compound. His unannounced arrival caused quite a stir amongst the Italian, Turkish and Pakistani troops guarding the main gate. As his motorcade of vehicles, the local Somalis call them "technicals" (their version of our Army humvys with mounted machine guns) approached our Grounds the Turkish soldiers across the street from our Embassy Compound thought they were coming to attack and opened fire. Quite a few volleys of bullets were in the air before the real purpose of his arrival was made clear. From my room, I heard the rapid gunfire out front but never associated it with anything to do with me.

Minutes later, an Italian guard came to our office just inside the American Embassy Compound walls and said a War Lord or somebody was out front and wanted to speak to me. I told him to frisk him like any other Somali entering our gates, and then send just him to our office, alone. Soon Osman Atto was standing before me with several Italian guards at his side. I told them to wait outside while we spoke.

Osman looked worried and timid; though I'm sure it was an act to win me over again. His first words were "papa, you made a mistake, I would never harm you. My fight is with Bob. You are my friend and we have been like brothers. Believe me I will never harm you." I replied back to Osman. I don't know who or what to trust right now and the best thing for me was to leave the country. I expressed my hope that either his Clan or the Mahdi Clan would kill Bob if he ever returned to Somalia but I wasn't going to wait around to see it happen.

I told Osman that I wanted to leave the embassy compound much like our office manager Donald had done the day snipers from across the road were shooting at us. I wanted to leave in the back of a heavy duty dump truck, with or without his "technicals" providing my safety en route. Here was his opportunity to get me if he wanted to but his children could soon be in the hands of my brother. I knew Osman didn't have satellite telephone link ups like we did, so there was no way he could find out about his children's safety for quite some time. He was worried and I could see it and feel it. At this meeting, he never spoke of the bank accounts but concluded by saying whatever I wanted would be done; and it was.

Some of our workers lowered my foot locker and suitcase into the rear of a big, steel dump truck and the vehicle departed the embassy compound gates. No other American was with me on that final trip, just one of our TCN, third country national drivers. Not once did I ever look over the top edge to see who or what was guarding my safety, if anyone; but there were no incidences of any type en route to the air port.

Stevie, one of Marr Bell's original three project managers arrived in Mogadishu and began crying and bitching there, much like he had done on Failaka Island back in Kuwait. Again the company sent this "vaginally whipped" guy someplace he was unprepared to go and his frail mental health kept him within compound walls at all times. His misery brought misery to others but for some reason Marr Bell seemed to feel they owed him something.

Just a few hours before my departure, I found out Stevie had sold all the food we had been given to distribute to our hired Somali laborers. When an American Army Company was returning Stateside, they gave one of our project managers Bill a truck and a half load of food supplies, can goods of all kinds, sugar, rice, tea, coffee and many other items that Bill and I personally loaded and stored and had started passing out to our laborers each day. They would always be taking food home as well as the money we paid them.

Stevie sold the supplies to another contractor within embassy walls. What he did with the money was unimportant. Whether he pocketed it for himself or gave it to Disaster Recovery didn't matter. He had no right morally or financially to do it. On the way to the airport, I cursed his family and hoped one day they would know true need for such items; my way of hoping "the sins of the father would be passed on to his sons".

I felt the big dump truck come to a brief halt before moving once again, we had now entered the airport's security front gates and was moving toward the terminal. The only affirmation to my location was hearing two guards speaking to one another as one climbed up and then the other peered over into the dump truck's bed to look down at me. Within two hours, I was once again aboard the International Red Cross executive jet headed to Nairobi, then Kuwait.

It turns out that I did get out just in the nick of time. If I thought conditions were bad while I was in Somalia, later, I would probably have lost my life.

In quick order, twenty four peacekeepers were killed and more than fifty were wounded. Either in retaliation or in error, some Pakistani Blue Helmet peace keepers thought they were being attacked, opened fire on the locals and killed about twenty. A week later the United States began conducting aerial raids against Somali weapon caches of both Clans and about twenty more locals were killed.

A month later, on and on and on: an American helicopter assault on War Lord Mahdi's stronghold killed fifty Somalis, a land mine killed four Americans, one American Black Hawk helicopter was shot down, and then Army rangers came to assist and were surrounded. Two more American helicopter gun ships were shot down in the attempted rescue in which the battle lasted ten long hours. Twelve American soldiers died and seventy more were wounded in that fabled clash.

The barbarism of that Black Hawk attack worsened as Somalis mutilated and dragged some of our United States' soldier's nude, bloodied bodies through the streets while throngs of civilians continued chopping and assaulting them.

After leaving Somalia, I tried to distance myself from as much of it as I could, however, I heard a few months later that my friend Aideed's men kidnapped 20 more UN relief workers and a journalist, then killed four other foreign journalist. Another surprise came when I was notified that Osman Atto had joined the opposition and killed his former boss Aideed. Now, Osman Atto himself is War Lord.

After Atto killed former war lord Aideed, Aideed's son who had been sent to Somalia as a United States Marine interpreter, stepped into his dead father's shoes and became the new opposing War Lord against Osman Otto. With Aideed's son's succession, came a new United States Marine saying, "The Marines in Somalia have a "Corporal to Dictator" program".

The only other thing I heard of passing interest about Somalia after leaving it was when three million dollars was missing from a safe inside the United Nations offices in Mogadishu. There was a familiar ring to the sound of that. Bob and I often frequented "said office" and it was he who continually talked about having to have a load of cash on hand as cash flow. He envisioned a scheme for aid organizations, foreign contractors and military business that needed money and necessities inside Somalia. I had on several occasions been to meet with Neil Reese-Evans, UNISOM's Chief Civilian Personnel Manager, and then went over to that same office where the money was kept. Once, Bob was with me. Often the safe was open and the money was in full view of anyone just coming in from other rooms. Not only was the safe a sorry excuse for it's own name but that office's door could be opened by little more than a linebacker pushing up against it. A simple credit card was but one other way to access approximately three million dollars of wrapped hundred dollar bills that got replenished into that safe each month.

Bob's bank never came into being, but he spoke of it often and how it would be great to have a secured bank within Embassy walls. I seriously never thought Bob would pull off such a stunt as robbing the UN offices, but he was full of surprises and had a bold crudeness about him. I felt anything was possible.

After fleeing for my life and getting to Mogadishu's Airport in one piece, I instructed my rescuing Lear jet's pilot to make a slight detour to Mombasa, Kenya. There I was going to attempt to empty the War Lord's account; after all, I was the one who had all those correct account numbers from the times I made his numerous deposits. Bank personnel knew me for what I had been doing but it was still unclear as to whether they would allow me to make the money go in the opposite direction. On several occasions I had taken money straight to Ossman Atto and other times only a portion of it went to Somalia while the rest went into the Mombasa accounts. Other times our company man Kitts delivered it.

With all the balls I could muster, I appeared before a bank officer and requested paperwork to put the money withdrawal in motion. From official to official I went back and around. I stayed calm and decisive and at no time did I think they thought I was putting one over on them. My efforts were unsuccessful however, for whatever reasons, but at least I tried.

A couple hours after the failed attempt, I landed safety at Moi International Airport again. En route, I made a telephone call to Maia at Marr Bell's office in Kuwait asking her to meet me in Cairo for a holiday. Following our landing in Nairobi, the International Red Cross jet pulled into a much smaller private terminal about a half mile from the other passenger terminals. Immigration was quicker and easier and totally accomplished within thirty minutes. I then headed for the Hotel InterContinental.

Business at the Marr Bell office in Kuwait was slow so Donald gave Maia a week off. Three days later, Maia and I met at the airport in Cairo, Egypt. We had been to Cairo several times before and had always enjoyed ourselves. They say "You either hate Cairo or you love it". We love it and could never get enough of it. Two of our friends had been posted as Ambassadors to Egypt. Margaret Scooby was a former friend in Kuwait and is now Madam Ambassador to Egypt.

Cairo is crowded, a little dirty, a lot noisy, quite exciting, very exotic and probably one of the best locations on earth to feel vibrant and alive within a culture that has lured travelers for thousands of years. Cairo has everything, good food, inexpensive clubs, gambling, great shopping, the pyramids, ancient Biblical locations, museums, palaces, crypts, and on and on. We'd done most of the other touristy things on previous trips to Egypt, so this time I surprised Maia by arranging a cruise on the Nile. First though, I booked us into a different hotel than we had ever stayed before. In the past with my Kuwaiti Royal hosts, I had always come to massive, opulent, private residences or to former Palaces now converted for State visitors into lodges. Together, Maia and I had stayed at a mid-city former palace of King Farouk's which is now a museum and a hotel, but this time I wanted something even more special than that.

The spectacular Mena House Oberoi had been built as a Royal hunting lodge in the mid 1800's by an Egyptian King. Its location was too far from mid city shopping areas or museums to walk but had more history than all the other places we had stayed in previously. The new Oberoi, at the foot of the great pyramids of Giza is young in the eyes of the thousands of years old structures that surround it, yet its not so immodest past has come to make it one of the great destinations of the affluent traveler of today. Since the 1860's, the Mena House Oberoi's guest list has included the world's most powerful, most learned and most moneyed clientele on earth.

Located right at the base of a short, steep plateau rise where the Sphinx and the great pyramids of Giza stand, few places on earth can classify the soil on which they sit more historically significant to mankind than the Mena House Oberoi. Its exclusivity, charm nor romance can adequately be ingested through literature alone. I wanted Maia and me to experience our stay there as well as its three thousand five hundred year old neighbors. First we had to arrive.

My plane from Nairobi, Kenya was early to land at Cairo's International Airport and Maia's was late so plan B went into effect. Maia and I would now meet at the hotel instead of the airport. I preceded her to the hotel, got checked in and situated in our suite, had a drink at the bar and waited while peering through my ice cubes toward the lobby as each new guest arrived. Our suite's superb appointments were in grand proportions. Not unlike the palaces of Saudi Arabia or Kuwait where oil money dictates extravagance, but inside Mena House Oberoi there's also an understated taste that replaces oil garishness.

There are flowing marble floors partially covered by exquisite Persian carpets, priceless anti-quities every where, and fourteenth century, dark, carved wood, arabesque windows inlaid with Moorish mushrabiya panels. The hotel's architecture accentuates its one of a kind Pharaoh's view from sweeping terraces. The personal touch comes with your own valet who calls you by name. How strange it seems that these things are less than three countries and barely a thousand miles away from Somalia but worlds apart from its chaos, blood letting and sniper fire.

In a few days Maia and I would sail the Nile but tonight amongst all this splendor, we'd dress formally, dine by candle light and sit at the piano bar looking toward the great pyramids of Giza, bathing in the Saharan night glow.

When one stays at the Mena House Oberoi, you're following in the steps of Sultans, Kings, Emperors and Presidents, and you feel it.

Our first full day back in Egypt together was spent sleeping in late, admiring and exploring res-toration work at the Sphinx and taking a camel ride over to the Great Pyramids of Giza. Later in the day, we mixed into Cairo's modern culture by emerging ourselves on traffic laden bridges spanning the Nile and down ancient city streets now crowded with throngs of turban and burkha clad pedestrians, pan handlers selling paintings of Cleopatra on papyrus, and the smells of spices, coffee's and roasting chestnuts and meat on the spit. There was no shortage of dancing bears, a gazillion taxis and cars; all blowing their horns while competing for the same traffic lanes.

Maia and I have always found Cairo a safe city and have never had any reason to feel differently. The only time a bad thing ever happened to me was once when I caught a man trying to pick my wallet from my back pocket. He apologized for more than five minutes. I had to threaten him with bodily harm if he didn't quit apologizing and get away from me.

As daylight became dusk, Maia and I departed the eight hundred years old bizarre district of Khan Khalili and had gotten as far as the hotel district of the Shepherd and the Hilton near the Nile. Some celebrating sounds of drums and women's tongue wailing lured us closer until we came upon a crowd surrounding a young couple who had just gotten married. In the Arab tradition, their wedding party had moved from indoors to the outside. In Egypt especially, it's a customary way of allowing passers by to join in the celebration of the bride and groom. The bride and groom gather around a band for the reception indoors, and then move with their band and all guests to dance out doors beside the street.

Many other people besides Maia and I gathered to listen to their small wandering minstrel of two Arabic drums, a flute making a duck quacking sound and a tambourine. The bride and groom danced with other well wishers while friends of the couple passed the hat around for money contributions.

This bride was dressed in full western style white bridal gown with lots of crinolines but her counterpart, the husband, wore no tuxedo, just a plain three piece suit with Turkish style fez atop his head. Crowds continually sounded their approval by applauding and occasionally some women brought their hands to their mouths and sung out the customary Lu lu lu lu lu lu lu.

While winding down our evening in a one horse carriage, Maia had an idea that while in Egypt, we should get married again Egyptian style. Later that evening, with a few toddies to the wind, the new plan became more and more involved. Before we knew it, we were planning a full scale, ship board wedding on the Nile. For the next full day until our ship sailed, both of us would shop for everything needed; wardrobe, presents for those standing up with us and lots of wedding paraphernalia to take aboard ship with us.

Our second morning in Cairo was leisurely passed by breakfast in bed, before dressing in casual clothing and heading to the tall "Cairo Tower" mid city for lunch. The revolving restaurant sits high atop a columned elevator, on a small island right in the middle of the Nile River, in the middle of down town Cairo. It's not that the food is so great up there, but the vistas alone are worth the inexpensive meal tickets.

From atop the Cairo Tower, you eat as the restaurant revolves. For a mere ten dollars, you dine on Beef Wellington and wine, see cruise ships and sail boats along the Nile, congested traffic on the streets below, several forty story apartment buildings of Mahdi in the distance, and an incomparable panorama of the desolate Sahara Desert on a horizon studded with the silhouettes of the pyramids of Giza and Memphis.

It was during this luncheon atop the Cairo Tower that we remembered an Egyptian friend of ours in Kuwait, Moussa Gouda who told us about another palace that had partially been turned into a hotel, and that his cousin Talal worked there. We'd look him up and get a few traditional wedding pointers from him.

Fortunately for us, Talal still worked at the Manial Palace and his boss was insistent that we make use of him on a shopping spree, though he was well aware we were not staying at his hotel. The hotel manager also called his lady friend to assist Maia that afternoon and they too were off to shop.

Moussa's cousin Talal could have been his brother in looks. They were both slender in build, dark black hair, olive complexion, both mustached, and both dressed immaculately with the same taste in clothing. Talal would be a good choice in helping me select traditional costuming for our wedding.

Neither Maia nor I saw much of our hotel that day. We stayed busy with our new companions preparing for the big event. Talal and I went to many shops toward the entrance of the Khan Khalili again, one of the world's oldest shopping malls in continuous use. The whole place was covered in wall to wall people, elbow to elbow with hardly any room for parcels in our hands. I think he said it was from the year 600 AD or six hundred years old, I really didn't understand which.

Talal complimented me on my Khaki "safari look" of tan epaulet shirt; multi pocketed pants and banana republic, "Indiana Jones vest", but said it would have to go for at least a few hours on the day of mine and Maia's remarriage.

That night, Maia and I dined with our new friends at our side, and then bade our host's good bye with promises of at least a short visit with them following the cruise.

Our cruise ship had just been newly outfitted by its new owners, Sheraton Hotels. The five hun-dred feet long ATON boasts all cabins as luxurious suites, and unsurpassed pampering. Maia and I had our own individual valets here too. For the true jet setter, there was also access to a business center with a secretary and a complete communications facility. All suites aboard the ATON dwarfed suites I'd seen on any of the ships I had worked on during my youth.

Our stateroom was on Tutankhamen deck where every picture, every wall mural and even the chairs and commode tables resembled artifacts recovered from the ancient boy king's tomb. Our private outside terrace came with Egyptian urns with swaying palm trees and blooming flowers. Best of all though was the ever changing view of the dark soiled, fertile Nile Delta shore line that was over shadowed by the creeping, barren, orange Sahara Desert that loomed in the distance.

Throughout the ship, the ancient Egyptian motif was used on everything from the elegant stem ware to the carpets we walked on. Glass Art Deco style light shades reflected brilliant etchings of ancient chariots and the ships gift shop was loaded with dainty Egyptian perfume bottles, vases and colorful jewelry engraved with hieroglyphics and 22k gold cartouches.

As we sailed from Cairo southward, we passed the busy metropolitan city center of Cairo, and then continued along the lush shoreline through the suburb of Mahdi and its towering, glass, high rise condominiums and beyond. Barely out from suburban Cairo, we passed several small, fertile, Nile Delta farming communities before nearing the ancient city of Memphis. From the ship's top deck, we could see the numerous pyramids of Memphis straining upward, as if to make sure we could catch at least a small glimpse of them and pay respect to their greatness like we had already done to their relatives at Giza.

Maia and I swore we had never seen a greener place on earth than the Nile Delta. Its rich coal black soil supported multitudes of elegant dark green date palm trees that slightly waved in Egypt's late season tropical breezes.

We began to see what had been part of that exotic, ancient Egypt that was more than just a past civilization to us but a real vibrant new one as well. From the ATON, we could see yet another of Egypt's contradictions, it's delicate balances in both human and agricultural terms; the extremes of new and old, rich and poor, the contradictions of fertile and arid, tranquility and urgency and they were all being presented to us at one glance. If I couldn't get some rest and relaxation here, then I couldn't get it any where.

Maia had brought two of my tuxedos to Cairo in case we decided to dress in the evenings as we usually do on vacations. She brought my white one and a black one, both of which would come in even handier now that we're vacationing aboard such an elegant vessel.

That night Maia's platinum blonde hair and Scandinavian features were stunning as she strutted her stuff in a three quarters multitier black gown. I was uncomfortable however, that she also brought along much of her 22 Karat gold bangles, earrings, sunburst pin and necklaces, and other jewelry items purchased since we'd been living in Kuwait. We're still almost neuvo riche and I can't bare the thought she'd ever loose any of it.

What else can a guy say about his clothes, other than I didn't wear white socks with my tux; I looked pretty good and felt pretty good.

As expected, dinner that evening was a European Arabic buffet served from silver chafing dishes amongst columns and murals of Cleopatra, Nefertiti and other ancients I couldn't name. As beautiful as the night was, it wasn't so different from that night about twenty years earlier when I met Maia for the first time aboard the M. S. Sun Viking in the Caribbean.

Back then, I was an Assistant Cruise Director out of the Port of Miami, Florida. Maia was a pas-senger with her recently widowed mother, and we were brought together on the dance floor. Tonight we'd dance again.

Even lazily floating down the Nile, cruises are not all love making and relaxation. The next morning was busy with the beginning of our daily tours. Maia and I scurried ashore with the other passengers to visit ancient ruins and try piecing together how all of this ancient stuff really fit together; which came before what and which was Upper Egypt and which was Lower Egypt. Was it before Cleopatra and after the great pyramids or before the Valley of Kings and Queens or after all of them?

About two and a half hours prior to departing our first stop, I decided to make use of the ships wonderful library and brush up a little on what came in which time period, and when and what we would be seeing next. The spacious reading room was very gentlemanly in appearance and well appointed with the exact literature I needed. I sat back in one of the high backed chairs, pulled up an ottoman and began to read. It would have been hard to please me more but my valet did. He found me reading and since I don't smoke, brought me a very large glass of ice tea, and with a little information most likely provided by Maia, also brought me several Hershey bars. That was enough to make me content, at least until time to dress for dinner that night.

If someone can say they spent a comfortable evening in tux and gown, we did. That evening was especially pleasant, enjoying the company of several new friends at the piano bar before turning in. The next morning, we met them again for breakfast and of course the buzz of the table was mine and Maia's forthcoming second nuptials. Our remarriage was now just hours ahead.

While still dining, our ship docked in the new city of Luxor, which surrounds the ancient city of Thebes where Cleopatra spent much of her reign. Most tourists from our ship and the other three in port were moving down the gangways into waiting taxis for the morning's tours. Maia and I had a lot to do. Many of our new friends said hopefully they would join us later for the wedding if their lunch hour cooperated. Maia and I waved good bye as they boarded their buses and taxis for the Valley of Kings, Hatshepsut's Palace and city of Luxor. We both had much to do.

To my surprise, I watched through the corner of my eye as an Italian movie company filmed an historical documentary. Of course I didn't know at the time, but they were wrapping up their final scenes. I was like a small child with sugar plums dancing in my head as I spotted their replica long Royal Barge.

Cleopatra herself would have taken pride in calling that vessel her own. It was the most fan-tastic elegant, sleek, beauty I'd ever seen. Bells went off in this crazy mind of mine and I thought, why not? What if we could get married aboard it?

No deal, the film maker in charge had already left for Rome and the remaining crew was wrapping things up so to speak. It would be impossible. They had no authority to allow the Royal Barge to be used for anything other than its original purpose. They graciously refused my offer to rent it for a couple of hours, but wished me well and bid me farewell.

Along with my indispensable ship valet, I headed into the city to hire a horse drawn carriage, a Coptic Christian Minister who would marry us, (not legally again of course), and to get some idea of what the site we had chosen actually looked like.

Everything done, Maia and I ate light lunches and began readying ourselves. Several ships' staff members, who usually take their time in Luxor to rest away from passengers, spent their time instead with the two of us trying to make our day unforgettable. About 12:30 pm, we were ready to disembark.

I exited the ship first and went straight from the gangway to the carriage where I awaited Maia. Her several cruise staff Ladies in Waiting made a real grand exit for her. They carried her flowers, veil and a small purse to the carriage, giggling all the while carefully helping to gather her gown and pushing it into the carriage behind her. I of course stood out of the way except to provide her with a gentleman's hand.

Maia's crème colored, satin gown with lace and caviar pearl bodice, billowed in the noon time breeze. She nervously clutched six white roses with matching ribbons, which she soon laid across her lap.

I felt pretty regal myself. I looked a little more traditional Egyptian than Maia, as men in Egypt tend to do more than their brides. I wore my white tuxedo shirt beneath something reminiscent of an Indian Nehru jacket from the nineteen sixties, not Indian of course, but in looks only. My groomsman wrapped my waist in a chic sash that corresponded to the colors of Maia's gown. My head was then topped with a burgundy colored fez, a very special gift from Moussa Gouda's cousin Talal. Talal had proudly given it to me only moments before we parted his hotel in Cairo, the day we went shopping together.

I couldn't say enough about the Fez. It was beautiful, dark burgundy cashmere, eight inches tall and sat much like an inverted flower pot atop my head. The fez' flat top had a button in the center from which a tassel hung down the side. The tassel was barely similar to those worn for graduation in that it was thicker, more intricately designed and far more expensive. It was made of twisted gold and burgundy braid. The fez was quite handsome and I wore it with pride.

Maia and I rode in our separate one horse carriages slowly through the streets of new Luxor, then to the edge of ancient Thebes where we would disembark. This was Cleopatra's southern capital, the Capital of Ramses, the boy King Tutankhamen and many others who reigned in unprecedented splendor for more than three thousand years. Much of their city still stands.

Maia's carriage and entourage followed closely behind mine. In eager anticipation of the event, Maia fidgeted with her roses and white silk ribbons while I savored the spectacle we were making and the throngs of people watching, applauding or shouting their best wishes as we passed.

There was neither a way nor the time to inhale the beauty of Thebes' ancient but gargantuan sized buildings, and columned edifices that now loomed above and before us. My eyes first glanced the wide pedestrian walk that lay before us, lined by carved stone lions guarding both sides of the entry of ancient Royal Thebes. How many ancient Royal parades had passed beneath these columns? Cleopatra and the others had many times seen what I was now seeing. Far away walkways all concluded into one ornately chiseled archway more than twenty feet high, where only Royals and their servants were allowed to pass.

Even further back and well within the "Royals only", courts was one of the few remaining tall, hand carved, obalisque of the ancient world. It's said that Cleopatra had it gold plated but through the years it has eroded and become the color of regular limestone again.

Within these surroundings and just outside the very entrance to Karnack Temple where Pharaohs and their queens, Cleopatra and Julius Caesar, Mark Anthony and Moses long ago stood, Maia and I stepped from our carriages. The Temple of Karnack was once the worship place for rulers and it was here Maia and I would be remarried.

As our carriage came to a complete halt, I jumped from the side nearest the great entrance and with my hand extended once again, assisted Maia's step. Throngs of people crowded and strained to see us and watch our event as it unfolded. To the crowd's approval, the Egyptian musical group I hired to play after the ceremony began an early rhythmic number as they strolled behind us, as we walked hand in hand toward the inner most sanctum of Karnack.

Past the next archway we moved hand in hand, as an even grander part of Thebes came into view, a street with one hundred twenty two columns, half along each side of the thoroughfare as far as we could see. At one time, this great columned street had been under roof. Each of its 12 feet thick, six storey tall columns were covered in hand carved hieroglyphic writings and symbols from top to bottom. Owls, chariots, grains of harvest and paintings of people adorned each one ton, carved limestone ceiling stone that till this day still remained perched far above our heads.

Our final turn into the Temple of Amon brought us to an alter from 1100 BC, which was the exact location Pharaoh Ramses II was married three thousand years ago. Like Ramses and his bride, Maia and I would recite from our own vows. As we both stood in humbled silence, I was pleased to let comparisons of that great ancient Pharaoh and I end there. Unlike Ramses II, I had no intentions of fathering more than one hundred children and building a columned street that would be topped with facial likenesses of each of my sixty sons.

Maia and I stood before the great altar in the blistering Egyptian noonday sun. Her satin, pearl gown glistened and slightly waved with each gentle Saharan breeze. Perspiration formed on my forehead as the local Coptic Christian Priest, who looked more the part of a Catholic Pope in Rome, began his part of the ceremony. He read translations from the original wedding text that Ramses II recited before his bride and High Priest. The words from Maia and I that followed couldn't equal the poetic verses that Ramses II murmured but ours were meant and vowed just the same.

Following our ceremony, the full band of drums, flute and tambourine played as onlookers cheered and occasionally Arabic women whaled with their tongues LU LU LU LU LU. We turned and faced the crowd then received the hand shakes and blessings of many of those close enough to get up front to greet us. We then turned and moved back in the direction of our carriage.

We returned to our ship, ATON, changed clothes, then joined a dozen or so of our new found, shipboard friends; many of whom had been present in Thebes for our ceremony. Maia and I had planned a special small buffet for those in attendance and were pleasantly surprised when the chef appeared, announcing with great pleasure, the buffet was being moved aboard the movie set's Royal Barge.

After Maia and I departed with our entourage to Thebes, the Italian movie production manager came to offer the boat for our pleasure. The chef and the movie production manager had worked out details of a two hour floating buffet for us and our guest at no charge.

I had been unable to rent the Royal movie barge but was now offered it for free, with all the trim-mings. How much better could the day get. What a spectacle and an impression upon us the wedding in the Temple of Amon had made, and only this could top it.

By two o'clock in the afternoon, twenty friends and crew joined us aboard the Royal Barge where we were too excited to do more than nibble at the scrumptious buffet prepared in our honor. The chef had his hands full as he sat at the barge's helm, commanding the thirty oarsmen who quietly glided the gilded ancient replica over the waters of the Nile. Cleopatra certainly traveled well if this was any semblance to the true life she led.

As the ship slid through the wave less Nile, Maia and I sat like true royalty, midship, on thrones of gold beneath a gently waving Royal red canopy. As wonderful as the Aton was the return trip aboard it to Cairo, and the rest of the trip in general was anticlimactic. The only thing even more anticlimactic was the reality that our return to Kuwait now lay only days away.

CHAPTER 24

Secret Passages

Maia had quit working at Marr Bell and had begun as a Secretary at the new building site of the American Embassy in Kuwait. The old shabby embassy proved not only vulnerable to attack because of its location but was also considered temporary from day one. It had been a great location down town near Dasma Palace and the Kuwait Towers but the property itself was owned by a foreign Prince who never allowed permanent buildings on the site. Now he wanted even the land back. The new embassy complex was to be located further into the suburbs and more inland away from the sea Instead of prefabricated trailers, this new one would be state of the art and far more massive.

The new American Embassy building, land and costs of construction were given to the United States by Kuwait, in appreciation for American help in liberating their country from Saddam Hussein. Additional grounds would provide housing for senior staff members and their families, as well as a palatial Ambassador's residence, swimming pools, tennis courts and a jogging track. This more secure compound built on the outskirts of town will be part of the American State Department's efforts to beef up security for all U.S. embassies worldwide. Kuwait's volatility makes it, what is known in State Department terms, a "flashpoint" country. This nation is not only in the Middle East, but has a pretty poor track record of insurrection and instability created in most part by their neighbors Iraq and Iran.

The latest in technology, bomb proof construction, security and a few unexpected surprises are included in the new Embassy compound's plans; not the least of which is a tunnel system linking it to Kuwait's Bayan Guest Palace.

Bayan Guest Palace and the new embassy complex grounds are nearly three quarters of a mile apart, but will be linked by a secret under ground passageway that could be used for escape in either direction or somewhere in between. In the event there is an attempt to bomb the American Embassy, staff would have a place to go. If there is another Iraqi invasion, coup against Kuwait's Royal Family or even future problems with Iran, key personnel could seek safety via the tunnel.

The land separating the new American Embassy and Bayan Palace is owned by Kuwait's Ruler, the Emir. In past years, except for the palace at one end, the land has remained baron and separated from the inhabited community of Bayan by fences and concrete guard posts.

For two years, a German Boring company has worked for the government of Kuwait, preparing the full length tunnel from the Guest Palace to the edge of the new American Embassy's grounds. The linkup will come sometime after the new U. S. Embassy opens for business. The same German boring company recently completed another secret passage way below Dasma Palace and will soon start their third and fourth such projects. These secret, subterranean passageways are recent after thoughts that have now become higher priorities than the original projects that brought the German Boring company to Kuwait. Originally, the Germans were hired to modernize the capital city's sewer system and the below ground tunnels at the Khiran and Doha Power Plants.

The first of these new high priority projects was the completion of an escape route from His Highness the Emir's residence and business offices at Dasma Palace, in Downtown Kuwait City. It had been started prior to the Iraqi invasion and scheduled for completion about three months after Iraqi occupation began. Unfortunately for the Kuwaitis, it was delayed and delayed again. Completion of the Dasma Palace tunnel was no longer possible for November 1990, a full two years after the first hole was knocked in a basement wall below the palace mosque. Now there were two more delays; the seven month Occupation by the Iraqis and the other, the rebuilding of the countries infrastructure following the Gulf War.

The new tunnel at Dasma Palace now runs from the mosque basement, beneath the palace's exterior walls, to a small unnoticeable stucco building on a side street, in the al Sharq District, nearly two blocks away. It was from this al Sharq location, the Germans began digging in the direction of Dasma Palace.

The TBM tunnel bore machine and blades used in Kuwait is similar, but considerably smaller than those used in the construction of the Channel Tunnel linking England to the European continent, and the ones used in carving out the $7 billion subterranean Saicon Tunnel System for bullet trains in Japan. This smaller version in Kuwait has nine feet in diameter rotor blades that bore while standing on end, much like the lid of a trash can with steel blades. The blades on the side facing into the dirt or sand (the Channel Tunnel machine bore into rock) gouge out the hole, while conveyor belts, called sand hogs, send the sand outward and upward for proper removal by men called muckers. More simple appendages to the bore machine's backside, allows interlocking steel ribs to be set in place forming the permanent tunnel wall that holds back the earth.

Because of the secretive nature of digging tunnels below the palaces, the operator of the bore machine and the muckers are always brought to the site blindfolded. Though most of these men have worked for the German company in their homeland and in Italy before Kuwait, they are never privy to engineers discussing the location of the excavation, nor of future projects.

Historically, a palace tunnel was used in Kuwait many years ago as a standby at Seif Palace. In olden days, when the original palace was on the hill near the Old Souks, the Emir had a tunnel built directly from his quarters connecting it to his favorite Diwaniya (men's meeting place). The old Emir visited the Souks and the Diwaniya daily, where he was open to visitation and requests from his close knit public. The old tunnel was not secret, but more of a private passageway away from the heat.

In the completely new, modern Seif Palace, the new "bore whole" tunnels have two exits. One leads to the basement of the Grande Mosque on the other side of a busy city traffic circle, outside palace grounds. The other connects several of Seif Palace' basements into one single maze exiting seaside. The one leading to the sea is the most sophisticated and well equipped except for one other at Bayan Palace, which has additional golf carts below ground to traverse the great distances between the Guest Palace at Bayan and the United States Embassy.

The prototype tunnel at Seif Palace combines not only escape routes, support equipment and food supplies, but elaborate safe refuge suites of rooms for both Royal Highnesses the Emir and the Crown Prince who have their new offices at Seif Palace.

Either of Kuwait's top leaders may enter the maze of tunnels from his personal Diwan at separate ends of Seif Palace, or from the master bathrooms of their private suites on the second and third floors of the main buildings. If the Amir or Crown Prince or anyone in their families wishes to stay hidden during another invasion, they can do so down there in comfort for an indefinite period of time.

To enter the underground passageways from Bayan Guest Palace, you must enter from beneath the curved staircase in the rotunda, on the main floor of each guest building. The escape door lies well hidden from view by impeccable faux marbling that blends with the inner walls of each palace's main rotunda and with its real marble floors, stairs, columns, cornices and lower wall trim.

Both Bayan Guest Palace and Seif Palace's underground mazes connect most main buildings inside palace walls to each other. Backup electricity for television monitors, special lighting, ventilation and cooling systems are provided by several hidden generators. The same generators make sure no Royal in hiding lives in less than regal comfort.

Each Royal underground chamber is furnished with marble floors, faux marble walls, large, comfortable, fat sofas and chairs, teakwood desks, King size "Murphy beds", gold and black onyx bathrooms, maids' and servant's quarters. There are enough guard's rooms, munitions, food and medical supplies down there to last quite a long time. Of Kuwait's five Palaces, only the Sha'ab and Doha Palaces have no hiding places below ground, nor plans to build them.

Soon after returning to Kuwait from Somalia, I returned to work at the Ministry of Information following my year and a half absence. Unbeknown even to me at the time, I began assembling a wide range of information concerning Ministry offices, types of communications and locations, Palace interiors, personnel itineraries of higher ups, new construction and inter personal feuds. I did all this without ever asking to see or hear anything. Knowledgeable Kuwaitis just wanted to impress me with what they knew and were quite proud of their accomplishments. I followed them around like a puppy dog. The only thing I did through my own initiative during these early days was to collect a full range of letterheads from each Ministry and authorizing stamps from throughout the country. Even this was done more like postage stamp collecting than anything sinister.

Kuwaitis, for whom I was now employed full time again, were always seeking my assistance in obtaining information about this that and the other. "The other" in this case was usually something having to do with my balls slipping through the border to get inside Iraq. Foremost on their list was whether the Americans were still lying to them about satellite information. Could I cross the desert into Iraq without passing through normal border check points? I knew of course it was no trouble for me. I had done before and would do it again. Of course I didn't tell them I was that confident because they would have felt my services weren't worth as much as I was charging.

It seems the Kuwaitis weren't the only ones out there that wanted assistance in gathering a little information. Royal Ordinance's Little Bob had aroused my interest in such forays when he introduced me to a Britt that needed to be taken behind lines so to speak. That went well and several more like it sort of opened me up to a new side career. So, I was at the disposal and eager to hear proposals from all who came.

The initial Kuwaiti requests seemed innocent enough; I gathered new information for them that more accurately detailed farm properties in the north of their country and the former Iraqi munitions storage facilities and bunkers that had been built on them. I also supplied them with information on farms and other structures and the new Iraqi bunkers and store houses that had been built just above the United Nations demilitarized zone inside Iraq. The British wanted me to continue transporting some of their men into Southern Iraq for unspecified reasons, and this I also did. At least for now I was employed by two governments doing menial tasks.

Farms are unnatural in Kuwait but several have existed for many years through the use of irrigation. Since the Iraqis destroyed Kuwait's water desalinization plants, neither drinking water nor affluent were available, so the farms dried up and reverted to sand. These farms mostly border the northern region adjoining Iraq, with the exception of some at the southern end of the country, near Wafra at the Saudi Arabian border.

It was these northern farms that Saddam Hussein's occupying armies transformed into storage facilities for their weapons and munitions. Following the Gulf War, coalition forces transformed them into bombed out, destroyed ammo dumps, littered with thousands of unexploded ordinances.

My mappings for the government of Kuwait were to detail the massive changes these facilities had undergone and their present conditions, since the war. Bangladeshi ordinance teams would later sweep these areas clean of explosives but right now they were still full of grenades, mines, and bombs. I really never understood why I got this job instead of a Kuwaiti, but perhaps it was because of all the exposed and unexposed live ordinance in the area.

American satellites detailed the farm land and structures from the skies but someone still had to see the insides of all the buildings and bunkers to complete the reports. For me it was a cake walk. These are the same farms, bunkers and destroyed areas I plundered while at Marr Bell. All I was doing differently was drawing maps and listing totals.

To my surprise, my future jobs became more interesting and farther afoot than I ever thought they would, even taking me as far as one of Saddam Hussein's Palaces on the western side of Basrah, Iraq.

It seemed as though all countries wanted more in depth, similar information about the same parcels of land and often my orders from Kuwait and the British overlapped. "Learn everything about the demilitarized zone between the two countries. Pay special attention to Kuwaiti farms within a triangle from the border station at Abdaly down to Sheikh Ali's (the Emir Sheikh Jabber's son) farm, on a dirt road north of the Rawdatain Oil Fields; then over the Iraqi line, one kilometer north of the Kuwait Naval and United Nations base at Umm Qasr."

I used to go to Sheikh Ali's farm to rest after putting in a long, hot day getting positions on the GPS, Magellan, Global Positioning Satellite equipment. I often relaxed while feeding the Sheikh's private collection of deer. Some had been killed during the Gulf War but had been replenished. Sometimes I went to another part of his farm to look for truffles. Kuwaiti truffles are also very expensive and taste good but Maia had to cook them a fairly long time to get the small sand content out.

Few people except Sheikh Ali's personal guests have ever seen his deer or even know of the truffles. The deer were exquisite, rare, little creatures in such a land as baron as this.

Once as a guest at the farm, I joined Sheikh Ali and several other family Royals, close friends and associates as they walked amongst the deer while planning a business deal for a sky scraper in Dubai, United Arab Emirates. Since that ti$359.04

$359.04

Me, I've always taken extra loaves of bread to feed the deer, while sitting under a canopy of cool trees. In latter times, I was an uninvited guest on a mission, so I made use of the farm refuge but steered clear of Sheikh Ali's residence.

Sheikh Ali's farm has a modern brick, one story structure that has a Diwaniya at the south end and sleeping quarters toward the rear. There is a large front lawn with green grass, a gazebo with several cooking grills and several automobile garages separated from the house. Sometimes while hiding, I was able to see a group of people on Sheikh Ali's front lawn, cooking goat and camel or just sitting in the gazebo.

Before going on some nocturnal excursions, I often waited on Sheikh Ali's farm, or over at the nearby farm of a Kuwait newspaper editor less than a half mile away. A third farm, that of former Parliamentarian, Sheikh Saleh was also nearby but more crude and too rustic for me. Sheikh Saleh had cattle, ducks and pigeons but no grass and few trees. His whole place was too hot, dusty and crude.

Once, Maia and I were guests for dinner at Sheikh Saleh's plain concrete block farm home. Maia sat behind a carved wood, mushrabiya screen eating privately as the only woman there, while I sat cross legged with Sheikh Saleh and two friends on the floor, eating atop newspapers. It was a large feast but I hardly ever get hungry when faced with feet and toes at the table. Sheikh Saleh is a nice quiet spoken man, but our views on many things differ considerably.

I learned long ago to be the first to serve myself at these eating functions and fortunately as the guest, I was expected to do so. I was told to begin before everyone else and I did without hesitation. I carefully put the amount of food on my plate I thought I would consume, because I knew I would never want seconds. By the time everyone had ripped apart

animal carcasses, eaten balled up rice and tomato sauce, licked their fingers several times and played with their feet, then returned these same fingers to dip into the food over and over again without use of silverware was too much for me.

I'm embarrassed that I didn't receive their hospitality more graciously, but there is something within me that makes my stomach uneasy at such dinners. I try hard to always sample all the foods and abide their customs, but I have an aversion to hot sweating people and dirty feet at close proximity to my food.

The convenience of Sheikh Saleh's farm to the Iraqi border was good, but I still remained uneasy hiding there. There were just too few trees and not enough comfortable cover. By moonlight, I would leave the safety of whatever cover I had chosen, to drive my tan Chevy Astro van over deserts or dirt roads over the border into Iraq. Though I often crossed the border in both directions, most often I'd cross near Umm Qasr, the Iraqi village north of the demilitarized zone. Umm Qasr is a divided town with Kuwait and the United Nations base occupying one side and the Iraqi village of Umm Qasr on the other.

To enter near Umm Qasr, I lay in wait near a line of wasted trees on Kuwait's side, until it was as dark as it was going to get, then I would abandon my van near some high brush and walk into Iraq. There were no trees or bushes at the cross over point, so I depended on my dark or beige clothing to blend in with the night sky or color of desert.

As soon as I was safely into Iraq, I walked around the nearly extinct post war village of Umm Qasr, summing up any information that might be deemed valuable to anyone. Even months after a sand berm was built between Kuwait and Iraq, and United Nation's soldiers took up positions along the neutral zone, I still managed to get through quite easily.

Despite Kuwait's latest move to widen and strengthen their border, there were still two locations west of the Umm Qasr Base, where breaks in the new berm posed no problem in crossing, at any time.

Two other Americans were caught in my area in 1996. Rumors that followed said they were running liquor back to Kuwait City for sale to expats and Kuwaitis, when caught by Iraqi soldiers. I had almost run into the same two men on two occasions. Whoever these guys were, they used much the same method I used, except they were more brazen and entered Iraq nearer the United Nations guard posts. They also used a white vehicle much like those driven by United Nations soldiers. I never brought liquor back from Iraq because I wanted no contact with anyone on either side of the border. I didn't even let those two guys know I had seen them. On the last of their trips, they were captured by Iraqi troops, and then taken to Baghdad where they were held in Al Gharib Prison.

I continued infiltrating through the same area the Americans were caught, but of course I took many precautions that apparently paid off. One was not to tell anyone exactly where I was going and not to have any contact with anyone from that area once I was there.

The Brits asked me to go once again and I told them Kuwait was using me for much the same stuff but not detailed information like them. For quite some time I didn't tell the Kuwaitis the Brits were also using me. While almost always alone and undercover, I carried out all tasks for both countries. The Brits this time wanted me to enter several hangar type buildings in the Iraqi Umm Qasr area and also some garage like sheds just outside town; all of which could be seen well enough by U2 spy planes from above. Also spying from above were two Greyhound bus size satellites that made twice daily elliptical orbits overhead. My job was to provide interior details of "cold" objects the satellites could not see.

Spy planes continually bombard the area with infrared heat seeking devices that can detect the human body, foot prints, car engines, mechanical equipment and the likes, and is even capable of detecting recent tire tracks in the desert; but when it comes down to it, they can't see equipment or weaponry inside unless it is running. With all this ingenuity, there are still times when people like me have to carry out on-site confirmations. Sometimes, but rarely, I'm asked to clear up questions that came through the British, for the National Reconnaissance Office back in the United States. Sometimes the information is shared with Kuwait and some times it is not.

There was only one real problem with trying to pass information on to people from my own United States. Many of the American operatives or agents, or whatever they like to be called in the field, don't like to be told anything they didn't discover themselves. On no fewer than twenty occasions, I went to the U. S. Embassy in Kuwait, or met with someone else from the American community at a desert base in Kuwait that didn't want me to tell them anything. Like Bob from Marr Bell, they already knew everything they wanted to know. Don't try to give intelligence to an intelligence person, because they tend to discount whatever you say. They are always smarter than you and know everything about everything; especially the American intelligence community.

The Brits and Kuwaitis however, were anxious for information. The United States is known for blunders because of poor or wrong information in foreign operations. We've seen missiles slam into buildings in Iraq, the Balkans, Sudan and other regions, only to find out it was now a school or a hospital, or didn't house what it was suppose to.

To the "real" field intelligence operatives, it was more important that their information not be questioned, rather than having someone else point out that it was in error. Perhaps their feelings got hurt or they felt they were the only ones intelligent enough to discover and pass on valuable information to Washington.

The American government admits that there is no substitution for a mole or a human spy, while at the same time refusing to finance or listen to anyone that hasn't sat down at one of their desks in Washington or been trained amongst them. There is also a "no touch" policy toward unsavory characters. When in fact, these "unsavory" people should be listened to. It is they or their acquaintances that are most likely the ones dealing in unsavory acts the United States should learn more about.

On a couple search and discover missions into Iraq, I made it all the way to the suburbs of Baghdad, more than three hundred miles away. My only regret was that I finally got to see the site of ancient Babylon, south of Baghdad, between the towns of Karbala and Hilla. Unfortunately for me, it was about two o'clock in the morning, mostly cloudy and no moon, so I didn't get to see much.

On one of my first long distance trips, I had been given permission to keep my car under cover at a farm near the Euphrates River, not too far from Babylon. On that trip too, I forayed at night only. I had binoculars of course, night vision goggles, several good topographical maps, maps of nearby villages, lots of iced tea in thermoses and traditional clothing, the Dishdasha and local black and white head gear to cover my clothing.

I wore both gray and light brown colors normally worn by local Iraqis during change of hot seasons into cooler or colder months. I tried to always keep a good distance between me and any locals for fear my light skin color might give me away.

Because of the extreme heat of Kuwait's summer, I had gotten use to wearing Arabic head gear under my hard hats while working at Marr Bell. The flowing white head piece covers the back of my neck well and keeps it from getting sunburned. When the outside temperature in Kuwait and Southern Iraq is 135 degrees, I needed to wear more than a turned around baseball cap. My friend Ghassan, a Palestinian/Jordanian always tried to get me to wear the black and white head piece like they wear, but inside Kuwait, I never thought it was a good idea to wear the colors of the enemy who sided with Saddam Hussein during the invasion and occupation of Kuwait.

Though I pretended each border crossing was easy, no trip inside Iraq was really a cake walk. There was always some event that was unaccounted for that made my adrenalin rush, but on each trip, I did try to foresee any problems that might arise or that I might create myself. I always carried food items from local Kuwaiti and Arab markets so any disposed or accidentally dropped wrappers or containers looked no different than their people might have brought into the desert with them. I didn't want anyone to find candy wrappers or containers showing U. S. Camp Doha price tags indicating an American or a soldier may have been prowling around. The most critical items I carried, of course, were cameras. I wasn't used to James Bond type gear and no one furnished me with anything that was exceptionally clever, but I did carry simple cameras, regular 35mm and VHS video.

All the while plundering in Iraq and enjoying it, I got paid very well indeed. Maia's career was not at a pinnacle, but she was enjoying her work with the five men of the Foreign Building Office of the new American Embassy in Kuwait. Each of the men in the FBO office was talented in his own right and Maia was there to do their typing and reports, much like what she did at Marr Bell; but at Marr Bell she had the added responsibility of helping Donald keep up payroll for thousands of foreign expatriate laborers in their own currencies.

The five men Maia worked for were the architects and engineers sent by the United States to execute proper construction of the new Embassy compound. They were as kind to Maia as they were talented. She was always treated as a lady, even in that hot small desert field office, and she always dressed the part. No sandals, tennis shoes or blue jeans for her. Maia had always and still continues to wear dresses, suits, jackets and high heels. Often she'd tell me of her high heels bogging down in the hot sand as she walked from one portable office building on the site to another, but not once did she ever change her dress code.

When the American Embassy excavation crews were digging a pit for the huge water storage area below ground, it surprised me they didn't hit or cave in the pretunnel passageway connecting Bayan Guest Palace to their site. I knew of it, but couldn't say anything as I watched heavy equipment moving dirt around, right above where I was pretty sure the subterranean water storage might have met the escape tunnel. I just didn't know if they knew about the entry. Surely they did!

J. A. Jones Construction Company won the bid to build the American Embassy but not the new Ambassador's residence. J. A. Jones set up portable offices next to the Foreign Building Offices where Maia and the five State Department planners worked. A Kuwaiti firm won the bid to construct the Ambassador's residence. They set up their own portable offices on the outside of the compound's walls with a small access whole in the western wall for workers.

The desert was coming alive with people and construction. Some of the new workers were old friends of ours. Several of our former Filipino employees from Marr Bell, switched their sponsorship over to J. A. Jones and continued seeing Maia on a daily basis.

With Maia's new position came some wonderful new friends. The wives of the five men Maia worked for were not quite what we considered movers and shakers, nor were they even friendly to us; but everyone else connected to the new construction site and the old Embassy downtown were great.

The American Embassy in Kuwait celebrates all the usual American holidays like Christmas, Fourth of July with a picnic, the annual Marine Corps Birthday Ball and fifties and sixties parties, as well as tennis tournaments, swimming parties and monthly receptions for American Embassy staff and their spouses, at the Ambassador's residence.

Since Kuwait is a Muslim country and doesn't allow pubs or nightclubs, even in hotels, the American Embassy also provides employees a social on the last day of each work week. It's quite a popular way of winding down the week's stresses with a little beer or wine, popcorn and hot dogs, good music and great companionship. No drinks were ever allowed to leave Embassy property and all screw tops and pull tabs on bottles and cans were taken off when served, so no one could go home with a purse full.

With the sterile environment of Kuwait, people had to make their own fun. There were quite a few parties each month. They differed from dinner parties like those given by Maia's two main bosses, to smaller get together, socials and barbecues at all our homes. There was country western dancing and drinks at Betty's and theme parties like Halloween and fifties and sixties at mine and Maia's penthouse, Thanksgiving at Barbara's etc.

Maia and I had a social life in Kuwait long before becoming one of the Embassy crowds, so we had more connection to the outside world, local flavor you might say. Embassy people tend to stick together and don't socialize very often with locals or other expats from other countries. Maia and I were careful not to offend, but we knew how to turn out a social list that kept everyone talking and coming back for more. We thought our blend made for more interesting conversations and presented more international life exposure.

Maia's boss, Howell Wood's dinner parties were more like coming home for Thanksgiving. Mr. Wood's wife Jolie cooked all day and had such an abundance of food that everyone ate well and still carried home something tasty. At the Howell's we sat back in comfortable chairs and on Arabic throw pillows on the floor, like we might have done at Mom and Dad's. Mr. Woods, a short burley, jovial man of sixty two years, with somewhat scarce white hair is a gentle character and never changes day to day or circumstance to circumstance. He is a rock you can count on. His wife of more than forty years, Jolie, originally from El Salvador in Central America is more temperamental. She was raised to cook and cook well. Jolie was a former beauty queen who met Howell while attending college in San Francisco. She is opinionated but sweet; motherly but don't come home too often; and loves to dress beautifully, but has become quite overweight and now uses a cane to get around.

There have been wonderful dinners at their home in the Kuwait City suburb of Mishref, where booze as well as food flowed freely. Their dog Chessy wore fad clothing and it wasn't unusual to see him dressed in a World War Two bomber jacket or in a Santa Clause suit. He enjoyed the crowds as much as the crowds enjoyed him. His favorite thing was to run up and down the staircase chasing small stuffed animals that guests threw from floor to floor.

Jolie has quite a collection of crucifixes from all over the world, as well as glass perfume bottles. Howell was quite the articulate builder and proudly showed his collection of framed pictures of palaces and Embassies he'd built.

There were two Jims Maia worked for, both sharp and great assets to the State Department. Jim Capen a fifty nine year old divorcee, architect, drew up plans for new Embassies, renovations and additions for others. His expertise was giving old Embassies a face lift. Jim was one of those people involved in the American Embassy conflict in Moscow, where all the walls and half the floors of the entire new complex were found to be giant listening devices. All was not well with moving into the Moscow complex and a big fight ensued with Washington demanding the antennas and listening devices be removed before the Russians could move into their new Embassy complex sitting on the best hill over looking Washington, D. C. The standoff lasted for years and the Americans finally gave in and moved into their new bugged offices while the Russians moved into their new buildings in Washington that the Americans had been forbidden to help construct. Jim was also a good party giver.

The other Jim, Jim Lehman was a very quiet forty two years old, probably the most talented of them all. He was of small stature, thin and wiry, no pun intended, though he was the wiring and plumbing master, who was the backbone of existence in most buildings. He and his wife Tanya of seven years were always seen hand in hand, though none of her warmth ever slipped our direction. Jim's talents were especially needed and sought after in such places as his next assignment in Rome, Italy, where the American Embassy is in a four hundred fifty year old Palace of a former Italian Queen.

After hundreds of years, that Embassy was ready for another remodel that would bring its heating, air conditioning and wiring systems up to date. Jim was the man chosen for the job. He had to worry as much about the priceless works of art in the building, as he did about the precious walls and floors he had to cut into. There had to be new air vents in walls not thick enough to hold them, or in some cases, they were too thick. The priceless works of art were too bulky and heavy to move but weren't allowed to get dust on, or be vibrated by construction equipment. His job in Rome was cut out for him, but Jim was the man for it.

Rob Browning, another of the gentlemen Maia worked for, was head of quality control for the Kuwaiti company building the new Ambassador's residence. That wasn't an easy project either. He had to oversee Kuwaitis who tried to under cut their own budgets, sneak in cheaper products, forego needed security and make a mockery of American building standards. The building upon completion was magnificent.

Maia's head boss, Tom Farley was a forty nine year old Floridian, whose wife either would not or could not for health reasons, join him in Kuwait. He was a big boy, a better than average golfer who looked more the part of a former football player. Tom played golf whenever and wherever he could, even on courses that were mostly sand like the ones in Ahmadi Township and along Fifth Ring Road south of Kuwait City. He also left the country for a good round of golf in neighboring Arab countries, but most enjoyed Dubai, United Arab Emirates.

One day, I went with Tom to Ahmadi, though I confess I was less interested in playing golf on the semi arid wasteland, than I was at looking over the remains of our British friends Guy and Shari's Tara Plantation home, or what was left of it. The home no longer existed as I knew it. It had been burnt to the ground by Iraqi invaders after they sacked it.

Actually, Guy and Shari almost had to flee the residence on two separate occasions. The first was shortly after the occupation of Kuwait began, when they thought Iraqi soldiers were readying themselves to occupy the residence as their headquarters. The tanks, Iraqi personnel carrier trucks and jeeps drove through the lavish front gates and up the circular drive. Several armed men with machine guns pushed their way through the front door and carefully gave the whole house a once over. Guy and Shari were sure the soldiers would return and confiscate it for one of their high ranking officers, but the Iraqis disappeared never to be seen again.

The time Guy and Shari actually fled their home was toward the end of Occupation. Without any prior warning, Shari saw Iraqi vehicles stop in front of the house, then burst through the front gates again. Trucks full of soldiers were jumping out with rifles in hand.

Shari was sure this time they meant business so she ran out the back door and down the alley to a friend's house. Later, she and the friend ventured along the front side of the street to get a better view of what was happening at her home. She was just in time to witness the soldiers throwing hand grenades and torching the house and much of its contents. Many of her most prized furnishings and possessions had already been loaded on the Iraqi trucks. Shari had fled without even retrieving her watch and wedding ring lying above the kitchen sink. Guy, Shari and their daughter remained hidden at friend's houses until they left the country on the third flight out after Liberation. That wasn't until the airport was reopened following Desert Storm.

Friends said Guy and Shari took one final drive by their house before departing to the airport on their final morning in Kuwait. Guy was silent and Shari cried as they held each other and their teenaged daughter while they all stared for the last time at the charred rubble they once called home.

Tom Farley continued playing through his round of golf at the Ahmadi course while I walked through the ruins of the grand ole house. Its front facade was scorched but still standing, the elegant southern white pillars looked like those in Atlanta must have appeared after Sherman's march to the sea. The mansion's roof had burned to a crisp and much of its ember beams and joyces had fallen. The beautiful marble fireplace and mantle were cracked from heat, and scorched almost beyond recognition.

There were no burnt Oriental Carpets because Shari had seen the soldiers roll them up and carry them away on Iraqi trucks. The winding Loretta Young staircase still had some spools extending downward from the rail, but its steps had burned and collapsed into a heap on the floor of the foyer. The rear and side walls of the mansion were in worse shape than the front. Many sections had caved in. The super bar and pool house had been leveled by hand grenades, and the fire that followed, left nothing identifiable. Even the swimming pool, we all used to enjoy together, was destroyed. Its water long ago evaporated and the bottom now covered in oil and debris from the house and sky. The bushes in the garden were fighting for life and lacked any semblance to their coifed looks prior to invasion.

CHAPTER 25

Cover Job for a Double Life

Nothing in Kuwait was the same as pre-invasion. I still hadn't returned to the direct employee of the Royal Family, but at least I was enjoying my newest jobs, reconnaissance for the Ministry of Information and the Brits. That would do for now. The snooping was fun and exciting but still left too much time on my hands, so I decided to add a new full time job to my already existing work schedule. It was recommended I try working for the Minister of Information in yet another capacity, a more public oriented job like television or radio. Whatever position I could get there, I'd take. It would probably be helpful sooner or later, and I needed even more contacts there. Many of my old ones were still out of the country. I needed to be around Kuwait's social elite once again.

In Kuwait, Diwaniyas are places where groups of men who rarely spend time with their wives, meet every night. Sometimes they just play cards, other nights they talk politics or business. Always they speak about ladies but continue spending their time with men. The whole while, they talk or whatever, they drink hot tea and smoke water pipes and cigarettes. The water pipes don't have hashish in them like most Americans think, but rather pear pits or peach pits or other concoctions that smell good. This smell, on top of burning sandal wood incense, makes the place smell like a candle shop inside a mall back home. I like it.

Kuwait has a non coed society except in attempts at procreation and then only sometimes its coed. The subject of women borders on the taboo, but that's precisely what they talk about most of the time. Boys in Kuwait attend separate schools from girls and can't even meet them privately until almost the day they're married. Boys and single men even eat in separate sections of McDonalds, Burger King and Pizza Hut so they don't lust for the women or make verbal or eye contact over the table. Muslim Secret Religious Police patrol most locations, trying to catch anyone violating the law.

Suddenly when men are adult enough, financially responsible enough and the family has approved, they can take a wife. A man's engagement and marriage takes place through deals made by the groom to be's father, uncles and other males within the girl's family. Now he goes from abstinence, masturbation or homosexuality to having a wife to care for. Since he has been unable to develop skills with women, has never been taught any in school, and has never had a personal relationship with a woman, he suddenly must become her keeper, protector, lover and soul mate all at once. He doesn't of course and continues his nightly gatherings with the boys at diwaniyas.

Diwaniyas are men's' familiar refuges away from their wives. These guys get stressed once they've taken their first wife because some time there after, they are expected to take another and another and another; four in all. This diwaniya refuge becomes more of a necessity than a social event once all the wives are producing all the children they're each expected to have. The average is probably six to nine children for each wife. For First Class Kuwaitis, the State contributes money monthly for the family's upkeep for the rest of their lives.

Male Diwaniyas are held on grand scales for the moneyed and Royal elites, and less so for the second class Kuwaiti and third class bedouin stateless Arabs in Kuwait. There are big ones once a week at places like the Minister of Information's home, and there are smaller ones in every home in Kuwait.

The places that house family diwaniyas are built onto homes like garages are in the United States. Most appear as living rooms full of sofas with their legs chopped off, with a few glass coffee tables strewn around the room, a chandelier in the center of the ceiling, a few Arabic throw pillows and water pipes lying around on the floor and possibly a television set with a VCR. There are no pictures on the wall, even of family members, and no plants, just an Islamic religious quote from the Holy Koran if anything. If the men play cards, it is done with their legs folded, sitting in the floor the same as during meal time.

After returning to work at the Ministry of Information, my social life took off again. The number of diwaniyas I attended increased dramatically. Above and beyond the secretive jobs I was doing for Kuwait and the British, I was now on radio as a news and weather man and Political Section Manager. Within two days of applying for the job, I got it. My extended duties came later when I began writing other programs for television and radio as well. At the beginning, the Kuwaitis wanted me to read on-air scripts handed to me already written by several Egyptians under the direction of a Kuwaiti.

The stories I first had been given contained all English words, but were written the way an Arab speaks, a way barely understood by a native English speaker. I demanded and won the right to start from the beginning, pulling the news from the wire services, doing the rewording myself and creating my own entire program. For the first time, Kuwait English News became a lot more like similar shows in America.

Everything that was news worthy world wide came into one office at the Ministry. The German, Arabic and Kuwaiti wire services came to the same room as Reuters, AP and the top global wire services. The Arabic ones especially would prove invaluable later. There is a lot they don't tell us westerners.

Several times daily, I tore the incoming teletype from the machines, rewrote them to fit my newscast time allowed, then typed them and broadcast them on-air without one Arab in the picture.

The norm in Kuwait is that nine out of every ten jobs is redundant. It certainly was the case at the Ministry of Information, for both radio and television. Their procedure before I came back was to have a Kuwaiti pull the service off the teletype machine, censor everything unfit to be aired for Muslims in an Islamic country, hand the remaining, mauled stories over to several Egyptians who then picked through each story trying to rewrite them, then hand them to yet another Egyptian to type from their long hand, then to another to retranslate back into English, then to yet another to retype the broadcast into English, then hand it to a news reader to go on the air with it. At this point, even the redundancy wasn't complete. An engineer then came into the studio to work the on-air switches, volume, lead-in music etc. for the announcer to just sit there and read.

I eliminated everyone, no censors were left, no rereaders, no typists other than me and no engineer. I broadcast what I wrote, which included local and international news, weather, sports and stock averages.

When first hired at the Ministry of Information, the Arabs in the news room people didn't want me around, so they put me at a desk outside their office in the hallway alone, much like what happened to me at Dasma Palace in the first days. I changed position here at the Ministry of Information as rapidly as I had at Dasma Palace, finally making it into the Crown Prince's office over there. Here, I ended up having my own office and broadcast studio, in which I kept CNN and BBC on while I wasn't on the air. From these two world wide services, I could get up to the minute coverage and immediately go "live" if there was a major story breaking.

People inside Kuwait who had cable television found my news from within the country refreshing, others like fundamentalist Muslims who refuse outside communications devices like cellular telephones and satellite dishes, hated what I did but listened to every broadcast so they could call me and complain. They kept me on the carpet because of phrases I used. Many things to them sounded blasphemous, so each time I said something that didn't suit them, I had to undergo lengthy interrogations about why I said it. Some times they'd demand the Minister of Information discipline me by deducting pay for each incursion. The Minister, like a lamb, bowed to Islamic fundamentalist pressure, and each time, I was reprimanded and forfeited some pay. I never quit because I felt for the first time, people were hearing real news inside the country.

Within the next few years, numerous battles took place in my studio, the outer offices or the Minister's office. It even came down to a race in the early mornings between me and the Kuwaitis who tried to outsmart me by censoring the wire service copy before I came to work. I just showed up earlier and earlier until a Kuwaiti couldn't come in at those times of the morning. After all, four thirty or five o'clock in the morning was usually about the time they would be going to bed.

Taboo subjects for radio or television were; sex, anything negative about Islam or the Islamic point of view, crimes inside Kuwait and stories about the Royal Family. There were other limits as well but you never knew when you crossed one of those lines until you had already done so. I couldn't even say "ole Bill Clinton played his saxophone last night at a White House dinner". They considered it degrading the President of the United States.

Once in my early days at the Ministry, I wrote, and then announced that "forty three Christians had their throats cut by Muslim fundamentalists yesterday in Algeria". For that story, I lost four hundred dollars and got an ass eating by several top Muslims the Minister of Information allowed to come into my office after me. There were times, I had so many confrontations and pay deductions that at the end of the pay period, I was afraid I would owe my employer money.

Another fight occurred over how I broadcast the Russian-Chechnya battles raging in Southern Russia. The Chechens are Muslims battling Russia for Independence, so anything I said had to be very carefully written. The Russians had to put the rebellion down in hopes of saving all other Southern Russian states from seeking independence as well. To the Arabs, it was simple Russia hated Muslims.

In other news casts, I couldn't say the names of Saddam Hussein, whom I had to refer to as the "Ferocious Iraqi Aggressor", or the "Iraqi Dictator". Another name I couldn't use on the air was puzzling to me at first; "Yasser Arafat". I was allowed to give the names of Israeli Presidents and Prime Ministers, but not the leader of the Palestinian Liberation Organization, PLO.

I later found out there were long standing deep animosities between Kuwaitis and Yasser Arafat. He lived in Kuwait for many years, and I'm told worked as an engineer in the suburb of Hawalli, where Ghassan and Ruba live. He originally got a lot of support for Palestinian causes from Kuwaitis but much later when he became head of the Fatah Organization, he failed to acknowledge and praise the Kuwaitis for all they had done. Now Kuwaitis officially say they support Palestinian causes but detest Arafat and his Fatah organization. Actually, the record shows Kuwait expelled four hundred fifty thousand Palestinians from Kuwait following the Gulf War. That shows how much they really love and support any Palestinian cause.

On my new job, I got into trouble several more times in quick succession. Over the next few years there were times, almost daily, when there were anti-American demonstrations around Kuwait City. The Kuwaitis were again protesting American military men and women from Camp Doha coming into the city's Souks and other shopping areas while in uniform. They said the uniforms made them feel like the Americans were occupying their country as conquerors and it was a disgrace to Islam to have soldiers on their soil (The same armies that saved their asses from Saddam Hussein were now not good enough to shop in their markets wearing the infidel uniform). I was angry and showed it in my broadcasts.

On a different subject matter, I got an ass eating that almost left with me no lower extremities at all. I was giving the weather forecast following the news. I said, "Cross your fingers for rain". All hell broke loose. I was prevented from leaving the radio booth until several people called for me in an Under Secretary's room, inside the main administration building of the Ministry. Already in the office were three television and radio executives, all al Sabahs from the Ruling Family, plus four Muslim Mullah religious leaders in fundamentalist clothing. I could hear a rapturous roar of voices from down the hall even before I got there. I knew it wasn't Ed McMahan in there to present me with a check for ten million dollars.

Most of the room was full of fundamentalists who still appear much as Muslims did several hundred years ago. They still wear shorter than normal Kuwaiti dishdashas (white robes), they have longer uncut beards, unpretentious sandals and old traditional head gear, (they wear the white gutra with black roping instead of just white).

In the presence of top ranking people from the Ministry, the Mullahs backed me into a corner for almost four hours. Each one screaming at the top of his lungs at the same time. They had no idea how easy it was to filter their annoying screeches out, but I found it humiliating that the three al Sabahs present took so much pleasure in watching the spectacle of an American being eaten alive as they entertained themselves, like Romans watching a lone Christian being eaten alive by the lions. One of them had such a smile on his face and wide open eyes that I pictured him being sexually aroused by my reaction to all the yelling; and he probably ejaculated before the encounter was over.

On that particular day, I tried over and over in my mind to remember back to the newscast and figure out what I had said, because in typical Arab fashion, in all the screaming, they forgot to tell me what I had said. I remembered that I had not said anything like Muslims cutting Christian throats again, so I was totally confused. More than two hours later they began calming down. I heard one of them say in English, "how dare you bring religion into the weather." I though hard for a minute and then remembered a little phrase I said following the weather, "Keep your fingers crossed for rain." They told me this was religious because of the word "cross". I tried to think of a word in Arabic that had more than one meaning but I wasn't thinking so well with all them yelling at the same time. I told them that the word "cross" had nothing to do with the crucifix. I often cross my legs and have no religious experience.

The al Sabahs present were quite well educated men and could have explained away the situation to their more fanatic, less intellectual brothers but they enjoyed the whole confrontation. From that day on, I saw even less in the Royals to respect, except the power they wielded because of their money.

I made it through another day but was far from being in the clear. Now the Arabic News Department was demanding four copies of everything I was going to say on the air, before I said it. I told them, since I come in every morning at five, five thirty or earlier and go on the air at seven o'clock, I hope someone will be here real early like at six o'clock to read and approve my copy. I knew that would halt them in their tracks because no Kuwaiti is up at that time of the morning unless he's been out partying with friends all night.

I was soon instructed just to leave a copy of each of my daily broadcasts with the senior boss before leaving work. That was easy so I did. However, even that didn't keep me out of trouble. I occasionally would forget, (on purpose some times) to read the Crown Prince's name without each of his titles. During news casts, I didn't like the repetition of names and titles to confuse the story I was trying to tell as Kuwaitis usually do. For instance:

"The Crown Prince and Prime Minister, His Highness Sheikh Saad Abdullah Al Salem Al Sabah today had audience with His Excellency Sheikh Saud Nasser Al Sabah, the Minister of Information at two o'clock. His Royal Highness the Crown Prince and Prime Minister Sheikh Saad al Abdullah Al Salem Al Sabah and his Excellency the Minister of Information Sheikh Saud Al Nasser Al Sabah spoke of preparations for the upcoming meeting with his Highness the Emir, Sheikh Jaber Al Ahmed Al Sabah along with whom they'll be meeting his Highness King Fahd Ibn Abdul Aziz, Custodian of the Two Holy Mosques. That meeting will be held at the Amiri of His Highness the Amir Sheikh Jaber Al Ahmed Al Sabah tomorrow at noon.

These run on sentences are considered normal in Arabic broadcasting but I didn't like saying them because they were boring and confusing. They easily lost the meaning of the paragraph being read, because you're concentrating on saying the same names and titles over and over. I told them I respect the people who have the titles but I think if they want me to effectively report news to the English speaking community, I have to eliminate a lot of the double talk and tell about the event. Now if the Ministry wishes me to report to a Kuwaiti audience who are just learning English, that is a different story altogether. I could put together another format and speak much more slowly.

I always rewrote everything they tried to slip by me, like that paragraph on King Fahd's meeting with Kuwait's Royals. I rewrote it simply:

"His Highness the Crown Prince and Prime Minister Sheikh Saad Abdullah Al Salem Al Sabah met today with the Minister of Information, Sheikh Saud al Nassir al Sabah. Together they spoke of their upcoming meeting with his Highness the Emir, Sheikh Jaber and Saudi Arabia's King Fahd ibn Abdul Aziz, the custodian of the Two Holy Mosques at the Amiri Tomorrow at noon".

It was still long but cut almost in half.

I was finally given permission to drop some repetitious names but not all wording. At least once during the news report I had to say all the titles and full names, but no longer had to repeat them over and over. It was a good compromise.

The Ministry of Information's wire service room gave me a lot of vital information not available to the Kuwaiti public, or to the Americans even in the Embassy. Though most stories originated outside the country, those that didn't were of great interest. Having this access or inside window on Kuwait brought me many bits of information the western English speaking community in Kuwait, including the American Ambassador or the

U.S. State Department could never hear or read. They could never hear communiqués of protests, about internal bombings of movie theaters showing western movies, information about Brotherhood (fundamentalist Muslims) and their priorities and preferences for upcoming Kuwait University elections etc.

Maia's job was coming along well and she was really happy working for the Foreign Building Office of the new United States Embassy. The first Embassy function we attended was a "Fifties and Sixties Dance". I got volunteered to be the Disc Jockey.

Around Kuwait, my interest in fifties and sixties music was well known. I developed a nostalgic program that would last about twenty minutes out of each of the four hours of the party and asked someone else to play more modern songs that were good to dance to for the remaining forty minutes. I asked my Lebanese friend Samir to back me up and share the "free" disc jockey position. Like younger people around the world, even Arabs like Samir was familiar with all the latest pop chart songs of the day, and was more than willing to DJ for the Embassy. Samir was the same friend that usually house-sat our penthouse while Maia and I went away on vacations.

Over the years, since my teen years, 50's and 60's music continued to be my favorite music, so I have vigorously collected tunes from that era all my adult life. I have almost fifteen hundred hits on tape, CD's and cassettes. I liked the 50's and 60's music because the singers were all high school kids like our selves. Kids singing to kids. Any one of them could have been in our high school class. They weren't an older generation singing to us.

As the party DJ, I played the hits and chimed in with lots of memorable trivia about some of the singers and groups. I had emceed 50's and 60's parties at class reunions in several cities around the United States, and met many of the performers in person while emceeing shows on Cruise ships like; "The Song of Norway", "Nordic Prince", "Sun Viking", (where I met my wife) and "The Boheme" years before.

This Embassy's 50's, 60's party was held at the old Embassy compound, around the same swimming pool where the diplomats had to draw their drinking water during Iraqi occupation. There were several hundred people in attendance and I reintroduced them to the hand jive, stroll, the cha cha, pony, limbo and other dances from that innocent time in our lives.

One of the first people I met that evening was an attractive blonde lady in her middle forties, wearing a pink poodle skirt, black and white saddle oxfords, a short pink scarf around her neck and her hair was in a pony tail. I watched her shag with several men through four songs and couldn't believe her dance style. The guys were no match for her but I knew I was. We danced the same. Finally, I put the record on, "Come Go with Me" by the Del Vikings and it was our turn to dance together. Everyone later said we looked like an ad for Coca Cola in the fifties. I was wearing tight jeans, penny loafers with white socks, a white tee shirt with a pack of cigarettes rolled up in my sleeve and my hair was slicked back in a duck tail, with something similar to Dipody Doo.

It was great fun and my wife and I joined the lady and her friends at their table while Samir DJ'd his part of the hour. Barbara Miller Vaughn and I shagged several more times that evening. I told her how it was amazing we danced the exact same steps. She said it was just the way she learned to dance in Savannah, Georgia. Now I couldn't believe what I was hearing. Savannah was also the place I learned to dance.

Within minutes, we were comparing notes about school. Both of us had attended Savannah High School in the early sixties, and then later she graduated from Jenkins High school where most of my friends went. The "Class of 64" was having a reunion amongst the camels in a Middle Eastern Desert.

Barbara was posted at the American Embassy, serving as Secretary to the Commanding General of American Troops in Kuwait. She was also as talented a singer as she was a dancer, singing the "Star Spangle Banner" and other songs at many of the Embassy and military functions. For a couple of years in a row, we celebrated "Fourth of July" together. The first was with Ambassador and Mrs. Ryan Crocker, several UNIKOM Generals and many of our other friends in Kuwait City; another in the remote desert of the demilitarized zone between Kuwait and Iraq at the Umm Qasr Base. Up there, Barbara sang to troops from more than twenty nations as we all danced in the stifling heat and humidity that only cooled to 105 degrees by late evening.

Betty McNaughton, another of our dearest friends from the American Embassy, was Secretary to Ambassador Crocker. Betty's husband was an Embassy Official before he died several years ago. For Betty, a fifty-seven year old widow with grown children, life was more complete with an Embassy family so she went to work full time for the State Department and continued taking posts in Washington and around the world.

My first impression of Betty was that of a delightful, funny, snappy dresser but somehow with a school marm look. It was her red hair, up in a bun that likened her to turn of the century days. I figured she sort of had one foot in each world today and yesteryear. Later I would revise my thought simply to "a foot solidly planted at home in the diplomatic corps and the other still back at her real home in Texas.

I remember her coming toward our table at the "fifties-sixties party". She was a nice looking, tall, lanky, red head who gracefully and very ladylike came to sit beside Barbara, only smiling toward Maia and I without having been spoken to first. I saw a strong gracious lady there. It didn't matter what the theme night was, it was still Texas in her heart.

Betty wore a long gaucho skirt with cow girl boots and her hair in the bun was like watching "Little House on the Prairie" meeting "Lavern and Shirley". She continued her silent listening and smiling and like a true lady, waited to be introduced before speaking. When Betty got on the dance floor, look out. She was one "dancing fool" "a Two Stepping Cowgirl". As much and as often as Betty loved to dance, she thought a lady always waited for the man to ask her. Without being mind readers many of us guys who were more than ready to dance sat around much like her, legs and feet dancing under the table with each new rhythm, while the top part of her body remained constrained above.

Betty was a pleasure to dance with, whether it was Country Western Two Step, the Shag, Cha or Macarena. I had to try to break Betty from that frame of mind her mama instilled in her, "A lady never asks a man to dance", and I told her "get over it, I like to dance too. "If I didn't ask her, she should come over and ask me. Later that evening, Betty did one of the best limbo's I'd ever seen and showed great spirit. Maia and I liked her happy energy. It took a few more gatherings but Betty did finally get over her shyness toward me and other guys to dance, and we had a ball at many more functions over the years. Fortunately, my sweet Maia was very understanding and knew it was just fun and dances. If Maia was jealous, it didn't show and I didn't notice.

Many other fifties & sixties party attendees showed enthusiasm for the period music I played that evening and wanted to know if we could do it again. We quickly organized a weekly instruction class for learning to dance fifties style. I taught the class and showed everyone what I remembered of the Stroll and Hand Jive. We even viewed my old American Bandstand and Bandstand Reunion tapes. Soon, we had our own fifties style line dances until the Macarena made it big. The group mostly dissolved when many of our friends and fellow dancers started leaving for their next embassy postings back in the States or elsewhere in the world.

Texas Betty McNaughton lived in the eighth tower of a major high rise apartment complex provided by the United States Department of State. Her building was less than one block away from the old Embassy complex, just inland from the Persian Gulf. Her three bedroom apartment with great views of the famous Kuwait Towers cost the American Government two thousand three hundred dollars a month. In her expensive pad, Betty threw some pretty good Country Western parties.

Betty's apartment, like most in Kuwait, are nice but Kuwaitis who own the buildings charge absorbatant prices knowing the American Government will always pay. Betty's great taste in furniture, bric-a-brac and paintings reflects her charm and personality. Her living room and dining room look like those pictured on the covers of "Better Homes and Gardens". For years, Betty has painted still life's in oil and water colors, some of which we admired within the surrounds of her other loves, candles, antiques and Jack Daniels toddies.

Betty is Betty; she even takes the elevator to her building's basement, gets in her car and drives the one block to work. She said actually, its because the Ambo (Ambassador) as she calls him often makes her work late and no way is she stepping out on a Kuwaiti street after dark for a little walk home.

Betty's love life consists of secretive interludes with a much younger man. These liaisons have been going on for more than a year but she is such a lady, she still tries to hide them from everyone; without much success I might add. The younger man is an American military officer who is also unmarried, but Betty still believes everyone thinks of her as a celibate "Snow White", so the secrecy continues.

Maia and Betty sit for hours talking about what I call fru fru; dresses and materials, seamstresses, ball gowns, antiques and gossip. Like all the other Embassy ladies, they compare notes about who wore what, where, and when and where did they have it designed or made. The subject gets especially heated near November when they begin planning what they'll wear to the Formal Marine Corps Ball, Christmas celebrations and New Years Eve Party, providing of course they'll be in the country during such times.

More than once, Maia has come from a "little" shopping spree with the girls and brought home more than five thousand dollars worth of Gold jewelry at a time. Maia jokes that if she dies first, for her final rest, she wants me to put all her gold jewelry on her so she can go out like Cleopatra. I told her she will. I'll see to it that she's laid out with all of it on her; but it took grave robbers centuries to tear it from around Cleopatra's body, whereas it'll only take me about two minutes to remove it from her just before the coffin lid closes. I told her "You're going to see one crying, fighting husband if one shovel of dirt hits that coffin before I've looted it. I also assured her the gold will be in a smelter before any one knows it, but I may put her name on the brick.

CHAPTER 26

Dedication of the "New American Embassy"

The Embassy, our friends there and the social life that emanated from it kept us busy. At Marr Bell, we had lots of visiting dignitaries like Princess Anne the Princess Royal, Prime Minister Margaret Thatcher and other lesser known Brits, but now at the American Embassy we were hobnobbing with the American Hierarchy; President Bush, President Clinton, Madeline Albright, Senators and Congressmen, Generals and the. Not so much that any of us here could ever get to be their friends, but at least they are Americans and at Marr Bell-Royal Ordinance the dignitaries were always British.

When George Bush came to Kuwait the second time, he was no longer President. His first time was in April 1993, while still President. Maia wasn't working for the American Embassy at that time but I steered her and several other friends away from any of the President's scheduled meetings or motorcade routes that day. My premonition of trouble turned out to be true. President George Bush Sr. had come to a country that was still infiltrated by people loyal to Iraq, Kuwaiti fundamentalist Muslims and others that were just anti-American in general. He was almost murdered on that visit.

Thirteen people, Iraqis and Kuwaitis were convicted of attempting to assassinate the American President by blowing him up with a bomb as his motorcade rode through Kuwait City.

The Ministry of Information was alive with information concerning the attempt to kill George Bush, but there were as many Kuwaitis running around the building trying to hush the incident up as there were people trying to find out exactly what happened. God! The most powerful man on earth was almost killed right under the Kuwaiti's noses and they didn't want their own people to know anything about it. A verbal command was issued that nothing more would be said of the matter at the Ministry of Information, because such talk would only destroy public confidence in Kuwait's government and damage their ties to America.

President Bush was hurried out of sight and secured at His Highness's Palace until all travel access to and from Kuwait City could be closed down, communication lines secured and Washington be advised of all up to the minute changes and investigations.

A bomb did go off in a crowd lining the motorcade's route and many people were injured yet not one word leaked out to the press. There was never anything on the news in Kuwait and I couldn't find out anything for several months until I vacationed back in the United States. Kuwaiti's whose news was forbidden to carry the story, remained uninformed and continued their lives as if nothing happened. Even the ones at the Ministry of Information who tried to bury the story, took the old Kuwaiti posture that surely they were not at fault for anything that happened, though one Kuwaiti was later sentenced to death along with five Iraqis for their involvement in the attempted assassination. Several other Kuwaitis received varying, lesser sentences of six months to twelve years in prison.

When I was sentenced to prison three years later, I was sentenced to three and a half years at hard labor for supposedly harming 3 percent of a Kuwaiti citizen's bird finger. MY SENTENCE WAS HARSHER THAN THE KUWAIT JUSTICE SYSTEM GAVE TO FIVE OF THE MEN WHO CONSPIRED TO MURDER THE MOST POWERFUL MAN ON EARTH, THE PRESIDENT OF THE UNITED STATES OF AMERICA, IN KUWAIT'S CAPITOL CITY. Perhaps those five attempted assassins were from good families tied to Kuwait's Royal Family, and they promised not to do it again.

Following Kuwait's trial concerning the attempted assassination of the world's top leader, all consequences for that monstrous act escaped the real Kuwaitis involved. Both the United States and Kuwait once again turned their revenge toward the Iraqis for plotting to kill President Bush. Kuwait again came out as the victim. President Bill Clinton hurried to retaliate against Iraq by sending cruise missiles into the Iraqi Capital, Baghdad. Iraq's Intelligence Headquarters was the target but some of the missiles missed, killing six civilians. Wrong intelligence again from someone who was sitting at a desk in Washington. What a surprise!

"The incident" was never reported on Kuwait television or in any media of any kind. Fortunately for the United States and the world, Former President George Bush was alive and well and as a civilian returned to Kuwait once again. The second well calculated and guarded visit came in May of 1996. This second trip was carefully orchestrated to entice Kuwaitis to show their admiration for him and open their golden but cheap purse strings. Presents given to the President of the United States while still in office have to be declared and turned over to the U.S. Government, but now as a civilian, George Bush could keep all the booty for himself.

President Bush landed in the early hours of the morning and was quickly ushered into the Royal reception terminal of His Highness the Emir. Almost every high ranking Kuwaiti with title or position was on hand to greet the former leader of the coalition forces that freed their country from Saddam Hussein. Accompanied by Kuwait's Crown Prince, President Bush's tremendously long motorcade wound through the streets of Kuwait City, first to Parliament, then to His Highness the Emir's Palace, then on to several other engagements. The normal visitations, speeches, luncheons and dinners continued for a couple of days, but the main purpose for George Bush coming to Kuwait was the dedication of the new United Sates Embassy.

While Mr. Bush made his way around first day visitations, State Department employees and their families picnicked and swam for the last time in the old Embassy compound grounds downtown. Maia and I sat pool side while we waited for Mr. Bush's arrival.

Security that day was unbelievable. There would be no replay of the last visit when a bomb, not a bullet nor a hale of bullets, but a bomb almost blew up the President of the United States.

On the eighteenth floor rooftop of the Safir International Hotel, across the street overlooking the entire old embassy compound, as well as on other lower profile buildings in the neighborhood, swat teams were in full sight dressed in Ninja black uniforms with machine guns. Some looked down on the complex; others looked back up toward all the windows and balconies of the hotel. The entire American Embassy compound itself was heavily surrounded by Kuwait military humvys, who's mounted M-60 machine guns, were always kept ready to fire. Two tanks, several Kuwaiti armored riot police, personnel carrier trucks loaded with armed men and foot patrols were stationed at all corners of the compound's grounds. Other Kuwaiti military units patrolled by foot every sidewalk and roadway in the neighborhood even fanning out as far as the Persian Gulf beach front, half block away.

Roadblocks on Gulf Road and in the surrounding B'neid Al Gar residential community started as far away as three blocks in all directions.

Some apartments like Betty's were used as vantage points for more security teams with cameras and phone headsets communicating to a control headquarters what they were seeing in and around the American Embassy grounds down below. All of this was in addition to the usual Jersey barricades and machine gun turrets that normally protect the Embassy's high walls and automobile accesses.

To enter the American Embassy compound that day, we all had to go through our normal identification check and electronic scanning, the same as usual, but access even into the small metal detector room was now single file only. One person at a time. Not even an American employed by the U. S. Embassy and their American spouse was allowed inside together. All other nationalities working for the American Embassy were excused for the day and unable to attend the "American only" gathering.

President Bush arrived and walked amongst the hundred or so Americans there, shaking hands and rattling off small talk before settling in with Ambassador Ryan Crocker and wife Christine. The former President then moved once again into the crowd of Americans, wishing everyone a happy Fourth of July, and expressed his appreciation for everyone serving their country abroad. Before departing for his next function with Kuwaitis, the civilian, former President George Bush spent forty five minutes more seeking out individuals for small talk. As he neared the end of the patio next to the swimming pool, he turned and waved and said he would see everyone again tomorrow at the dedication ceremony of the new embassy compound in Bayan.

The next morning at work, in the Ministry of Information's main building, I received a deluge of reports over KUNA, Kuwait News Agency wire service, regarding all the speeches and gatherings Bush had attended the evening before. He and his entourage had been hosted at the Emir's palace for dinner, and the lengthy reports listed by name each Kuwaiti and foreign dignitary in attendance. Those reports acknowledged many of Kuwait's cream of the crop citizens, Royalty, Parliamentarians, Ministers and others; who in turn gave accurate and detailed blow by blow descriptions of their personal experiences with George Bush, the man who led the world coalition of armies that freed their country in the Gulf War.

I would not have liked to be the fly on the former President Bush's shoulder during all that elbow rubbing and cheek kissing, but I would like to have been on the jacket of the men who stood behind him receiving, and stuffing away all the presents being given to the former President. Two men stood next to a number of two feet by two feet boxes that were being filled with the likes of solid gold swords, solid gold Dhows (replicas of Kuwaiti fishing boats and a symbol of the country), gold medallions, gold ink pens, exquisite watches and even more importantly, monetary contributions.

This most enriching evening should go down as one of the most lucrative ever spent by a President or ex President. All in all, $72,000,000.oo in cash, that's seventy two million dollars and tens of thousands of dollars in gifts were tallied and boxed. The money of course was designated for the new George Bush Library being constructed on the grounds of a university in Texas.

Bush is one of my favorite Presidents and I wish he would have been allowed to serve another term in office, so I don't begrudge him the cool, calculated way his trip was planned as a civilian instead of a sitting President. But even to me, he pulled off quite a feat. It was dazzling to think of all that money and gifts would have ended up in the pockets of the United States Government, had he still be in office.

On the morning of the dedication of the new United States Embassy in Bayan, I went to work as usual and did the 7 o'clock, 9 o'clock, and noon news programs, and then headed to join Maia and other Embassy and FBO staff already in Bayan. The ceremony scheduled for 2 o'clock in the afternoon was going to be during the hottest time of day, so I quickly headed through all the security and into one of the large hospitality tents set up inside the compound's walls, near the front entrance.

On the noon news, I announced it was already 106 degrees, climbing toward the expected high temperature of 117 degrees, but I was sure by now it was already that or above.

Impressive was the first word I thought when I saw the way the grounds inside the compound looked. The new "Inman" style, secured Embassy was dressed and readied for its first official function. All the very tall, stately, matching height date palm trees, pregrown hedges, flowering planters and the rolled out grass sod lawn were manicured to perfection.

The new embassy's three fountains, the one in the central courtyard, the one in the entry foyer and the one in the inner courtyard were bubbling with crystal clear water that cascaded over sky colored, Moroccan influenced tiles with an Arabic motif. All the water and tall date palms, grass and shrubs were certainly in sharp contrast to our semi arid wastelands just outside the gates.

All Embassy employees, their families and Kuwaiti guests, spent time before the dedication sipping cold sodas and juices, eating finger foods and licking ice creams under expansive canopies and tents. The floors of the tents were filled wall to wall with expensive Persian carpets, which added just a little regional flavor to the event. Most of the crowd remained near the central courtyard's fountain and esplanade, beneath the tall, wide canopied date palms. The perfectly matched trees didn't appear to have been planted only a few days ago. Instead, they looked as if they had all been there for months if not years. Several of the original plantings had died and as late as two days ago, a huge crane was brought across the lawn to hoist and stand them in place. As in all new Embassies, every minute detail had been taken care of.

Suddenly, about 1:45 p m, in a barrage of clicking cameras, applause and whistling, former President George Bush, Ambassador Ryan Crocker, His Highness Sheikh Saad, Kuwait's Crown Prince and Prime Minister rounded the corner into an appreciative crowd. A second entourage of American diplomats in business suits and Kuwaitis in traditional white dishdashas with flowing white head pieces followed. A few Royals were wearing their brown, ceremonial, sheer muslin robes trimmed in gold brocade over their traditional ones. George Bush Sr. always looks good and wore a simple but nice dark suit for the occasion. I looked closely at Ambassador Crocker's shoes while he was seated to see if he was still wearing the ones with the holes in the soles or wearing white socks, fortunately he wasn't, but had he, it wouldn't have been the first time.

Maia's boss, Tom Farley stood beside Ambassador Crocker, President Bush and the Crown Prince for the ribbon cutting ceremony. Naturally there were plenty of speeches, but fortunately short ones, because of the intense, hot, desert sun beating down upon us.

Following the ceremony, the most important guests left the outdoor heat for more comfortable air conditioned private quarters inside while the rest of us toured the entire new facility. Maia and I were later pulled aside and asked at Betty McNaughton's urging, to ride in the Presidential motorcade that would return President Bush back to his waiting 747, on the tarmac of the Royal Terminal. Soon Betty, Maia and I were being whisked by security men into a limousine of their picking. (With President Clinton, Maia and I rode a bus in the motorcade; this was a step up for us.)

Maia and I sat in the limousine's rear seat while Betty rode facing us in the jump seat. A small group of Embassy employees and their families rode the 47 passenger bus to the airport. Of the twenty-four vehicles long motorcade, fifteen were steel reinforced Suburban security cars and police cars, not counting of course, the more than two dozen motorcycle police at both ends.

When we arrived at the airport, we stood aside in a special small roped area apart from the several hundred other well wishers who had assembled to bid the former President goodbye. The President said his farewells to his Kuwaiti hosts and to Ambassador and Mrs. Crocker then waved to the larger contingent of well wishers who in turn were shouting and waving American and Kuwaiti flags. President Bush came to our area, shook several hands and thanked everyone present again for their service to the United States overseas and praised the employees for their diligent work and support. He then turned and walked toward the red carpet where His Highness the Crown Prince and Prime Minister and a handful of other Kuwaitis were waiting to see him off. There were more handshakes then George Bush alone ascended the staircase toward the open door reflecting the Presidential seal of the United States of America. The former President waved one final time to everyone at the Royal Terminal and to his hosts then turned and walked inside Air Force

One. Booty and entourage aboard, the giant blue and white plane taxied briefly then climbed steeply into the sky.

Our new group of friends from the Embassy began expanding and becoming closer at the same time. Barbara and Betty often came over to our penthouse for dinner and wine, and we rotated dinner parties between their residences as well. When Betty came to our apartment, she always enticed me into dancing the Country Two Step, I did for her but I remained loyal to my fifties and sixties style dancing. Sometimes, there were only six or eight of us at these cozy dinner parties but you would think there were three times more people. We danced, sang and laughed and had a few alcoholic drinks in defiance of Kuwaiti laws forbidding it.

I've never seen someone with as many western outfits as Betty. The outfits changed but her red hair in a bun didn't. Barbara and I continued sneaking in Shags and Beach Boy tunes between Betty's country hits but Maia and the other Country Western fans out voted Barbara and I most of the time.

Maia and I were happily entwined with our new embassy "gang" but we still spent time and longed for even more with our original friends from Marr Bell days and all the off shoots of acquaintances from that period. Many of us had been together through rough times and good times, deaths, prisoners of war and happier occasions; like holiday vacations and birthdays, weddings and births.

One of our "original gang" friends we continued staying close to was Janelle, the Lebanese-American mother of three who was kicked out of Kuwait when her Kuwaiti husband died. Janelle was a real sport and a lot of fun. Janelle was at full strength whether battling cancer, throwing a great party or battling former in-laws for her kid's inheritance.

After her husband died, she came back and fought for millions of dollars and their former home. Like the rest of us, Janelle has had a lot of ups and downs. Iraqi Occupation was bad for all of us and people in Kuwait have had more than a few roadblocks in life to contend with much less coming back to a country that had been destroyed by mines, bombs, torture and fires. Janelle was the one who made that transition for most of us a little easier.

Janelle returned to Kuwait from the United States shortly after Desert Storm and she's happy giving parties once again. She left Kuwait shortly after Occupation began and returned shortly after it was over. Her home suffered some damage by vibrations from exploding bombs and Iraqi troops and from the oil clouds, but most of it was easily repaired. For the most part, her family escaped the worst part of war by leaving the country before Saddam Hussein had completed the real clamp down. Janelle's older son, Haythem continued attending university at San Diego State in California and her second son, Mish returned to Kuwait with the American Military as a guide. Many other half Kuwaiti half American young people returned like Mishal did and helped the American forces, where ever and when ever they could.

After the war, Mish began working for Kuwait Airways the same as his father had but of course Mish was not a pilot but a male steward. Janelle's only daughter Miriam disappointed her mother by marrying at the ripe old age of eighteen. She always thought Miriam's young husband was trying to legally take her share of the fortune but so far has been blocked from doing so. In Kuwait he is now legally entitled to all her money.

The biggest news about Janelle was that she had recently remarried, this time to an Egyptian attorney named Jalal. The new husband is a sixty two year old practicing lawyer with a Kuwaiti firm. Another big surprise to our group was that she didn't mind sharing her husband with his other wife in Cairo. Jalal seems caring, quite nice and thoughtful but he is an attorney. That alone awakened terrible distrustful feelings inside me because of my loathing for that profession in any county, Kuwait even more so. He came to Janelle with plenty of baggage. Unlike our friends Boudran and Linda out in Jahra contending with another wife and children, Jalal lives in Janelle's home several months at a time, then rotates to the other wife and his several grown children in Egypt. Boudran at least has another wife in the same town and only has to be missing from Linda's bed while he has weekly conjugal visits at the other wife's residence.

When Janelle married Jalal, she made an agreement to share him with the other wife so Jalal returns to Egypt for fun and frolicking with the other wife on a regular basis with Janelle's blessing. With Jalal added to "our original gang", we have again grown with yet another real character, as if we didn't already have plenty.

Another of our closest friend's was Joseph Territo, an Italian-American former intelligence officer for the United States Army, now retired. His most recent adventures have led him to be part owner of a diamond mine in Sierra Leone, Africa, gold mines in another African country and confidante and close personal friend to some rather dubious former Presidents throughout Africa, Central and South America. Joseph has been imprisoned in two countries for who knows what reasons and now he's like the rest of us, "carpet bagging" in Kuwait. He made millions and lost millions. He also lost his family because he never went home to Virginia to see them. He just kept sending them money. When the money was gone, they felt no other attachment to him and quit writing.

Joseph Territo, a mid sixty something year old Italian-American with bald head and lollipop could easily be confused with Kojak. He always wears military style khakis, safari vests, shirts with epaulets but instead of boots, he wears flip flops. Except for his feet, he looks like an ad for senior citizen's wearing Banana Republic clothing. Joseph's numerous adventures during and since the rebuilding of Kuwait led him to a rendezvous with a wretched woman who has become his second wife and sort of a friend of ours, Kathleen Youngkin.

Kathleen, a self described talented artist of notable fame was brought to Kuwait for the restoration of several Royal Palaces. Her resume boasted of her renowned reproductions of marble, faux marble, tromp loile, tiles, mosaics, cornice work and etched glass, put her into a select global class who travel the world to remodel and rebuild such places as Windsor Castle after the fire and massive desert palaces of Arab Royals in Saudi Arabia and United Arab Emirates. We however never saw anything remotely great that she did and figured she extremely stretched her qualifications to get jobs rebuilding those burned out palaces in Kuwait. Kathleen brought her two teenage children to Kuwait where they attended the private English School. Renee, the younger of the two was an honor student and Billy showed great promise as an artist but less toward the academic world. He tended to be bored easily in school except for subjects he truly enjoyed. One day, no doubt he'll be a great artisan like his mother always thought she was.

Joseph's suave, debonair charm and Kathleen's are a strange dynamic couple who loves, fights and works at peeks and valleys few of us can understand or survive.

Joseph, before his marriage to Kathleen, maintained a three story bachelor apartment and business office in downtown Kuwait City. His place was always "a happening". Journalist, expat school teachers, college professors, contractors, Kuwaitis, Americans and probably ten other nationalities were always either at Joseph's or they were on their way. There was always someone over the stove cooking for the crowd or he was preparing the big ethnic Italian meal himself. Joseph served tasty pastas made by his own hands, along with home brewed red and white wines aged several weeks in plastic tubs in his own bathroom "still". As a resourceful man, he always had liquor, ham, bacon and pork chops in this Islamic land where pigs and alcohol are forbidden.

About every weekend there was a party and dance at Joseph's apartment, where the music was a concoction of American and Arabic contemporary hits. During business days, Joseph preferred low key music like the Muzak in elevators but on weekends he cranked it up with songs by Boys II Men, Michael Bolton, Guns and Roses, etc. All parties lasted until two or three in the morning. Joseph's place turned out to be the number one meeting place for most of our friends in Kuwait.

When Joseph died, shock and grief were hardly the words to describe the emptiness our gang felt. For the party scene, it was a catastrophe and for Kathleen a personal devastation.

Joseph had been battling cancer for about a year but almost all signs of it had disappeared after intensive chemotherapy and radiation. What actually killed him were tainted mushrooms, consumed at a local restaurant. The mushrooms normally wouldn't have had a serious affect on Joseph except to make him sick, however the radiation and chemotherapy had weakened his immune system so much that he couldn't fight off the poison.

For almost a year, Kathleen was in deep depression and kept in limbo about her status in Kuwait. She and her children like most unmarried women except school teachers and nurses are unwelcome to live amongst Muslim society. Through some strange event or circumstance, it was easier for Kathleen and the kids to remain if they were living as part of mine and Maia's family so three more people came to live with us.

Kathleen was using large doses of sleeping pills and antidepressant medications that didn't seem to work and when she went out to run errands or take the kids to school, she put Joseph's cremated remains in the passenger seat next to her and strapped him in.

You see, Joseph had to be cremated and since Kathleen and her family had been in the Middle East for many years, she didn't have a place stateside to bury Joseph, so she took his body out of Kuwait, went to a crematorium in India, and brought him through customs again as grey plaster of paris in a clear bag. Soon after, she encased him in a gorgeous, foot long, silver and stone inlaid Moroccan vase.

Now we had five "live" people, one "dead" person and four cats living in our apartment. At least now, Kathleen could have Joseph nearby and felt much closer to him even during short drives to the market etc.

Any ways, during one of Joseph's socials, more than two years prior to his death, we met Betty Lippold. Betty came to Kuwait for adventure and instead became a top notch reporter for the largest English newspaper in Kuwait, THE ARAB TIMES. Her retired military husband, Lt Colonel Carl Lippold tagged along with the more energetic Betty, while enjoying his retirement from the United States Air Force. Carl and Betty's zest for an adventurous life came to Kuwait like the rest of us for a more secured retirement.

Carl doesn't seem to mind being the husband of someone who constantly keeps things stirred up and lively. Not that Betty "rules the roost" but Kuwait is obviously her choice of habitats, not his.

Ever since Carl's retirement from the Air Force quite some years ago, they've both continued moving from place to place. Betty is no spring chicken but acts like one. Really, she's a sixty two year old flower child of the sixties who has the energy and looks of a woman half her age. It is mostly Betty and Joseph that keep all the parties jumping. They keep everyone on the dance floor and when everyone else tires, they dance together or alone.

In that ole girl body, lurks an amorous young sexual lassie. Only recently has our gang started noticing Betty's developing close relationship with a young Iranian semi-pro tennis player, Abdullah. They dance the night away at the parties and who knows at what other times.

Before Betty and Abdullah, our close knit gang has always stayed close as friends only. There has never been anyone else who has ever crossed over that line between friendship and lover but for them it seems to be working. Because of everyone's love for Betty, her attraction to young Abdullah has never been a subject of conversation. After all, everyone really cares for Abdullah too.

What is there not to like? Abdullah is a vibrant, six feet two inches tall, good looking guy who can build a car engine, press your clothes, cook your meals, play a killer game of tennis, water ski, dance, write English, Farsi or Arabic poetry, take great photos and on and on and on. Anyone who needs anything done, Abdullah can and will do it.

Betty is a wiry blonde whose long blonde hair and style of clothing are a throwback to her days in San Francisco and the Haite-Ashbury District. Through the years, she has aged but her mind and energy haven't gotten the message. We all love her and her free spirit. She is feisty and full of life and spends each long ten hour workday seeking out stories only Betty can get away with writing in a censored country like Kuwait. Whenever I'm in her apartment, I always look for Geritol bottles or anything that can give me a clue to what gives her all that great energy.

Abdullah is tall, good looking, trim and strong and only twenty eight years old. He's not dark like most Iranians but rather fair with light brown hair. Best of all, Abdullah gloats over Betty who is at least thirty seven years his senior. To understand that relationship, one only has to know both of them. They are both caring and articulate and seem to mold their personalities into one. No one has ever actually said they are sleeping together because it never comes up. They obviously fill a need in each others lives with a relationship that has gone far deeper than a bedroom.

When Betty fell down some stairs in a building she had just completed a news story in, Carl was back in the United States. It was Abdullah who took care of her and nursed her back to health after a very complicated surgery that left her in a cast then a cane for the better part of a year. Abdullah, whose schedule of work and social activities is already exhaustive, returns to Betty's side later in the day and evenings to help her in hers. He carries her in his arms up flights of stairs and takes pictures and whatever else is needed. He has the patience of a lamb whose temperament is as endlessly good as his many talents.

Betty's husband Carl is a wonderful man but still retains his independence and freedom in the ways an older military man might require. He still loves Betty and its obvious but he is in a more scholarly world of books, writing and travel. Carl often boards military transport planes through Europe and the United States traveling to see his children and grand children, old retired friends and business trips (probably to invest all the money they save because neither Betty nor Carl have ever spent any of the money they've earned through retirement pensions or from Betty's work in Kuwait). Abdullah as proxy husband lives in the same apartment as Betty and Carl.

Betty, Carl, Abdullah and Betty's son Randy from her first marriage, opened an upscale art gallery in St. Augustine, Florida and continue selecting and sending beautiful paintings, rugs, tapestries and sculptures to it while still residing in Kuwait.

The long list of our friends is evident of our busy social life and we have a great one. Maia and I consider ourselves very fortunate we have friends of every walk of life, every social class and creed but we seem to have been derelict in choosing one that is introverted, lacks opinion or is uninteresting.

Our friend Ekaterina is hardly the latter. Katia as we call her is a former Russian KGB agent whom we met at Joseph's apartment. She's a bio-chemist at a local Kuwait Government lab. As the months passed since our first meeting, we've seen more and more of Katia. She's never made "out of bounds" inquiries from us as Americans nor has she ever asked Maia anything about American Embassy work. Though our closeness is reciprocal, there is still a maintained distance on subjects that might cloud our relationship.

At times, Maia and I had our doubts to whether the rumors about her being a KGB agent were true or not. We didn't really know whether to trust her or not, nor whether she was aggressive in gathering some kind of spy information or not. She certainly always acted like a real normal human being, who worked, laughed, joked, danced, cooked and liked to dine out while raising two kids as a single Mom.

After knowing Katia for more than two and a half years, Maia and I were having dinner with her one evening at a local revolving restaurant high atop a building in the Al Sharq District of Kuwait City. I came right out and asked her if she was a KGB agent, a Major in fact. First, with sort of a sheepish grin then dabbing her lips with a cloth napkin, she said "Who told you that?" I said just about everyone. She continued to fuss with her napkin as her smile grew bigger and bigger. Then she sheepishly said "A past has a way of catching up with you doesn't it." She went on by saying, "Yes, I had been trained and worked for quite some time for the Soviet Government in the branch you call KGB." I then asked what kind of cases she had. She said "you would not understand about them, most were internal situations in my hometown in the Ukraine.

"When I got married", Katia said, "I strayed further and further away from my job, until they only called on me once a year or so. When the Soviet Union broke up, the KGB did also. The Government was unable to keep track of us as easily as they had in the past because they had a lot of problems of their own. I just sort of evolved out of it."

I asked Katia had she had any cases since coming to live in Kuwait and she replied "Your wife works for the United States Embassy and I haven't asked her any questions about her work there or yours and I don't mean yours at the Ministry of Information or Dasma Palace." "I understand that you are fairly busy in your own activities that I bet you wouldn't want to discuss right now." With that line, it was my turn to look sheepish and turn a slight shade of blush."

In her Russian-English accent, she said, "If you want to know about spies and intrigue, you should ask Nesim Abadi but I suspect you already know about him." Nesim Abadi, an Iranian, frequents many of the same parties we attend at the Turkish and other Embassies around town as well as having attended a few parties at our own apartment.

I asked Katia, "Why, what does he do?" She said "Now that man is connected." We didn't get into details about Nesim Abadi because I was still more interested in hearing about Katia from the source, Katia herself. In such a small country like Kuwait and an even smaller expatriate community, one hears many stories about ones own acquaintances. Some of the other things I had heard about Katia were burning my tongue not to ask but I thought I'd be pushing too hard prying farther into her personal life.

Even more importantly than the KGB spy question I asked Katia was the other more delicate subject matter. Katia always had lots of money and I heard the way she came about much of it through a Russian prostitution ring in Kuwait. It was no secret Katia acted like a "Madam" to many of the girls in question. It was also well known, Katia threw some pretty good parties at the Russian Embassy in Kuwait when their Ambassador was out of the country.

Those parties were not the type Maia and I, nor most of our friends were ever invited to. They were little more than sanctioned orgies, linking up Kuwaiti men to Russian girls. Maia never believed any of the stories but I knew several men who had attended such parties.

Our three hour dinner with Katia wound down by mostly she and I bantering back and forth over dessert about other friends we both thought were less than above board in their personal activities.

Joseph was one of those subjects that night and on many occasions since. He is another of our inner circle of friends Katia and I get a kick out of discussing. Both of us had lots of stories to share about him, mostly involving Africa, Spain, Italy and Iraq. Though Joseph is an American, he has been involved with the American and British Intelligence communities and farmed out to other governments on the side. Even the Ministry of Information where I work is aware of him. Twice I came across papers naming him specifically.

No doubt, the list of friends and characters met at Joseph's parties are impressive and nearly endless. Another of those whom we met at one of his parties was Hashim, a cousin of Nesim Abadi whom Katia brought up.

Hashim was the first cousin of the Shah of Iran. At the time we met him, he was rotating coasts in the United States as a small time movie producer mostly living in New York City. He was visiting relatives married into Kuwaiti families here in Kuwait City, when he attended Joseph's party. Hashim thoroughly enjoyed networking at Joseph's very international assemblages of friends. After all, attending Joseph's parties was tantamount to putting your name on an endless party and dinner roster of "Who's Who" of the Expatriate World inside Kuwait.

Putting all our friends together from old Marr Bell Royal Ordinance days, Maia's Embassy group, and my Kuwaiti contacts from the Ministry of Information, Dasma Palace and Joseph's group, our plate was full. Most of our friends are personable and generous to a fault as well as being diverse in cultures, customs and traditions. Each get together, whether big or small, was a learning experience. This combination also led to reciprocal parties in palaces, holidays aboard yachts and vacations with friends in far away places. With all the hoopla and staying on the go, we still always managed quality time for close personal relationships with many of these people.

Nothing is better than hanging out at a friend's house, learning their traditional dances, eating their food and hearing their jokes and about their way of life. With some, we play scrabble, monopoly and guessing games and with others, we look at photographs, play with their babies or debate "the three forbidden subjects" Religion, Politics and Sex. Life with our proxy families can't get much better.

David and Sharon Gugliandolo are two of our newest friends but rapidly becoming two of our dearest. David is a thirty four year old "wheeler dealer" with a Doctor's degree in something. He's a Sicilian with good manners, quick wit, light complexion and dark fast growing beard. He's from a financially well-off family who permitted him the luxuries of "finding himself", while being educated where he wanted and traveling and working where he wanted, any time he wanted.

Similar to me but even more so, David worked on cruise ships out of Miami, Florida, in hotels in London and Paris, restaurants in India and Hong Kong and back packed through many countries around the world.

David's young wife Sharon is a native of India with a very British education. She has been living in Kuwait with her family for many years so also speaks the local Arabic dialect as well. She and David met at Joseph's office where the consortium David works for has an office. He and Sharon rapidly fell in love and got married. Sharon has dark hair, dark complexion and a beautiful petite figure. Their newest arrival, son Sean is definitely a cross somewhere in between the Sicilian and the Indian but at this point looks more like a tanned Winston Churchill than either of them.

David and Sharon travel often and enjoy purchasing fine art and cultural things from countries around the globe. David often goes on business trips to marble quarries and mosaic tile factories and takes Sharon along so each trip becomes another small vacation. Both are fun and witty and Maia and I spend many evenings with the two of them dining out on our penthouse terrace over looking Kuwait City and the Persian Gulf or at their home near the old American Embassy. David and Sharon as well as being two of our favorite dinner partners are our favorite scrabble partners.

Sharon is a part time Secretary for the Safir International Hotel across from the old American Embassy and only two blocks from where she and David live. Sharon is a good cook but David is much better, unlike me and Maia. I'm not much of a cook and Maia didn't find out where the kitchen was in our house, until we had been married around a half dozen years. The four of us often dine at the newest eateries in Kuwait City whether they are Indian, Iranian, American, French, Chinese, Thai, Arabic or whatever. I can't say if we've ever eaten at a British restaurant though. From what I've tasted on each trip to Britain, I don't think any one can export it and stay in business long.

Once when David and Sharon were passing along Gulf Road near our apartment, they looked up and saw me dangling off the side of the building with ropes extended from the penthouse roof. They delayed their shopping to come see what I was doing. I explained that the building maintenance workers only washed down our windows once every three months and Maia and I like clean windows. What's the use of having a penthouse with floor to ceiling windows if they're always covered in sand or watermarks?

Within the first week of living in our place, I learned how to rig a contraption that would allow me to climb off the side of our building from our roof, drop to our windows and use a garden hose and squeegee to clean the windows. David said I must be crazy, he thought it was awfully brave and stupid. His exact expression was "What are a few dirty windows in Kuwait?"

Little did David and Sharon know nor would they ever learn that hanging outside my windows from the top floor of our building was not as brave or stupid as some of the other things that were taking place in my professional life at that same time.

David and Sharon also liked to go furniture antiquing with Maia and me. During such forays, I've picked up some reproduction Louis XVI pieces, several carved wardrobes, many mirrors, ancient urns, Sultan's trunks and Bedouin carpets and camel throws.

The most fun shopping in the Kuwait City area is the giant Friday (Juma) Iranian flea market where more than a thousand stalls are sprawled over a vast parking lot. Anything you want at any price you want is there. You just have to find it. When the day time temperatures in the summer are almost 130 degrees we don't go, but in the fall and winter as well as early spring we go almost weekly.

One particular area of the Iranian Market is filled with stalls of Arab barkers selling old silver jewelry, serving trays, brass trunks, swords and daggers, hand blown lamps, Persian carpets, coins and much more. This is the part where we spend most of our time.

CHAPTER 27

Marine Corp Ball

Someone we often see at Friday Juma Market is Linda, my coworker at the Ministry of Information Super Station Radio. Her husband Badran, the former Kuwait Army Officer was the one taken prisoner during the Iraqi invasion of Kuwait. On the morning Saddam Hussein's troops invaded Kuwait, Jahra and Badran were in the invasion's direct line. About three o'clock in the morning on August 2, 1989, Badran and Linda were awakened by loud pounding on their front door. They were told the Iraqis were attempting to cross the border in force and Badran had to leave for work at the Ali Al Salem Air Base, west of town. Deep down they thought it was only a military exercise but Badran told Linda he'd call later and let her know what was really happening.

Since Jahra is mostly Bedouin and Fundamentalist Muslim, the building they lived in was not allowed the use of televisions or cellular telephones. Without being able to inform Linda of his whereabouts, Badran and Linda's separation were going to last for a long time and each not knowing the others safety, dead or alive. Witnesses said Badran fired missiles that morning at approaching Iraqi helicopter gun ships but was quickly overrun.

Linda and their twelve year old daughter Miriam waited for news about Badran but none came. Each day passed into a week and each week into months. Word would not come for more than a year by which time Linda and daughter Miriam would be in the United States. During occupation,

Linda sought help from the American Embassy to get her and Miriam out of the country and return them to the United States. Linda was able to get whatever travel documents she needed but could not be helped in getting out of occupied Kuwait. Most borders were closed within the first few weeks and only the one to Baghdad remained open.

Linda and Miriam sought freedom by traversing the desert roads of Iraq in a car with several other people. They arrived safely in Baghdad and proceeded on to Amman, Jordan before boarding a flight to the United States. Linda had little family left in the United States, so after a brief visit to El Paso, Texas, she took Miriam to Washington, D.C. where they remained until occupation and Desert Storm were over. Badran would not be heard from for more than a year.

Talk about a social change. To Miriam who was almost a teenager, Washington was like a new wonderland. She and Linda could walk through a mall without being in black Abaya and face veil. The United States and Kuwait Governments financially assisted those fleeing Kuwait, who made it to our shores, so Linda and Miriam had no worries about finding or paying rent for a place to live. The United States helped them obtain temporary housing and got the children enrolled in school, and the Kuwait Government handed out monthly allowances from their foreign bank accounts to pay for housing, an automobile and necessities like additional clothing that would take them through a Washington winter.

These Kuwaiti families and others dislocated in London, Cairo, Paris, Washington and many other cities sat out the rest of Occupation and Liberation with most creature comforts.

Linda and Miriam were thrilled with their new surroundings in Washington but one of the most important parts of their lives was still unaccounted for. They didn't know whether Badran was alive or dead. For a long time there was no word of his fate. Linda stayed in touch with the Kuwait Embassy in Washington almost daily where the Kuwait Ambassador during that time was Sheikh Saud Nasser Al Sabah, later mine and Linda's employer as Minister of Information.

Linda and Miriam received a call one day from the Kuwait Embassy in Washington saying they had new information pertaining to Badran. Linda rushed there and was told he was alive but being held prisoner in Iraq. Linda was still unable to contact him but at least she felt slightly comfortable in the knowledge he was alive. Even knowing prisoners were alive in Iraqi jails was no reason to celebrate. Iraqis and Iranians are known for detaining prisoners for many years after their wars or conflicts are over.

In the case of Iraq, they recently released many Iranian prisoners more than seven years after the Iraq-Iran war was over. The Iraqis repeatedly denied the existence of any more prisoners, yet seven years later they were freed. Now almost six years after the Iraq-Kuwait war, the Iraqis are still holding Kuwaitis.

Linda and Miriam arrived back in Kuwait late 1991 and were immediately surprised when reunited with Badran who had been one of the few lucky people freed from Iraqi prisons. Badran's other wife; a Bedouin had stayed in Kuwait during Occupation and Liberation and knew scarce more information during that time about Badran's whereabouts than Linda did. In fact Linda probably knew more.

Since returning to Kuwait from prison, Badran's citizenship has been in question. Like most Bedouins, his loyalties to Kuwait were in question about whether he had cooperated with the enemy as had other Bedouins and Palestinians. Even though Badran had proof and eyewitness accounts of his valor and of his commitment in helping captured wounded Kuwaitis during their imprisonment in Iraq, he became part of a post war "witch hunt" by first class Kuwaitis who had to find someone else to blame for everything that had gone wrong. Palestinians sided with the enemy, many Bedouin stateless people and second class Kuwait's as well as other expat laborers sided with Saddam Hussein quite willingly.

Due to these circumstances, first class Kuwaitis categorically lumped everyone together. Their witch hunts included Kuwaiti posse's who began gunning down other civilians on the streets of Kuwait City and its suburbs, kidnapping and torturing others and denying any favored positions in the Kuwait military, Government jobs and in the private sector to anyone under the slightest suspicion. In other words Badran can't legally work in Kuwait any more so Linda has set out to earn her family's living by being a Disc Jockey on the morning wake-up show at the Super Station FM 92.5 with me. In order for them to return to America, Badran would have to denounce one wife and three or four children which he says he will never do.

Linda's morning "Breakfast Show" on the Super Station FM 92.5 has taken off like a lightening bolt. The listening audience loves her and what she does. No one can tell Linda isn't an old pro DJ from an American station. Linda's on-air voice and presence is beautiful and it is funny for me sometimes to sit back and watch the ease and control she has with the new show. I broadcast the news, weather and sports on the hour then programming goes back to Linda for more good listening.

Linda's booth is separated from mine by an eight foot wide, thick, vacuum sealed, glass window. From either side, we control the next song coming up or bring the station to "Live Studio" for talking or for going to commercials. We often banter back and forth about when a particular "Oldie and Goldie" song was popular or who did it. Linda's audience is loyal and very responsive by telephone and fax. It didn't take long before everyone in Kuwait knew the two of us from the Super Station, and not unusual for me to ride and elevator where someone will say, "I know your voice, you're Charles Petty." This happens at the laundry, the auto repair shop and parties. Super Station listeners even more so than the television audiences make us feel famous.

United States Embassy personnel are use to entertaining themselves and others with whom they work but not often with others not within the Embassy fold. There are times, very few times when everyone willingly jumps at the chance to be entertained by a few of the well-to-do private Kuwaiti citizens who open their guest palaces and beaches to foreign Embassy personnel. Recently was one of those times. Maia called my studio and eagerly announced that this coming Friday the Al Marzouks are hosting every Embassy in the country at their bi-annual beach and swim party.

Ambassadors and their families and Embassy staff members come to the Al Marzouk's huge summer guest palace on the beach in Fintas, south of Kuwait City for lots of food, frolicking on the beach, jet skiing and swimming.

September is still very hot in Kuwait and most people are tired of the heat but there's little they can do about the temperature. It's best to lay back and try to enjoy it as best you can. Most Kuwaitis are still out of the country, escaping the summer heat but most foreign staff members of Embassies have to stay in Kuwait even during the worst summer days. The Al Marzouks give some respite to those terrible, long hot days by ingratiating themselves and their huge summer complex to all those who will come and enjoy. More than two hundred fifty persons from more than twenty countries arrived at this summer's picnic luncheon and swim party.

The Al Marzouk's summer complex has three main buildings, each two stories high. The entire complex with tennis courts, swimming pool, and private beach, fishing pier, jet skis and vast parking is well secured by heavily guarded privacy walls except along their personal three hundred foot long stretch of beach front.

Mostly the children swam in the Persian Gulf and the pool but a few American soldiers joined in as well. The rest of us sat around tables under ramadas eating delicious food and downing soft drinks and ice cream sundaes.

The Al-Marzouks are intermarried to the Al Sabah Ruling Family but are considered just wealthy first class Kuwaiti citizens. They're wonderful hosts and always make everyone feel so comfortable and special. Mr. and Mrs. Al Marzouk who are in their late thirties or early forties dress and look as sestern as most of their guests. They continued walking amongst them speaking of Country Western Music, their personal favorite and of vacation destinations other guests also frequent. They're both interesting and interested in knowing many of us personally.

Get togethers, like the day with the Al Marzouks, are wonderful for making new acquaintances and reacquainting yourself with nice people you met at other Embassy parties throughout the year. At times, many of us are disappointed in Kuwait and Kuwaitis but at least we will always be able to look back on days like the one with the al Marzouks and know we have fond memories of Kuwaitis also.

Our table that day was a bee hive of activity the whole three hours we were guests at the Al Marzouks guest palace. Maia, Barbara and Betty sat discussing several other guests and where they had seen them before. One would say, "oh there is the beautiful lady from Hong Kong who wore the exquisite dark blue gown at the British Embassy formal three months earlier; or would giggle and point out others that had stood out at parties in the Turkish, German, French, Japanese or Italian embassies like the Russian and Polish hookers who claim to be personal trainers.

One of the preoccupations of Maia and other close lady friends is checking out the gold being worn by the others at gala events. Maia and Betty or Barbara or Betsy find out where it was purchased or designed then plan trips to Dubai, United Arab Emirates or Manama, Bahrain to hunt for similar items. All of us guys just sit around discussing the last time we went to Bahrain or Dubai on business or layovers, and what hotel we stayed in or disco we went to. We talk about the pool and bar at the Chicago Hotel in Dubai, a favorite of everyone's especially the Brits, Americans and Canadians and other clubs and restaurants.

The al Marzouks thoughtfully left four jet skis on the beach for the guests to enjoy and we did. Several of the guys and I took off for a little trip down the beach and back. As we skimmed over the blue green waters of the Persian Gulf passing mansion after mansion that dotted the coast line, pictures ran through my mind of what everything looked like only a few years ago during and after Iraqi Occupation. This time, there was no sign of the concertina wire and trenches dug full length of the beach, the huge Iraqi cannons and machine guns nests everywhere aimed out at the sea or the rotting bird and fish carcasses or slicks of oil that polluted the waters.

The skies have cleared, they are no longer filled with oil and the Gulf's waters team with life, not floating mines. In some way I feel those memories are allusions from someone else's mind or in a past life.

That summer as most was uneventful in Kuwait and Maia and I managed to make it through another hundred fifty scorching hot days. By the time fall rolled around, it was time for everyone to begin planning the holiday season and the long awaited coming of cooler weather. The holiday season usually kicks off a barrage of picnics, parties and annual balls that start with mine and Maia's Halloween party, the American Embassy's Marine Corps Ball, then comes Thanksgiving, several other functions at the Embassies in Kuwait, Christmas and all the parties associated with it and then the welcoming of the New Years and Eid, a Muslim holiday that lasts a month. By the end of Eid, we're already well into Kuwait's short winter.

Temperatures finally level off to a tolerable maximum about two weeks before the November Marine Corps Ball at the United States Embassy and start rising again late February. The Ball is a yearly affair celebrated worldwide in American Embassies and on U.S. military bases. In Kuwait, it is a prized event. Only the most fortunate and influential are allowed to attend. Even other Americans within the country can't attend unless they are a guest of a marine or an embassy staff member. Officials of the host government and persons belonging to other Embassies all try to be on the exclusive short list of invitees but it is the hottest ticket in town and most don't make it.

This year, the 221st Marine Corps Birthday Ball was held on Thursday November 14th, 1996. It was the finest of the several years we had been attending. All invitations had gone out and preparations had been completed by early November. This year the ball was held amongst the fountains and beneath the forest of date palms in the inner courtyard of the new American Embassy in Bayan for the first time.

About 7:45 p.m., Maia and I arrived at the heavily fortified Embassy and entered the first checkpoint though still well away from actual Embassy grounds. Army tanks guarded the surrounding expanse of desert while several Kuwait military humvys with mounted m-60 automatic weapons were stationed at intervals closer in and around the compound grounds. Cars were lined up almost a half block just waiting for their turn to be waved through the final of three checkpoints and into the parking lot outside embassy grounds. Foot patrols and guard towers kept visual account of all activity inside and outside the perimeter. Nepalese Ghurka security guards checked each automobile for explosives as it pulled into the rear of the line more than a block away.

As Maia and I got closer to the gate, one Ghurka guardsman shoved a roller device similar to a mechanic's jack beneath the car to view the undercarriage for any possible bomb while another Ghurka hoisted the hood and carefully, visually scanned the engine. A third Ghurka checked the trunk and opened our car doors to better check the inside floor, glove compartment and side panels for any packages or oddities.

Next, we parked within the walled perimeter, exited our cars and waited for the next series of personal security screening at the foot gate which opens on the other side into the main complex. One person at a time was brought into the small bulletproof room, scanned with a wand, body searched and ladies' purses were checked, then we were in.

The inner compound was beautiful and tranquil at night, certainly not reflective of all the commotion going on outside the fortress walls. The long majestic date palm lined promenade was beautifully lit with each tree having its own accent light. The sculpted gardens and horizontal sidewalk level fountain bubbled in colors of blue and green. Even the beautiful new sculpture recently dedicated to those persons killed in a terrorist bomb blast here in Kuwait, was lit.

As we entered the main doors, Ambassador Crocker and wife Christine greeted us. The Ambassador wore a simple but sharp black tux. I couldn't tell but hoped he wasn't wearing those old shoes with the holes in the soles again (I still always check for them at each function). Fortunately for him, he was wearing proper black ones that night. Christine who looks a lot like Meredith Vihar on "The View" was wearing a simple black three quarters length gown with only a simple pair of earrings. Christine is more of a charming, down-to-earth First Lady, obviously more at home at a smaller more personable embassy posting than perhaps the more formal embassies of Paris, London, etc. I was happy to see that night that Mrs. Crocker appeared in better health and more rested than usual.

The rest of the reception line was made up of Marine Corps Gunny and seven other marines (the entire contingent of Marines the U.S. Embassy in Kuwait.) They all looked especially regal in formal Marine dress uniforms with all their spit and polish medals and braid. The last Marine in the reception line handed each lady arriving, a long stemmed red rose.

Lyle Dittmer, the Embassy's Administrative Officer who runs the daily operations of the Embassy and his wife Rashida looked well and quite elegant as they received their personal friends in a separate line at one end of the rotunda just past the lavish Arabic ceramic tiled fountain. Rashida always looked lovely and tan, coifed and elegant but tonight especially so. Her full length dark gown shimmered beneath the large overhead chandelier. Maia and I passed from the Ambassador's and Marine's reception line to the Dittmer's. We all air kissed each other on both cheeks and moved along to a group of our other friends who had already assembled near one of the three wet bars.

Barbara Vaughn, Betty McNaughton, Betsy Gorlay, Mike and several of our other friends had already arrived and were toasting each other in the massive two storey mauve, beige and sky blue southwestern looking corridor the staff members refer to as the Souk (an Arabic word for shops). Two of the liquor bars were set up either side of the grand staircase leading upstairs to the Ambassador's secured office. A third bar was set up in the ballroom where everyone will later dance.

Looking around at all the elegant gowns, visible cleavages, jewels and truck loads of gold in the room became my pastime as I circulated at Maia's side air kissing, back slapping and hand shaking. Probably the most interesting thing to me was a small group of American men assigned to one of the military's special units. They were wearing kilts. I didn't know we Americans had such a group. One soldier wore a kilt with a "Mounties" style hat and brandished a special sword at his side. The only other men who stood out from the normal black tuxedo were the British attendees who wore scads of sashes and medals on their tuxedos.

Maia looked more beautiful that night than at any of the previous Balls. She was wearing a gown specially designed for her last year in Thailand where we attended the King's birthday celebrations near Bangkok. She hadn't worn that gown at any local functions because it was very formal, more so than most functions we attended. Maia has always loved pearls, so naturally the dress was developed around the use of hundreds of small ones. Her gown is sea blue with hundreds if not thousands of small pearls individually sewn into intricate shimmering bead work. The dress's bodice is heavily beaded in three coordinating sea tones giving the appearance the upper part of the gown changes colors under different lighting. It is full length and fairly tight, only taking some fullness just a foot before the gown touches the top of her feet. On the right side, there's a two foot long split where she reveals a little leg but modestly. Maia's light blonde hair really sets her gown off. Her gown was so intricate that she chose to wear tiny accessories that were modest in comparison. Her not so modest accents were the 6 ct. solitaire diamond ring she wore with her wedding ring and her matching full carat diamond earrings inside a diamond loop on each ear.

There isn't much to say about me and my tux, except I must have still looked somewhat like a model after all these years because several professional photographers taking the official pictures at the Ball asked me if I was really a former international model for Calvin Kline (maybe they though I looked like shit and just couldn't believe I really ever was in the big time). Someone had told the photographers the former model was here and after they checked out all the guys at the ball, they though it must be me (of course I was flattered and hoped it was because I still looked pretty good, though I was the one who had spread the rumor in the first place).

My tux had a form fitting vest that flattered my shape. I wore Maia's deceased Father's jeweled cuff links and her Grandfather's beautiful pocket watch with the new gold phaub engraved with my initials. My scarf and handkerchief were silk Co Co Chanel with back to back CC almost obscurely woven into the silk fabric. I was surprised my accessories seemed to be of great interest, oddly enough to the guys as much as the ladies.

Betsy, Betty and Barbara all wore exquisite gowns, either imported or designed elsewhere and made by seamstresses here in Kuwait. Betty McNaughton who busily stayed beside Ambassador Crocker the first part of the evening probably wore the most unique gown of all present. It was scarlet velveteen showing a little Country Western flare. The dress was fairly low cut instead of the usual high neck, puffy sleeved and full skirted to the floor. She purposely designed the gown's bodice to accentuate her heirloom cameo that rested comfortably between her breasts. Imagine that, the sheepish lady actually had some and had pushed those puppies out there for all to see.

Barbara's gown was "hot" and coquettish for the blonde with the figure to wear it. It was floor length, full and midnight black. Her waist was drawn tight, fitting like Spandex. Her waistline looked like a twelve year old school girl's but moving upward there were no doubt that those bosoms was part of a fully developed woman. Her back was exposed almost all the way down to her lowest lumbar. Barbara like most other ladies that night wore either fabulously designed gold or was dripping with diamonds. Her tear drop diamond earrings and necklace whether real or imitation glistened and sparkled in the Souk's mellow lighting. Several women present were influenced by the British, who wore small tiaras like those that have become fashionable since Princess Diana's wedding and gala appearances.

Betsy's Parisian black designer gown was more sophisticated than all the others and shorter, almost at cocktail length. Betsy's parents were assigned to the embassy in Paris on two different occasions while she was a young impressionable adult and the dress reflected the French culture still in her. Paris is still Betsy's second home and recently she purchased the dress while she and her two sons visited.

There was one word to be said about that night, TITs, everybody that had them, showed them. They were pushed up, pointed out, exposed and admired. I'm not a prude but even the Reverend Jerry Falwell who had frequented some harlots in Louisiana before his "I've sinned confession" would have thought there was just a little over abundance of Tits that night.

That night, Betty, Ambassador Crocker's Secretary was escorted by her secret boy friend who wore Army dress uniform prominently displaying all his service ribbons. Barbara that night was accompanied by an American Army General and Betsy's escort was our good friend mike, the British aircraft technical engineer. Most guys were dressed not so differently than me. Again what else can you do to a black tuxedo?

Several American and Kuwaiti Generals and wives, a few Kuwaiti Princes and their girl friends, a few Ambassadors and their significant others and several high ranking State Department officials rounded out the short list of that night's selected invitees.

After the reception line completed its function and everyone had freshened their cocktails, the crowd followed Ambassador and Mrs. Crocker into the new Embassy's inner courtyard that opened under a canopy of tall date palm trees and bright stars. About two dozen round tables of eight were tastefully decorated in the red, white and blue

Marine Corps theme. Each table was dressed in white table cloth and topped with a beautiful floral centerpiece of carnations, baby's breath and votive candles while the place settings were nicely coordinated in silver, crystal and china with the usual complimentary wine glasses, engraved "Simper Phi" the Marine Corps Motto.

The official Marine Corps ceremony kicked off celebrations with a procession of Marines forming the Ceremonial Arch of raised swords under which Ambassador Crocker entered. The Marine Colors and American flag were then presented to the guests and the official birthday greetings read by His Excellency Ambassador Crocker.

The birthday cake was about two feet by three feet rectangular and decorated as an American flag. Ambassador Crocker and the lead Marine, Gunny used a ceremonial sword to cut the cake, presenting the first piece to the Ambassador, the second to the oldest American Marine present and the third to the youngest American Marine present, an eighteen year old.

After all the ceremonies were complete, we dined to music by a Philippine orchestra. Later that same orchestra became a pretty good band playing some oldies and new popular songs. Most surprising was seeing everyone get up to line dance to the Macarena. Generals, Colonels, Princes and Mrs. Crocker, Maia and a hundred others were on the floor wiggling butts, flapping hands and turning to the music.

CHAPTER 28

Moon and Rain over the Euphrates

While The British Royal Ordinance was in Kuwait and housed in our camps, I developed close relationships with several of their 2-5 squadron soldiers who taught me how to use the Magellan (Global Positioning Satellite) service. This would become a valuable tool now and in the years to come, when I went on foraging and information gathering trips into Northern Kuwait and across the border into Southern Iraq.

Royal Ordinance used the Magellan or GPS to accurately pin point locations of explosives, bunkers, heavy cannons, mine fields and other things in Kuwait and I would begin using it to pinpoint locations of munitions dumps inside Southern Iraq as well as several other items and sites I came across.

During an extended period of time, perhaps the first nine months following Iraq's defeat, Saddam Hussein was still licking his wounds so I was able to use the time to plunder the southern end of his country.

When I wasn't in Northern Kuwait or Southern Iraq, I was back out on Failaka Island with Royal Ordinance taking care of their camp while they removed mines, bombs and any other explosives from the island. It was with a couple of their top explosives experts one day that I saw the GPS used for the first time, to pinpoint what they believed to be a mass grave. They said it had all the "tell tale" signs, like a drive path running along both sides of the long rectangular fill area and three markings. One marker was in the middle and one at each end. The location of the possible mass grave was reported to the Kuwait Government but was never followed up, at least that I know of.

The first time I'd use the Magellan, GPS was shortly following Liberation when Bob, Marr Bell's executive Officer in Kuwait told me to find some ten-by-twenty feet long steel, ISO shipping containers for use as shops and storage at our Messila Beach camp, thus opening up my first opportunities for recent exploring of Kuwait's north and Southern Iraq. Often at great danger to myself, these treks led me through areas where coalition aircraft had dumped large amounts of ordinance, some exploded yet still much of it strewn but unexploded. While everyone else went to work the next day, I headed straight for Northern Kuwait and the border region now known as the Demilitarized Zone.

On that first trip, I was alone just riding around seeing stagnant lakes of oil, oil wells with their caps blown, oil fires in all directions and bombed and destroyed tanks and other military vehicles along the road and in the deserts while also trying to find Iso containers. There were quite a few dried up farms from lack of irrigation and many destroyed or partially destroyed Iraqi munitions storage facilities amongst the farms but few containers.

I left Kuwait and crossed over the border into Southern Iraq near the former Abdaly Customs Check Point that had been totally destroyed by Iraqi forces at 2 o'clock the morning of invasion.

Now only a month after the Liberation of Kuwait, I could still easily cross from one country to the other on a lonely stretch of paved highway that used to be the main route from Kuwait City to Basrah or its fork off to Baghdad.

Destroyed military trucks and tanks littered the way here as well as all the way from Kuwait City northward. The tanks and armored vehicles on the paved areas were surrounded by a tremendous amount of small rockei holes blown into the concrete and surrounding desert sands by cluster bombs from allied air craft.

Crossing at the Abdaly Check Point was no challenge at all. There wasn't really anything left to stand in my way. I later came to know this as one of the easiest crossing points even much later after it became modestly guarded by Kuwaitis and Iraqis again.

In April 1991, almost two months since multinational Liberation tanks from Desert Storm rolled into Kuwait freeing the country from Iraqi occupation, I made that first crossing into Iraq on a pillaging run. United Nations soldiers had not taken up positions yet along this frontier or any others in the newly demarcated Demilitarized Zone. In fact, locations for their housing sites were still in the planning stages.

Even several other crossing points to the west and northwest of Kuwait were still easily accessible into Iraq. The war had not been long over and the Kuwaiti soldiers assigned to border posts were timid and scared of their own shadows, as were the beaten and bewildered Iraqis on the other side. Where ever I wanted to cross, I crossed. Whatever I wanted to do, I did.

At first, I tried a conservative approach, trying to talk to the Kuwaiti guards on the border to set up some kind of rapport that would enable me to come back into the area again and again without suspicion. They were hospitable enough. That wasn't the problem. They were more interested in wasting my time having tea with them than letting me get on with what I came to do.

Within the first few miles after crossing over the border near the former checkpoint at Abdaly, I found several 20 feet long metal shipping containers in good shape and returned to Messila Camp to make preparations for the next day when I would try to retrieve them. I needed and got approval from Bob to take two low bed trucks and a crane to the border for the containers. By nine o'clock in the morning, our small convoy rolled from Messila Camp and headed west along Sixth Ring Road past the bedouin community of Jahra then turned north through the endless expanse of deserts and northern oil fields up to the Kuwait-Iraq border.

What a difference a day made. This time, there were three checkpoints instead of one, the first at Muttla Ridge, now known as the Valley of Death; another at a fork in the road just before the northern oil fields and the other at Kuwait's border with Iraq. Each check point was manned by about four Kuwaiti soldiers. Luckily, I was prepared and looked so official, at none of the three was our little caravan stopped.

My Red Land Rover with British flags on the sides and the Munitions and Oil Field stickers in the right front window looked as though we had authorization to do anything, anywhere at any time.

Once again there was no trouble crossing from Kuwait into Iraq at the Abdaly Check Point. I did however stop and carry on about a five minute conversation with the Kuwaiti guards, still trying to build some kind of rapport. One guard told me that an Iraqi on the other side kept pointing his rifle at him and could I tell the Iraqi to stop when I passed him. I told the Kuwaiti soldier, "aim your damn rifle and shoot him."

I got back into my Land Rover and motioned for my small convoy to press forward. When we got the hundred yards or so to the Iraqi soldiers, I gave them a quick wave then proceeded without question or incident. They just looked puzzled but raised no weapons. I knew they probably wouldn't try to stop us because at this point they were still intimidated by anything we might do.

I just passed and gave them a stare like "What the hell are you looking at?" At the least they had to assume I was either crazy or some big official with this caravan of trucks and crane driving through "no man's land" into a newly destroyed, hostile Iraq.

We drove about six miles into Iraq paralleling a high hill on our left. At that point, we turned right and headed several more miles in a northeasterly direction through dry farm land until we relocated my yesterday "find". Our guys got out, did a little shoveling of blown sand from around the sides of the ISO containers, and then lifted them by crane on to the low bed trucks. We then took the slower two hours and fifteen minutes trip back to Kuwait City.

Returning through the border was no different than going. A courteous wave and a nod and we were headed home again.

Several more trips for similar types of containers soon followed and my guys and I felt absolutely no hesitation about taking on any future assignments in Northern Kuwait or Southern Iraq. This early into my Iraqi explorations, it was just fun and games. I had no serious plans of making crossings into Iraq a part time business.

For now crossing into Iraq was just for recreational purposes but life has a way of evolving, making use of our latest learned talents and knowledge. In this case and without my becoming aware of it, my curiosity of Iraq was setting me up for a life change.

Knowledge from these almost insignificant little trips transformed my innocent explorations into the darker profession of intelligence gathering or spying as some would call it; I never called it that.

Several times I headed up to the same border region on a day off, just to hunt for AK 47 Kalashnikov rifles and 9 mm pistols. On each trip, alone in my red Land Rover or with one other person, I became more acquainted with the roads west, north and east. I learned everything about the little side roads far beyond where their pavement ended, and I learned where there was refuge from the scorching desert heat in abandoned block farm houses and where there were metal sheds, well preserved or half dilapidated that may be of use to shelter me and my car from the extreme heat. I also became more acquainted with time factors and how long it would take me to go from a destroyed factory about fifteen miles southwest of Abdaly to several locations beyond the first, landmark, large hill inside Iraq.

I journeyed farther north and west on each occasion; then north and east. Once after driving probably two hours past the border, I saw a large river. On the bus trip to Baghdad while escaping occupation, I was neither interested in nor looking for rivers or any other land marks. Now under quite different circumstances, I was interested in everything I saw.

In Kuwait we had no rivers, yet here inside Iraq not extremely far from Kuwait's border, it was almost like finding a part of the world yet unseen by our guys back in Kuwait City. The river was much bigger than I would have imagined. There were even green farm lands and trees nearby. Even the farm land in Kuwait was only sand that had been irrigated to the point where potatoes, onions, melons and a few other crops could be grown.

Here on the shores of the Euphrates River were real rich, black dirt and even a slight bit of marshland along its southern banks. I could see several small livable structures around but I made no attempt to let anyone see me (ya right! in my bright red Land Rover).

An exciting moment came several months later when I set my mind to and finally did journey within view of Basrah, Iraq, fifty miles from Kuwait's border and only about fifteen more from Iran. From the Abdaly Check Point, I had driven about ten miles along the Iraqi side of the border to the small Iraqi community of Umm Qasr, testing my way in that direction. Like all the other places I had ventured, the almost deserted stretches of desert west of Umm Qasr village was easily crossed without fear of running into any locals or Iraqi Army. Few Iraqi farmers and villagers had returned to the region since the end of the Gulf War and Saddam Hussein was still licking his wounds and hadn't gotten very brave yet so there were no military encumbrances to deter me.

Other than a few burned out Iraqi Army tanks, and some rockei potholes in the road, there wasn't much to see. At Umm Qasr, there were a lot of concrete buildings in disrepair, a few minarets and small mosque domes that looked undamaged and utility poles that still appeared ok, not destroyed by Desert Storm.

I had the nicest vehicle in town, an almost new forty thousand dollars all perks British Land Rover, so I didn't want to draw attention and let the locals think they had a tourist. I stayed as far away from people as I could. Earlier, before coming this far into Iraq, I decided this exploration may take more than one afternoon or one day so I brought some edible supplies. I brought lots of water, potato chips and candy bars as well as dried fruit packs.

For this trip, the dangers would be increased so I took a little precaution at letting someone know where I was headed. Captain Pun, the head of our Nepalese Ghurka munitions experts at Marr Bell-Royal Ordinance camp wasn't around when I left so, I handed a letter in a sealed envelope to one of his subordinates. I told him "give it to Captain Pun to give to Mr. Bob" if I hadn't returned in two days.

The only other thing I did was charge my movie camera battery and put some film in my small Nikon camera. I had taken a movie camera with me each time in the past but I had never been so far inside Iraq exploring before, so now I became just a little paranoid about getting caught as a spy rather than an inquisitive American with no real purpose for being in the area.

This time, I did take a little precaution to at least bare some semblance to being an Arab, at least from a distance. The Arabic head gear I took with me was red and white like Saudis and some Iraqis wear rather than just white like Kuwaitis. This wouldn't really disguise me but it would get me by in any situation where a little distance was involved.

I left Umm Qasr in the Demilitarized Zone and headed north then east passing over a war damaged highway interchange, well before nearing some swamp lands and high grass. I saw more of the latter as I turned southeastward, straying too far from the main road. I ran into more and more swamp lands as I headed farther and farther east. I hampered my own progress to Basrah by getting further into the swamps. I then had to retrace my tracks back to the main road before being able to once again head toward my primary objective.

The only information departed on me from that little back tracking foray was seeing flocks of elegant, pink flamingos in the savanna grasses. I was shocked such birds lived around there. Most were off pink or white but I had never seen anything like this in Kuwait and never imagined any would be near such an arid area as Kuwait.

Often, I drove without fear of Iraqi troops spotting me but occasionally and usually out of the blue, we nearly came face to face. While leaving the marshlands heading back toward the main highway, there was one such event.

There was only one road heading in and out of the area I had been exploring. Suddenly ahead, I spotted several Iraqis. It was too far yet to tell whether they were civilian or military or whether they had spotted me. I was fairly deep into enemy territory so it was best I put all my self preservation tactics into use.

First, I lay low and hoped they hadn't spotted me yet. After a few minutes realizing they must not have, I had to make my play first.

I thought to myself, "Self, there's one way in and one way out". Since they appear to be walking in my direction, I could wait for them to come upon me or I could at least with some element of surprise floor my gas peddle and plow full speed ahead through them. I did, and it worked. It was over before they knew what hit them (figure of speech). Six men flew like birds in a trap shoot as I neared them with everything my car's horse power could give. They dove to the side like bowling pens slapping each other down before the ball got to them.

By the time I had assured my safe distance from them, I turned ever so slightly to my rear to peer at the uninjured but muddy Iraqis who were probably just hunters. What ever, I had lucked out and my car beat their rifles to the draw.

Further up the main road, I saw more large areas of bomb wholes blown into the pavement by rockei cluster from our coalition forces bombers.

The majority of these cluster bombs exploded on or near bridges where Iraqi military tanks and trucks were either trying to advance or retreat.

I finally got to the outskirts of a community I figured had to either been Basrah or a suburb. There would be no security for me if I got closer so I pulled off the road and took a little time to figure out my next move. From here on in, there would be too much traffic and people along the sides of the roads so I was afraid I couldn't stay undetected much longer. I turned and headed back to Kuwait.

Most often on these little trips I saw no Iraqi military or compounds at all and on this trip to Basrah, I only saw three soldiers in the far distance and they were at less than alert status. It didn't even frighten me coming within a hundred yards of them. I figured if they saw my red Land Rover and British flags on the side, they would probably figure I must know what I'm doing and where I'm going because otherwise, I would probably have to be nuts to be there.

The trip back to Messila Camp was uneventful and of course just made me feel even more confident there were few or no hazards awaiting me on future trips inside Iraq; whether Bob needed me for one or if I wanted to do a little exploration on my own.

Word had gotten around camp that I'd been making these journeys and several people came to watch the videos I made. I guess my adventures became the topic of a conversation somewhere in England too. It was on a Wednesday afternoon that one of Royal Ordinance's top men came to me and asked could I take him to the Iraqi side of Umm Qasr. I readily agreed, feeling this time it was a little more like a command performance, legitimizing what I'd been doing all along for fun and adventure.

Brumley, a squatty, slightly rounded, short man from RO said he just wanted to see the lay of the land and whether there was the possibility of reclaiming the steel from all the destroyed vehicles in the desert. I told him I'd seen hundreds and hundreds of destroyed military trucks and tanks all over the desert in every direction. I told him I knew where the heaviest concentrations of destruction were and I'd show him if he was comfortable enough to venture a little farther than Umm Qasr.

On his first occasion accompanying me, Brumley was more interested in how easily I navigated my way through the Kuwaiti and Iraqi checkpoints. He could see for himself that my method of looking very preoccupied by talking on the car radio and waving to the Kuwaiti guards got me an uncomplicated admittance to the next sector or over the border. He was slightly ill at ease a few times but admitted we had come farther, easier than he ever believed possible.

This was to be only the first of several such trips for the two of us together. In each of his next trips, I took him pretty much to the same places I had gone alone before, north and east.

One day while heading in the direction of Baghdad, (still a couple hundred miles away) Brumley wanted to keep going. We ended up passing to the other side of the Euphrates River more than a hundred miles from Kuwait. We then drove another forty miles before finding shelter in an abandoned shed where we parked the Land Rover and stayed part of the night. At first, we settled down and talked over the day's events and plans for future trips. He brought his Magellan and was constantly pinpointing first the big hill then a grouping of Iraqi military buildings, then a war scarred area of abandoned destroyed vehicles and tanks then several more locations.

We had no maps because he said he really never believed we would get this far. After lying low in our protective shelter for a few hours, I could see he was as antsy about seeking out the next unknown territory as I was. I said if we go another fifty miles without complication, we could still make it back to the Kuwait border by dawn, even if we stop-ped again for a few hours of "shut eye".

Brumley suggested we use our jug of water to make a little mud to smear on the British flags on the car doors and on the license plates, front and back. We did so and then ventured further. For me, this time seemed more like a real adventure than all those other times. We were now well behind enemy lines and presented ourselves as spies no matter how you looked at it.

About 9:30 p.m. we drove through a small village community but continued to be unimpeded by any locals. Neither of us at this point felt danger nor concern that we were already more than a hundred fifty miles inside Iraq.

Until now, our gas supply had held out but we were close to a point of no return. We'd soon have to turn back so at that moment, I made the decision for the both of us, we'd turn around and head for Kuwait.

Nearly fifty miles of back tracking and we were in trouble. A small unit of Iraqi soldiers lay ahead with several vehicles off to each side of the roadway. It was not a road block but more like a small convoy taking a break before traveling on to their assigned destination.

The signs ahead indicated a fork in the road that I interpreted as one direction heading toward the more barren southwest wastelands and the other following south and east, the exact way we wanted to go.

So far none of the Iraqis had spotted us yet; I guess our one vehicle was less easily spotted than their convoy. On instinct, I wisp my long flowing ghutra head piece around the lower part of my face; only exposing my eyes. I appeared Arab enough but I looked over at Brumley and barreled out laughing.

When we entered Iraq earlier in the day, I instructed Brumley how to wear the ghutra and what to do in case we may be discovered but obviously in a panic he had forgotten. Instead of leaving his head dress on during the entire course of the day, he had removed his. Now in desperation he was attempting to put it back on the way I had shown him but without much success. He was a scream. The way he was rewrapped was more like a kerchief tied under the chin of a fat lady. Brumley looked more like a granny back home in the UK than a Brit in disguise as an Arab behind enemy lines.

At least for now we seemed safe. Though it was no time for humor, I figured if we were caught, I may not fare so well but Brumley may get mounted. I took the near capture by the Iraqis with an air of impunity but Brumley soon put those extremely dangerous, relaxed feelings to rest by reminding me that the vehicle we were traveling in was fire engine red with British flags on the doors on both sides, although mud supposedly covered the flags.

"That could be a tip off, you think?" he said. It was true and then the seriousness of the situation set in on me too. The men just ahead are real soldiers with real weapons and real ammunition. There was nothing we could do if seen but surrender or go down in a hale of bullets. Both our hearts raced; mine so much now that I no longer felt like laughing or even talking.

We remained unspotted and regarded this as our lucky day. We soothed our souls and found a sufficient clutter of trees and shrubs to hide in until we could continue or journey back to Kuwait. Quietly we coasted head first into the bushes and turned off the engine. We'd rest for as long as it took.

About three hours later, we arrived back at the little community of Samawa in South Eastern Iraq. We had driven part of the way through the small mostly adobe village when again we saw Iraqi military soldiers just ahead. Without panicking, we turned down a side street and found a really dark area near some water and trees. Again we thought it best to stay for a few hours until the soldiers and locals went to bed.

It was just after one o'clock in the morning when we rolled back through the main streets of Samawa heading homeward. We continued our journey along the banks of the Euphrates River in a slight rain. The mud covering the British flags on the doors had long ago washed off. Luckily until now, we hadn't been seen by anyone who acted the least bit interested in us so we continued our way back toward the Kuwait-Iraq border pleased with our accomplishments.

By daybreak, we were several miles back on the Kuwait side of the border. The trip far inside Iraq was fairly uneventful and again I had a tremendous feeling of pleasure with myself for having gotten so far in and out again without incident.

My Royal Ordinance friend Brumley turned client when he asked if I could get a different car or truck in which we could make more trips. I told him I had already sent for my tan color Chevrolet Astro van from the United States. It would arrive in about two weeks. He said he appreciated what I had done for him and promised he would reimburse me the $1,250 shipping cost of my van to Kuwait. Just two days later he came across with KD (Kuwait Dinar) 400. (A little more than $1,300. US).

Maia was less than happy about my escapades and voiced her opinions but never gave me an ultimatum. She of course kept saying we had to be extremely careful and would rather I find a hobby like fishing or something less dangerous. I told her if I started fishing, I'd probably want to go to the Euphrates River or maybe the Tigris near Baghdad. The subject of fishing never came up again.

Maia just about lost her cool one day when I came home with the guy from Royal Ordinance. We were both carrying all kinds of gadgets and equipment. She half heartedly laughed and scowled at the same time. Here we sat on the living room floor sorting camera gear, Magellan's, two of them now and a small Japanese movie camera. My movie camera was the big old Panasonic type, about a 1975 version. The smaller one would be less conspicuous if anyone ever approached us. I joked several times that my friend was making me feel just a little like James Bond, but of course I didn't mind. I guess to him, it was more than apparent I was a most willing participant. In the future he would certainly use this eagerness to place us within the reach of Saddam Hussein himself.

CHAPTER 29

Terrorist Funding in America

Along with my escapades into Iraq, my life was evolving in another direction as well. I got involved with another friend, this time an American named Phillip who'd been trying to prove that Kuwait was involved with radical Middle Eastern groups in other parts of the world, either in funding or training. Knowing Kuwait as I did, I doubted the latter was true but Kuwaitis funding such groups was certainly within plausibility.

Perhaps it was sometime following my involvement with this hunt for information that Kuwait's Minister of Information became knowledgeable of my endeavors and started harassing me at work and even occasionally having me tailed.

My friend said he had heard of a mosque downtown in Safat District, Kuwait City that could be the center for businessmen in Kuwait funneling money to Islamic militant groups around the world. He knew of a money exchange process called al Taqua that these groups use to transfer funds around the world. It's similar to the way banks transfer money, only without a paperwork trail.

Kuwaitis, but not the state of Kuwait, have also been known to hide terrorists like Abu Nidal in their homes. He was the one who planned the take over and murder of passengers on a cruise ship in the Mediterranean. They've also been known to hide close associates of Osama ben Laden like Ramzi Yousef, one of the masterminds of the first World Trade Center bombing in 1993. Possibly even then, he was already within the new al Qaeda Organization supported and probably run by Osama ben Laden.

On September 11, 2001, ben Laden and his al Qaeda organization's quad hijacking of American passenger airliners sent the world into shock as they cowardly and despicably murdered almost four thousand people. These terrorist who stormed the cockpits and aimed three of the four hijacked aircraft into the World Trade Center twin towers and the Pentagon as well as the downed airliner in Pennsylvania resulted in the highest death tolls ever caused by an enemy on American soil and the most financially costly incident in American history.

All total, terrorism against America has been adding up at a staggering pace including those killed by a five thousand pound bomb blast at the American housing building, Khobar Tower in Saudi Arabia. Nineteen Americans killed there and then the East African embassy bombings in Kenya and Tanzania that killed another 223 persons followed by the American Naval ship Cole docked in Yemen.

Much of the al Qaeda terrorist network's funding passes through paperless channels like the al Taqua money exchange in Kuwait, Saudi Arabia, Pakistan, and mostly other Arab countries but much of their financing passes right under our noses here in the United States from even more unlikely sources like the American "Discount Coupons" fraud.

As far back as 1993 the United States Government has been alerted to the coupon fraud and has done nothing but monitor it while hundreds of millions of dollars has been scammed from it and sent overseas to finance fundamentalist Muslim organizations like the al Qaeda, Hamas, Islamic Jihad and others. In Kuwait it's no different.

Several mosques within Kuwait City were suspected of having ties to subversive anti-western groups and according to Phillip, it's going to have to be up to someone like me with all my ties in Kuwait to prove or disprove involvement by Kuwaitis. The Kuwait government doesn't feel they need to help cover up activities by such groups but feel it is not the place of a westerner like me to get involved in such personal matters. They on the other hand feel there is nothing to investigate and will be of no help to outsiders in such matters.

Phillip lay out proof to me that certain groups and individuals even within Kuwait, especially in Jahra and at the University should be watched or at least worth keeping my ear to the ground for some insight into what they're up to.

A terrorist scam, American dollars from American people to finance terror against Americans. Abu Nidal has been linked to the Hamada Super Market coupon scam in Brooklyn, New York. Bulk sales of discount coupons can be found even on the Internet. Special agents of the U. S. Government have tripped over piles of still usable discount coupons during investigations into Arab and Muslim organizations within the United States. Each of these piles could be redeemed for dollars and used toward recruit of bomb makers, purchases of chemical or biological weaponry or simply for travel and living expenses for terrorist while in the United States.

Possibly up to two hundred million dollars worth of these coupons have already been converted into cash and distributed amongst Islamic cells inside the United States and abroad. In a sense, we're financing terrorism against ourselves.

In South Florida, hundreds of millions of dollars in food stamp fraud money has been sent to the Palestinian backed Hamas and the Iranian backed Hizbollah. In one such Florida case, a Muslim by the name of Adnan Bahor has been charged. In Texas, the Holy Land Foundation, Muslim's largest source of contributions in America has been monitored for more than eight years while Americans poured funds into the organization they thought was helping children Of the Holy Land when in fact the monies have been solely used to finance the Palestine Liberation Organization's radical Hamas wing. They in turn have used the contributions to school youth in Gaza in fundamentalist teachings of the Qur'an and the belief that bomb making, suicide for the cause and the destruction of Israel and the West should be their main goals in life.

Islam itself is not the blame but some Muslims in a distortion of theology are acting within their own broad interpretations to impose a reign of terror against the West. No one must forget that Islam is not so much a religion of peace as it is a religion of war. According to Islam, in the Holy Qur'an 4:29; it is forbidden to kill innocent people or to commit suicide. Shaheed suicide as it is known (bomber suicide) is also forbidden in Qur'an 4.29 as well, but these same extremist who advocate it have also set up a social safety net for families of those who have sacrificed themselves in a suicide bombing. Financially, the families are provided for and they are also told the act by their martyred loved one has put them on a direct path to heaven.

Ben Laden and other Islamic Fundamentalist usurp parts of the Koran without using the verse or adjoining verses in their full context. For instance in Qur'an verse 3.89 it says "Slay your enemies where you find them"; however directly following is the second part of that statement 3.90 "But if they let you be, let them be".

Ben Laden, the Saudi Arabian dissident millionaire who now heads a vast spider web network of terrorist camps and organizations known as the al Qaeda has been mostly headquartered amongst the fundamentalist Taliban Muslim's in Afghanistan. Until their recent purge during the Afghan War, they controlled about ninety five percent of that country but their terror network still spreads to more than fifty other nations. Within none of these countries are they known for educating the masses, building the infrastructure, boosting the economy nor even providing the slightest necessities for life to those who follow.

Kuwaitis and many other moderate Arabs continue financially supporting groups like these as well as others like the Palestinian Hamas, Fatah and other Arab causes like Hizbollah, Islamic Jihad and The Brotherhood Organization just because they are Muslim and anti-western or Christian, not necessarily because they are violent.

These same moderate Arabs are the first ones to scream to the Western free press that America and the entire West, categorize all Muslims into one group and we shouldn't; but when they do the same, it is permissible. They also fail to follow up their demand for freedom inside our western countries with their endorsement for us to have the same freedoms in their Muslim countries. There, we are not even allowed to fly through the airport in some cities like Mecca if we are not Muslim, and we can be flogged on the street in their country for simply walking down the street at the wrong time of day, not observing their holy times of prayer.

In these Muslim societies, we westerners who live amongst them are forbidden the right to eat the foods we wish like pork, observe our prayers at large gathering places, wear a crucifix, or have our women dress as they wish.

As these Islamic groups grow more in strength within the United States they may even go so far as to not allow church bells to ring unless the call to mosque over boisterous loud speakers can also be heard throughout all our cities five times a day.

A scary phrase I heard even moderate Muslims in Kuwait repeat over and over again was "It is the duty of all Muslims to perform JIHAD (holy war) by HEART, HAND, TONGUE or SWORD against the West and its infidels." Speak to one in the United States and he will categorically deny this. Muslims conveniently also have a word al Takeea which allows them to lie if it benefits Islam. The next time you're around a Muslim ask him or her about Islam and the first word out of their mouth is that Islam is a "tolerant" religion when nothing about it seems so. Funny that precise word was taught to them.

In the time period between this book's writing and its publication, President Obama introduced into the American Health Care Bill on page 107 a truly Muslim diktat. He is specifically using the word "Dhimmitude" which is the taxing system used by Muslims in their own countries for tolerating the presence of non-Muslims. The Islamic concept of Dhimmitude under Sharia Law is taxes non-Muslim residents of their countries just for being there. All Americans are mandated to purchase insurance; however, the Muslims within America are exempt from purchasing the same insurance or from being penalized for not purchasing it because in Islam Insurance is considered to be "gambling," "risk-taking," and "usury." All other Americans would have crippling IRS leans placed against their assets including real estate, cattle, accounts, and receivables, and could even face hard prison time if they refuse to buy this health care insurance or pay these penalty taxes. Lewis Farrakhan and all other Muslims will have no such penalties, but will have 100% of their health needs paid for by this de facto government insurance that all non-Muslims are paying for care[1].

It was for the above reason and for a lot of others that I agreed to get more involved with Phillip in helping get financial paper trails or information concerning radical groups inside Kuwait. Where else better than from within their midst and who better than me; someone who already has access too many of the places and people necessary to reach this goal. I could start by snooping around, finding out if more radical Kuwaiti politicians and Parliamentarians, most of them from fundamentalist neighborhoods were involved in such activities.

I immediately started sending out feelers to many persons I thought might know something. The first to respond was an Arab student/friend at Kuwait University that told of a group called the Brotherhood on campus being financed by businessmen within and outside Kuwait. They were powerful enough to win almost every student body seat they wanted. Another student gave me several leads, the first concerning the Saudi Arabian branch of Hizbollah headed by Abdul Kareem al Nasser. They also had influence on campus in Kuwait City but less than the Brotherhood. The second bit of information given me by this student sent me to a disgruntled Dutch woman who claimed to be the secretary of a Mosque where money was sent supporting some legitimate and some

---

1   http://theamericanjingoist.net/index.php/2010/04/10/american-dhimmitude/

not so legitimate groups in Lebanon and Palestinian occupied territories, as well as a newly reorganized renegade upstart group in Afghanistan.

If I could help hide the Dutch woman in my apartment for a few days while she flees her Kuwaiti husband, she would possibly hand some informative papers over to me. It was a done deal. Maia and I agreed even to help her exit Kuwait.

The more I dug into her papers and the organizations mentioned in them and their clandestine fund raisers, the more sophisticated and complex they became.

This mosque in the Safat District of down town Kuwait City was but one of four sending huge amounts of money to Mujahedeen and other guerrilla networks. There was no shortage of places and causes where the money would be funneled to; Northern Africa, Pakistan, Afghanistan, several other places and groups like Hamas and Fatah inside the Middle East, to Islamic fundamentalist groups in the Philippines, Somalia and Sudan and other subversive groups in Peru, South America and even in the United States.

It was about this time I first stumbled over information regarding a big daddy of anti-western, anti-American criminal masterminds. Of course the name meant nothing to me when I first saw it but the frequency and use of the name Imad Mugniyah was a most prominent one.

It was through some Arabic papers translated into English that I had my first proof that large amounts of money were leaving Kuwait for these subversive organizations and others and the recruitment of extremist even back home in the United States. Most papers concerning the United States mentioned organizations already in place in such cities as Dearborn, Michigan near Detroit, Los Angeles, Tampa-St. Petersburg, Hollywood and Vero Beach, Florida and of course New York and New Jersey. One address was even in Evansville, Indiana. The name Imad Mugniyah was on more than a couple of these papers.

As I said, the name Imad Mugniyah didn't sound familiar but to my friend Phillip, it was music to his ears. A connection was now being made directly between a flow of money and the man who masterminded two terrorist attacks in Lebanon against the United States. The first was when a Shiite Hezbollah group bomb killed 63 Americans and the second was the Marine Corps barracks bombing that killed 241 American soldiers.

Mugniyah was also involved in the 1985 TWA 847 hijacking which ended in the brutal murder and dumping of the body of an American Navy Seal. Mugniyah also masterminded the bombing of the Israeli Embassy in Argentina that left 115 dead. With the information I was now uncovering, I was proud to finally be contributing in some small way to the crackdown on terror.

From mentor Imad Mugniyah's insane ideology and his violent acts, Osama ben Laden received inspiration. Mugniyah began his rise to power by fighting on the side of the Afghan military against the Russians. He then became instrumental in training rebels in the Central Asian country of Chechnya who were seeking their independence from Russia. Though he has been less successful there, it enabled him time to develop his own skills in leadership and assemblage of a loyal military chain of command below him.

The money trails I followed from inside Kuwait to ben Laden and other organizations were next to impossible, they ended up being more by word of mouth than anything else. Each month a group of Islamic fund raisers and philanthropist met at the Al Sharq Kuwait City Mosque to funnel money through to certain groups. Most was cash but what little paperwork there was from those meetings most often went to an Atlantic Avenue address in Brooklyn, New York and one other in Jersey City, New Jersey. It was later verified through the American Embassy that these were addresses of Osama ben Laden's administrative and recruiting headquarters inside the United States.

Though I haven't seen him personally, I know for a fact that one of Osama ben Laden's fastest rising lieutenants Jamal Ahmed Al Qaeda was seen at least at one of these meetings in Kuwait City and inside the United States a week later.

Another location in New York is that of more recent notoriety, the Mojid al Salam Mosque where the blind Muslim Cleric Sheikh Omar Abdel Rahman and his followers have been extremely active in anti-American causes and implemented in several terrorist bombings on American soil.

Most of the men hired through these offices were designated for guerrilla training by mercenary fighters who had fought in Afghanistan or were destined to be linked to more sophisticated types of terrorism studies involving their professional careers, pilots, finance, group organization leaders, clerics, etc. Some of the discount coupon fraud money was used for these purposes.

These New York offices and others known by the American Government were never closed, though one even became implicated in the financing and recruitment of terrorist who blew up the World Trade Center Buildings in 1993. In that bombing, Ramzi Yousef may have been the mastermind but American born Abdul Yasim from Indiana made the explosives that killed six employees of the World Trade Center and caused a half billion dollars in damages.

It is said that "our intelligence evolution against terrorism is usually one step behind the terrorist". How well I knew that because any time I tried to share information with the U.S. Embassy while over seas, other than to Phillip, I was discouraged and told mind my own business.

Kuwait has continually put on the "victim" image to the world while privately and underhandedly financing groups that sought to destroy the very western infidels who saved Kuwaiti asses and freed their country from Saddam Hussein. Their victimization has been with the blessings of the United States whose diplomats and intelligence services in the field have all but made it impossible to complain or provide information to. Their lack of coordination amongst themselves and lack of recruitment in the field of persons who are in position to provide good legitimate information is in itself, criminal.

I tried unsuccessfully to give Ambassador Crocker information about these organizations at a few of Howell and Jolie Woods dinner parties but the Ambassador was less than interested and purposely left me no opening to begin a real conversation with him about them or even to say hello.

I was even warned by someone where I worked at the Ministry of Information not to say anything to Ambassador Crocker because of the Ambassador's close ties to the Minister of Information, Sheikh Saud Nassir Al Sabah, one of my bosses.

Phillip asked me to find out if Ramzi Ahmed Yousef who had been charged with masterminding the 1993 World Trade Center bombing in New York had ever lived in Kuwait. Kuwait had earlier been allusive about Yasser Arafat's involvement there and was probably now lying about Ramzi Yousef's rumored visits to Kuwaiti mosques.

The United States believed information they were given was correct that Ramzi Yousef was in Kuwait a few months before the World Trade Center bombing in New York. It was indeed possible some contributions from wealthy Kuwaitis went toward Osama bin Laden's organization al Qaeda and in-directly helped finance the first World Trade Center bombing.

As for Yasser Arafat, the leader of the Palestinian Liberation Organization, PLO had also lived in Kuwait for many years. He was an electrical engineer in Hawalli near where my friend Gus now lives. I was always told never to say the name Yasser Arafat on radio. I could say the leader of the PLO or use other terminology but never his name. Part of the reasoning behind this was because the PLO supported the Iraqi takeover of Kuwait in August 1990. Even further back however, Kuwaiti businessmen and friends of Yasser Arafat helped bankroll his budding Fatah Organization many years ago. The Kuwaitis felt slighted by Arafat and his organization as it grew in political influence and power. Still they poured money into his Fatah Organization and later changed to supporting the Hamas instead because of Arafat's continuing arrogance of not properly thanking his Kuwaiti benefactors.

When fundamentalist Osama bin Laden visited Kuwait, he didn't stay in Jahra where most fundamentalist live but rather in a prosperous Kuwaiti neighborhood just off Fourth Ring Road in the heart of Kuwait City.

Kuwait's official propaganda machine is the Ministry of Information where I worked. It is there that news is censored or changed or even eliminated. Unfortunately for the censors, while I was there, they had their problems with me. They had never had an American amongst them before, especially one that was no puppet. We often verbally battled over untrue or slanted stories that I knew should have gone out to their population without editing but my paycheck was paid by them and I bowed to them because after all, it was their country and their people.

Many wealthy Kuwaitis, including members of the Royal Family financially supported Hamas, the Hizbollah and the Brotherhood openly. After a suicide bus bombing in Tel Aviv, Israel, I would listen to some Parliamentarians and even a few Ministers praising the barbaric murders, then go on television denouncing them publicly so as not to lose the sup-port nor rile the United States.

When I first came to work at the Super Station FM Radio, I wasn't use to writing as if I were on the other side of Palestinian or fundamentalist causes, so I dove head first into hot water with some of my statements. Several staff directives came down through the Ministry of Information forbidding me to say such phrases as "Hizbollah guerillas" in Southern Lebanon and Syria launched attacks against Israeli soldiers. They said first of all they weren't considered guerrillas. They were freedom fighters fighting against the Israeli occupying army.

I've seen American officials interviewing Middle Eastern officials from Kuwait and other countries on television. The Americans asked Arabs (point blank), "Do you support Hizbollah guerillas?" they answer truthfully

"No". To the Arab, he answered correctly because of the terminology used by the interviewer. Hizbollah are not GUERILLAS, they are freedom fighters seeking the destruction of Israel and infidel countries of the West.

The way American and western linguists hone in on specific words or phrases, so do Arabs. The Arabic language has many more words or phrases that sidestep direct definition. For instance, we have the word horse and several more similar. A gelding is still a horse and so are studs, pintos, palominos and quarter horses and about a dozen more words. These words are more specific than the actual definition of "horse" but they still mean a horse. Arabs use truthful words but in deceptive ways.

Some Kuwaiti businessmen openly support Osama ben Laden who after being stripped of his Saudi Arabian citizenship in 1994 went more extreme in fighting western culture and religion. He supports a more radical Islamic state even in his own country that opposes the Royal Family of Saudi Arabia.

Osama ben Laden had personally organized as many as twenty five other splinter groups in London, Paris and other places throughout Europe before beginning his clandestine and hidden life style. Soon after he was implicated in the Khobar Towers bombing in Saudi Arabia that killed nineteen Americans and wounded hundreds more, his influential family had the Saudi Royal Family squelch rumors of his involvement and impeded United States investigations into the bombing.

At every turn, the Saudis refused to share information on what knowledge they knew of the bombers or bombing. The Saudis tried, convicted and sentenced several men to death for the bombing without ever allowing the United States investigators access to the men or to what other information the Saudis may have obtained. The men were beheaded and the Saudis closed the case. Hundreds of interviews outside Saudi Arabia indicated ben Laden was instrumental in at least the planning of that bombing attack at the Khobar Towers but we'll never be able to prove it through information coming out of Saudi Arabia because ben

Laden's family controls more than a billion dollars of wealth and remains influential there.

It was in Osama ben Laden's guest house in Pakistan that Ramzi Ahmed Yousef was hiding when he was commandeered away by an American ninja style Strike force. First contact between Ben Laden and Ramzi Yousef was probably in Kuwait City, well before Kuwait City or New York. American secret agents found Yousef's whereabouts, and then went in on a swat type exercise that snatched him and brought him to America to stand trial for the 1993 bombing of the 110 storey buildings.

American interrogations of Ramzi Ahmed Yousef also revealed a plan to blow up 11 American airliners around the world as a "Jihad" Muslim fundamentalist strike against the infidels of the United States. One 747 barely missed being destroyed en route to the Philippines.

Much of the terrorist movement in the world is not only against America but indirectly created by America. This was the case with the United States supporting Saddam Hussein financially with billions of US dollars and with biological weapons for use against Iran in their eight years war against each other. Our side poured unaccountable amounts of money into Saddam Hussein's coffers and set up his laboratories to build germ and chemical weapons. We checked the progress on the Iraqis building their facilities, and then supplied the scientists and the germs needed. We did the same thing in Afghanistan.

In Afghanistan, we poured billions of dollars into weapons and trained guerillas inside the country to sustain the war against the occupying Russians. A Texas Congressman was instrumental in getting the U. S. to bankroll almost the whole war, made available missiles, rifles, tanks and training to any fundamentalist or extremist who would take up arms. The same men completed their war in Afghanistan and since they had no more Russians to fight, they exported their mercenary services to Bosnia, Egypt and any other country they felt comfortable creating disturbances in. These Muslims then came together in a final cohesion of Islamic fundamentalism and began their movement against all Arabs' nemesis, the West and in particular their benefactors, the United States.

Ben Laden used his training and the equipment to send radical pro Islamic troops into Algeria against the government there, to Bosnia on the side of the Muslims being driven out by the Serbs and Croats, to Sudan to bolster the radical Islamist there, to the Philippines to continue massive insurrections on Islands, to Egypt to overthrow the Egyptian Government, to Jammu and Kashmir to fight the Indians and carry out guerilla attacks preventing India from clamping down on the region, to Pakistan to help disrupt the non Muslim population and to Lebanon, Syria, Palestinian occupied territories, Indonesia, the Philippines and many more regions of the world.

When Afghanistan's two main warring parties led by the President and opposed by a former General kept internally fighting long after the Russians were defeated, a group of Muslim students emerged from the University system and gradually took over the entire country. With the blessings of the United States and my sincere broadcasts daily, these students eventually commanded an air force and large armies who would do their bidding even against the hand that fed them.

The United States again supported extremists because selfishly the U. S. wanted the students who were religious to halt the poppy flower growing and harvesting of drugs. But unfortunately, though religious, the Taliban continued the growing and production of which in term brought them even more money.

The United States wanted stability in the region and a government they could deal with. I was one who desired the same. Daily reports came through my office how Afghanistan was being torn apart by a military General and the President of the country. I favored the religious Taliban because at first I too thought they would be the remedy needed to halt the destruction of the country.

Instead, the Taliban destroyed even the University system they stemmed from and forced all the men in the country to begin wearing beards and following strict Muslim law as only the students saw it.

The Taliban students forced the women off the streets and out of the work place, forbidden to be schooled, work in hospitals and even halted the women's public saunas and baths which were the only places many women had to wash in Afghanistan because running water no longer ran to the homes in the Capital city of Kabul or any other. Women were flogged for showing the slightest amount of skin, even at the ankles; their finger nails pulled out if they used nail polish and were beaten severely if they laughed in public. They were shot in the head, execution style for infidelity and for an unwanted pregnancy; they were buried up to their necks and stoned to death. It's illegal to even play soccer or fly a kite.

The Taliban students and their extreme fundamentalist interpretations of Islam then destroyed the entire country's infrastructure so they could start again, but never have.

Osama ben Laden became the man behind the movement and accepted the Taliban's cover while providing them with cash, training and purpose. Osama ben Laden became the man many governments would like to interrogate.

Ben Laden was no longer welcome in Saudi Arabia where his citizenship had been revoked and he had few countries where he could remain independent and yet have full complicity from the local government to carry on planning and training for his extremists views. Afghanistan became his home once again.

The Taliban no longer had financial supporters like the United States so they needed someone with money. The Taliban Organization was still unrecognized as the legitimate government of Afghanistan by the United Nations and the world so no world aide of any kind was forth coming.

Osama ben Laden, the rich man without a country became Taliban's main financier.

Osama ben Laden was welcomed into Afghanistan this time as a wealthy benefactor and allowed to set up huge fundamentalist Islamic guerilla training bases in the exact same mountain encampments once run by the CIA. From there, he would export thousands of well trained terrorist world-wide.

The Kuwaitis, who contribute to these kinds of organizations and groups, consider them charitable causes. They say many of these fringe organizations have a true purpose for existing. For instance, I detest the Hamas organization. They're despicable in their need to destroy Israel and to murder as many Israelis as they can in bus bombs throughout Israel, however, Hamas schools in the Gaza strip fulfill a great need for education where there is none.

These schools however go too far to the extreme. Hamas not only supports the much needed school but indoctrinates small 8, 9, and 10 year old children into radical Islamic ideology which the children find hard to grasp but learn through rote memory.

The children learn lessons in math, religion and the need to kill Jews and westerners. They learn it's good to plan a bombing against Jews and if they become a small martyr, it would please their parents and all Palestinians.

Islamic fundamentalists are told for every person they kill in a suicide bombing, they will be helping another loved one into the kingdom of Allah in the hereafter. One West Bank Palestinian, who recruited suicide bombers said he asked children to test the greatness of their faith to Islam, then promised them one hundred wives after martyrdom.

Hamas schools embellish and develop hatred and tell stories to the small children of how they too can one day elevate their family in the community's eyes.

A mother can show great loss but great pride also that her son killed as many people as he could on the streets of an Israeli city. Many of those supporting Hamas say true, the organization has a bad side but they also provide electricity in Gaza and occupied areas to many who have been without, and they provide sports events and facilities and some housing. They provide schooling where the Fatah Organization of Yasser Arafat has failed too, even though he has billions of dollars of funding provided by the international community.

We have to wonder why the Fatah Organization under Yasser Arafat doesn't provide these services. His group is funded by Arab and non-Arab alike. He has billions of dollars earmarked for his Palestinian state, yet he has no book work showing where all the money goes and his organization accounts for little or none of the money coming to them from the international community. Surely, we can see by visiting Gaza and several other places; they don't get the money there.

Yasser Arafat has no heir apparent or Vice President nor anyone else who even knows where all the money his Palestine Liberation Organization gets is kept. He and he only have one small book that is always carried on his person with facts and locations that he may refer to at any given time. Only following the crash of his aircraft in 1992 did the book leave his hands temporarily. During the crash, the pilot and several others died but Arafat was cushioned by his personal guards, wrapping their arms around his body hugging style to protect him from almost certain death. He lived of course but suffered a brain tumor which had to be removed several days later. The shaking and trembling seen on Arafat now is not Parkinson's disease but rather results of this tumor. His personal financial control book was returned to him immediately following his condition improving several days after the crash.

It's hard getting evidence on Kuwaiti individuals or businesses supporting moderate or radical organizations and even more difficult handing the evidence over to the United States or our Ambassadors because they don't want to rock the boat with their fragile Arab alliances.

Kuwaitis don't just write a check and an organization cashes it. They have fund raisers where the money passes through religious groups that show little if any accountability. I often found lots of circumstantial evidence but little or no physical evidence. Our world banking system has a lot of loopholes that radical Islamists like Osama ben Laden utilize quite efficiently. No one is left accountable or outside the law on money transfers, even to the United States for persons the U. S. knows has radical ties. We also know most money used within the United States by Islamic fundamentalist isn't brought in from outside the country anyway but rather through the discount coupon and food stamp scams here at home.

On each covert, night time, exploratory visit to a mosque or business, I ran into the same U. S. addresses. The Atlantic Avenue address in Brooklyn, New York, Florida, Michigan, New Jersey and on the last little snooping raid, I found a new address in Arlington, Texas.

Each time I went digging for information and seemingly went undetected, I received a visit from someone at the Ministry of Information, on The Minister Sheikh Saad's behalf. The visit always began pleasantly and went down hill from there. It was like each of the different people who came to me had been taught the same rhetorical phrases and warnings to say. I was to stay away from certain places and people. They warned me how easy it would be in Kuwait to ruin my reputation or to cause bodily harm to me or my wife without fear of prosecution. Kuwait is not a Democratic society and proof isn't needed.

An Under Secretary to the Minister of Information said he heard I joked about the extreme amount of homosexual activity in Kuwait and how someone should write to Gay magazines worldwide saying how Gays should vacation on the beaches here instead of the Caribbean or somewhere else. One of Kuwait's Under Secretary's said it would be easy to publish fabrications about me and send it to every household in Kuwait and America if he felt it was necessary to destroy me. He said with Kuwaitis thinking all western women are loose whores, it would be equally as easy to destroy the reputation of my wife or pit her against me or he could simply include me in promiscuous homosexual activity locally.

While I continued trying to get bits and pieces of information about radical groups and finances, I made a few more trips back into Iraq. The Royal Family, the Emir and Crown Prince had returned in March 1991 to Kuwait but still weren't in need of my services at Dasma Palace yet. As time moved along and the Royal Family's diwaniyas became more active, I was more frequently invited back. I've always kept abreast of most political situations inside Kuwait and in nearby countries and at these diwaniyas, I was often asked what Americans felt about each subject, if anything.

The Kuwaitis still wanted to hear my thoughts and decided it was again a good time to hire me for any information I might be able to give them concerning my visits inside Iraq.

I asked my Royal Ordinance friend, Brumley whether it was a good idea or not to let some Kuwaitis in on our Iraqi activities. I told him the Kuwaitis I had talked to without revealing too much information about our escapades seemed quite interested and said they would pay me for any first hand reports I made to them concerning their security, or knowledge I had concerning Saddam Hussein or his recent movements.

It appeared to me that what intelligence reports were being given to Kuwait's Royals wasn't being passed down to the rest of the higher ups within the country so they wanted my info.

My friend Brumley spoke with British Intelligence and returned to me with an overall "OK" but with a little reservation. Obviously, sooner or later there would be a sensitive subject that would be more for the eyes and ears of my own government and Britain than to an Arab country. I was told to remember my own loyalties and allegiances first.

That was fine with me. When I talked to Maia, we both agreed that I was never to turn over information to Kuwait that would be inconsistent with the U. S. or British policy in the region. My country would always be first and long after Kuwait is no longer an ally, nor perhaps even a country; I can walk tall and proud for having stayed a loyal American. I also told my RO friend if it was a problem, I wouldn't give any information to the Kuwaitis at all.

Brumley again returned to me about a week later and said it would be interesting to find out what the Kuwaitis would request of me, knowing I was already doing intelligence runs for other governments. I was to tell the Kuwaitis I was at their disposal for any runs inside Iraq in exchange for allowing certain border passages and crossover points at the newly constructed trenches and berms to remain open.

It was shortly after this time that Kuwait, through an advisor of the Crown Prince and Prime Minister put me on their payroll. Monthly, I received additional payments automatically deposited in the same account I was paid in by the Ministry of Information for my Radio show.

CHAPTER 30

I've Stayed Too Long

About five o'clock one afternoon, my Royal Ordinance friend Brumley that had been going with me into Iraq, came to our apartment and introduced me to a man he called Jake. Jake, an American, said he worked with a lot of Brits and Americans gathering needed intelligence about Saddam Hussein and a few other matters. He said satellites have proven invaluable to the United States and others but there are still things that need to be verified on the ground. He asked if I would be interested in taking him to some sites that needed further verification.

Brumley had already told me that Jake had a job that needed taken care of within the next week so I didn't have much time to think it over. He'd appreciate it if I would take him into Iraq and sit with him for a while looking some maps over. This new guy Jake had heard about several of my other trips and had decided that his Arab friends who were "in place" were possibly playing both ends of the fence and always wanted, or demanded more and more for the privilege of him working with them. He grew to distrust them while at a Diwaniya one night several of the man's friends spoke openly of what was supposed to have been guarded knowledge.

I assured Jake I didn't even tell my wife everything except about when I would be leaving and how long I'd probably be gone. I also gave her a run down on where I was going but not why. Jake and his friend and I decided it was best to keep Arabs completely out of what could easily be construed as direct covert activity. Kuwaitis often played both sides of the fence with Iranians and Iraqis and neither Jake nor I was sure whether a Kuwaiti would carry the line for us one day if trouble came.

My Chevrolet Astro van arrived at the port in Schuwaikh two days before our next trip and I had already gotten my license plates and insurance papers. I also felt comfortable the van's crème color would be an asset in the desert terrain we'd be crossing and hiding in.

The next crossing was again easy and Jake was almost amused at the way I busily waved to the guards on both sides of the border and mocked speaking on the CB radio. I wasn't sure whether the Kuwaitis had been instrumental in my next border crossings as promised, so I continued playing it by ear, usually through intimidation or sneaking through.

Jake and I wasted no time heading directly toward the town of Basrah. We tried staying off the main road as much as possible and made our way more carefully around the area we had seen Iraqi soldiers on the last visit. It had been raining quite a lot lately and everywhere seemed to be flooded or too marshy to travel off the main roads. The low wet-lands area that was normally swampy, were more like lakes now and it was difficult to leave the main road at all. Jake wanted me to drive to three or four places along Southern Iraq's rail lines and that was what we were attempting to do, but it was difficult. I wasn't familiar with the areas he wanted to go but I had accidentally strayed through two of the villages on earlier occasions so I had some knowledge of how I had gotten there and which way I should go from there.

Jake began gathering bits and pieces of information as soon as we entered an industrial area south and west of Basrah. From here we rode back and forth toward the coast taking notes and positions, and then following roads that looked as though they led to factories. Most of what we saw was textile mills, but several other buildings were huge chicken farms, cement block companies and automobile wrecking yards.

The first day inside Iraq, we even felt so adventurous we wandered through a couple of heavily populated streets in Basrah's suburbs while wearing our traditional headgear and Dishdasha. We tried never to get close enough to anyone that they'd suspect we were westerners. We had taken the front and back Iraqi license plates from a car along side the road north of Umm Qasr and replaced my new Kuwaiti ones with them. I was not privy to what we were going into Iraq for, or when we expected to find it. I continued more as a chauffeur than any informed person knowing what I was looking for.

Within hours of crossing the border, we had already found the rail line northwest of Basrah and determined it was indeed the one going in the direction Jake wanted. He said we needed to continue driving to a village quite far from there called An Nasiriya. From there, we would continue along that rail line north and west. For most of that first day, we stayed within sight of the Euphrates River whenever possible; occasionally taking a road and bridge that crossed to the opposite side. It was very fertile along the riverbanks and we passed not only agricultural land but also groves of lush date palms that appeared so much more hospitable than Kuwait's hostile arid environment. Even in Basrah, we were both surprised at the amount of trees in the city.

We had driven quite some time before Jake determined the village before us was An-Nasiriya. He pointed to a satellite photo and said we should start looking for the two long partially dilapidated metal sheds pictured along side the rail line. It was at this time that I started hearing reasons why we were there. Jake indicated his bosses believed the two sheds may be drop off points where both Iraqi soldiers and their supplies usually left Iraqi Army military trains. From there, the Iraqi military units would head over roads further south and southwest into the low grazing lands in the direction of Saudi Arabia and Kuwait but still more than a hundred miles from the border.

Jake's bosses suspected the Iraqi soldiers were carrying chemical or viral materials to these further camps. Our job was to go to the off-loading docks adjoining the dilapidated metal sheds and do what Jake called the Castle Meyer Swab Test to check for any residue possibly left there as proof chemicals or germ agents had made it that far. We'd swab the area down with special gloves and Q-tips, and then bag them for lab testing back in Britain or the United States.

Not long after we saw a sign in Arabic saying An Nasariya, Jake seemed to have recognized something ahead. He suddenly said "go that way". Sure enough, within five minutes we were looking straight toward the long metal buildings. There had been several people walking and visiting each other along the road next to the buildings so we felt a little uneasy. I parked the van and we waited in near silence behind some high growing bushes and ragged looking trees for about an hour and a half. As daylight turned to dusk, Jake said we couldn't wait any longer; he needed some sun light in order to see his way around inside the sheds. He switched from shoes to Arab sandals more like the natives then left the van.

First Jake went inside one building then the other. He stayed in the second one until well after dark. It really wasn't a lot of time, maybe twelve or thirteen minutes total but it felt longer to me. He came back carrying two plastic bags with some regular looking cotton ear swabs inside one and a simple pair of white cotton gloves in the other. He said these may give us the evidence we need. The items now sealed in plastic would be sent back to a laboratory that would check for traces of whatever had been moved along the platforms and carts inside and outside the two metal sheds. This task completed, we moved to the next.

We headed in a northwesterly direction again. Jake said we had to make some time now to get near a place called Samawa. I told him I remembered being there once before with his friend so I thought I knew that road fairly well. It was night the last time I was there too.

It took us another hour or so to get there then cross to the other side of the Euphrates River. This time, we drove more northerly through the tiny village of Rumaithiya then stopped just short of the community of Ad Diwaniya. We had gotten off on the wrong road and ran into another surprise, more rice fields and too much water to go further. We parked beside a mosque and Jake took a reading from his Magellan. He said we still had to find another road that turned West before we could reconnect with the rail line. He said since I read Arabic a little, I was to look for any signs that said An Najaf.

We stayed directionless for a short time then felt quite sure we were on the right road again. According to the compass, we were at least heading in the right direction and we were also back on a paved road, a big improvement. It didn't take us too long to get to An Najaf nor to locate the rail line. The building Jake wanted to find was equally easy to locate. He did about the same thing he'd done at the other location. Jake went inside, spent a few minutes, wiped a few places with swabs and gloves then returned. Until this point, I had the feeling we were on a regular scavenger hunt some place else in the world other than a hostile, enemy country but our luck was running out. We had gotten back onto the main road that ran from Basrah through a lot of little towns and villages all the way to Baghdad, almost three hundred miles from one end to the other.

If caught now, there would be hell to pay. Jake and I knew from satellite photographs of the area that there were quite a few Iraqi troops stationed nearby in several directions. It certainly wasn't without concern that some of these seasoned Iraqi soldiers could be traveling from one site to another and run smack dab into us. We could be shot if I reacted wrong and started to flee or we could be apprehended and interrogated, which knowing the reputation of Iraqi interrogators could result in a lot of pain and suffering to both of us. Still we proceeded.

Two or three miles north of An Najaf, Jake asked me to see if the building in the small 5X7 inches photograph was the same as the one about fifty yards ahead on the right. It certainly appeared to be. The clincher was the Arabic Coca Cola sign on a lean-to near the front door. In Arabic Coca Cola looks nothing like it does in English but with its backward looking K still has a very recognizable, distinct look. The mud adobe shack with crumbling, wooden lean-to looked a lot like it had been a small store a long time ago but had been converted to a substandard living quarters. Jake told me to pass it then pull to the side and wait.

About three minutes after Jake got out of the van, an Iraqi appeared from the right side of the building with Jake. Both were speaking in English. Jake and the man came to the car, got into the back bucket seats and turned the overhead light on. I turned to get a better look at what they were reading or looking at. It was a map. After a few minutes, Jake turned off the overhead light and I kept only the van's parking lights on. As we proceeded, Jake told me to continue heading down the same darkened road in the same direction we traveled prior to arriving at the small building.

Jake said he and the man were looking for a set of berms and bunkers in a field just beyond a line of trees and bushes. The area we were in now was more for goat, sheep and camel grazing than any of the well vegetated areas we had been driving through earlier, but there were still some trees. Worst of all was the closer we came to the berms and bunkers, obviously the closer we would be getting to Iraqi soldiers. Because there wasn't a lot of vegetation, it was easier to see further distances but easier for someone else to spot us as well.

Jake said we were looking for two of the fifty bunkers Saddam Hussein had built since Desert Storm. These were the only two bunkers outside Basrah and Baghdad that have been abandoned by the Iraqi army. Because of the similarity of construction of all fifty bunkers, it was important to find out how well these two were built and what characteristics they shared.

Jake had to enter both of them to find out how deep they were, how thick the ceilings between floors were, whether steel rebar was used in their construction and the consistency of the concrete. He said often, when a nation was having hard economic times like Iraq, the concrete was more watery and thinner than at other times. Steel rebar may be used but not as extensively as when economic times were better. The information he got that night may be important in the programming of cruise missiles to hit similar targets in the future. Most likely the similar bunkers around Iraq including Baghdad would have to be taken out by American "Bunker Buster" smart bombs.

Five thousand pound Bunker Buster missiles are in use by five Desert Storm Coalition allies. They can penetrate the protective shells of heavily armored bunkers and set off a massive explosion after the final target on the lowest level is reached. They can penetrate more than one hundred feet of rocky soil or at least twenty feet of solid concrete. The trick here is for the missile to get inside the bunker without the main detonator going off until it broke through several floors of concrete and iron. The payload level is determined by intelligence reports such as ours prior to the cruise missiles being programmed.

The cruise missile would be programmed on an aircraft carrier or at a base before it's placed on a B 52 bomber or launched from a ship. The missile will explode several times, the first as an impact to the outer crust of the bunker then again each time another floor is reached. The final massive incinerator explosion destroys the real target that is actually buried as far as sixty to eighty feet down.

Only Jake and I would be going on from here. The Iraqi that helped lead Jake to the site wouldn't be going with us. Getting across the berms would be our first problem, the second getting inside. Maybe the Iraqis reconnaissance hadn't been very reliable. Maybe there are Iraqi soldiers in or around the bunker. Maybe it was a set up. All these things entered my mind but failed to deter us just the same.

From our nearly totally exposed position, we could see no soldiers but there was as seen on the satellite photo a fence then one small and one larger structure nearby, then the bunker. Our report said the site is presently believed to be unmanned but we didn't know that for sure and wouldn't be taking any chances.

At first Jake crept toward the fence alone, cutting the gated entry with a big commercial weight steel cutter. I soon caught up to him and in an all out race, foot before foot almost to the point of tripping, we both ran. Still there was no sign of anyone around the small, seemingly deserted site. We two, brave men with our hearts pounding loudly in our ears first stormed the interior dirt berms then with almost no hesitation continued on to the side of the huge concrete structure. From our vantage point now looking back in the direction of our vehicle, the situation seemed more in control and we both began relaxing if you could call it that.

Jake got nearest the door first with me in quick pursuit. He used a can of spray first to freeze the lock then Jake hit it pretty hard a few times until the lock fell to the ground. The world to the outside of the thick steel door and the bunker's inside was the sharpest of contrast. Outside was lit by the moon, inside the darkness was total.

Jake and I pulled our small battery operated lamps down from atop our heads, turned them on and lowered them to our foreheads. After hastily but precisely pacing about, Jake determined the bunker to be three floors deep with a maximum of forty five feet in depth. Jake used his pick ax to continue breaking away samples of the concrete and we spoke and walked. He was looking for rebar but failed, as expected, the bunker had been built during a time of tight money and was built quite inferior with no rebar and probably watered down concrete.

Jake handed me two hands full of concrete chips in a plastic bag and told me to label them with my ball point pen. He then pulled out his Magellan GPS and tapped in his code signal, communicating our where abouts and the results to an orbiting satellite. Now if we were caught, the result of our little escapade was already known to the outside world.

Jake said spy satellites cross this region three times daily for photographic reconnaissance and listening in on emissions and signals from Iraq's Communications networks. These satellites fly over at varying altitudes according to their function. The photographic recon flights were in lower orbits of ten miles while the satellites listening to electronic emissions from Iraqi emitters or communications networks were much higher in an elliptical orbit. The lower flying satellites mostly observe and take pictures of Iraqi military movements, construction sites and day to day activities of a sensitive nature. They're essential in letting the U. S. and other countries know what Saddam Hussein and his forces are up to.

From their orbit, certain satellites can read the print on a newspaper's headlines from ten miles up, but cannot see under structures or sample harmful or menacing particulates like anthrax or other viruses or chemicals. That's where Jake and I come in. Jake runs the operation and I'm more or less just a chauffeur with balls.

Jake first took a reading from the Magellan to establish to the NRO, National Reconnaissance Office that we were there, and then a few yards away did it again to recheck the first reading. When we were finished at the bunker site, we still had one more location to find that night before completing this mission.

We took the Iraqi man back to the same place we'd picked him up two and a half hours earlier then we were off, deeper into the night and enemy territory. This time as we drove the lonely roads, with even our full headlights on, Jake divulged he worked for the NRO, the United States National Reconnaissance Office outside Washington, D.C. (as I suspected). He used to work at the super top-secret Lockheed-Martin plant on the outskirts of Denver, but gotten bored and asked to be reassigned. Jake used to advise builders of American spy satellites on what their technology had to cover. He only came to Kuwait for a break in routine but said deep down he'd rather stay in the field where the work was more "hands on" than ever going back to his old work in Colorado again.

We drove about forty more miles as we talked. Jake said the second abandoned bunker site we had to locate was actually on the way back toward Kuwait and he knew what he was looking for now and pretty much where it was.

We had reentered the area of Iraq where the vegetation was pretty thick and the night was pretty dark. At times, we talked freely without thinking of danger while playing tapes of our favorite music. Our luck had been so good; we had gotten a false sense of security. All that security left us in the flash of a moment.

About one mile from where we dropped the Iraqi off, we rounded a corner straight into an Iraqi roadblock. It wasn't a military checkpoint but it was local police. After the initial shock set in, self preservation was heightened in each of us. My first thought was to plow through the roadblock and run over anyone in our way. My reactions however hadn't caught up to my thoughts and I had already begun slowing down.

What a roadblock was doing out in the middle of nowhere was beyond either of us. Trees and darkness all but concealed the little portable roadblock and its three local gendarmes who seemed as surprised as we were. Obviously they had been snoozing. The little shack they called their office was something they could put on a truck and move to an-other location. The long white wooden plank that leveled across the street to halt traffic was also portable. It had two concrete blocks hanging by a rope on one end. When someone needed to go through, the policeman would push on the blocks and the plank would go up. The police were very haggardly dressed but appeared to each have the same uniform on and of course they each had Kalashnikov rapid fire AK 47's. For this reason only did I halt and remain steadfast as two of the men approached and the other moved to guard our rear.

It was almost insane how I didn't become fearful when stopped but handled it matter of factly with cool collected thoughts. I would congratulate myself later but for now I still had to get us out of this potentially dangerous situation. I must admit though, it was a lot harder to think when the muzzle of a machine gun is aimed between your eyes.

The policeman nearest me ordered me to roll down my window and began pointing with his rifle for me to step from the van. We spoke as best we could, no English on his part and only passable Arabic coming from my mouth. I wasn't at ease like back in Kuwait where my thoughts were really on translating and remembering words. I was now watching the rifles of three men more than I was trying out my Arabic vocabulary.

I could tell Jake was more uneasy and having a hard time trying to figure out what the policemen said to me and I said back to them. During my discussion with the policeman, I tried to make it look as easy as a breeze so Jake wouldn't feel the need to panic. The policemen told me I had to have special travel "Haweea" legal papers. I told them I had some but wanted to know why they needed them. "These papers are for the people in Baghdad" I told them, "and no one else". "I want to know if your commander is on duty or awake now. Our situation is too complicated for you and we can't afford to be delayed from our important meeting with officials in Baghdad."

The policemen seemed a bit on edge and I surmised we were probably the first foreigners these guys had ever seen and probably pretty important ones at that.

The highest ranking policeman came closer toward me while lowering his rifle to a less threatening position. He said his supervisor was at home with his family so we should wait for permission to continue on to Baghdad. I told them I was angry because now we were losing time and had to be in Baghdad at nine o'clock in the morning. We were to meet with Iraqi Government officials and the United Nations Mission there on very important matters. They said no problem (mo mushcala); we can go after the commander comes to speak with me.

The scrawny policeman motioned to the north side of the roadblock where he wanted us to park. I told him I will not wait for the supervisor but I would rather hurry, by going to the supervisor's house to save time. The little Iraqi policeman said "O K, please come with me and we'll go to his home together." I told Jake to sit in the back seat and let my policeman friend sit up front with me. Jake looked alarmed as he slipped into the back armchair, at the same time I motioned for the Iraqi to come sit in the front seat. I said "Taal, Nachnu roh enta bait maodir" I explained to Jake, the policeman is coming with us to his boss's house.

I noticed the little uniformed man had unguarded himself by putting the rifle in a position between the seats that was as accessible to me as it was to him. He came with us for about two miles before I turned to him and said, "We're alone now, I must kill you." From my door I pressed the automatic door lock down at the same time I spoke. "You die."

Suddenly it was as if there was no air in the car at all. My heart for the first time was pounding loudly and by turning and facing Jake in the back seat, I could see his fear was no less than mine. The only weapon inside the car was in the hands of the Iraqi and all three of us knew it.

I could feel my hands weaken slightly while I trembled, most visibly from my upper chest. I told the Iraqi policeman "Now I'm late for my meeting in Baghdad with very important people." (I didn't know whom I was scaring most, Jake or the policeman.) Only part of my threat was in Arabic so I didn't really know whether the policeman had gotten my meaning or not but he had. He began trembling and apologizing.

The Iraqi continued apologizing for several minutes and at one point I was afraid he was going to pee on the seat. I told him if it's OK with my important friend in the back seat, I'd let him go but if he called his commander or other police and we got stopped again before we reached Baghdad, I would make sure his own people would come back to kill him. He could not know how important this meeting was. He'd suffer for any part he played in our delay. Why else would I be on this road hundreds of miles from Kuwait City unless it was most important to my government and his. He apologized again and shook my right hand with both his hands. I could feel the moisture stay on my hands even after his sweaty ones pulled away.

I told him I was so sorry he was the one who delayed me but I hoped he and his family stayed well. He was even apologizing after he was out the door and the whole time Jake was getting back into the front seat.

I left the little rag tag policeman beside the road shaking with tears in his eyes. I had to stop a second time to throw his rifle out. He was so anxious to leave, he had forgotten all about it. He was one grateful man and I was such a beast.

Now I needed to comfort Jake. I actually felt sorry for the little local man and Jake. The ragged little policeman from a small poor agricultural area where probably nothing ever happened was no match for me. Most likely he was illiterate and knew almost nothing of the world outside his own community. Then from the dark of night, he thought he was going to be killed by this crazy foreigner. For the next hour, I thought of how many different ways I could have handled the situation but the end result was what I had hoped for and we were free. I knew I had to frighten him to prevent more people from getting involved.

Now all Jake and I had to do was keep our eyes peeled for another roadblock. If the man squealed, this one may actually have our names on it. We were a couple hundred miles from our border now and I wasn't sure what we'd do if we were caught or pursued this far from our own familiar turf.

Jake and I rode in silence for a while before Jake said "go over there, we need to get some sleep." The area he pointed to was so dark, I was really unsure of where we were spending the night. It appeared we had turned into a grove of trees that could have been on someone's property. Perhaps we'd be found during the night or before we woke up in the morning. I slept very uneasily. The only way I felt better was after I got out the van and walked around for a while. I then saw we were pretty much alone for at least several hundred yards in all directions. Even if someone went down the main road, I didn't think we could have been seen so the next few hours I rested better.

In the morning, Jake surprised me, it was as if he had forgotten last night and was ready for today's adventure. He never once brought up last night again. We awakened slightly after the sun came up and drove a few miles before we saw people. I never worried too much about running out of gasoline because we were carrying five, five gallon cans but I was still a little worried about the policeman telling someone else we were on the road to Baghdad and of course at this point, we still were.

Jake fixed our position several times on the Magellan and told me we had to go further west or northwest. We made our way to the spur rail line villages of Karbala and Hindiya where we again followed each of the rail lines from where they separated to their end. Jake did a few swabbing downs and writing on plastic baggies before dusk, then we headed back toward Hilla. Again I was near the ruins of the ancient city of Babylon but Jake said it would be dangerous to walk around there. Even though it was once again night, he said there were probably either archeologists or soldiers there. I think it was pretty obvious to both of us that most likely tourists weren't around, especially at this time of night or even inside Iraq during these troubled times.

The first time I came to ancient Babylon was in the wee hours of the morning and here we were again in the wee hours of the morning. I still wasn't going to be able to see it this time either.

We sat in the van, ate our snacks, talked an awful lot and even played the radio though Jake didn't appreciate any Arabic tunes. I didn't like most of them either but there was one played often on the Super Station Radio that reminded me of Janelle and the parties at her house. We heard that one hit and it was uplifting for me but the rest of the music sort of rambled like an unrehearsed orchestra tuning up. Each piece in the band seemed to be playing their own thing. I'm a Beach Boys, Jan and Dean kind of guy. I like Frankie Valli and the Four Seasons, Three Dog Night, Sonny and Cher and the Supremes; for those, we played cassette tapes.

The Iraqis could chase me or play hide and seek as long as I had my music. Even if worse came to worse and we were captured, maybe the Iraqis would allow me to listen to my tapes in a prison cell.

I had the ear plugs in while we visited our next bunker site. Jake told me to turn off on a little dirt road that leads directly to some chain link gates outside a clearing about ten acres wide. We sat a long distance away while we looked for anyone who might still be patrolling the site or for any activity from surrounding areas. There was none and we never saw anyone, just a small building nearby. Like the other bunker site before, there was a mound of dirt, though this one was a little taller.

Moments earlier though it seemed a half hour had passed since I watched as Jake exited the van and headed for the perimeter gates while I stayed behind the wheel; ready to move forward to collect him in the event someone entered the picture. Within seconds he had the gates open and waving his hands for me to follow his lead.

Last time I left the van where it was, but this time, quietly, I rolled the van forward inside the perimeter until he motioned for me to get out and head toward the ten foot high dirt berms that lay before us. First he climbed to the top of the dirt while staying as low as possible in the event anyone in the surrounding area might see him. From the top of the mound, he motioned for me to come. As both of us lay on our stomachs straddling the rounded top of the berms, he said "ready, set, go". Both of us ran toward a small doorway on the side and toward the bottom of the bunker. From opposite sides, we approached the doorway.

There were a few signs in Arabic around that I couldn't read but assumed said "warning stay out" or something similar. There was a cheap Chinese version of a steel Yale lock securing the heavy metal doorway. It was easily breached, posing no problem to Jake. While he checked for any possible alarm device he pulled a few little wires from a lock picking set he bought in a spy shop in Phoenix, Arizona and the lock opened. We entered the musky smelling dark concealed concrete bunker.

Jake with me in tow, did the same "in depth" exploration there as he had done alone at the previous site. We must have looked a sight, both of us creeping through totally dark, concrete vacated bunkers deep within enemy territory, wearing small coal miner type head lamps from Home Depot, carrying small hammers and pick axes.

I had Diana Ross and the Supremes playing "Baby Love" and other hits in my ears the whole time. I probably missed half of what Jake was telling me as I sang along with "My world is empty without you Babe", "Stop in the name of Love", "Some day we'll be together again", and a few others.

All was not fun and song though, Jake kept showing me what he had done at the first bunker and said he'd like me to learn to do the same type procedures here. He measured the room we were in, then found the stairs and made a few markings on a paper he was carrying. We then moved to the next level and took another measurement from ceiling to floor before he started picking away at concrete on the walls. He showed me the best place to take samples was from the corner where two walls meet. I could chip out a piece of concrete relatively easily there and continue picking at it until I found out whether there was any re-bar near the corner.

To make our measurements, we both carried simple carpenters' retractable rulers. We both continued our measuring and chipping until we had completed all three levels. We laid the bags of concrete chips and notes down and moved on to the next procedure. Jake put on a pair of special cot-ton gloves and wiped down the room in the first level while I watched. He then put the gloves in a plastic bag, sealed it shut and proceeded to do further wiping in corners and edges of the room with q-tip swabs for the Castle Meyer Test. He completed that task and put the swabs into a plastic bag and marked them all with number ones. He then handed me a pair of gloves, swabs and plastic bags and asked me to follow the same procedure on the second level down while he did the third.

When we left the bunker, it was well toward morning and if anyone was inside the little building they were surely sound asleep now. We removed our miner hats with lights before climbing back over the berms and quietly returned to our van and out the fence opening. Just then, the sun started coming up. I was proud of the help I was to Jake but his only words were "We stayed too long."

CHAPTER 31

Behind Enemy Lines Again and Again

Jake was worried the road back would be in total daylight and our chances for getting caught this late in the game were too great. I was less concerned about the Iraqi side than I was of the Kuwaiti. I hoped we could steel through the Iraqi-Kuwait border with minimum interference or chase. The United Nations soldiers were daily expanding their control over the Demilitarized Zone and I was more uneasy about avoiding them in the middle than either side. I was even more surprised when Jake said we only had a few more locations to go to and a few more chores to perform before heading home. We both remained quiet for the next hour except when Jake told me where I should be driving.

We arrived back at the rail line once again, and Jake swabbed down some more buildings and platforms, took a satellite position reading, put the swabs and gloves in more bags and marked them. As we began heading back toward Kuwait City, Jake took out a group of labels and a black magic marker. He was again marking the bag's labels and adding a few more details to each. It was a long trip home and since we were in broad daylight, we were especially careful looking ahead as well as behind us at all times. Avoiding small villages and thoroughfares where a number of people were walking was almost impossible. We just kept our Iraqi head pieces on and hoped no one could see the pale faces behind them.

Later that day about fifty miles on the Iraqi side of the border, we stumbled onto a really important military staging area of giant cannons, several tanks and troop carrier trucks. We were sure the satellites had already followed the movement of this equipment, but we took a few readings on the Magellan and some photos any ways. Iraqi troops had probably been brought South during the night on the same rail lines we were testing for chemical or biological traces. Jake made a special note of our positions with the Magellan and we both described to the best of our knowledge how many pieces of arms we saw and how many military trucks were there and if we saw troops.

We did see troops two separate times. We didn't see any with the cannons but we did see several Iraqi soldiers near a convoy of troop carrier trucks and two tanks. It appeared to us there were only a few Iraqi soldiers watching the tanks and vehicles, but probably many more were inside tents avoiding the intensity of direct sun.

The way back became more and more familiar and even though we were still inside hostile territory, my feelings of relief took over and I actually felt jubilation. I enjoyed the strange trip even though much of the time my adrenalin level was very high; it felt great just not having the rush continue any longer. Much of my desire to know what was far north of Kuwait was certainly satisfied on this trip, so I told myself I wouldn't be returning that far into enemy territory again if I was lucky enough to get all the way back to the safety of my wife, cats and apartment. I was mentally drained and would be happy when the entire trip was over and we were beyond detection and confrontation by Iraqis, United Nations troops or Kuwaiti guards. Unfortunately or fortunately, this would be the first of many more such nights deep within enemy lines. I had now learned a new trade and would often be sent alone.

Just South of the border, now inside Kuwait, I calmed down enough to sing along and harmonize with my Beach Boy tapes just like I always did riding down the streets in Savannah, Georgia or near our other home in Tempe, Arizona.

A couple years after Liberation, Kuwait began securing their border with Iraq. The overall plan called for a trench to be dug along the entire border as a final buffer between the two countries. They also built high berms full length of the border beside the trenches. A later phase will one day flood the trenches making all of Northern and Western Kuwait cut off by a moat from Iraq.

The first phase created a United Nations Demilitarized Zone and buffer within months of its conception. Several lookout towers were erected and modest security once again returned to the Kuwait-Iraq border. The propaganda war of words from the Ministry of Information started about this same time. Kuwait newspapers and television shows often reported on the electronic detection devices in place along the border and stories of all the Iraqi infiltrators being caught. Surely if such a system was in working order I would have been caught a number of times when I breached it in both directions. Construction on the Kuwait border security was hap hazard at best and posed no problems for future trips into Iraq.

In the beginning, I passed easily through guards on the main highways right into Iraq but never felt confident about coming back the same way. I didn't know why but I always tried to find a different way back. After the roadblocks became harder to pass through I began using the open desert routes more often. When the trenches and berms were con-structed, I resorted to the few openings left in them. When I made my reports to the Kuwaitis, especially the Minister of information, I always mentioned which holes in the border I used in crossing for that mission. They never told me to limit it to one place nor did they ever admit they were aiding my crossings. I never shared all information with him or any other debriefer. With the British and sometimes an American, it was a different story. I gave the details.

As Kuwait began returning to normal everywhere else in the country, the border became more secured and access even to the main roads into Iraq was made harder. You had to have a lot of documentation to cross from the Kuwaiti side then several yards further you had to have a lot of documentation to be allowed further passage into Iraq. Most of the time I avoided the whole mess, but in the event I had no recourse but to cross at an official checkpoint, that's where the Kuwaitis came in handy. They supplied me with reasonable papers.

At first I used the main roads then as complications grew, I resorted to zig zagging over desert terrain so much that my path sometimes sent me in directions I would rather not have gone, but it was still doable with a fare amount of ease, just a little inconvenience. Next came my discovery of two breaks in the berms near Umm Qasr and that remained my preferred route of travel for ever more.

Sometimes while driving quite fast across some hardened sand, I left billowing clouds of dry dust in the air that could be seen for miles. Obviously had there been more lookout towers in that period of time, I would have been a sitting duck. Fortunately, there were only a few times I crossed the neutral zone between Kuwait and Iraq like that in broad day-light.

The only time my passenger and I had trouble returning to Kuwait was once when a UNSKOM vehicle spotted us but I outran it. The driver of that car fooled us though by radioing ahead to have another UN car pull us over about two miles down the road. We stopped and told the Russian or Eastern European that we had strayed across the border at another location where there was no berms. We had come through by accident and didn't realize we had entered Iraq until it was too late. We got scared of Iraqi soldiers who might have seen us and had to make a run back to Kuwait's border. When we saw the other UN car, we thought it was Iraqi soldiers after us, so we drove as fast as we could to outrun them. We were sorry to hear they were UN cars.

Though we were pursued and caught this time, the next several times I crossed into Iraq or came back into Kuwait alone or with someone else, we used the same whole in the berms near Umm Qasr. It had an uncanny familiarity about it and of course I knew all the check posts, guard posts and UNSKOM patrol routes for several miles in all directions.

Long ago the Kuwaiti higher ups had indicated to me that they would aid my crossings but I was never quite sure that was happening so I relied on my own instincts which I trusted more. Usually the crossings were done right under the United Nations noses, mostly at dusk but a few times on rainy days with visibility limited, I crossed in broad daylight.

There could possibly be other reasons for the openings in the berms and the undug portion of trench. The Iraqis had a lucrative booze market in Kuwait with influential moneyed Kuwaitis being the main go between. It wasn't only two Americans bringing booze back across the border. On several occasions I saw Kuwaitis driving small double cab Toyotas or Mitsubishis back across the same undug portion of trench with a truck bed loaded in liquor cases with Johnnie Walker and Jack Daniels labels.

Of course, there was one final possibility of why breaches still remained in the border berms, and that was that the Kuwaitis wanted it left that way for reconnaissance missions of their own to the north and east like I was doing for Jake, the British, the Americans and the Kuwaitis. Whatever the reason, I made full use of them as if they were my own private little bridge and wholes.

On the occasions I crossed the border after dusk, I waited in the farmlands about 10 miles away, then crept closer as darkness fell. I kept my lights off and cruised toward the United Nations camp at Umm Qasr, staying just out of binocular range to the west.

Slowly, I inched toward the North until I came along the trench. I then turned east and continued till I got to the fifteen feet wide undug portion. The dirt berms were next. The dirt was piled very high along the division except for a twenty feet opening at that point and another fifteen feet wide opening a half mile away. From there I got out of my crème colored van and crawled up the high dirt embankment, looked back on the surveillance trails and over to the lights of the Iraqi town of

Umm Qasr. If everything was clear for miles around, I then drove through the berms and headed north, first slowly then faster over the moderately smooth desert until I was west of the town.

I continued driving north. A few miles further I came to the now ever familiar interchange north of the village. On the map it looked like a freeway interchange in the United States but it was a poor substitute for one. At the interchange, I could head in two directions, toward Basrah or toward Baghdad.

Once, when I came through during the day, I remembered seeing all the pitted wholes from cluster bombs dotting the bridge and highway, so at night I always had to wing my way carefully so as not to damage my tires. This was another location in which Iraqi tanks and armor tried hiding from allied aircraft which still saw it and pitted the area with cluster bombs. Now all that remained was remnants of wreckage. Most had been cleared and hauled away.

The only times I didn't go prowling around the borders or over into Iraq was when there was a buildup of Iraqi troops. During those times, both sides were more alert and a lot more people were in the area. Once I was asked to go during that type situation but I refused and was never asked again until conditions improved and fewer soldiers were on both sides.

I got a call from Jake one morning saying he'd like for us to go to Iraq again on Tuesday. I told him it might interfere with my work schedule at the Ministry but he said it was most important, so I rescheduled my work to only miss three newscasts. I was always the one who had taken everyone else place at work, it was about time someone paid me back by taking my shift. I arranged to switch one workday with a coworker named Mazan Al Ansari, who actually owed me many make up hours but then again he was a Kuwaiti so felt no obligation to repay the hours or cover for me. As with most Kuwaitis everything was for free. I finally talked him into covering for me only if I did as he asked and talked to Maia about his girlfriend. An important mission had to be on hold while I had to take care of a Kuwaitis problem with his girl friend.

Mazan was dating a girl employed by the American Embassy. Maia and most of her friends felt this young Kuwaiti girl was a trouble maker and passed Embassy information on to Kuwaitis without a "need to know", so Maia and fellow workers were unfriendly to her. Mazan wanted me to talk to Maia about becoming friends with her and helping her get closer to other female Embassy workers. In Kuwait any influence that can be rendered in such ways in normal, in fact so normal that it even has a name "Wasta". Wasta is one of the only ways anyone can get anything of importance done in Kuwait.

I told Mazan, Maia seldom spoke of such things to me but I had witnessed her making a slight snub at the girl at Embassy functions before but there had to be a reason for it. Maia is strong willed and anything I might tell her about Mazan's girlfriend would probably go in one ear and out the other. I probably would have no influence on her at all.

When I told Maia about Mazan's demand before he would fill in for me, she was even more perturbed at the girl. Maia said several other coworkers and she had noticed it seemed that every time something was going on at the Embassy or was planned for in the future, Mazan had all the information first. Much of it was not public knowledge and she and the others resented my coworker always coming around them at parties letting them know how much he knew about Embassy affairs.

I told her I'd noticed he did the same thing at the Ministry. He always told all the information to everyone at the Ministry before Maia even talked to me about it. If one of our Presidents was coming to town, Mazan had the schedule sooner than anyone else and let everyone in town know it. I later told Jake I didn't want to get the Embassy involved yet but I thought Mazan was the one instrumental in giving the exact scheduling of President Bush's motorcade to the Kuwaiti public. I think he either read the information on one of his radio or television shows or he gave the Arabic news office the schedule and let them include it on the radio. It was well within the time frame that would have allowed the men attempting to assassinate President Bush to plan the hit against him.

I told Jake I wanted some information on this Kuwaiti. He said no problem. Within three days Jake was on the phone saying Mazan was a loud mouth who dated the girl for two reasons, she must be having sex with him and he gets information from her easily. I thought in most countries that were considered spying on the Embassy of another country. If I'm to believe all that I hear, Mazan's father or Uncle was a former Kuwait diplomat who had not only lived in the United States but also Russia. Jake said what Mazan was doing seems to run in the family. A senior member of Mazan's family had also been more than friendly to people at the U. S. Embassy in Moscow. He also was familiar with someone in the U. S. Embassy secretarial pool there, and was known for "pumping" them for information.

Former President Bush barely escaped the assassination attempt against him in Kuwait because of such a leak. In my opinion there appeared more than a slight connection there.

Now that my schedule was being cared for by Mazan, Jake and I grabbed the necessary supplies needed and began our next journey into Iraq. First we stopped in Jaberiya just off Fourth Ring Road where we picked up a Brit who was obviously of Arab decent. He brought with him a lot of information concerning several of Saddam Hussein's dozen palaces in the Basrah area. Today, it was our job to get close to the largest of the seventy-eight fortified complexes Saddam considered palaces. Forty-eight of the complexes, mostly in the Baghdad area were considered Presidential.

It wasn't for another month that I would find out the true purpose of that run behind Iraqi lines. I found out our passenger had a two fold mission. United States intelligence believed the Russians were selling the Iraqis instruments vital to the growing of germs for germ warfare. Jake's friend had mentioned something to him about a huge tank the size of a car the Russians had probably sent by ship within the past week via the United Arab Emirates "Baghdad Dock" to Basrah. The tank could have dual use purposes. It was a large piece of equipment designed for being used in fertilizer plants but could also be used in developing deadly agents for germ warfare.

U. S. Intelligence said they believed the big tank was reloaded at the "Baghdad Dock" in Dubai on Monday. The United States and British intelligence always kept an eye on that particular dock in Dubai. It was the same one used for vehicle and tire shipments to Saddam's forces in Iraq. This dock was used by the Russians, North Koreans and Chinese among others to service the insatiable Iraqi desire to gain technology and equipment for purposes of developing chemical and germ warfare. All those countries would ship it to that dock then a rouge ship would put it in their cargo and head along the Iranian coast until it arrived at the docks in Basrah, Iraq.

Jake's friend's job was to find out more about the shipment to Basrah, Iraq and possibly even locate the tank if it had already arrived there. Jake and our other passenger's knowledge and expertise's were way beyond mine and I was glad I was only the driver.

Jake's friend expected the palace site where we were going would be heavily guarded, so we would have to make our approach carefully. The Arab-Brit carried satellite photos showing the palace sitting far away from town, alone on a hillside. Our passenger pointed to the map and said "we have a few places to go first but when we return, over there is where I'll be getting out." He pointed to a small group of dilapidated buildings probably two or three miles from the main complex and down hill from the palace.

I was first shocked to find out he wasn't coming back with us, then I was further shocked to find out Jake was going to stay with him. Now it made sense, the amount of stuff each was carrying in their nylon back packs was for the additional time they were going to be there.

Earlier that evening following dusk, entering into Iraq, we used the Umm Qasr route and as usual we waited near Abdaly at Sheikh Ali's farm feeding deer until it was time to cross over. We had no problem passing through the Demilitarized Zone, west of the village or the interchange before taking the Basrah cutoff. Within the next half hour we were again in the swampy wetlands of Southern Iraq. This time it was rainy and the runoff was overflowing everywhere. That whole trip for the most part remained uncomplicated, except for some rain delays. We detoured twice to see what was under two other sheds satellite photos couldn't see, before proceeding to our intended destination.

In the first shed there was nothing but some messed up Iraqi military vehicles. They looked as though they were being cannibalized (parts taken off to use on other vehicles). In the second place, I was more help than the two of them. We opened a small door to the side of an old rusting warehouse and immediately spotted a brown almost dirt colored semi truck trailer. I told them this was the same kind I found a long time ago near Kuwait's border and had filmed it for my boss. I told Jake and his friend I was so impressed with the trailer because it was built like a steel safety vault. The whole trailer was steel. I actually dragged it all the way to Kuwait City.

Jake said he had heard that my truck was the first and only mobile chemical lab truck ever found and analyzed. He even said he had pictures of it himself. They were both shocked to find out it was me who had taken it all the way to Kuwait City before my boss made me abandon it. He asked me a few questions about the insides and I told him about the lights being specially adapted with tubes covering them and sealed into the metal walls. I described the thickness of the steel on the doors and flooring. The floor also had small metal runners like the whole interior could be slid in and out on them.

In the shed that contained the chemical lad truck, we tried to get closer but there were a couple of men in a little office at the front of the warehouse. Jake said it may be easier if two of us wiped down the most likely areas of the truck while the third man watched the men in the office. It was about midnight so the guards appeared to be quite laid back and maybe even ready to go to bed. They'd been sitting on the floor around a late meal for at least the thirty minutes we'd been there.

I wore a black silk jogging suit under my dishdasha and Jake wore a beige colored one so I was the one selected to go with the Brit-Arab to do the rub down. Jake watched the warehousemen from a crouched position inside the warehouse almost opposite them. He stayed beneath a work table in dark shadow as we did our work.

The two of us put on gloves that were just removed from protective plastic and headed to the truck. When we arrived at the back side, our nameless friend pointed for me to stay where I was. I should wipe all the areas around the door including the handle and the steel step. He then proceeded to the dark side of the vehicle where the trailer's front door was located. He wiped it down as I finished doing the same in the rear. He indicated he had a couple more pairs of gloves and wanted to continue wiping the metal shelves and table tops to the rear and opposite side of the trailer as well. When everything was accomplished, we had taken about twenty additional minutes.

The Iraqis ate and had tea, never noticing our intrusion. Jake used the Magellan to pinpoint the warehouse's position again and marked it down along with information about our find. He also noted something on a small map.

One of the conversations Jake and the man carried on was about all the chicken feed factories we had seen on another trip. Jake's friend said chicken feed factories as well as milk factories and fertilizer plants were three of the easiest locations in which to hide dual usage equipment for chemical and germ warfare processing. Then Jake's friend told us about one of the chicken feed factories he had visited inside Iraq on another occasion. He said the Al Hakim factory in another part of Iraq was Iraq's largest endeavor in growing and testing germs for warfare. He had been there about two months' earlier and found particles of Anthrax, Aflatoxin and Botchalianum as well as drying and milling equipment.

These things made little sense to me but my friend told me how the process worked, but of course it was over my head and I only retained part of it. Something about collecting and separating microscopic pores that aided the germs into becoming deadly biological agents. He said the hardest project was actually in the distribution of the deadly agents after they were developed. They had to be delivered by shooting them at a target or spraying them out. The Iraqis were still trying to develop a super aerosol spray that would disperse the deadly agents in the most deadly fashion.

If these agents were put in a capsule on a missile, usually the heat made them lose most of their deadly agents. That is why the Iraqis were persistent in their efforts to develop an aero spray.

Aero sprays were more effective because they were much more deadly at ground level. One of the Iraqi tests was on their own people, the Kurds in Northern Iraq. Thousands of them died when an aerosol spray of chemical agents was released on their villages. The Iraqis were presently perfecting a spray and a missile delivery system for use on a larger scale.

Jake went on to tell me that the anthrax and other germs the United States sent to Iraq during the late 1980's would someday come back to haunt us. He said each of these diseases has a fingerprint that is different and one day after Saddam Hussein follows through with poisoning America we'll be able to trace it back to our own agents and germs we supplied him. For instance, two different components in anthrax are Bentonite or Cilica (used by the United States). By diagnosing which is present in the anthrax, it is more possible to narrow down who owns it. Most Anthrax is held in two facilities, the Center for Disease Control in Atlanta, Georgia and a site in Russia. There however other locations in Eastern Europe, Iran, North Korea and of course all that we gave to Iraq.

Jake and I continued talking above my head for a while longer and after a little maneuvering up and down some side roads, we arrived at our drop off point where Jake and the other guy got out. As they stepped from the van, I said "I'll see you back in Kuwait whenever." They said they felt sure I'd have no problems on the way back I couldn't handle. I also felt quite comfortable about the trip home.

CHAPTER 32

Germ Warfare and Propaganda

I'm alone now and still in hostile territory. All the way back to Kuwait I've been thinking how much trouble everyone is going through to find out information about some germs that were once ours to start with. The United States first introduced them to the Iraqis and then taught them how to manufacture more. The reports Jake carried indicates the United States had approved the export of seventy shipments of Anthrax and other disease causing pathogens to Iraq between 1985 and 1989. Now he's out looking for the site the Iraqis use to manufacture those same germs, or whatever you call them.

President Bush finally halted the shipments to Iraq's scientists in 1989, barely a year and a half before the Iraqis invaded Kuwait. Iraq's large pool of more than 7,000 Scientific or Technical experts, Nuclear Scientists and Engineers is due to our support and cooperation during Iraq's long war with Iran.

Nobel Prize winning geneticist Joshua Lederberg chaired a board of directors at a Rockville, Maryland Company that supplied at least seventy shipments of these disease causing agents to Iraq. At that time, Joshua Lederberg personally helped the Iraqis with any problems they might have. I've heard by rumor that he is now the one heading a Pentagon panel that is dismissing links between biological weapons in Iraq and the "Gulf War Veterans Illness". Where is their reasoning in that? To which side do you think he's tilting?

He's possibly the man that exported to Iraq all those deadly Anthrax and other agents of which spores can remain lethal for decades, and now he's denying any connection of these diseases to the illnesses now plaguing our own American troops. Since he has a Pentagon position, or at least had one when all the hoopla started over "Gulf War illnesses". Did he and our government just cover their own asses by dismissing the possibility of any "Gulf War illness"? Surely if falling allied bombs destroyed munitions and aircraft on the ground, some loaded with chemical or biological agents near our men, I suppose some of our soldiers could have been exposed. What if we hit some factory or lad or storage facility near Al Jabal or Kamasiyah? Kamasiyah was blown after the war ended but still in time that American troops were still in the area. We know that within Saddam Hussein's Presidential Guards, there is a unit devoted to nothing more than moving these chemicals and biological elements from place to place around the country. Did we miss all of them?

We know through CIA reports that as far back as 1991, just after the Gulf War ended, our inspectors found a lot of military equipment and as many as 2,160 rockets stored at an Iraqi site at Kamisiyah. Even with just this one find, we know that chemical arms were in separate storage facilities surrounded by berms southeast of that main ammunition dump. More than 500 rockets containing Sarin and Cycloserine gas were found by our inspectors. Remember Sarin gas and its deadly results in the Tokyo subways?

Heading out on this trip into Iraq was preceded by a warning. It could be dangerous because of Iraqi soldiers, and it could be dangerous because if we find what we're looking for, it may be a tremendous health hazard. I hadn't guessed we were talking about germs and biological warfare agents, but for months we'd all been hearing about what Saddam Hussein had probably been doing in milk and chicken factories; so it came as no surprise.

I remained undeterred. It wasn't like I chose to become a secret agent or whatever I am; but it has evolved and I've just gone with the flow. It's been nerve racking, but I'm eating it up like pancakes for breakfast.

His Highness the Crown Prince's Advisor again came to me yesterday and said he was pleased not only with my work in the field (inside Iraq) but also with my radio show in the morning. I had a good speaking voice and the westerners and Arabs enjoyed listening to me. He said he himself listened each morning to my broadcast because his English is limited, but I speak very clearly and my accent is better than the British ones he had been trying to listen to on British Broadcasting Company, BBC. He wanted me to do the formatting and be the chief writer and supervisor of a new propaganda broadcast that would be aired daily to the people of Iraq. He said Kuwait would have its own little "Radio Free Iraq". He had a little trouble convincing his cousin, the Minister of Information, Sheikh Saud that I was the one to write the new program. He said for some reason the Minister never came out and rejected me, but he did keep throwing other names out of people he preferred to do the writing. He said the Minister wanted to keep all those persons involved Kuwaitis, though he admitted I was the best writer by far.

I decided to take the new job because again, it would add a little more money to my pay and add a lot more to the knowledge I'd be receiving about Iraq and even about the Kuwaitis "of what" and "how" they think. My new work schedule would change very little. My regular radio news job was in the same location as the new broadcast station, just down the hall. The hours I'd be writing propaganda would be between the nine o'clock and twelve o'clock news and weather show I was already doing for FM 93.5. Each morning, I'd have to come in about an hour earlier and stay an hour later. That's all. Since it was being cleared by the Minister of Information, it still wouldn't make any demands on me that would impede my time for cross-border excursions. Both higher ups knew I had to go and could take some of the next broadcasts.

The first few months at the new propaganda broadcast was informative and it was obvious the Kuwaiti hierarchy was really getting into it. We still weren't sure whether we were getting through to the Iraqi person on the street and in these beginning stages were still ironing out some writing problems between me and the Kuwaitis who wanted to put lots of irrelevant and out right false information into reports. I persisted and kept everything moving toward a broadcast that would be informative, truthful and most of all believable.

I eliminated a lot of Kuwaiti personal views of Saddam Hussein and tones of admonishing the Iraqi public for following him. I figured we should put the real information out there for the Iraqi public to hear and make their decisions from. If we lectured them on their evil ways, the Iraqi public would just turn the broadcasts off then it would be just Kuwaitis listening to themselves talk.

As time passed even the Crown Prince who is also Kuwait's Prime Minister became more involved with the broadcasts. Our morning briefings moved from the Ministry of Information where the radio station was to the Dasma Palace office of the Crown Prince. He wasn't always there but he or his advisors tried to sit in on each intelligence briefing that laid the ground work for that day's propaganda broadcast.

Several men from Kuwait's CID, Secret Police usually came to the meeting, as did someone representing the American Military; British intelligence MI6 and two of us from the Ministry of Information, a Kuwaiti and me. I took notes and accepted written reports from which I could rewrite each AM broadcast. Finally, the group as a whole became more aware of the importance of a "Radio Free Iraq" and an abundance of real information began rolling in.

The Kuwaiti who was in the Ministry of Information with me, translated documents I couldn't fully read in Arabic, and he translated my written words into Arabic for broadcast to the Iraqi people.

I was very good at condensing news reports down to a "Readers Digest" version very quickly. Before I left the Crown Prince's office, I already had the outline, if not the exact wording of the propaganda on quickly scribbled paper. I read it aloud and listened to any critique that came from those assembled. Most of the time it was minimal and I obviously felt I had captured the most important messages that should be put out to the Iraqi public.

I was the one who insisted on having the main structure and message written before I left the room, because as I read it back to those present; there was little chance the Kuwaiti who was to complete the translation would add to the report or take away from it. I put him in position that he had to translate only what had been heard around the room instead of letting this man that I trusted very little, throw his own two cents in at the end. In the actual broadcast, the Kuwaiti and I both went on the air together. First in Arabic and English we welcomed our Iraqi listening audience and bantered back and forth a little about the day's weather to put everyone at ease.

Another thing I insisted on was that we closely monitor the weather for Southern Iraq as far north as Baghdad; so that when we gave it, they would consider it the best weather report they were going to get for the day. Iraqi television has no access to Western satellite technology and don't even pull their weather reports from CNN or BBC. When we went on the air, we gave the Iraqi public information and weather they could trust; right under Saddam Hussein's nose.

I spoke almost no Arabic on the broadcast because The Ministry and Crown Prince's Office said my speaking English added authenticity to it. We went "ON AIR" with three different types of broadcasts. One telling of rebellions against Saddam Hussein's armies, another telling of assassination attempts; and another telling the world community views on Iraqi current events.

For instance report type no. 2:

"The eldest son of Saddam Hussein, Huday has been shot in a brave assassination attempt. Huday lies near death in a hospital unit of the Hashemite Palace in Amman, Jordan. His wounds to the neck and abdomen are critical. The people of Iraq are showing their uneasy alliance with Saddam Hussein when members of Saddam's own family turn against him. One of Huday's own guards, Iyada Deham was hired by Huday's Uncle Watban Takriti to kill his own nephew. Watban Takriti is Saddam Hussein's half brother who is also married into Saddam's wife's family. The guard that shot Huday is none other than a relative of another of Saddam's family, Barzan Al Takriti who represents Iraq at the United Nations in New York. The near lifeless body of Huday was driven by ambulance ten hours over the open desert to Jordan late yesterday. Hussein Kamel Al Majid one of Saddam Hussein's personal consultants are with Huday under the roof of King Hussein of Jordan."

In other broadcasts, we showed other tensions within Saddam Hussein's family. We used lengthy reports condensed down to easy listening ones that spoke of Saddam's oldest son Huday who also disliked another of his uncles, Barzan Takriti whose main job was Ambassador to Switzerland. Takriti controlled all the secret bank accounts of Saddam's family. Huday suspected Barzan had been stealing money so he wanted him killed, but Saddam was afraid of losing his other half brother's support and all the money he controlled, so Huday was forbidden to kill his Uncle.

Huday also wanted to kill another uncle, Watban Al Takriti whom he actually got fired from his Minister of Interior post. They both began plotting assassinations against each other. Watban had allowed conspiracies against Saddam to get close enough that he almost allowed Saddam Hussein to be killed more than once. Huday knew that part of their family's joint profits from oil deals through Kurdish territory into Turkey had also been skimmed by Watban. The family shared $700 million annually from there.

Watban's failure in keeping assassination attempts from Saddam Hussein caused the Iraqi dictator to employ a Praetorian Guard of all armed

Iranian exiles not Iraqi. Saddam still needed Watban to keep charge of the Kurdish oil or he too would have been killed.

The middle of August 1996 was deadly within Saddam Hussein's family. Two of his daughters fled Iraq to Jordan with their husbands to seek asylum. These were not merely sons-in-laws of Saddam. These were Lt. General Hussein Kamel Hassan, who was trusted by Saddam Hussein who allowed this favorite son-in-law to become the architect of Iraq's Advanced Weapons Program. With the General and Saddam Hussein's daughter fleeing to Iraq with their children was the General's own brother who was also married to another of Saddam Hussein's daughters. This son-in-law was Commander of Saddam Hussein's Presidential Guard (a very highly trusted position). (I believe these were two of the men I met in Jeddah, Saudi Arabia three days before Saddam's forces invaded Kuwait).

After the foursome, their children and a few others defected to Amman, Jordan, they began freely giving information about Saddam's regime and his nuclear testing abilities to the outside world. Lt. General Hassan said Iraq was only three months away from testing an atomic bomb when Desert Storm broke out. Saddam Hussein thought he still had time to test the bomb before going to war against the allied forces but the atomic bombs weren't ready yet. The other chemical tipped bombs that were to be used against Kuwait, Israel and American troops were readied and loaded onto 15 planes at the Al Bakr Air Base northeast of Baghdad.

Saddam said he didn't want to "use them up" on the first couple days of war, so he was keeping them waiting but Allied bombing missions over that base were so intense that the planes were kept grounded for fear they'd lose them. Saddam Hussein's own soldiers were in such fear the bombs would be set off amongst them by allied bombings that they felt safer by moving them from populated areas near the capital Baghdad, far out into the desert and only left a few men to guard them.

Another piece of information Lt. General Hassan broke to the 10 American interrogators sent to Amman, Jordan was that initially Saddam Hussein's forces had been instructed to capture 5,000 American soldiers. The men would be put tied on the fronts of Iraqi tanks much the same as hunters put a dead deer across the hood. Their live bodies would be used as human shields. This plan was also delayed, and then dropped; when his forces stayed more on the retreat than on the offense.

Saddam Hussein lured his daughters and their husbands back from Amman, Jordan with the promise of amnesty. Both men were executed hours after they crossed back into Iraq.

Saddam Hussein also killed one of his brothers-in-law. His wife's brother was an Air Force General who wanted to help Iraq move from isolation to reenter the world community. Saddam killed him also, but that death caused another coup attempt against Saddam Hussein again. Saddam Hussein's wife's family, the Dulaimiu Tribe took the execution news of Air Force General Ahmed Mazllum Dulaimiu, Saddam's wife's brother badly. Another of Saddams wife's brothers, General Turki Ismail Dulaimiu led a mutiny in the Army against Saddam Hussien. A big battle was fought in Abu Ghareeb twelve miles north of Baghdad. It took hundreds of Saddam Hussein's top troops and many tanks to quell the rebellion. It was finally put down through the Dulaimiu tribe's elders. Saddam Hussein gave them "blood money" of $5 million in cash and 500 racing camels. Half the camels were female (an even better prize). The feud halted.

In another report, we spoke of Tariq Aziz. We often saw Iraqi Deputy Prime Minister Tariq Aziz, a Christian, as Saddam Hussein's spokesman on television at the United Nations. He was also in trouble with Huday, Saddam's son. Recently since Huday's recuperation, he lashed out at Tariq Aziz because of his attitude about complying with UN terms. Huday didn't like Tariq Aziz being a Christian and having ideas of taking Iraq out of isolation nor his views on compliance, so he wanted him killed. He managed to remove Aziz's bargaining powers at the United Nations and put another man, Foreign Minister Saleh Mohammed Sahhan in charge. Aziz is now just a mouth piece and messenger boy with no bargaining power.

There was an old joke in the United States saying if President Bush was killed, there would have to be a second bullet to hit Dan Quayle. In Iraq there was a similar saying that if Saddam Hussein was shot, there had to be three bullets, the second for Huday, Saddam's son and a third for Tariq Aziz.

Another type broadcast we radioed was similar to this:

"American and other aircraft carrier ships have reentered waters near Iraq's Southeastern Coast. They are on alert with the probability of attacking several installations in and around Baghdad. Saddam Hussein's continued policy of building and testing chemical and Biological weapons deems it necessary for United States smart missiles to again overfly Iraqi cities. Only destruction can follow such confrontations. Most Iraqis are tired of living with such tough economic hardships but until Saddam stops his secretive weapons ambitions, there can be nothing but disdain from the world and more hardships for the Iraqi people."

"Fifteen years ago, Iraq enjoyed close relations with the West, the United Nations and OPEC, Oil Producing Exporting Countries as well as the Arab League. At that time, Iraq sold $28 billion of oil a year to the world community allowing the Iraqi economy to be strong and the market places full. Today, Iraq has to beg permission to sell only $4 billion in oil a year, the economy is at bottom with all Iraqis except those close to Saddam Hussein being asked to endure hardship for the President while he continues waging wars and political battles. Daily he parades in front of children's schools, government buildings and before his troops. He congratulates you on denying your children necessities so his troops can stay strong. He builds palaces of glitter and gold, yachts that will never sail and fifty storey towers that bear his name. The people of Iraq are shunned by the world, even your Arab brothers and sisters. You are starved into submission and cut off from their Arab nations who prosper. War costs billions of dollars.

The loss of friendships and allies costs even more. The cost of Saddam Hussein's 200 meter yacht alone would put incubators and medicine in the hospitals. The cost of one new palace would provide millions of dollars for milk and food for all the children of Iraq. Why then are Iraqis content with supporting a mad man who treats his own people with such disregard and abandonment?

"Saddam Hussein says the world has turned against Iraq. He tells you other nations are starving your babies and stealing Iraq's wealth. This same man disregards the lives of your women and children so much that he calls for them to lie down in the halls of palaces and buildings he believes are targeted for bombings. Where is he during this time? Is he lies with you and your babies holding their hands?"

Broadcast type number three tells of troops who unite in mutiny. They tell of opposition groups planning to take back control of their regions to rebuild their own economies without help from Baghdad or Saddam Hussein. These broadcasts also tell of the world's plans to assist Iraq in rebuilding their torn country once Saddam Hussein is toppled. It mentions the lifting of the embargo and all sanctions in place. It tells how a new government will be formed that will align itself with the world community, and begin exporting record amounts of oil. Aid agencies from around the world will enter Iraq to begin feeding the hungry. Iraq's new armed forces will unite rather than stay splintered and they will rebuild their strength while maintaining their borders. Disputes will be settled with the Kurds in the North and Shi'ites in the South. They will receive assurances from the United Nations that no nation will move militarily against Iraq during its time of reorganization and Iraq in return will no longer move against its neighbors. Iraq will get back to educating its young people instead of preparing them for war. A new and better Iraq awaits, only one thing stands in the way. Saddam Hussein, the mad man who fears for his safety so much he must always sleep with trusted guards only a few feet away.

The Kuwaitis had a way of not leaving well enough alone. They wanted to actually begin broadcasting information that would stir up rebellion within Iraq or incite Iraq to once again attack Kuwait. I was against any such broadcasts and said so in no uncertain terms. They wanted to create another conflict and again be the bystanders, with hired troops at least from the United States to again come save their asses and destroy Saddam Hussein.

I found out that Kuwaitis behind the scenes had been meeting for months to discuss possibilities of getting foreign troops back into the region and how far they would have to go to make it happen. The dual purposes also included getting the Americans out of their pocketbooks.

Chapter 33

Kill the Americans

Kuwaitis wanted to rid Iraq of Saddam Hussein and they wanted to rid Kuwait of the United States always dipping into their country's pockets. The most plausible solution so far was to set America up for some kind of deadly strike from inside Iraq. So far the scenario would play out like this: American troops always come in the spring for military exercises in Kuwait's desert region nearest the border with Iraq. After about a month, Kuwaiti soldiers join the exercises for a joint military maneuver. The "kill" should be done when only the Americans were up there.

Kuwait had gone so far as to select one of their own military generals to plan such an attack. He would command a unit of most trusted soldiers to smuggle through the demilitarized zone a scud missile that would be used in the attack. The launch would be done with one of Saddam Hussein's own missiles that had been captured during the Gulf War, and brought into Kuwait to be stored in a secure munitions depot.

The target had already been selected as well. Kuwait had been advised that a contingent from Fort Stewart, Georgia would be in the region first and the longest. They will do. Since scud missiles are not easily aimed, it would have to be fired with the utmost intelligence report on the largest concentration of Fort Stewart soldiers.

A surprise to me was that I was to become part of the set up for the kill. "Radio Free Iraq" (meaning me), would deliver a blistering antagonistic statement to Saddam Hussein; then follow it up by boasting about the newly arrived Americans and their strength numbers and fairly exacting locations. The Kuwaitis would have no qualms about leaking all this intelligence data to put their plan into action. They could always apologize for it later.

In this same propaganda news cast I was also suppose to relate approximate positions of U. S. Navy vessels in the Persian Gulf nearest Kuwait's shores. I was to further antagonize the situation by saying it was possible these troops would move against Iraq's southern border and push farmers from their land to create a wider buffer zone similar to the way the Israelis had done in Southern Lebanon. I was to say the present Demilitarized Zone allows too many infiltrators into Kuwait and the new zone will station military units from the United States, Kuwait and Great Britain inside the new buffer zone on Iraqi territory.

The unprovoked, surprise attack would no doubt cause the Americans to go back into Iraq and finish what they should have done to start with, kill Saddam Hussein. Once this is done, the Kuwaitis could get off the hook for billions of dollars each year for defensive Patriot Missiles and other expensive military hardware the Kuwaitis wouldn't need any more against a beaten, non threatening neighbor.

I refused to have anything to do with the broadcast and wouldn't even write it for someone else. I wanted nothing more to do with the Ministry of Kuwait's radio station if they were continually trying to get American men and women killed by targeting them. I was told I should not be so touchy, chances are Saddam couldn't hit them anyway because scuds are unreliable and better yet, the end result would show Saddam Hussein the Americans and British are in the region to stay, fully supporting the Government and people of Kuwait.

When I left the Ministry's tall administrative building that day, I was sure I no longer worked for the AM Kuwait Radio Station. I left the Ministry of Information's main building and walked through the glass skywalk over to the Radio Building to continue my normal Super Station news programs on the FM band. In the days and weeks that followed, I never once turned the AM broadcast on to hear if they had gone ahead with it. From that day on, that station was dead for me. Several Kuwaitis asked me to return but I never did and gradually the program went off the air.

Once at an American Embassy function held in Ambassador Crocker's residence, I ran into the American military officer with whom I had several meetings at the Crown Prince's Office. I asked him what explanation the Kuwaitis had given him why the broadcasts stopped? He said they simply told him they were reorganizing the program's format and they would contact him in the future when the show was to begin airing. I then told him what had transpired on my end and how I wanted no part in setting up Americans to be killed by Iraqis or Kuwaitis.

I told him I felt so strongly that the Kuwaitis persistence was so abnormal they scared me into believing it was entirely possible the Kuwaitis would target our American soldiers just to make it look like Saddam Hussein had done it. They would do it to anger the American public so the American people would force Washington into returning to Baghdad to finish off Saddam Hussein like they should have done in the first place.

The military man and I spoke only a few minutes more and both of us explained our own reasons why the United States saved Saddam Hussein. I knew one reason was because the Saudi Arabians and Kuwaitis hadn't paid their Gulf War bills yet, so we had to keep Saddam in power until they came across with all they were expected to pay. (Keep the wolf at the door, so to speak.) The military man said maybe the United States should have allowed the Israeli Masaad to go in for him. (My sentiments exactly.) The Israelis wanted to take out Saddam because of the scuds he lobbed into Israel during Desert Storm. The United States even stopped the Israelis in their tracks instead of letting them take care of business like they normally would have.

The United States should have killed Saddam when he visited Salmiya, Kuwait on November 15, 1990, during Occupation. Satellites tracked him all the way home as he traveled in a Winnebago motor home the entire 450 miles back to Baghdad.

The past week at work lay heavy on my mind and it was time for a little R&R, rest and recuperation. Barbara Vaughn's dinner that afternoon would be perfect timing. I needed the break to see friends again and to ease Maia's concerns. She was upset that I'd been so upset. Maia and I could have a good time, unwind and maybe get back to feeling good about living in Kuwait again. We agreed not to say a word to anyone at Barbara's about what had been going on between me and people at the Ministry of Information.

As usual, the second we entered Barbara's apartment, we could smell the turkey in the oven almost like it was Thanksgiving. Often there were twenty five to forty people stopping over at Barbara's for special evenings, eating and having a good time, watching Armed Forces Television and talking. Barbara lives in what is called the Silver Towers. Like Betty, Barbara lives alone in an American Government-paid two story apartment with more than 2,200 square feet.

Barbara's apartment reflects the way most of us who live overseas collect artifacts from all the different regions and countries we've visited and lived in. There are carpets from several countries, silver tea services and carved items from other places and pictures showing our families back home; and our travels and friends of days gone by. I immediately went over and found the 1964 Savannah High School and Jenkins High School year books of our graduation on the coffee table. Of course she had laid it there especially for me. Maia and I visited a few minutes with Barbara, and then sat down together while I pointed out pictures of friends and activities from those school years. I was quiet in those days and was in none of them except the unassuming yearbook picture.

Our night at Barbara's was a little out of the ordinary as had the whole week been. Barbara had the regular military people from Doha base as well as a few American school teachers and other American Embassy friends over to share the evening. She also introduced all of us to a man whom we had been reading about in the local Arab Times Newspaper. He was a Kuwaiti who wanted to change his religion, no easy task in a

Muslim country like Kuwait. Hussein Qambar Ali sat on the sofa casually speaking with several people from Barbara's Bible study group. Hussein said he wanted to become a Christian, to convert from Islam, but his family and the Kuwait legal system was making it extremely difficult. He had been kicked out of his own home by his wife and three children, outcast from his wife's family and his own and was now staying on the run fearing for his life.

Even his automobile had been taken away and no lawyer in the country wanted to represent him because of the difficulties faced in trying to convert away from Islam. Kuwait is an Islamic nation where even Parliament says there is no law that could force his imprisonment nor can he be put to death legally, however, conversion is a crime against Islam and Parliament says it will do nothing to prevent the sentence of death from being carried out. The official charge against Hussein Qambar Ali is "Apostophy".

Barbara and several others from her Church had been hiding the Kuwaiti until he could reach safety from religious persecution in the United States. That night at Barbara's, he seemed to be a nice enough person but I got the feeling he wasn't telling the whole truth about his situation.

Barbara and several other women including Maia were in the kitchen putting the finishing touches on dinner while the rest of us watched television and talked. The fellowship of friends, the sounds of many people talking at once, the smell of turkey in the oven and all the other great eats in the air made me feel so comfortable that I truly enjoyed every minute of that day, as if it were a major holiday instead of just a get together of friends, months before the holiday season even started.

Barbara is always a busy person and fills her time away from Embassy work with religious activities and choir rehearsals with the "Kuwait Singers". It's a group made up of English-speaking expats from six countries that enjoy putting on singing programs for the public throughout the year, especially around major holidays like Christmas. Barbara had been having a great time going to rehearsals several evenings weekly, but always had time for others, her Christian work and cooking a great meal.

The dinner at Barbara's was a good time for several of the ladies to discuss their ball gowns for the coming season, while the guys sat glued to the television watching sporting events on the Armed Forces Network Television.

The next big American Embassy Marine Corps Ball was just over two months away, in November and the ladies were again busily swapping names of material shops and seamstresses to make their gowns. Maia imported her gown from India, where she saw it on one of our trips and fell in love with it right away. She wouldn't be having another made this year. Betsy bought another one on her last trip to Paris, where she will return to live soon. It was her first choice for change of Embassy duty and she got it. Betsy was partly raised in Paris by her parents who were assigned to the American Embassy there, while she was a teenager. Now she had the opportunity of having her two sons live in Paris about that same period of time in their lives.

We guys have holiday dressing so easy. Not much choice in what a tuxedo will look like. I have two black ones, one white one and several different cumber buns, vests and shirts. This year I was lucky to pick up some fine formal scarves in Paris and Rome, either of which would look nice around my neck at this year's Marine Corps ball. Maia liked the CoCo Chanel scarf best, but I had worn it last time, so maybe that would be one of the only changes I made. My studs and cuff links are heirlooms from Maia's father that I'd worn at gala events in Saudi Arabia, on the Royal train across India, in Rome and in Cairo and on the Orient Express and other occasions and will probably be worn again for the next one.

Betty McNaughton, Betsy Gorlay and Betsy's British friend Mike arrived late at Barbara's and did the normal air kissing of cheeks around the room before heading in different directions to mingle. Betsy was cute as ever with her pixy dark hair and slender build and Mike the typical

Brit, slightly under dressed but full of fun and ready for a slice of that American turkey bird and a drink.

Mike's a great guy and hopefully he and Betsy will be married before her posting to the Embassy in Paris. The two of them come to our apartment occasionally and we always have fun laughing and talking for endless hours. When Betsy was in the United States and Paris recently, Mike continued coming over and sharing a bottle of fine wine while we discussed the difficulties in training Kuwaiti aircraft specialist on how to keep American built, Kuwaiti owned fighter aircraft repaired and in the air.

Mike said his position as trainer sounds good but all the reports recently in Kuwait's newspapers about the faulty aircraft sold to Kuwait by the United States is a lot of baloney. He says the Kuwaitis are always saying they have been sold inferior planes, when all that is wrong with them is their maintenance program. He said Kuwait hired him as a teacher not as the aircraft mechanic. Most of the time he has to do both because Kuwaitis show up for work or school whenever they feel like it, not as per schedule.

That means if Mike doesn't carry out the repairs himself, then the aircraft is "down". He says he and many other guys like him have such trouble getting Kuwaitis to come to work that quite a few aircraft are "down" at any given time. Kuwaitis think once aircraft or equipment is sold to them. It is perpetual care like in a cemetery.

Dinner at Barbara's was exceptionally good as usual and everyone settled down to hot tea and television. Betty McNaughton, the Ambassador's Secretary came over with her small entourage and they quickly spread to mingle. Betty as usual looked extremely well and as meticulously dressed as always but her hair was a mess. Never had I even seen one hair out of place on her, let alone see it rough looking like it was that day. Betty noticed me looking at her hair with surprise and I didn't even get the word hello out before she said in her Texas accent "I know I look like I've been ridden hard and put up wet, but the Ambo (Ambassador Crocker) has been working me to the bone." "I can't follow that man to his next assignment to Syria because he's going to kill me." Within a few more minutes, Betty had settled down and was relaxing with a drink in her hand like almost everyone else.

Maia and I hadn't been back at our apartment twenty minutes before I got a call. My Royal Ordinance friend Brumley wanted me to take him back inside Iraq. Three weeks ago, the Kurdistan Democratic Party (Saddam Hussein's Northern Kurdish allies) militia seized several opposing Kurdish militia bases and captured the Northern Iraqi village of Arbil. Now the Kurds of the KDP are in control. Saddam regained his military strength over the North and now wants to move south into Shiite territory once again. My friend said a Southern Iraqi opposition group called the Islamic Revolution in Iraq wanted to show the two of us what they think are chemical warheads ready to be mounted on missiles. They're afraid the warheads may be used against them.

It was September 14, 1996. The opposition said Saddam Hussein's forces were preparing to use the railroad again from An Nasiriya to reenter the southern marshes to destabilize Southern Iraq and possibly Kuwait. Brumley and I had to go meet with the Iraqi opposition leaders now before more units of the Republican Guard arrived in the area. My friend said there was new evidence also of another underground bunker in the desert southeast of Samawa, south of An Nasiriya, north or northwest of As Salman that we needed to check. The bunker site had been recently abandoned like the other two we investigated before but this one may still hold valuable traces of VX nerve gas that is 10 times more deadly that the Sarin gas used by the Japanese Aum Shinrikyo Cult.

I knew the Iraqis used to have some missiles in this area but only now did intelligence from the American NRO, and British MI 6 or whoever, acknowledge something of a more problematic nature exists there. Now all of a sudden, they're sending us needed confirmation on what they believe is the contents of this next bunker and in the surrounding berms. We will be going into Iraq, meeting with some of Saddam Hussein's opposition, looking over the abandoned bunker and at the missile site the group is suspicious of. Satellite photos are being sent to us, so we'll have a better idea what the United States knows and what the inside berm area looks like. This information will help us lay out a plan for how we enter the bunker site and what Iraqi guards we may have to confront once there. Perhaps the most danger we face is if an Iraqi buildup is taking shape and moving south toward us. We may get caught up in it. The last bit of information we received from the NRO also contained a warning passed along by the CIA: AT NO TIME ARE YOU TO BE ARMED DURING THIS ASSIGNMENT.

The warning didn't make sense. We may not be CIA personnel but if we're doing a job that puts us in hostile territory and there is a high likelihood we'll be confronting some Iraqi soldiers, I think that warning is a little out of line. What if we are ready to break our way inside the bunker and an Iraqi soldier spots us? We can't ask him to stand aside or unlock the door. My small pocket knife has no chance against a bullet fired from a Kalashnikov.

I had decided to do something that I had already secretly sworn to Jake I wouldn't do. Arm myself for this trip inside Iraq. I'd do it with a weapon Jake had given me first to care for, then to actually keep as my own. He proudly told me of the specialness of this weapon, and then made me promise that it would never see the light of day (nor night) because the ramifications to me and others who might be traced to me could be devastating. Without really knowing or understanding its significance, I armed myself anyways.

Jake had described my gift as a Dan Wesson revolver which meant nothing to me at the time. With its silencer, it was regarded as the small version of the Delisle commando carbine silencer, considered by everyone as the mother of all silencers. It was used by the United States for assassinations like the one attempted against Ugandan Dictator Idi Amin in 1971.

My new revolver was near perfectly quiet when fired due to its special construction for venting the gas to the rear of the bullet chamber, had no muzzle flash (even if fired next to you in the dark), and was small;

with only about an eight inch silencer chamber extending out the front of the revolver's muzzle.

When Jake gave me the weapon, he showed me all I needed to know about it but hoped I would keep it as a memento of our occasions in the field only. He went on to tell me how the Soviets had what they called their version of the revolver and the carbine rifle called the Dragonov. It was a 7.62 caliber sniper weapon used by the KGB and special Soviet operatives in Viet Nam. It was accurate and silent up to one thousand yards. It had been perfected as one of the more secretive, less traceable, new methods of kill since the old Russian NKVD had become the KGB.

Since the first day Jake had given me the weapon, I had delusions of using it against Saddam Hussein. Sometimes, I dreamed about it at night. I wouldn't try to kill Saddam Hussein for any glory or celebrity; I'd just do it because maybe I could. Saddam Hussein had come to Kuwait and the border region several times after occupation of Kuwait. One time he was only about a block from me. If the circumstances ever presented it again and would allow me the time to prepare a little, I think I would have at least tried to Kill Saddam. Perhaps if violently confronted today or any other day after crossing behind enemy lines into Iraq again, maybe I'll still get the chance to try it and begin getting some experiences needed to become an assassin.

I think I've always known I had many of the characteristics British Intelligence says are needed to become an assassin: an expert shot, can keep my cool in close quarters, take good initiative, have no feelings of regret for deed done. In the United States, political or government orchestrated assassinations were called "Executive Actions", in Britain following World War Two they were called them "Converting to His Majesty's Custody". I'm sure I can do it.

Thursday afternoon about four o'clock, Jake and I and our new associate started toward the border. We didn't get very far north of Jahra when our third friend's mobile phone rang. Satellite pictures show a heavy concentration of Iraqi troops moving into the area we're headed for.

They are getting off at railheads of three small towns then moving south. Several more minutes elapsed while we continued our drive toward Kuwait's border with Iraq. The telephone rang again and this time we were told to abandon plans for entry today and for some time to come.

Within days of our attempted trip to Iraq, Reuters Wire Service reported many Iraqi troop movements in our direction. Everyone I talked with thought it was strange that Saddam's forces were becoming confrontational at this particular time. So far, we couldn't logically find a reason for it. Our logic was usually a lot better than all the scholars we occasionally watched on American television, giving their ideas on what was happening with Saddam Hussein and why. Jake and I came to the conclusion that Saddam was jealous of President Clinton's lack of attention.

Saddam Hussein was losing his importance in the daily life of the American President who was now getting involved with affairs of North Korea. Saddam Hussein has been witnessing in the past few weeks President Clinton crumbling to Pressure from the North Korean President. The North Korean leader wants to keep his country's old nuclear reactors and the byproducts for making nuclear bombs, or make the United States and Japan rebuild North Korea's economy and build billions of dollars worth of nuclear power plants. And so on and so on.

Saddam Hussein sees his situation much like those blackmail demands by the North Korean President and wants President Clinton to offer rewards likewise to him to be a good boy. In order to achieve a similar deal, Saddam Hussein may even raise the stakes by showing he is ready to mass his troops on the border to scare the Clinton White House into bargaining with him. A negotiated withdrawal as part of a bargain may also force the Uni-ted Nations to ease sanctions against Iraq or even lift the embargo all together.

It became clear to us Saddam Hussein was creating a faux crisis to get negotiations going in his favor. Sure enough within the next month, there was a huge buildup on the border with Kuwait and a new crisis was at hand.

My "outside" activities the month of September accelerated, I'd been working my normal job at the Super Station and had my arm twisted to once again getting involved with the AM Kuwait propaganda broadcast station. I had also returned inside Iraq once again with Jake. Conditions for Jake and me in Kuwait were about to heat up. He showed me a docu-ment that I had a terrible uneasy feeling about. It showed Kuwait was building "safe" bunkers below several locations. The document had been translated in England and named both Jake and me mentioning our investigative work on Iraqi bunkers. The document explained how Kuwait one day would need to protect themselves not only from the Iraqis or Iranians but against people like Jake and me who clearly could compromise or get almost any information we were after, either far inside Iraq or here in Kuwait.

The document echoed one of my earlier statements that one day our host country Kuwait and the United States may be on opposing ends, and the Kuwaitis were already beginning to distrust the two of us. I knew the Kuwaitis better than most people from the West, even those who call themselves authorities, and I have been concerned for a long time the Kuwaitis may turn against the bearers of the intelligence reports (Jake and I) instead of the information we brought. What's that expression "shoot the bearer of the news"?

In this report Jake or someone else found, the Kuwaitis wrote about their secret bunkers in fairly graphic detail and that we probably already knew about them also. If that was true, perhaps there had been a breach of Kuwait security by the two of us and if true, what could be done about it?

The document astounded us and gave us information there were five new bunker sites inside Kuwait similar to those we found inside Iraq but far better constructed and deeper. It would take a "Bunker Buster" missile to penetrate these prized payloads for sure, but what would the Kuwaitis be hiding down there? Jake and I decided not to follow up on the report because if we did something to either prove or disprove the Kuwaitis had such bunkers; we may be falling into a trap. Perhaps this was all misinformation, hoping to snare us on a mission inside Kuwait where we could be caught trying to pinpoint one of their bunker locations or perhaps there is even a more sinister plot to harm Jake and me.

Supposedly, the bunkers here in Kuwait were three floors down reaching almost sixty feet in depth. They had been built since the Liberation of Kuwait to insure the safety of top members of Kuwait's military and Royal family. Three of the four were supposedly located at Seif Palace, Doha Palace and below the Ministry of Defense complex. Well I knew about the tunnels if that's what they were talking about. I had been shown them by Royal family Ministers, so didn't think I'd be in danger for now having that knowledge.

The deepest and most complex bunker was built on the backside and below the Operations Center at Jaber Base southwest of Jahra. The one at Seif Palace was built for possible shared use of the Emir and the Crown Prince. It was built with a lot of specialized, luxurious features like the secret tunnels I already knew about. This bunker supposedly was real large, half the size of the interior Ceremonial Courtyard of the old Seif Palace. It is located between the Amiri Diwan to the east and the Crown Prince' Diwan on the west and constructed of four extra reinforced concrete and steel slabs eighty two feet below a recessed two story seaside building.

The bunker's walls and ceilings had been built explosion retardant. That meant the walls and ceilings had blast absorbent partitions built in at forty feet intervals throughout. Nearly the same type construction is being used in all the newest American and British Embassies in troubled regions of the world. "Bunker Buster" bombs would be about the only weapon that could take the entire structure out with ease. The document also proves the Kuwaitis are now using the building techniques perfected by the United States.

Jake and I had been wrestling several of our own demons lately concerning jobs we had done and jobs we were still doing, and this latest document makes my skin crawl. Who knows what the future holds for Jake and me in Kuwait. For now, there is nothing we can do but wait and hope the seriousness of the matter just goes away.

I used my day off this week to go with Jake on what he calls a fishing trip. Actually Jake invited me to join him at a "special" invitation only activity right here in Kuwait City within sight of Seif Palace. Jake says together, we've done a lot of dangerous things and for this one day at least, we can have some fun. He asked how would I like to go with some guys on an assignment where they'd be actually doing some vital tests but having fun right here in our own backyard so to speak? I'd just be along for the ride and adventure.

Though Jake's word "adventure" brought some disturbing thoughts to mind, I replied "sure, I'll go". Jake and I called on two American Sea Bees at the Holiday Inn Farwaniya and loaded into their oversized van for the short drive to the shoreline just west of the Schuwaikh Port near downtown Kuwait City.

We all got into wet suits, flippers and goggles and had a little briefing while sitting on some rocks half submerged in the bay. We were instructed to follow these Sea Bees out into the water about twenty yards, where they would be setting some "Alligator Mines" on the bottom and watch their results. The five mines we had with us were FFE, Free From Explosive but otherwise had all their normal characteristics (if that was what you could call them). The mines were to be laid on the bottom of the bay by one of the Sea Bees, and then activated. One of the Sea Bees said he would put the first one in fairly shallow water so we can stay nearby and watch it become active.

The Sea Bee had programmed the "Alligator Mine's" memory with specific information relative to the size and weight of the large container vessel we saw coming toward us. We all submerged to be near it as it came alive. As the ship came nearer and nearer, the mine rose off the bottom then hesitated as if waiting for further instruction. The mine then moved in the direction of the big cargo ship gaining speed as it closed in on its target.

We hurried back to shore while trailing it with a small electronic tracking device. All of a sudden . . . BANG or rather THUD. The mine had reached its target and hit the side of the cargo ship with such force that had it been armed with explosive, it would have blown a huge whole in the bottom of the ship. Even disarmed, it hit with enough force we could hear it several hundred yards away. We laughed and cheered. Wow, what a new experience for me. This was great, thanks Jake and guys.

We waited a few more minutes and one Sea Bee said "how would you like to see how easy it would be to sink that Iranian passenger ferry with hundreds of people aboard"? He then armed another mine and headed off alone for a few minutes.

We all sat mostly submerged in the clear blue bay water discussing the targeted ship. The Iranian ship was probably the most beautiful modern vessel in the Persian Gulf at the time. It was about five hundred feet long, beautiful gleaming white with a sleek design like a billionaire's yacht. Twice weekly, the same ferry transports Kuwaitis and Iranians back and forth across the Persian Gulf from Kuwait City to a small port in the south of Iran about three and a half hours away.

After returning to our side, our Sea Bee friend said "watch this", and then proceeded to press two buttons. He said "keep your eyes and ears peeled. You'll hear the kill". Within forty seconds, BANG or rather THUD again. This time we cheered but I didn't cheer as loudly as the first time. I was thinking how strange this game is we are playing with weapons designed to destroy. Here we are toying with explosive devices on a massive container ship and a passenger ferry loaded with people. It just wasn't funny any more.

These guys said during the Gulf War, hundreds of Alligator Mines were thrown overboard along the Iraqi coast. They were programmed to destroy any known Iraqi vessels and in some cases even Iranian ships.

After our time out together, Jake said he'd like me to take one of these guys into Iraq next month. He said the man would need to test the waters along the southeast Iraqi coast near Basra.

When I got home, there was an urgent call from our newspaper friend Betty. She wanted to know if we had heard of the fire at the Patterson's apartment today. I hadn't and didn't understand the urgency in her voice on our message recorder.

I immediately tried to call our friends the Patterson's but got no answer. When I called Betty, she was crying saying the Patterson's eighteen year old son burned to death in their apartment today. Kevin was a really nice looking blond headed young man with probably a future in the National Basketball League in the States. At eighteen, he was already six feet three inches tall and had been playing basketball on his Kuwait High School team for more than a year. Now he was a senior and hoped to catch the eye of University scouts stateside. He really wanted to go back to the States to the University of South Carolina or some place near his grandparents and the rest of the family.

Kevin's good looks and blond hair had endeared him to many young teenage American and British girls living in Kuwait who attended the same school. Kevin's is one of the only co-ed schools in the country and life there is as close to normal as any school in a Muslim country can be.

Kevin's father works for Kay & Associates, an American firm that trains Kuwaiti mechanics to maintain U. S. aircraft sold to the Kuwaitis. His mother is a real worrywart and always keeps pretty close eye on Kevin and his twenty one year old sister, but tries to let them have some freedoms as well. American young people sometimes have it difficult living in a society without dating, movies and dances with opposite sex; so parents often have trouble steering them away from activities Kuwaiti boys participate in like drag racing and hanging out in large groups, raiding local carnivals and going to male only dances.

Kevin is a handsome, wholesome, friendly guy, popular with almost everyone at the school but his whole life has now come to an end without ever knowing the pleasures of living in a society where he can meet a nice young lady, take her to the movie or to a dance or have a double date. His life has ended with all the promises for a great future unfulfilled. He is returning to America in a coffin in the cargo section of a plane instead of sitting with the family at a window seat as usual.

The Pattersons are staying at another friend's apartment until Kevin's body is released by Kuwaiti red tape. As expected, the family has literally gone into seclusion. They lost their household goods, their furniture, their clothing, and Kevin, their only son. Fortunately, someone from his father's employment is taking care of a lot of the footwork involved in getting through the Kuwaiti legal paper trail for release of Kevin's body.

Betty Lippold and I are talking often now. She is one of the only people getting any information to or from the family. She's covering the story for the Arab Times and I'm covering it for the Radio. I was warned it would not be appropriate to include the story in any of my broadcasts because it might show unfavorably on Kuwait. The circumstances are not good and should not be reported according to the Ministry of Information.

Fire started on a lower floor and quickly spread to the upper floors of the building. The Pattersons lived on the fifth floor. Very black smoke filled the hallways and stairwells before Kevin became aware of the fire. Someone on one of the lower floors had taken the elevator down and had failed to close the door properly; so it stayed there. Kevin was heard hollering loudly to people fleeing the lower floors, but they were not really listening to him, they had their own agenda of fleeing. Kevin tried a few times to come down to the fourth floor but was sent rushing back up because the stairwell was acting like a chimney.

Kevin was the only one home in their family at the time of the fire because his father was at work and his sister and mother had gone grocery shopping. Usually Kevin came down to help them carry all the bags up in the elevator as soon as they beeped the horn after arriving. This time, Kevin again waited near the sliding glass doors adjoining the small terrace and balcony when he felt it was near time for them to get home. The day of the fire was no different and Kevin had the glass sliding doors open as he watched television nearby.

The fire trucks didn't take long to get to the apartment building but the firemen were inexperienced in working the fire truck. They tried several times unsuccessfully to operate the ladder but couldn't figure it out. The fire truck wasn't new, the firemen weren't new, they were just Kuwaitis. They are a people who have done few things for themselves and something as important as "life and death" may at times be just a little beyond their abilities.

When Mrs. Patterson and her daughter arrived home from grocery shopping, they were told everyone was out of the building but they soon saw Kevin on the balcony above. Smoke was pouring from the apartment's open sliding doors behind him but he appeared to be safe for now. His father arrived on the scene within minutes of the mother and sister. They all shouted to Kevin and he returned replies back to them for almost twenty minutes.

The father told Kevin the firemen were preventing him from trying to help rescue him and the firemen were also unwilling to go up the stairwell because they said it was too dangerous and the boy was too big. They had all the necessary equipment, the fire retardant suits and the air breathing canisters but not the will to go into the fire. Kevin's father told him he would try to drive a vehicle up near the building for Kevin to jump down on but again the firemen were angry and resorted to actually restraining Mr. Patterson and leading him away, down the street.

Soon, the Father returned and Mother, Father and sister continued talking to Kevin for what seemed to be hours until he appeared weaker and his voice was fading. The strength was being drained from him by the extreme heat and nearby flames. The smoke had all but engulfed him. He hung over the balcony and at times only spoke above a whisper as his family strained to hear him before shouting back hope. Kevin's Mother and sister were screaming as time was running out. They all knew without firemen going into the flaming building there was little hope for Kevin to stay alive. Within minutes, Kevin only stood and peered over the balcony at his family while everyone's tears filled their eyes so much they couldn't see his last gulps for breath. Kevin slumped down beyond the concrete balcony wall and lay unconscious as the fire and smoke raced through the building.

While his Father and Mother shouted for Kevin to reappear and jump any ways, he never answered back. Their son and brother had died before them while Kuwaiti firemen directed traffic and restrained the victim's family. The firemen seemed moderately unfazed by the loss of Kevin and while still on site of the blazing building, they half jokingly talked about which of them would have been big enough amongst them to help carry that big boy down the stairs on a ladder any ways.

The family was of course devastated and returned to Beaufort, South Carolina for Kevin's funeral. Those of us left in Kuwait held a small memorial service at the one, small, allowed Christian Church in Kuwait City.

CHAPTER 34

Kicking Ass and Taking Names

The Kuwaitis and I enjoyed a mutual hospitable relationship for several more months. I progressed to other assignments within the Ministry of Information and at Dasma Palace. At the Ministry, the Minister of Information, Sheikh Saud Al Nassir Al Sabah was moving ahead with the rebuilding of Kuwait radio from the ground up. He had a seemingly unlimited budget for purchasing new equipment, adding new programs, hiring new personnel and picking out prime space for him and his cronies to hang out in the new seventy storey communications tower being constructed almost across the street from the present Ministry of Information Complex.

The new tower isn't really all that new. Almost half of it had been built prior to the Iraqi invasion of Kuwait but was left as a damaged giant in the city's center for almost six years before construction toward completion restarted. Kuwait is soon to boast the structure as one of the tallest on earth, a needle-like tower stretching almost eight hundred feet tall with five floors of offices, a restaurant, communication centers and a play club for Royalty way up near the top. "More stylish and much taller than the Space Needle in Seattle and technically more sophisticated than any other communication center in the entire Middle East", is how my bosses describe it.

The Minister of Information's secret propaganda radio station toward the Iraqis is said to be gaining some popularity inside Iraq but it is obvious to me, it is just a lot of bucks for very little bang. I am no longer writing for them but occasionally consult. While the Ministry is bustling with new people and more dollars, my job at the Ministry is changing modestly. The Minister of Information still likes to call on me for problem solving and creating new material but is sticking to our mutual decision of me no longer writing for the propaganda station full time, which he knew I had liked to do prior to our differences over what I saw as a real threat to American soldiers security. Though we were getting along well enough, there remained a barrier between us over another of my extra curricular activities concerning money trails and possible alliances between some Kuwaitis and radical Islamic groups like Hizbollah, Brotherhood, Hamas, al Qaeda and Islamic Jihad. The Minister hasn't been outright reprimanding me but the coolness is there. My other little ventures for him and his government still continued each time I was asked to go somewhere for someone. With all these little nuances, life for Maia and I continued unabated.

Information I gathered on financial support for Muslim extreme organizations was adding up, but as far as written proof was concerned most of it remains just hear say; nothing in writing. Supporting my claims though, still didn't seem to be as hard as finding out who to give my information to. The Kuwaitis are offended I'm looking, the Americans, certainly not at this embassy have any interest. Is there anyone wanting to hear what I've found out.

The jealousy within departments and offices of the United States government is almost more than I can deal with. If you try to turn in some information you've learned to the United States Embassy, then you may or may not get heard. Other times they almost fight over your information. There seems to be a lack of coordination or a lack of policy, even within offices of the same organizations as to what they want to hear from you; and what they don't want to hear.

It appears everyone wants to take credit or deny they didn't already have the information. It's a competitive world. No wonder we Americans still have foul-ups on the ground in foreign countries even though the United States has "FORTY ONE AGENCIES" involved in counter intelligence. The Justice Department falls over the FBI and the FBI and the CIA don't share information and the NSO and the NRO claim they had the information all along and so it goes on and on. Fortunately, I don't have to pass on much information because Brumley and Jake do most of that. I just remain their glorified taxi driver most of the time.

For things happening at the Ministry of information, at Dasma Palace or diwaniyas concerning money trails, information, etc. that's a different story. If it's not me who will be passing crucial information along, then who will it be? I can't think of any other American in the Middle East in the exact position I'm in.

It seems as though the al Qaeda Organization of Osama ben Laden is the largest and probably the most sophisticated terrorist network of its kind in history. His complex web contains many levels like a fortune five hundred corporation in the industrialized nations, but each leg of it has the ability to act unilaterally in the interest of al Qaeda, when ever and how ever it deems necessary.

In direct succession to Osama bin Laden are top Lieutenants Ayman al Zawahiri and head of Military Operations Mohammed Atef. Next, there are four governing committees.

Al Qaeda has a planning and support base, military operations council, religious and legal council, finance council, media council of which a Kuwaiti is the head spokesman; and many individual pan-Islamic cells of fighters numbering up to five thousand in more than fifty countries. A number of Kuwaitis from all classes are included in the upper councils and in the lower cells of most.

These al Qaeda groups are not to be confused with the more numerous Taliban in Afghanistan which is almost totally supported by al Qaeda and bin Laden as well.

I keep looking for money trails but their banking and investments cover the globe and are far from my reach and expertise; their greatest revenue producers are cleverly disguised as charitable funds from wealthy organizations and individuals of oil rich countries like Kuwait, Qatar and Saudi Arabia.

I've continued making slow progress on the funding trails local but my regular job at the Super Station and my expanded jobs inside Iraq and within the walls of Dasma Palace steal most of my time. I've already thought it out and if any of my jobs has to be forfeited in the name of time, I'll drop the one at Super Station 92.5 broadcasting the news, weather and sports, even though I really enjoy it. Money wise it also isn't the big payer like the others.

Dasma Palace is where the Emir of Kuwait use to live and the offices of both he and the Crown Prince and Prime Minister were until the new grand Seif Palace reopened. While their offices were still at Dasma, I began to be requested there more often and for longer periods of time. Perhaps this was someone's way of keeping my nose out from places it shouldn't be.

To me, it seemed a reward; all my earlier work rewriting communiqués between the Kuwaitis and the American Embassy had paid off. Only a native English speaker can tell that I have no formal training in writing and don't do it as well as they think I do. However, one thing I do is writing as pointedly as I speak; and that has been a problem in the past. My straight forwardness has been appreciated by the higher ups at Dasma Palace and reflected by increased wages, and increased time spent in the Crown Prince's Office. Along with my new position more closely related to the Palace's inner circle comes an increased list of social dos. I am now also allowed to attend the most powerful diwaniyas in the country. Few First Class Kuwaitis enjoy the access and privileges I'm afforded, even as a foreigner.

At the Crown Prince's Diwan, normal discussions evolve around Middle East policy, Kuwaiti relations with the West and military strategy concerning the border region joining Iraq. One piece of information I gathered from these inner circle of all males is Kuwait's arrogance and distrust they show for other Arab organizations like the Gulf Cooperation Council of States (Kuwait's brotherly nations of Bahrain, United Arab Emirates, Saudi Arabia, Qatar, Oman and Yemen) and the Arab League (the most distrusted of the two due to that body's stand taken not to condemn Saddam Hussein after he invaded Kuwait).

To the world and to other Arabs, the Kuwaitis speak of their affection for the Arab League and their appreciation for the Arab states who joined with the West in Liberating Kuwait from Iraqi occupation. Behind the scenes however, the tune plays a lot differently. The Royal Offices are often outraged at another League opinion or suggestion and threaten never to attend any of their meetings again. I suspect Kuwaitis see mirror reflections of themselves in the pettiness and sniveling that often goes on at those conferences. Kuwaitis hate to admit it but remember deep down that their own GCC and the Arab League of States both wavered and never made any decisions concerning freeing them from the powerful Iraqi tyrant President Saddam Hussein. These brotherly policy making bodies quivered in their shoes at the mere thought of offending Saddam Hussein.

Some of these Arab states did try to prevent Saddam Hussein from invading Kuwait but others only joined coalition partners when they knew the whole world was going to fight Saddam together; then they came on board. Only Saudi Arabia is seen as an Arab power house with enough to lose that they committed early on to whatever was needed to halt Baghdad's ambitions.

Kuwait's Royal offices still burn with humiliation each time they recount the Cairo Conference in which the Arab League failed to condemn Saddam Hussein for occupying Kuwait. Often since those days long ago, I've witnessed explosions of anger that are bent on passing along retribution toward those Arab states when the right time comes.

Since His Highness, Kuwait's Crown Prince and Prime Minister, Sheikh Saad Abdullah al Ahmad al Sabah often finds it too time consuming to sit in and listen to all daily briefings from the CIA and MI6, and even the occasional tri-monthly ones from Masaad of Israel, he delegates that task to me. That arrangement didn't happen over night or by him simply walking into the office one day saying "Charles take over the intelligence briefings", it was a lot more subtle and less direct than that.

Like most Kuwaitis in the country, key personnel in the Emir and Crown Prince's Offices go on Summer holiday elsewhere. Those who normally receive intelligence briefings with His Highness are no different. Often those few left with His Highness hearing what the CIA and MI6 had to say, didn't really know what was being said by the Americans and Brits. They often came asking me questions and telling me phrases saying "what does that mean"? Finally it struck one of them; it would be more convenient to have Charles sit in on the briefings with them.

My role in that capacity widened and during much of the Summer months, no one even bothered coming to the briefings at all, just me. It was all left in my hands. When necessary, which was often, the CIA came to me at ten o'clock in the morning and lectured or showed satellite photos, copies of documents and occasionally even videos of intelligence gathered in the region, most of which had to do with Saddam Hussein and Iraq. The same thing would happen again at eleven o'clock or eleven fifteen in the morning for about thirty minutes with British Intelligence MI6 either attending or following with one of their own when necessary. Not always but usually every third month, on the first Tuesday, even the Masaad of Israel came to fill us in on joint interest reports they had received over the last thirty days concerning Iraq.

Each morning following the nine o'clock News, Weather and Sports, I quickly compiled all materials for the Super Station's Noon News, Weather and Sports broadcast; then made a mad dash through the streets of downtown Al Sharq and Kuwait City to get over to Dasma Palace to hear, then prepare a short Readers Digest version of the intelligence briefing for His Highness or send any important communiqués to him elsewhere if he was outside the country. I'd then rush back to the Ministry of

Information to read the noon news weather and sports that I had earlier prepared.

Most of what I heard at those intelligence briefings was nothing out of the ordinary and I considered some of the field information either rumor or other people's opinions. Some of the information was good and there were even days it was exciting. If satellite photos showed Saddam Hussein's troops had made sudden movements toward Kuwait's border or specialized equipment was photographed being taken by train from Baghdad southeast toward the Persian Gulf toward Basrah, then the excitement for me grew.

Most briefings were repetitious or redundant of the other intelligence services. What the Americans had, the British also had. In most instances one briefing would have sufficed instead of one from each. I didn't have to tell this to His Highness because he already knew that, and in some part I guess this was the reason he allowed me to be the one briefed. What I got from the briefings was much more in depth than what a Kuwaiti could have gotten from the same words. I could see a little more in the actual wording of sentences than a non English speaking native could. Often I'd say, "This information seems to be true because both agencies, the CIA and MI6 said it, but in some cases just the CIA would say something that I felt was misinformation or an outright deception. In those cases, I weighed what I perceived the reason was behind the Americans stating such information. If I thought the United States had reason to cause fear in the Kuwaitis or reprimand them, I reported it without change.

I found the Americans especially would warn the Kuwaitis that their going along with other Arab countries on certain issues would cost them. I made no attempt at softening the reprimand to them but rather made sure the Kuwaitis knew there was a price to pay. Heed the warning or the Americans will allow Saddam back on the border real soon.

In more diplomatic terminology of course like the time I reminded His Highness that he stuck his foot in his mouth at the last conference in

Cairo and the U. S. is now telling him to be more careful in what he says to other Arab States.

There were several times I felt a squeeze play on the Kuwaitis by the Americans or the British but did little to soften them either. My hosts are not known for paying their financial debts and it was obvious the United States and even Great Britain occasionally had to use strong arm tactics on them to get what was due. For instance, I had just come from more than two hundred miles inside Iraq where I had seen almost no movement on the rails or main highways, yet all satellite photos and briefings from the United States showed renewed aggression by the Iraqis. They were again coming toward the Kuwait border in great numbers. This erroneous information was corroborated by British Intelligence. I knew differently but held my tongue. My briefing to advisors of His Highness told of the build up, not what I knew to be fact. The United States and Britain was entitled to their protection money and arms sales payments in a timely fashion and it wouldn't be me who'd say anything different.

The most fun I had in the briefing room was during each crisis or mock crisis. Names of ships arriving in the region were charted, troop arrivals were detailed, practice exercises were planned, communiqués were flying left and right and endless platters of food were brought in so we wouldn't miss a hectic moment. It was times like these that I learned more about the United States and its readiness in the region, it's evacuation plans for American dependants and the true control the U. S. had over the entire situation. Kuwaitis, even their top guys were sort of redundant.

If there was going to be any action, the United States would plan it, then inform the Kuwaitis what might be best for them to do. The Kuwaitis may or may not be able to follow up with their own preparations according to how many high ranking Kuwaiti officers were still at Disney World in Florida, over in the Philippines buying new maids or having indiscriminate sex orgies in Bangkok.

Through times of crisis and others, the Kuwaitis depended on me and me on them. Little disturbing things continued happening though that I didn't like but in those times, everything was workable until once again I overheard some Kuwaitis, this time at Dasma Palace tossing around the idea of putting American soldiers lives at risk. It was more apparent to me than ever that planning the attack against the Americans hadn't simply gone away.

In October, 1994, I heard four members of parliament and several other men I didn't recognize, telling how the Americans were continuing to bleed their country's banks and it was time Kuwait should act against them. Someone should take the lead in making the Americans get rid of Saddam Hussein like they should have done in the first place. "That should finally stop both the Americans and Saddam from attaching Kuwait's purse strings" said one. They reminisced how good it use to be with only the Brits on their soil and how at least back then, the Brits were contributing to Kuwait's coffers by creating and increasing their oil production and sales instead of trying to extract money from them constantly like the Americans.

Again I began hearing of that nightmare scenario about finding a way the Americans could be pushed into getting rid of Saddam Hussein. Again similar discussions were being tossed around by some high ranking Kuwaiti Generals who mentioned the plan to hit the American soldiers. I thought that whole notion had been killed but obviously it hasn't and even some of these men seem to know about it. This time a little more information was leaked. Someone had actually been going through munitions storage catalogs trying to find out whether the American company CMS or which of the other companies; or whether their own Ministry of Defense was now in charge of the former Iraqi scud missiles needed to kill the American soldiers.

Hearing such talk from high ups in the Kuwaiti Government once again riled me badly and it was about this time that I decided to really turn against the Kuwaitis in full force. Who else but someone in my position could hurt them with a knife to the heart and still be around to watch them squirm. I had no real plan how to do it except that my well placed employment within their ranks was bound to present the right time and way to get back at them sooner or later.

At first I just started fooling around with a couple of phrases in the intelligence briefings. Not just occasionally omitting a few pertinent facts like before but really carefully rewording them to change their meaning now. Neither Sheikh Saad nor any of his men seemed any the wiser. Next, I stretched the truth on a few briefings to find out how gullible they might be, and then proceeded even further from there. Again every thing went smoothly and I was now giving the Kuwaitis misinformation, my way, successfully.

Within weeks, I was literally giving the Kuwaitis intelligence briefings that bore little resemblance to the ones I was getting from the CIA and MI6. The over-all photographs were there but I reinterpreted them for the Crown Prince's and advisor's briefings. For instance, the CIA would say:

"The Iraqis appear to be pulling back from their forward positions so reconnaissance flights are going to be reduced. A confrontation is no longer probable."

Even without changing the satellite numerical information at the bottom and to the side of each photo, I continued telling the Kuwaitis the latest photographs were present photos of the region and compared to several others seen recently, it should be obvious to them a buildup was taking place. I went on to tell them how the American CIA briefer was a little concerned the Kuwaitis weren't taking the situation as seriously as they should and the Kuwaitis should be acting more aggressively, bolstering their border with Iraq; like taking more initiative in their own troop movements, perhaps by trying to put more of their own men between the American soldiers in the desert and the Iraqi border.

The next CIA briefing wasn't until three days later. I could see it on the Americans faces. They were dumbfounded by Kuwait's sudden erratic behavior and their troop movements near the border but didn't really see it as a problem yet. Kuwait's top Generals were, after all, present during most of these American theater exercises. Surely they know what is and are not expected of them; and for now it were to leave the field, let the Americans hold their own exercises alone first. "Strange!!" was all that was said by the American intelligence agents "but how can we think like an Arab?"

The Kuwaitis were not suppose to interfere with present American deployment in the region and were to stay out of the Americans way until joint exercises were to be held between the two countries a couple months later.

The next time I briefed the Kuwaitis, I told them the Americans were surprised to see Kuwait taking the initiative but were even more surprised to see how rapidly they had taken action, good work guys. I further told the Kuwaitis, the Americans wanted the Kuwaitis to conduct small training maneuvers on their own to further show the Americans their willingness to do what ever is necessary to secure their own borders if the Americans ever decide to leave.

In just over a week, I had created a whole new border situation in which the Kuwaitis were getting in the Americans way and the Americans began reprimanding them for it. Then the Kuwaitis would talk over the situation saying the Americans were crazy. First the Americans say they want the Kuwaitis to take more initiative, and then reprimand them for doing so. "You can't win with these Americans; they want to control everyone everywhere." The Kuwaitis would say things like "Soon the Americans will be placing moral demands on Kuwait to further alienate them from other neighboring Arab brotherly states and push for equal rights for women, new labor laws and constraints on the Muslim clerics who preach against western music, wrestling matches and hooliganism of Kuwaiti youths who follow western ways. After all, violence by Kuwaiti youths has risen markedly since the youth started listening to western pop music, holding more dances, hanging out at McDonald's and watching televised shows like "Bay Watch" and police and crime shows."

While I began enjoying my new role of inserting disinformation then sitting back watching the results, I was being hurt in the worst way you can hurt me, financially. Again and again I checked my bank account to see if I was seeing correctly, there was still no payment for the past several months from the Ministry of Information since that time the Minister and I had our differences about Radio Free Iraq. I was still working for him doing all the radio shows daily and even seeing him on occasion and all he would say is, "something must be wrong" and he'd check into it. That was not a new phrase from him.

The matter was obviously growing more serious each day, yet I kept working. When I inquired through the payroll office, I received the same explanation, "Your account will be credited within a few days. Everything is OK."

Maia and I had plenty of money in our Kuwaiti checking and savings accounts, after all I had been tax free from the United States for several years and much of the money had been piling up in this account because I wasn't sure how to get it back to America without Uncle Sam taking a huge chunk of it. I'm patriotic to Uncle Sam but want his hands to stay out of my pockets and up to eighty five thousand dollars a year tax free, he did. After that, my purse strings were free game.

I wasn't really worried whether my Super Station pay was accredited a day later or two weeks later but the "run around" I was getting perturbed me and I wasn't going to stand for it without doing what I was now learning to do well, retaliate.

After four months, I presented a bill of thousands and thousands of dollars to the Ministry of Information for all the work I had done at the Super Station for as far back as a year earlier for the AM propaganda radio station and another radio show, that began airing each evening more than five months ago. I helped format and totally wrote the new evening show and Mazan Al Ansari was now the on air person and the only one getting paid for it. Earlier I had never sought retroactive pay for these hours because I knew sooner or later my talents, time and efforts would be noted and the money promised would arrive.

Handing the Ministry copies of all my detailed time schedules and (supposed) earnings didn't seem to be working. Kuwaitis are like children, they have to have limits set on them; otherwise they will abuse anyone who allows them selves to be abused. Working at both establishments, the Ministry of Information and Dasma Palace, I saw ample reason why I should halt them in their tracks before they did to me what I had seen them do to others. These people are rich, rich, rich, but CHEAP, CHEAP, CHEAP with capital letters. I wasn't just anybody else, I had the ammunition to fire back "hard" and I did.

My frustrations with both the Ministry and Dasma Palace built up and then were calmly eased time and time again by them trickling small amounts of cash to me but never any sizable monies.

During an altercation with the Minister of Information, I questioned him while he sat three feet in front of me. "You say my back pay is forth coming, is there any reason I should think you're not telling me the truth right now?" "Oh Charles" the Minister replied in the fashion and tone of the villains in the old silent movie days, "Everything will be settled soon, it's been all a big misunderstanding". Little did he realize that I was setting him up for a few more misunderstandings of my own? My secret retribution against Dasma Palace continued and even increased and now I've added the Minister of Information to my DIS LIST. I felt it unwise to alert either of my employers so I refrained myself and never took the pleasure to tell them I was countering each of their insincere moves with bigger and better ones of my own. Why put either of them or anyone else on to what I was doing?

The money issue was now becoming a disturbing problem, but I continued taking assignments for Dasma Palace inside Iraq that I was getting paid for as well as going whenever National Reconnaissance or the British wanted me to. These assignments weren't just lucrative; they were exhilarating, scary and "fun?" I had always taken on all Iraqi cross-border assignments from the Crown Prince's Office without concern for my own safety, even when I knew my assignment would take me far into enemy territory.

I had always been pleasant and smiling and everyone liked me enough to invite me to their weddings, their holiday feasts and even on their yachts and vacations, yet all that was beginning to change. Situations at work were becoming more confrontational and the money issue was still out of hand with few if any logical explanations coming from the Minister of Information's office. A pivotal point had been reached and I knew both sides had gone too far. It would only be time before something radical would happen to me. I figured if I had to leave Kuwait, I would give my final efforts into making my presence missed (the old Nixon adage can be used here, "They won't have me to kick around any more").

I threw myself into gaining more security secrets, tracking money from Kuwaitis to Muslim fundamentalists, misinformation about satellite photos and briefings, purposely rewording papers being forwarded from Dasma Palace to the United States Embassy and other western agencies and pinpointing buildings and future targets inside Kuwait that can be used against Kuwait for many years to come. It was now me and the West against them. They had broken the special relationship I once enjoyed with them and now I'm lashing out to make sure they feel as hurt by the end result as me.

Often at night I lay in bed getting more and more pissed off about my financial problems and the run around I was getting from the Ministry of Information. The more pissed off I got, the more creative and vindictive I got. My retaliatory plans were probably all formulated between midnight and four in the morning. Each day, I had a plan and a goal. Each day, I would copy some documents, ask questions of someone I wasn't suppose to or purposely give misinformation. It was difficult to aim my displeasure straight at one or two of the men I knew were the heart of all my problems, so I just aimed in their direction and shot from the hip. Damn anyone who gets in my way.

Like the dangerous game the Kuwaitis played against Saddam Hussein at the Jeddah meeting three days before the invasion of Kuwait, I knew my game now was high stakes too. It may cost me like it did Saddam in the Gulf War, but It'll cost the Kuwaitis too. My inside knowledge and position is like having at least a few wild cards up my sleeve. I'm playing to win, but I know I could just as easily lose, maybe even my life.

The Minister of Information and possibly even the Crown Prince and Prime Minister will feel my wrath sooner or later. Daily, I continued my personal rage with a smile on my face and pleasant demeanor. This smile is no longer from the heart but from the parting of the lips. My teeth are now ready to eat some ass. Charles has now become someone I don't even know.

I knew my boldness would sooner or later eliminate me from my favorable employment positions so; I had to continue being satisfied daily with just taking little nibbles of tail instead of outright bites. I also knew that they were beginning to distrust me but with the good track record I had, they had no real reason to believe their own sixth sense. The way they saw it, I was doing very good work on my radio shows, excellent work developing new shows and spots for television and radio, had always done their dirty work inside Iraq. They still appear to be thankful I've taken the burden from His Highness of sitting in on all the intelligence briefings from the West.

By late 1995, I had come a long way from my first acts of defiance against both my employers which had started innocently enough. The Minister of Information whom I considered a cold snake was first in my next move. I purposely waited until Tuesdays of each week to conduct further acts against him. Each Tuesday, the Minister of Information attended his Parliamentary duties and was out of his office all day. If on rare occasion he did come in, it was very late in the afternoon or early evening; I'd try not to be there then.

If the Minister wouldn't see me in his office, I'd see his office without him. When the Minister isn't in, the floor receptionist is scarce, Fallah abu Rashed (his kiss-ass man servant assigned to him as a Royal since youth) was usually out wandering the malls, and the only other two people on the floor, Sheikh Khalid al Sabah, the Minister's cousin who had no real job and the Minister's Secretary; The Turkey (as I called him), was also often scarce. The floor's receptionist whose desk was near the elevators and stairwell was usually out with the Bangladeshi tea boy doing who knows what most of the time, so when the Minister wasn't in, the mice were out playing. The snake really had no one minding his rock. The Minister's door was unlocked and only too easily entered. His door was as secure as the Ministry's gates the morning the Iraqis came in August 1990.

The first time I entered the Minister of Information's office was just to prove to myself I had the run of the place, but other than that I had no real purpose in mind. I still had hopes of my salary problems straightening out and I would again become satisfied with my superiors and my job, thus I'd never have to go so far as I was now planning. My distrust for Kuwaitis didn't come natural nor was I predisposed to distrust them; I learned how and why I should, over a period of time. After my exposure to these people for more than seven years, I had the opportunity of seeing their deviant, cheating, lying selves at work, up front and personal, against not only their foreign adversaries but their own families and business acquaintances as well.

If I was going to be one of their adversaries, I wouldn't be lying down like their other ones waiting for them to stick something up my butt. I'd prove my worth and stand equal to them in any confrontation that may one day come. I already knew my opponent's well, now it was time to know their files.

When I first started my payback several months ago, the workload I brought upon myself and had been given by others had become chaotic. I hadn't lost control, but I was juggling more than a handful of jobs and at least two sideline missions or investigations at the same time. My discontent with Kuwait and Kuwaitis was becoming more apparent and my motives turning more and more sinister. I would have been great full had the situation gotten better but the loss of pay was really starting to add up. By mid October it was already in arrears by tens of thousands of dollars.

I began responding the only way I felt I could. I subtly put everyone on notice. If they play with fire, more than my ass will get burnt. My deceptive smiles kept everyone off guard. I was already playing hard ball with them and they didn't know it. Even after confrontations, they never put anything off limits to me in the Palaces or the Ministry. I'd make them sorry for that mistake.

I was certainly the person from the Western World who knew more about Kuwaiti dealings, character flaws and internal information than anyone else. My credentials were in order. Who else from America, Britain or anywhere in the West had ever been in such informative positions inside Kuwait and privy to such knowledgeable facts about the people who ran the country? Now that I had a few grudges to settle and I was sure they weren't going to be settled through talking calmly, I would react in the only way Kuwaitis would understand.

CHAPTER 35

A Royal Confrontation

I went about my business, juggling work schedules on radio and working within the walls of Dasma Palace, while carrying out my personal vendettas against each. At least for now, I didn't have to try to fit Jake and more trips into Iraq into my work schedule. It had been quite a while since my cross border friend Jake had contacted me and it was just as well. Most of the information we procured together inside Iraq had been turned over to the Kuwaiti's at the same time the United States and Great Britain got it.

I was certainly in no mood to help the Kuwaitis gather intelligence against their enemy Iraq any longer. If they wanted any further information about the Iraqis, let them send their own teams over if they have the balls.

I often thought to myself, if I'm expendable, let's see which First Class Kuwaiti household my new replacement will come from. I don't see any foreigner on the horizon. If someone else will be risking his life for the benefit of Kuwait, let it be a Kuwaiti.

October was running out and almost on a daily basis I tried to resolve my pay matter with the Ministry or even through Dasma Palace by entering their offices and politely requesting to speak to the Minister or His Highness the Crown Prince. No one ever seemed to be in for me any more so my personal animosity toward at least the Minister of Information grew even deeper. Each brick wall I ran up against or denial I encountered, my resolve became stronger. I'd have to do it my way.

I continued going to his office during his days off. I was still doing my work and my security clearances were still good to get me into the Ministry complex. No one further down the chain of command appeared to know a rift had surfaced between me and the higher ups there. Guards readily allowed me into all gates, anytime I showed up. I knew most of them anyway and with a few "Kaif Haliks" and "Shlonics" ("How's it going?)" I was welcomed inside. Internal security guards were no different. Access everywhere was easy.

No key was ever needed to the Minister of Information's private elevator because all I had to do was climb the stairwell to the thirteenth floor. At first I peered at all the papers on the Minister's desk and even made some copies. I got braver each Tuesday and as time passed I became quite familiar with his four drawer file cabinet. Only a few desk drawers were locked and I would wait till I had run out of other papers to copy and drawers to open before I started trying to pick locks there.

The Minister's office was wonderful. I never had to leave the premises with anything. He had one of the finest fax machines and Turkey's office had one of the finest copiers in the world. I'd use one or both machines each visit, depending on whether I wanted to keep copies for myself or whether I just wanted to fax information to other machines inside Kuwait or as far away as the United States. None of the tea boys or lower staff ever questioned my presence or what I was working on; if they happened to be there at all.

Any papers I found of interest but didn't want to spend time nor effort trying to get someone to later translate, I saved for much later. I shoved them inside my shirt flatly against my chest. This way I had no bulges that could be seen while walking the corridors within the Ministry of Information Complex.

I became more aggressive in forwarding information to International Human Rights Groups and to Philippine authorities as well as the Governments of India and Sri Lanka concerning maid mistreatment. I also wrote letters to newspapers in Amman, Jordan concerning bad treatment of Palestinians in Kuwait. I named names and cited dates and events. I even sent several articles that appeared in Kuwaiti newspapers to Yasser Arafat at PLO Headquarters. That was an Arab organization that wasn't too fond of Kuwait either but still enjoyed taking their contributions.

If news copy passed my desk concerning stories of abuse, I passed them along. When internal articles came to be censored at the Ministry, I made copies before they were changed then sent them out of the country where they could do the most good. I left copies in place and took the originals home.

Several times, Kuwaiti men at Diwaniyas around the city would tell me reasons why the Americans should either reduce their influence in the region and in Kuwait specifically, or tell me how the Americans are behind every plot in the Middle East and were probably behind Iraq's invasion of Kuwait as well. Ambassador April Glaspie's name would often come up and say how she allowed Saddam Hussein to think taking Kuwait by force was not only possible but within his reach without the Americans getting involved between neighboring Arabs.

Several times I told the Kuwaitis reasons Saddam Hussein should come back. Most of the time though, Instead of immediately lashing out at them which would have shut their mouths and shielded me from future plans and information, I decided just to listen and as always got an ear full. Part of their conversations reflected anti-American sentiments but there was some dissention amongst them as well, more positive to the United States and the West. An Under Secretary at the Ministry of Information, whom I've loved to quote on several other occasions for his "foot in mouth" expressions, did it again. He said certain decision making should be left only to smart men like his boss, the Minister of Information. The Under Secretary (also an Al Sabah within the Royal Family) said unlike many of his other cousins, the Minister of Information even more so than the Emir and the Crown Prince is cleaver (a word I've often found interchangeable in Kuwait with liar, but to a Kuwaiti still an honorable tradition).

The young man seemed to think it would be better to allow people like the Minister of Information to make certain decisions like killing the American soldiers than allowing more incompetents like those ruling the country to do so. The whole discussion was senseless with only Arab reasoning.

I disagreed with almost every word out of the young man's mouth, except those reflecting the cleverness of the Minister. I too feel he is very cleaver and I would trust him like I would a rattle snake. The Minister of Information may have won the hearts of a lot of Americans when he was Ambassador to the United States during the Gulf War, but reality is that he is more of a quiet, ruthless character who doesn't like any ones opinion to differ from his. He is cool, even tempered and never buries his fangs into you in argumentative fashion, he just gets even with you in other ways. When he asks your opinions or explains he will take care of matters, he is only feeling you out for the tender place in your neck to lock his jaws onto.

Back at work, the battle of wills between my employers and me continued unabated and I expanded my retaliation against them to almost every aspect of my work. I used all the information that flowed to me from within their own walls. I prided myself on forwarding only information that was derogatory, true and correct. There was enough of that. I never had to resort to untruths. I continued sending reports to the Philippines concerning the already explosive situation of maid abuse in Kuwait and I sent more recent abuse clippings to Sri Lankan, Bangladeshi and the Egyptian press.

One of my earliest acts of defiance paid off very well indeed and in short time. It pitted Saudi Arabia's Royals against Kuwait's Royals and even mentioned another of my similar retranslations concerning Bahrain. Several articles about my deed even made into the Kuwaiti English newspaper Arab Times; (Though the article rambles and fails to get directly to the point like Arabs speak, it served my purposes none the less): It read:

SAUDIS SOUR ON REPRINT

Kuwait City; January 23, 1996 Highly informed sources said that the Kuwaiti leadership has succeeded in averting a major crisis with Saudi Arabia over a translated press report on Saudi internal affairs.

The sources said that one of the reasons for the visit by Deputy Premier and Foreign Minister Sheikh Sabah al Ahmad to Saudi Arabia three days ago was the translated report which leaked out from the Kuwait National Assembly.

The report has been published in a London newspaper at the end of November last year. It was translated and printed on official letterhead of the foreign relations committee of the Assembly.

The sources said the translation of the report angered the Saudi authorities, especially the large number of copies that were printed. Saudi Second Deputy Premier and Defense Minister, Prince Sultan bin Abdul Aziz sent a letter in this connection to His Highness, Kuwait's Crown Prince and Prime Minister.

As a result, the Council of Ministers discussed the issue for one hour and the Cabinet members assigned the Prime Minister to discuss the matter with speaker of the National Assembly Ahmad al Saadoun.

The Cabinet also decided to advance an already scheduled visit by Sheikh Sabah to Saudi Arabia in order to inquire about the health condition of the Custodian of the Two Holy Mosques, King Fahd bin Abdul Aziz and discuss the demarcation of borders between the two countries. (Finally a sentence that starts getting closer to the real subject. All the rest was just run-on.)

The sources added that the Kuwaiti Council of Ministers expressed anger over another leak concerning the behavior of the National Assembly and pointed out similar practices by a number of MPs who signed a memorandum to the Emir of Bahrain regarding the ongoing incidents there. (Some of my doing too.) The Council of Ministers considers the

Kuwaiti memorandums acts of interference in the internal affairs of Bahrain.

I also sent Bahrain a communiqué that showed a new treaty between Kuwait and Iran about Kuwait would not interfere with Iran's on going efforts to destabilize Bahrain from factions within.

The Council also called for the putting an end to such practices which may spoil strong relations with sisterly countries, especially Saudi Arabia and Kuwait.

All it took for me to get two Arab allies pissed at each other was twenty letters on stolen letterhead sent to various locations and institutions around London. The story was also totally true. Members of Kuwait's Parliament had been back stabbing their Arab allies much the same as Kuwaitis do the Americans. I just felt it was my duty to inform the outside world that Kuwait's Parliamentarians were at it again. Kuwaitis think everyone is at fault for everything that happens to Kuwait outside the country as well as within. They absolutely take no responsibility for anything they say or do that hurts allies.

Many areas of Kuwait's government are corrupt but you would never hear it from them. They can't criticize themselves. For instance, slavery in Kuwait is still unofficially sanctioned by the Government and their Government Ministries are the biggest dealers in the slave market; brutally housing the majority of Indians, Bangladeshis and Egyptians in the country.

One story I sent to the world press via Reuters and Kuwaiti run Human Rights Organizations got absolutely no response from the latter because the Human Rights Organization within Kuwait run by Kuwaitis only is tantamount to allowing the wolves to cull the chickens in the hen house at will.

Only yesterday from the neighboring country of United Arab Emirates came the story of slave laborers being railroaded and imprisoned for their Kuwaiti Master's ill dealings.

Reports indicate an entire shipping transport container loaded with hundreds of thousands of dollars in liquor was discovered on a United Arab Emirates dock before its shipment to Kuwait. All the "Bills of Laden" were in names of Bangladeshi and Pakistani workers employed for years in Kuwait City as street sweepers earning less than one hundred dollars a month. The Kuwaiti Government was tipped off and the inbound shipment of liquor was seized. Someone had to go to prison. The Kuwaiti "Sponsors" of the street sweepers accepted no part of the blame and the expat laborers were sentenced by Kuwaiti Courts to very long prison terms at hard labor. In this Muslim country where Islam forbids the drink of alcohol, one bottle of liquor sells for at least a hundred dollars. The shipment was worth more than a million dollars. Half those laborers were unable to read or write yet the Kuwaiti public and their Government sentenced the poor laborers to long sentences of almost certain death.

No matter, outsiders were blamed and sentenced and the matter lay to rest with no discipline befalling Kuwaiti citizens who bankrolled and shipped the liquor. Everything wrong inside Kuwait is easily blamed on migrant workers or Western influence. Pre war Kuwait was no better than it is now. Kuwaiti vices of boozing, homosexuality and cheating in business haven't changed nor increased but radio and television programming has.

American influence was non existent before Saddam Hussein invaded Kuwait but since Liberation it is quite prevalent. Cable television in the country is now almost an institution except in fundamentalist homes. New programming is from American, British, Australian, Hong Kong English and Indian television shows. Naturally almost all popular American exports are violent cop shows, violent movies, missing children shows and seductive shows with sexual overtones.

Even before these changes, Kuwaitis believe and have been taught all American women are sluts, the men are violent and our police have to get in a couple good gun shots each day before leaving work. Now with the influence of television programming from the West, the Kuwaitis can use the Americans especially as scapegoat for all their own troubles and short comings; again without assuming any responsibilities themselves. Kuwaitis speak of themselves in Saintly terms prior to the Gulf war, and say the American assault on Iraq was seconded by the cultural assault on Kuwait.

I can't wait to see who Kuwaitis blame for their own perversions and wrong doings when the Iranians or Iraqis take them next time and their brotherly Arab states fight alone to Liberate them or rather don't fight. Of course I know they'll probably buy our military once again and we'll save them again then wait for payment again.

Kuwaitis spend more time blasting sexual overtones from the Barbie Doll than radical Islamic movements that sponsor terrorism from their soil. They fear Barbie's anatomically incorrect body more than they fear terrorist recruitment within their own University. In 1995, Barbie Dolls were banned in Kuwait because young Kuwaiti boys "lusted" over their seductive female figures while the Islamic Brotherhood movement made great advances on their University campus. "Barbie Dolls lead to sexual crimes with women" the Kuwait Government says. (In the worse case scenario, boys in Kuwait began dreaming of women instead of other little boys.)

The newspapers were full of stories about boys who wanted to riot and rape after watching the first two fashion shows with live female models ever inside the country. Negative newspaper stories so outraged the Kuwait public that the incidents and protests that followed lead to the banning of those types of "sexual" appearances.

For the month of October, I continued working my regular radio job but was less frequently needed at Dasma Palace. I regularly checked whether any bank transfers were made into my account but none had. Apparently my discontent with Kuwait was minor compared to their discontent with me. In typical Kuwaiti fashion though, their discontent was done secretively rather than through personal confrontation. Few differences in Kuwait are settled face to face. It bears great resemblance to their sexual habits.

I knew my time in Kuwait was nearing an end but there was always some hope everything would work itself out and things would return to almost normal. Before all this, I enjoyed my work and friends in Kuwait but like most things, you only see what you want to see. I was blind to many things because I wanted to be. Now that times are bad, I see the seedier side of everything. There is no sense living in a bubble anymore even if it had been lined in money (which of course now, it isn't).

Even prior to all my problems with them, it was not uncommon for about a hundred dollars to be missing from our salaries at the Ministry and Dasma Palace one month, then two hundred dollars another month. When you asked why the difference in pay, they'd say Parliament said they had too many financial obligations and their payments to the United States had to be assisted by all foreign workers in the country who involuntarily had given up a percentage of their wages for that month or several months in a row to help clear the debt. There was never any use arguing with them that was the way it was done and that was that. Rich Kuwaitis were not expected to put in their share and none working at the Ministry could show me where they had deductions taken out either.

Lack of will to pay debts stems from the top of Kuwait society to the bottom. I still say one main reason the United States and Britain let Saddam Hussein live following the war was so they could continue defending Kuwait and getting paid for it. Kuwait would have no choice but to continue paying the piper or their worst dreams would come true again. The big bad wolf can reappear at their door anytime. In the past, Kuwait and Kuwaitis have financially screwed everyone who has ever dealt with them and for the first time, coalition partners have been able to force Kuwait into a more subservient financial standoff by keeping Saddam Hussein only a few kilometers away.

Being as close to some of the royals as I was, put me within earshot of the next information that I would use as a bullet. From within the Ministry complex I fired off the shot that was heard by all England.

It seems the Kuwait Royal Family had fled in the middle of the night from a London hospital without paying their bill. A member of the Royal Al Sabah Family and his entourage had been flown to London via Kuwait Airways to have emergency surgery for his daughter who stayed hospitalized for nearly six weeks. When the daughter was getting well, Kuwait Airways flew them home. I ruffled some flowing white robes by bombarding the British tabloids with continual jabs.

One article read:

June 4, London (Reuter) senior staff at a London hospital is angry at the early opening of a new wing to accommodate the Kuwaiti Royal Family while a Princess is in intensive care.

The Newspaper Independent reported.

It said, the hospital's staff were upset because the new 140 million pounds ($210 million) wing at Guy's Hospital; described as the most advanced hospital building in Britain had not yet cared for any Patient under Britain's National Health Service.

It quoted a Kuwait Embassy official as saying:

Princess Miriam, eldest daughter of Crown Prince and Prime Minister Sheikh Saad al Abdullah al Sabah was on a life support machine at Guy's after suffering severe head injuries when her jeep overturned in Kuwait Last week.

At that report, The Independent did not say whether the Kuwait Royal Family was paying for the accommodation in the new government-funded and charity-funded wing at Guy's, but did say the Princess was a private patient.

Simon Hughes, a member of Parliament for the Opposition Liberal Democratic Party was quoted as saying it was ironic, "one of the richest families in the world are benefitting from the best buildings in the National Health Service while thousands of British patients were denied treatment there".

Several private donors and charities have canceled their donations or asked for their money back, said the Independent.

Somehow, the Kuwait Government convinced the British Government the Al Sabah would be better off in a hospital to her rather than one treating common British people. One whole wing of the hospital was opened for the single guest. It was fully staffed, fully furnished and fully equipped to cater to every whimper and need of the Al Sabah patient and her family.

Staff members who went out of their way for the care of the patient and those who waited on His Highness' large entourage "hand and foot" were constantly told they would be compensated for their services. Payment was expected but it wasn't going to come from the Kuwait Royal Family who slipped out of the hospital in the dead of night without so much as even thanking the doctors and nurses who so diligently attended them. No money was forth coming.

Again, I was relentless in sending many communiqués to various tabloids in England about the whole affair and the British people got the last laugh. They constantly blasted the Royal al Sabah's in their infamous tabloid newspapers so much and for so long that the Emir of Kuwait finally donated a million Pounds Sterling ($150 million) to the London Zoo. You can bet the gesture came very difficult for the billionaire family who even cheated laborers and contractors who restored and rebuilt their own palaces inside Kuwait after Saddam Hussein destroyed them.

That hospital story has become all too familiar in specialty hospitals within the United States too. The hospitals that have fallen prey to the Kuwaitis are specialists in heart operations and transplants, optical surgical hospitals, cancer treatment facilities and pediatric care hospitals. In Ohio, New York, Massachusetts, California, Georgia and Minnesota the Kuwaitis have fled in the night aboard chartered planes to get out of paying their hospital costs. The American Embassy in Kuwait says such notices of collection from Hospitals and automobile companies in America are numerous but are considered non collectable. The U. S. taxpayer is stuck with the bill.

The United States Embassy doesn't even bother notifying the Kuwaitis that notices came concerning their debts because no one in the households seem to ever know what the Embassy is talking about when they call. The Kuwait government says such incidents if true are not within their jurisdiction and it is easy for other people to impersonate Kuwaitis. The United States also refuses to pull their final trump card on those Kuwaiti individuals who perpetrate such schemes because they say forcing them to pay through the courts is near impossible and canceling their ten year multi entry visas will not have a "positive effect" on relations.

Reading the British tabloid responses made my heart feel better that others now knew them for what they were but not even these stories helped my personal situation which continued to deteriorate. Each day when I reported to work at the Ministry of Information, I was greeted either by silence or by tension that could be cut with a knife. No one outright taunted me but they obviously had been told by someone in higher position to keep an eye on my activities and not get into any heated discussions or controversies with me.

The Minister of Information had really become scarcer and I could never get in to see him for another of those rare face to face discussions about pay or anything else. The more he kept this line of action up, the more I justified my actions of search, seizure and copy. I had now expanded my spook activities throughout the Ministry complex, faxing and copying more than three hundred documents and choice stories.

Working for the Crown Prince was only slightly different from working for the Ministry of Information. On the few occasions I was summoned back to do a little work at Dasma Palace or to finalize something, I tried to carry on conversations with higher ups there and let them know my financial problem. They've been kind but appear unwilling to intercede on my behalf. I in turn have decided they would start getting what they pay for. I purposely use these now infrequent jobs to guide them in wrong directions. If they ask my suggestions on wording for a paper an office is sending to the American, British or German Embassies, I change the wording around to make it less clear, or change the meaning of what they really want to say. The changes are very subtle and I'm sure none of their staff can find anything wrong with the way the information is written.

In November 1995, I decided to make a face to face confrontation that would solve the situation one way or the other.

I asked His Highness did he intend to continue leading me on or would he do the manly thing by cutting me loose to seek employment elsewhere? I also asked him had he placed a travel ban against me at the airport. He muttered something like he hoped the situation with me could be resolved but at that time he didn't want to talk about it. I asked him would he have his secretary set up an appointment for a time when we could talk about it. His hee hawing was insolent and I decided to keep the confrontation going. I told him I had apprized several people at the United States Embassy that I believed the Minister of Information was capable of having me killed. Does he think that could be true?

The Crown Prince's response was hostile. "If he wanted to kill you, you would already be dead." I told him I had been sending documents from his office and the Minister of Information's to several safe places outside the country. I told him their inability to resolve the outstanding pay issue with me would cost him more than my back services in the long run. He shot back "if you had left certain situations alone, you'd still be getting your pay." I said I suppose that clarifies that one or both of them had put a stop payment on my monthly salaries. He didn't reply.

I said "You know if you don't kill me and you don't fire me, I can send documents any where in the world concerning all our little sideline information gathering and you'll be the one who will be exposed. You didn't take action against Saddam Hussein but I know what you did against Bahrain and the United Arab Emirates. I have copies of all papers from two files you passed on to Iran which were given to you in confidence by Bahraini officials on their visit here while trying to drum up your support

against the Iranian Shi'ite insurrections taking place in their country."
(I brought up this particular point because I knew the Crown Prince and
Prime Minister were recently rebuked by several of their Gulf allies over
the incident and he remained touchy about it.)

I told His Highness "You were disloyal to the Bahrainis who were one of
the allies that freed Kuwait from Iraqi occupation. By this time I was
being towed from the premises, a Kuwaiti guardsman under each arm. I
continued shouting from just a short distance but was sure he couldn't
hear me so why continue. He should remember I was with his advisor
when he turned over the documents on the Bahraini internal findings
to their enemy Iran? I also remember how a nights him squirming during
a televised questioning by Bahraini reporters in Manama that wanted
him to tell how Kuwait was helping them in their time of crisis? They
were demanding the Kuwaitis offer their undying support for the Bahrain
government on "live" television and all Kuwait's Crown Prince said in
about ten different ways was "things are happening behind the scenes".
"Indeed they were, but against their ally Bahrain. The Kuwaitis were
aiding their enemy Iran during Bahrain's time of trouble."

Don't they know that people like me can cause great interest in Bahrain
and the United Arab Emirates with what we know about harmful things
Kuwait has done to neighboring nations they regard as "brothers".

What if I told the United States and the United Arab Emirates that Kuwait
offered the Iranians their support over Abu Moussa and the other two
islands in the Straits of Hormus, if the Iranians would stop infiltrating
Kuwait through Failaka Island and Sabahiya? At times Kuwait has become
a traitor to their allies and have probably even listened entertained
arguments for killing American troops from Fort Stewart, Georgia in their
country's interest to rid Iraq of Saddam Hussein."

Sometimes in the past, one of the Minister of Information's high ranking
staff and I argued and he either left the room and slammed the door or
I did. On this occasion, I also heard a Kuwaiti again ranting and raving
about how the Americans just want to keep bleeding Kuwait's finances

and didn't really want to get rid of Saddam in the first place. He said "The U. S. has always wanted ports and bases in Kuwait and now they have them and it's not enough. They want all our money too." This time I was prepared for a fight and I was standing fast and it was his time to slam the door and end the conversation once again.

If the world wants stories about Royalty, Kuwait is a good place to start the presses rolling. Everyone hears about the Arab oil wealth, how they would like to hear about the Sultans and Emir and Sheikh's private lives. In the West, America, Britain or France, they can't even stir up a good sex scandal like Royal Kuwaitis consider normal life. If they think the Sultan of Brunei has sex scandals in his Palace from hiring and kidnapping people like former Miss Americas and other highly paid models, then enslaves from around the world should hear what goes on around here.

Once in a while to further annoy the Minister of Information, I'd ask questions about what I thought were scandalous behavior by them and their family. I'd ask about His Highness the Emir's private sex life. How many children does he really have, Does he really keep at least one wife position open for new arriving wives. What is the youngest age his sleeps with? Why do men dressed as women attend Kuwait ladies parties and spy for beautiful young virgins? What do they really do with the women who use to be married to the Emir when he's finished with them? I've heard the new ones are as young as twelve years old. When they are damaged goods, they can never remarry again for the rest of their lives.

I would ask them to tell me about the latest incident in which the Emir Sheikh Jabber's newest twelve year old wife wanted to kill him because she didn't want to marry the old man in his late sixties. He took her from the Bedouin community of Jahra through a deal with a semi-nomadic tribe leader.

The Emir of Kuwait openly and often uses the Islamic "Temporary Marriage Law" as his own private way to impregnate and get any lass he wants in the country. He keeps the women on a rotating basis that always stays within Islamic law of four wives at the same time by denouncing one of them immediately upon finding another. It has happened as often as weekly for this man known for his sexual appetite and the name of "The Wednesday Marrying Royal." Fortunately I can credit the Crown Prince for his decency and loyalty to his wonderful small family. It's good to see he is not following in the tradition of the old Emir.

Considering the old Emir is one of the only truly heterosexual men in the country, his work is cut out for him and he knows it. If having a hundred children is his goal to replenish his nation riding a virtual tidal wave of immoral men, then he is well on his way.

If he desires, women are procured from ladies private parties which his spies plan and attend. There's no courting or foreplay. Each new girl is a business deal. Some require more gold dowry or land for the family than others and some bare children faster than others and become favored for doing so. Others are assigned a new husband like our friend Hazel because her husband wanted to get rid of her so he can move onto the next. He even took her home and her children away from her.

Sometimes to piss off the high and mighty in Royal circles, I ask about someone's health I know has a liver disease due to drinking taboo alcohol or someone's drug habit which is also very taboo in Kuwait. An expat worker with such ailments or habits would be imprisoned under Islamic law or worse. The Kuwaiti Royal Family and first class Kuwaitis have a different code of ethics and punishment for their own, much more like us in the West. The abuser is often sent to a private estate in Cairo with enough money to have a rip roaring good time out of the sight of Kuwait's palaces.

Another touchy subject is to ask if anyone still has a video copy of the Kuwaiti Sheikh and his wife who made pornographic tapes. I would say "I lent someone mine while I was in the United States and I need another copy". This was the same tape Saddam Hussein's forces found in the Royal Family member's home while his troops were pillaging, shortly following invasion. The Iraqis showed it around to all the soldiers and made many copies for distribution to other Kuwaitis who could then see how their illustrious leaders really behaved. I heard Saddam's men felt it was against Islam to run it over the television so they stopped short by making sure everyone in Kuwait saw the tapes by making many of them available to the public. Almost every young boy aged fourteen has a copy or shares one with his friends.

Since my standoffs have gathered momentum, I've gradually started shipping small boxes of papers, newspaper articles and audio and visual tapes from Kuwait through American Embassy mail. I had been doing it all along but stepped up my postal endeavors as rougher times between me and them has became more confrontational. I suspect they'll conduct a search of our apartment at any time so I want nothing incriminating left lying around. It was at this time that Maia and I devised a code that I would use if I called her on the telephone and was telling her to "sweep" the apartment or "get out".

CHAPTER 36

Walking With a Zealot

I hadn't heard from my intelligence gathering buddy Jake in several weeks, and thought either he was staying away from me because of my problems or he had already left the country; which was what I really suspected. Even without Jake, two groups of people he introduced me to continued contacting me from outside the country. Perhaps they didn't know what was going on in my life or didn't care, but either way they needed a little more information concerning a Kuwait mosque that had been connected to the Atlantic Avenue address in Brooklyn, New York where renegade Saudi financier Osama ben Laden had operations.

An American group wanted me to enter the Mosque and search for several papers that had letterhead like the one they sent me as a sample. Late night entry into the mosque would be no problem because the buildings are always open to the public, but often have a lot of people in or around the main building.

For three days, I spent several hours each day sitting in my van about a hundred yards away in a parking lot watching movement in and around a particular mosque. I left work and headed straight to the mosque. I parked and watched worshipers following the five "Call to Prayers" over the loud speakers and I again watched the building in early morning before I went to work and once again late at night. If I can get inside the building and do any looking for papers in files or on desks, it obviously will have to be done at night because too many people are around during the day.

One day, I entered as a guest of a Mullah for a tour of the facility. The Mullah had been working and living there for several years conducting mostly Friday services. He was very pleasant and instructive, pointing out where he and two others slept in adjoining quarters near the side entry and showing me around the main prayer room; which has six large chandeliers and probably thirty or more Oriental and Persian carpets and throw rugs covering the entire floor. As is customary, there are no chairs in the prayer hall, only a few small ornate X shaped wooden stands in which worshipers can place their Qur'an as they kneel and bow on the carpets in prayer.

In the States we always say Muslims face east when in fact they face Mecca. It's strange that in Kuwait they do the same toward Mecca, but the direction for prayer is south-southeast. Even inside grocery stores are marked accordingly.

To the rear and left of the main prayer hall is a room upstairs. Up there, behind a wall of mushrabiya carved wooden spindles is the area veiled women watch religious readers during service.

This Mullah is a quite and educated man and says if I ever want to come over and talk or learn about Islam, I am welcome. He says sometimes a few other friends stay late in the evening and perhaps I will join their diwaniya one night. He says unfortunately they will have to end before midnight because one or two of them has early morning duties before four thirty a.m. (That was good information to know.) On another day, I stopped in again and brought chocolates and told the Mullah I would be in to visit with him within a week or so. I wish times had been more pleasant because I would actually like to have gotten to know him.

It was still during the middle of the week on Arab calendars, Monday, when I decided to enter the mosque on my fact finding mission. I knew the "lay of the land" so to speak and the hours the Mullah and the other mosque workers kept, and I had a feel for whether the men were passive or violent and whether they were moderates or fundamentalist. Perhaps now was the time to enter.

Shortly after two o'clock a.m. I entered the courtyard and found most doors of the mosque closed but unlocked. I entered through the regular front gate which had been left open, then walked to the side of the white block and adobe building where worshipers slipped out of their shoes. The Mullah's sleeping quarters was off to the left and dark. From the courtyard near the shoe racks beside the main doors, I quietly entered. I pulled at one of the two very old four inches thick wooden doors with dark, aged iron hinges and door handles and it opened without as much as a creek.

The first large room inside the mosque was where worshipers come to meet each other and exchange niceties before going into the main prayer room. I really only needed to enter two more doors after that, one to a two-room office that lay in the opposite direction worshipers went to pray; and the other off to the side of the second room where I spotted a fax machine on my surveillance visit.

So I wouldn't have to carry a flashlight, I brought along the same Home Depot miner's light with spot lamp that I used in the Iraqi desert inside Saddam's bunkers. The head light frees my hands and minimizes the area lit at the same time. There were no drapes in the office windows nor ornamental block or mushrabiya, so I had to be particularly careful of any light escaping. For this purpose I brought along a three sided, two feet tall light weight folded cardboard that I had painted black. The cardboard could easily be refolded back to one size two feet by one foot. I fixed a shade over the miner's lamp, so it only showed downward instead of radiating light outward that could easily have been seen out toward or through the windows.

The mosque's office walls were lined with sets of books like one might see in an attorney's research office and had lots of other religious material in various degrees of disorganization on desk tops and tables etc. The floors were marble tile as are all floors in Kuwait and echo any sound, so I slipped off my shoes just inside and behind the front courtyard gate. As I softly and silently glided through the dark, I passed a long conference table and two smaller round ones, before coming along side the first of two desks in the room. One desk was a typical U. S. military issue metal desk with a simple gray padded roller chair, while the other was far more substantial. It was a grand wooden desk that had seen a lot of years. My guess was that it was for someone with more authority than the Mullah I met. There was only one small three-drawer file cabinet in the first office but several small cabinets and boxes sitting behind and to either side of the first smaller desk.

I carefully ruffled through the top of the big wooden desk first, but found no letterhead like I car-ried for comparison. The desk drawers were locked but the file cabinet wasn't. I was afraid I would never finish skimming all the papers filed in one of the drawers but when I did, I was surprised to find out the other two drawers had almost nothing in them. I still hadn't found any of the right letterhead yet, but I was certainly well on my way to eliminating where it might be. I quietly walked the five or six feet back over to the smaller desk and began quietly shuffling papers there. Of course nothing on top was of interest, so I began going through each unlocked drawer and the wooden cabinets.

Taa daa, I found a couple papers with the correct letterhead. They were not placed in an area that showed they were of any real interest or importance to the secretary or whoever sat at that desk. They were just bunched up in a stack of other papers, and only stood out because they had several staples and paper clips that kept them all together as a group. I just took the whole bunch.

As quietly as a cat walks, I exited the mosque and hurried the papers home, then placed them in the elevator shaft equipment room of my building near our penthouse terrace door temporarily; until I could find out what all I had. If they were what I was looking for, I didn't want them inside our apartment in the eventuality there would be a raid. By now it was four fifteen a.m. and I had to be at the Ministry of Information Complex within an hour to start rounding up news copy from the Reuters and KUNA Wire Services. Feel like it or not, my first news show aired at seven o'clock.

My three morning broadcasts have gone well and since I no longer have to race through the streets to get to Dasma Palace, at noon I headed back to our apartment for some well deserved rest. I was getting use to not having to lose sleep any more and hoped last night's adventure yielded what was necessary to end any more inquiries from the Americans or Brits, and give me back my nights at home in my own bed with Maia.

Following the noon broadcast that day, I went back to the penthouse and rested most of the afternoon until just before five o'clock. Finally, I went outside to the elevator shaft room and got the papers I collected the night before from the mosque. I was pleased to see two of the papers had the exact letterhead I was supposed to look for and there appeared to be a lot of other important paperwork attached to them. I threw the whole bunch into a manila envelope and had Maia take it with her to the Embassy for mailing the next morning.

On Tuesday of the following week, I received a fax from two different people at two different places in the United States saying "well done". I didn't know what I sent them because I don't read Arabic that well, but it seemed to please them; so I was pleased. It was apparent the information I sent back to the United States had been shared with other interested parties. One fax said, please go to the Embassy and tell them I'm expecting a "clear line call" Wednesday at five o'clock p.m.; which was fine with me because that was the same hour Embassy employees like Maia, Betty, Betsy, Barbara and all the others finished their work week and went pool side for our social hour of beer, hot dogs and popcorn. It was the social start of our weekend.

That Wednesday, I arrived at the American Embassy about 4:45 p.m., so I didn't have time to say hi to Maia or anyone else before going into the Embassy Communications Room for the call. The telephone rang and the Embassy employee answered it and exchanged some pleasantries with the party at the other end before handing the telephone over to me. This was the first time I had ever spoken to anybody requesting information. Communication had always been through Jake.

I carried on about three minutes of casual conversation with the party at the other end and even asked what happened to Jake. The man said Jake was out of the picture for right now and hopefully he and I could exchange stories again one day. I left it there and didn't ask any further questions. The man who identified himself as Mr. Merchant said the information I gathered for them was explosive. He said in their dreams they couldn't have wished for something that good that proved their suspicions were correct. Just from information from him, I could read through the lines. Some Kuwaitis were involved in an operation of purchasing false United States ID's for Muslims who were to be entering the United States through Mexico.

Mr. Merchant said he wouldn't go into detail about the papers I furnished but said they had direct correlation to a long time investigation that tied Arabs and Mexicans into illegal cross border entries. He did say however that the numbers of illegal's crossing wasn't insignificant but a fairly large number, all with less than above board reasons for entering the United States in such a manner.

Mr. Merchant and I talked nonchalantly for a few more minutes then he dropped the boom. Would I be willing to reenter the mosque a second time and relook for more documents in the same area I found these and send him as many as I can? Of course I agreed. I didn't do so because it was a fun game for me, but I did like the feeling I had direct contact with someone who was important enough to make me feel I was important for what I was hanging my head on a limb for.

Over a period of the next two weeks, I avoided the mosque and Mullah at all times but reentered the premises twice more. I couldn't say it was easy each time, but with my heart pounding loudly in my mouth, I did manage to get several more pieces of paper out without being apprehended.

By the third call between Mr. Merchant and me, he began letting loose with a little more of the information from his end; I guess in a sort of thank you, ease your conscience sort of way. He said there are more than fifty terrorist groups operating inside Canada alone, most involved in just fund raising and recruiting. That border between the U. S. and Canada is more than double the length of ours with Mexico but the U. S. Mexican border is far more porous.

Mr. Merchant said Middle Easterners from Lebanon, Iraq, Iran, Yemen, Syria, Pakistan and Afghanistan have a steady ant stream of routes they take into the United States from Mexico. Mexican citizens make lucrative amounts of money as forgers, drivers and guides getting these radical illegal Arabs across the border.

In the two months alone preceding the November 11, 1993, World Trade Center blast, U. S. Government agents caught 80 illegal Arabs armed with forged ID's and passports entering through Cochise County, Arizona. Mexicans arranging the entries collected tens of thousands of dollars just in a few months for their assistance.

Those Mexicans arrested were bold enough to say there is no way of stopping them in the future; they not only know the easiest routes but how many U. S. border agents are working each shift, when shift changes occur and what time they have their coffee breaks. Mr. Merchant said funding was coming from three places that he can see and Kuwait is one. I told him that the only way I could see money getting put into such hands as this mosque would be through Friday donations from affluent families that may not actually attend services there; all other worshipers at this mosque appear to be lower to bare minimum income workers from Bangladesh, India, Pakistan and Egypt. I know from personal dealings, being around moneyed Kuwaitis that do handle and give out big money. They do it without any paper trail to follow.

I wanted a little more praise and wasn't ashamed to let him know that I was still quite uneasy doing what I was doing. He reassured me once again and said he was happy to have reliable people like me working with him. He said for instance, someone not so different from me prevented some Arab extremists from assassinating the Pope five or six years ago. A Filipino working with him had been gradually closing in on a radical group in Manila when the final break came. A fire had accidentally started in an apartment there and inside; the firefighters and police found several clerical robes, false ID's, escape routes and time tables.

Mr. Merchant said "Charles, you're doing very well but remember that any time you get too nervous or feel you can no longer work with us without bringing harm to yourself, quit. We'll have been happy to have had you with us and forever in your debt." "Take care of yourself and I hope to talk to you again someday."

The only other time I used the "safe line" at the Embassy was when I had over heard something rather than actually having proof of it in writing. Word had been going around at the Ministry of Information and at Dasma Palace and several diwaniyas that terrorists were going to strike at the heart of America. The only part that differed was whether the intended target was a cruise ship or a theme park.

Whoever I spoke to this time on the "safe line" said they were pleased with this information and I was to avoid any further conversation about the subject and "by the way avoid that mosque you've been going to like the plague." "You're not to ever return there again", but the man at the other end said I should draw out as detailed a floor plan as I could concerning the mosque's layout and its dimensions and fax that back to them as soon as possible. "Do not for any reason go there again", even the GPS location was unimportant at this point.

When I ended the conversation and hung up, I felt a little put off. Again I was getting a mixed message from whoever I was talking to in the United States; more in the tone of voice at the other end that in words themselves. It seemed to me that someone within the same office as Mr. Merchant didn't share his same enthusiasm for my information and that I should not bother them with any other leads. I couldn't believe I had scored big like a real spy one time and seemed use-less or put down the next.

I didn't say much to Maia about my little nighttime escapades and follow up "clear line" phone calls through the embassy, but I felt somewhat let down and I guess I did reflect it in my voice. For the first time, I really began telling Maia some of the things I'd been doing and we finally got to the point she didn't want to hear any more. It was scaring her. It wasn't enough that I had some of the most powerful men in the country angry at me already; but now I'm getting into yet another area that could get me killed.

Maia admonished me from doing such things and didn't want to hear of anything else like that for the rest of my life. She said "Just go do all those damn crazy things" and leave her out of it. If I wanted to "get killed" that was my business, She said "too bad you think more of that stuff than you do about living a normal life with no explosions going off in our apartment, or bombs under our car; or people who will probably one day walk up and shoot you on the street."

Few words were spoken between us for several hours but the whole while, I day dreamed and rationalized about the pleasantries Mr. Merchant and I shared, and the opposite way I felt with whomever I had just spoken.

That night I lay in bed, certain I had already made the connection of what targets the terrorists had in mind. Later that night I tried to tell Maia the scenario I was putting together in my mind but she said I should be thankful she was still talking to me but still wasn't ready to hear "that stuff".

Several days later, I received another fax saying return to the American Embassy at five o'clock p.m. for another "clear line call". This time Mr. Merchant wasted no time getting straight to the point. He said an American was en route to Kuwait by the name of McAllister. He may or may not use that name in Kuwait, but he thinks that is his real name and he'll feel secure enough to use it. It is possible he will have contact with the Embassy while there, but most likely not. Mr. Merchant said someone from the Embassy will be making some inquiries locally to assist me in trying to locate the man after he arrives. I'm to keep an eye on the man or befriend him but keep a slight distance, allowing him to go where he needs to go and do what he came to do without my interference. If asked, I should tell him I still work for Marr Bell Construction Company. He won't know the company closed its doors in Kuwait several years ago. It was better the man not find out I work for high sources in Kuwait or my wife works for the American Embassy.

Additional statistical information about McAllister followed by fax to the American Embassy the same day. There was a copy of his passport, a physical description in case he used another name and a little bio on the man. He was from Little Lake, Arkansas and was considered a dangerous man who had in the past been involved with several fringe racist organizations wanting to topple the American Government.

McAllister was a character who left his job as a train engineer out west to ramble from one group to another. He had no criminal record but was considered dangerous because of his affiliations. He had been implicated in a train wreck in the deserts of Western Arizona several years ago but never indicted. During the telephone conversation, Mr. Merchant said it was possible McAllister was coming to Kuwait to link up with fundamentalist who would finance the operation he spoke to me about before. Mr. Merchant didn't have to tell me that such an interaction between Arabs and Americans if true, would transform the terrorism base within the United States.

Terrorism in America would take a turn for the worst to be sure, and those executing it would use this opportune time to stretch their anti U. S. Government muscles. It would be perpetrated by American citizens and funded by Islamic fundamentalist groups who also wish to disrupt the American way of life; or cause huge distracting problems for our Government.

Again following my call and departure from the Embassy, I told Maia the latest on the mosque papers situation. Over the past five days, she did allow me to clue her in on a few details but was still leery of hearing any dangerous information. Not being a real spy or having lived a secretive life before, I didn't know how to keep this kind of information from my wife. She and I never had a communication barrier between us before, and it was hard to put up one now. Maybe everyone else who normally does what I've been doing for only a short time are more comfortable holding everything inside them, but I wasn't.

When I told Maia I believed the targets were Walt Disney World and the Disney cruise ship, she was really concerned and began saying how horrible such an act would be. Think of all the ramifications from such a one-two punch. American theme parks all over the country may become targets with assistance of other Americans. Again our great nation would suffer a monstrous deadly blow and reap economic instability on us as well. Terrorism in 1993 wasn't just some 747's blowing up a half way around the world. It has already come to American cities and now may even hit the establishments we send our children to for fun.

There were few hours in the next days and weeks that I didn't think of a Disney bombing and I was angry at the Kuwaitis, fundamentalist or not, who were obviously financing or plotting to create turmoil and death in the United States. I could now only hope Kuwait would start policing their own organizations involved in exporting terrorism or money used for similar purposes, but of course I knew that would be impossible. Their system of government is geared against external forces that might cause problems. They themselves are incapable of policing each other.

The Communications guy Gerald at the Embassy said he would be working with Kuwaiti authorities on American suspicions about McAllister and for their concern for his where abouts at all times in Kuwait. I was to just sit around and wait for a call when I would be needed. It could come today or two days from now. Go about life as usual and they'll contact me again when McAllister arrives. I knew it would be unwise to go to hotels and start inquiring as to whether McAllister had reservations, because someone there may unintentionally tip him off that another American was looking for him. I had jobs to do and errands to run, so I made no further effort to wait for the call.

The weekend was upon us when I finally got the call from Gerald. McAllister arrived on a plane from the United States about 11:30 last night and checked into the SAS Hotel about six miles further down Gulf Road than where we live. He was staying in one of the hotel's bungalows facing the sandy beach of the Persian Gulf. I made no effort to go to the SAS before taking a little nap after work. I had gotten off the "Air" about a quarter after twelve noon and needed a few hours rest before trying to personally confirm it was him.

I entered the SAS Hotel main lobby and wandered around for a while hoping he'd also be coming through the same busy area soon. For more than two hours, I stood watching the marble bowling ball water fountain where the ball appears to levitate and rotate atop a thin layer of water. I then had a slice of pie, milled around the gift shop and continually walked back and forth between the beach side pool and the lobby, for another hour and twenty minutes. Not once did I catch a glimpse of McAllister, so I went home and returned again around dinner time. I had several more hours this evening I could spend waiting to confirm it was really him.

Around eight forty five in the evening I spotted a man in the distance that could be McAllister so I moved rapidly toward the coffee shop for a better look. It was McAllister all right and he had done nothing to alter his appearance from the photograph I received via Embassy fax. He was about six feet one inch tall, sandy haired with graying near the temples, rugged complexion and wearing tan colored trousers and a light blue button down collar shirt. He certainly looked American enough I could have spotted him amongst twenty five Brits or Europeans.

I began my movement toward casually meeting McAllister when I got tapped on the shoulder by another man. When I turned, I half recognized him but didn't really associate where I had seen him or what his name was. He said "You're that radio/television guy aren't you?" I answered affirmatively and followed by saying I knew him but couldn't place where I knew him from. He said he was present when I interviewed Rolf Ekeus several months ago. The chief inspector for Iraqi weapons disarmament was due back in Kuwait soon, but there was no timetable for his arrival yet. He was on his way back to Baghdad and would return to Kuwait following meetings there. This man, a Norwegian was in Kuwait making other meeting arrangements for Ekeus's visit to this country.

The Norwegian wanted to know more about Kuwait and said he'd like to buy me dinner, but I told him I was waiting for a pilot to check in and would be happy to join him later for conversation but right now I had better wait around the lobby. We parted company and he headed toward the Chinese restaurant adjoining the main lobby, while I resumed my position toward the coffee shop; but McAllister was gone.

Within minutes I spotted McAllister again standing in the hotel rear entrance toward the swimming pool. I moved in his direction and as soon as I was within five feet, I asked was he Ted Arthur of the Morrison Shand Company? I rapidly followed by introducing myself and saying I was instructed to give Mr. Arthur a tour of the town. I used my real name because I was so well known in Kuwait I didn't want someone to come up or holler my name and cause doubt in his mind about whom I really was. He was congenial and in an educated southern drawl said "no", he wasn't Mr. Arthur but didn't say who he was. I apologized and said it was a shame because I was going to show him a few places tonight then give him the grand tour of the burned and gutted Iraqi Embassy tomorrow, along with highlights of damage done during the Iraqi occupation and other points of interest in Kuwait City.

I told him Kuwait City wasn't exactly a tourist destination but it would still hold interest for anyone who had never been to the Middle East before. He continued the conversation with me as though he were totally uninhibited about who he was or who I might be. The conversation continued and I described to him what the Hotel looked like shortly after occupation and what the beach he was looking at, looked like with long trenches and layers of barbed wire, while the Iraqis resided here.

McAllister was amused that I had lived in Kuwait during invasion and occupation and wanted to know what in the world would possess me to move permanently to a place like Kuwait. I told him "Money" pure and simple. In addition, I told him how nice it was for my wife and me to travel to other nearby countries where we could have the vacations of our lives. I told him we'd already visited more than eighteen countries like India, Egypt, and Russia etc.

McAllister said he was in Kuwait to work with some men programming computers and if it wasn't for that he wouldn't ever want to come to this part of the world. He said he lived out west where the trees are tall and where there is some pretty good contour to the land. I said "Yes, but look what you're missing by not living here, insolent Arabs, desert sand, dusty choking winds, camels and high rent payments but cheap gasoline. He chuckled and said he thought he could forego getting use to such attractive daily life features.

When my parents were in Amway, they were taught to present their information and then before trying to sell it to you; you should withdraw the offer to make the other person want it more by taking it away from them. I was about to find out if that method worked. I told McAllister he'd have to excuse me, I have to go ask at the front desk whether my bosses' pilot friend had arrived yet, then I would be going home. I have all day tomorrow off so perhaps I'd run into him again when my wife and I have lunch at the hotel as usual about two o'clock. I walked away and didn't turn and watch his reaction, nor where he wandered to after that. Contact had been made and I hoped Amway was right.

The next day I lured my wife to the SAS Hotel Chinese Restaurant and told her just in case this McAllister guy happens to make his presence known to me, she was to act like our luncheon at the SAS was routine for us every Thursday at Two. When we arrived at the hotel, we waited around in the lobby for a while but didn't see McAllister. Maia and I went in and slowly dined for almost two hours. Amway steered me wrong, maybe I should have tried harder to reel him in last night.

Shortly after I returned Maia home, I told her I had to return to the Hotel and try again. She asked why someone else couldn't be doing all this crazy stuff. She said "All we're going to get out of it is association with psychopaths and bombers." "This is not what I followed you overseas for."

As soon as I returned to the Hotel, I hadn't even gotten through the front doors before we spotted each other. McAllister waved and said "How's it going today?" I said I had just dropped off the pilot and was heading back toward home. How was he today? He said he had finally gotten enough sleep, but the nine hour adjustment in time was really doing him in. He said during the middle of the night. He sat in bed watching television but when daytime came, he fell asleep.

I asked had he eaten lunch yet and he said no. I told him hop in we'll go to one of the main shopping districts that has more than a dozen restaurants and fast food joints. We went to Salmyia, where we walked through Sultan Center Market for a while then stopped at Johnny Rockets for a typical 50's style American meal of hamburgers, fries and coke. He said he wished the place was nearer the hotel, but he wasn't staying in Kuwait long enough to worry about food too much. I told him we didn't have Johnny Rockets in Savannah but I had grown fond of it here. He said there wasn't one near him that he knew of either but when I mentioned Georgia, he said he was looking forward to returning to the States and stopping by to visit his daughter in South Carolina that was next to Georgia, right? He would probably be leaving in two or three days. I said oh, your daughter is going to become a southern lady like my mother if she stays there too long. He said she loves it where her husband is stationed near Greenville or some city like that. I told him yes, there is a Greenville. He said she was a smart girl and takes after him in love of computers. She use to work in a travel agency in California but now she is enrolled in a school that trains staff members for work on Cruise ships and in Cruise offices. He thinks the school is in a little town near by Greenville.

I never asked leading questions or said anything out of the normal because I didn't know what else a spy or agent or officer, or whatever they're called would ask him. I did however try to make contact with Gerald through his Embassy number last night but there was a recording on the other end that had nothing to do with Gerald. I left my number anyway and told him I'd let him know how far the situation had progressed with our visitor yesterday. Obviously, I'd have a lot more to tell Gerald the next time I talked with him.

After leaving Johnny Rockets, I showed McAllister a little of the city and he asked about the Kuwait Towers. We went to Kuwait Towers and rode the elevators to the lower level revolving observation and snack bar deck; where I pointed out Failaka Island in the Persian Gulf, the ships entering the Bay of Kuwait on their way to the port of Schuwaikh and the Amir's Dasma Palace down below. I showed him the old American Embassy grounds and the only hills in Kuwait, Mutla Ridge, where all the bombing sorties killed thousands of fleeing Iraqis in the Valley of Death.

He said he should return to the hotel because someone was going to be picking him up at eight o'clock this evening for a business meeting. He said he appreciated my informative tour and said perhaps before he leaves the country, my wife and I could join him for dinner. After dropping him back at the SAS, I never saw or heard from him again, but the story wasn't over. When I got home, Maia said Gerald had called and wanted to speak with me as soon as I returned.

Gerald said he would be able to take the information of McAllister's pending eight o'clock appointment and move on it. He thanked me and I didn't hear from him again either for the next couple days.

About three days later I received another call from Gerald at the Embassy wanting to meet with me alone, not in my apartment if Maia was there. We agreed to meet at Sizzler Steak House over looking the sea at Fashion Way Mall next to where I lived. As we sat in a booth overlooking the Persian Gulf and Arabian Gulf Road, he began filling me in on what had been learned over the past several days about our American visitor. He said normally he didn't think I should know any more than I had to, but since the next part of our assignment could be dangerous, I had the right to know a little more about what we were up against.

As you can tell by now, I can shoot a line of crap with ease and even convinced Gerald to let me in on what was happening.

It appeared a member of Kuwait's High Society but not of the Al Sabah Royal Family was about to make a name for himself in fundamentalist circles of the Middle East. Like renegade Saudi multimillionaire and terrorist financier Osama ben Laden, this moneyed Kuwaiti had planned what could be one of the most deadly terrorist alliances in history and a project that would catapult him into world fame.

Gerald said his sources weren't sure how the Kuwaiti became the possible new benefactor of the American, but it was believed his name was pulled from a prime list of wealthy supporters of Islamic causes and anti-Western sentiments. He may or may not know what he's getting involved in. Gerald said it was best I didn't know the man's name, but rather what activities he had been up to. The man had recently formed an alliance with the American that also had grandiose dreams. They had been communicating through different means back and forth for more than three months and a visit by the American; obviously McAllister would help solidify their means to each other's goals.

The American McAllister was involved in what is called "leaderless resistance" in the United States. He shunned larger racist and anti-American Federal Government groups and organizations where he always felt subjugated. He desired his own following for his own accomplishments and preferred at this time to remain a phantom cell rather than part of any group he'd joined in the past, then left.

McAllister at one time or another had been involved in the Ku Klux Klan, Identity Christians and several other larger groups but always left them to join smaller cadres or groups in which he could have more authority. He religiously visited fringe group meetings and larger group's headquarters. His views and doctrine were formulated from brochures, pamphlets, videos, audio tapes and lectures purchased through racist catalogs like MOD and conferences he attended in Montana, Hayden Lake, Idaho where the Freeman Organization is located and Estes Park, Colorado where several similar type groups had what was termed a Rocky Mountain Rendezvous.

McAllister had been a passing acquaintance of Louis Beam, another Arkansan who had once been acquitted of sedition charges by the Federal Government. It was from Beam, McAllister first heard of the desire to form unions with Middle Eastern factions or organizations, but Beam had nothing to do with what was going on with McAllister now. Years ago Beam vowed to unite the racial right in the United States like the KKK, Identity Christians, Posse Comitatus and other such groups with anti-Jewish racial groups in the United States and abroad. He wanted to form a coalition with international groups and organizations that had similar ambitions of overthrowing the United States Government, but for very different reasons.

McAllister's contacts had been made from his Little Lake home in Arkansas to the PLO, Palestinian Liberation Organization of Yasser Arafat, Islamic Jihad in Syria and Iran and Hezbollah, Party of God in Syria and Lebanon. In exchange for a very large amount of money, his benefactors would have a new terrorist front opened within the borders of America without implication of Arabs or their organizations. He and his group would immediately become a force to be dealt with, and the Arabs would no longer have to have their own organizations within the United States to do anything; but continue their fund raising efforts. The partnership between McAllister and any accepting group or organization would become a more than one-time alliance.

Gerald handed me a sheet of paper photocopied from a letter stateside that had been sent to him. The letter highlighted writings from a book by Howard L. Bushart, John R. Craig and Myra Barnes, PH.D. Called SOLDIERS OF GOD. According to their plan, the unions of such groups would have the capacity for a tremendous amount of social and political disruption and a great deal of damage within the United States. "The radical racial right in America will parallel in many ways the Islamic fundamentalist cause world wide." "The racial right would herald in a new American era in which will be reflective of their concepts of the "old America" in which the Constitutional Republic would not be separate from the church. If the government is to be successful for a nation of Aryan Israelites (it read), it must include the laws of God and no laws of man may supersede these divine sanctions. In no way should the Church's true gospel be excluded from the state."

Gerald said within the past few days, the same American group's Internet chat site has been busy boasting of a faster return to a Constitutional Republic than ever thought possible. He quoted the Internet page saying "A great wave of awakenings was near. The faded and tarnished Glory of our Founding Forefathers will once again be based on the Christian Church. American school children will once again have prayer in school and they will learn the morals of Bible teach-ings."

The moment I heard Gerald's words about "teaching children morals and returning prayer to school", I had two separate thoughts. I too would like to see prayer restored to schools as it had been in my youth. With all the shootings of children by children in schools around the nation, something had to change but with moderation; lest we find ourselves no different than Middle Eastern Islamic fundamentalist. Their hate and radical perceptions dominate their lives and seek to destroy others. I could hear the same words spoken from Palestinians who want more schools and closer religious ties for their children in the Gaza Strip and West Bank.

CHAPTER 37

Night Crawling

Since this McAllister character had come to town, Gerald and I had been on a treasure hunt for information and we were getting bundles of it. Gerald said the day I called him from the SAS Hotel and told him McAllister had an eight o'clock meeting; he was there to follow him. A Kuwaiti with an Indian driver picked him up and they drove to a Kuwait City commercial suburb called Schuwaikh. He followed them until the Kuwaiti and McAllister got out of the car and entered a furniture store. Gerald quickly parked and was able to see which of the rooms in the rear of the store they went in. Their meeting lasted just more than two hours, and it appeared no one else entered nor left the room the whole time.

Gerald returned to the store a little later to see what type security it had, and whether the premises could easily be breached late at night. Without giving me details, he said he entered the furniture store's rear office and found a few things of interest after it closed. Gerald proceeded to tell me several documents appeared to be incriminating and he wanted me to enter once again with him that night. Gerald was sure there were still many papers of interest in the rear room but it would take him a week if he continued entering and searching alone.

When I told Maia I was going to be out during the wee hours of the morning, she said "Oh great" now you have linked up with another Jake."

"If you get killed robbing some place, what do you think the Embassy is going to do with me?" "You've already got the Minister of Information and the Crown Prince pissed at you, how much further up the ladder do you think you can go before they chop both of our heads off?"

Her thoughts were comforting. A blade to the neck for my efforts. I can't say her little speech didn't make me a lot more leery that night than I would have been had she not given it to me.

Gerald and I had no problems reentering the office but had a terrible time trying to figure out what could be useful. When I entered one file cabinet drawer that hadn't been checked by Gerald yet, I found several books in English. One was titled "American Extremists" by John George and Laird Wilcox and two others called "The Militia Movement" and "Hate Groups in America" by Gary McCuen and "Gathering Storm, America's Militia Threat" BY Morris Dees with James Corcoran. A militia news letter called "Taking Aim" was between two of the books. Of course, I didn't have time to look through them, but out of curiosity it was worth spending a little time to see why the Sheikh and his friends might be interested in them.

The only other things we found that night were faxed letters from McAllister to someone named Hashim Nesimabadi, a name that would come up again in the future. I had never heard the name and neither had Gerald, but I told him the name was Iranian. It wouldn't be unusual to have a name like that in Kuwait though because many Kuwaitis are descendants of Persians or Iranians.

The next item we found was something that posed a big question in our minds and we couldn't figure why two different money orders were clipped to exteriors of American Federal Express envelopes. Gerald was afraid they'd be missed, so we didn't take either of them. For the most part, that night had presented several things for us to photograph but nothing we could carry when we left the office. Gerald told me I had a few more minutes while he was taking pictures of the letters; so now might be a good time to glance through the books to see if any particular pages were marked or corners bent.

The only things I readily spotted were hand written circles around a lot of organization names, militia group names, locations in the United States and names of individuals. To really see what the Arabs were looking for would take more time.

While waiting for a response from Gerald's upper chain of command in the United States about the stuff we found that night, we reentered the same office three more times in as many days. Each time, we took nothing from the scene but came away with rolls of film to be developed. During the process of screening the literature at hand more carefully, I found a radical rightist two hundred pages militia training manual called M.O.D. It obviously had been printed by a racist or far right group in the United States. Its contents provided details of how to form militias and prepare them for war. The manual outlined the Biblical and ideological justification for a guerrilla war in the United States and listed actions that could be taken such as:

. Raiding armories to seize arms, ammunition and explosives

. Coordinating sabotage attacks to cripple the economy of the U. S. Agricultural or industrial production, transport and communications systems, the military and police systems.

. Conducting a campaign of domestic terrorism that includes actions "usually involving the placement of a bomb or fire explosion of great destructive power capable of affecting irreparable loss against the enemy.

. Executing spies, government officials and anyone else who of their own free will go to the police to supply clues and information and finger people in paramilitary groups. Another part of the same book "Gathering Storm" was highlighted in pink magic marker that read: Arab Islamists are Ethnocentric. Their bias expresses their own race, religion, culture and nations are superior. They judge others by their own standards and values. In parts of the Middle East, there is no separation between church and state because their countries follow religious lines. (Sentiments many Islamists and American militias share)

The markings also drew through a few paragraphs in the book "The Militia Movement and Hate Groups in America": One underlined section read: Revitalization movements can have positive effects as in the Middle East. The Islamic revival has fueled a surge in religious faith and strengthened the family. Ironically, though, because of its widespread social approval of the values of the movement, it is difficult for the non violent majority to keep the extremists in check. Martyrdom is proof of sincerity, arrest and execution of these individuals is not a deterrent.

Also, the following statements were marked by magic marker: The World Trade Center bombing was a predictable out growth of official United States policy. Largely uncritical American support for Israel alone has been enough to turn the United States into an international target. Though murderously misdirected and morally monstrous, terrorist attacks are a natural response to Washington's determination to make everyone else's conflicts its own by continually meddling in foreign squabbles and seemingly condoning most any injustice perpetuated by most any ally. Consider the 1983 bombing of the Marine Corps barracks in Beirut, Lebanon. The United States sent soldiers into the middle of a civil war, sided with one of the warring parties and shelled Muslim villages as a show of strength. How then could anyone have been surprised when a suicide bomber reversed the direction of death making 241 young American Marines pay the supreme price? The United States intervened in a distant conflict for no cause and terrorized people with whom it had no quarrel, providing everything but an engraved invitation to revenge-minded killers. Unfortunately American policy-makers shared responsibility with foreign terrorist for the soldier's deaths.

Next to a couple paragraphs titled "War on Islam" were several stars that again had magic marker through each line. They read: Especially dangerous today is the American Government's campaign to make an enemy of every living Muslim Fundamentalist wherever he or she resides in the world. There's no doubt that Islam poses a serious challenge to Western culture and values but the United States can do little to halt its spread and has no reason to intentionally antagonize Muslims who otherwise wouldn't think about America, yet Washington is speaking of alliances with African nations and others throughout the world that most policy-makers, let alone citizens can't find on a map in order to contain an ancient religion that has endured for centuries.

It continued: Declaring a de facto war on Islam invites retaliation and the most likely victims will be innocent Americans like the children in Oklahoma City, workers at the World Trade Center and the Marines in Lebanon. Yes, the United States must respond to terrorism. Part of the solution is improving detection, prevention and punishment but the United States must also reduce the manifold justifications as perverse and warped as they are, for terrorism that has needlessly been provided to those with seared consciences and murderous intentions. So long as Washington tolerates, encourages and worse engages in one or other variations of terrorism, it will risk repetitions not only of Oklahoma City, New York City and Washington but also of the plethora of other bloody attacks around the globe in recent years.

Another pamphlet found was from the Nation of Islam in the United States. Several markings on each page seemed to question the Nation's interpretations of Islam and there were lots of notes about Louis Farrakhan, the head of Nation of Islam.

When Gerald and I finished getting what we could in the furniture store's rear office, we were departing from the back exit when a car pulled alongside Gerald and asked in Arabic what we were doing there? Of course we both stumbled for words because we were caught totally unprepared to face anyone. I know I hadn't even taken time to prepare something to say if we had been caught. Gerald just looked at me and I knew we were up the creek. I told the man who looked Syrian or Lebanese, my friend and I were embarrassed because we were having a homosexual encounter when he spotted us and we were sorry. We would leave and never return there again. (I knew in Kuwait that would be likely but not between two Americans) The man appeared to buy the story but all the while interrogating us, he came closer and closer. We had to answer a few more questions for him while he fondled me first then Gerald then asked did we want "this", Using his hand to grip his crotch, then fingers to outline his semi stiff cock. Without either of us showing the least bit interest in him or his cock, he drove away after giving us one more good look over.

Gerald dropped me off at my apartment, where I had to awaken again for work in barely two hours. Instead of reclining for a brief sleep, I continued thinking of the parts of articles I had just completed reading from the American books. My first impressions were that they rambled a little too much for me to comprehend their exact messages, but I figured that was probably the way racist and militia doctrine read.

Being an American overseas gave me a unique perspective from which to read these paragraphs. First I thought those militias have no idea how well they have it in the United States. There are few countries in the world that are as free and tolerant as the American Government. Surely if each of the authors and their followers spent their yearly vacations in a different country each year, they'd be happy to return to the Good ole imperfect but great United States.

Secondly, I was worried fundamentalist Arabs were probably reading and believing each written word as they hung on to each phrase that these American authors were including in their books against their own government. The Arabs, who circled, placed marks next to and highlighted these and other paragraphs, phrases, names and locations were probably thinking how they could use this information in subversive ways against the United States; and even those who wrote them. I'm sure they had no way of knowing the books were written by authors about racist extremists in America and such paragraphs the Arabs were paying most attention to were not written by the books authors, but were quotes or excerpts from literature they were quoting from racist and hate groups.

I knew the Arabs could care less whom the authors were, who wrote those lines and phrases because all they really wanted to do was read that Americans were also discontent with their government and wanted to topple it.

I can guarantee after living in an Arab and Islamic society for as many years as I have, these naive Americans way of life would never be as good as it is now if they allowed Muslim extremists to help them topple our existing government. Most, if not all their freedoms would be wiped out. These same Arabs would teach these right wing American separatists, seditionists, militaristic Christian groups what loss of freedom and government control really is if the Federal Government of the United States was overthrown.

Many Arabs profess by 2020 to subjugate the American military and indirectly the American people within our own land. They hope to continue building their Islamic support through new mosques and Islamic organizations and Islamic Centers in the United States and throughout the American military. They support, though have doubts about the Nation of Islam here, but are happy to see its influence in American prisons. They are also supporting fellow Arabs who reside in the United States in their demands that the American Government soften their tone and rhetoric against Arabs and Islam. Arab-Americans are now crying victimization every time anyone says a derogatory remark about them.

We can't do the same in their countries no matter how long we live here. We can't have citizenship here in Kuwait or rights as one; or even purchase property in most Islamic countries. I have been unable to even buy a truck in Kuwait because it is considered subversive.

Soon the National Association of Arab Americans will have their Washington lobbyist gain support and legislation against any outspoken words against them in film, television, radio talk shows and newspaper articles. To be politically correct we are not even allowed to show discontent against Arabs in America, in our own country.

I wish such an organization of Americans or lobbyist was permitted in Arab countries of course but that will forever be impossible. Perhaps such pro Arab legislation should be passed in the United States only if it is reciprocal toward Americans living in the Middle East. Many of these are not even privileges, much less rights for foreigners in Muslim countries. This is usually when they say "Yes but that is what makes America so great and makes us want to live and work there."

A call I received from Gerald later in the afternoon almost floored me. He said he hated to speak on "open unsecured lines" but we hit pay dirt and I had to meet him now. I told Gerald Maia wasn't home and it would be best if he came to our apartment. Within fifteen minutes he was there. Because Gerald was about to tell me something extremely important, he even said he wouldn't speak indoors in case it was bugged. (He knew of my recent troubles with the Minister of Information and the Crown Prince.)

Gerald began to talk as we leaned over the roof top rails. Amongst the paper work we procured from the mosque in downtown Kuwait City were what we had figured were U. S. money orders. They were anything but real. They were samples of counterfeit U.S. money orders the Freemen group from Mussel Shell County, Montana was hoping to flood into world markets. Somehow, perhaps through McAllister they had gotten hold of them.

I was told someone had been using them inside the United States to pay bills but now someone is trying their luck on the world market. It now appears such an alliance of Islamic Fundamentalists and American Freeman groups would be trying to do the same thing Iran had tried to do after the Ayatollah came to power; try to destabilize the American economy worldwide by mass counterfeiting the American dollar.

Gerald told me how Iran had printed billions of dollars in U. S. Twenty and Hundred dollar bills and tried to flood the world market with them. The same thing had been tried by numerous other renegade governments and groups but never by an American one. He said the scale of the forgery was probably due to the latest efforts of these present day Islamic Fundamentalists Arabs. He said this is more of a problem than guys like me and Gerald could possibly imagine.

Gerald and I stayed away from the furniture company's rear office for almost a week, while we continued reading the fallout of our find. As I read the reports sent to Gerald from the United States, they got worse and worse and I began having doubts as to whether I wanted anything else to do with the situation any longer. It would surely turn dangerous if any of our intelligence gatherings was stumbled upon by a Kuwaiti. After all, the other night was a close call. Both Gerald and I continued to speak carefully and out of doors each time we met following "the break ins". Each time we met the news got worse.

The latest reports we received indicated Federal agents in the United States had been following McAllister and a few of his militia friends for almost a year. They were still allowing him to continue his contacts in Kuwait and with other Arabic groups, while trying to gather even more evidence against him.

No worse follow up messages could have come than arrived the last week of November 1995. Federal agents confirmed plans by McAllister and several other men to conduct terrorist acts on three U. S. Targets. Unlike any terrorist acts before on American soil, they planned two explosions and one chemical attack near simultaneously. The influential Kuwaiti would be providing a large portion of the sixty two million dollars required by McAllister to carry out the terrorist acts.

Border restrictions were still lacks in the United States but were finally under more scrutiny by our government, so Arab men and anyone looking Arab was subject to more critical review. There was no doubt in my mind that Arabs would soon feel the heat and they would turn to their sisters to carry out fundamentalist plans against the United States. Their women are not highly scrutinized in the United States and have easy access to universities stateside and to visitations to other family members already inside the United States.

Now for the first time, I was finding out that U. S. Federal agents had uncovered a two year plan by McAllister and his friends that even called for introducing the deadly poison Ricin to dessert silverware on the "Disney Magic" Cruise ship in Florida. The poison was to be put on the silverware on the first night out of port. The poison Ricin may be made from the innocent castor bean plant, but when treated correctly, one mere speck of it on a sharp object or introduced into the mouth is six thousand times more potent than cyanide and twelve thousand times more deadly than rattlesnake venom. Terrorism would not have to come from overseas anymore, it would have its roots right here in the United States.

The Soviets had used the same poison on an umbrella tip to kill a Bulgarian diplomat in 1978. A canister of the white Ricin powder was brought through the Canadian border from Alaska by an American in 1995. He was arrested and the poison was seized. However it was not the only Ricin to enter the United States or to be made on American soil. Undoubtedly McAllister managed to find enough to kill everyone on the ship several times over and now he's looking for financing that'll pay him for the privilege of bringing more terrorism to our shores.

The second phase of McAllister's multi-terrorist attack was to take place in the most crowded restaurant inside the gates of Disney World in Orlando, Florida. This explosion would take place the following day around noon when the restaurant would be at its busiest.

A third attack was to take place within hours after reports were aired by the American news media, of the Disney World bombing in Orlando and only one hour after the Carnival Cruise ship "Destiny", at the time the largest cruise ship in the world, departed the port of Miami. To provide a grander spectacle, the crowded cruise ship with more than three thousand persons aboard would still be within site of Miami Beach as it blazed and sunk.

These three terrorist acts would send a nation and a world into shock and literally destroy the tourism industry of Florida. Even if someone worked in a factory in Florida, they would feel vulnerable to terrorists and would always be looking over their shoulder for bombers. The multi-billion dollar cruise ship industry would be dead, at least in Florida where more cruise ships are based than any where else in the world.

Following our discoveries, Gerald decided we should lay low and not talk about what we found to anyone inside Kuwait including Maia, but the bad news only got worse. The night Gerald and I were caught behind the furniture store's office, the Syrian man turned us in by calling the police and giving them Gerald's automobile tag number. It had taken more than a week for the Kuwait police to approach the American Embassy with their information.

Gerald was notified by his superiors and was warned of problems such incidences could cause between relations of the two countries if further information was leaked about what we had really been up to. Gerald said the Syrian man had no idea who the man was with Gerald, but someone at the Ministry of Information or the Crown Prince's office must have put two and two together. Three days after talking to Gerald about the incident, the Crown Prince's office called me in.

CHAPTER 38

A Bomb for Halloween

In everyone's life there is sun shine and happier days. I had my troubles and knew things for better or worse would come to a head sooner or later, but I figured as long as Maia's job remained secure at the American Embassy, time was still on our side. Deep down, I was really confident this little private war between me and the Ministry and Dasma Palace would be resolved. It wasn't the first time we had our differences, and they had always been patched up pretty easily but this time; so many situations were intertwined that I did really fear there could be no resolving such vast differences.

For the next couple of days, I wasn't going to allow any of that to get in my way. Maia and I had just gotten our Christmas flight reservations confirmed for the United States, and the up coming holiday season with our friends in Kuwait would help me weather my troubles for a while longer. Mine and Maia's Halloween party is considered the first kick off of the holiday season.

Halloween had never been celebrated to any degree in Kuwait before Maia and I arrived. There had been two stores that sold masks and a few costume oddities but overall, there was no place to wear them in Kuwait even if you bought them. In November 1991, Maia and I started our first annual Halloween Party. Over the years it grew into an evening we were proud of and known for. Our guests started with the people we worked with at Marr Bell and Royal Ordinance, and then expanded to include my radio station and Ministry of Information co-workers, Dasma Palace employees and American Embassy friends as well as Ambassadors of several other embassies around town. From these friends, there evolved a diversified group of party goers.

The Halloween party of 1995 was to be the biggest and best yet. Like the Marine Corps Ball at the American Embassy, mine and Maia's Halloween party became the social ticket of the pre-holiday season. Limiting the amount of guests was the hardest part. No more than two hundred of our closest friends could come due to space. Though we live in a penthouse with two large out door terraces, there has to be ample room for the event to flow smoothly with all the banquet tables etc. Outside, and down below in the parking lot; it looked like another embassy ball in Kuwait City. All the number 1 national auto tags with flagged limousines and chauffeurs signified a strong contingent of Ambassadors from countries around the world to Kuwait were present.

This year the party was to be held on a Thursday night, so the maximum amount of our closest friends and colleagues could attend. Thursday night in Kuwait is in the middle of the Islamic weekend, the same as Saturday night is in the Western World.

The first year we gave a Halloween party, anyone who wanted to could attend and even bring along another friend or two. As the years passed and the party became more successful, the square footage of the penthouse didn't grow consistent with the amount of people we became acquainted with. It became necessary to limit the invitees. The number of guests had grown from 30-35 to well over 200.

In 1995, we sent out invitations with RSVP to our closest friends first. We then waited to see what kind of number we had from those wishing to attend before expanding the guest list. Next, we invited people we considered additional characters we thought would make the party interesting and keep conversations moving. Thirdly, we invited persons from several other companies and Ministries we had become acquainted with from other parties over the year.

All in all, we ended up with a fabulously diverse crowd of dear friends, movers and shakers, whits, spies, Generals, media persons, Sheikhs, Diplomats and back stabbers. Back stabbers were interchangeable with any of the previous groupings. Security of course had to be increased dramatically when prominent guests like Ambassadors and their spouses were in attendance.

I had arranged internal and external security for this year's Halloween party from two close Kuwaiti friends, Captain Hassan at Kuwait CID Secret police and Captain Khalid of Traffic Police. Captain Hassan himself worked our apartment building's single ground floor entry for the first few hours and Captain Khalid's patrols kept eye on the parking lots and party goers entering and leaving from the street. Each Ambassador was usually driven by his own chauffeur-guard who stayed near their autos, even after the Ambassadors had come up to the penthouse. American Ambassador Crocker and wife Christine never attended.

Our penthouses' roof and rooftop balconies were covered in lighted pumpkins and pumpkin lanterns, full size standing scare crows, a dance floor and lots of seating and dinner tables. The guest list was so big this year, we even had workers come in to dismantle our beds so those rooms could also be used by the Farah Restaurant caterers serving the food; and for the disc jockey's booth. All rooms including the bedrooms had glass from floor to ceiling and wall to wall like the living room, so people who had never been to our apartment prior to that evening would probably have no idea they were standing in what was usually our bedroom.

Dance music was played by a well known Kuwaiti party man and friend of ours, Dr. Taib. When he wasn't spinning tunes, he was involved in research. From research Doctor to friend and Disc Jockey to later becoming a radical Islamic Fundamentalist. We never saw Dr. Taib after that.

Guests were encouraged to go all out in costuming themselves for our party, and they did. Janelle came as a fortune teller with crystal ball, her new husband Jalal came as an Egyptian Pharaoh and son Mishal came as a convict with ball and chain, (some real stereotyping here) Joseph was Kojak, Betty Lippold who also covered the event for the Arab Times was a sixties hippy (which she was), Abdullah was a Russian Sailor, Carl was teddy bear, our Lebanese mechanic Mustapha who had eight children, came for the third year in a row as a rabbit (which he was), Ghassan and Ruba came as Sonny and Cher, Embassy Betty as Calamity Jane, Barbara as a Can Can dancer, Ali was a Maharaja, David was the King of Siam, Sharon was a Maharani, Mike and Betsy were Caesar and Cleopatra, Saleh, Kuwait's Don Juan was Lion King, Samir was Elvis Presley and our Iraqi friend Mayada was Jackie Kennedy and looked just like her with the pink dress, pill box hat and hand bag and Maia's chauffer came as a flying monkey.

Maia was Cinderella with tiara and wand and I was a cowboy Sheriff with badge, ten gallon hat, boots and spurs. Maia was lovely and I looked like my shining, modeling days. Linda and Badran showed up late because Linda was doing an "on air" hit tunes dedication show on radio prior to arriving. She and Badran made great gypsies and their costumes were fabulous. Also in attendance were some really unique costumes of Statue of Liberty, an American school teacher, two mermaids, kings, a Genie, one Yasser Arafat, a bag piper, and a grown baby in diaper with a giant sucker, Fidel Castro and many more.

The music played, the people danced, food was plentiful and there were a hundred and ten bottles of house wine and champagne for everyone who wanted it. A former advisor to the Crown Prince, Issa Al Asfoor parked his chair in the middle of the floor and sipped his jack Daniels straight from the bottle as he enjoyed all those who passed. Bodies passed him at crotch level and Issa's head never looked upward at anyone's head or down toward their shoes. He just kept staring straight into everyone's mid sections.

Russian, University professor and former KGB spy, Alexandra danced to the rhythms as did ex CIA agent Joseph, Kathleen, Janelle, both Betty's and Abdullah. Though Abdullah is Iranian, he was determined to show everyone he could do Russian squat dancing and did a pretty good job of it. Even the two Russian Diplomats present, joined in cheering Abdullah on.

All was going more than well, when I received a muffled call about 10:15 p.m. It was an Arabic speaking caller who simply said in broken English "A bomb will explode at 10:30 p.m." I used the intercom button to call Captain Hassan who said to immediately get everyone out of the building. His men would evacuate other residents still on other floors.

While everyone was being orderly evacuated down the stairs and penthouse elevator, I received a second telephone call. This time I could barely make out what was being said. I stuck a fingertip in my opposite ear to hear the message better. It sounded like the voice of my Royal Ordinance friend Jake but inside an echo or from the other side of a large room. His voice said "get out" twice then went silent.

Within minutes the building was surrounded. There were police cars, lights, noise and people everywhere. I was told by Captain Hassan that a bomb squad was en route so Maia and I should stand outside with the crowds until either the bomb went off or the calls were proven a hoax. Maia and I stood with Janelle and Jalal, Mike and Betsy and Betty, Carl and Abdullah. I told Betty we were just about ready to go "live" with a broadcast from the Super Station's "Love Line Show" and Talal Yagoot the show's host, when the bomb threat came.

I guessed Betty would have a good story for the Arab Times Newspaper tomorrow, if they let her print it. She said she would submit two reports, one with the usual social commentary and the other as a bombing or bomb scare, whatever happened. She was sure however that the latter would never be allowed to be printed.

Salmyia, where Maia and my apartment was, was the liveliest of the elite shopping districts in the greater Kuwait City area and that night, the normal weekend crowds had already started filling the streets. All our guests were evacuated in costume so there were hundreds of people standing around three sides of the building and across the street along the beach, attracting even more people. Traffic along the six lane Gulf Road came to an almost stand still while passers by gawked at people dressed in strange costumes and flashing police car lights.

Over flow crowds had to be kept away by a newly roped off perimeter more than fifty yards out from our building. Any further out and we would have been in the Persian Gulf waters or all the busy restaurants and shopping malls would have had to be evacuated also. Everyone who knew what was going on waited at 10:30 for the building to blow up. The time came and went as did the bomb team. I was given the "all clear" and asked to walk with Captain Hassan and the bomb squad Captain around my apartment prior to allowing everyone back in. As I appeared on the roof top terrace with police, a chant rang from the streets in three directions "Charles, Charles, Charles, Charles." I waved to the crowd in a manner befitting the British Royal Family and then returned to the ground level entry to inform my guests the party was "on".

Next, it seemed like a cast of thousands tried to enter the apartment for the wildest Halloween party ever. The only people who didn't return that evening were Embassy personnel from several Western countries. They felt the security risk was too high, so gave their apologies to Maia and me before departing.

I assumed position next to Captain Hassan at the single entry, ground level to help sort out those wanting to come in and those who we had never seen before that wanted to crash the party. Kuwait police seemed to think the bomb scare was a hoax too, but if our guests wanted to re enter, it was all right with them. A beefed up police force would however keep a very visible profile near our building, in the parking lots and in the adjoining shopping district; where there were three gold markets and boutique Malls, the busiest market in Kuwait the Sultan Center, a and probably ten eateries.

For the next thirty minutes our front door was like gaining entry into "Planet Hollywood" or "Studio 54" in New York. Thankfully there were more than enough people wanting to return to drink the hundred or more bottles of champagne and wine left and eat the platters of falafels, dana kebab, shish kebab, Indian curry chicken, chicken and beef shawarma, rice, fries and humus.

Friday morning was time for Maia and me to sleep in late to recover from the three o'clock a.m. departure of our last party goers. About nine thirty, we received another call from the police telling us a bomb squad had been recalled to our building because an explosive device had been seen by some Filipino elevator repair men a few minutes earlier.

Maia and I quickly scrambled off our mattress on the bedroom floor. (I had brought the mattress in from the rooftop storage after all the guests had gone. We slept on the mattress because it was too late last night to reassemble our bed before crashing from fatigue.)

Maia and I dressed as best we could and hurried down the stairs, then out of the building with our three cats in carry cages. Several policemen had already started blocking off the roads once again and were steadily evacuating the few persons who lived in our building. Our Dutch friends, Monique and Marcel who lived below us and whom we didn't have a chance to talk to during the party last night, stood outside with us. The building next door was also evacuated this time because obviously the danger was very real and explosives had been seen. Even the Italian Ambassador's residence in front of us and the larger Zahra apartment high-rise building was evacuated.

Shortly after the bomb squad rushed inside our building, they sent word three sticks of dynamite were taped on a metal bar just above the removable elevator roof light panel. Fortunately the dynamite was disarmed and removed without incident.

No newspaper is printed in Kuwait on Friday (Arabic Sunday) morning, so we had to wait for Saturday morning's newspaper to see which of Betty's articles had gotten printed. It was a hoot. Almost one full page was dedicated to pictures of Maia and me and our costumed guests, but no mention was made of the bomb scare or the sticks of dynamite found in the elevator's roof.

For several days, I tried to follow up the bomb scare through my policemen and CID friends but continually got passed from telephone number to telephone number and never learned any information concerning the device, why it hadn't exploded or if anyone had been arrested in connection with it. Most of the people at the police stations I talked to acted as though they knew nothing about a bomb. Even my two friends were of no help resolving the matter. Neither ever seemed to have any information concerning who targeted us, nor if we were really targets at all.

Because of our bomb ordeal, a Ghurka from the American Embassy who specialized in bombs and booby traps was sent over. I went with him to a child's toy store where we purchased a small yellow and orange plastic toy lawnmower, probably meant for a toddler two or three years old. When we got back to the parking lot where my van was, he showed me how the toy lawn mower could easily be rolled beneath my van to help me make some of my own safety checks in the future. Once the center orange portion that simulated where a motor would be was taken off, he laid a foot long, ten inch wide mirror atop the little toy and slanted it, so that I could see the undercarriage of the van. After attaching the mirror with duck tape, he walked with me around the van shoving the little rolling mirror under at several different locations. He showed me where a bomb was most likely to be placed below my van in the event my vehicle and I were the bombers next targets.

Each day before climbing into my van and starting the engine, I made a routine bomb check by shoving my little rolling mirror under the van and checking for dynamite or plastic explosive. I never found any bombs or anything suspicious but, two weeks later we had another bomb scare at our apartment. Unlike last time when the call came directly to our apartment, this time it was received by the live-in Egyptian building maintenance manager, Mohammed. He was scared. We Americans were causing too much trouble for his two buildings and he remarked how happy he'd be when we moved somewhere else.

CHAPTER 39

Prison Indignations

During the first week of December 1995, I continued working at the Superstation Radio as usual; but behind the scenes, up in the Minister of Information's office things continued getting worse for me. Little did I know that wheels were already in motion to "contain and silence" me. Several events were taking place simultaneously within the government of Kuwait that had a lot to do with what was to become of me, and how. The foremost had to do with a Kuwaiti family. They were pressuring the Crown Prince's office to lobby Washington hard against their son's imprisonment in Boston.

My boss, Kuwait's Minister of Information and former ambassador to the United States during the Gulf War had been asked by the Kuwaiti family to rally a powerful support team to free him. It would be up to the Minister and a group of attorneys and judges to become lobbyist against the American Justice system. After all, the young Kuwaiti was only doing what is legal in his own country and that was to own and enslave his maid.

Maia and I planned to go on Christmas vacation December 7th. Our scheduled departure aboard Olympic Air to the United States via Athens, Greece and Paris, France departs Kuwait International Airport at 11:30 p.m. Until that time, it appeared we were on schedule and ready to go.

My immediate supervisors at the Super Station went so far as or guarantee me everything would be straightened out with the finances when I returned the first week of January 1996. Permission for exit had been given and I had already picked up my exit papers.

An expatriate worker in Kuwait cannot depart without receiving these exit papers from his employer. The Department of Immigrations pulls all computer files and checks all grievance and unpaid bills the person leaving must settle before departure. These bills can include such incidentals and rent, phone bills, traffic tickets etc. A Kuwaiti may simply by his word, place a travel ban on anyone and it has to be resolved in the Kuwaiti's favor before the non Kuwaiti is allowed to exit the country's borders.

To say my arrest on the morning we were to depart for the Christmas holidays was a shock would be an under statement. Had it come a few days or weeks earlier and for different reasons, we would have understood. It would have still been a surprise but not a shock. There are several different ways the Minister of Information or His Highness could have dealt with my situation, but I guess to them my dilemma was a difficult one.

They could arrest me and take a chance that I would open a can of worms with clandestine information I knew, or they could take me into the desert never to return; or they could wait and find out whether all the information I have about them would be severely damaging if leaked to the public. If I was to be killed I could assure them that many little secrets would have already been in the right hands, and leaked to the public; theirs and ours back home. Hopefully when such information is released, some of the public's perception of Kuwait always as a victim would change. In any future show down between Kuwait and its neighbors, Kuwait may have to depend on her own Brotherly Arab States for protection and we all know how that would turn out.

The simplest thing would have been for them to have paid me for work already done. The worst scenario would be for me to end up disappearing in the desert late one night. Dead is so final.

Oh they kept saying they'd put me on trial for espionage and spying and they actually had gone so far as to hold my espionage pretrial in absentia. They also knew by the time I told the U.S. all the details; they'd have to come to my rescue and Kuwait would look like the fools they are.

All along I had been hoping Senator Daniel Patrick Moynihan was acting on the information that I had given him almost one year earlier about how Kuwait wanted to kill American soldiers and make it look like Saddam did it. Though, I still suspected that shortly after telling Senator Moynihan in New York of the Kuwaiti plans, he must have been the one that let the information slip back to the Kuwait government about what I had told him. Only two weeks following our meeting, I returned to Kuwait and everything started going down hill from there. I was later advised that a touchy subject had been breached, and Kuwait had investments in New York City and especially in the ports of New York. It was my guess that I had been sold out by my own side, once again for money.

I did think the Kuwait government might halt my reentry into the country following Christmas holiday vacation, but they had neither reason nor the ability to halt Maia from returning to her job at the United States Embassy. For this reason, we were content with leaving the pent house, our cats, vehicles, personal belongings and our bank accounts.

We weren't feeling threatened enough to transfer our non interest bearing, but non reportable hundreds of thousands of dollars to stateside accounts.

The way things turned out, the Kuwaitis followed their line of least likely scenario from the right thing to do. Like the show down with the Iraqis at the Jeddah Conference three days before invasion, they became their own worst enemy and chose to be lambs at the slaughter.

At that time, the Crown Prince remained hard headed against Iraqi demands rather than conceding a little money from his tight fist. Back then he caused the invasion of his own country by poor decision making. With me as with the Iraqis, the Kuwaitis remained arrogant and I felt made another poor decision. With them now in full pursuit of me there remained little for me to do other than continue my attack 'Damn all consequences, full steam ahead."

In 1990 the Crown Prince's bad decision resulted in the Gulf War, thousands of people killed including many of his own countrymen, thousands taken hostage, his country's economy totally wrecked and debts in the billions of dollars; but the Kuwaitis remained arrogant and played the role of victim throughout. For such influential men in many countries it would have caused the person who screwed up so badly to commit "Hara-kiri" or jump from a skyscraper but not a Kuwaiti, life just went on normally without any shame. This was the mentality I was up against.

The first time, their huge wallets and their American and British friendships saved their asses. They ended up with their nation restored to them, their palaces and their bank accounts back under their control and someone else, not Kuwaitis fought their battle for them. In their case with me, the consequences won't be anything like having another Gulf War befall them, but I'll make sure it will cost them plenty.

The Kuwaitis carried out their little plan to arrest and imprison me and use me as a chess pawn to free their young rich slave Master from the Boston prison. The Kuwaitis flexed their muscle at Ambassador Crocker and cast me as the bad guy, and won.

Ambassador Crocker was knowledgeable of only what the Kuwaitis were willing to tell him and it was enough for him. Not once did the Ambassador request a meeting with me to find out if there was another side to the story, nor any extenuating circumstances. To him, I was an embarrassment to the Embassy, a trouble maker who wanted to be paid by a Kuwaiti and then had a fight. Representation of my side through the Embassy Counselor Section stayed in a "containment" mode without ever investigating what really caused my imprisonment. It was easier for the Embassy to believe I was a bad boy beating up people who owed me money. Actually all Kuwaitis owe people money and usually get away without paying. It's the Kuwaiti way. I just took them to task for it; I didn't come here for the scenery.

Kuwait had to have an American in prison before there could be a prisoner swap for their guy in Boston. It didn't take a genius to figure out which American it would be. Outside of Linda Lou at the Super Station and the ambassador, I was the most well known American in the country. My bosses could solve so many problems at one time. Had they put me on trial as a spy, a lot of legal and illegal activities the Kuwaitis were involved in would become public. To imprison me on the simpler charge of "assault" squelched any chance I had of the Embassy rescuing me. It left me with little I could say because I knew the situation could have been much worse. I could have been executed by firing squad as a spy or beheaded at the mosque next to the Governorate. None of this could happen if I was brought up on just "assault" charges. It would not be in my best interest or my good friend Ghassan's who was arrested with me to start throwing out a lot of accusations or revealing high profile illegal activities now. If I started fighting dirty, there was no doubt in my mind Ghassan would be the first casualty. The Kuwaitis would probably have killed him and used it as a warning to me.

In Kuwait, a bad boy like the Minister of Information in such high position is dangerous. He controls censorship within the country much the way the former Soviet Union used to. Everything, including all stories and news on television, radio, newspapers and magazines as well as what is stated publicly an Universities and in all social groups and organizations is approved or allowed to pass only by the grace of the Minister of Information. The people of Kuwait only get to know what he and his staff wants them to know. With that kind of power, is it hard to believe he and his cousin, the next ruler of the country contrived such charges against me and blew them out of proportion?

While the young Kuwaiti sat comfortably in a prison near Boston, his family and Government steamrolled over their sympathetic ally the Ambassador and the United States Embassy. The charges brought against me were true but the facts and the wronged party was changed to favor the Kuwaiti. It was true a Kuwaiti Advertising Agency owner owed me money, and it was true he started a fight with me in his office but it wasn't true that he was the wronged party. He lied to his family and he lied to his own legal system. The fight between me and the Kuwaiti seven months before my arrest was not only settled and forgotten, but was reopened solely as a maneuver to gain a bargaining chip for the Kuwaiti's prison release. The wealthy Kuwaiti family had to try everything to get their son out of prison in the United Stated. I was just a pawn; my destiny was of no consequence to them at all.

My Palestinian friend and former coworker, Ghassan Abu Omar, a Civil Engineer who was arrested with me was a tragedy of injustice. Ghassan was innocent from day one. He was purely a victim of circumstance by a Government who hates Palestinians and Jordanians. Ghassan was with me when the Kuwaiti started the fight but I whipped the Kuwaiti alone. Ghassan and I knew it would have been impossible for a Palestinian in Kuwait to raise a hand to a Kuwaiti. I neither asked him for help, nor did he give it. We both knew they would have chopped his head off after prayer services at the mosque on Friday or he would have been killed in an accident arranged for him by the police.

Ghassan and Ruba's family suffered all the inconveniences, dangers, and financial downfalls associated with imprisonment of a loved one in Kuwait, and for no reason other than his association with me; and that he happened to witness the fight. I had never divulged one piece of sensitive information to Ghassan of my work for the Americans, Brits, or the Crown Prince nor of my trips into Iraq or investigating Islamic Fundamentalist. It wasn't that I didn't trust him, but such things are not heaped upon friends like you might on a wife. Even all our Embassy friends had no idea I was involved in such a wide range of activities.

I will always believe Ambassador Crocker received warnings about my dangerous intelligence gathering activities. He had to have known I received and placed calls through the Embassy back to other organizations for whom I was providing information. If he wasn't standing up for me now, there was no reason to believe he would; even if I turned over a lot of relevant information to him after my imprisonment. I never felt I could trust him. He had a job to do, bring money into the United States Treasury, and he was doing it. He had to associate closely with Kuwaitis in powerful positions to keep billions of dollars in arms sales rolling in. It was his responsibility to boost revenues for the American Commerce Department. It is yet another matter to try to collect all debts owed by Kuwait.

I was told by the Counselor Section of the American Embassy less than a week after my arrest, if it was between winning my freedom or the United States continuing to bring in billions of dollars in arms sales and contracts to Kuwait; which one would win.

The attorney that was recommended to represent Ghassan and me was already part of the larger Kuwaiti plot even before we got him. Those owing me money and those wanting to clear the Kuwaiti in an American prison were the same. They were creating the situation and controlling it. The United States Embassy laid back and rode it. My attorney Sheikh Salem al Tamimi was either told never to go on the offense or never to implicate higher ups; or he learned not to do it on his own.

I was in prison and primed for a prisoner swap, the Kuwaitis had silenced me and kept the monies they owed me; which is anti Islamic (you are always to be paid for good work done). Our side had even allowed me to be discredited to our own embassy in an effort to rollover. Everything was in favor of the Kuwaitis now and I was just where they wanted me. They didn't however count on me becoming ill.

During the seventeenth day of my suffering the effects of cold weather, torture, verbal abuse, legal setbacks and squallered conditions, my body started shutting down. It was a degrading shock for me knowing that my mental intentions of staying resolute and fighting were being sabotaged by my own body. Even as early as ten days ago, my body started contradicting my will.

June, the Medical Officer from the United States Embassy came to see me that morning with another embassy official Paul Blankenship. They were quite concerned over the amount of weight I had lost is such a short period of time and the swelling from my thigh down. I had had a hip replacement on that side several years earlier. My leg had swelled so much; circulation was being cut off by my pants.

June's portable scale showed I had lost more weight than any of us had suspected, down from 188 to 139. I had told them days ago about the occasional chops the policemen would give me to the throat and upper chest, but now maybe they could see for themselves it had an effect on my eating. June also suspected an infection because my temperature stayed at 103.

I had mentioned to June that a Kuwaiti doctor was administering shots to me nightly and warning me they contained aids virus and cancer but she shrugged it off like she thought I was delusional. I expected that she had been programmed by the embassy to keep me a little at bay. She was very nice and comforting but when I told her things the Kuwaitis had done, she didn't even ask follow up questions or make any following conversation.

Little did June or I realize at the time, that within the next several hours, my temperature would spike and I would lie down on the hard filthy floor of my jail cell and never feel like getting up again. A medical team (I forget now whether they were Kuwaiti or American) came to my assistance and prepared me once again for transport to al Razi Hospital.

Fearing it would be the last time I would have a combination of physical assistance and personal strength, I asked to make what I thought would be my final telephone call to Maia. She was already in New York and it would take longer to contact her so I sent for Betty Lippold the Arab Times reporter friend. I wanted her to know what was going on while imprisoned. Under guard, I made the call to Betty from an ambulance stretcher in the prison office.

The telephone call and subsequent transfer to the prison office and the hospital came after policemen came into my cell, shackled my ankles and cuffed my writs, and then lifted me by the chains like a sow on a spit onto the awaiting stretcher.

Betty and Abdullah headed straight for the al Razi Hospital Emergency Room. While the guards manhandled me, I was still chained and in a wheelchair. Betty and Abdullah kept asking questions and photographing me. There has never been any doubt that Betty played an integral part in making the public inside Kuwait aware of my captivity and dilemma. Her story and Abdullah's picture made front page of the Arab Times the next day.

On December 19, 1995 the Arab Times front page read:

The American Charles Petty formerly broadcasting the news every morning on Kuwait's Super Station Fm 92.5 before being arrested on assault charges was hospitalized last evening for the second time in two days. He was taken to Mubarek al Kabir Hospital Tuesday complaining of severe pain to the right leg and hip. The following day as the medication wore off, the pain returned. Petty was taken by ambulance to the al Razi Hospital Orthopedic Ward where he will remain under police custody. He is scheduled to return to court again on December 23 for further sentencing in the al Enzi versus Petty abu Omar.

Unfortunately many Kuwaitis don't read the English translated paper and many things in the Arabic version are deleted as subversive.

Betty said when the photo of me desperately ill, chained, sitting in a wheelchair returned to her office and the editing desk after being developed, it had a note attached saying it would not go to print. Warnings in Kuwait are not to be taken lightly, but Betty worked later than almost the entire newspaper staff just so she could sneak it in.

As I lay ravenous and delirious with fever, prison guards remained at my bedside. The shackles and hand cuffs had been removed. Only the chafed and rubbed raw imprints remained. Two guards remained bedside and another two just outside either side of the door.

Some of the guards were quite pleasant and others wanted little or no conversation with me. Most of the time, I just lay there rotating between sleep and a drowsy awareness. When I felt well enough to speak to a few of the guards, I did so and enjoyed their company. All of them were quite inquisitive about how an American came to be in a situation like this. They like most Arabs were unaware of why I was here, but were well aware of the Kuwaiti prisoner being held in Boston.

While speaking with the guards, I was careful not to incriminate the Royal Family or the Minister of Information, because it would only alienate me twenty four hours a day. Any battle I would wage against my foe would be done later, if I survived at all.

When I felt better and ready to sit up, the guards became friendlier and began asking questions (in Arabic of course) about my wife and family and about life in the United States; life before now in Kuwait and how I liked the Royal Family. I had to skirt that last part because I knew a lot more about their royals than they did; after all, Kuwaiti Royals have very little to do with their common public.

My rapport with them grew better as time passed. One morning one of them even brought me a special tool to unscrew the windows, for me to make a prison break. I told him thanks a lot but I was so weak that I'd have to have someone outside the window to drag me away on a sheet because I couldn't walk. We both got a pretty good laugh out of picturing that escape.

Three Kuwaiti policemen came to the hospital just after noon and told the nurses that I had to go somewhere. As I tried to over hear their conversation, I thought they said someone from my embassy wanted to meet with me. The nurse on duty obliged the policemen and brought in my civilian clothes to be dressed on me by the Indian attendant.

My right thigh was still terribly swollen but not as much as a few days earlier before being admitted to al Razi Hospital. The policemen though pleasant shackled me and cuffed me and anchored them together with a leather belt around my waist and chained them all together. The policemen then threw each of my arms up and over their shoulders and we were off to the awaiting squad car.

Soon after departing the hospital, the squad car turned away from the intended route of either the American Embassy or the Courts Building downtown and I knew I was in trouble. I also knew I had no way to neither halt, nor even delay what was coming. Momentarily, we entered a side street that led to the north entry of the Police Academy.

They wasted no time slapping me in the face and dragging me first by the chains and later by my shirt collar. I was slammed down stomach first on the cold ceramic tiled floor, and then as I haphazardly tried to struggle to my feet, I was body slammed to the floor once again, this time much harder. Just moments after being slammed horizontally, one of the policemen grabbed my ear and pinched it so hard I thought he'd cut it. He proceeded to drag me a short distance by a grip on the ear and one handful of hair on my head. I don't know which hurt most.

In what seemed like the next few minutes, I was dragged to an almost barren, darkened, four walled concrete room where two ten feet tall A-framed ladders and four policemen stood. The ladders stood side by side and reached almost to the concrete ceiling, where a lone steel hook protruded downward. Two of the already waiting policemen laughed and gestured with those bringing me in. Their sign language seemed to be mimicking that I was to be hoisted up the ladders or something.

My assumption was correct. Two policemen took my legs and the other two stretched me out by taking hold of the upper torso. They lay me flat on the cold, damp concrete where they detached the chains, leather waist band, the cuffs and leg irons. I began freezing and shivering as they stripped me of my clothing and began wrapping me in additional chains that could easily have been use to moor or anchor a fair sized boat. They had already reattached the wide leather waistband to me, and the new chains started around the neck and kept wrapping until they reached my ankles.

Now mummy style, they carried me a few feet in horizontal position and then in unison hoisted me toward the ladders. They slung my body upwards above their shoulders then two pushed while two carried me to the top. One pair of hands balanced my upper body while the other attached my big steel bindings and leather waistband to the hook on the ceiling.

Nude, wrapped in steel mummy style and freezing, I hung from my stomach for a mercilessly long time. First my guts wrenched and then contorted from the weight as I stretched outward in a feeble attempt to stop the arching of my back. Soon there was no fighting and no strength left and nothing in my bowels. I rotated from swimming dizziness to blackout.

I convulsed and quieted only to convulse again and again. There were intervals of excruciating pain shooting throughout my body, the groin area and my right side; especially where I had many surgeries following an automobile crash in 1984 in Arizona. My toes felt as though they were wrapped in ice.

Strangely enough, time was the key factor. My body fell at rest, almost peacefully. Opposite ends of my body hung lifeless, drooping downward toward the floor in an arch. The blood within me filled my head so it felt like pilots might feel while experiencing negative G forces. My eyes protruded and the ears barely functioned' barely auditing muffled sounds.

When I was finally taken down, I convulsed one final time as my body came to rest on the cold ceramic floor. Several minutes into my recuperation, I looked up at the standing policemen who had been joined by another man familiarly similar to the doctor who nightly administers the syringes. Up to his old tricks again huh, and I was out.

I don't remember being returned to my hospital room but when I became conscious; I lay exhausted and wrenched with a blinding headache. They could have unloaded me into a trash dumpster and I would have been content. I remembered over and over again a policeman telling me "You speak of doctor and we make for Falistini same same.

That night was my worst since being jailed. I became delusional and dreamed the nurse came in and made me stand in the bed. She held my legs as I attached my hands to a trapeze and began swinging. I swung higher and faster as the crowds cheered and cool breezes surrounded me. I yelled to the crowds that my grand finale would be to somersault into the giant ice cream sundae.

Of course the next morning, I asked the Filipina nurse what happened because everyone was acting so normal. She said I had a rough night tossing and turning and moaning loudly. She said my fever stayed around 105 for awhile but it appears the medication was working and it has dropped quite a bit now. The IV drip they had put during the night had been torn out and I bled a lot but everything was going just fine now. The IV would remain in until my body recovered some more. Obviously, the Kuwaiti guards suppose to be watching me neither saw all the blood; or didn't care. I choose to think they were on the floor beside me sleeping on duty.

Paul Blankenship from the Embassy Counselor Section and several other American Embassy people showed up the next morning saying they came to inform me the al Enizi Klan had an agreement drawn up that would exonerate Abdul Kareem and the Klan against future lawsuits brought by me. The agreement stated our good intentions toward Abdul Kareem and the al Enizi family.

It turned out Ghassan's physical condition was better than mine but his plight and daily life in Kuwait Central prison was worse.

The first break in my assault case came after the al Enizi heard I was preparing defense by a group of high powered American lawyers. They were also intimidated when word got out that the United States State Department was getting involved. I told the judge in front of Abdul Kareem's father that I no longer wanted the money he owed me but I am pressing for a travel ban against the al Enizi family entering the United States twice a year. I want their relationship with the mosque and family in Michigan stopped.

The United States Embassy didn't hang me out to dry, but wanted little to do with my case other than end it. They constantly badgered me to end this vendetta for money. They understand how Kuwaitis are and that's that. Money leaving the Kuwaitis fist is hard to get even if by Islamic law you have earned it.

The U. S. Embassy just wanted me to get healthy and move on. Sign the Exoneration Agreement, and move on.

My only immediate reward was to find out that the Kuwaitis efforts had been unsuccessful in getting their client al Zanki out of prison in Boston. He would have to serve the entire sentence on slavery charges until June 5, 1997. According to the agreement, the Al Enizi Klan was not to receive from me or the State Department a demand of $185,000. ransom. However at this time we did not know that Mine and Maia's entire bank account At Kuwait National had already gone missing. Neither of us had signed any document legally releasing it nor access to it so therefore it had to be some high official usually an Al Sabah Royal family member who stole it and made it look as though it never existed. Even worse than having hundreds of thousands of dollars wiped out was that our safety deposit boxes were also gone with more than a million to two million in gold bars, coins and Dowry jewelry.

All our savings from seven and a half years work and all the gold we had acquired were gone with no explanation. Kuwaiti citizens control foreigner's entry or exit with a phone call and now I found out they can do the same with something as personal as a private bank account.

The primary objective remained to get Ghassan and me out of prison and get my health back. The battle for our bank account, my back pay and whatever else I wanted to do legally would have to come at a later time.

The American Embassy Counselor Section made the final solution sound so easy: first I should sign the document saying I would not legally seek retribution against the Al Enizi Klan, then the prison doors would magically fly open. The only other thing that had to be done was go to the Courthouse in a couple of days, appear before a judge, resign the same document in front of him and we'd be free. Everything sounded so easy but it wasn't.

The Bastards had won on all points; I was imprisoned for assault by a Kuwaiti who attacked me. There is still no payment forthcoming from the Ministry or Dasma Palace, our bank accounts have been emptied and my health is gone.

Some of this could have been avoided if I knew the rules by which I was playing. That's important in third world countries the same as in second and in super power nations like ours in the United States. The Egyptian District Attorney seven months earlier had advised me not to press charges (unknowing at the time, in Kuwait if you do not press charges this is seen as admission of guilt on your part). Though Kuwait has a legal president on paper that says the accused is to receive notice, charges were filed against me, a court date had been scheduled and held and yet there had never been a posting of any notice of any kind. The Criminal Investigations office which was headed by my attacker's father saw to it that we were never aware of anything going on. And now, to contest any part of the "Exoneration Agreement" would result in me and Ghassan having to immediately begin our three and a half year prison sentence at hard labor; this time with American Embassy's blessings.

Kuwait was going through another one of their legal-illegal systematic robberies of foreigners who had come to work for them. Not only had our bank account and deposit boxes been emptied, but the Ministry of Information automatically dropped all past salary disputes because of unauthorized days of work I missed while imprisoned.

The Ministry of Information went even further to slam the door on me and my past salary grievances. They drew up paperwork showing in the years of my employee there, I had never worked full time for them, though I averaged forty five hours each week as opposed to the average Kuwaiti putting in less than thirty hours weekly which was considered full-time. Part-time employment also meant that at termination, neither the Minister of Information nor Dasma Palace had to pay my three months severance pay.

During my hospitalization, I had been permitted to place several international calls back to the United States. I called Maia in New York and my family in Savannah, Georgia. Maia had the best communications of all. She was constantly being apprised of my situation and the court proceedings by some of our dear friends at the American Embassy and by the Charge D'Affair Georgia DeBell and Counsel General Kevin Richardson. Not just our friends, but the Embassy itself was very good about sending Maia faxes with daily updates and relaying hers to me. Only my brothers in Georgia and my father knew what was happening to me in Kuwait and had been keeping mother in the dark about the whole situation, because she was delaying heart surgery for Maia and me to be there with the rest of the family.

No one but me really knew what was going on and there was little reason to complain or upset anyone else. All I could do is bare it and hope I'd be freed before my health became even worse. Three more days of torture followed. Each day the weight of the chains met less resistance. By the third and fourth days, my back easily slipped into its arched position allowing the weight of the chains to thrust my head and feet toward the floor nearly making my feet touch the back of my head. Each day as the one before, my bowels released and the stench in the room was almost as bad as my original prison cell of unwashed slaves. Each day the policemen would come in to get me and the nurses would prepare and dress me as if I was being taken for a meeting with Embassy staff.

The policemen would haul me away in chains and cuffs. Each day they took off my clothes. Lay me on the hard cold floor of the Kuwait Police Academy, wrap me in heavy cold chains, hoist me up the ladder and make lewd comments and gestures while I hung suspended by my stomach from a ceiling hook. Each day I would black out from the pain, convulse several times, loose my bodily functions, receive injections and return to my hospital room looking only a little paler and more tired from my troubles. Each time, the policemen carried me back to their car deposited me in a wheelchair at the hospital and casually rolled me back to my guarded but warm room.

Chapter 40

"I am Beaten"

It was an upside down world for me. The policemen would torture me and the doctors would help me get well enough to be tortured some more. My doctors would x-ray me, give me IV medications and would try to stabilize my weight loss. They brought my fevers under control and provided me with a clean, warm bed in which to sleep. Then the whole process would repeat itself again.

For obvious reasons the swelling in my hip and leg refused to go down. Between the second day of my incarceration and the beginning of the second week I had been punched in the stomach so often and chopped in the throat that I found it quite hard to swallow and digest food. Actually, I was so sore in the chest and stomach cavity that it was just easier not to eat, although once in a while I did. I have no doubts that Kuwaiti policemen are taught how, when and where to punch people in the abdomen without evidence of severe bruising. Their expertise in this area became familiar to me on a regular basis, but once again the technique of my torture would change.

The fourth day at the Police Academy was different. First the policemen put a dental x-ray bit in the lower half of my mouth and forced me to bite down. With one policeman's hands holding my mouth shut so tight that I felt the bit cut into my lower gums. Within a short time I began tasting blood in my mouth but was unable to remove the policeman's hands and spit, so I swallowed it. This continued for about a half hour while my hands remained cuffed behind me and my leg irons stayed in place on my ankles. At times I almost gagged to death but the policeman's hands continued their relentless crushing to my head and jaw even as I radically threw my head back and forth. By now the blood was coming from my upper gums as well.

When the policeman finally let go, I thought my troubles were over but he swung around and with great force slugged me in the stomach and I projected in his direction the dental bit, saliva and blood that had filled my mouth. It was worth getting the next punch in the abdomen just to see his look in horror at his own blood spattered uniform. That punch was not the last that day, nor the last I'd receive over the next couple mornings to come.

The hospital was only too cooperative with Kuwait's policemen each morning in taking me away to the Police Academy and I remained silent for Ghassan's sake. Word from him said he wasn't doing well mentally. The ordeal was taking a great toll on him and his family. I knew they couldn't kill me, but they could still kill Ghassan, so I endured what was necessary to help repay my obligation to him.

One afternoon, my doctor returned with the latest x-rays of my right foot, leg and hip. He said I'd probably have to have another hip replacement and a knee operation but the main thing at this time was to get the fever and swelling in both areas down.

By now, I was having even more trouble eating but I had come to the reality I must not grow weaker for my own sake. I must force myself to eat. If the punches to my stomach, the hanging by my stomach muscles were painful, surely eating couldn't be so bad. I began eating at least part of everything brought to me. Hopefully soon after I signed the "Exoneration Agreement", I would be allowed to leave the prison and head to America. I sure didn't want any delay in that happening. Food became my priority.

The day of the initial signing of the "Exoneration" documents before the Counselor Section came. Paul Blankenship from the Embassy came with Fathi, the Embassy's interpreter in tow. I signed and shed some tears and the first part of the ordeal was over. The next signing would take place whenever the Al Enizi Klan and their judge felt the time was right.

Prison security guards remained at my bedside and on either side of the doorway to my hospital room even though the case was supposed to be over. Because they remained, I thought the signing of the papers could be yet another Kuwaiti trick.

Things started looking up though. A steady stream of visitors began pouring in to see me and wish me well. Ghassan was still in the hell hole Central Prison and I felt terrible for him and Ruba, but for me at least there appeared to be an end to all the madness. Ruba came daily to visit me as her normal cheery self, bringing McDonald's hamburgers and French fries but of course I couldn't really eat much of them, just nibble at them to show my gratitude. Ruba didn't show her hardship outwardly, but I knew she and Ghassan lost a lot of money because of this whole incident in which Ghassan was never guilty to start with.

In the true "Kuwaiti Way," Ghassan's Kuwaiti sponsor used the imprisonment to gather what riches he could. He demanded Ghassan sign legal papers stating all monies collected from rental of Gus's heavy equipment (bulldozers, 966 loaders and dump trucks) would be collected by the sponsor (his legal partner according to Kuwaiti Law). Several of the bigger, costlier pieces were working the Sabaiya Power Plant Project across the bay from Kuwait City. The sponsor "swore to Allah" he would bring all the money to Ghassan's wife Ruba. In typical Kuwaiti style though, he used the delegating paper to collect the money legally, then confiscated it for the Embarrassment Ghassan brought upon him. The sponsor had already brought in a little over eight thousand dollars and kept it all.

The Kuwait continued using the dateless "Power of Attorney" letter for more than four more months after Ghassan was freed. The total kept from Ghassan and Ruba by the Kuwaiti was over thirty-two thousand dollars.

The sponsor then had the audacity to beg Ghassan's forgiveness for his greed and please allow him to remain his "sponsor" collecting his normal 1.5 percent of all Ghassan's income following release from prison (of course he would be unable to return any of the already collected money). Ghassan knowing he would be thrown out of the country and his equipment seized and given by the State of Kuwait to the sponsor, accepted the Kuwaitis apology and continued his indentured servitude to him. This was also the time for another "Power Play" by the Kuwaiti, so another paper was delivered to Ghassan's address requiring him to sign for an additional boost of 1.0 percent income to the Kuwaiti or life for Ghassan and his family would become unbearable now that Ghassan had a prison record. This new raise in the Kuwaitis income would provide his children a better lifestyle, "The Kuwaiti Way" at someone else's expense.

On the morning of December 17, the United States Embassy council staff of Paul Blankenship and the interpreter came to the hospital early. They told me the hospital staff would soon be making me ready for release and travel to the United States but first I had to make the final court appearance. I should soon begin getting dressed because the Court expected to hear my case that morning.

It was raining and cold outside. The nurses said since I didn't have a jacket or anything heavy to wear they'd tell the policemen to allow me to keep the hospital blanket around me. The nurse removed my IV drip before bringing my clothes and a male nurse assistant helped me dress. The nurse came back in to take my temperature while the policemen put my hands in cuffs and my ankles in leg irons. Then they wrapped my waist again in the wide leather belt and attached both the handcuffs and leg iron chains to it.

My temperature was still 103 and my cough was terrible and deep, so I should be kept warm during transport said the nurse. The doctor came in for a minute also and said he told the policemen to allow me to lie down in the patrol car seat because I was still unable to sit up for long periods of time.

Within minutes the policemen lead me through the hospital's main exit into an awaiting police car. I walked slowly because it had been more than a week since I had stood for more than a couple of minutes, much less walked. I felt the weight of the leg irons as if I was dragging several bowling balls. I continued to walk especially slowly because the cold irons were also rubbing my sockless ankles raw.

Once the two policemen and I arrived at the squad car, they removed my light blue wool blanket and left it beside the curb in the parking lot. For the few minutes it took them to unlock the car doors, recheck my chains and step on my foot I was nearly frozen. I knew through their procrastination, I was in trouble again. I stood along side the police car getting wetter and colder while they sat inside talking over something. A soaking rain ran down my back and into my pants. My hair had already been wet a little from the sweats that morning so within minutes I felt like someone was making me wear a bag of melting ice atop my head, and inside my underpants.

Soon after being shoved into the back seat of the squad car, I asked "Could I have some heat please?" The policeman sitting on the passenger side of the front seat turned and said to me "I am al Enizi." That said it all; he was part of the family I was imprisoned for. Before another word came out of his mouth, he turned on the air conditioner and put the fan on high. He and the other policeman then directed their air vents in my direction for maximum effect toward the back seat. The al Enizi said "you like this?" I said did you like Saddam's visit to Kuwait?" "I hear the Americans are going to pull out and Saddam is coming back, ha ha."

We rode through several miles of city streets while I froze. I shivered in silence without giving them the satisfaction they so patiently listened for; but I'm sure my teeth's chatter gave away my silent agony. All I had on was a tee shirt, trousers and coverlets on my feet. No long sleeve shirt, no jacket, no socks, only hospital slip-on shoes.

As we arrived at the rear of the Security fenced Courts building, my driver pulled within fifty feet of what appeared to be a loading dock for tractor trailer trucks. It didn't take long for me to figure out the boys had a little more discomfort in mind for me. After pulling me from the car and taking my hospital slippers away, the policemen told me to lie across the hood of the car. When I didn't put my chest down on the cold wet hood, they pushed me down on it until full contact was made. Now I was brutally cold and really wet.

The outside temperature was cold enough for me to see my breath, but felt much colder because between abuse and torture, I had been sequestered in a warm hospital room for quite some time. The winds picked up a little, driving the bone chilling weather further into my body like knives searching for a waterbed heater. I was kept alone, standing beside the car for almost twenty minutes as the rain got harder and then quit. Then it got harder again. Both men stood under the loading dock's overhang enjoying what they were seeing as I got more and more drenched and more and more frozen. They carried on a conversation with another man in dishdasha as I strained to hear them. All I could hear though was laughter, then a little more talking; then the sound of more rain drops hitting my ear.

Soon, I began shivering uncontrollably. I was then brought indoors but kept in a passageway where the outgoing draft was like a chimney.

The man I was sure was an al Enizi told them to take me somewhere, but I couldn't hear where. I thought it couldn't be worse than the other places I'd been; so I gladly followed them, shivering, teeth chattering and limping badly; I followed them while I dragged my chains.

The room where the Kuwaiti man in dishdasha put me adjoined the delivery bay, and had iron bars and a small gate to a cage; where prisoners could remain in temporary lockdown. The Kuwaiti with the two policemen in tow led me to the cell; then spat in my face (Kuwaitis are real spitters) then gave me a swift knee into my hugely swollen right thigh. It was as if a giant bumblebee had bitten into the muscle. There was an immediate charley-horse effect, dropping me to the cell floor.

Just as I began regaining my composure and getting to my knees the Kuwaiti administered another right knee to the side of my head. I lay dazed but conscious as my hospital shoes were thrown at me with instructions to put them on before I leave. I would be going upstairs to the court room within an hour. For the duration of that remaining time, I sat on the cold floor of the room with my back against the wall just trying to get my sense back. The Kuwaitis spit was now making its way further down along my cheek and I was too tired and hurt to do anything but stay pushed into the cold cinder blocks.

The abuse for now was over and the spit and clothing were drying from my body heat and what little heat was in the cell. Regaining my composure was taking a little more time following each set back. The great urge to vomit passed and came again.

For several minutes, maybe a lot longer, I remained disoriented but could ascertain that getting me up to the court room was fully under way.

I was sure everyone would see my swollen head and partially wet condition as soon as we entered the court room, but apparently no one did; or they didn't care. This time I grew angry at the ambassador himself because at first I could see him and he just kept looking away; not wanting to see me or the condition I had been delivered in. I couldn't understand if he wasn't here for me, then why had he come at all?

Instead of taking the elevator up in the Justice Building, they made me climb the stairs to the fourth floor. It was on this climb I realized there was permanent damage to my hip and something else.

Not only was my leg unprepared for that stairwell ascent, but for the first time I realized how really deep my cough was getting too. I coughed and coughed and coughed some more. It was on my way up the stair well that I also first learned to play a little game in my head. Each time I felt a kick or a blow to the head or the cough hurt too much, I played like it was a reality game on a computer. It could happen there without really happening to me personally. Maybe crazy now, but I think it made me feel better then. In reality now, I would play that same game but with soldiers from Saddam Hussein's army torturing Kuwaitis.

Kuwaitis have a whole history of cruelty to those who serve them and that barbarism was repaid when Saddam's troops entered Kuwait City for the first time. The Bedouins and the Filipinas, Palestinians, the Egyptians and the Indians and Bangladeshis turned in their Masters to the Iraqis to deal out some torture or some vindictiveness of their own. I can't believe the world sided with Kuwait and the Occupation of the country only lasted seven months.

I entered the court room dragging my chains ahead of the two policemen. I could see Ghassan had already been brought into the room and was sitting in a chair in the holding cell, behind bars; in the front of the court room off to the Judges right side. The U. S. Embassy Counselors and my attorney sat inattentively in the second pew only partially acknowledging my entry, and certainly making no effort to visit with me a moment before the trial started.

I was extremely weak now and I wanted to pass out or throw up, I didn't know which. It turns out I was only there to witness one more cruel act by my captors. In full view of the entire court room, the al Enizi policeman motioned for me to lie on the cell floor instead of sitting like Ghassan and the other prisoners. Actually I was relieved, because I don't know how much longer I could have set up right if I wanted to.

My first sight of Ghassan was sickening. I barely recognized him. He appeared like a fundamentalist Muslim. His eyes were very dark and recessed and his head had been shaven, his beard had grown unattended, he was wearing a dirty white robe and sandals; and he too had lost a lot of weight.

Sometime during the court hearing, I started moaning for Paul Blankenship from the Counselor Section to come help me. Instead, Fathi, the interpreter from the embassy came to the cell to look at me, but never inquired as to why I lie cuffed to the floor instead of being sat upright like the other prisoners. I told him the men had been torturing me again and he said "look, you're going to make things a lot worse for yourself if you tell Paul and he has to tell the Ambassador once again how you're acting. Ambassador Crocker told us before we left the Embassy that He didn't want any more trouble out of you."

I said "I don't think you understand, He said" I think you don't understand. The Ambassador is pissed at you Charles for all the trouble you've caused and you'd better get one thing straight. The embassy doesn't stand behind you on your problems and the Ambassador says we should make you sign the paper ands get you the hell out of the country. He then walked away.

I remembered the judge and several others talking after the room was called to order, but I didn't really understand what was going on. I continued being dizzy and disoriented and also moaning. Finally the judge ordered someone (I don't remember who) to uncuff me and walk me to his chambers behind the court room. I also slightly remember passing by the front of those assembled to accuse me.

Within a few minutes, the judge and all participants showed up to resolve our differences in favor of the Kuwaitis behind closed doors. He said "are you all ready to sign this binding agreement?" I said "I'm forced to do so or I fear that your people will kill me". He said "nonsense" and passed the papers for both of us to sign.

One thing the Kuwaitis really believe in is the "evil eye". When Abdul Kareem was asked to show no hard feelings after winning, he tried and I refused to shake his hand. I told him in a low voice "The evil eye is for you and your family".

Again the judge asked everyone to shake hands and again I refused. I didn't want Abdul Kareem's shit wiping hand on mine now or ever.

Following the signing of all legal documents by all parties, I was returned to the Hospital via the same two policemen and police car that had done all the little tortures on me. Before I left the judges chambers, I once again tried to talk to Paul Blankenship and he again pulled away. The Kuwaitis on this day had another glorious day in court.

Following an uneventful return to the hospital, my turncoat Kuwaiti attorney al Tamimi showed up asking a very unusual favor of me. He said "now that differences have been resolved, could you speak personally with Ambassador Crocker about posing for pictures with all the male members of the al Enizi male Klan members. I laughed hysterically and ask him if he knew what "fuck off means in Arabic"?

The next morning's Arab Times front page read:

Litigants sign to forgive and forget

The article read:

An agreement was signed Saturday between Abdul Kareem al Enizi, Charles Petty and Ghassan abu Omar for the first party to drop all charges against the other two parties. Neither party is to pursue the case any further, nor is the two accused to be deported from Kuwait. Lawyers for the defense and prosecution have been meeting daily in negotiations with their parties (which wasn't true) since the retrial hearing last Monday. Yesterday's hearing was held in the Court of First Instances under the jurisdiction of Judge Amiani. The judge met privately with each of the three litigants. He is expected to rule next Monday to allow both imprisoned parties to be released. Charles Petty and Ghassan abu Omar's sentences of three and a half years at hard labor are to be suspended with the unconditional dropping of charges with nothing in return. Until Judge Amiani makes his ruling official, both Ghassan abu Omar and Charles Petty will remain in custody. Mr. Petty is presently incarcerated at the al Razi Hospital and Mr. Omar is currently in Central Prison,

Upon my return to the hospital, I began speaking to the nurses about what the policemen had been doing to me. The nurses warned me to be very careful. Kuwaitis are vengeful people, with quick tempers and of limited education. "Always think it's not over yet." Sometimes they here at the hospital treat other foreigners for very serious wounds done to them in prison or by their Kuwaiti sponsors; but most of those injured are from third world countries and never come back. Some were so brutalized that the nurses knew they didn't just get better and go home.

As the Filipina and Indian nurses fussed over me, trying to take my temperature, freshen my water and juice pitchers and tuck my bed and fluffing my pillows, they each gave me their thoughts. They said never trust the al Enizi Klan, they're known as a group of men with a mob mentality who within the past several months sanctioned the gang style murder of the boyfriend of one of their young nieces. He was riddled with bullets in a neighborhood Bayan Co-op parking lot by several of the young al Enizi. Word on the street is that they openly boasted of their kill.

The nurses said it is not unlike Kuwaitis from families like the al Enizi to be financially supportive of those carrying out murderous vendettas against other nationalities while being bank rolled by the more business like al Enizi.

Even the doctor who talked to me about my ordeal reminded me that al Enizi and the al Sabah are close Klan's and frequently do anything they can get away with and cover each others backs, legally and illegally.

One of the stories a nurse told me while she attempted to straighten my covers was quite interesting. That nurse and several others had watched a television program in which Abdul Kareem al Enizi was being interviewed following my imprisonment. Abdul Kareem said he was enjoying the celebrity it was causing as was his father. He at one time also mentioned his recent trip to America and said while on business there, he was also given the opportunity to speak to a congregation in Detroit, Michigan and share with them the problems Muslims face at home with Americans and other nationalities trying to upset the moral fiber of an Islamic country. He said Americans should be forced to stay on Doha base and not allowed to interrupt the daily life of the good people of Kuwait.

I told them I would have thrown up if I would have heard such garbage. She said the second broadcast he appeared in Kuwait was with the backing of the young brother hood at the University of Kuwait where they too oppose Americans getting their hands on all the lucrative contracts and bases and port in Kuwait. They obviously didn't remember who just four years earlier had saved their asses and purse strings. It wasn't the Muslim Brotherhood or any other Muslim group or nation. It was our American men and women who fought the Gulf War to Liberate Kuwait. It was Americans who believe in God, we're not infidels as they call everyone from the West. Our God was omnipotent six hundred years before their Mohammed was even born.

By evening, the hospital was quiet and I was calming down from the day's events and the mistreatment outside the Justice Building. It was then that it entered my mind for the first time that I might be going home soon. Maia had called the hospital from New York about 8 p.m. Kuwait time. I explained some of the day's events to her, but of course I left out the part of the abuses. Maia said some of our best friends from the Embassy in Kuwait had been keeping her well informed on what they knew about twice a day. The Embassy would contact her about once a day to update her on the legal battles and about me in the hospital.

Maia said she was still trying to contact Senator Daniel Patrick Moynihan's office but was having no luck. They were either avoiding her calls or had left for the holidays. She assumed since we hadn't heard from him over the past year and even suspected it was he who had turned me in to the Kuwaitis; it was the first.

Maia said the next day she was going to a travel Agency in New York City to purchase an airline ticket for our trip to Savannah, Georgia once she learned the date. She said she would make them for the third of January in hopes that I would be there by then.

CNN representatives came to the hospital. Earlier they had been persistent about getting in to see me and about getting mine and Ghassan's story out. I however did my self an injustice and wouldn't allow them in. I knew that mother's life in the United States was hanging by a thread in the hospital, and news of my imprisonment on television would possibly be too much for her. I signed a document provided through the American Embassy halting any contact by CNN. (Big mistake)

The next morning, the Arab Times front page showed a picture of me lying in a hospital bed. It read:

COURT 'FREES' PETTY, ABU OMAR

RELEASE WITHOUT BAIL

Kuwait City . . . American Newscaster for the Kuwait Super Station Charles Petty and his Civil Engineer friend Ghassan abu Omar arrested on December 6 on criminal assault charges were released Monday afternoon on their own recognizance after a brief hearing in Judges Chambers. Judge Amiani told the Arab Times that both men were released without bail and he will be making his final decision on the matter December 25, Christian Christmas Day. Petty was helped from the prisoner's cage into the judge's private chambers while his friend Ghassan abu Omar remained seated in the cage.

The article went on to tell more about the judge's decision and what the prospect was for the present ruling to stand and the case to be dismissed.

For the next few days I remained hospitalized, warm, clean, pampered by the Filipina and Indian nursing staff and an IV drip continued as well. I continued getting stronger each day but my cough remained really bad and deep. The throat stayed inflamed and it remained difficult to carry on much of a conversation unless the other person was prepared to do most of the talking.

As expected, I received word from the court, the judge officially cancelled the three and a half years at hard labor sentence, and the doctor's news was equally good. In a few days, I'd be ready to travel. He reiterated "ready to travel, not well".

Ghassan was released a few days before me and was finally home with Ruba and their two young children. He of course was feeling much better. When he visited me in the hospital, we spoke of the luxury of taking warm showers and shaving again, but never spoke of the ordeal we had just been through. This adventure would surely bind us together though, for the rest of our lives.

On his second visit, Ghassan's description of where he was kept in Central Prison was atrocious. Much worse than where we started out together. He said he couldn't even accurately describe the squalled and horrid conditions and things that went on inside that prison. He said all the prisoners and the guards at Kuwait's Central Prison followed our trial closely and many prisoners had passed him notes with information and stories for me to take back to America. They hoped I'd be able to one day get the stories to the International Human Rights Organization that we were unable to see inside Kuwait.

One of mine and Ghassan's early cellmates had just been freed from Kuwait's Central prison and came to see me. He was a well educated Syrian who was transferred to the worst prison until he made amends to his Kuwaiti sponsor. A sponsor is sort of a Kuwaiti who owns part of you and your income while in Kuwait. Everyone has to have one. He was eager to personally tell me the story of a young Bangladeshi boy about twelve years old who was one of those serving "hard time" along side all the older males in the prison. He said in Central Prison, younger children stay with their mothers who are serving time but the youth about ten years old and older are thrown in with all men. The young Bangladeshi had no one inside Kuwait that could protect him from the greed, ruthlessness, and sexual appetite of his Kuwaiti sponsor.

At nine years old, the little boy had been sold by his parents to a Saudi Arabian who turned him into a camel Jockey. (A normal deal) Part of his contract said that a percentage of his winnings would be sent to the parents for each race won. With the Saudi, the contract had always been abided by; but the boy was sold for a very high price to a Kuwaiti following the year's biggest race, of which the boy had won. The Saudi kept up his part of the contract by sending the boys parents a part of the winnings, however, his Saudi sponsor sold the boy to a Kuwaiti for a premium price. The boy was brought to Kuwait where he worked for his sponsor for more than a half year. He jockeyed in several smaller races inside the country and in the United Arab Emirates but failed to win. The failure was not the fault of the boy but his Kuwaiti didn't own quality stock.

After never receiving any money from the Kuwaiti for all the races he had been in, the boy made demands on his Master. The Kuwaiti not only depended on the boy for the races but for sexual purposes in his chalet vacation house on the coast near Nuwaiseeb border with Saudi Arabia. The boy had no choice in the matter but to continue servicing his Master's friends as well. When he rebelled, the Master taught him a lesson by putting him in Central prison on Administrative hold; until he felt satisfied the boy repented enough. There was no date set for the little boy's release which is a Kuwaiti custom while on hold.

Within days of being thrown in with grown men, the boy had been shared by the majority of male inmates in his cell block. His pleas for help fell on deaf ears. They had been met by laughter and hostility. The guards had even taken their turns as they had with me in beating him and sodomizing the little boy. The child became lifeless and just sat or laid around against the walls after each time he was returned to the cell. He spoke to no one, not even lifting a hand in self defense. Another young Bangladeshi boy treated the same as this one was found lying in a pool of blood with his neck broken and genitals amputated two weeks prior to this Syrian's release. The Syrian told me that the little twelve years old was still there when he left.

Sexual abuse is not only tolerated but condoned by Kuwaiti's womanless society until the men reach twenty six to thirty years of age. They learn in early school days that they are to service the older boys and one day their turn will come to be the older boy. Most men do switch to more heterosexual behavior after marriage, but of course old habits die hard.

With no pomp or circumstances I was released from Kuwait prison custody at noon. The guards just disappeared without a word said. The last thing I knew was one handing me a handkerchief as I coughed up some blood; then he wasn't there any more.

I gathered my few belongings and called reporter Betty Lippold. Her husband, American Air Force Colonel retired, Carl Lippold came to take me on my ride to freedom. Doctors in their final meeting cautioned me to continue all medications until I could get to some physicians stateside. Now I would be leaving Kuwait, even if I had to crawl.

I gathered my packet of x-rays and a large amount of medication along with my few toiletries and walked very slowly down the hallway between all the nursing and doctor staff bidding me farewell and God speed. They had all been wonderful amongst the hell. Perhaps it was their knowledge and steadfast for me that kept the Kuwaitis from taking me into the desert never to be seen again. I stood at the hospital's Orthopedic Wing doorway for a few minutes alone in the quiet with no one around me talking.

Carl was on time and happy to see me packed and ready. We drove slowly and I enjoyed sitting and looking out the window at bland Kuwait City. We passed nearby the former Iraqi Embassy is Sha'ab district where the Colonel, Betty and Abdullah live and I couldn't help but wonder whether the next time I drove down this boulevard, (not in the near future of course) whether it would still be Kuwait or Iraq once again. I know one thing, if I hear Saddam is on the way, the American forces may be against me but I'll be acting as a tour guide showing the Iraqis in.

Since Kuwaitis have learned nothing from their past they are destined to repeat it. Carl dropped me off at the pent house and allowed me to be alone, but the telephone never stopped ringing. It was still hard for me to carry on my end of the conversation because of my inflamed throat but I did so and thanked everyone that called wishing me well.

A knock at the door sent chills running down my spine, several Kuwaiti's were there. The one nearest my full glass view, I recognized from the office of His Highness the Crown Prince and Prime Minister. I was already beaten, what more could they possibly want now?

"Sheikh Saad sends his regards Charles" said the nuisance visitor. "I'll bet he does" I responded bitterly. The little entourage of traditionally clothed Arabs welcomed themselves inside and promptly parked themselves around our sprawling eighteen seat sofa in the living room before their next words were uttered. This time I gave no customary pecks on the cheeks and certainly shook no hands. Surely the men in impeccable white dress dishdashas and white head scarves had an agenda and I wanted them to get to it. I didn't think they were here to check on my health; in that case they came very late.

His Highness expresses great sadness that such terrible events have estranged you and him (you think?) His highness Sheikh Saad always thought of you as his brother and can't understand how two brothers could come so divided. (The story of Cain and Able entered my mind.)

"Brothers have not always fared well with other brothers in Kuwait's Royal family" I stated. I remember only a few ago when some wished to have the Minister of Defense killed because he was becoming too powerful. One had his eye plucked out if you remember correctly and sent him in exile to Egypt and then to England. "Remember" I said,

"This man is now the man who is the Crown Prince and Prime Minister." "Remember also the one who was ousted from his line of succession because he wed an American?" Sniping barbs and half witted chuckles bounced off each of us for another few minutes before the emissary for His Highness got down to business. Like the al Enizi Klan they wanted everything to be resolved and forgotten but forgot to speak of money.

I let the men know the Crown Prince and his cousin the Minister of Information were behind my imprisonment and the emptying of my bank account and one day, maybe far in the future they would pay for that. After being handed an envelope which I never opened, I sounded my parting warning for the men "if you or your employers think they are going to place a fatwa (a religious death edict) on me, then let it be said now that I have worked for them a number of years and have many papers in possession of people out side Kuwait who will use them to help destroy whoever kills me. You had better pray I don't get hit by a car in the future or crash in a plane because Kuwait will have a hundred times more damning secrets unveiled than the ones I will use in a book.

I relayed to one that I knew his temperament and was sure at this time he wished to push me over the railings of my apartment, but he should be warned my death would result in many things to come in the future.

What they all should remember at the Ministry and at Dasma Palace is that those who wish me harm now or in the future is that enough papers have been stored and sent around that there'll be some back lash. As for this envelope they gave me, I don't want to know what is in it. I don't want money now. In the future I wish to have our country's sever relations. I have never even seen a grateful Kuwaiti buy a coca cola for American servicemen and they have advised them that they don't even want the Americans to come to town shopping.

It was Christmas Eve in the Middle East, which to an Arab only means that the infidels are celebrating. This year instead of being overwhelmed with peace and Joy, I'm embittered and seek revenge.

I backed up and looked; I was standing in the same floor to ceiling glass picture windows I had watched Kuwait City burn and now I'm hoping it will burn again. This time I intend to be a formidable assistant for those coming to plunder.

Breaking my thought was another telephone call. This one was from Barbra Vaughn, my new, old high school friend from Savannah High in Georgia. She and Betty McNaughton were having a party with all their friends over for a Christmas dinner. I had already missed Janelle's Christmas party but I guess I was glad anyways. Not once did she come about me in prison, but at least her son Mish did. Early on, he brought me a box of Kit Kat chocolate bars that I shared with all my cell mates. At Barbara's that evening, we watched Armed Forces Network Television and everyone ate and ate and ate. I, not so much. I had a few problems trying to get anything down but appreciated the invitation and the camaraderie. At least my eyes ate a lot for me.

There was a great attendance with people from the American Embassy, Barbara's Bible study and Choral group the "Kuwait Singers" and many of Betty McNaughton the Ambassador's secretary's friends and boy friend.

My low spirits got a great boost by listening to caroling with good friends, rounded out by visiting with the third of my angels during captivity Betsy Gorlay. It was during dinner I tried to convey to them all that I was now looking forward to mine and Maia's future and the flight home to the States. I thanked all of them from the bottom of my heart, Barbara, Betty and Betsy especially.

Conspicuously missing that evening was Barbara's friend Hussein Qambar Ali, the Kuwaiti friend who decided to convert from Islam to Christianity, which is no sin but still punishable by death if done by the family.

Several of us wanted to hear the latest on him. Barbara embarrassingly obliged by saying the story had really taken on a life of its own since we all spoke with him in this same apartment several months earlier. It seemed the whole reason Hussein Qambar was converting to Christianity was that he wanted to be closer to young American lady from Colorado who had lived in Kuwait while she taught school.

Qambar recently appeared of Kuwait Arabic television and in newspapers renouncing Christianity and saying the Christians and women had plied him with liquor and tried to brainwash him against Islam and Allah. He escaped from his Colorado captors wrathful hands and returned to Kuwait and the arms of his loving wife and children. At least that was his tale.

Barbara said it wasn't quite the way it really happened. He renounced his one wife and children and religion to become the companion of the American mistress in Colorado where he took up residence. He was persuaded to travel about on speaking engagements to local churches and possibly a nationwide tour renouncing Islam. When he didn't get the money he wanted and the free car and apartment, he grew impatient and angry and that he had renounced his wealthy family in Kuwait, and now would not be wealthy or famous in the United States.

Hussein Qambar flew back to Kuwait renouncing publicly the whole adventure in the United States and the infidel Christians he associated with and all Americans that had befriended him in Kuwait. He was now a pretty famous speaker in mosques throughout Kuwait city and inside Saudi Arabia and had celebrity and fame in his own right with many television appearances scheduled. He told of his pain in the grips of the Americans and Christians and only Allah helped him endure his personal hell.

By late evening, I was very tired and ready to see my apartment and cats possibly for the last time. I bid everyone farewell and in turn they said they would be praying for me and Maia.

Two of mine and Maia's dear friends we got to know through Janelle, Joy and Heyman were kind enough to want to bid me fare well and take me to the airport. We visited for a while, and then we were off.

Just two and a half hours following Barbara's party, and I was sitting at Kuwait International Airport Terminal Two, not far from the Royal

Terminal I was use to. There was no problem in the Customs and Immigration line neither with my Residency papers nor with permission to leave the country; but several Airport Security Guards with machine guns approached and formed a contingent surrounding me with one offering to carry my lone briefcase. They all, as in a protective circle around me escorted me straight to my Air France boarding Gate, where they held me for a few minutes until the pilot and a number of his crew came forward to claim me.

As soon as I was turned over to them, the French pilot introduced himself. He said "My wife and I have been following your story very closely as have a lot of our friends". He said "I don't live in Kuwait City but your story has been in all the French papers too." He said I was told by Immigrations that you would be boarding this flight to Paris and I'd like to know if there is anything you would like me or my staff to do for you?" I'd like later to come back and speak with you if I may". He then escorted me to a first class bulk head seat and introduced me to several more of his staff as they applauded me. "Bon Jour" several said and they took turns tucking me in and feeding me for the rest of the flight. The pilot did come back to talk later and invited me to spend Christmas with his family near Paris or join him there later if I was going to ever be coming back that way.

The planes engines revved up and I felt the wheels leave the tarmac. Suddenly the feeling of being lifted was not only from the plane's ascent but from all the troubles of my imprisonment and the tortures I'd endured now being left behind. Without any one else noticing, I peered out the window and flipped Kuwait the bird then closed my view.

ABOUT THE AUTHOR

Former prankster, businessman and model, Chuck, as he prefers to be called, has moved through life according to where his heart has dictated rather than where others would have led. The native of Stoughton, Wisconsin, grew up in his adoptive hometown of Savannah, Georgia. Lifes' lessons began in lower middle-class housing where money for travel and holidays were the exception; thus his philosophy became "work in great destinations where others pay to play." Following his insatiable desire for excitement and danger expanded his philosophy to be "when there is a world crisis at hand, see it firsthand." Experience in war and travel to more than 70 countries had him living at both the top and bottom ends of the socio-economic scale, from palatial penthouses on Miami Beach to a sleeping bag on the desert floor. Chuck feels as though he has packed several lifetimes into one. His exploits during his first 60 years have been fun, yet dangerous at times. He feels equally blessed for all those times and the present, as he retreats into suburban life and the mundane.